The Complete History of

The Holocaust

Other Books in
The Complete History of Series:

American Slavery
Ancient Greece
The Death Penalty

The Complete History of

The Holocaust

Mitchell G. Bard, *Book Editor*

David L. Bender, *Publisher*
Bruno Leone, *Executive Editor*
Bonnie Szumski, *Editorial Director*
Stuart B. Miller, *Managing Editor*

Greenhaven Press, Inc., San Diego, California

Every effort has been made to trace the owners of copyrighted material. The articles in this volume may have been edited for content, length, and/or reading level. The titles have been changed to enhance the editorial purpose.

Library of Congress Cataloging-in-Publication Data

The Complete history of the Holocaust / Mitchell G. Bard, editor.
     p.   cm.
  Includes bibliographical references (p.   ) and index.
  ISBN 0-7377-0373-3 (lib. bdg. : alk. paper)
  1. Holocaust, Jewish (1939–1945) I. Bard, Mitchell Geoffrey, 1959–

D804.3 .C6498   2001
940.53'18—dc21
                                                    00-056046
                                                       CIP

Cover photo: Hulton Getty Picture Library

Printed in the USA

Contents

children was particularly great as they eventually were banned from schools and clubs.　.

CHAPTER 2: THE FINAL SOLUTION

CHAPTER 4: VICTIMS

CHAPTER 5: RESISTANCE

CHAPTER 6: THE RESCUERS

Introduction

The Holocaust was not a sudden act of mass murder. It was a gradual process that began with relatively minor restrictions on Jewish behavior and gradually escalated over a period of nearly a decade to the point where the official policy of the Nazis was the extermination of every Jew in Europe.

The Germans were not content with just killing people, however. They tortured, dehumanized, and humiliated them. Prisoners' heads were shaved, their names were replaced with numbers, and, in Auschwitz, their arms were tattooed. The most sickening methods were used to kill people—gassing, hanging, clubbing, heart injections, driving inmates into electric fences, burying them alive—and prisoners were used as guinea pigs for medical experiments. Some of these experiments involved seeing how often bones could be broken before they could no longer be reset, observing how the body would react to extremes of heat and cold, and using X-rays for sterilization.

A number of factors allowed the Nazis to pursue the systematic escalation of the persecution of the Jews. Anti-Semitism in German society; the need for a scapegoat for Germany's loss in World War I and subsequent economic woes and humiliation; and the fears and weaknesses of average Germans, most of whom were unprepared to stand up to the goose-stepping Nazi bullies who took control of the nation.

Singling Out the Jews

At the time Hitler came to power, Germany was regarded as the most civilized country in the world, and Jews were among its most prominent citizens, holding positions of influence in every field. Jews had also fought with distinction in World War I, and veterans considered themselves as German as anyone else. Though many Jews remained committed to their faith, many others assimilated, partly because they believed this would make it easier for them to be accepted by their non-Jewish neighbors. It therefore came as quite a shock when a boycott against Jews was initiated early in 1933. This boycott was not only directed against Jewish businesses but also professionals such as doctors and lawyers. Jewish civil service employees, with the exception of World War I veterans, were dismissed from their posts.

The persecution of Jews in other ways and in other professions followed. In May, Nazis burned books written by Jews and opponents of Nazism. In July, a law was passed revoking the naturalization and cancelling the citizenship of Jews who had immigrated to Germany after 1918. Toward the end of the year, Jewish writers, artists, and journalists lost their jobs. A few months later Jews were denied the right to health insurance. By 1935, posters began to appear in the windows of shops, restaurants, and other public places that read, "Jews not wanted."

The legislated persecution of the Jews culminated in the adoption of the Nuremberg Laws in 1935. These laws were the basis for the exclusion of Jews from all public business life and for the reclassification of the political rights of Jewish citizens. Under the National Citizens Law, Jews were denied voting rights and were forbidden to hold public office. Any remaining Jewish civil service employees, including World War I veterans, were dismissed. The Law for the Protection of German Blood and German Honor prohibited the marriage of Jews to non-Jews. Other bans prevented Jews from using the same facilities as non-Jews.

Virtually every institution of the government contributed to the anti-Jewish policy of the Nazis. Among the most important were the press and propaganda ministry. Throughout the early years of Hitler's rule, as his Nazi Party came to dominate the nation, the German people were fed a steady stream of anti-Semitic propaganda through official government channels and publications. The most vitriolic attacks on the Jews were issued by Hitler's minister of propaganda and public information, Joseph Goebbels, who also supervised a weekly publication, *Der Stürmer*, which was devoted primarily to promoting hatred against the Jews. Its motto was, "The Jews are our misfortune."

Looting Jewish Possessions

During the early years of Hitler's rule, persecution of Jews was limited primarily to denying them certain rights and jobs. In 1937, however, the Nazis began to take away the possessions Jews had acquired. Jewish businessmen, for example, were forced to sell their businesses, usually at below-market prices. Industrialists and other wealthy property owners were required to register with the government and to declare their holdings. Professionals, most of whom had already lost their jobs, were stripped of their licenses in 1938. Doctors, for instance, were only allowed to serve as nurses, and then only for Jewish patients.

During the course of 1938 the Germans also continued to isolate Jews by instituting new methods for branding them. They were given identity cards, their passports were confiscated, and new passports identifying them as Jews were issued—at least to those who managed to navigate the bureaucratic obstacles created to make it more difficult. Jews also had their driver's licenses taken away and were required to change their names, adding either *Israel* for men or *Sara* for women to their names.

The Germans found still more rights to take away and limitations to place on Jews: Children were expelled from school, Jews were banned from cultural and sporting events and associa-tions, and other limits were placed on Jews.

All of these various measures were based on Hitler's anti-Semitic views and his desire to ultimately rid Germany of Jews, but they were not simply edicts from one man. The vast array of prohibitions was devised, implemented, and enforced by a growing number of people in an ever-expanding bureaucracy devoted largely to what became known as "the Jewish question."

Nazis Turn to Violence Against Jews

The level of persecution against the Jews was ratcheted up significantly in 1938. As disconcerting, humiliating, and discriminating as the measures had been, they had not yet posed a physical danger to the well-being of German Jews. This began to change with the destruction of synagogues in Munich and Nuremberg and the Night of Broken Glass, *Kristallnacht*. On November 9–10, the government organized attacks by mobs that destroyed 191 synagogues and looted 7,500 shops. At least ninety-one Jews were killed.

Another alarming new development was the arrest of more than 26,000 Jewish men, who were then imprisoned in concentration camps at Dachau, Buchenwald, and Sachsenhausen. Though concentration camps are associated with the murder of Jews, the first one, Dachau, was actually established in June 1933 for non-Jewish opponents of the Nazi regime and other "criminals." After *Kristallnacht,* however, the camps increasingly became prisons for Jews.

After *Kristallnacht,* there was a respite in the violence against the Jews, but the Nazis found other ways to torment them, including making them pay for all of the damage done during the pogrom. Ominously, the Germans also began to impose anti-Semitic measures against non-German Jews as they seized control of Austria and Czechoslovakia. The importance of "the Jewish question" was also reinforced by the creation of a new bureaucracy, the National Central Office for Jewish Emigration, with central offices in Vienna and Prague.

Ghettoization

Germany's invasion of Poland on September 1, 1939, marked the unofficial start of World War II. One of the reasons Hitler said he went to war was to make room—Lebensraum ("living space")—for Germans. He believed that Eastern Europe had to be conquered to create a vast German empire with a greater population and new territory to supply food and raw materials.

Hitler's objective was complicated, however, by the fact that the conquest of Poland brought another 2 million Jews under his authority. The Nazis wasted little time in applying their anti-Semitic laws against the newly conquered Jews, but, once again, they escalated the severity of the measures. These people needed to be removed to create German "living space." Toward that end, Heinrich Himmler created special task forces within the SS, the *Einsatzgruppen*, which were charged with liquidating all political enemies of the Reich. By the end of the war these mobile killing units would liquidate approximately 1.4 million Jews. Initially, however, the mass murder of Polish Jews was not practical, so while Hitler planned the creation of special camps for the extermination of the Jews, he decided to isolate them in ghettos.

The ghettos were enclosed areas—barbed wire at Lodz, a brick wall in Warsaw and Krakow—guarded by German soldiers. Living conditions in the ghettos were horrible. Malnutrition was widespread and death by starvation and disease was a daily occurrence.

Each ghetto was administered by a Jewish council (*Judenrat*), which was composed of influential members of the Jewish community. This was one of the many diabolical inventions of the Germans. The council members represented the Jewish community to the Nazi authorities, but their primary role was to implement German policy. They were put in the position of having to decide whether to help the Nazis or risk being murdered for their refusal. Many Jews believed they were in some way helping to improve the plight of Jews in the ghetto, but ultimately they were often the ones who had to choose who would be deported to the death camps. In the end, cooperating with the Nazis did not spare the *Judenrat* from sharing the same fate as the other Jews.

The ghettos provide yet another example of the unprecedented effort the Nazis devoted to disposing of the Jews. It was an enormous bureaucratic and logistical task to organize the segregation of more than 2 million people, who were spread throughout Poland, and later to transport them in the most efficient manner to the death camps.

The Final Solution

Throughout 1940–1941, the German army marched through Europe, invading one country after another and, in the process, absorbing more and more Jews. Anti-Jewish laws would almost immediately be instituted, but this did not solve the problem of creating "living space," so the Jews were rounded up and deported to the growing number of concentration camps.

By the beginning of 1942, hundreds of thousands of Jews were already dead. Still, the head of the SS, Heinrich Himmler, recognized that it would require greater coordination among the various Nazi institutions and officials to accomplish the goal of achieving the Final Solution to the Jewish question, namely the extermination of the 11 million Jews he believed to be living in Europe. On January 20 a meeting was held on the shores of a Berlin lake called Wannsee for this purpose. Afterward, the liquidation of the ghettos and the deportation of Jews from the occupied territories became a much more systematic process.

From that point until the surrender of Germany, the Nazis followed the course laid out at Wannsee and proceeded to murder approximately 6 million Jews as well as an almost equal number of non-Jews. And the killing continued unabated even when the course of the war turned against Germany. When every German was needed to fight, when food, oil, and transportation were in short supply, resources continued to be used to kill Jews rather than to be diverted for military use. As Emil Fackenheim has written, "The killing of Jews was not considered just a part of the war effort, but equal to it." It is an overstatement to say the Germans lost the war because of their dogged commitment to the Final Solution, but there is no question that the extermination campaign was a drain that weakened their ability to fight.

Ordinary Men

Jews did not dehumanize themselves. Ordinary Germans and people from countries the Nazis occupied assumed positions in the bureaucracies that implemented the anti-Jewish legislation; they became members of the army, the secret police, and other military and paramilitary organizations that harassed, arrested, tortured, and murdered Jews, and with all too few exceptions, they stood by and did nothing to help the Jews.

The Germans also spared no effort in creating an enormous bureaucracy and devoting scarce resources which would have been better used in the military campaign against the Allies, to the task of carrying out the Final Solution. It is a tribute—a strange word to use in the context of mass murder—to German efficiency that the Nazis could round up millions of Jews, segregate them, imprison them, and finally kill them.

It is not an easy task to kill 6 million people, but the Germans were determined to find practical ways to kill as many people as quickly as possible. More than 1 million Jews were killed by mobile killing squads—the *Einsatzgruppen*—and in other actions that involved little more than lining men, women, and children up in front of ditches and machine-gunning them. Shooting people was not good enough for Hitler because it was too slow and messy, so the Nazis figured out how to use poison gas—first in vans, later in gas chambers—to kill larger numbers of Jews. At first bodies were simply dumped in pits, later they were cremated. The Germans even studied how to get the bodies to burn faster.

The magnitude of the atrocities makes it easy to forget that most of the murders were carried out by individual Germans, often men with wives and children who were "ordinary men." Some Nazis were undoubtedly sociopaths, but most were not. They were more typically people who sat home petting their dogs, reading bedtime stories to their children, and listening to Mozart after spending the day shooting mothers and infants. Moreover, the atrocities these men (they were almost entirely men) committed were not the type of antiseptic killings portrayed on television. Shooting a Jew at point-blank range, as Nazis often did, meant getting blood and brains splattered on them. In the death camps, the Germans could kill people with gas rather than their own hands, but then they had to look at masses of bodies and smell burning flesh in the crematorium. The horrific images that we can see in old photographs and movies do not capture the smells and sounds. Still, "ordinary men" committed these atrocities day after day.

Victims

The principal targets of the Nazi extermination campaign were the Jews. True, Hitler started out by arresting his political enemies and murdered thousands of Communists, "asocials," and other non-Jews, but these groups did not pose the threat to Aryan blood that the "parasitic" Jews did. The other group the Nazis sought to exterminate was the Roma, or Gypsies. Ironically, the Gypsies were Aryan, but since they did not conform to the Nazi stereotype, they also needed to be eliminated. Jehovah's Witnesses were persecuted for their failure to cooperate with the regime, but they could gain their freedom by recanting their faith; few if any did, but at least they had an option other enemies of the state did not. Gays also were victims because they were viewed as degenerates who could contribute to the destruction of the pure Aryan breed.

American citizens were also among the victims of the Nazis. Thousands of Americans were trapped in Europe during the war, and many wound up in concentration camps. American soldiers captured during the fighting were usually sent to prisoner-of-war camps; however, a few instances are known where Jewish (and sometimes non-Jewish) soldiers were sent to concentration camps.

Jews were not only murdered in concentration

camps. Thousands were killed while employed as slave laborers. In some instances, the labor was primarily designed to kill the prisoners; in others, it was meant to aid the German war effort. We are still learning the extent of the involvement of some of the largest German companies and the German subsidiaries of foreign companies in the exploitation of Jewish slaves.

The Germans were diabolical in their effort to conceal their intentions. Who could have suspected that a shower would be anything but a place to get clean? With hindsight it is difficult to appreciate what it was like for people who had no idea where they were going and what fate awaited them. When Jews got off trains that took them from their homes or ghettos, they were whisked into an alien environment before they had time to adjust. Their possessions were taken away, and they were faced with snarling dogs, armed soldiers, and officials barking orders at them. Before they could realize they were headed to their deaths and could decide to resist, their clothes were taken and they were standing naked in a shower.

It took luck and determination to survive. Those who lived to tell the tale have incredible stories: people who lived underground in caves for years, who hid in latrines to escape, who were sent to monasteries and pretended to be non-Jews. Inside the camps, a prisoner had to stay healthy enough to work, and that often required "organizing"—the phrase prisoners used for stealing, trading, or otherwise acquiring the necessities of life, from food to clothing. Survival often depended on the age and sex of a prisoner. A young child had little chance of survival; more than 1 million children were murdered in the Holocaust. The same was true of the elderly. Women were more likely to be killed than men because they were less able to perform hard labor and because they could not be allowed to live and produce more Jews.

Resistance

Jews did not all go like lambs to slaughter, though. Many instances of resistance are recorded, from the extraordinary uprising in the Warsaw ghetto to the escape from Sobibor to the blowing up of the crematorium at Auschwitz. Many more examples were less dramatic and not the subject of books or movies. Prisoners who refused to give in to the dehumanization of the camps displayed a different type of resistance that was reflected in secretly organizing religious services or classes.

Resistance was rarely an option, even if Jews had the desire to revolt. By the time most prisoners figured out they were likely to be killed, they were too sick and weak to do anything about it, never mind the fact that they had no weapons and that any act of defiance would usually lead to the punishment of not only the resister but other innocent prisoners as well.

In hindsight, it is easy to criticize the Jewish councils, the *Judenrats*, the Germans created to administer Jewish affairs in the ghettos, but did they really have a choice as to whether to help the Nazis? Failure to do so would have probably been futile. They would have been killed, and others would have been found to take their place. Now we know that even those who cooperated with the Nazis were killed in the end anyway. At the time, though, many Jews honestly believed that cooperating with the Nazis would help save lives.

What Did We Know?

It is hard to believe the press did not make the murder of millions of Jews a bigger story and stimulate government efforts to rescue. The truth is that many reports of what was happening to the Jews *did* appear, but they were often buried deep in newspapers and were written in a way that detracted from their credibility. Though the Allies had plenty of evidence to prove the mass murder of Jews, the press and general public found the reports too hard to believe. It simply was not possible to believe that hundreds of thousands of people could be murdered in a single place. This reluctance to accept what turned out to be the truth was also a result of experience from World War I, when the participants routinely accused each other of atrocities, many of which, people later learned, had been fabricated to stimulate support for the war and hatred of the enemy.

The Failure to Act

From the beginning of his political career, Hitler made no secret of his intentions regarding the Jews. Though it would later be said that the concentration camps carried out their murderous deeds behind a carefully orchestrated veil of secrecy, Hitler repeatedly made public remarks that left little to the imagination, such as his January 1939 speech to parliament predicting the "extermination of the Jewish race in Europe" in the event of war.

Despite Hitler's openness about his objective, governments around the world were reluctant to take his words seriously, even after he went to war and began to carry out his stated goal of exterminating the Jews. The U.S. government knew what was happening to the Jews in Germany throughout the 1930s and learned about the Final Solution by 1942. Still, a combination of factors led the Franklin Roosevelt administration to actively prevent Jews from being rescued in some instances and to passively do so in others.

The late 1930s and early 1940s were a time when the United States was just coming out of the Great Depression and the general public was anti-Semitic and xenophobic. Little support existed for admitting refugees, especially largely penniless ones, to compete for already scarce jobs. For most of the war, U.S. officials made it difficult and sometimes impossible for Jews to enter the country to escape Hitler. Of course, exceptions were made for people who were famous or could help the war effort, such as scientists, literary notables, and artists. What made the situation worse was that the United States set an example that was followed by virtually every other country in the world, leaving the targets of the Final Solution at Hitler's mercy. One of the most dramatic examples involved the *St. Louis*, a ship full of refugees who were trying to escape Germany and were bound for Cuba in 1939. When the *St. Louis* was prevented from landing in Cuba, it sailed along the Atlantic Coast of the United States, but Roosevelt would not allow it to dock in any American port.

Late in the war, Roosevelt did create the War Refugee Board, which took modest measures to rescue Jews, but it was too little too late. The administration was also urged to use the military to slow down or try to stop Hitler's killing machine, but defense officials rejected suggestions to bomb the concentration camps. In the end, Roosevelt believed the best way to save the Jews was to devote all of the nation's energies to winning the war. Undoubtedly, the Allied victory saved Europe and millions of lives, but 6 million Jewish lives were still lost.

The Righteous Ones

Discussions of the Holocaust inevitably focus on the millions who died and the fact that most Germans and citizens of other Nazi-occupied countries cooperated in the Final Solution. Still, many Jews survived, in part because of the often heroic acts of non-Jews who risked their lives to save them. Thousands of "righteous persons" did everything from providing shelter to food to documents to Jews in danger. Oskar Schindler is perhaps the most famous rescuer thanks to Steven Spielberg's award-winning film *Schindler's List*. Diplomats such as Raoul Wallenberg and Chiune Sugihara also helped thousands of Jews escape by giving them visas. In a few instances, whole towns shielded Jews from their tormentors, as was the case in Le Chambon, France. In a way, it is one of the most perverse aspects of the Holocaust that people who acted morally should be considered heroes. It is the murderers who should have been the exceptions, not the rescuers.

Justice?

The question of what to do about the Nazis who perpetrated atrocities during the war was not as easy to answer as one might expect. Hitler and several of his top aides committed suicide to avoid arrest and prosecution. A strong sentiment existed among the Allies, especially the British, to simply execute leading Germans on the spot, but eventually agreement was reached to try those viewed as war criminals. This, too, presented a dilemma. Logistically, the thousands of Germans who had participated in the various actions against Jews and others could not be tried, so a decision had to be made as to which Nazis should be held responsible. The twenty-two highest-ranking officials were tried at Nuremberg, but hundreds of other trials were held for camp guards and others involved in war crimes. Low-ranking officials claimed they were only following orders and should not be held responsible for their actions, but one of the most important conclusions of the war crimes trials was the rejection of this excuse. Both those who gave orders to commit atrocities, though they may not have pulled the triggers themselves, and those who pulled the triggers because they had been given orders, were found guilty.

Many Nazis were executed for their crimes, but a shocking number had their sentences reduced or commuted. Others were never tried and escaped to countries in Latin America, and elsewhere, where they lived quiet lives under assumed names. The United States actually actively recruited some Nazis who they believed could help in intelligence operations against their newfound enemies in the Soviet Union. A number of Nazi hunters, Simon Wiesenthal being the most famous, have tirelessly pursued the Nazis who escaped justice, and to this day, war criminals are being found and tried. Of course, the most dramatic case was that of Adolf Eichmann, one of the architects of the Final Solution, who escaped to Argentina and was found and abducted by Israeli agents who took him to Israel, where he was tried, convicted, and executed for his crimes against humanity.

Life After the Camps

The men and women who survived the camps at the end of World War II cannot escape their memories. As one former Buchenwald inmate said, "For forty years, when I shaved in the mirror, I could see the pile of bodies in the mirror."

A remarkable thing that you learn from survivors is that one of the most powerful feelings they have is not fear but shame or guilt. They ask themselves, "Why did I survive?" Many cannot accept that they lived while others—friends, family, even strangers—died.

Survival often required people to do shameful or distasteful things. For example, this book contains stories about people who took the clothes from corpses because the dead did not need them anymore. Elie Wiesel tells the story of people stealing food from his sick father and being told he should do the same. People had to make inhuman choices, such as which of their children should live and which should die. The memories of these choices continue to haunt them.

Conclusion

It is important to study the Holocaust because the events of World War II are quickly becoming ancient history. Soon no one from the generation that fought in that war or lived through the torment of the Holocaust will be alive to tell their stories. The period will take up less and less space in history books and teachers will devote less time to teaching about it. Even today, many high school history texts spend only a paragraph or two on the Holocaust, so students can hardly be expected to appreciate its significance.

On the Internet and many college campuses, revisionists try to convince people that the Holocaust did not happen at all, that it is exaggerated or that it is something Jews dreamed up to get sympathy. When the witnesses have all died, who will stand up with the mountain of evidence in books like this to confront them and say, "You are lying!" Pseudoscientific arguments suggesting that Jews were not gassed or could not have been murdered in such large numbers may sound plausible to the uneducated or naive. After reading this book, however, you will be neither.

Many survivors dislike books and, especially, movies about the Holocaust. They believe the Holocaust is incomprehensible to anyone who did not live through it. Paradoxically, the more you learn, the more incomprehensible it seems. After all, how can anyone explain why Germans did what they did or how Jewish prisoners survived the physical and psychological torture they endured? This book contains clues, but not answers to these questions. The goal is not to make the incomprehensible comprehensible, it is simply to shed light on a very dark subject.

This book documents what many people saw and heard, but only part of it. For most of it, there are no words.

Background to the Holocaust

Chapter 1

Introduction

*I*n many countries, dictators come to power by leading the military to overthrow the existing government. It may seem remarkable now, but this was not the case at all in Germany. Adolf Hitler rose to power through the democratic process; that is, he was elected. Of course, once his party gained power through the electoral process, he skillfully manipulated the system to dominate the government and, ultimately, to declare himself the nation's supreme leader. Even that decision, however, was ratified by the German parliament.

Hitler's ascent to power was also extraordinary because he had started out as a member of a tiny, inconsequential party of rabble-rousers. When he first attempted to gain power, during the Beer Hall Putsch, he ended up in jail. In less than a decade, however, he recovered from that failure and built a formidable organization that slowly won support from the people. In 1928, the Nazi Party won just 12 seats in the Reichstag, Germany's parliament. Two years later, they won 107, and became the second largest party in the government.

Hitler was not even a German citizen until 1932, when he decided to run for president. Hitler lost that election, but his party won 230 of the 670 seats in the Reichstag. A year later, Hitler became chancellor. Though the Nazis used the democratic process to assume power, they never won a majority of the German vote. In the last free election before the war, the party won only 43 percent of the vote.

Once Hitler assumed power he gradually began to impose regulations that persecuted the Jews and introduced his racist ideology in which Aryans were supermen and Jews were parasites. The fact that the Austrian-born Hitler was nothing like the blond-haired, blue-eyed German example of perfection that he championed did not dissuade the German people from allowing him to lead them to ruin.

This chapter looks at the life of Adolf Hitler, how he came to power and the first steps he took to turn the Jews in Germany from citizens to outcasts.

Selection 1

What Is the Holocaust?

Richard Rubenstein and John Roth

This chapter offers an introduction to the Holocaust. In this excerpt, some of the terms that will be used later are defined for the first time, especially the word Shoah *and what is meant by the term* Holocaust. *Richard Rubenstein has taught religion at Florida State and served as President of the Washington Institute for Values in Public Policy. He is an ordained rabbi and author of several books. John Roth has taught philosophy at Claremont McKenna College and is a prolific writer of books and articles.*

On 23 February 1930 a twenty-one-year-old law student died in Berlin. Like many other young men in the Germany of his day, Horst Wessel, a Lutheran preacher's son, had rebelled against his bourgeois upbringing and joined the "Brownshirts" (*Sturmabteilung,* Storm Detachment) of the *Nationalsozialistische Deutsche Arbeiterpartei,* the National Socialist German Workers' Party, better known as the Nazi party. Wessel's political activities included participation in bloody street battles with Communists. Of greater significance, Wessel was in love with a former prostitute and had moved in with her. Abhorring notoriety, their landlady sought to evict them by enlisting help from a Communist gang. One winter night the gang broke into the couple's room. Much to the landlady's dismay, a former intimate of Wessel's girlfriend gunned him down.

History frequently pivots around small events. Horst Wessel's demise is a case in point. His death would have been inconsequential had he not written a poem sometime before. Entitled "Raise High the Flag," it had been set in march-time to a Viennese cabaret song from the turn of the century. As Wessel was dying, Joseph Goebbels, the mastermind behind Nazi propaganda, saw an opportunity to turn a lovers' triangle into political power. Wessel's lyric immortalized those who had given their lives for the Nazi cause. Arranging to have the "Horst Wessel Song" sung at the conclusion of a Nazi meeting, Goebbels envisioned that it would become "the hymn of the German revolution." He was correct.

Excerpted from Richard L. Rubenstein and J.K. Roth, *Approaches to Auschwitz.* Copyright © 1987 John Knox Press. Reprinted with permission from Westminster John Knox Press.

That same February a Jewish doctor, Sigmund Freud, went about his work in Vienna. Only a few weeks earlier he had finished a small book that would be among his most famous. In English it is called *Civilization and Its Discontents.* Among its final words are these: "Men have gained control over the forces of nature to such an extent that with their help they would have no difficulty in exterminating one another to the last man." Freud was also correct. Horst Wessel's song would help to prove the point.

As the Nazis sang in the Berlin *Sportpalast* that February night in 1930, an infant destined to be at least as well known as Freud was fast asleep. The revolution glimpsed by Freud's premonition and rallied by Wessel's song would profoundly mark this Jewish girl, Anne Frank. Years later she lived for months in her Amsterdam hiding place writing the diary that is still read by millions. One of its last entries, dated 15 July 1944, testifies: "I see the world gradually being turned into a wilderness, I hear the ever approaching thunder, which will destroy us too." Anne Frank also affirmed "that people are really good at heart," and she went on to say that her gloomy forecast would not be the last word. "If I look up into the heavens," she wrote, "I think that it will all come right, that this cruelty too will end, and that peace and tranquillity will return again." Anne Frank was correct, too, but how far is not clear. She was right about the gloomy part. As for the rest, perhaps the best one can say is that the jury is still out.

Horst Wessel, Sigmund Freud, and Anne Frank—these people never met. Yet they are linked together in ways that must be grasped if we are to comprehend what it means to live in the late twentieth century. What links them is an event now called the Holocaust.

What Is Meant by the Holocaust?

The Third Reich's system of concentration camps, murder squadrons, and killing centers took more than fifteen million defenseless human lives. All of these deaths were tragic and should be mourned. Between five and six million of them were Jewish, and it will bear remembering that the Jews were the only group that Hitler targeted for extinction. Not every Nazi victim was Jewish, but the Nazi intent was to rid Europe, if not the world, of Jews. Hitler went far in fulfilling that goal. Two-thirds of Europe's Jews were dead by the end of World War II. Thus, the Holocaust refers—not exclusively, but primarily—to the Nazi destruction of the European Jews. It also refers to more than that sentence can suggest. Some further references to Freud, Wessel, and Anne Frank will clarify that fact and illustrate the scope of meaning reflected by the word "Holocaust" in the following chapters.

The event designated as the Holocaust is named by more than one term. Many of Horst Wessel's peers, for example, took part in what the Nazis called the Final Solution, *(Die Endlösung)*. Wessel's friends had lived through a period when hopes for imperial expansion were shattered by Germany's humiliating defeat in World War I. The aftermath was one of political and economic instability coupled with yearnings for a renewed sense of German identity. Nazi political instincts capitalized on these conditions. Their tactics included an ideological campaign that implicated the Jews in all of Germany's problems. Jews, the Nazis proclaimed, were unnecessary, unwanted, undesirable. In short, they were superfluous. Nazi propaganda accorded Jews this status not because they were impoverished. Nor were Germany's Jews uneducated, unskilled, or unproductive. People can be considered redundant for those reasons, of course, and some of the Nazis' Jewish victims fitted into such categories. Most, especially in Germany, did not. On the contrary, they were able men and women. Thus, the Holocaust reveals that it is as easy for talented people to lose their places in the world as it is for those who cannot cope with the complexities of technological civilization, Even those who facilitate and adapt to the modern world may be spewed out by it. A surplus or redundant population, therefore, is not simply a matter of numbers. It can be any population that for any reason can find no

viable role in the society where it lives. The Nazis were determined to put Jews into that category. They succeeded. . . .

The Nazis planned brutal treatment for groups they labeled "subhuman," such as Slavs and Gypsies, but to advance their aims they degraded Jews to "nonhuman" status. After experimenting with various techniques that failed to achieve the desired results, the National Socialists unblinkingly embraced the most radical alternative: systematic, state-sponsored total annihilation. . . .

Two Hebrew words, *Churban* and *Shoah,* also name the Holocaust. Both signify catastrophic destruction. According to Uriel Tal, the term *Shoah* was used by Polish Jews as early as 1940 to designate their plight under Hitler. The roots of this word, however, go back much further. Indeed, they are biblical. The term is found in the Psalms, in Isaiah's prophecies, and in Job's lamentations. Its meanings are multiple. Sometimes it refers to dangers that threaten Israel from surrounding nations; at other times it refers to individual distress and desolation. If catastrophic destruction is signified in each case, Tal argues, "all Biblical meanings of the term *Shoah* clearly imply Divine judgment and retribution." Those ancient meanings, however, are called into question by the Final Solution. In contemporary usage, *Shoah* conveys the old sense of destruction but adds a profound element of doubt and even despair where religious tradition is concerned. . . .

How Shall We Interpret the Holocaust?

The Third Reich lasted from 1933 to 1945. Auschwitz, which epitomizes the Holocaust, functioned as a labor and death camp from 1940 through 1944. But these momentous years were centuries in the making. It is crucial to keep this question in mind: why did the Holocaust fail to occur before the 1940s? . . .

Since the triumph of Christianity in the fourth century, Raul Hilberg emphasizes, there have been three fundamental anti-Jewish policies: conversion, expulsion, and annihilation. "The sec-

German Expansion

North Sea · DENMARK · SWEDEN · LATVIA
Baltic Sea · LITHUANIA
GREAT BRITAIN · Polish Corridor · Vilna
EAST PRUSSIA
Braunschweig
NETHERLANDS · Danzig · Bialystok
O Berlin · Warsaw
BELGIUM · POLAND
LUXEMBOURG · GERMANY · SUDETENLAND · BOHEMIA & MORAVIA
RHINELAND · Weimar · Breslau
SAARLAND · Nuremberg · CZECHOSLOVAKIA · SLOVAKIA (To HUNGARY 1939)
FRANCE
Munich · Vienna · ROMANIA
SWITZERLAND · AUSTRIA · HUNGARY
U.S.S.R.

Legend:
- Germany 1933
- Areas annexed 1936–1939
- Areas occupied 1940–1941

ITALY · Adriatic Sea · YUGOSLAVIA
Mediterranean Sea

ond," says Hilberg, "appeared as an alternative to the first, and the third emerged as an alternative to the second. . . .The missionaries of Christianity had said in effect: You have no right to live among us as Jews. The secular rulers who followed had proclaimed: You have no right to live among us. The German Nazis at last decreed: You have no right to live." This dynamic will become evident as we move through the Middle Ages to the eve of the French Revolution. . . .

The unification of Germany under Bismarck in 1870, coupled with the Russian pogroms of 1881, formed one fateful watershed for Europe's Jews. World War I created another. More than inaugurating the twentieth century as one of mass death, it also proved mass extermination to be a politically acceptable method for modern states to use in restructuring society. In addition, when the Germans interpreted their own defeat as a "stab in the back" fomented by a Jewish world-conspiracy, the stage was set for the beginnings of the Nazi party and the emergence of its political messiah, Adolf Hitler. As the Great Depression struck, European nationalism never waned. Fascism was on the rise, and Jewish circumstances became increasingly problematic. Particularly in Poland, which had by far the largest Jewish population of any European nation between the two World Wars, the situation for Jews worsened every year. Gradually caught in the closing vise between a Poland that wanted its Jews to leave and a Germany that would eventually murder them, millions of eastern European Jews learned to their sorrow what the Jewish political scientist, Hannah Arendt, would mean when . . . she referred to Jews as a pariah people. . . .

When the Nazis came to power in 1933, their commitment to antisemitism was clear, but their practical policies toward Jews were not. It is one thing to have antisemitic feelings and quite another to make those feelings effective in a political regime. Hence it took time for the Nazis to work out a coherent anti-Jewish program. From 1933 to 1938 hoodlum violence mixed with "paper violence," but increasingly the latter proved decisive in ways that the former could not. With the help of an expanding bureaucracy to expedite such matters, German Jews were dismissed from government positions, eliminated from professions and from commerce, and stripped of basic legal protection. The objective behind this paper violence was not harassment and degradation for their own sake but rather to drive Jews out of Germany, albeit with as little as possible in their possession. With the help of the emerging power of the SS (*Schutzstaffel* or protection unit), Hitler created refugees.

The outbreak of World War II in September 1939 required new strategies because it foreclosed opportunities for expulsion of Jews and at the same time brought millions of Jews under German authority in eastern Europe and the Soviet Union. From the Nazi viewpoint, this war was a racial struggle aimed at giving the Germanic peoples their rightful dominion over the European continent. Populations that did not belong were either to serve Germans as slaves, or to be eliminated, or both. As mobile death squadrons (*Einsatzgruppen*) fanned out with advancing Nazi troops all along the eastern front, attention behind the lines was given to a strategy of ghettoization, which would ultimately feed the death and slave labor camps of the Reich. The Nazis sacrificed countless victims—for example, Slavs, Poles, Gypsies, Russian prisoners of war, homosexuals, the handicapped, and the mentally ill—but the Jews, ranking lowest in Hitler's racial hierarchy, were especially targeted. The Nazi policy toward these people, aimed at total domination, was symbolized by orders "to dig mass graves, strip, climb into the graves, lie down over the layer of corpses already murdered and await the final *coup de grâce*.". . .

Although the Nazis did not parade their death camps openly, the extermination of the Jews was no secret either. It bears remembering, however, that awareness of the Final Solution involved numerous stages and decisions. On all sides, they were momentous. Dissemination of news about the Holocaust, for example, was complicated not only because the Nazi regime suppressed the truth but also because such reports as did exist could not readily be repeated with impunity or seemed so horrible as to be beyond belief. In short, one could learn the truth and yet disguise, doubt, dismiss, or deny it; and even when one surmised or knew that a report was authentic, questions remained about what, if anything, should be done. . . . Although exceptions exist, a majority of Christian institutions and individuals either stood by as the Holocaust unfolded or actively contributed to the Jews' demise. But if Christian complicity is part of the catastrophe represented by Auschwitz, religious institutions were not alone in failing to do all that they could to alleviate the plight of persecuted minorities. Western governments knew about "the Jewish problem," even talked about it during the thirties, but generally did little to relax restrictive immigration policies in favor of Jewish refugees. Intent though they were on refusing Hitler victory during the war, serious questions remain as to whether they did everything possible to minimize the Nazi toll on the Jews. Nor were business communities and the professions left with clean hands. Granted new freedom to experiment by the Nazis, German science made unprecedented use of human subjects, destroying most of them in the process. Under Hitler, German industry capitalized on the fact that profit can be made from human misery. It modernized slavery, finding ways to get the most for the least by working people to death. Moreover, the Nazi experiment proved that a highly advanced society, steeped in music, art, philosophy, and literature, is not immune to propaganda that teaches people to kill. . . .

The Meaning of Genocide

One thing that can be done is *genocide*, which was an all-but-inevitable consequence of the National Socialist emphases on antisemitism,

German nationalism, and conquest of new territory for the German people. Often used in conjunction with the Holocaust, genocide is a recent term, coined by Raphael Lemkin in 1944. Significantly, as Lemkin defined it to mean "the destruction of a nation or of an ethnic group," he observed that genocide denoted "an old practice in its modern development." Lemkin saw that the plight of the Jews under Hitler was not a simple repetition of past historical patterns. Yet precisely what was new and unprecedented in these circumstances? Far from resolving that issue to everyone's satisfaction, Lemkin's discussion initiated a continuing debate about whether the Holocaust is better understood as an instance of genocide or whether it is a singular event that belongs in a category all its own.

The problem is that genocide covers a multitude of sins. The destruction of a nation or of an ethnic group can happen, for example, through deprivation of the means to live and procreate or through killing them outright. In short, the methods of genocide can be diverse. Even killing can be slow and indirect—starvation, for instance—as well as quick and immediate. The destruction process, moreover, can be as subtle as it is prolonged. Procedures to curtail birth rates and to increase mortality can have a genocidal effect over time. Eventually a people can also disappear if their culture is decimated by eliminating intellectual leadership, dismantling institutions, and suppressing literacy.

Variations on the theme of genocide also include another basic distinction. There is a difference between genocide understood as the annihilation of a national, religious, or ethnic identity, and a more radical form that makes no exceptions for the giving up of such identity through assimilation or conversion. . . .

The Jews were permanent Nazi targets. They lacked any options for changing their identities to guarantee their safety within the Third Reich. Nazi propaganda portrayed the Jews as less than subhuman, in fact as not human at all. They were considered disgusting parasitic vermin and at the same time the embodiment of absolute evil that must be eliminated to complete the Nazi drama of salvation. Hence they were the only group Hitler destined for *total* destruction by unrelenting, mass murder. . . .

Consider two modern attempts at population elimination to clarify further some similarities and differences. First, as Americans sought their own *Lebensraum* by expanding westward in the nineteenth century, millions of Native Americans were destroyed—more than 40% of the population died. Nevertheless, this genocide was not on a par with the fate of the European Jews under Hitler. Missionizing efforts toward the Indians and the establishment of reservations show that American intentions stopped short of a truly Final Solution. Such points are made not to minimize the destruction of Native American life in the United States, but rather to clarify how civilization has "advanced" to new levels of destructive consciousness in our own day.

A second important benchmark is found in the early twentieth-century case of the Armenians. . . . This crumbling Turkish regime, which once stretched from Persia to Hungary, was a congeries of nationalities without an adequate base of unity that could enable it to compete with the nationalistic consciousness that were rising in other European states at the time. The Armenians, a Christian minority in this predominantly Muslim culture, had long been present in the empire, but in the late nineteenth century, as they began to assert themselves collectively, they became increasingly the targets of pogroms and massacres.

The empire's decline greatly concerned an enlightened group of Turkish officers whose party achieved a 1908 victory—welcomed by Muslims, Christians, and Jews alike—under the promise of "Freedom, Justice, Equality, Fraternity." Political instability was unrelieved, however, and by 1911 a dominant faction emerged with the conviction that a strong and unified Turkey was incompatible with a continuing acceptance of minority demands, including those of the Armenians. . . .

Uneasy about losing power to Russian influence, Turkey went to war as Germany's ally. By the winter of 1915, the Turks were in combat against Russian units, many of which were Armenian, along a front that included Turkish provinces with a substantial Armenian population. The stage was set to take a decisive step in the Turkification process. Thus, under the pretext of Armenian disloyalty, the government informed the governors of certain border provinces that a decision had been taken to exterminate all Armenians living in Turkey. There could be no exceptions, for those Armenians innocent today might well be guilty tomorrow. Thus an estimated two-thirds of the 1.8 million Armenians living in Turkey in 1914 were either annihilated outright or marched off to die in the desert.

The scale of Turkish ambitions was more modest than those of the Nazis later, and the Turks lacked some of the detailed biological and demonizing ideology that informed Hitler's policies toward the Jews. But present in the Turkish-Armenian encounter was a calculation of means and ends in which premeditated genocide of a radical kind emerged as the remedy of choice. . . .

The Armenian disaster happened because the calculating rationality of the "Young Turks" in power determined that the most cost-effective way to modernize the Turkish state entailed extermination of a minority group. The Nazis made similar calculations to facilitate their aims for the Third Reich. The difference was that their efforts reached far beyond established German frontiers and sought a Europe—ultimately a world—that would be *Judenrein,* free of Jews altogether. That goal was practically conceivable only through a sophisticated, bureaucratic orchestration of modern technology and transportation. The Nazis were ready when the twentieth century brought the required elements together in an environment of economic upheaval and mass warfare in which everything was permitted. . . .

Study about the Holocaust can provide some understanding of what happened in a particular time and place, why it happened, and how that happening fits into a broader historical pattern. Such understanding, unfortunately, does not constitute a map for the present and the future, at least not one to guarantee that people will stem the tides that kill.

Selection 2

A Brief History of the Holocaust

Holocaust Memorial Center

This article offers an overview of the history of the Holocaust, which traces its beginning to 1933, when Hitler came to power. It describes all of the elements of what we now call the Holocaust, starting with anti-Jewish propaganda and steadily escalating to the isolation of the Jews and the decision to exterminate them. This introduction was taken from the website of the Holocaust Memorial Center in West Bloomfield, Michigan.

*T*he Holocaust (also called *Shoah* in Hebrew) refers to the period from January 30, 1933, when Adolf Hitler became chancellor of Germany, to May 8, 1945 (VE Day), when the war in Europe ended. During this time, Jews in Europe were subjected to progressively harsh persecution that ultimately led to the murder of 6,000,000 Jews (1.5 million of these being children) and the destruction of 5,000 Jewish communities. These deaths represented two-thirds of European Jewry and one-third of world Jewry. The Jews who died were not casualties of the fighting that ravaged Europe during World War II. Rather, they were the victims of Germany's deliberate and systematic attempt to annihilate the entire Jewish population of Europe, a plan Hitler called the "Final Solution" (*Endlösung*).

After its defeat in World War I, Germany was humiliated by the Versailles Treaty, which reduced its prewar territory, drastically reduced its armed forces, demanded the recognition of its guilt for the war, and stipulated it pay reparations to the allied powers. The German Empire destroyed, a new parliamentary government called the Weimar Republic was formed. The republic suffered from economic instability, which grew worse during the worldwide depression after the New York stock market crash in 1929. Massive inflation followed by very high unemployment heightened existing class and political differences and began to undermine the government.

On January 30, 1933, Adolf Hitler, leader of the National Socialist German Workers (Nazi) Party, was named chancellor by president Paul von Hindenburg after the Nazi Party won a significant percentage of the vote in the elections of 1932. The Nazi Party had taken advantage of the political unrest in Germany to gain an electoral foothold. The Nazis incited clashes with the communists, who many feared, disrupted the government with demonstrations, and conduct-

Reprinted from the Holocaust Memorial Center, "A Brief History of the Holocaust," an online article found at www.holocaustcenter.com. Reprinted with permission.

ed a vicious propaganda campaign against its political opponents—the weak Weimar government, and the Jews, whom the Nazis blamed for Germany's ills.

Propaganda: "The Jews Are Our Misfortune!"

A major tool of the Nazis' propaganda assault was the weekly Nazi newspaper *Der Stürmer* (The Attacker). At the bottom of the front page of each issue, in bold letters, the paper proclaimed, "The Jews are our misfortune!" *Der Stürmer* also regularly featured cartoons of Jews in which they were caricatured as hooked-nosed and ape-like. The influence of the newspaper was far-reaching: by 1938 about a half million copies were distributed weekly.

Soon after he became chancellor, Hitler called for new elections in an effort to get full control of the Reichstag, the German parliament, for the Nazis. The Nazis used the government apparatus to terrorize the other parties. They arrested their leaders and banned their political meetings. Then, in the midst of the election campaign, on February 27, 1933, the Reichstag building burned. A Dutchman named Marinus van der Lubbe was arrested for the crime, and he swore he had acted alone. Although many suspected the Nazis were ultimately responsible for the act, the Nazis managed to blame the Communists, thus turning more votes their way.

The fire signaled the demise of German democracy. On the next day, the government, under the pretense of controlling the Communists, abolished individual rights and protections: freedom of the press, assembly, and expression were nullified, as well as the right to privacy. When the elections were held on March 5, the Nazis received nearly 44 percent of the vote, and with 8 percent offered by the Conservatives, won a majority in the government.

The Nazis moved swiftly to consolidate their power into a dictatorship. On March 23, the Enabling Act was passed. It sanctioned Hitler's dictatorial efforts and legally enabled him to pursue them further. The Nazis marshaled their formidable propaganda machine to silence their critics. They also developed a sophisticated police and military force.

The *Sturmabteilung* (S.A., Storm Troopers), a grassroots organization, helped Hitler undermine the German democracy. The Gestapo (*Geheime Staatspolizei*, Secret State Police), a force recruited from professional police officers, was given complete freedom to arrest anyone after February 28. The *Schutzstaffel* (SS, Protection Squad) served as Hitler's personal bodyguard and eventually controlled the concentration camps and the Gestapo. The *Sicherheitsdienst des Reichsführers SS* (S.D., Security Service of the SS) functioned as the Nazis' intelligence service, uncovering enemies and keeping them under surveillance.

With this police infrastructure in place, opponents of the Nazis were terrorized, beaten, or sent to one of the concentration camps the Germans built to incarcerate them. Dachau, just outside of Munich, was the first such camp built for political prisoners. Dachau's purpose changed over time and eventually became another brutal concentration camp for Jews.

By the end of 1934 Hitler was in absolute control of Germany, and his campaign against the Jews in full swing. The Nazis claimed the Jews corrupted pure German culture with their "foreign" and "mongrel" influence. They portrayed the Jews as evil and cowardly, and Germans as hardworking, courageous, and honest. The Jews, the Nazis claimed, who were heavily represented in finance, commerce, the press, literature, theater, and the arts, had weakened Germany's economy and culture. The massive government-supported propaganda machine created a racial anti-Semitism, which was different from the long-standing anti-Semitic tradition of the Christian churches.

The superior race was the "Aryans," the Germans. The word Aryan, [according to author Leni Yahil in *The Holocaust: The Fate of European Jewry*] "derived from the study of linguistics, which started in the eighteenth century and at some point determined that the Indo-Germanic (also known as Aryan) languages were superior in their structures, variety, and vocabulary to the Semitic languages that had evolved in the Near East. This judgment led to a certain conjecture about the character of the peoples who spoke these languages; the conclusion was that the 'Aryan' peoples were likewise superior to the 'Semitic' ones."

The Jews Are Isolated from Society

The Nazis then combined their racial theories with the evolutionary theories of Charles Darwin to justify their treatment of the Jews. The Germans, as the strongest and fittest, were destined to rule, while the weak and racially adulterated Jews were doomed to extinction. Hitler began to restrict the Jews with legislation and terror, which entailed burning books written by Jews, removing Jews from their professions and public schools, confiscating their businesses and property and excluding them from public events. The most infamous of the anti-Jewish legislation were the Nuremberg Laws, enacted on September 15, 1935. They formed the legal basis for the Jews' exclusion from German society and the progressively restrictive Jewish policies of the Germans.

Many Jews attempted to flee Germany, and thousands succeeded by immigrating to such countries as Belgium, Czechoslovakia, England, France and Holland. It was much more difficult to get out of Europe. Jews encountered stiff immigration quotas in most of the world's countries. Even if they obtained the necessary documents, they often had to wait months or years before leaving. Many families out of desperation sent their children first.

In July 1938, representatives of 32 countries met in the French town of Evian to discuss the refugee and immigration problems created by the Nazis in Germany. Nothing substantial was done or decided at the Evian Conference, and it became apparent to Hitler that no one wanted the Jews and that he would not meet resistance in instituting his Jewish policies. By the autumn of 1941, Europe was in effect sealed to most legal emigration. The Jews were trapped.

On November 9–10, 1938, the attacks on the Jews became violent. [On November 7] Hershel Grynszpan, a 17-year-old Jewish boy distraught at the deportation of his family, shot Ernst vom Rath, the third secretary in the German Embassy in Paris, who died on November 9. Nazi hooligans used this assassination as the pretext for instigating a night of destruction that is now known as *Kristallnacht* (the night of broken glass). They looted and destroyed Jewish homes and businesses and burned synagogues. Many Jews were beaten and killed; 30,000 Jews were arrested and sent to concentration camps.

The Jews Are Confined to Ghettos

Germany invaded Poland in September 1939, beginning World War II. Soon after, in 1940, the Nazis began establishing ghettos for the Jews of Poland. More than 10 percent of the Polish population was Jewish, numbering about three million. Jews were forcibly deported from their homes to live in crowded ghettos, isolated from the rest of society. This concentration of the Jewish population later aided the Nazis in their deportation of the Jews to the death camps. The ghettos lacked the necessary food, water, space, and sanitary facilities required by so many people living within their constricted boundaries. Many died of deprivation and starvation.

The "Final Solution"

In June 1941 Germany attacked the Soviet Union and began the "Final Solution." Four mobile killing groups were formed called *Einsatzgruppen* A, B, C and D. Each group contained several commando units. The *Einsatzgruppen* gathered Jews town by town, marched them to huge pits dug earlier, stripped them, lined them up, and shot them with automatic weapons. The dead and dying would fall into the pits to be buried in mass graves. . . . In addition to their operations in the Soviet Union, the *Einsatzgruppen* conducted mass murder in eastern Poland, Estonia, Lithuania and Latvia. It is estimated

that by the end of 1942, the *Einsatzgruppen* had murdered more than 1.3 million Jews.

On January 20, 1942, several top officials of the German government met to officially coordinate the military and civilian administrative branches of the Nazi system to organize a system of mass murder of the Jews. This meeting, called the Wannsee Conference, "marked the beginning of the full-scale, comprehensive extermination operation [of the Jews] and laid the foundations for its organization, which started immediately after the conference ended."

While the Nazis murdered other national and ethnic groups, such as a number of Soviet prisoners of war, Polish intellectuals, and gypsies, only the Jews were marked for systematic and total annihilation. Jews were singled out for "Special Treatment" (*Sonderbehandlung*), which meant that Jewish men, women and children were to be methodically killed with poisonous gas. In the exacting records kept at the Auschwitz death camp, the cause of death of Jews who had been gassed was indicated by "SB," the first letters of the two words that form the German term for "Special Treatment."

By the spring of 1942, the Nazis had established six killing centers (death camps) in Poland: Chelmno (Kulmhof), Belzec, Sobibor, Treblinka, Maidanek and Auschwitz. All were located near railway lines so that Jews could be easily transported daily. A vast system of camps (called *Lagersystem*) supported the death camps. The purpose of these camps varied: some were slave labor camps, some transit camps, others concentration camps and their sub-camps, and still others the notorious death camps. Some camps combined all of these functions or a few of them. All the camps were intolerably brutal.

The major concentration camps were Ravensbruck, Neuengamme, Bergen-Belsen, Sachsenhausen, Gross-Rosen, Buchenwald, Theresienstadt, Flossenburg, Natzweiler-Struthof, Dachau, Mauthausen, Stutthof, and Dora/Nordhausen.

In nearly every country overrun by the Nazis, the Jews were forced to wear badges marking them as Jews, they were rounded up into ghettos or concentration camps and then gradually transported to the killing centers. The death camps were essentially factories for murdering Jews. The Germans shipped thousands of Jews to them each day. Within a few hours of their arrival, the Jews had been stripped of their possessions and valuables, gassed to death, and their bodies burned in specially designed crematoriums. Approximately 3.5 million Jews were murdered in these death camps.

Many healthy, young strong Jews were not killed immediately. The Germans' war effort and the "Final Solution" required a great deal of manpower, so the Germans reserved large pools of Jews for slave labor. These people, imprisoned in concentration and labor camps, were forced to work in German munitions and other factories, such as I.G. Farben and Krupps, and wherever the Nazis needed laborers. They were worked from dawn until dark without adequate food and shelter. Thousands perished, literally worked to death by the Germans and their collaborators.

In the last months of Hitler's Reich, as the German armies retreated, the Nazis began marching the prisoners still alive in the concentration camps to the territory they still controlled. The Germans forced the starving and sick Jews to walk hundreds of miles. Most died or were shot along the way. About a quarter of a million Jews died on the death marches.

Jewish Resistance

The Germans' overwhelming repression and the presence of many collaborators in the various local populations severely limited the ability of the Jews to resist. Jewish resistance did occur, however, in several forms. Staying alive, clean, and observing Jewish religious traditions constituted resistance under the dehumanizing conditions imposed by the Nazis. Other forms of resistance involved escape attempts from the ghettos and camps. Many who succeeded in escaping the ghettos lived in the forests and mountains in family camps and in fighting partisan units. Once free, though, the Jews had to contend with local residents and partisan groups who were often openly hostile. Jews also staged armed revolts in the ghettos of Vilna, Bialystok, Bedzin-Sosnowiec, Cracow, and Warsaw.

The Warsaw Ghetto Uprising was the largest ghetto revolt. Massive deportations (or *Aktions*) had been held in the ghetto from July to September 1942, emptying the ghetto of the majority of Jews imprisoned there. When the Germans entered the ghetto again in January 1943 to remove several thousand more, small unorganized groups of Jews attacked them. After four days, the Germans withdrew from the ghetto, having deported far fewer people than they had intended. The Nazis reentered the ghetto on April 19, 1943, the eve of Passover, to evacuate the remaining Jews and close the ghetto. The Jews, using homemade bombs and stolen or bartered weapons, resisted and withstood the Germans for 27 days. They fought from bunkers and sewers and evaded capture until the Germans burned the ghetto building by building. By May 16 the ghetto was in ruins and the uprising crushed.

Jews also revolted in the death camps of Sobibor, Treblinka and Auschwitz. All of these acts of resistance were largely unsuccessful in the face of the superior German forces, but they were very important spiritually, giving the Jews hope that one day the Nazis would be defeated.

Liberation and the End of War

The camps were liberated gradually, as the Allies advanced on the German army. For example, Maidanek (near Lublin, Poland) was liberated by Soviet forces in July 1944, Auschwitz in January 1945 by the Soviets, Bergen-Belsen (near Hanover, Germany) by the British in April 1945, and Dachau by the Americans in April 1945.

At the end of the war, between 50,000 and 100,000 Jewish survivors were living in three zones of occupation: American, British and Soviet. Within a year, that figure grew to about 200,000. The American zone of occupation contained more than 90 percent of the Jewish displaced persons (DPs). The Jewish DPs would not and could not return to their homes, which brought back such horrible memories and still held the threat of danger from anti-Semitic neighbors. Thus, they languished in DP camps until emigration could be arranged to Palestine, and later Israel, the United States, South America and other countries. The last DP camp closed in 1957.

Below are figures for the number of Jews murdered in each country that came under German domination. They are estimates, as are all figures relating to Holocaust victims. The numbers given here for Czechoslovakia, Hungary and Romania are based on their territorial borders before the 1938 Munich agreement. The total number of six million Jews murdered during the Holocaust, which emerged from the Nuremberg trials, is also an estimate. Numbers have ranged between five and seven million killed.

Country	Number
Africa	.526
Albania	.200
Austria	.65,000
Belgium	.24,387
Czechoslovakia	.277,000
Denmark	.77
Estonia	.4,000
France	.83,000
Germany	.160,000
Greece	.71,301
Hungary	.305,000
Italy	.8,000
Latvia	.85,000
Lithuania	.135,000
Luxembourg	.700
Netherlands	.106,000
Norway	.728
Poland	.3,001,000
Romania	.364,632
Soviet Union	.1,500,000
Yugoslavia	.67,122

Selection 3

The Life of Adolf Hitler

Robert S. Wistrich

Perhaps no man has had more written about him than Adolf Hitler, yet we still do not understand how he could become the greatest threat to the world since Napoleon and the architect of the Final Solution. Ironies abound in his life story. Consider, for example, that this short, dark-haired, relatively unathletic man succeeded in championing a theory of a master race consisting of blond-haired, blue-eyed supermen. He also came to represent Germany though he was born in Austria and did not become a German citizen until 1932 when he decided to run for president. Throughout Hitler's rise to power and prosecution of the war in Europe, he made no secret of his intentions and yet leaders of the Allied nations consistently underestimated him and ignored his declarations. He was one of the most honest politicians of our time, doing in most instances precisely what he said he would do. This is particularly evident in his treatment of the Jews whom he repeatedly promised to exterminate and then set about accomplishing that goal. More than fifty years after his death, writers continue to crank out books on Hitler in hopes of explaining what may be unexplainable, how a man can become so evil. This brief biography is taken from Robert S. Wistrich's book profiling the major figures in Nazi Germany. Wistrich is the Jewish Chronicle Professor of Jewish Studies at University College, London, and holds the Neuberger Chair of modern European history at the Hebrew University of Jerusalem.

Founder and leader of the Nazi Party, Reich Chancellor and guiding spirit of the Third Reich from 1933 to 1945, Head of State and Supreme Commander of the Armed Forces, Adolf Hitler was born in Braunau am Inn, Austria, on 20 April 1889. The son of a fifty-two-year-old Austrian customs official, Alois Schickelgruber Hitler, and his third wife, a young peasant girl, Klara Poelzl, both from the backwoods of lower Austria, the young Hitler was a resentful, discontented child. Moody, lazy, of unstable temperament, he was deeply hostile towards his strict, authoritarian father and strongly attached to his indulgent, hard-working mother, whose death from cancer in December 1908 was a shattering blow to the adolescent Hitler.

After spending four years in the Realschule in Linz, he left school at the age of sixteen with dreams of becoming a painter. In October 1907 the provincial, middle-class boy left home for Vienna, where he was to remain until 1913 leading a bohemian, vagabond existence. Embittered at his rejection by the Viennese Academy of Fine Arts, he was to spend 'five years of misery and woe' in Vienna as he later recalled, adopting a view of life which changed very little in the ensuing years, shaped as it was by a pathological hatred of Jews and Marxists, liberalism and the cosmopolitan Habsburg monarchy.

Existing from hand to mouth on occasional odd jobs and the hawking of sketches in low taverns, the young Hitler compensated for the frustrations of a lonely bachelor's life in miserable male hostels by political harangues in cheap cafes to anyone who would listen and indulging in grandiose dreams of a Greater Germany.

In Vienna he acquired his first education in politics by studying the demagogic techniques of the popular Christian-social Mayor, Karl Lueger, and picked up the stereotyped, obsessive anti-semitism with its brutal, violent sexual connotations and concern with the 'purity of blood' that remained with him to the end of his career. From crackpot racial theorists like the defrocked monk, Lanz von Liebenfels, and the Austrian Pan-German leader, Georg von Schoenerer, the young Hitler learned to discern in the 'Eternal Jew' the symbol and cause of all chaos, corruption and destruction in culture, politics and the economy. The press, prostitution, syphilis, capitalism, Marxism, democracy and pacifism—all were so many means which 'the Jew' exploited in his conspiracy to undermine the German nation and the purity of the creative Aryan race.

Hitler Fights in WWI

In May 1913 Hitler left Vienna for Munich and, when war broke out in August 1914, he joined the Sixteenth Bavarian Infantry Regiment, serving as a despatch runner. Hitler proved an able, courageous soldier, receiving the Iron Cross (First Class) for bravery, but did not rise above the rank of Lance Corporal. Twice wounded, he was badly gassed four weeks before the end of the war and spent three months recuperating in a hospital in Pomerania. Temporarily blinded and driven to impotent rage by the abortive November 1918 revolution in Germany as well as the military defeat, Hitler, once restored, was convinced that fate had chosen him to rescue a humiliated nation from the shackles of the Versailles Treaty, from Bolsheviks and Jews.

Hitler Joins the Party

Assigned by the Reichswehr in the summer of 1919 to 'educational' duties which consisted largely of spying on political parties in the overheated atmosphere of post-revolutionary Munich,

Excerpted from Robert S. Wistrich, "Who's Who in Nazi Germany," an online article found at www.routledge.com/who/germany/hitler. html. Reprinted with permission from Taylor & Francis Books, Ltd.

Hitler was sent to investigate a small nationalistic group of idealists, the German Workers' Party. On 16 September 1919 he entered the Party (which had approximately forty members), soon changed its name to the National Socialist German Workers' Party (NSDAP) and had imposed himself as its Chairman by July 1921.

Hitler discovered a powerful talent for oratory as well as giving the new Party its symbol—the swastika—and its greeting 'Heil!'. His hoarse, grating voice, for all the bombastic, humourless, histrionic content of his speeches, dominated audiences by dint of his tone of impassioned conviction and gift for self-dramatization. By November 1921 Hitler was recognized as Fuhrer of a movement which had 3,000 members, and boosted his personal power by organizing strong-arm squads to keep order at his meetings and break up those of his opponents. Out of these squads grew the storm troopers (SA) organized by Captain Ernst Rohm and Hitler's black-shirted personal bodyguard, the Schutzstaffel (SS).

Hitler focused his propaganda against the Versailles Treaty, the 'November criminals', the Marxists and the visible, internal enemy No. 1, the 'Jew', who was responsible for all Germany's domestic problems. In the twenty-five-point programme of the NSDAP announced on 24 February 1920, the exclusion of the Jews from the Volk community, the myth of Aryan race supremacy and extreme nationalism were combined with 'socialistic' ideas of profit-sharing and nationalization inspired by ideologues like Gottfried Feder. Hitler's first written utterance on political questions dating from this period emphasized that what he called 'the anti-semitism of reason' must lead 'to the systematic combating and elimination of Jewish privileges. Its ultimate goal must implacably be the total removal of the Jews.'

The Beer-Hall Putsch

By November 1923 Hitler was convinced that the Weimar Republic was on the verge of collapse and, together with General Ludendorff and local nationalist groups, sought to overthrow the Bavarian government in Munich. Bursting into a beer-hall in Munich and firing his pistol into the ceiling, he shouted out that he was heading a new provisional government which would carry through a revolution against 'Red Berlin'. Hitler and Ludendorff then marched through Munich at the head of 3,000 men, only to be met by police fire which left sixteen dead and brought the attempted putsch to an ignominious end. Hitler was arrested and tried on 26 February 1924, succeeding in turning the tables on his accusers with a confident, propagandist speech which ended with the prophecy: 'Pronounce us guilty a thousand times over : the goddess of the eternal court of history will smile and tear to pieces the State Prosecutor's submission and the court's verdict for she acquits us.' Sentenced to five years' imprisonment in Landsberg fortress, Hitler was released after only nine months during which he dictated *Mein Kampf* (My Struggle) to his loyal follower, Rudolf Hess. Subsequently the 'bible' of the Nazi Party, this crude, half-baked hotchpotch of primitive Social Darwinism, racial myth, anti-semitism and lebensraum fantasy had sold over five million copies by 1939 and been translated into eleven languages.

The failure of the Beer-Hall putsch and his period of imprisonment transformed Hitler from an incompetent adventurer into a shrewd political tactician, who henceforth decided that he would never again confront the gun barrels of army and police until they were under his command. He concluded that the road to power lay not through force alone but through legal subversion of the Weimar Constitution, the building of a mass movement and the combination of parliamentary strength with extra-parliamentary street terror and intimidation. . . .

The Growth of Nazi Power

In January 1925 the ban on the Nazi Party was removed and Hitler regained permission to speak in public. . . .

Though the Nazi Party won only twelve seats in the 1928 elections, the onset of the Great Depression with its devastating effects on the middle classes helped Hitler to win over all those strata in German society who felt their economic existence was threatened. In addition to peasants, artisans, craftsmen, traders, small businessmen, ex-officers, students and declasse intellectuals, the Nazis in 1929 began to win over the big industrialists, nationalist conservatives and army circles. . . . Hitler played on national resentments, feelings of revolt and the desire for strong leadership using all the most modern techniques of mass persuasion to present himself as Germany's redeemer and messianic saviour.

In the 1930 elections the Nazi vote jumped dramatically from 810,000 to 6,409,000 (18.3 per cent of the total vote) and they received 107 seats in the Reichstag. . . . Hitler officially acquired German citizenship [in 1932] and decided to run for the Presidency, receiving 13,418,011 votes in the run-off elections of 10 April 1931 as against 19,359,650 votes for the victorious von Hindenburg. . . . In the Reichstag elections of July 1932 the Nazis emerged as the largest political party in Germany, obtaining nearly fourteen million votes (37.3 per cent) and 230 seats. Although the NSDAP fell back in November 1932 to eleven million votes (196 seats), Hitler was helped to power by a camarilla of conservative politicians led by Franz von Papen, who persuaded the reluctant von Hindenburg to nominate 'the Bohemian corporal' as Reich Chancellor on 30 January 1933.

Once in the saddle, Hitler moved with great speed to outmanoeuvre his rivals, virtually ousting the conservatives from any real participation in government by July 1933, abolishing the free trade unions, eliminating the communists, Social Democrats and Jews from any role in political life and sweeping opponents into concentration camps. The Reichstag fire of 27 February 1933 had provided him with the perfect pretext to begin consolidating the foundations of a totalitarian one-party State, and special 'enabling laws' were ramrodded through the Reichstag to legalize the regime's intimidatory tactics.

With support from the nationalists, Hitler gained a majority at the last 'democratic' elections held in Germany on 5 March 1933 and with cynical skill he used the whole gamut of persuasion, propaganda, terror and intimidation to secure his hold on power. . . .

Germany Becomes a Dictatorship

The destruction of the radical SA leadership under Ernst Rohm in the Blood Purge of June 1934 confirmed Hitler as undisputed dictator of the Third Reich and by the beginning of August, when he united the positions of Fuhrer and Chancellor on the death of von Hindenburg, he had all the powers of State in his hands. . . .

During the next four years Hitler enjoyed a dazzling string of domestic and international successes, outwitting rival political leaders abroad just as he had defeated his opposition at home. In 1935 he abandoned the Versailles Treaty and began to build up the army by conscripting five times its permitted number. He persuaded Great Britain to allow an increase in the naval building programme and in March 1936 he occupied the demilitarized Rhineland without meeting opposition. He began building up the Luftwaffe and supplied military aid to Francoist forces in Spain, which brought about the Spanish fascist victory in 1939.

The German rearmament programme led to full employment and an unrestrained expansion of production, which reinforced by his foreign policy successes—the Rome-Berlin pact of 1936, the Anschluss with Austria and the 'liberation' of the Sudeten Germans in 1938—brought Hitler to the zenith of his popularity. In February 1938 he dismissed sixteen senior generals and took personal command of the armed forces, thus ensuring that he would be able to implement his aggressive designs.

The Road to War

Hitler's sabre-rattling tactics bludgeoned the British and French into the humiliating Munich agreement of 1938 and the eventual dismantlement of the Czechoslovakian State in March 1939. The concentration camps, the Nuremberg racial laws against the Jews, the persecution of the churches and political dissidents were forgotten by many Germans in the euphoria of Hitler's territorial expansion and bloodless victories. The next designated target for Hitler's ambitions was Poland (her independence guaranteed by Britain and France) and, to avoid a two-front war, the Nazi dictator signed a pact of friendship and non-aggression with Soviet Russia. On 1 September 1939 German armies invaded Poland and henceforth his main energies were devoted to the conduct of a war he had unleashed to dominate Europe and secure Germany's 'living space.'

The first phase of World War II was dominated by German Blitzkrieg tactics: sudden shock attacks against airfields, communications, military installations, using fast mobile armour and infantry to follow up on the first wave of bomber and fighter aircraft. Poland was overrun in [*sic* less than one month], Denmark and Norway in two months, Holland, Belgium, Luxemburg and France in six weeks. After the fall of France in June 1940 only Great Britain stood firm.

The Battle of Britain, in which the Royal Air Force prevented the Luftwaffe from securing aerial control over the English Channel, was Hitler's first setback, causing the planned invasion of the British Isles to be postponed. Hitler turned to the Balkans and North Africa where his Italian allies had suffered defeats, his armies rapidly overrunning Greece, Yugoslavia, the island of Crete and driving the British from Cyrenaica.

The crucial decision of his career, the invasion of Soviet Russia on 22 June 1941, was rationalized by the idea that its destruction would prevent Great Britain from continuing the war with any prospect of success. He was convinced that once he kicked the door in, as he told Jodl (q.v.), 'the whole rotten edifice [of communist rule] will come tumbling down' and the campaign would be over in six weeks. The war against Russia was to be an anti-Bolshevik crusade, a war of annihilation in which the fate of European Jewry would finally be sealed. At the end of January 1939 Hitler had prophesied that 'if the international financial Jewry within and outside Europe should succeed once more in dragging the nations into a war, the result will be, not the Bolshevization of the world and thereby the victory of Jewry, but the annihilation of the Jewish race in Europe'.

America Enters the War

As the war widened—the United States by the end of 1941 had entered the struggle against the Axis powers—Hitler identified the totality of Germany's enemies with 'international Jewry', who supposedly stood behind the British-American-Soviet alliance. The policy of forced emigration had manifestly failed to remove the Jews from Germany's expanded lebensraum, increasing their numbers under German rule as the Wehrmacht moved East.

The widening of the conflict into a world war by the end of 1941, the refusal of the British to accept Germany's right to continental European hegemony (which Hitler attributed to 'Jewish' influence) and to agree to his 'peace' terms, the racial-ideological nature of the assault on Soviet Russia, finally drove Hitler to implement the 'Final Solution of the Jewish Question' which had been under consideration since 1939. The measures already taken in those regions of Poland annexed to the Reich against Jews (and Poles) indicated the genocidal implications of Nazi-style 'Germanization' policies. The invasion of Soviet Russia was to set the seal on Hitler's notion of territorial conquest in the East, which was inextricably linked with annihilating the 'biological roots of Bolshevism' and hence with the liquidation of all Jews under German rule.

At first the German armies carried all before them, overrunning vast territories, overwhelming the Red Army, encircling Leningrad and reaching within striking distance of Moscow. Within a few months of the invasion Hitler's armies had extended the Third Reich from the Atlantic to the Caucasus, from the Baltic to the Black Sea. But the Soviet Union did not collapse as expected. . . . Underestimating the depth of military reserves on which the Russians could call, the calibre of their generals and the resilient, fighting spirit of the Russian people (whom he dismissed as inferior peasants), Hitler prematurely proclaimed in October 1941 that the Soviet Union had been 'struck down and would never rise again'. In reality he had overlooked the pitiless Russian winter to which his

Adolf Hitler

own troops were now condemned and which forced the Wehrmacht to abandon the highly mobile warfare which had previously brought such spectacular successes. . . .

Hitler now assumed personal control of all military operations, refusing to listen to advice, disregarding unpalatable facts and rejecting everything that did not fit into his preconceived picture of reality. His neglect of the Mediterranean theatre and the Middle East, the failure of the Italians, the entry of the United States into the war, and above all the stubborn determination of the Russians, pushed Hitler on to the defensive. From the winter of 1941 the writing was on the wall but Hitler refused to countenance military defeat, believing that implacable will and the rigid refusal to abandon positions could make up for inferior resources and the lack of a sound overall strategy.

Convinced that his own General Staff was weak and indecisive, if not openly treacherous, Hitler became more prone to outbursts of

blind, hysterical fury towards his generals, when he did not retreat into bouts of misanthropic brooding. His health, too, deteriorated under the impact of the drugs prescribed by his quack physician, Dr Theodor Morell. Hitler's personal decline, symbolized by his increasingly rare public appearances and his self-enforced isolation in the 'Wolf's Lair', his headquarters buried deep in the East Prussian forests, coincided with the visible signs of the coming German defeat which became apparent in mid-1942.

The Collapse of the Third Reich

Rommel's defeat at El Alamein and the subsequent loss of North Africa to the Anglo-American forces were overshadowed by the disaster at Stalingrad where General von Paulus's Sixth Army was cut off and surrendered to the Russians in January 1943. In July 1943 the Allies captured Sicily and Mussolini's regime collapsed in Italy. In September the Italians signed an armistice and the Allies landed at Salerno, reaching Naples on 1 October and taking Rome on 4 June 1944. The Allied invasion of Normandy followed on 6 June 1944 and soon a million Allied troops were driving the German armies eastwards, while from the opposite direction the Soviet forces advanced relentlessly on the Reich. The total mobilization of the German war economy under Albert Speer and the energetic propaganda efforts of Joseph Goebbels to rouse the fighting spirit of the German people were impotent to change the fact that the Third Reich lacked the resources equal to a struggle against the world alliance which Hitler himself had provoked.

Allied bombing began to have a telling effect on German industrial production and to undermine the morale of the population. The generals, frustrated by Hitler's total refusal to trust them in the field and recognizing the inevitability of defeat, planned, together with the small anti-Nazi Resistance inside the Reich, to assassinate the Fuhrer on 20 July 1944, hoping to pave the way for a negotiated peace with the Allies that would save Germany from destruction. The plot failed and Hitler took implacable vengeance on the conspirators, watching with satisfaction a film of the grisly executions carried out on his orders.

As disaster came closer, Hitler buried himself in the unreal world of the Fuhrerbunker in Berlin, clutching at fantastic hopes that his 'secret weapons', the V-1 and V-2 rockets, would yet turn the tide of war. He gestured wildly over maps, planned and directed attacks with non-existent armies and indulged in endless, night-long monologues which reflected his growing senility, misanthropy and contempt for the 'cowardly failure' of the German people.

As the Red Army approached Berlin and the Anglo-Americans reached the Elbe, on 19 March 1945 Hitler ordered the destruction of what remained of German industry, communications and transport systems. He was resolved that, if he did not survive, Germany too should be destroyed. . . .

On 29 April 1945 he married his mistress Eva Braun and dictated his final political testament, concluding with the same monotonous, obses-sive fixation that had guided his career from the beginning: 'Above all I charge the leaders of the nation and those under them to scrupulous observance of the laws of race and to merciless opposition to the universal poisoner of all peoples, international Jewry.'

The following day Hitler committed suicide, shooting himself through the mouth with a pistol. His body was carried into the garden of the Reich Chancellery by aides, covered with petrol and burned along with that of Eva Braun. This final, macabre act of self-destruction appropriately symbolized the career of a political leader whose main legacy to Europe was the ruin of its civilization and the senseless sacrifice of human life for the sake of power and his own commitment to the bestial nonsense of National Socialist race mythology. With his death nothing was left of the 'Greater Germanic Reich', of the tyrannical power structure and ideological system which had devastated Europe during the twelve years of his totalitarian rule.

Selection 4

The Nuremberg Laws

Lucy S. Dawidowicz

Looking back on World War II, it is typical to think of Hitler as a dictator who seized power and ruthlessly murdered the Jews. It is important, however, to remember that Hitler was democratically elected. The Nazi Party was supported by a significant proportion of the German people. Moreover, Hitler used legal means to concentrate power in his hands (of course, he also used terror to eliminate his opponents). In January 1933 Hitler became chancellor. When a Dutch Commu-nist set fire to the Reichstag, *the German parliament building, Hitler blamed the fire on the Communists, outlawed their party, and arrested their leaders. The following month Germany held its last free election. The Nazis won only 43 percent of the vote; nevertheless, the Reichstag passed the Enabling Act, which gave Hitler dictatorial powers. He used them to abolish trade unions, dismantle all competing parties, and eliminate his political opponents. Though terror was also used against the Jews, persecution in the early years was done primarily through increasingly restrictive legislation that prevented them from working, attending school, or functioning as normal members of German society. This excerpt discusses the anti-Jewish legislation adopted by the Nazis, which foreshadowed the extralegal measures taken later. The late Lucy S. Dawidowicz was one of the leading Holocaust authors. She taught modern Jewish history at Yeshiva University, Stanford, and the State University of New York at Albany. She wrote several books on the Holocaust, including the seminal work from which this excerpt is taken.*

*T*he legislation that Hitler's government began to enact sanctioned what violence had already accomplished to a considerable extent—the elimination of Jews from government service and public life. On April 7, two days after Hitler's letter to [President Paul von] Hindenburg promising a "legal" solution to the "Jewish problem," the first anti-Jewish law in the Third Reich was promulgated. Eventually, some four hundred laws and decrees were enacted, inexorably leading to the destruction of the European Jews. The first decree, entitled "Law for the Restoration of the Professional Civil Service," authorized the elimination from the civil service of Jews and political opponents of the Nazi regime. "Civil servants of non-Aryan descent must retire," and honorary officials "must be discharged." Hindenburg's objections were met in a paragraph exempting "officials who were already employed as civil servants on or before August 1, 1914, or who, during the World War, fought at the front for Germany or her allies, or whose fathers or sons were killed in action in the World War."

A companion law, promulgated at the same time, canceled the admission to the bar of lawyers of "non-Aryan" descent and denied

Excerpted from Lucy Dawidowicz, *The War Against the Jews.* Copyright © 1975 Lucy Dawidowicz. Reprinted with permission from Henry Holt & Co.

permission to those already admitted to practice law, with the Hindenburg exemptions. In rapid succession came similar laws excluding Jews from posts as lay assessors, jurors, and commercial judges (April 7), patent lawyers (April 22), panel physicians in state social-insurance institutions (April 22), dentists and dental technicians associated with those institutions (June 2). On April 25 the Law Against the Overcrowding of German Schools and Institutions of Higher Learning was promulgated, limiting the attendance of "non-Aryan" Germans to a proportion to be "determined uniformly for the entire Reich territory." An accompanying executive decree set that ratio for the admission of new pupils at 1.5 percent until the proportion of "non-Aryans" would be reduced to a maximum of 5 percent. On May 6 the Law for the Restoration of the Professional Civil Service was extended to affect honorary professors, university lecturers, and notaries. With the promulgation of three more laws—the first forbidding the employment by government authorities of "non-Aryans" or of persons married to them (September 28, 1933); the second establishing a Reich Chamber of Culture (September 29, 1933), which saw to the exclusion of Jews from cultural and entertainment enterprises (art, literature, theater, motion pictures); and the third, the National Press Law (October 4, 1933), placing political newspapers under state supervision and applying the so-called Aryan paragraph to newspapermen—the Nazi regime had accomplished a cardinal objective toward which German professionals and academicians had striven as far back as 1847: the exclusion of Jews from public life, government, culture, and the professions.

To simplify and clarify this procedure, a decree defining a "non-Aryan" promulgated on April 11. A "non-Aryan" was anyone "descended from non-Aryan, especially Jewish, parents or grandparents." Descent was "non-Aryan" even if only one parent or grandparent was "non-Aryan": "This is to be assumed especially if one parent or grandparent was of Jewish faith." Thus, in cases of "racial" ambiguity, the religious affiliation would be decisive. Every civil servant had to prove "Aryan" descent, through submission of the appropriate documents—birth certificates and parents' marriage certificate. (Eventually, elaborate genealogical questionnaires had to be answered.) Finally, to deal with ambiguous or exceptional cases, the decree provided that "if Aryan descent is doubtful, an opinion must be obtained from the expert on racial research attached by the Reich Minister of the Interior."

What Is a Jew?

The Nazi definition was simple: a Jew is a Jew is a Jew—that is, down to the third generation. The files of the Ministry of the Interior probably bulged with legal formulas defining who was a Jew. . . .

Three other laws were promulgated in 1933. . . . On April 21, a law was promulgated banning *shehitah*, Jewish ritual slaughtering animals for food. . . .

The Law on the Revocation of Naturalization and Annulment of German Citizenship, promulgated July 14, canceled . . . naturalization of "undesirables," which had been granted during the lifetime of the Weimar Republic. The law's executive order (July 26) specified East European Jews as political undesirables, even if they had committed no offense. On September 29 the Hereditary Farm Law was issued, stipulating that only those farmers could inherit farm property who could prove that their ancestors had no Jewish blood as far back as 1800. . . .

With German thoroughness, the laws had seen to it that the Jews were dismissed from all positions in public life—government, professions, and all of Germany's social, educational, and cultural institutions. Both instrumental and affective purposes were served by the enactment of this legislation. For one thing, thousands of jobs became available. Furthermore, the ouster of the Jews brought high elation, solidified party loyalty, and augmented party strength. What had begun as popular anti-Semitism, when the taste of victory had stimulated the taste for blood, now received complete legal sanction. . . .

More Terror

At the end of March 1935 acts of terror and boycotts of Jewish businesses were renewed. All local and national NSDAP [Nazi] party organizations and their associated institutions joined in a massive discharge of hate and violence. During the summer of 1935 Jews were prevented from going into cinemas, theaters, swimming pools, resorts. Small businesses were paralyzed by boycott and by violence, particularly in Berlin's main shopping street. Jewish newspapers were forced to suspend publication for periods of two to three months. . . .

A 1935 photo of a German road sign reads "The Jews Are Uninvited Guests."

As once before in 1933, so now in 1935, the violence of anti-Semitism was channeled into law. On the occasion of the annual NSDAP congress in Nuremberg, new anti-Jewish laws, the so-called "Nuremberg Laws," were adopted unanimously by the Reichstag, on September 15, 1935. These laws legitimated racist anti-Semitism and turned the "purity of German blood" into a legal category. They forbade marriage and extramarital relations between Germans and Jews and disenfranchised those "subjects" or "nationals" of Germany who were not of German blood. . . .

Anti-Jewish Legislation

Before long the Law for the Protection of German Blood and German Honor . . . was completed. Its preamble declared:

Imbued with the insight that the purity of German blood is prerequisite for the continued existence of the German people, and inspired by the inflexible will to ensure the existence of the German nation for all times, the Reichstag has unanimously adopted the following law, which is hereby promulgated.

The provisions were simplicity itself: marriage between Jews and "nationals of German kindred blood" was forbidden; extramarital relations between the two groups were forbidden. Jews were forbidden to employ female domestic help under forty-five years of age who were of "German or kindred blood." Finally, Jews were forbidden to fly the German national colors, but could display "Jewish" colors.

Then Hitler asked them to prepare a basic Reich citizenship law. . . . This law gave the Jews a special status as subjects in Germany. . . . The Reich Citizenship Law distinguished between a subject *(Staatsangehörige)* and a citizen of the Reich *(Reichsbürger).* A subject was anyone who enjoyed the protection of the Reich and was therefore obligated to it. A Reich citizen was a subject with "German or cognate blood" and acquired a "Reich certificate of citizenship," a reward that Hitler had already conceived in *Mein Kampf.* . . .

The Reich Citizenship Law perpetrated a fantastic hoax upon the Germans. The Reich citizen was declared to be the "sole bearer of full political rights." But rights no longer existed in Germany. There were no political parties, no elections, no freedoms, no protection. The only right a citizen had was to give his assent—by shouting himself hoarse at mass rallies or by voting *"Ja"* in one of the five plebiscites that Hitler had substituted for political democracy. For unless the Reich citizen was *kadavergehorsam* [slavishly obedient], he would more likely be cadaver than citizen.

The Jews, however, were not hoaxed. The law and its thirteen supplementary decrees (the last published July 1, 1943) set the Jews apart from the Germans legally, politically, socially. Henceforth, they would be outside the protection of the state. Eventually, they would be completely at the mercy of the secret police, without access to law or courts. Indeed, the *Sachsenspiegel* [a thirteenth-century authoritative legal code in northern Germany] had been far more humane in the protection it afforded the Jew as alien.

The centrality of "blood and race" that obsessed National Socialism was transformed with bureaucratic fastidiousness into legal racial categories. While drafting the Law for the Protection of German Blood and German Honor, the legal experts proposed certain distinctions among different categories of *Mischlinge,* the "mixed" offspring of Germans and Jews. Hitler had rejected these at the time, but left their legal clarification for supplementary decrees. After week-long conferences of legal and racial experts (Hitler had himself called a meeting on this subject), the Ministry of the Interior finally arrived at a set of definitions of the different categories of Mischlinge. The basic definition of a Jew, supplanting the definition of April 11, 1933, was published November 14, 1935, in the first supplementary decree to the Reich Citizenship Law. Later regulations defined categories of Mischlinge that did not come under the rubric of "Jew."

Briefly, the categories were: (1) Jew, (2) Mischling, first degree, and (3) Mischling, second degree. A Jew was anyone with at least three full Jewish grandparents. Also legally to be regarded as a Jew was someone who had two full Jewish grandparents and who belonged to the Jewish religious community when the law was promulgated September 15, 1935, or who joined later, or who was married to a Jew then or later, or (looking to the future) who was the offspring of a marriage contracted with a Jew after September 15, 1935, or who was born out of wedlock after July 31, 1936, the offspring of extramarital relations with a Jew. Anyone who was one-eighth or one-sixteenth Jewish—with one Jewish great-grandparent or great-great-grandparent—would be considered as of German blood.

More complicated was the status of the "part-Jews." A person with two Jewish grandparents, who did not otherwise fit into the group defined as Jews, that is, who was not affiliated with the Jewish religious community, who was not married to a Jew, etc., was designated as "Mis-chling, first degree." A person with only one Jewish grandparent was designated as "Mis-chling, second degree." For the time being, these distinctions affected marriage and offspring of that marriage. Within a few short years they were to decide between life or death.

The Nuremberg Laws completed the disen-franchisement of the Jews of Germany. The first stage of the National Socialist program had been achieved. Hitler himself, in introducing the laws to the Reichstag assembled at Nuremberg, hinted at a forthcoming change in anti-Jewish policy. The Law for the Protection of German Blood and German Honor, he said, was "an attempt to regu-late by law a problem that, in the event of repeat-ed failure, would have to be transferred by law to the National Socialist Party for final solution."

Selection 5

Jews in Germany: From Citizens to Outcasts

Saul Friedländer

Adolf Hitler never hid his attitude toward the Jews or his intention to exterminate them. One of the incredible aspects of the Holocaust is how he put his goal into practice in a coun-try considered the most sophisticated and civ-ilized in Europe, and where Jews played such a prominent role in virtually every part of so-ciety. Whatever his desires, Hitler could not immediately begin the "Final Solution" after coming to power in 1933. A slow, methodical process was required to make respectable German Jews outcasts and to dehumanize them to the point where they could be mur-dered with impunity. This excerpt describes how the persecution of the Jews escalated from banning Jewish musicians from per-forming to taking away their citizenship and ultimately their lives. Saul Friedländer grew up in Nazi-occupied France. Considered one of the leading authorities on the Holocaust, he teaches at the University of California at Los Angeles and at Tel Aviv University.

The exodus from Germany of Jewish and left-wing artists and intellectuals began during the early months of 1933, almost immediately after Adolf Hitler's accession to power on January 30. The philosopher and liter-ary critic Walter Benjamin left Berlin for Paris on March 18. Two days later he wrote to his col-league and friend, Gershom Scholem, who lived in Palestine: "I can at least be certain that I did not act on impulse. . . . Nobody among those who are close to me judges the matter differently." The novelist Lion Feuchtwanger, who had reached the safety of Switzerland, confided in his fellow writer Arnold Zweig: "It was too late for me to save anything. . . . All that was there is lost."

The conductors Otto Klemperer and Bruno Walter were compelled to flee. Walter was forbidden access to his Leipzig orchestra, and, as he was about to conduct a special concert of the Berlin Philharmonic, he was informed that, according to rumors circulated by the Propaganda Ministry, the hall of the Philharmonic would be burned down if he did not withdraw. Walter left the country. Hans Hinkel, the new president of the Prussian Theater Commission and also responsible for the "de-Judaization" of cultural life in Prussia, explained in the April 6 *Frankfurter Zeitung* that Klemperer and Walter had disappeared from the musical scene because there was no way to protect them against the "mood" of a German public long provoked by "Jewish artistic bankrupters.". . .

Albert Einstein was visiting the United States on January 30, 1933. It did not take him long to react. Describing what was happening in Germany as a "psychic illness of the masses," he ended his return journey in Ostend (Belgium) and never again set foot on German soil. The Kaiser Wilhelm Society dismissed him from his position; the Prussian Academy of Sciences expelled him; his citizenship was rescinded. Einstein was no longer a German. . . .

As peripheral as it may seem in hindsight, the cultural domain was the first from which Jews (and "leftists") were massively expelled. . . . Thus, even before launching their first systematic anti-Jewish measures of exclusion, the new rulers of Germany had turned against the most visible representative of the "Jewish spirit" that henceforth was to be eradicated. In general the major anti-Jewish measures the Nazis would take from then on in the various domains were not only acts of terror but also symbolic statements. . . . The regime's initiatives engendered a kind of split consciousness in a great part of the population: For instance, people might not agree with the brutality of the dismissals of Jewish intellectuals from their positions, but they welcomed the cleansing of the "excessive influence" of Jews from German cultural life. . . .

Jews Stay Calm

A benefit for Jewish handicrafts had taken place at Berlin's Café Leon on January 30, 1933. The news of Hitler's accession to the chancellorship became known shortly before the event began. Among the attending representatives of Jewish organizations and political movements, only the Zionist rabbi Hans Tramer referred to the news and spoke of it as a major change; all the other speakers kept to their announced subjects. Tramer's speech "made no impression. The entire audience considered it panic-mongering. There was no response." The board of the Central Association of German Citizens of the Jewish Faith (Zentralverein deutscher Staatsbürger jüdischen Glaubens) on the same day concluded a public declaration in the same spirit: "In general, today more than ever we must follow the directive: wait calmly." An editorial in the association's newspaper for January 30, written by the organization's chairman, Ludwig Hollander, was slightly more worried in tone, but showed basically the same stance: "The German Jews will not lose the calm they derive from their tie to all that is truly German. Less than ever will they allow external attacks, which they consider unjustified, to influence their inner attitude toward Germany."

By and large there was no apparent sense of panic or even of urgency among the great majority of the approximately 525,000 Jews living in Germany in January 1933. As the weeks went by, Max Naumann's Association of National German Jews and the Reich Association of Jewish War Veterans hoped for no less than integration into the new order of things. On April 4, the veterans' association chairman, Leo Löwenstein, addressed a petition to Hitler including a list of nationalistically oriented suggestions regarding the Jews of Germany, as well as a copy of the memorial book containing the names of the twelve thousand German soldiers of Jewish origin who had died for Germany during the World War. Ministerial Councillor Wienstein answered on April 14 that the chancellor acknowledged receipt of the letter and the book with "sincerest feelings." The head of the Chancellery, Hans Heinrich Lammers, received a delegation of the veterans on the twenty-eighth, but with that the contacts ceased. Soon Hitler's office stopped acknowledging petitions from the Jewish organization. Like the Central Association, the Zionists continued to believe that the initial upheavals could be overcome by a reassertion of Jewish identity or simply by patience; the Jews reasoned that the responsibilities of power, the influence of conservative members of the government, and a watchful outside world would exercise a moderating influence on any Nazi tendency to excess.

Even after the April 1 Nazi boycott of Jewish businesses, some well-known German-Jewish figures, such as Rabbi Joachim Prinz, declared that it was unreasonable to take an anti-Nazi position. For Prinz, arguing against Germany's "reorganization," whose aim was "to give people bread and work . . . was neither intended nor possible." The declaration may have been merely tactical, and it must be kept in mind that many Jews were at a loss how to react. . . .

For some Jews the continuing presence of the old, respected President Paul von Hindenburg as head of state was a source of confidence; they occasionally wrote to him about their distress. "I was engaged to be married in 1914," Frieda Friedmann, a Berlin woman, wrote to Hindenburg on February 23: "My fiancé was killed in action in 1914. My brothers Max and Julius Cohn were killed in 1916 and 1918. My remaining brother, Willy, came back blind. . . . All three received the Iron Cross for their service to the country. But now it has gone so far that in our country pamphlets saying, 'Jews, get out!' are being distributed on the streets, and there are open calls for pogroms and acts of violence against Jews. . . . Is incitement against Jews a sign of courage or one of cowardice when Jews comprise only one percent of the German people?" Hindenburg's office promptly acknowledged receipt of the letter, and the president let Frieda Friedmann know that he was decidedly opposed to excesses perpetrated against Jews. The letter

was transmitted to Hitler, who wrote in the margin: "This lady's claims are a swindle! Obviously there has been no incitement to a pogrom!"

The Jews finally, like a considerable part of German society as a whole, were not sure—particularly before the March 5, 1933, Reichstag elections—whether the Nazis were in power to stay or whether a conservative military coup against them was still possible. . . .

Hitler Becomes Dictator

The primary political targets of the new regime and of its terror system, at least during the first months after the Nazi accession to power, were not Jews but Communists. After the Reichstag fire of February 27, the anti-Communist hunt led to the arrest of almost ten thousand party members and sympathizers and to their imprisonment in newly created concentration camps. Dachau had been established on March 20 and was officially inaugurated by SS chief Heinrich Himmler on April 1. In June, SS Group Leader Theodor Eicke became the camp's commander, and a year later he was appointed "inspector of concentration camps": Under Himmler's aegis he had become the architect of the life-and-death routine of the camp inmates in Hitler's new Germany.

After the mass arrests that followed the Reichstag fire, it was clear that the "Communist threat" no longer existed. But the new regime's frenzy of repression—and innovation—did not slacken; quite the contrary. A presidential decree of February 28 had already given Hitler emergency powers. Although the Nazis failed to gain an absolute majority in the March 5 elections, their coalition with the ultraconservative German National People's Party (Deutschnationale Volkspartei, or DNVP) obtained it. A few days later, on March 23, the Reichstag divested itself of its functions by passing the Enabling Act, which gave full legislative and executive powers to the chancellor (at the outset new legislation was discussed with the cabinet ministers, but the final decision was Hitler's). The rapidity of changes that followed was stunning: The states were brought into line; in May the trade unions were abolished and replaced by the German Labor Front; in July all political parties were dissolved with the sole exception of the National Socialist German Workers Party (Nationalsozialistische Deutsche Arbeiterpartei, or NSDAP). Popular support for this torrential activity and constant demonstration of power snowballed. In the eyes of a rapidly growing number of Germans, a "national revival" was under way. . . .

Anti-Jewish violence spread after the March elections. On the ninth, Storm Troopers (Sturmabteilung, or SA) seized dozens of East European Jews in the Scheunenviertel, one of Berlin's Jewish quarters. Traditionally the first targets of German Jew-hatred, these *Ostjuden* were also the first Jews as Jews to be sent off to concentration camps. On March 13 forcible closing of Jewish shops was imposed by the local SA in Mannheim; in Breslau, Jewish lawyers and judges were assaulted in the court building; and in Gedern, in Hesse, the SA broke into Jewish homes and beat up the inhabitants "with the acclamation of a rapidly growing crowd." The list of similar incidents is a long one. There were also killings. . . .

Much of the foreign press gave wide coverage to the Nazi violence. The *Christian Science Monitor*, however, expressed doubts about the accuracy of the reports of Nazi atrocities, and later justified retaliation against "those who spread lies against Germany." And Walter Lippmann, the most prominent American political commentator of the day and himself a Jew, found words of praise for Hitler and could not resist a sideswipe at the Jews. These notable exceptions notwithstanding, most American newspapers did not mince words about the anti-Jewish persecution. Jewish and non-Jewish protests grew. These very protests became the Nazis' pretext for the notorious April 1, 1933, boycott of Jewish businesses. Although the anti-Nazi campaign in the United States was discussed at some length during a cabinet meeting on March 24, the final decision in favor of the boycott was probably made during a March 26 meeting of Hitler and Goebbels in Berchtesgaden. But in mid-March, Hitler had already allowed a committee headed by Julius

Streicher, party chief of Franconia and editor of the party's most vicious anti-Jewish newspaper, *Der Stürmer*, to proceed with preparatory work for it.

Jews Are Boycotted

In fact, the boycott had been predictable from the very moment the Nazis acceded to power. The possibility had often been mentioned during the two preceding years, when Jewish small businesses had been increasingly harassed and Jewish employees increasingly discriminated against in the job market. . . .

Hitler informed the cabinet of the planned boycott of Jewish-owned businesses on March 29, telling the ministers that he himself had called for it. He described the alternative as spontaneous popular violence. An approved boycott, he added, would avoid dangerous unrest. The German National ministers objected, and President Hindenburg tried to intervene. Hitler rejected any possible cancellation, but two days later (the day before the scheduled boycott) he suggested the possibility of postponing it until April 4—if the British and American governments were to declare immediately their opposition to the anti-German agitation in their countries; if not, the action would take place on April 1, to be followed by a waiting period until April 4.

On the evening of the thirty-first, the British and American governments, declared their readiness to make the necessary declaration. . . .

In the meantime Jewish leaders, mainly in the United States and Palestine, were in a quandary: Should they support mass protests and a counterboycott of German goods, or should confrontation be avoided for fear of further "reprisals" against the Jews of Germany? [Nazi minister Hermann] Göring had summoned several leaders of German Jewry and sent them to London to intervene against planned anti-German demonstrations and initiatives. Simultaneously, on March 26, Kurt Blumenfeld, president of the Zionist Federation for Germany, and Julius Brodnitz, president of the Central Association, cabled the American Jewish Committee in New York:

WE PROTEST CATEGORICALLY AGAINST HOLDING MONDAY MEETING, RADIO AND OTHER DEMONSTRATIONS. WE UNEQUIVOCALLY DEMAND ENERGETIC EFFORTS TO OBTAIN AN END TO DEMONSTRATIONS HOSTILE TO GERMANY. By appeasing the Nazis the fearful German-Jewish leaders were hoping to avoid the boycott.

The leaders of the Jewish community in Palestine also opted for caution, the pressure of public opinion notwithstanding. They sent a telegram to the Reich Chancellery "offering assurances that no authorized body in Palestine had declared or intended to declare a trade boycott of Germany." American Jewish leaders were divided; most of the Jewish organizations in the United States were opposed to mass demonstrations and economic action, mainly for fear of embarrassing the president and the State Department. Reluctantly, and under pressure from such groups as the Jewish War Veterans, the American Jewish Congress finally decided otherwise. On March 27 protest meetings took place in several American cities, with the participation of church and labor leaders. As for the boycott of German goods, it spread as an emotional grass-roots movement that, over the months, received an increasing measure of institutional support, at least outside Palestine. . . .

In principle the boycott could have caused serious economic damage to the Jewish population as, according to [historian] Avraham Barkai, "more than sixty percent of all gainfully employed Jews were concentrated in the commercial sector, the overwhelming majority of these in the retail trade. . . . Similarly, Jews in the industrial and crafts sectors were active largely as proprietors of small businesses and shops or as artisans." In reality, however, the Nazi action ran into immediate problems.

The population proved rather indifferent to the boycott and sometimes even intent on buying in "Jewish" stores. . . .

The lack of popular enthusiasm was compounded by a host of unforeseen questions. How was a "Jewish" enterprise to be defined? By its name, by the Jewishness of its directors, or by Jewish control of all or part of its capital? If the

A sign reading "Germans! Defend Yourselves! Don't Buy from Jews!" hangs outside a shop during the Nazi boycott of Jewish-owned businesses.

enterprise were hurt, what, in a time of economic crisis, would happen to its Aryan employees? What would be the overall consequences, in terms of possible foreign retaliation, of the action on the German economy? . . .

The possibility of further boycotts remained open. . . .

At the same time it was nonetheless becoming increasingly clear to Hitler himself that Jewish economic life was not to be openly interfered with, at least as long as the German economy was still in a precarious situation. A fear of foreign economic retaliation, whether orchestrated by the Jews or as an expression of genuine outrage at Nazi persecutions, was shared by Nazis and their conservative allies alike and dictated temporary moderation. . . .

According to the German Communist periodical *Rundschau*, by then published in Switzerland, only the smaller Jewish businesses—that is, the poorer Jews—were harmed by the Nazi boycott. Large enterprises such as the Berlin-based Ullstein publishing empire or Jewish-owned banks—Jewish big business—did not suffer at all. What looks like merely an expression of Marxist orthodoxy was in part true, because harming a Jewish department-store chain such as Tietz could have put its fourteen thousand employees out of work. For that very reason Hitler personally approved the granting of a loan to Tietz to ease its immediate financial difficulties. . . .

In March 1933, when Hans Luther was replaced by [Hjalmar] Schacht as president of the Reichsbank, three Jewish bankers still remained on the bank's eight-member council and signed the authorization of his appointment. This situation did not last much longer. As a result of Schacht's proddings and the party's steady pressure, the country's banks banished Jewish directors from their boards. . . .

During the first years of the regime, however, there are indications of a somewhat unexpected moderation and even helpfulness on the part of big business in its dealing with non-Aryan firms. Pressure for business takeovers and other ruthless exploitation of the weakened status of Jews came mainly from smaller, midsized enterprises, and much less so, at least until the fall of 1937, from the higher reaches of the economy. Some major corporations even retained the services of Jewish executives for years. But some precautions were taken. Thus, although most Jewish board members of the chemical industry giant I.G. Farben stayed on for a while, the closest Jewish associates of its president, Carl Bosch, such as Ernst Schwarz and Edmund Pietrowski, were reassigned to positions outside the Reich, the former in New York, the latter in Switzerland.

Highly visible Jews had to go, of course. Within a few months, the banker Max Warburg was excluded from one corporate board after another. . . .

Aryanization

When the Nazis acceded to power, they could in principle refer to the goals of their anti-Jewish policy as set down in the twenty-five-point party program of February 24, 1920. Points 4, 5, 6, and 8 dealt with concrete aspects of the "Jewish question." Point 4: "Only members of the nation may be citizens of the State. Only those of German blood, whatever their creed, may be members of the nation. Accordingly no Jew may be a member of the nation." Point 5: "Non-citizens may live in Germany only as guests and must be subject to laws for aliens." Point 6: "The right to vote on the state's government and legislation shall be enjoyed by the citizens of the state alone." Point 8: "All non-German immigration must be prevented. We demand that all non-Germans who entered Germany after 2 August 1914 shall be required to leave the Reich forthwith." Point 23 demanded that control of the German press be solely in the hands of Germans.

Nothing in the program indicated ways of achieving these goals, and the failure of the April 1933 boycott is a good example of the total lack of preparation for their tasks among Germany's new masters. But, at least in their anti-Jewish policy, the Nazis soon became masters of improvisation; adopting the main points of their 1920 program as short-term goals, they learned how to pursue them ever more systematically.

On March 9 State Secretary Heinrich Lammers conveyed a request from the Reich chancellor to Minister of the Interior Frick. He was asked by Hitler to take into consideration the suggestion of State Secretary Paul Bang of the Ministry of the Economy about the application of "a racial [*völkisch*] policy" toward East European Jews: prohibition of further immigration, cancellation of name changes made after 1918, and expulsion of a certain number of those who had not yet been naturalized. Within a week Frick responded by sending instructions to all states (*Länder*):

> In order to introduce a racial policy (*völkische Politik*), it is necessary to:
>
> 1. Oppose the immigration of Eastern Jews.
> 2. Expel Eastern Jews living in Germany without a residence permit.
> 3. Stop the naturalization of Eastern Jews. . . .

The measures taken against the so-called

Eastern Jews were overshadowed by the laws of April 1933. The first of them—the most fundamental one because of its definition of the Jew—was the April 7 Law for the Restoration of the Professional Civil Service. In its most general intent, the law aimed at reshaping the entire government bureaucracy in order to ensure its loyalty to the new regime. Applying to more than two million state and municipal employees, its exclusionary measures were directed against the politically unreliable, mainly Communists and other opponents of the Nazis, and against Jews. Paragraph 3, which came to be called the "Aryan paragraph," reads: "1. Civil servants not of Aryan origin are to retire. . . ." (Section 2 listed exceptions, which will be examined later.) On April 11 the law's first supplementary decree defined "non-Aryan" as "anyone descended from non-Aryan, particularly Jewish, parents or grandparents. It suffices if one parent or grandparent is non-Aryan.". . .

For the first time since completion of the emancipation of the German Jews in 1871, a government, by law, had reintroduced discrimination against the Jews. Up to this point the Nazis had unleashed the most extreme anti-Jewish propaganda and brutalized, boycotted, or killed Jews on the assumption that they could somehow be identified as Jews, but no formal disenfranchisement based on an exclusionary definition had yet been initiated. The definition as such—whatever its precise terms were to be in the future—was the necessary initial basis of all the persecutions that were to follow. . . .

In 1933 the number of Jews in the civil service was small. As a result of Hindenburg's intervention (following a petition by the Association of Jewish War Veterans that was also supported by the elderly Field Marshal August von Mackensen), combat veterans and civil servants whose fathers or sons had been killed in action in World War I were exempted from the law. Civil servants, moreover, who had been in state service by August 1, 1914, were also exempt. All others were forced into retirement. . . .

By the end of March, physical molestation of Jewish jurists had spread throughout the Reich.

In Dresden, Jewish judges and lawyers were dragged out of their offices and even out of courtrooms during proceedings, and, more often than not, beaten up. . . . At the same time local Nazi leaders such as the Bavarian justice minister, Hans Frank, and the Prussian justice minister, Harms Kerrl, on their own initiative announced measures for the immediate dismissal of all Jewish lawyers and civil servants. . . .

The Justice Ministry had prepared a decree excluding Jewish lawyers from the bar on the same basis—but also with the same exemptions regarding combat veterans and their relatives, and longevity in practice, as under the Civil Service Law. . . . .

Because of the exemptions, the initial application of the law was relatively mild. Of the 4,585 Jewish lawyers practicing in Germany, 3,167 (or almost 70 percent) were allowed to continue their work; 336 Jewish judges and state prosecutors, out of a total of 717, were also kept in office. In June 1933 Jews still made up more than 16 percent of all practicing lawyers in Germany. These statistics should, however, not be misinterpreted. Though still allowed to practice, Jewish lawyers were excluded from the national association of lawyers and listed not in its annual directory but in a separate guide; all in all, notwithstanding the support of some Aryan institutions and individuals, they worked under a "boycott of fear."

Nazi rank-and-file agitation against Jewish physicians did not lag far behind the attacks on Jewish jurists. . . .

Hitler was even more careful with physicians than with lawyers. . . . He suggested that measures against them be postponed until an adequate information campaign could be organized. At this stage, after April 22, Jewish doctors were merely barred de facto from clinics and hospitals run by the national health insurance organization, with some even allowed to continue to practice there. Thus, in mid-1933, nearly 11 percent of all practicing German physicians were Jews. Here is another example of Hitler's pragmatism in action: Thousands of Jewish physicians meant tens of thousands of German patients. Disrupting the ties between these physicians and a vast number of patients could have caused unnecessary discontent. Hitler preferred to wait.

On April 25 the Law Against the Overcrowding of German Schools and Universities was passed. It was aimed exclusively against non-Aryan pupils and students. The law limited the matriculation of new Jewish students in any German school or university to 1.5 percent of the total of new applicants, with the overall number of Jewish pupils or students in any institution not to exceed 5 percent. Children of World War I veterans and those born of mixed marriages contracted before the passage of the law were exempted from the quota. The regime's intention was carefully explained in the press. According to the *Deutsche Allgemeine Zeitung* of April 27: "A self-respecting nation cannot, on a scale accepted up to now, leave its higher activities in the hands of people of racially foreign origin. . . . Allowing the presence of too high a percentage of people of foreign origin in relation to their percentage in the general population could be interpreted as an acceptance of the superiority of other races, something decidedly to be rejected."

The April laws and the supplementary decrees that followed compelled at least two million state employees and tens of thousands of lawyers, physicians, students, and many others to look for adequate proof of Aryan ancestry; the same process turned tens of thousands of priests, pastors, town clerks, and archivists into investigators and suppliers of vital attestations of impeccable blood purity; willingly or not these were becoming part of a racial bureaucratic machine that had begun to search, probe, and exclude. . . .

In September 1933 Jews were forbidden to own farms or engage in agriculture. That month the establishment, under the control of the Propaganda Ministry, of the Reich Chamber of Culture, enabled Goebbels to limit the participation of Jews in the new Germany's cultural life. (Their systematic expulsion, which would include not only writers and artists but also owners of important businesses in the cultural domain, was for that reason delayed until 1935.) Also under the aegis of Goebbels's Propaganda Ministry, Jews were barred from belonging to the Journalists' Association and, on October 4, from being newspaper editors. The German press had been cleansed. (Exactly a year later, Goebbels recognized the right of Jewish editors and journalists to work, but only within the framework of the Jewish press.)

In Nazi racial thinking, the German national community drew its strength from the purity of its blood and from its rootedness in the sacred German earth. Such racial purity was a condition of superior cultural creation and of the construction of a powerful state, the guarantor of victory in the struggle for racial survival and domination. From the outset, therefore, the 1933 laws pointed to the exclusion of the Jews from all key areas of this utopian vision: the state structure itself (the Civil Service Law), the biological health of the national community (the physicians' law), the social fabric of the community (the disbarring of Jewish lawyers), culture (the laws regarding schools, universities, the press, the cultural professions), and, finally, the sacred earth (the farm law). The Civil Service Law was the only one of these to be fully implemented at this early stage, but the symbolic statements they expressed and the ideological message they carried were unmistakable.

Seeing the Future

Very few German Jews sensed the implications of the Nazi laws in terms of sheer long-range terror. One who did was Georg Solmssen, spokesman for the board of directors of the Deutsche Bank and son of an Orthodox Jew. In an April 9, 1933, letter addressed to the bank's board chairman, after pointing out that even the non-Nazi part of the population seemed to consider the new measures "self-evident," Solmssen added: "I am afraid that we are merely at the beginning of a process aiming, purposefully and according to a well-prepared plan, at the economic and moral annihilation of all members, without any distinctions, of the Jewish race living in Germany. The total passivity not only of those classes of the population that belong to the National Socialist Party, the absence of all feelings of solidarity becoming apparent among those who until now worked shoulder to shoulder with Jewish colleagues, the increasingly more obvious desire to take personal advantage of vacated positions, the hushing up of the disgrace and the shame disastrously inflicted upon people who, although innocent, witness the destruction of their honor and their existence from one day to the next—all of this indicates a situation so hopeless that it would be wrong not to face it squarely without any attempt at prettification."

Persecution Spreads

The City of Cologne forbade the use of municipal sports facilities to Jews in March 1933. Beginning April 3 requests by Jews in Prussia for name changes were to be submitted to the Justice Ministry, "to prevent the covering up of origins." On April 4 the German Boxing Association excluded all Jewish boxers. On April 8 all Jewish teaching assistance at universities in the state of Baden were to be expelled immediately. On April 18 the party district chief (Gauleiter) of Westphalia decided that a Jew would be allowed to leave prison only if the two persons who had submitted the request for bail, or the doctor who had signed the medical certificate, were ready to take his place in prison. On April 19 the use of Yiddish was forbidden in cattle markets in Baden. On April 24 the use of Jewish names for spelling purposes in telephone communications was forbidden. On May 8 the mayor of Zweibrücken prohibited Jews from leasing places in the next annual town market. On May 13 the change of Jewish to non-Jewish names was forbidden. On May 24 the full Aryanization of the German gymnastics organization was ordered, with full Aryan descent of all four grandparents stipulated. Whereas in April Jewish doctors had been excluded from state-insured institutions, in May privately insured institutions were ordered to refund medical expenses for treatment by Jewish doctors only when the patients themselves were non-Aryan. Separate lists of Jewish and non-Jewish doctors would be ready by June. . . .

For young Hilma Geffen-Ludomer, the only Jewish child in the Berlin suburb of Rangsdorf, the Law Against the Overcrowding of German Schools meant total change. The "nice, neighborly atmosphere" ended "abruptly. . . . Suddenly, I didn't have any friends. I had no more girlfriends, and many neighbors were afraid to talk to us. Some of the neighbors that we visited told me: 'Don't come anymore because I'm scared. We should not have any contact with Jews.'" Lore Gang-Salheimer, eleven in 1933 and living in Nuremberg, could remain in her school as her father had fought at Verdun. Nonetheless "it began to happen that non-Jewish children would say, 'No I can't walk home from school with you anymore. I can't be seen with you anymore.'" "With every passing day under Nazi rule," wrote Martha Appel, "the chasm between us and our neighbors grew wider. Friends with whom we had had warn relations for years did not know us anymore. Suddenly we discovered that we were different." . . .

The Genetically Inferior Should Die

The Law for the Prevention of Genetically Diseased Offspring (*Gesetz zur Verhütung erbkranken Nachwuchses*) was adopted on July 14, 1933, the day on which all political parties with the exception of the NSDAP were banned and the laws against Eastern Jews (cancellation of citizenship, an end to immigration, and so on) came into effect. The new law allowed for the sterilization of anyone recognized as suffering from supposedly hereditary diseases, such as feeble-mindedness, schizophrenia, manic-depressive insanity, genetic epilepsy, Huntington's chorea, genetic blindness, genetic deafness, and severe alcoholism.

The evolution leading to the July 1933 law was already noticeable during the Weimar period. Among eugenicists, the promoters of "positive eugenics" were losing ground, and "negative eugenics"—with its emphasis on the exclusion, that is, mainly the sterilization, of carriers of incapacitating hereditary diseases—was gaining the upper hand even within official institutions: A trend that had appeared on a wide scale in the West before World War I was increasingly dominating the German scene. As in so many other domains, the war was of decisive importance: Weren't the young and the physically fit being slaughtered on the battlefield while the incapacitated and the unfit were being shielded? Wasn't the reestablishment of genetic equilibrium a major national-racial imperative? Economic thinking added its own logic: The social cost of maintaining mentally and physically handicapped individuals whose reproduction would only increase the burden was considered prohibitive. . . . Although the draft of a sterilization law submitted to the Prussian government in July 1932 still emphasized *voluntary* sterilization in case of hereditary defects, the ideas of *compulsory* sterilization seems to have been spreading. It was nonetheless with the Nazi accession to power that the decisive change took place. . . .

Paragraph 12, section 1, of the new law stated that once sterilization had been decided upon, it could be implemented "against the will of the person to be sterilized.". . . It seems, though, that even before 1933, patients in some psychiatric institutions were being sterilized without their own or their families' consent. About two hundred thousand people were sterilized between mid–1933 and the end of 1937. By the end of the war, the number had reached four hundred thousand.

From the outset of the sterilization policies to the apparent ending of euthanasia in August 1941—and to the beginning of the "Final Solution" close to that same date—policies regarding the handicapped and the mentally ill on the one hand and those regarding the Jews on the other followed a simultaneous and parallel development. These two policies, however, had different origins and different aims. Whereas sterilization and euthanasia were exclusively aimed at enhancing the purity of the *Volksgemeinschaft* [community of people united by German blood], and were bolstered by cost-benefit computations, the segregation and the extermination of the Jews—though also a racial purification process—was mainly a struggle against an active, formidable enemy that was perceived endangering the very survival of Germany and of the Aryan world. Thus, in addition to the goal of racial cleansing, identical to that pursued in the sterilization and euthanasia campaign and in contrast to it, the struggle against the Jews was seen as a confrontation of apocalyptic dimensions.

Selection 6

Jewish Children in Germany

Marion A. Kaplan

When the Holocaust is discussed, the focus is usually on what happened in Germany and the occupied territories after the beginning of World War II. The seeds for the Final Solution, *however, were sown much earlier, certainly by the time Hitler came to power, if not when the Nazi Party was formed. German Jews lived good lives and many were among the country's elite, holding prestigious positions in universities, politics, and industry. That all changed with Hitler. While many of the most obvious anti-Semitic measures were directed against adults, children also suffered greatly. The seriousness of their plight grew year by year as the Nazis implemented ever harsher restrictions, ultimately resulting in Jews being banned from schools. At first many young people responded by trying to fit in or by "turning the other cheek," then large numbers abandoned public schools for Jewish ones, and eventually thousands fled the country. This excerpt by Marion A. Kaplan, a history professor at Queens College and the Graduate Center of the City University of New York, describes what it was like for children during the prewar years. Kaplan's own parents escaped Germany.*

*I*n 1933, approximately 117,000 Jewish children and youth between the ages of six and twenty-five lived in Germany. Compared with their elders, whose loss of jobs and businesses proceeded erratically, the younger generation faced a more drastic deterioration in conditions at public schools and among non-Jewish friends, often finding their first safe haven in a Jewish school. They also experienced a drastic reduction in their aspirations and lived in tense homes with families on edge. . . .

Jewish Children in "Aryanized" Schools

Nazi legislation of April 1933, euphemistically entitled the "Law Against the Overcrowding of German Schools," established a quota of 1.5 percent total enrollment for Jews. Where Jews made up more than 5 percent of the population, schools could allow up to 5 percent of their pupils to be Jewish. Exemptions included Jewish pupils whose fathers had served during World War I, children of mixed marriages (with

Excerpted from Marion A. Kaplan, *Between Dignity and Despair: Jewish Life in Nazi Germany.* Copyright © 1998 Marion A. Kaplan. Reprinted with permission from Oxford University Press, Inc.

no more than two Jewish grandparents), and Jewish children with foreign citizenship. Elementary school (the *Volksschule*) attendance remained, for the time being, required for all. . . .

Because children spend so much time in school, unprotected by family, Jewish children continually met with the blatant repercussions of Nazism there. Well before Jewish children were expelled from German public schools, the majority lost the rights of non-Jews. They often had to sit apart from classmates. The curriculum isolated them further. In German class, one Jewish teenager had to study literature on the need for German expansion. . . . In English class, the same girl read news articles from a British pro-Nazi tabloid. Teachers often required essays on Nazi themes. Jews, however, were prohibited from addressing these topics and, instead, were given arbitrary topics that had never been discussed in class. No matter how well an essay was written, a Jewish child seldom received a top grade.

School administrators and teachers barred Jewish children from school events, whether inside or outside school. When Nazi movies were shown, Jewish children could not attend but afterward had to listen while other children discussed the film. Denied school subsidies, they were forbidden from going to swimming pools or sleeping in dormitories on class trips. A mother described her daughter's unhappiness about missing special events: "It was not because she was denied going to the show that my little girl was weeping . . . but because she had to stay apart, as if she were not good enough to associate with her comrades any longer." On Mother's Day, Jewish children had to take part in the school festivities but were not allowed to sing along. When they protested, their teacher responded haughtily: "I know you have a mother . . . but she is only a Jewish mother." On the rare occasion when Jewish children could take part, the "Aryan" children would show up in their Nazi youth group outfits, making it clear who did not belong. . . .

The pain of children—who often faced anti-semitism from classmates and teachers—disturbed both women and men profoundly as parents, but women coped with their children's distress more directly than did the men. Children told their mothers the latest incidents. Principals summoned mothers to pick up their children when they were expelled from school—often more than once—and mothers then searched for new schools. Mothers were usually the ones whom teachers phoned when children were excluded from class events or received grades beneath their actual achievement level. . . .

Sympathetic teachers were not uncommon in the early years. Yet the threat to job security made those who had earlier shown sympathy more careful later on—behavior that was multiplied a thousandfold in the German population. When a Jewish girl had to leave public school in Wiesbaden, she asked her teacher to write a few lines in her autograph album. The teacher happily complied for her favorite pupil, but a few days later the principal asked to see the girl's mother. He feared that the teacher's affection for a Jewish child could endanger her career if the authorities found out. Clearly ashamed of himself, he asked that the girl remove the page from her album and give it to him. . . .

Little ones found it agonizing not to be part of the group. When asked in late 1933 what he would wish for, a seven-year-old answered "To be a Nazi." When his father asked what would happen to the rest of the family, he responded that he wished they could be Nazis too. This is the same child whose teacher noted that he flinched every time the Nazi flag was raised. Another little boy, referring to his circumcision, confided to his father that he wished he were a girl. Then the other children would not know immediately that he was a Jew. . . .

In one small town, the elementary school teacher insisted that Jewish children give the Nazi salute. The parents advised the children not to do so. The teacher threatened the Jewish children with the wrath of their "Aryan" schoolmates: "'I am not responsible if the children turn against you.'. . . And then, after a short time, we went along, cooperated, and didn't mention it at home.". . .

Jewish Schools

Harassment, as well as expulsions from public schools, provoked many families to enroll their children in Jewish schools. In 1933, there were about 60,000 school-aged Jewish children (between the ages of six and fourteen) in Germany. As a result of the Nazi takeover, the proportion of Jewish children attending Jewish schools leaped from 14 percent in 1932, to 23 percent in 1934, and to 52 percent in 1936. To keep up with demand, the communities provided 130 schools by 1935 and 160 (with over 1,200 teachers) by 1936. In 1937, Jewish schools peaked at 167, serving about 60 percent of Jewish children (23,670). Still, a significant proportion of Jewish children between the ages of six and fourteen remained in the public elementary schools, subject to torment by teachers and other children, until the Nazis barred their attendance in November 1938. . . .

Recalling his relief at entering a Jewish school as a fifteen-year-old, one man later wrote: "There was no longer a picture of the *Führer*. . . no unfair brawls and no Nazi fighting songs. Liberated, I was allowed to breathe freely.". . .

About two-thirds of Jewish children and youth left Germany between 1933 and September 1939. One Jewish school in Berlin exemplifies the enormous changes Jewish children had to face. At the end of 1932–33, 470 children attended the Jewish middle school on Grosse Hamburgerstrasse. Two weeks later, at the beginning of the new school year, the enrollment burgeoned to 840, and one year later it rose to 1,025. Then a rapid decline set in. As families fled, attendance dropped to 380 by the spring of 1939. . . .

Ruth Klüger's experience in Vienna was typical of many children. Born in 1931, she attended eight different schools between the ages of six and ten. The decreased enrollments as children and teachers emigrated forced Jewish schools to merge. She recalled that what most interested her when she arrived at school each morning was how many other pupils had vanished. Then the remaining pupils would be transferred to another school and would have to get used to new teachers, as they, too, emigrated. . . .

Jewish Teens

In 1933, about 58,000 Jewish "youth," between the ages of sixteen and twenty-four, lived in Germany. Adolescents and young adults needed and had more freedom than children but faced new challenges. . . .

Increasingly, Jewish youth groups became an important source of camaraderie, distraction, and hope for young people. Before 1933, many Jewish children and youth had belonged to non-sectarian groups, with Jewish organizations appealing only to a minority. In 1932 about 26,000 people, or 25 to 30 percent of Jewish youth, belonged to Jewish associations. . . .

By 1936, 50,000 youths between twelve and twenty-five, about 60 percent of the total, had joined. From early on, their realm of action was limited: members could no longer camp in public places, wear uniforms, or appear in group formation. In addition, the groups were in constant flux as members emigrated or left for apprenticeships and agricultural training centers. Nevertheless, they played an important role, providing teens with a haven from work, school, or tense families. They also helped some teens question the political judgments of parents who hoped to remain in Germany, making the younger people more eager to flee. . . .

This coming together of Jewish youth both reflected and intensified a generation gap with parents. Young people saw no future for themselves in Germany, whereas many parents clung to whatever they still had. . . .

Regardless of parental disapproval, Jewish youth thrived on the activities and institutions set up by private or community groups. For example, when it became clear that Jews were either unwelcome in or prohibited from using German youth hostels, "Haus Bertha" was founded in July 1934 in cooperation with the League of Jewish War Veterans for use by Jewish groups. In the midst of forests and heaths twelve miles outside of Gelsenkirchen, it lasted until 1937, when the Nazis closed it. The visiting teenagers played sports, took hikes, and attended lectures on Jewish themes. According to the lodgers, the hostel was "a ray of hope . . . if only for a short time." Another sixteen-year-old boy believed his training there gave him the "backbone" to overcome the enormous adjustments of emigration. One visitor summed up the short three-year existence of the hostel by commenting that it gave "many hundreds of Jewish boys and girls" vacations which they could not have had anywhere else in Germany.

Half-Jewish teens, or "*Mischlinge*," often had a harder time finding a circle of friends than did Jewish teens. Excluded from most "Aryan" clubs and activities, they were also isolated from Jewish activities. At first, many children and young people of mixed background attempted to deny their part-Jewish origins. They could no longer hide their origins by the age of ten, however, when most "Aryans" entered Nazi youth groups, Christian groups had the same requirements as the Nazi groups. . . .

Jewish teens could also expect a dismal future in the German economy. The limits set on Jews at trade and vocational schools, as well as their exclusion from universities and institutions of higher learning, restricted employment possibilities. . . . In addition, Jewish job training programs were limited, and Jewish businesses, where a teen might have apprenticed, were closing down. . . . Also, decrees time and again eliminated career choices. For example, by 1935 some provinces had declared that women teachers of agricultural home economics could only be "Aryans" and that only "Aryan" women could take exams to qualify as midwives, social workers, or physical therapists. While before 1935 Jewish girls would have looked forward to business or professional careers, by mid-1935 the apprenticeship office for Jewish girls reported that half were applying to become seamstresses. By 1937, when young women had shifted their focus to jobs useful in countries of emigration, 24 percent of graduates from Jewish schools planned to learn a craft. They largely preferred tailoring (20 percent), because, as one woman maintained, "sewing knows no language." Sixteen percent trained for domestic service, 13 percent for commerce, and 12 percent for social work. By the end of 1937, about thirty institutions offered some training in home economics. And, lest girls harbor unrealistic notions about continuing at a university abroad, they were warned "that Jewish girls in and out of Germany have almost no chance to study [at the university]. The few scholarships available are only for young men."

What a narrowing of career prospects meant in practice can be seen through the experience of Annemarie Scherman, aged sixteen in 1933. Originally she had wanted to become a goldsmith, but because she was a *"Mischling"* she could no longer apprentice in Germany. So she learned about pediatric nursing, passing the course exam with commendations, but was prohibited from taking the state exam. When she tried to enroll to study medicine at the university, she had to sit on a bench for Jewish students and carry student identification with a yellow stripe across it. Unhappily, she tried to become a medical assistant but found that this pursuit was barred to Jews and *"Mischlinge."* Finally, she took a business course, learning stenography, typing, and other secretarial skills. She passed her exam in 1938 but could not find a job because every application form asked her "racial" history. She finally found a job at a newspaper for a brief interlude and then worked as an assistant to a doctor who opposed the regime. . . .

Children Leave Home

Between 1934 and 1939, thousands of parents made the agonizing decision to send their children out of Germany and into the unknown, either on what were called "children's transports" (*Kindertransporte*) or by themselves. At least 18,000 "unaccompanied children" left Germany. Many teenagers departed, often for Switzerland or England, as parents with means found study opportunities for them. Other teens headed abroad on their own after preparing at agricultural training centers. Some of these centers were founded outside Germany, such as the agricultural training center for Jewish apprentices, Werkdorp Nieuwesluis, established in Holland in 1934. By 1936, there were centers in ten other European lands, where 843 young men and 288 young women trained for agricultural careers, the women mostly in home economics.

Still others managed to get out as menial laborers, for girls and young women generally as household servants or apprentices. Typically, they saw their departures as permanent, with few expecting to return. . . .

Even before the November Pogrom [*Kristallnacht*], British rescue groups, including the Quakers, brought German-Jewish refugee children to England, but the numbers were small. Spurred into more intense action by the pogrom, these groups formed the first major transports of children, leaving Berlin, Hamburg, and Vienna in December 1938. Zionists also increased their efforts after the pogrom, bringing more agricultural apprentices into Palestine than ever. The *Kindertransporte* took between 8,000 and 10,000 children to England (after November 1938), 3,400 to Palestine, and some to other European countries and the United States. There they received foster care or, in the case of Palestine, lived on kibbutzim or in children's homes until their parents could join them. Many parents never made it.

The children who went to Palestine did so under the auspices of Youth Aliyah. Pioneered by Recha Freier in Berlin and supported financially by Hadassah, the Zionist women's organization in the United States, it rescued over 3,200 children from Germany. It required 60 percent boys and 40 percent girls because of what its leaders considered the division of labor on the collective farms where the children would work.

For children, the *Kindertransporte* could be a terribly wrenching experience, a considerable adventure, or both. Feelings of adventure crop up in men's memoirs of their teen years. Charles Marks wrote: "To me it was an adventure; to [my parents] it must have been agony." Some children went abroad in one direction while their parents fled in another. In a letter to relatives abroad, one woman worried that her friends were heading toward Shanghai while their children traveled to England on a *Kindertransport* but conceded: "None of this devastates us anymore, we are used to much worse."

For parents, the decision to send off a child was the most excruciating moment of their lives. . . . One woman recalled that when she received her papers at eighteen to emigrate to England as a governess, her mother fainted. Many mothers on their own, with husbands either abroad or in concentration camps, made the agonizing decision to send their children out of Germany, and they suffered intensely from the loss of daily initimacy. Herta Beuthner, whose husband was in Argentina, sent their son to Palestine to avoid his induction at fifteen into forced labor: "The separation from my only child was heartbreaking. For many days and nights I lay in my bed, crying, and I didn't want to live anymore."

Some mothers could not bear the thought of parting from their children. Almost fifty years later, Miriam Gillis-Carlebach recalled that when she told her mother that she wanted to leave for Palestine, Lotte Carlebach covered her face and cried, "My only Miriam." The teenager tried to console her: "But Mommy! Eight children will remain at home with you!" Her mother would not be comforted. "Each child is my only child. I yearn for you already." Whereas Lotte Carlebach sympathized with her daughter's desires and approved of her emigration, Ruth Klüger's mother showed no such un-derstanding. As a result, both mother and daughter wound up in Auschwitz. Both sur-vived, but even late in life, Ruth Klüger re-called her frustration when her mother refused to let her join a children's transport. A young man from the Jewish community had told her mother there was one last chance to send her child to Palestine:

> My heart pounded, for I would have loved to leave, even if it had been a betrayal of her. But she didn't ask me or even look at me once, rather she said, "No. One does not separate a child from her mother." On the way home I struggled with my disappointment, which I could not express to her without hurting her. I believe I never forgave her for this. . . .

By 1939, 82 percent of children aged fifteen and under and 83 percent of youth aged sixteen to twenty-four had managed to escape Germany. The remaining Jewish children and teens had fewer and fewer friends. . . . Opportunities for those increasingly nervous and frightened chil-dren who remained—the *Kindertransporte*, like other exits, were never sufficient—continued to dwindle. By July 1941, about 25,000 Jewish children and youth under age twenty-five still lived within the borders of pre-1938 Germany.

<hr>

Selection 7

Hitler Robs the Jews

Richard Z. Chesnoff

The Nazis slowly excluded Jews from every as-pect of German society. They not only perse-cuted the Jews, but also stole from them. Long before the killing began, Jewish property was stolen, sometimes blatantly; other times, it was done so under the guise of some bureau-cratic regulation. In one of the more diabolical aspects of the Holocaust, the Jews actually were forced to pay for their own destruction. It began when Hitler required the German Jew-

ish community to pay for the damage the Nazis caused on Kristallnacht. *Ultimately, money confiscated from Jews was used to help pay for the war effort and the Final Solution. Much of the money, jewelry, artworks, and other valuables plundered by the Nazis were transferred to places like Switzerland and were hidden in secret bank accounts. Today, a global hunt is under way to locate Jewish assets and return them to their rightful owners. This excerpt discusses the measures taken by the Nazis prior to the onset of the war to strip the Jews of their possessions. Richard Z. Chesnoff is a senior correspondent for* U.S. News & World Report *and a columnist for the* New York Daily News.

*B*erlin's main boulevard was not the best place for a young Jewish boy to be on the morning of November 10, 1938. But to the crowds that quietly packed the Kurfürstendamm the day after *Kristallnacht,* the thirteen-year-old, blond-haired, blue-eyed youth in short pants and knee socks seemed the perfect "Aryan." Six decades later, Michael Blumenthal still remembers every detail of the Nazis' infamous orgy of anti-Semitic destruction and looting. "I have never forgotten the sight," says the Holocaust survivor who went on to become an American Secretary of the Treasury. "Every Jewish store had been wrecked, glass from shop windows littered the sidewalks, . . . and from the direction of the major synagogue on the Fasanstrasse I could see rising clouds of smoke. . . . No one helped. People just stared. There was a kind of strange silence."

For Adolf Hitler and his most willing executioners, Jews were a cancer on society, a malignancy that had to be surgically but brutally excised with no anesthesia: The Jews of the world, declared Hitler, are "vermin."

But for the Führer and the clique of officers and technicians who helped him mastermind the mechanics of the Holocaust, Jews—particularly Europe's Jews—represented much more: They were also a golden cow to be milked dry and eventually melted down for the greater glory and profit not only of the Reich but of those who fanatically supported it.

This state plunder was part and parcel of a coalescent ideology of exclusions, expropriation, and finally extermination. And in that wicked process of exclude and annihilate, the Reich managed to amass many of the multimillions needed to finance the brutal war it launched in 1939 and fought to defeat in May of 1945. . . .

A Passing Madness

Amazingly, Nazi anti-Semitism provoked little panic among German Jews. In 1933, fewer than 38,000 of Germany's 525,000 Jews chose to read the writing on the wall and leave Germany voluntarily. In the four years that followed, fewer than 100,000 more chose exile—tragic testimony to an overwhelmingly delusional German-Jewish conviction that Hitler and Nazism were merely a "passing madness.". . .

Still others who might have considered departing were frightened away by the enormous economic cost of emigration—not to mention the scarcity of visas from countries to go to. Jewish-owned property could be sold only at increasingly lower prices. And while the Reich maintained that it was eager to be rid of its Jews, transferring whatever was left of their funds overseas became more and more expensive. The emigration tax on "capital flight," already high, had been raised by the Nazis. And waiting did not make it less expensive. With each month of the Nazi regime, prices dropped on Jewish property—both personal and communal, and especially in rural areas. In December 1935, the Austrian *Reichspost* gleefully reported from Germany that an "Aryan" farmer in Franconia was able to purchase an abandoned synagogue for 700 marks and convert it to grain storage. By the same year, in certain areas of central Germany, 40 to 50 percent of all Jewish businesses had been liquidated.

As if that were not bad enough, exchange rates offered for the purchase of foreign currency became progressively lower. Until 1935, emigrating Jews were entitled to exchange their Reichsmark at 50 percent of their face value. It then dropped to 30 and finally, on the eve of the war, to 4 percent. . . .

The Cost of Kristallnacht

"It was Kristallnacht," says Holocaust authority Avraham Barkai, "that marked the transition to open and undisguised robbery of Jewish property in Germany by official institutions of the Nazi regime." This was followed by a new series of regulations that completely forbade any independent economic activity by German Jews. It was the beginning of the Final Solution.

But the atrocities of Kristallnacht also brought the Reich a potential financial hangover. [*Reichsmarschall* Hermann] Göring already worried about foreign retribution, still angrily bemoaned the loss of property that might have fallen into the Reich's—and his—hands. "I wish you had killed two hundred Jews instead of destroying such valuables!" he shouted at SD [SS intelligence operation] chief Reinhard Heydrich. But the biggest problem was paying for the damage. According to [historian Saul] Friedlander, "a representative of German insurance companies, Eduard Hilgard, estimated it in the multimillions. Just the windows destroyed in Jewish shops were insured for about $6 million. And because the glass was Belgian, at least half of this amount would have to be paid in foreign currency"—still in short supply. It represented half the Belgian glass industry's total yearly production.

Faced with that prospect, the Nazis dreamed up a solution that almost matched the evil of the Kristallnacht pogrom: The Jews themselves were ordered to bear the costs of repair, while the Reich would confiscate German insurance payments of more than 250 million Reichsmark. As if that were not odious enough, a special decree was promulgated ordering German Jews to "contribute" a one-billion-mark *Sühneleistung*, or "atonement payment." It would consist of 20 percent of the declared capital of every German Jew owning more than 5,000 Reichsmark. Germany's Jews were even ordered to repair their own damaged synagogues,

lest they prove a "public danger."

The same order, issued by Göring at Hitler's behest, commanded the cessation of all Jewish business activity as of January 1, 1939. Jews would have to "sell" their enterprises as well as any land, stocks, jewels and artworks. *Treuhänder*—Reich-appointed fiduciaries—would help them complete the transactions within the allotted period.

To drive the point home, the order also forbade Jews to drive or have cars, to ride in trains, to go to theaters or cinemas. They were banned from city districts containing government offices—unless summoned there. Special measures were reserved for Berlin's Jews, who were officially banned from all concert and conference halls, museums, fairs, exhibit halls, and sports facilities—especially public swimming pools. A November 29 order from Heydrich's office even prohibited them from owning carrier pigeons.

Stealing from the Jews

As Avraham Barkai points out in his landmark study of the Reich, Nazi economic policy had two stages: The first dates from 1933 to 1938, when Jews, facing a rising tide of exclusion and discrimination, "voluntarily" sold or disposed of their businesses—usually at greatly discounted prices. The second period, which followed Kristallnacht, lacked even the pretense of volunteer sale. Under direct order of Hitler via Göring, Germany entered the final phases of the *Entjuden der deutschen Wirtschaft*—the dejudaization of the German economy. It was among the central points Göring announced on November 12, 1938, in his program "to exclude the Jews from the economic life of Germany." Much had already been swallowed up by the voracious economic masters of the Reich—and both Austria and the Sudetenland had proved rich plunder fields. Now it remained, says Barkai, "to liquidate the little that was left in a single stroke and within the space of a few weeks."

The November laws also triggered the organized confiscation of any Jewish-owned property. Directors of state collections were ordered to undertake "the safekeeping of works of art belonging to Jews." In exchange, the owners were issued meaningless receipts. A Reich Legal Notice of January 16, 1939, designated municipal pawnshops as the Öffentliche Ankaufstellen—the Public Acquisition Offices—where Jews were to hand over art objects and jewelry. A follow-up February memo from the Reich's Economic Minister required all Jews to deliver "any objects in their ownership made of gold, platinum or silver, as well as precious stones and pearls." That included scrap precious metals, and even fillings, the memo notes. "A refusal of the offer by Jews can no longer be considered." Even holy objects were prey. In Frankfurt, the Nazi-sponsored Research Institute on the Jewish Question became a repository for priceless plundered Judaica, much of it centuries old.

Jewish businesses that still existed were placed under the control of a government-appointed *Treuhand*, who earned sizable fees and commissions for Aryanizing an enterprise. In some cases, huge industrial plants, such as the Simson armaments factory in Suhl, had already been confiscated without any compensation. Other firms were now grabbed by high-ranking members of the party—or by hitherto loyal employees who had fortuitous connections to senior and not so senior Nazis. . . .

Paying for Their Own Deaths

Though the Nazis often used Aryanization as a way to reward party stalwarts, Hitler became increasingly anxious to exercise his own prerogatives. By December 10, 1938, Göring moved to ensure that most if not all the illicit profits from "dejudaization" flowed directly into Hitler's coffers—to finance the regime and its rapidly growing war machine. "[Jewish] assets have to flow into the hands of the Reich," Göring told a closed-door meeting of his inner circle, "not serve as a source of riches for incompetent party members."

Just how much was stolen? The value of Jewish property—liquid and real—in Germany, Austria, and the Sudetenland was estimated in 1933 to be anywhere between 10 and 12 billion Reichsmark [RM] ($2.5 and $3 billion). Most of the property of the 140,000 Jews who were still able to emigrate from Germany between 1938 and 1941 went directly into official Nazi coffers in the form of what Barkai calls "legal" levies, such as the notorious Reichsfluchtsteuer, the "escape tax." The balance was deposited into blocked accounts that the holders never saw again. Experts such as Barkai estimate that only "a small fraction" of the RM 8 billion ($2 billion) in assets declared by the Jews of Germany and Austria in April 1938 ever left Germany with them. The approximately 170,000 Jews who remained behind had their funds taken from them in early 1939. German emissaries had already begun to transfer funds to Switzerland and Sweden—special slush funds of plundered Jewish wealth. . . .

When the full-scale deportations of Germany's remaining Jews to Theresienstadt Camp in occupied Czechoslovakia began in 1941, the Reich forced all deportees to sign over their homes and insurance policies to the Reichsvereinigung. In exchange for these "home purchase agreements" and the deposit of a minimum of 1,000 RM to the Reichsvereinigung, the German government cynically undertook to take care of the deportees "for the rest of their lives." Most would have little time left. . . .

By 1943, when the deportations to the extermination camps were virtually complete, the special blocked accounts all had been confiscated by the Gestapo through the Reich's Treasury. By direct order from [SS leader Heinrich] Himmler, the funds were to be used to finance the Final Solution. The Jews would pay for their own murders.

Kristallnacht

Ben Austin

When Hitler assumed power, the measures he took against the Jews were primarily administrative and legislative, denying them various rights enjoyed by other Germans. Some Jews recognized that their future in Germany was no longer secure, but few could foresee that the Nazis would escalate their campaign from persecution to extermination. It was not until late 1938 that Jews were given a reason to worry about their safety. The organized attacks that were mounted against Jews on November 9 and 10—Kristallnacht—were a warning that the situation was going to get much worse before it got better. Of course, it is much easier to see this with the gift of hindsight; many Jews still did not realize that the night of murder and vandalism was only the prelude to a campaign of genocide. Ben Austin, a sociology professor at Middle Tennessee State University describes in this article what happened on Kristallnacht *and what that event meant.*

*a*lmost immediately upon assuming the Chancellorship of Germany, Hitler began promulgating legal actions against Germany's Jews. In 1933, he proclaimed a one-day boycott against Jewish shops, a law was passed

Excerpted from Ben Austin, "Kristallnacht," an online article found at www.us-israel.org/jsource/Holocaust/kristallnacht.html. Reprinted with permission from the author.

against kosher butchering and Jewish children began experiencing restrictions in public schools. By 1935, the Nuremberg Laws deprived Jews of German citizenship. By 1936, Jews were prohibited from participation in parliamentary elections and signs reading "Jews Not Welcome" appeared in many German cities. . . .

In the first half of 1938, numerous laws were passed restricting Jewish economic activity and occupational opportunities. In July, 1938, a law was passed (effective January 1, 1939) requiring all Jews to carry identification cards. On October 28, 17,000 Jews of Polish citizenship, many of whom had been living in Germany for decades, were arrested and relocated across the Polish border. The Polish government refused to admit them so they were interned in "relocation camps" on the Polish frontier.

Among the deportees was Zindel Grynszpan, who had been born in western Poland and had moved to Hanover, where he established a small store, in 1911. On the night of October 27, Zindel Grynszpan and his family were forced out of their home by German police. His store and the family's possessions were confiscated and they were forced to move over the Polish border.

Zindel Grynszpan's seventeen-year-old son, Herschel, was living with an uncle in Paris. When he received news of his family's expulsion, he went to the German embassy in Paris on November 7, intending to assassinate the German Ambassador to France. Upon discovering that the Ambassador was not in the embassy, he settled for a lesser official, Third Secretary Ernst vom Rath. Rath, was critically wounded and died two days later, on November 9.

The assassination provided Joseph Goebbels, Hitler's Chief of Propaganda, with the excuse he needed to launch a pogrom against German Jews. Grynszpan's attack was interpreted by Goebbels as a conspiratorial attack by "International Jewry" against the Reich and, symbolically, against the Fuehrer himself. This pogrom has come to be called *Kristallnacht*, "the Night of Broken Glass."

On the nights of November 9 and 10, rampaging mobs throughout Germany and the newly acquired territories of Austria and Sudetenland freely attacked Jews in the street, in their homes and at their places of work and worship. At least 96 Jews were killed and hundreds more injured, more than 1,000 synagogues were burned (and possibly as many as 2,000), almost 7,500 Jewish businesses were destroyed, cemeteries and schools were vandalized, and 30,000 Jews were arrested and sent to concentration camps. . . .

The official German position on these events, which were clearly orchestrated by Goebbels,

Passersby look at the smashed window of a Jewish store after Kristallnacht, *a government-sanctioned rampage of violence against Jews.*

was that they were spontaneous outbursts. The Fuehrer, Goebbels reported to Party officials in Munich, "has decided that such demonstrations are not to be prepared or organized by the party, but so far as they originate spontaneously, they are not to be discouraged either."

Three days later, on November 12, Hermann Goering called a meeting of the top Nazi leadership to assess the damage done during the night and place responsibility for it. Present at the meeting were Goering, Goebbels, Reinhard Heydrich, Walter Funk and other ranking Nazi officials. The intent of this meeting was twofold: to make the Jews responsible for *Kristallnacht* and to use the events of the preceding days as a rationale for promulgating a series of antisemitic laws which would, in effect, remove Jews from the German economy. An interpretive transcript of this meeting is provided by Robert Conot, *Justice at Nuremberg,* New York: Harper and Row, 1983:164–172:

> "Gentlemen! Today's meeting is of a decisive nature," Goering announced. "I have received a letter written on the Fuehrer's orders requesting that the Jewish question be now, once and for all, coordinated and solved one way or another.

> "Since the problem is mainly an economic one, it is from the economic angle it shall have to be tackled. Because, gentlemen, I have had enough of these demonstrations! They don't harm the Jew but me, who is the final authority for coordinating the German economy. If today a Jewish shop is destroyed, if goods are thrown into the street, the insurance companies will pay for the damages; and, furthermore, consumer goods belonging to the people are destroyed. If in the future, demonstrations which are necessary occur, then, I pray, that they be directed so as not to hurt us.

> "Because it's insane to clean out and burn a Jewish warehouse, then have a German insurance company make good the loss. And the goods which I need desperately, whole bales of clothing and whatnot, are being burned.

And I miss them everywhere. I may as well burn the raw materials before they arrive.

> "I should not want to leave any doubt, gentlemen, as to the aim of today's meeting. We have not come together merely to talk again, but to make decisions, and I implore competent agencies to take all measures for the elimination of the Jew from the German economy, and to submit them to me."

It was decided at the meeting that, since Jews were to blame for these events, they be held legally and financially responsible for the damages incurred by the pogrom. Accordingly, a "fine of 1 billion marks was levied for the slaying of Vom Rath, and 6 million marks paid by insurance companies for broken windows was to be given to the state coffers."

A Turning Point

Kristallnacht turns out to be a crucial turning point in German policy regarding the Jews and may be considered as the *actual beginning of what is now called the Holocaust.*

1. By now it is clear to Hitler and his top advisors that forced [e]migration of Jews out of the Reich is not a feasible option.
2. Hitler is already considering the invasion of Poland.
3. Numerous concentration camps and forced labor camps are already in operation.
4. The Nuremberg Laws are in place.
5. The doctrine of *lebensraum* [living space] has emerged as a guiding principle of Hitler's ideology. And,
6. The passivity of the German people in the face of the events of *Kristallnacht* made it clear that the Nazis would encounter little opposition—even from the German churches.

Following the meeting, a wide-ranging set of antisemitic laws were passed which had the clear intent, in Goering's words, of "Aryanizing" the German economy. Over the next two or three months, the following measures were put into effect:

1. Jews were required to turn over all precious metals to the government.
2. Pensions for Jews dismissed from civil service jobs were arbitrarily reduced.
3. Jewish-owned bonds, stocks, jewelry and art works can be alienated only to the German state.
4. Jews were physically segregated within German towns.
5. A ban on the Jewish ownership of carrier pigeons.
6. The suspension of Jewish driver's licenses.
7. The confiscation of Jewish-owned radios.
8. A curfew to keep Jews off the streets between 9:00 P.M. and 5:00 A.M. in the summer and 8:00 P.M. and 6:00 A.M. in the winter.
9. Laws protecting tenants were made non-applicable to Jewish tenants.
10. [Perhaps to help insure the Jews could not fight back in the future, the Minister of the Interior issued regulations against Jews' possession of weapons on November 11. This prohibited Jews from "acquiring, possessing, and carrying firearms and ammunition, as well as truncheons or stabbing weapons. Those now possessing weapons and ammunition are at once to turn them over to the local police authority."]

One final note on the November 12 meeting is of critical importance. In the meeting, Goering announced, "I have received a letter written on the Fuehrer's orders requesting that the Jewish question be now, once and for all, coordinated and solved one way or another." The path to the "Final Solution" has now been chosen. And, all the bureaucratic mechanisms for its implementation were now in place.

It should be noted that there is some controversy among Holocaust scholars as to the origin, intent and appropriateness of the term *Kristallnacht*. The term, after all, was coined by Walter Funk at the November 12 Nazi meeting following the pogrom of November 8–10. The crucial question is whether the term was a Nazi euphemism for an all-out pogrom against German Jews and whether the Nazis used the term in a derisive manner. There is considerable evidence that both of the above questions have an affirmative answer. . . .

What's in a Name?

[Editor] Walter Pehle makes the following observation:

It is clear that the term Crystal Night serves to foster a vicious minimalizing of its memory, a discounting of grave reality: such cynical appellations function to reinterpret manslaughter and murder, arson, robbery, plunder, and massive property damage, transforming these into a glistening event marked by sparkle and gleam. Of course, such terms reveal one thing in stark clarity—the lack of any sense of involvement or feeling of sympathy on the part of those who had stuck their heads in the sand before that violent night.

With good reason, knowledgeable commentators urge people to renounce the continued use of "Kristallnacht" and "Reichskristallnacht" to refer to these events, even if the expressions have become slick and established usage in our language.

So, it appears, the term "Kristallnacht" or "Crystal Night" was invented by Nazis to mock Jews on that black November night in 1938. It is, therefore, another example of Nazi perversion. There are numerous other examples of this same tendency in the language of the Nazi perpetrators: Sonderbehandlung ("special treatment") for gassing victims, Euthanasia for a policy of mass murder of retarded or physically handicapped patients, Arbeit Macht Frei (Work Makes You Free) over the entrance to Auschwitz. When the Nazis launched their plan to annihilate the remaining Jews in Poland in the fall of 1943, they called it "Erntefest," or Harvest Festival. While this may have been a code word, . . . it had the same grim and terrible irony that is reflected in Kristallnacht as in so many other instances of the perverted uses of language in the Third Reich. Perhaps most cynical of all is the use of the term, "Endloesung der Judenfrage" (Final Solution of the Jewish Question), for what is now known as the Holocaust. Goebbels frequently used such terminology to amuse his audiences (usually other Nazi officials) and to further demoralize his victims.

On the other side of this controversy are those who argue that the term should be retained. In the first place, it is the term which has been used now for fifty years and connotes significant meaning to those who study the Holocaust. As [Holocaust scholar] Froma Zeitlin observes:

> But I would like to point out that whether or not the name came into existence as a Nazi euphemism or not, the event itself and what it has come to signify has transformed an "innocent" name into one of unforgettable and dramatic meaning. The term is permanently out of circulation for any other use whatsoever. Can you imagine us now using "Kristallnacht" to refer to some street riot or another, no matter how extensively the streets were littered with broken glass? Certainly not. Moreover, what disturbed the German populace was less the sight of synagogues burning (fires take place all the time, after all—it depends on the scale) than of the savage and wasteful vandalism that confronted bystanders everywhere, disrupting the clean and orderly streets (to say nothing of consumer convenience). What was indeed memorable was the sheer quantity of broken glass. A third point was the economic outcome of this massive breakage. Germany didn't produce enough plate glass to repair the damages (synagogues did not have to be replaced—quite the contrary). The result was twofold: the need to import glass from Belgium (for sorely needed cash) and the outrage of indemnifying the Jewish community to pay for the damages. So the broken glass came to assume yet another outrageous dimension in the wake of the event.

The Final Solution

Chapter 2

Introduction

Hitler made no secret of his desire to exterminate the Jewish people. Still, the Nazis did not begin by murdering the Jews. The level of persecution slowly escalated as the German people were indoctrinated with the idea that Jews were subhuman and therefore not worthy of being treated humanely. Jews were killed even before World War II began, but the conscious decision to murder every man, woman, and child did not come until the Wannsee Conference in 1942.

Many people have tried to explain how ordinary Germans became killers, how it could be that a camp guard could ruthlessly murder women and children during the day and then go home to his own wife and children in the evening, play with the dog and listen to Beethoven. Two authors in this chapter, Christopher Browning and Daniel Goldhagen, offer their theories.

When discussing the Holocaust, it is often easy to get caught up in the magnitude of the number of victims. Each individual had his or her own life, his or her own stories. In some cases they were simply shot, but, in others, they were tortured. The Jews were not considered human, they were guinea pigs, and therefore could be used for hideous experiments. Some of the ghastly experiments carried out in the name of medicine are described in this chapter. Among the most notorious were those conducted on twins in Auschwitz. These selections are not easy to read, but they have been included because it is impossible to appreciate the impact of the Holocaust without learning about the worst of its horrors.

Selection 1

The Nazi "Euthanasia" Program

Michael Berenbaum

Jews were persecuted in Germany from the early 1930s on, but they were not murdered in large numbers until after the war began. Even when the the war began, however, the immediate victims were not Jews. Hitler's first targets were the disabled, the mentally ill, and the infirm. Today, euthanasia *is associated with mercy killing. Allowing people to "die with dignity" when, for example, they have terminal illnesses and are in great pain.*

For the Nazis, however, the program was designed to eliminate people they did not believe were worthy of life. It was during the campaign to murder the unworthy that the Nazis learned to use gas chambers. This excerpt describes the Nazis' euthanasia program. Michael Berenbaum taught at Georgetown University and has served as project director of the U.S. Holocaust Memorial Museum and as president of Steven Spielberg's Shoah Visual History Foundation.

*m*ass murder began with the death of a few individuals. In September 1939, Hitler signed an order empowering his personal physician and the chief of the Führer Chancellery to put to death those considered unsuited to live. He backdated it to September 1, 1939, the day World War II began, to give it the appearance of a wartime measure. In the directive:

> Reich leader Philip Bouhler and Dr. Brandt are charged with responsibility for expanding the authority of physicians, to be designated by name, to the end that patients considered incurable according to the best available human judgment of their state of health, can be granted a mercy killing.

What followed was the so-called euthanasia program, in which men, women, and children who were physically disabled, mentally retarded, or emotionally disturbed were systematically killed.

Within a few months, the T-4 program (named for Berlin Chancellery Tiergarten 4, which directed it) involved virtually the entire German psychiatric community. A new bureaucracy, headed by physicians, was established with a mandate to "take executive measures against those defined as 'life unworthy of living.'"

A statistical survey of all psychiatric institutions, hospitals, and homes for chronically ill patients was ordered. At Tiergarten 4, three medical experts reviewed the forms returned by institutions throughout Germany, but did not examine any patients or read their medical records. Nevertheless, they had the power to decide life or death.

Patients whom it was decided to kill were transported to six killing centers: Hartheim, Sonnenstein, Grafeneck, Bernburg, Hadamar, and Brandenburg. The members of the SS in charge of the transports donned white coats to keep up the charade of a medical procedure.

The Gas

The first killings were by starvation: starvation is passive, simple, and natural. Then injections of lethal doses of sedatives were used. Children were easily "put to sleep." But gassing soon became the preferred method of killing. Fifteen to twenty people were killed in a chamber disguised as a shower. The lethal gas was provided by chemists, and the process was supervised by physicians. Afterward, black smoke billowed from the chimneys as the bodies were burned in adjacent crematoria.

Families of those killed were informed of the transfer. They were assured that their loved ones were being moved in order to receive the best and most modern treatment available. Visits, however, were not possible. The relatives then received condolence letters, falsified death certificates signed by physician, and urns containing ashes. There were occasional lapses in bureaucratic efficiency, and some families received more than one urn. They soon realized something was amiss.

A few doctors protested. Heinrich Bonhoeffer, a leading psychiatrist, worked with his son Dietrich, a pastor who actively opposed the regime, to contact church groups, urging them not to turn patients in church-run institutions over to the SS. (Dietrich Bonhoeffer was executed by the SS just before the end of the war.) A few physicians refused to fill out the requisite forms. Only one psychiatrist, Professor Gottfried Ewald of the University of Göttingen, openly opposed the killing.

Doctors did not become killers overnight. The

transformation took time and required a veneer of scientific justification. As early as 1895, a widely used German medical textbook made a claim for "the right to death." In 1920, a physician and a prominent jurist argued that destroying "life unworthy of life" is a therapeutic treatment and a compassionate act completely consistent with medical ethics.

Soon after the Nazis came to power, the Bavarian Minister of Health proposed that psychopaths, the mentally retarded, and other "inferior" people be isolated and killed. "This policy has already been initiated at our concentration camps," he noted. A year later, mental institutions throughout the Reich were instructed to "neglect" their patients by withholding food and medical treatment.

The Economy of Murder

Pseudo-scientific rationalizations for the killing of the "unworthy" were bolstered by economic considerations. According to bureaucratic calculations, state funds that went to the care of criminals and the insane could be put to better use, for example by loans to newly married couples. Incurably sick children were seen as a burden for the healthy body of the *Volk*, the German people. In a time of war, it was not difficult to lose sight of the absolute value of human life. Hitler understood this. Wartime, he said, "was the best time for the elimination of the incurably ill.". . .

The killing centers to which the handicapped were transported were the antecedents of the death camps. The organized transportation of the handicapped foreshadowed mass deportation. Some of the physicians who became specialists in the technology of cold-blooded murder in the late 1930s later staffed the death camps. All their moral, professional, and ethical inhibitions had long been lost.

During the German euthanasia program, psychiatrists were able to save some patients, at least temporarily, but only if the psychiatrists cooperated in sending others to their death. In the Jewish communities of the territories later conquered by the Nazis, *Judenrat* leaders, Jews appointed by the Germans to take charge of the ghettos, had to make similar choices.

Gas chambers were first developed at the handicapped killing centers. So was the use of burning to dispose of dead bodies. In the death camps the technology was taken to a new level: thousands could be killed at one time and their bodies burned within hours.

The Roman Catholic Church, which had not taken a stand on the Jewish question, protested the "mercy killing." Count von Galen, the Bishop of Münster, openly challenged the regime, arguing that it was the duty of Christians to oppose the taking of human life even if this were to cost them their own lives. It seemed to have an effect.

On August 24, 1941, almost two years after the euthanasia program was initiated, it appeared to cease. In fact, it had gone underground. The killing did not end; mass murder was just beginning. Physicians trained in the medical killing centers went on to grander tasks. Irmfried Eberl, a doctor whose career began in the T-4 program, became the commandant of Treblinka, where killing of a magnitude as yet unimagined would take place.

Selection 2

The Final Solution

John Toland

Hitler had spoken often about his disdain for the Jews. His views could easily have been discerned long before he assumed power; yet, even after World War II began, many people did not take seriously his explicit calls for the extermination of the Jews. Within the Nazi Party itself, some of the highest-ranking officials were unaware initially that the orders for the killing of Jews were issued directly by Hitler. Though the Jews were persecuted in Germany before the war and began to be killed from its outset, the official policy of pursuing a "final solution of the Jewish problem" was not laid out until the January 1942 Wannsee Conference. From that point on, the campaign to eliminate the Jews became a top priority, at times seeming to be more important to Hitler than winning the war. This selection illustrates that Hitler made no effort to hide his intentions and that his subordinates were happy to carry out his wishes. John Toland is a Pulitzer Prize–winning author who has written numerous books. His biography of Hitler, from which this excerpt is taken, is considered one of the best.

wo days after the invasion of the Soviet Union the man responsible for the deportation of Jews, Reinhard Heydrich,

complained in writing that this was no answer to the Jewish problem. . . . It was fitting, therefore, that on the last day of July Heydrich received a cryptic order (signed by [Hermann] Göring upon instructions from the Führer) instructing him "to make all necessary preparations regarding organizations and financial matters to bring about a complete solution of the Jewish question in the German sphere of influence in Europe."

Behind the innocuous bureaucratic language lay sweeping authority for the SS to organize the extermination of European Jewry. As a preliminary step, Heinrich Himmler [the chief of the SS and the director of the extermination campaign] . . . asked the chief physician of the SS what was the best method of mass extermination. The answer was: gas chambers. The next step was to summon Rudolf Höss, the commandant of the largest concentration camp in Poland, and give him secret oral instructions. "He told me," testified Höss, "something to the effect—I do not remember the exact words—that the Führer had given the order for a final solution of the Jewish question. We the SS, must carry out that order. If it is not carried out now the Jews will later on destroy the German people." Himmler said he had chosen Höss's camp since Auschwitz, strategically located near the border of Germany, afforded space for measures requiring isolation. Höss was warned that this operation was to be treated as a secret Reich matter. He was forbidden to discuss the matter with his immediate superior. And so Höss resumed to

Poland and, behind the back of the inspector of concentration camps quietly began to expand his grounds with intent to turn them into the greatest killing center in man's history. He did not even tell his wife what he was doing.

Hitler's concept of concentration camps as well as the practicality of genocide owed much, so he claimed, to his studies of English and United States history. He admired the camps for Boer prisoners in South Africa and for the Indians in the wild West; and often praised to his inner circle the efficiency of America's extermination—by starvation and uneven combat—of the red savages who could not be tamed by captivity. . . .

In mid-October [1941], after lecturing on the necessity of bringing decency into civil life, he said, "But the first thing, above all, is to get rid of the Jews. Without that, it will be useless to clean the Augean stables." Two days later he was more explicit. "From the rostrum of the Reichstag, I prophesied to Jewry that, in the event of war's proving inevitable, the Jew would disappear from Europe. That race of criminals has on its conscience the two million dead of the First World War, and now already hundreds and thousands more. Let nobody tell me that all the same we can't park them in the marshy parts of Russia! Who's worrying about our troops? It's not a bad idea, by the way, that public rumor attributes to us a plan to exterminate the Jews. Terror is a salutary thing." He predicted that the attempt to create a Jewish state would be a failure. "I have numerous accounts to settle, about which I cannot think today. But that doesn't mean I forget them. I write them down. The time will come to bring out the big book! Even with regard to the Jews, I've found myself remaining inactive. There's no sense in adding uselessly to the difficulties of the moment. One acts shrewdly when one bides one's time."

One reason Hitler had delayed implementing the Final Solution was hope that his implied threat to exterminate the Jews would keep Roosevelt out of the war. But Pearl Harbor ended this faint expectation and Hitler's hope turned into bitterness, with extermination becoming a form of international reprisal.

The decision taken, the Führer made it known to those entrusted with the Final Solution that the killings should be done as humanely as possible. This was in line with his conviction that he was observing God's injunction to cleanse the world of vermin. Still a member in good standing of the Church of Rome despite detestation of its hierarchy ("I am now as before a Catholic and will always remain so"), he carried within him its teaching that the Jew was the killer of God. The extermination, therefore, could be done without a twinge of conscience since he was merely acting as the avenging hand of God—so long as it was done impersonally, without cruelty. Himmler was pleased to murder with mercy. He ordered technical experts to devise gas chambers which would eliminate masses of Jews efficiently and "humanely," then crowded the victims into boxcars and sent them east to stay in ghettos until the killing centers in Poland were completed.

The time had come to establish the bureaucracy of liquidation and the man in charge, Heydrich, sent out invitations to a number of state secretaries and chiefs of the SS main offices for a "Final Solution" Conference, to take place on December 10, 1941. The recipients of his invitation, aware only that Jews were being deported to the East, had little idea of the meaning of "final solution" and awaited the conference with expectation and keen interest. . . .

The Wannsee Conference

At about 11 A.M. [on January 20, 1942] fifteen men gathered in a room at the Reich Security Main Office at number 56-58 Grossen Wannsee. There were representatives from [Alfred] Rosenberg's East Ministry, Göring's Four-Year Plan agency, the Interior Ministry, the Justice Ministry, the Foreign Office and the party chancellery. Once they had seated themselves informally at tables, Chairman Heydrich began to speak. He had been given, he said, "the responsibility for working out the final solution of the Jewish problem regardless of geographical boundaries." This euphemism was followed by a veiled and puzzling remark which involved Hitler himself. "Instead of emigration," he said "there is now a further possible solution to which the Führer has already signified his consent—namely deportation to the East."

At this point Heydrich exhibited a chart indicating which Jewish communities were to be evacuated, and gave a hint as to their fate. Those fit to work would be formed into labor gangs but even those who survived the rigors would not be allowed to go free and so "form a new germ cell from which the Jewish race would again arise. History teaches us that.". . .

Thirty copies of the conference record were distributed to the ministries and SS main offices and the term "Final Solution" became known throughout the Reich bureaucracy yet the true meaning of what Heydrich had said was fathomed only by those privy to the killing operations, and many of this select group, curiously, were convinced that Adolf Hitler himself was not totally aware that mass murder was being plotted. SS Lieutenant Colonel Adolf Eichmann, in charge of the Gestapo's Jewish Evacuation Office, for one knew this was a myth. . . .

A few days later Hitler confirmed in spite of himself, that he was indeed the architect of the Final Solution. "One must act radically," he said at lunch on January 23, in the presence of Himmler. "When one pulls out a tooth, one does it with a single tug, and the pain quickly goes away. The Jew must clear out of Europe. It's the Jew who prevents everything. When I think about it, I realize that I'm extraordinarily humane. At the time of the rules of the Popes the Jews were mistreated in Rome. Until 1830, eight Jews mounted on donkeys were led once a year through the streets of Rome. For my part, I restrict myself to telling them they must go away. If they break their pipes on the journey, I can't do anything about it. But if they refuse to go voluntarily I see no other solution but extermination." Never before had he talked so openly to his inner circle and he was so absorbed by the subject that on the twenty-seventh he again demanded the disappearance of all Jews from Europe.

His obsession with Jews was publicly expressed a few days later in a speech at the Sportpalast on the ninth anniversary of National Socialism's rise to power. "I do not even want to speak of the Jews," he said, and proceeded to do so at length. "They are simply our old enemies, their plans have suffered shipwreck through us, and they rightly hate us, just as we hate them. We realize that this war can only end either in the wiping out of the Germanic nations, or by the disappearance of Jewry from Europe.". . .

Killing Jews Becomes Paramount

Hitler always took time to oversee the Final Solution. In this matter he neither needed nor took advice. He made this clear in his message on the anniversary of the promulgation of the party program in late February. "My prophecy," he said, "shall be fulfilled that this war will not destroy Aryan humanity but it will exterminate the Jew. Whatever the battle may bring in its course or however long it may last, that will be its final course." The elimination of Jewry overrode victory itself.

Despite such open hints, few had yet been initiated into the secret. [Propaganda minister Joseph] Goebbels himself still did not realize the enormity of the measures being prepared. One of his employees, Hans Fritzsche, did learn about the Einsatzgruppen killings from a letter sent by an SS man in the Ukraine. The writer complained that he had suffered a nervous breakdown after receiving an order to kill Jews and Ukrainian intelligentsia. He could not protest through official channels and asked for help. Fritzsche immediately went to Heydrich and asked point-blank, "Is the SS there for the purpose of committing mass murders?" Heydrich indignantly denied the charge, promising to start an investigation at once. He reported back the next day that the culprit was Gauleiter Koch, who had acted without the Führer's knowledge, then vowed that the killings would cease. "Believe me, Herr Fritzsche," said Heydrich, "anyone who has the reputation of being cruel does not have to be cruel; he can act humanely."

Only that March did Goebbels himself learn the exact meaning of Final Solution. Then Hitler told him flatly that Europe must be cleansed of all Jews, "if necessary by applying the most brutal methods." The Führer was so explicit that Goebbels could now write in his diary:

> A judgment is being visited upon the Jews that, while barbaric, is fully deserved. . . . One must not be sentimental in these matters. If we did not fight the Jew, they would destroy us. It's a life-and-death struggle between the Aryan race and the Jewish bacillus. No other government and no other regime would have the strength for such a global solution of this question.

By spring six killing centers had been set up in Poland. There were four in [Hans] Frank's Generalgouvernement [German-occupied Poland]: Treblinka, Sobibor, Belzec and Lublin; two in the incorporated territories: Kulmhof and Auschwitz. The first four gassed the Jews by engine-exhaust fumes but Rudolf Höss, commandant of the huge complex near Auschwitz, thought this too "inefficient" and introduced to his camp a more lethal gas, hydrogen cyanide, marketed commercially under the name of Zyklon B. . . .

No Room for Sentiment

Perhaps the most diabolical innovation of the Final Solution was the establishment of Jewish Councils to administer their own deportation and destruction. This organization, comprising those leaders of the community who believed that co-operation with the Germans was the best policy, discouraged resistance. "I will not be afraid to sacrifice 50,000 of our community," reasoned a typical leader, Moses Merin, "in order to save the other 50,000."

By early summer the mass exterminations began under the authority of a written order from Himmler. Eichmann showed this authorization to one of his assistants, Dieter Wisliceny, with the explanation that Final Solution meant the biological extermination of the Jewish race. "May God forbid," exclaimed the appalled Wisliceny, "that our enemies should ever do anything similar to the German people!"

"Don't be sentimental," said Eichmann. "This is a Führer order." This was corroborated by Himmler in a letter to the chief of the SS Main Office at the end of July: "The occupied Eastern territories will be cleared of Jews. The implementation of this very hard order has been placed on my shoulders by the Führer. No one can release me from this responsibility in any case. So I forbid all interference."

What Kurt Gerstein learned, as head of the Technical Disinfection Service of the Waffen SS, had already driven him to despair. "He was so appalled by the satanic practices of the Nazis," recalled a friend, "that their eventual victory did not seem to him impossible." During a tour that summer of the four extermination camps in the Generalgouvernement, Gerstein saw with his own eyes what he had read about. At the first camp he and two companions—Eichmann's deputy and a professor of hygiene named Pfannenstiel—were informed that Hitler and Himmler had just ordered "all action speeded up." At Belzec, two days later, Gerstein saw these words translated into reality.

"There are not ten people alive," he was told by the man in charge, Kriminalkommissar Christian Wirth, "who have seen or will see as much as you." Gerstein witnessed the entire procedure from the arrival of 6,000 Jews in boxcars, 1,450 of whom were already dead. As the survivors were driven out of the cars with whips, they were ordered over a loudspeaker to remove all clothing, artificial limbs, and spectacles and turn in all valuables and money. Women and young girls were to have their hair cut off. "That's to make something special for U-boat crews," explained an SS man, "nice slippers."

Revolted, Gerstein watched the march to the death chambers. Men, women, children—all stark naked—filed past in a ghastly parade as a burly SS man promised in a loud priestlike voice that nothing terrible was going to happen to them. "All you have to do is breathe in deeply. That strengthens the lungs. Inhaling is a means of preventing infectious diseases. It's a good method of disinfection." To those who timorously asked what their fate would be, the SS man gave more reassurance: the men would build roads and houses; the women would do housework or help in the kitchen. But the odor from the death chambers was telltale and those at the head of the column had to be shoved by those behind. Most were silent, but one woman, eyes flashing, cursed her murderers. She was spurred on by whiplashes from Wirth, a former chief of criminal police in Stuttgart. Some prayed, others asked, "Who will give us water to wash the dead?" Gerstein prayed with them.

By now the chambers were jammed with humanity. But the driver of the diesel truck, whose exhaust gases would exterminate the Jews, could not start the engine. Incensed at the delay, Wirth began lashing at the driver with his whip. Two hours and forty-nine minutes later the engine started. After another interminable twenty-five minutes Gerstein peered into one chamber. Most of the occupants were already dead. At the end of thirty-two minutes all were lifeless. They were standing erect, recalled Gerstein, "like pillars of basalt, since there had not been an inch of space for them to fall in or even lean. Families could still be seen holding hands even in death." The horror continued as one group of workers began tearing open the mouths of the dead with iron hooks, while others searched anuses and genital organs for jewelry. Wirth was in his element. "See for yourself," he said, pointing to a large can filled with teeth. "Just look at the amount of gold there is! And we have collected as much only yesterday and the day before. You can't imagine what we find every day—dollars, diamonds, gold! You'll see!"

Gerstein forced himself to watch the final process. The bodies were flung into trenches, each some hundred yards long, conveniently located near the gas chambers. He was told that the bodies would swell from gas after a few days, raising the mound as much as six to ten feet. Once the swelling subsided, the bodies would be piled on railway ties covered with diesel oil and burned to cinders.

The following day the Gerstein party was driven to Treblinka near Warsaw where they saw almost identical installations but on a larger scale: "eight gas chambers and veritable mountains of clothing and underwear, 115 to 130 feet high." In honor of their visit, a banquet was held for employees. "When one sees the bodies of these Jews," Professor Pfannenstiel told them, "one understands the greatness of the work you are doing!" After dinner the guests were offered butter, meat and alcohol as going-away presents. Gerstein lied that he was adequately supplied from his own farm and so Pfannenstiel took the former's share as well as his own.

Upon arrival in Warsaw, Gerstein set off immediately for Berlin, resolved to tell those who would listen of the ghastly sights he had witnessed. A modern Ancient Mariner, he began spreading the truth to incredulous colleagues. As a rock thrown into a pond creates ever widening ripples, so did the tale of Kurt Gerstein.

Selection 3

The Wannsee Conference

Arno J. Mayer

The persecution of the Jews began with Hitler's rise to power. The Nazis did not begin to systematically murder the Jews, *however, until after the war began. Even then the preference was toward deportation and ghettoization. Though Hitler made no secret of his interest in exterminating the Jews, no formal decision to do so was made. The situation began to change by the beginning of 1942, in part because of setbacks Germany was suffering on the battlefield. When the German army was defeated at Moscow and was forced to retreat, it marked a turning point in the war, ending an unbroken string of stunning political, diplomatic, and military victories. Hitler would retain delusions about the prospects of victory, but, after the entrance of the United States into the war after the December 7, 1941, bombing of Pearl Harbor, it became increasingly clear that Germany could not win the war. Hitler might have surrendered and cut Germany's losses, but he was determined to fight to the end. As the military situation grew more bleak, the Nazis' determination to solve the "Jewish question" became more resolute. Finally, on January 20, 1942, at a meeting of relatively low-level Nazi bureaucrats, the decision was made to devise a "final solution" to the Jewish problem. Chaired by Reinhard Heydrich and attended by Adolf Eichmann, the meeting established the administrative apparatus for accomplishing Hitler's dream of a Europe free of Jews. This excerpt discusses the decisions made at the Wannsee Conference. Arno J. Mayer is the Dayton-Stockton Professor of History at Princeton and the author of several books on the history of Europe.*

On November 29, 1941, Reinhard Heydrich sent invitations to a number of government and SS officials for a meeting to work out a coordinated plan for the solution of the "Jewish problem," now that Jews from the Reich were being banished to the east, where conditions were tempestuous and chaotic. If Heydrich spoke of a "total" or "final" solution in this summons, he certainly did not spell out what he or his superiors understood by this term. The conference was to be held on December 9 in Berlin, at the headquarters of the International Criminal Police Commission at Grosser Wannsee 56–8.

Reinhard Heydrich

At the last moment this meeting was put off for six weeks, until January 20, 1942. . . .

Heydrich chaired the meeting. The other fourteen participants were officials of Heydrich's subordinate rank, or lower. As the objective was to coordinate the solution of the "Jewish problem," there were delegates from both spheres of the dual state. There were three functionaries from traditional ministries, all of them party members or declared Nazi sympathizers: Dr. Wilhelm Stuckart, state secretary for legal affairs in the Interior Ministry; Dr. Roland Freisler, state secretary and second-ranking official in the Justice Ministry; and Martin Luther, deputy state secretary and close associate of [Joachim] von Ribbentrop in the Foreign Office. An additional four participants came from Nazi-created state administrations: Gauleiter Dr. Alfred Meyer and Dr. Georg Leibbrandt, state secretaries in the Ministry for the Occupied Eastern

Excerpted from Arno J. Mayer, *Why Did the Heavens Darken?* Copyright © 1988 Arno J. Mayer. Originally published by Pantheon. Reprinted with permission from the author and Rosalie Siegel, International Literary Agent, Inc.

Territories; Dr. Josef Bühler, state secretary and first adjunct to Dr. Hans Frank in the General Government; and Erich Neumann, state secretary in the Office of the Four-Year Plan. One delegate may be said to have come from the nerve center of the dual state: Ministerial Director Wilhelm Kritzinger, sitting in for Dr. Hans Heinrich Lammers, chief of the Reich Chancellery, who had frequent access to Hitler.

The remaining six delegates, all of them SS officers, spoke for the party side of the state: SS Colonel Dr. Gerhard Klopfer, chief of the Third (political) Division of the Party Chancellery, headed by Martin Bormann; SS General Otto Hofmann, director of the Bureau of Race and Resettlement in the Reich Central Security Office (RSHA); SS Major General Heinrich Müller, head of Section IV (Gestapo) of RSHA; SS Lieutenant Colonel Adolf Eichmann, chief of Division B-4 (Evacuation and Jews), also Section IV; SS Colonel Dr. Karl Schöngarth, commander of the Security Police and Security Service in the General Government; and SS Major Dr. Rudolf Lange, commander of the Security Police and Security Service in Latvia, who also represented his superior, the security chief of Reichkommissariat Ostland.

Eight of the fifteen participants at Wannsee, including three of the SS leaders, were university graduates. Without exception, all fifteen were versed in the "Jewish question," each from his own specialized perspective. Moreover, all must have known about the worsening plight of the Jews throughout the eastern territories, including Poland. How many of them were informed about the anti-Jewish ravages of the Einsatzgruppen and the regular SS is unclear. But at the very least, Heydrich, Lange, Bühler, and more than likely Stuckart, had firsthand information which they had no reason to keep to themselves. This is not to say that for any of these officials, even Heydrich, the massacres outside Kiev and Riga were necessarily rehearsals for a "final solution" of liquidation to be systematized and streamlined at Wannsee. Even so, there could be no doubt for any of them that they were assembled to increase, not alleviate, the torment of the Jews.

A Preview of the Final Solution

Hans Frank had assigned Bühler to represent the General Government at Wannsee, and apparently had sent him to Berlin for a preliminary briefing. On December 16, 1941, while the conference was on hold, Frank addressed the top members of his administration in Cracow. On this occasion he expressed ideas which were probably widespread in the higher political echelons in the east and reflected his deputy's report on the temper in the capital. Frank's own words must be quoted *in extenso*.

> Let me tell you quite frankly: in one way or another we will have to finish with the Jews. The Führer once expressed it as follows: should Jewry once again succeed in inciting a world war, the bloodletting could not be limited to the peoples they drove to war but the Jews [themselves] would be done for in Europe. . . . As an old-time National Socialist I must say that if the Jewish tribe survives the war in Europe while we sacrifice our blood for the preservation of Europe, this war will be but a partial success. Basically, I must presume, therefore, that the Jews will disappear. They must go away. To that end I have started negotiations to expel them to the east. In January this issue will be discussed at a major conference in Berlin, to which I am sending State Secretary Dr. Bühler. . . . In any case, there will be a great Jewish migration.

> But what is to become of the Jews? Do you think that they will be settled in villages in the conquered eastern territories? In Berlin we have been told not to complicate matters since neither these territories [nor our own] have any use for them [i.e., the Jews], we should liquidate them ourselves! Gentlemen, I must ask you to remain unmoved by pleas for pity. We must annihilate the Jews wherever we encounter them and wherever possible, in order to maintain the overall mastery of the Reich here. . . . Anyhow, we must find a way [other than a legal one] to achieve this goal, and I am perplexed as to how to proceed.

For us the Jews are also exceptionally damaging because they are being such gluttons. There are an estimated 2.5 million Jews in the General Government, perhaps. . . [even as many] as 3.5 million. These 3.5 million Jews, we cannot shoot them, nor can we poison them. Even so, we can take steps which in some way or other will pave the way for [their] destruction, notably in connection with the grand measures to be discussed in the Reich. The General Government must become just as *judenfrei* ["free of jews"] as the Reich.

Unlike before, Governor-General Frank was no longer satisfied with keeping his captive province from becoming the main dumping ground for unwanted Jews from farther west. He now saw an opportunity to rid it of its own Jews—whose numbers he exaggerated greatly—by either expelling them eastward or doing away with them in other ways. . . .

Apparently, Eichmann, the lowest-ranking official at Wannsee, took the minutes which, after review by Heydrich, became the official "protocol" of the proceedings. Naturally, this text reveals nothing about the private conversations of the participants before and after the meeting. . . .

On January 20, 1942, in his opening statement at Wannsee, Heydrich noted that Reichsmarschall Göring had charged him "with preparing the *Endlösung* [final/definitive solution] of the Jewish question in Europe," and that he had summoned this meeting to "clarify some of the fundamental issues." Göring's request for a draft proposal for the necessary "administrative, practical, and financial" arrangements called for prior consultation with all interested government agencies. Having established the source of his authority, Heydrich went on to claim that "without regard for geographic boundaries" in the main Himmler and he himself were responsible for the "implementation of the final solution."

A Review of Nazi Accomplishments

Before turning to what needed to be done, Heydrich reviewed what had been achieved since 1933. After being deemancipated and subjected to restrictions within Germany, the Jews had been urged and pushed to emigrate. Eventually, in January 1939, Goring had ordered him, Heydrich, to set up and direct a special emigration office to speed and organize the extrusion of Jews "by legal means." There being no other solution, this office proceeded to force emigration in the face of both domestic and foreign obstacles. All told, and despite numerous stumbling blocks between January 30, 1933, and October 31, 1941, some 537,000 Jews had left the Old Reich, Austria, and the Protectorate. In the meantime however, "in view of the risks of emigration in wartime and considering the [new] possibilities in the east," Himmler had forbidden all further emigration. Then Heydrich came to the core of the agenda.

> To rake the place of emigration, and with the prior approval of the Führer, the evacuation of the Jews to the East has become another possible solution
>
> Although both courses of action [emigration and evacuation] must, of course, be considered as nothing more than [so many] temporary expedients, they do help to provide practical experience which should be of great importance in view of the coming *Endlösung* of the Jewish question.

Needless to say, as it stands, and considering later developments, this statement was full of "warnings, and portents and evils imminent." But from the protocol it is not clear whether or not Heydrich amplified his proposition by discussing the disastrous plight of eastern ghettos like Riga and Łódź, which was being aggravated by the arrival of Jewish deportees from Germany. Did he himself have a clear idea of what he meant by *Endlösung?* Did he use coded language, confident of being understood by the assembled initiates?

All Jews Are Targets

Heydrich was, in any case, breaking altogether new ground. Until this day, the Nazi persecution of the Jews had been confined to the Jews of Germany, Austria, and the Protectorate, as well as of the territories conquered—and still to be conquered—in the east. Now, however, Heydrich broadened the range, in that he meant his projected *Endlösung* to apply to all of Europe. He circulated a table listing the Jewish populations of the entire Continent as well as of England and Ireland, for a total of over 11 million Jews. He claimed that this figure was on the low side, the count of Jews being based on confessional rather than "racial" criteria in many countries. To implement the *Endlösung,* Heydrich proposed "to comb Europe from west to east," beginning with German lands.

Heydrich envisaged that "under proper direction . . . and in an appropriate manner" the Jews would be put to work in the east. His idea was to form the Jews who were fit to work into "large labor columns, separated by sex," to be marched to the eastern territories, where they would build roads. Doubtless a great many Jews "will fall by the wayside from natural exhaustion." In turn, however, the "surviving remnant" would certainly consist of the "toughest" elements. In as much as the members of this residue would be the product of "natural selection," they would have "to be dealt with appropriately, [for] upon being freed they will constitute the embryo for the reconstruction of Jewish life (see the lessons of history)."

The idea was to make a clear distinction between Jews fit for hard labor and those unfit for it, with the expectation that many of those declared fit would be marked for early death by virtue of being unsuited for backbreaking work. . . .

Apparently, the unfit—children, many women, the infirm, the elderly—were to be evacuated "to so-called transit ghettos, for transportation further east from there." Heydrich saw a need to divide all potential evacuees into different categories and allow for exceptions. The Nuremberg Laws would be the basis of this projected operation. Certain half-Jews would be given a choice between, on the one hand, sterilization and staying in Germany, and, on the other, deportation. Jews over sixty-five years of age "would not be evacuated but sent to a ghetto for the aged," most likely to Theresienstadt, along with badly wounded

and heavily decorated Jewish war veterans. . . .

According to the protocol, not a single voice was raised to protest even the most egregious and unconscionable provisions of Heydrich's proposal. . . . Martin Luther of the Foreign Office noted that while there might be difficulties in removing Jews from the "northern [Scandinavian] countries," where they were rare in any case, he foresaw none for "southeastern and western Europe." To avoid "endless red tape," Wilhelm Stuckart of the Interior Ministry recommended that the sterilization of half-Jews be made not voluntary but compulsory. Erich Neumann of the Four-Year Plan urged that Jews "working in vital war industries not be evacuated until replacements were found," to which Heydrich agreed. For his part, Josef Bühler, Hans Frank's emissary, asked that "the final solution of this question" begin in the General Government, which could guarantee that there would be no local transportation and economic difficulties.

> Jews should be removed as rapidly as possible from the territories of the General Government, in particular because as carriers of disease they are a great danger to society at large and as incorrigible black they are undermining the economy of the country. Besides, of the 2.5 million Jews, the majority was unfit for work.

Bühler concluded with the plea "that in this territory the Jewish question be solved as quickly as possible." Apparently, Bühler, along with Alfred Meyer of the Ministry for the Occupied Eastern Territories, took the lead in the closing discussion of "different types of possible solutions" *(die verschiedenen Arten der Lösungsmöglichkeiten).* Both advocated "the immediate implementation of certain preparatory measures in the affected territories, care being taken not to disquiet the [local] populations." Given their responsibilities, Bühler and Meyer were mainly concerned with the eastern territories.

The War and the Jews

There was nothing definitive about the Wannsee Conference, nor could there be. Whatever its origin, it was held at an unexpectedly trying moment in the history of the Third Reich. War policy was in extreme flux, and so was Jewish policy. At the same time that Nazi Germany's leaders decided to go to any length in pursuit of the war against the Soviets, they resolved to step up the war against the Jews. With emigration to European countries and Madagascar foreclosed, they fixed upon the east as holding the key to victory over not only their military enemies but also the Jews. For them, the two campaigns were closely and fatally intertwined. For a while some Nazis continued to look to the defeat of the Soviet Union to provide space for the resettlement of Jews deep in the interior of Russia. Paradoxically, in this perspective military victory was the precondition for Jewish survival. To be sure, the Jews would in that case have suffered cruelly and disproportionately while the war lasted. Still, victory would have kept open the historical possibility of a significant remnant of Jews enduring, if only to be ghettoized in a distant reserve, or to be used as a pawn in bargaining for a negotiated settlement with the Western Powers. In fact, the faster and easier the victory, the larger this remnant and the better the chances for contingent survival would doubtless have been. Conversely, the longer and harder the fighting and the more ineluctable the defeat, the more catastrophic the consequences for the Jews. Such was, after all, Hitler's grimly insistent private and public prophecy.

On January 25, 1942, five days after the Wannsee Conference, Hitler held forth bluntly in the presence of Himmler and Lammers.

> The Jew must get out of Europe. Otherwise we will get no European understanding. The world over he is the chief agitator against us. . . . All I say is that he must go away. If, in the process he is bruised, I can't help it. If he does not leave voluntarily, I see no solution other than extermination.

. . . In this same diatribe Hitler wondered "why I should see a Jew in a different light than a Russian prisoner [of war]." He declined all responsibility for "the many [Russians] who are dying in prison camps." Instead, he blamed the Jews

for "having driven us into this situation," and once again asked, rhetorically, "why the Jews incited this war."

Two days later, on January 27, in another monologue at his Wolf's Lair headquarters in East Prussia, Hitler reiterated that "the Jew has to disappear from Europe," including from Switzerland and Sweden. On this occasion he said nothing about extermination, limiting himself to declaring that "it would be best if [the Jews] went to Russia." At any rate, he had "no pity" for them. . . .

On January 30, 1942, he addressed a rally in Berlin's Palace of Sports. . . .

> We fully realize that the war can only end either with the extermination of the Aryan peoples or the disappearance of the Jews from Europe. While I guard myself against making rash prophecies, on September 1, 1939, I declared in the German Reichstag that this war would not end, as the Jews suppose, with the extermination of the European-Aryan peoples, but with the destruction of Jewry. For the first time the ancient Jewish maxim will be put in practice: "an eye for an eye, a tooth for a tooth."

Certain that anti-Semitism would spread with the protraction of the war, Hitler predicted that "the hour would come when the most evil world enemy of all time will be put out of action for at least a thousand years.". . .

On February 24, 1942, he returned to this same theme. . . .

> My prophecy will be fulfilled: this war will not destroy Aryan humanity, but will exterminate the Jew. Such will be the ultimate outcome of this conflict, whatever its repercussions and no matter how long it lasts.

The world simply could not be at peace until after "the liquidation of this parasite."

In the meantime, Hitler kept reiterating his animus in private. During the night of February 3–4 he asserted that after many false starts in the persecution of Jews through the centuries, "this time they will disappear from Europe." On February 17, in the presence of Himmler, the führer charged that just as the Jews had once used Christianity to subvert the natural order of things, in which "the fittest rule," not the meek, so now they had recourse to bolshevism to advance their world conspiracy. Clearly, "the more thoroughly the Jews are thrown out, the faster this danger will be removed." According to Goebbels, in mid-February Hitler also spoke to him about the need to be unsparing with the Jews.

> There is no room for sentimentality. The Jews deserve the catastrophe in which they are caught up today. They will experience their own destruction along with the destruction of our [other] enemies. We must hasten this process impassively, and in so doing render an inestimable service to humanity which has suffered at the hands of Jewry for thousands of years.

Implementing Wannsee

. . . At the Wannsee Conference the switches were set for the deportation of Jews from German-occupied Europe west of the Warthegau to the ghettos and transit camps east of that line. The result would be not only the overcrowding of ghettos but also the concentration of all Jews in the most ill-starred lands of the Continent. Europe's Jews risked being trapped in the most politically tyrannized, economically wasted, and militarily vulnerable zone of German-occupied Europe. The Jews would have been gravely imperiled in this precarious region even without having violence deliberately done to them during and after their roundup and deportation in overcrowded railway cars. The idea was to use their evacuation and resettlement to decimate them, but not without concurrently exploiting their labor for the war effort. The result was a chronic but not irreconcilable tension between liquidation and productivity. Although Heydrich proposed to impress Jews for road-building, he put decimation through forced labor ahead of economic output. . . .

But Himmler, his immediate superior and overall head of the incipient "Final Solution," had a more far-reaching view of the function and place of the security services in the regime. . . . He now proposed to harness the labor of an expanding concentration-camp system for the war economy of the embattled Behemoth. To be sure, Himmler was not at Wannsee and he seems not to have alerted Heydrich to this new turn before January 20. But within less than a week after Wannsee, on January 26, 1942, he sent a wire to SS Major General Richard Glücks, chief inspector of concentration camps, prefiguring a radical change in the population as well as the purpose of the camps.

> Since no Russian prisoners of war can be expected in the near future I will send many of the Jews and Jewesses to he evacuated from Germany to the camps. Prepare the concentration camps to take in 100,000 Jewish men and 50,000 Jewish women next month. In the coming weeks the concentration camps will receive great economic contracts and assignments. SS Major General Pohl will provide you with necessary details.

By instructing Glücks to follow Pohl's orders, Himmler signaled the rising importance of the newly chartered Central Economic and Administrative Office (WVHA) within the SS. Paradoxically, Himmler's telegram did not distinguish between Jews fit and unfit for work, nor did it hint at any hoped-for decimation. There was either a hidden agenda or, more likely, the process of "selection" was to grow out of the iron exigencies of concentration camps and ghettos, which became total institutions of forced dehumanization, exploitation, and liquidation. . . .

Pohl's WVHA was charged with raising the largest possible Jewish labor force for hyperexploitation, either within concentration camps and ghettos or in private industry outside. . . .

Simultaneously, Heydrich's RSHA undertook to make all but Slavic Europe *judenfrei* "by combing it [of Jews] from west to east." For the moment these Jews, many of them highly assimilated and acculturated, were to be sent to the occupied eastern territories to be crammed into ghettos as well as concentration, labor, and transit camps, pending resettlement farther east.

Selection 4

The Einsatzgruppen: Mobile Killing Squads

Yale Edeiken

The Nazis devised many diabolical ways to murder their victims, from cruel experiments to the gas chambers. In the concentration camps, prisoners were killed slowly by backbreaking work, mistreatment, malnutrition, and disease. Approximately 1.5 million were murdered quickly by Germans who lined men, women, and children in front of ditches and machine-gunned them. The cold efficiency of the operations were thoroughly documented in detailed reports that helped war crimes investigators prove the guilt of the perpetrators. What is not explained here is how anyone could have stripped women and children and then shot them in the back of the head. The mobile killing squads, or Einsatzgruppen, assigned to commit these horrendous acts are the subject of this essay by Yale Edeiken.

The Einsatzgruppen were four paramilitary units established before the invasion of the Soviet Union for the purpose of "liquidating" (murdering) Jews, Romany [Gypsies], and political operatives of the Com-

Excerpted from Yale F. Edeiken, "An Introduction to the Einsatzgruppen," an online article found at www.pgonline.com/electriczen/documents/introduction.html. Reprinted with permission from the author.

munist party. Ultimately three of these groups (Einsatzgruppen A, B, and C) were attached to army groups taking part in the invasion. A fourth group (Einsatzgruppe D) was sent to the Ukraine without being attached to any army group. All operated in the territories occupied by the Third Reich on the eastern front. Most of the crimes perpetrated by the Eisnsatzgruppen took place in the Ukraine and the Baltic states of Latvia, Estonia and Lithuania. . . .

In effect the Einsatzgruppen were almost always operationally independent taking their orders directly from Heinrich Himmler and, until his death, Reinhard Heydrich. While there were plans to establish similar units in other territories controlled by the Nazis (Ohlendorf; Nuremberg testimony), these plans were never implemented. . . .

The most succinct description of the purpose of the Einsatzgruppen was given at the trial of Adolph Eichmann by Dr. Michael Musmanno, Justice of the Pennsylvania Supreme Court, who presided over the trial of 23 of the leaders of the Einsatzgruppen. He stated "The purpose of the Einsatzgruppen was to murder Jews and deprive them of their property." SS General Erich von dem Bach-Zelewski confirmed this at the main Nuremberg Trial when he testified that "The principal task [of the Einsatzgruppen] was the annihilation of the Jews, gypsies, and political commissars.". . .

Tracing the process by which the orders of the Einsatzgruppen to eliminate the Jews in the captured territories were developed is difficult. The process seems to have begun in March, 1941, while the plans for Operation Barbarossa (the invasion of the Soviet Union ordered by Hitler on December 18, 1940) were being made.

The decision to use units from the SD (security services) to perform special political actions was made early in the planning stages of the invasion. . . .

The initial policy was orally communicated to the officers of the Einsatzgruppen. They were later embodied in the "Commissar Order" issued by Heydrich Himmler and never revoked. The Commisar Order issued on July 17, 1941, called for "the separation and further treatment of . . . all Jews.". . .

The Composition of the Einsatzgruppen

There were approximately 600 to 1000 men in each Einsatzgruppe, although many were sup-port staff. The active members of the Einsatzgruppen were drawn from various military and non-military organizations of the Third Reich. The bulk of the members were drawn from the Waffen-SS, the military arm of the SS. . . .

Each of the Einsatzgruppen were further broken down into operational subunits known as Einsatzkommandos or Sonderkommandos.

The Victims of the Einsatzgruppen

The overwhelming proportion of the men, women, and children murdered by the Einsatzgruppen were Jews. The Einsatzgruppen also murdered Romany (gypsies), those identified as functionaries of the Communist Party, those accused of defying the occupying armies of the Third Reich, and those accused of being partisans or guerilla fighters against the invading armies. In all cases the murders were contrary to accepted law.

Although an exact figure will never be known, approximately 1,500,000 people were murdered

Members of an Einsatzgruppe execute Soviet civilians kneeling beside a mass grave in Kraigonev in the U.S.S.R. in 1941.

by the Einsatzgruppen. The Einsatzgruppen submitted detailed and specific reports of their actions to their superiors both by radio and written communication; these reports were checked against each other for accuracy at Heydrich's headquarters. According to those reports approximately 1,500,000 people were murdered. In evaluating this large number Justice Michael Musmanno, who presided at the trial of the Einsatzgruppen, wrote:

> One million human corpses is a concept too bizarre and too fantastical for normal mental comprehension. As suggested before, the mention of one million deaths produces no shock at all commensurate with its enormity because to the average brain one million is more a symbol than a quantitative measure. However, if one reads through the reports of the Einsatzgruppen and observes the small numbers getting larger, climbing into ten thousand, tens of thousands, a hundred thousand and beyond, then one can at last believe that this actually happened—the cold-blooded, premeditated killing of one million human beings. . . .

When the U.S. Army captured the headquarters of the Gestapo they found hundreds of written reports from the Einsatzgruppen dispassionately listing their activities. . . .

Other than the evidence provided by the reports, there is direct testimony from those who committed the crimes and some of the bystanders who witnessed them. These witnesses testified at two criminal trials held concerning the crimes of the Einsatzgruppen. The first of these was the trial of Otto Ohlendorf and 22 other defendants who commanded the Einsatzgruppen in 1947. This was a trial before a Tribunal of five judges at which the U.S. laws of evidence and substantive law were applied. The second notable trial was of members of Sonderkommando 4a (attached to Einsatzgruppe C) for 33,771 murders committed at Babi Yar on September 29-30, 1941. This trial was held in Darmstadt pursuant to German law in 1967-8. In both cases the courts heard direct evidence of the crimes committed and convicted the defendants. . . .

The Crimes of the Einsatzgruppen

The only possible interpretation of the reports that the Einsatzgruppen made to Heydrich is that the majority of those men, women, and children were murdered and robbed because they were Jewish. There is no other reason evident from the reports or the defenses that were presented at the various trials.

One of the most notable of these reports is the "Jaeger Report" which details the murders committed by Einsatzkommandos 8 and 3, attached to Einsatzgruppe A in the Vilna-Kaunas area of Lithuania from July 4, 1941 through November 25, 1941. This lengthy report describes the murder of over 130,000 people in that short period of time. This report consists of six sheets listing the murders of Einsatzkommandos 8 and 3 and concluding: "Today I can confirm that our objective, to solve the Jewish problem for Lithuania, has been achieved by EK 3. In Lithuania there are no more Jews, apart from Jewish workers and their families." Most of the report consists of entries such as:

29.10.41	Kauen-F.IX	2,007 Jews, 2,290 Jewesses, 4,273 Jewish children (mopping up ghetto of superfluous Jews)
3.11.41	Lazdjai	485 Jews, 511 Jewesses, 539 Jewish children
15.11.41	Wilkowski	36 Jews, 48 Jewesses, 31 Jewish children
25.11.41	Kauen-F.IX	1.159 Jews, 1,600 Jewesses, 175 Jewish children (resettlers from Berlin, Munich, and Frankfurt am main)

Jaeger report Sheet 5,
which contains 11 such entries.

The reports also give detailed information about the money and other valuables stolen from the victims. The scope of these activities is illustrated by "Operational Report No. 73" dated September 4, 1941 (NO-2844) and "Operational Report No. 133" dated November 14, 1941 (NO-2825). Both of these reports describe the activities of Einsatzkommando 8, a subunit of one of the Einsatzgruppen. The first of these reports states "On the occasion of a purge at Tsherwon 125,880 rubels were found on 139 liquidated Jews and were confiscated. This brings the total of the money confiscated by Einsatzkommando 8 to 1,510,399 rubels." Two months later the same sub-unit was able to report that they had stolen an additional million rubels: "During the period covered by this report, Einsatzkommando 8 confiscated a further 491,705 rubles as well as 15 gold rubles. They were entered into the ledgers and passed to the Administration of Einsatzkommando 8. The total amount of rubels so far secured by Einsatzkommando 8 now amounts to 2,511,226 rubels."

Nor was this thievery limited to their victim's money. Watches, jewelry and even clothing were even plundered. One particularly callous act of murder was described by Justice Musmanno in his decision:

> One of the defendants related how during the winter of 1941 he was ordered to obtain fur coats for his men, and that since the Jews had so much winter clothing, it would not matter so much to them if they gave up a few fur coats. In describing the execution which he attended, the defendant was asked whether the victims were undressed before the execution, he replied: "No, the clothing wasn't taken— this was a fur coat procurement operation."
>
> *Judgment,* p. 36.

Other Participants

The Einsatzgruppen did not act alone. They had help. The Einsatzgruppen could call on the Wehrmacht for assistance but far more important were local militia groups willing to cooperate in the massacres. At Babi Yar where 33,771 Jews were murdered on September 29-30, 1941, there were two Ukrainian "kommandos" assisting Sonderkommando 4a. In Lithuania Operational Report 19 (July 11, 1941) states that "We have retained approximately 205 Lithuanian partisans as a Sonderkommando, sustained them and deployed them for executions as necessary even outside the area." In the Ukraine the Einsatzgruppen frequently welcomed the participation of local militia both because they needed the help of these auxiliaries but because they hoped to involve the locals in the pogrom they were conducting. (Operational Report 81, from Einsatzkommando 6, September 12, 1941).

There are many known instances of these local militias assisting the Einsatzgruppen. During the "Gross Aktion" of October 28-29, 1941, at Kaunas in Lithuania during which 9,200 Jews were murdered, Lithuanian militia worked with the Einsatzgruppen (100 F.3rd at 308). Other examples are Zhitomir on September 18, 1941, in the Ukraine where 3,145 Jews were murdered with the assistance of Ukrainian militia (Operational Report 106) and Korosten where Ukrainian militia rounded up 238 Jews for liquidation (Operational Report 80). At times the assistance was more active. Operational Report 88, for example, reports that on September 6, 1941, 1,107 Jewish adults were shot while the Ukrainian militia unit assisting them liquidated 561 Jewish children and youths.

In many cases the militia that assisted the Einsatzgruppen were paid from the money and valuables stolen from the victims. . . .

When put on trial for his life Otto Ohlendorf, Commander of Einsatzgruppen D, did not use the excuse that the victims were "partisans." Instead he gave the Court a far different rationalization for the murder of the children:

> I believe that it is very simple to explain, if one starts with the fact that this order did not only try to achieve a temporary security (for Germany) but also a permanent security. For that reason, the children were people who would grow up and surely, being the children of parents who had been killed, would constitute a danger no smaller than that of their parents.

When he made this statement Ohlendorf was not speaking just as an individual and a dedicated national socialist; he was repeating the statements of his superior, Heinrich Himmler. Himmler and Ohlendorf were close associates and, in fact, were travelling together when they were captured after the collapse of the Third Reich. In his famous speech to a gathering of SS officers at Posen on October 6, 1943, Himmler made comments remarkably similar to those of Ohlendorf:

> We came to the question: what to do with the women and children? I decided to find a clear solution here as well. I did not consider myself justified to exterminate the men—that is, kill them or allow them to be killed—and allow the avengers of our sons and grandsons in the form of their children to grow up. The difficult resolve had to be taken to make this race disappear from the earth. . . .

(Translation by Gord McFee.)

The Methods of the Einsatzgruppen

The Einsatzgruppen shot people. It's as simple as that. Using various pretexts they rounded up their victims, transported them to a central killing ground and shot them.

At Babi Yar the Jews of Kiev were informed by placards posted around the city by Ukrainian militia for Jews to assemble at 8:00 a.m. on September 29, 1941, at a cemetery near a railroad siding for "resettlement." They were told to bring with them food, warm clothing, documents, money, and valuables. The scene was described by one officer at his trial in 1967. He stated "It was like a mass migration . . . the Jews sang religious songs on the way." At the railroad siding their food and belongings were taken from them and:

> Then the Germans began shoving the Jews into new, narrower lines. They moved very slowly. After a long walk, they came to a passageway formed by German soldiers with truncheons and police dogs. The Jews were whipped through. The dogs went at those who

fell but the pressure of the surging lines behind was irresistible, and the weak and injured were trod underfoot.

> Bruised and bloodied, numbed by the incomprehensibility of their fate, the Jews emerged onto a grassy clearing. They had arrived at Babi Yar; ahead of them lay the ravine. The ground was strewn with clothing. Ukrainian militiamen, supervised by Germans, ordered the Jews to undress. Those who balked, who resisted, were assaulted, their clothes ripped off. Naked bleeding people were everywhere. Screams and hysterical laughter filled the air.

Dawidowicz, "What is the Use of Jewish History?" pp. 106–107

After this brutal processing, the victims were lined up at the edge of the ravine and gunned down by teams of machine gunners. By the time they were finished on Spetember 30, 1941, 33,700 people had been killed.

Otto Ohlendorf testified about the methods used both at his own trial and the trial of the leaders of the Third Reich at Nuremberg. At Nuremberg he told the court that Jews were gathered for mass murders "on the pretext that they were to be resettled." He then told the Tribunal: "After the registration the Jews were collected at one place; and from there they were later transported to the place of execution, which was, as a rule, an antitank ditch or natural excavation. The executions were carried out in a military manner, by firing squads under command." Not all of the groups committed their murders with the military precision of Ohlendorf's. As he testified "Some of the unit leaders did not carry out liquidations in the military manner, but killed the victims singly by shooting them in the back of the neck."

After December, 1941, the Nazis experimented with vans designed by Dr. Becker using lethal gas, exhaust from the motors. Not only was this method slow but, according to Otto Ohlendorf, it was not popular with his men because "the unloading of the corpses was an unnecessary mental strain." Almost all of the victims of these experiments were women and children and, throughout the Einsatzgruppen's reign of terror, shooting was the primary means of execution. . . .

There Is No Way to Rationalize and Justify These Crimes

There are some who would try to deny or justify the murders committed by the Einsatzgruppen. The most benign explanation for this denial was given by Justice Michael Musmanno—an experienced judge and hardened combat veteran—who presided at the trial of the Einsatzgruppen. Shocked and sickened by the evidence which he heard, Justice Musmanno wrote:

> One reads and reads these accounts of which here we can give only a few excerpts and yet there remains the instinct to disbelieve, to question, to doubt. There is less of a mental barrier in accepting the weirdest stories of supernatural phenomena, as for instance, water running up hill and trees with roots reaching toward the sky, than in taking at face value these narratives which go beyond the frontiers of human cruelty and savagery. Only the fact that the reports from which we have quoted came from the pens of men within the accused organizations can the human mind be assured that all this actually happened. The reports and the statements of the defendants themselves verify what otherwise would be dismissed as the product of a disordered imagination.

Judgement of the Tribunal, p. 50.

Selection 5

Nazi Medical Experiments

Robert Jay Lifton

One of the distinguishing characteristics of the Holocaust is that people were not just murdered in unprecedented numbers but were also tortured and killed in the most sadistic ways imaginable. Some of the most sickening photographs from the Nazi period are those the Germans took to record their medical experiments. The pseudoscience of the Nazi doctors was aimed at advancing the ideology of the regime in some cases and, in others, advancing a research interest of a particular doctor. Their experiments included the steril-ization of men and women, the breaking of bones, and the injection of diseases into healthy people. This excerpt from the most authoritative book on the subject offers an overview of some of the more barbaric experiments conducted by the Nazis and rationale used to justify them. Robert Jay Lifton is a professor of psychiatry and psychology.

Excerpted from Robert Jay Lifton, *The Nazi Doctors.* Copyright © 1986 Robert Jay Lifton. Reprinted with permission of Basic-Books, a member of Perseus Books, L.C.C.

*n*azi doctors are infamous for their cruel medical experiments. And no wonder: those experiments killed and maimed; as tangible medical crimes, they were given considerable prominence at the Nuremberg Medical Trial. Yet they were no more than a small part of the extensive and systematic medicalized killing.

And it is that aspect of the experiments—their relation to the Nazi biomedical vision—that I shall mainly discuss.

Generally speaking, Nazi medical experiments fall into two categories: those sponsored by the regime for a specific ideological and military purpose, and those that were done *ad hoc* out of allegedly scientific interest on the part of an SS doctor.

For example, extensive sterilization and castration experiments in Auschwitz, conducted mainly by doctors Carl Clauberg and Horst Schumann, were encouraged officially as a direct expression of racial theory and policy; the experiments with typhus contagion (injecting people with blood from others with active typhus) and with the effectiveness of various preparations of sera (in treating experimentally induced cases of typhus) were connected with military concerns about typhus epidemics among German troops and civilian personnel in the East; while the study of pre-cancerous conditions of the cervix reflected a scientific interest of Dr. Eduard Wirths, the chief SS Auschwitz doctor, and his gynecologist brother Helmut. But the categories overlapped. . . . Here we shall focus on the extensive sterilization and castration experiments, in which Auschwitz more or less specialized, and which were a direct extension of the biomedical vision, but also mention other forms of experimentation and a scientific enterprise, including the establishment of a museum collection of Jewish skulls provided by Auschwitz.

Block 10

The center for these experimental projects was the notorious Block 10, a place that could be considered to be quintessential Auschwitz. Made up mostly of women prisoners, it was located in the men's camp, and the windows were kept closed and shuttered or boarded so that communication with the outside was totally cut off. . . .

At the same time, inmates on the block were completely vulnerable to visits and surveillance of various kinds by SS doctors and, on occasion, by nonmedical officers: "A continuous coming and going of SS . . . [so that] we never felt safe."

For any visit could mean new danger, and inmates therefore "awaited with impatience . . . the evening when we would be locked up as animals in a cage but . . . nonetheless felt freer."

Another woman prisoner doctor, Adelaide Hautval, told of the five hundred women "guinea pigs," all Jewish, from various countries in Europe, who were usually selected directly from transports, according to the needs of the Nazi physician experimenters: "Some required married women, others young girls, a third a mixture of all the categories." Overall conditions were superior to those in the women's camp, because there the "guinea pigs . . . would have died before the results of the experiments could have been assessed." Inmates suffered from hunger, nonetheless, and from the constant uncertainty about "What will it be this time?" For they had absorbed the Auschwitz principle that *anything is permitted.* At the same time the women deeply feared a transfer to Birkenau, where they knew death was more likely, because in Block 10 there was at least a hope that "maybe they will still let us live after this," though few believed that possible. . . .

Sterilization by Injection: "The Professor"

Block 10 was often known as "Clauberg's block," because it was created for him and his experimental efforts to perfect a cheap and effective method of mass sterilization. He was Block 10's figure of greatest authority, "the main man for sterilization.". . . He began his Auschwitz work in December 1942 in Birkenau; but after persuading the authorities that his important research required a special block, he transferred his experiemenial setting to Block 10 in Auschwitz in April 1943.

His method was to inject a caustic substance into the cervix in order to obstruct the fallopian tubes. He chose as experimental subjects married between the ages of twenty and forty, preferably those who had borne children. And he first injected them with opaque liquid in order to determine by X ray that there was no prior blockage or impairment. He had experimented with different substances, but was very secretive about the exact nature of the one he used, probably intent upon protecting any "medical discovery" from research competitors. . . .

The injection was done in three stages over a few months, though some women later described four or five injections. The goal of injecting the caustic substance was to create adhesions in the fallopian tubes that would cause them to be obstructed within a period of about six weeks, as would be demonstrated by subsequent X rays. Clauberg had a prisoner nurse, Sylvia Friedmann, observe the women after the injections for symptoms of any kind.

Despite the terror induced in women victims, Marie L., a French prisoner physician, stressed that many so feared being sent back to Birkenau (where one would be "awaiting death standing in frost, mud, and swamps . . . without water or care") that they could view Block 10 as "a piece of luck and the possibility of survival." Clauberg himself encouraged this hope by his reassurances that he planned not to send them back to Birkenau (meaning the gas chamber) but to take them to his private research clinic at Königshütte, just a few kilometers from Auschwitz. . . .

Clauberg eventually had as many as three hundred women under his control on Block 10. The experiments were supposed to be highly secret, and there was an attempt to isolate women who had been injected from those who had not. Accounts differ about the fate of the women he experimented upon. Those who refused to be experimented upon, or who were considered for one reason or another unsuitable, were sent back to Birkenau and usually gassed—as were those women who became extremely debilitated. Most women experimented upon remained on Block 10, though a considerable number developed fever and various forms of peritoneal infection.

There was the constant fear of being killed because of knowing too much. They also feared both sterilization and artificial insemination. . . .

Descriptions by women experimented upon begin to tell us in human terms what Clauberg was really up to. A Czech Jew named Margita Neumann told of being taken into a dark room with a large X-ray machine:

> Dr. Clauberg ordered me to lie down on the gynecological table and I was able to observe Sylvia Friedmann who was preparing an injection syringe with a long needle. Dr. Clauberg used this needle to give me an injection in my womb. I had the feeling that my stomach would burst with the pain. I began to scream so that I could be heard through the entire block. Dr. Clauberg told me roughly to stop screaming immediately, otherwise I'd be taken back at once to Birkenau concentration camp. . . . After this experiment I had inflammation of the ovaries.

She went on to describe how, whenever Clauberg appeared on the ward, women were "overcome with anxiety and terror," as "they considered what Dr. Clauberg was doing as the actions of a murderer.". . .

Imprisonment of Clauberg

Clauberg . . . was captured by the Russians on 8 June 1945. Imprisoned in the Soviet Union for three years before being tried, he was then convicted of war crimes and sentenced to twenty-five years' imprisonment. But following Stalin's death (in 1953), and various diplomatic agreements, Clauberg was repatriated with other Germans in October 1955. . . . When interviewed by the press, he spoke proudly of his work at Königshütte and Auschwitz and claimed, "I was able to perfect an absolutely new method of sterilization . . . [which] would be of great use today in certain cases."

After various pressures from survivor groups and others, Clauberg was arrested in November 1955; but for a considerable time, the German Chamber of Medicine, the official body of the profession, resisted action against him that would divest him of his title of doctor of medicine. . . . The German Chamber of Medicine finally did remove Clauberg's license. But when he died, suddenly and mysteriously, in his prison cell on 9 August 1957, the general belief was that he was in the process of naming names at the top of the Nazi medical hierarchy and that, consequently, medical colleagues helped bring about his death. . . .

X-Ray and Surgical Castration

Horst Schumann differed from Clauberg in being not a renowned specialist but a reliable "old Nazi doctor" (he joined the Nazi Party and the SA in 1930) who was available for ruthless medical enterprises. Schumann had been a leading figure in the "euthanasia" program as the director of the killing center at Grafeneck. When that center closed, he took over the one at Sonnenstein. . . .

In this case, [Heinrich] Himmler played an even greater role in formulating the experiments, together with Viktor Brack, the Chancellery official active in both the "euthanasia" project and the establishment of the death camps. In early 1941, Himmler and Brack were already exchanging memos in which they shared a vision of "sterilization or castration . . . by means of X-rays" on a massive scale. Brack later claimed

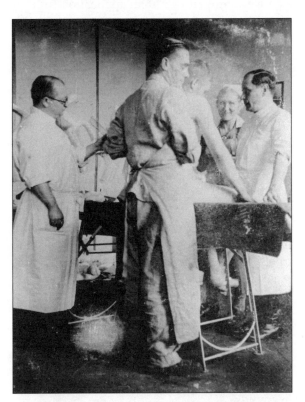

Dr. Carl Clauberg (far left) in the operating room of Block 10. Clauberg used Auschwitz prisoners as guinea pigs in his sterilization experiments.

that the idea originated with Himmler for application to Jewish populations, especially in Poland, and also implicated Reinhard Heydrick, the most ruthless voice around Himmler, but at the same time admitted that Himmler's words "made a great impression on me.". . .

By June 1942, at the height of the German military penetration into Russia, Brack became more specific and programmatic. Referring to consultations with his superior and with the head of the area in Poland where the greatest number of Jews was concentrated, he spoke of the necessity of carrying through "the whole Jewish action [the Final Solution]" but estimated that two million to three million of the ten million Jews in Europe were fit enough to work and therefore should be "preserved" but at the same time "rendered incapable of propagating." Ordinary sterilization methods being used for hereditary diseases would take too much time and be too expensive, but "castration by X-ray . . . is not only relatively cheap, but can be performed on many thousands in the shortest time.". . . Himmler, ever the scientist, insisted that "sterilization by X-rays . . . [be] tried out at least once in one camp in a series of experiments." Schumann was chosen for the task and, by late 1942, was at work on X-ray castration on Block 30 in Birkenau. . . .

His experimental policies were brutal and unrestrained. He worked on Block 30, in the women's hospital in Birkenau, in a large room containing two expensive X-ray apparatuses and a small booth for him, which had a window and was, of course, insulated with lead plates to protect him from radiation.

Experimental subjects—relatively healthy young men and women in their late teens or early twenties, who had been obtained by a previous day's order from the camps—were lined up in a waiting room and brought in one by one, often completely ignorant of what was to be done to them. Women were put between plates that pressed against abdomen and back; men placed penis and scrotum on a special plate. Schumann himself turned on the machines, which hummed loudly; and each "treatment" lasted "several minutes" according to Dr. Stanislaw Klociziński, "five to eight minutes" according to Dr. Alina Brenda, another prisoner physician. Many of the women emerged with what Marie L. called "substantial burns," which could become infected and take a long time to heal; and many quickly developed symptoms of peritonitis, including fever and severe pain and vomiting. Not long after the X rays, the women's ovaries were removed surgically, usually in two separate operations. . . . The ovaries were sent to laboratories to determine whether the X rays were effective in destroying tissue. . . .

Schumann's experiments with men had a parallel course, as described by Dr. Michael Z. in a written report: First, the rumor that "Jews were being sterilized with X-rays" by "an air-force lieutenant-physician"; then a visit by Schumann to a male medical ward during which he ordered them to prepare for forty inmates on whom they were to keep records of medical observations; the arrival of the experimental victims with burn erythemas [red areas] around the scrotum ("From their description, we recognized the X-ray machine"); the victims' later accounts of their sperm being collected, their prostates brutally massaged with pieces of wood inserted into the rectum; their exposure to an operation removing one or two testicles, and in some cases a second operation removing the remaining testicle (conducted with "noticeable brutality" and limited anesthesia: patients' "screams were frightening to hear"); "disastrous" post-operative developments including hemorrhages, septicemia, absence of muscle tone from wounds, so that "many . . . would die rapidly, weakened morally and physically" and others would be sent to work "which would finish them." But "their deaths mattered little since these guinea pigs have already served the function expected of them."

Dr. Erich G. told of the psychological pain of experimental victims and of their questions to him ("Will I [be able to] be a father? Can I [have relations with] females?") but admitted that at the time that was not the greatest emotional stress ("To survive was more important than to be mutilated or even castrated"); and the fear was that experimental victims would be killed ("It was impossible to believe that they would allow people to live after the war to be a witness"). . . .

Dr. Klociziński writes of as many as 200 men being subjected to X-ray castration, and of about 180 of those to amputation of at least one testicle, 90 of these operations taking place on one day, 16 December 1942. While overall statistics are uncertain, the general estimate is that approximately 1,000 prisoners, male and female, underwent X-ray sterilization or castration, and about 200 of these were subjected to surgical removal of testicles or ovaries. Whatever statistics are available derive from the Auschwitz policy of keeping relatively accurate surgical records of these experiments.

Like Clauberg, Schumann continued his experiments in Ravensbrück, there victimizing thirteen-year-old Gypsy girls.

After the war he managed to live obscurely in Germany—although recognized at Nuremberg as a war criminal—until an application for a license for a hunting gun led to his being identified. He fled Germany precipitately, traveled extensively, and eventually settled in Khartoum in the Sudan as head of a hospital. There for about seven years he apparently became something of a Good Samaritan. . . . He fled to Ghana, from where he was eventually handed over . . . to representatives of West Germany. By then, he had become weakened from chronic malaria and other illnesses. In custody for several years, he was convicted for his involvement in direct medical killing or "euthanasia"; but because of his heart condition and generally deteriorating health, he was released without having stood trial for his sterilization and castration experiments. He died in Frankfurt in 1983.

Specimens for a Museum

Block 10 played an important part in a form of "anthropological research" that was among the most grotesque expressions of the Nazi biomedical vision. Dr. Marie L. tells of its Auschwitz beginnings:

There appeared [on Block 10] a new protagonist of racial theories. He chose his material by having naked women of all ages file . . . in front of him. He wanted to do anthropological measurements. . . . He had measurements of all the parts of the body taken ad infinitum. . . . They were told that they had the extraordinary good fortune to be selected, that they would leave Auschwitz to go to an excellent camp, somewhere in Germany . . . [where] they would be very well treated, where would be happy. . . .

These women were taken to the concentration camp at Natzweiler, near Strasbourg, which although not designated as an extermination camp, nonetheless possessed its own gas chamber with the usual false showerheads as well as one additional feature: a one-way mirror that allowed those on the outside of the gas chamber to observe those inside. This mirror had been installed because the gas chamber itself had been constructed as part of the necessary research equipment.

A prisoner doctor reported that the group of Auschwitz women (thirty-nine of them according to other records) were given a sham physical examination for reassurance, then gassed, and that the corpses were immediately transported to the anatomy pavilion of the Strasbourg University Hospital. A French inmate, who had to assist the project's director, SS Captain Dr. August Hirt, told how "preservation began immediately" with the arrival of bodies that were "still warm, the eyes . . . wide open and shining." There were two subsequent shipments of men, from each of whom the left testicle had been removed and sent to Hirt's anatomy lab. . . .

Toward the end of the war, there was apparently some confusion about whether and how much to continue with research procedures, and eventually the evidence was ordered to be destroyed. But that process could not be completed, and French forces liberating Strasbourg found in Hirt's dissection room "many wholly unprocessed corpses," many "partly-processed corpses," and a few that had been "defleshed . . . late in 1944," and their heads burned to avoid any possibility of identification—with "special care taken to remove the number tattooed on the left forearm." Hirt himself disappeared at that time, and is now known to have killed himself shortly afterward. . . .

The Sick Doctor

Dr. Johann Paul Kremer . . . was fifty-nine years old when he arrived [in Auschwitz] in August 1942. . . .

Kremer had a long-standing research interest in problems of starvation, which he pursued by seeking debilitated inmates selected for death, whom he later termed "the proper specimens." After he had a patient "placed on the dissection table," where he took a history focused on weight and weight loss, an SS orderly injected phenol into the person's heart: "I stood at a distance from the dissection table holding jars, ready for the segments [organs] cut out immediately after death . . . segments of the liver, spleen and pancreas." On some occasions, Kremer arranged to examine these patients or have them photographed prior to their murder. We may say that he made maximally pragmatic use of the death factory for his own scientific aims. Dr. Jan W. told how, if Kremer spotted a prisoner whose cranial shape seemed unusual, or who interested him in any way, he would order that prisoner photographed and injected with phenol for his collection of "fresh corpse samples of liver and other organs," and concluded that "Kremer looked upon the prisoners as so many rabbits."

Dr. Kremer became notorious for a diary he kept (which was eventually discovered and published), with such sequences as:

September 4, 1942. . . . Present at a special action [selection] in the women's camp. . . . The most horrible of horrors. . . .

September 6. . . . Today, Sunday, an excellent dinner: tomato soup, half a chicken with potatoes and red cabbage (20 g. of fat), sweet pudding and magnificent vanilla ice cream. . . .

October 10. . . . I took and preserved . . . material from quite fresh corpses, namely the liver, spleen, and pancreas. . . .

October 11. . . . Today, Sunday, we got for dinner quite a big piece of roast hare with dumplings and red cabbage for 1.25 RM.

Kremer was imprisoned for ten years in Poland, and again tried back home in Münster, where he was sentenced to another ten years, considered already served. He died in 1965. . . .

Human Guinea Pigs

There is an additional Auschwitz research function: that of the camp as a constant source of victims for research done almost anywhere. Besides the Auschwitz prisoners taken to Strasbourg to be made part of Professor Hirt's skeleton collection, there are many other examples: eight prisoners from Auschwitz sent to Sachsenhausen for experiments with epidemic hepatitis, in which the possible death of the inmates was an accepted part of the arrangement; and the notorious sequence of twenty Jewish children, ages five to twelve, transferred from Auschwitz to Neuengamme in Hamburg, where they were subjected to injections of virulent tubercular serum and to other experiments, until they were removed from Neuengamme and secretly murdered just before the arrival of Allied troops. Auschwitz was not just a medicalized death factory but a source of "raw materials" for everyone's deadly medical experiments

Prisoner physicians could speak with bitter accuracy about the specific way in which their and other inmates' humanity was negated by Nazi experimenters. One observed that "man was the cheapest experimental animal. . . . Cheaper than a rat." Another declared that the experiments "had no scientific basis, and . . . that the main interest they had for those who performed them was to give Berlin, in their detailed reports, the illusion of important and continuous work, so that these brave 'researchers' might be kept far from the front in a position of sinecure."

We know that Nazi doctors partly justified the experiments by their sense that Jews were in any case doomed. While prisoner doctors made no such justification, their emotions were also affected by the Jewish death sentence. Dr. Jacob

R. could remember a feeling that "the experiments were of considerably less import than the whole inferno I was viewing there."

The experiments represent, among other things, a removal of medical limits. Ordinary medical behavior is predicated upon maintaining life—and refraining from actual or potential killing or maiming one's patient in the name of enhancing the life of one's own group or people. Paradoxically, that medical vision of social cure contributed directly to using medicine to kill or injure. Hence the array of Auschwitz experiments, and others done elsewhere including artificially inflicted burns with phosphorous incendiary bombs; experiments on the effects of drinking sea water; experiments with various forms of poison, by ingestion as well as in bullets or arrows; widespread experiments on artificially induced typhus, as well as with epidemic hepatitis and with malaria; experiments in cold immersion ("in freezing water") to determine the body's reactions and susceptibilities; experiments with mustard gas in order to study the kinds of wounds it can cause; experiments on the regeneration of bone, muscle, nerve tissue, and on bone transplantation, involving removal of various bones, muscles, and nerves from healthy women. All of the experiments were related to the Nazi biomedical vision, whether they directly contributed to cultural genocide (as in the case of sterilization) or were the work of German physicians taking a leading role in biological and genetic purification.

In experiments in sterilization, of course, the ideological source and goals are clear. But all the other experiments as well reflect the Nazi image of "life unworthy of life," of creatures who, because less than human, can be studied, altered, manipulated, mutilated, or killed—in the service of the Nordic race, and ultimately of remaking humankind. One experiments without limit in order to "gather together the best blood" and "once more breed over the generations the pure type of Nordic German." The task is never accomplished, so one must continue experimenting. All of Auschwitz becomes not only a vast experiment but an unending one.

The Twins of Auschwitz

Lucette Matalon Lagnado and Sheila Cohn Dekel

Perhaps the most notorious of the Nazis was Dr. Josef Mengele, "the Angel of Death," who conducted monstrous medical experiments at Auschwitz. Though he conducted "research" in the name of science, most of his work had little or no scientific basis and resulted in the torture and murder of many innocent people. This selection focuses on the work he did on twins in an effort to reinforce Nazi genetic theories by proving that most human characteristics were inherited. Some of the survivors of his experiments describe what happened in sometimes gruesome detail. Ironically, the twins suffered terribly because of Mengele, but many also survived because he protected his subjects. Lucette Matalon Lagnado is an investigative reporter and columnist and coauthor Sheila Cohn Dekel is a writer, lyricist, educator, and the widow of one of the twins whose story is told in their book Children of the Flames.

MAGDA SPIEGEL:
   A few hours after arriving at Auschwitz, I asked some people, "Where is my little boy?" My son was only seven years old. I was very worried about him.
   "You see these chimneys?" they replied, point-

ing toward the crematoriums. "Your child is there. Your parents are there. Your entire family is there. And one day, you will also be there."
   This was told to me the same day I had come—the same day.
   Dr. Mengele was the only person who was always standing there when the trains came. He was constantly making selections.
   The sky was red—red—the whole sky was red!
   It was the last year of the transports, and the Germans were putting masses—masses and masses—of people into the crematorium.
   It was like watching a movie.

Even early in the morning, the sky over Auschwitz looked opaque and foreboding, as if it were covered by a vast blood-soaked sheet. An oppressive smell permeated the air—soot and burning flesh, fumes from the crematoriums, and smoke from the arriving trains.

After the trains had pulled in and the cattle-car doors were opened, exhausted cargoes of Jews tumbled out. As SS men shouted, "Faster! Faster!," hordes of people were pushed this way and that by the uniformed guards. Women cried as their husbands were taken away from them. Old men clutched their wives in a final embrace. Small children huddled closer to their parents, sad and subdued. And the Nazis stomped around, cracking their whips on anyone who stood in their way, and even on those who were merely standing.

VERA BLAU:
When I arrived at Auschwitz in April 1944, my

Excerpted from Lucette Matalon Lagnado and Sheila Cohn Dekel, *Children of the Flames*. Copyright © 1991 Lucette Matalon Lagnado and Sheila Cohn Dekel. Reprinted with permission from Harper-Collins Publishers, Inc.

first impression was that it was very crowded.

My twin sister, Rachel, and I were eleven years old. We had come with our mother and little brother, and both of us started crying when we were separated from them. Then a woman from Czechoslovakia came over to us. She had been in Auschwitz a long time.

"Do not cry, children, do not cry," she said to us. "You see, they are burning your parents."

I did not believe her. I did not want to believe her.

What is universally known today as Auschwitz is in fact something of a misnomer. Auschwitz was the slave-labor camp in which murder was an everyday phenomenon, but, in fact, the Polish place name became the umbrella word for several camps. Although the slaves largely labored at Auschwitz, it was at Birkenau, a couple of miles away, that many of them were executed. And although the world lexicon came to equate Auschwitz with the gas chambers, it was Birkenau that was the actual extermination center. It was Birkenau where the ovens never stopped flaming and where SS physicians regularly dispatched inmates to the crematorium; and it was Birkenau where Dr. Mengele worked in his laboratory, and where his beloved twins were barracked, and where so many of them inevitably perished.

The Selections

Just one year after arriving at the death camp, Mengele was thoroughly absorbed in his research, the first step of which was selecting his subjects. Every morning, at the crack of dawn, he could be seen in the area where the transports disembarked, scanning the new arrivals.

Standing there in his perfectly tailored SS uniform, white gloves and officer's cap, Mengele looked impeccable—a host greeting guests arriving at his home. He sometimes stood for hours without flinching a hint of a smile on his face, his elegantly gloved hand beckoning the prisoners to the right or to the left. Often, he whistled softly as he worked, the *Blue Danube* waltz, or an aria from his favorite Puccini opera.

Mengele even engaged some of the new ar-

rivals in friendly conversation, asking them how the journey had been, and how they were feeling. If they complained of being sick, he listened with a sympathetic ear—and then sent them straightaway to die in the gas chambers. He actually seemed interested in hearing all the gruesome details: how uncomfortable the trip had been, how cramped and stifling the cattle cars were, how many Jews had died along the way.

Occasionally, Mengele pulled aside inmates and asked them to write "postcards" to their relatives back home. He seemed to take a special pleasure in dictating these notes, describing how lovely Auschwitz was, and urging everyone to visit. But once the postcards were prepared, their authors were summarily dispatched to the gas chambers.

Only when an interesting "specimen" came along did Mengele really spring to life. He urgently motioned to a nearby guard to yank the new arrival out of the line. SS guards were ordered to watch for any unusual or striking genetic material—the dwarfs, the giants, the hunchbacks—and to bring them immediately to Mengele. But most important of all to him were the twins.

ZVI THE SAILOR:

My twin brother and I were marching toward the gas chambers when we heard people yelling, "Twins! twins!" We were yanked out of the lines and brought over to Dr. Mengele. . . .

He was making the selections, deciding who would go to work and who would go to the gas chambers. He used his finger. He motioned everyone in my family in the direction of the crematorium.

As we marched to the crematorium, our mother told us, "You must not cry."

To this day, I do not know who told the Germans we were twins and had us removed from the line.

MENASHE LORINCZI:

Nobody knew whether it was good or bad to be a twin. Although the SS guards were going around asking for twins, families were afraid to volunteer their children.

Many twins died because their parents didn't

want to be separated from them. Mothers walked with their twins straight into the gas chambers. . . .

Once separated from their parents, the twins were marched through the camp, where they witnessed scenes of unparalleled horror. Piles of corpses were everywhere. Lying next to them, and virtually indistinguishable, were men and women thin as skeletons. These were the "Mussulmans"—the half-dead, with no strength or will to live, who were simply awaiting being carted to the gas chamber. A foul odor permeated the camp, which, combined with the heat, made it difficult to breathe. It was an absolute assault on the senses. Children clung to their twin, their last remaining links with the families they had lost.

The twins' initiation into Auschwitz formally began when they, like all new inmates, were showered and branded. They cried out in pain as numbers were etched into their flesh with searing metal rods. But unlike the other prisoners, who were given camp uniforms and whose heads were shaved, the twins were allowed to keep both their clothes and their long hair. These differences made them immediately recognizable as "Mengele's children.". . .

EVA MOZES:

In the early evening, we were finally taken to our barracks. There, we met other twins, some of whom had been at Auschwitz a long time. . . .

That first night, we went to the latrines. They were just holes in the ground, with waste in them. There was no running water. Everything stank.

I remember seeing three dead children on the ground. Later, we would always be finding dead children on the floor of the latrines.

From our barracks, we could see huge smoking chimneys towering high above the camp. There were glowing flames rising from above them.

"What are they burning so late in the evening?" I asked the other children.

"The Germans are burning people," they answered.

Mengele's Children

But the new twins also learned that, as protégés of the powerful Dr. Mengele, their own lives in this kingdom of death were guaranteed. Mengele made sure that his twins would be generally well-treated, at least by Auschwitz standards. They were spared the beatings and punishments inflicted on other inmates. Because they "belonged" to Mengele, no one, not even the most brutal camp guards, would dare lay a hand on them. In addition to keeping their clothes and hair, some of the twins, especially the boys, recall receiving somewhat better food rations than the other prisoners. Although all the twins say they were ravenously hungry throughout their stay, several remember having access to potatoes and slices of bread, which enabled them to survive. If caught stealing food—as many did, on a regular basis—they were not severely punished because of their protected status. Most important, the twins were not subjected to the terrifying random selections that adult prisoners faced. As long as they stayed healthy and useful to Dr. Mengele, they would be kept alive. . . .

Mengele's overall aim. . . was to test various genetic theories in support of Hitler's racial dogmas. Like other Nazi scientists, Mengele hoped to prove that most human characteristics, from the shape of the nose to the color of the eye to obesity and left handedness, were inherited. In addition, it is believed Mengele was searching for ways to induce multiple births, so as to repopulate the depleted German Army. The ultimate goal was to produce an ideal race of Aryan men and women endowed with only the finest genetic traits, who would rapidly multiply and rule the world.

For the sake of his experiments, Mengele tried to create an atmosphere that was, in sharp contrast to everything else taking place in Auschwitz, as close to normal as possible. He installed a small furnished office at one end of the twins' compound to help him monitor his child guinea pigs. He decreed that guards were to be held accountable if any of the twins fell ill or died, hoping this would motivate them to look after the children. If a twin died during the night, Mengele would storm through the compound in the morning, screaming at the guards, demanding an explanation. He also implemented a strict routine to regulate the twins' lives. Every morning at six o'clock, they were to be up for roll call in front of their barracks. Then came breakfast, a mug of tepid, muddied water the Germans called coffee, and perhaps a slice of moldy bread. Then Mengele would appear at the compound shortly thereafter for an inspection tour. . . .

Human Guinea Pigs

Typically, Mengele gave daily orders to have several of the twins "prepared" for experiments. He would ask Twins' Father [the man placed in charge of twin boys] or other adult supervisors to get the children ready by taking them to be bathed and cleaned. Special trucks emblazoned with fake Red Cross insignia arrived to pick up the youngsters and deliver them to Mengele's laboratories. Depending on the type of tests, the twins were driven to any one of several locations either within Birkenau or at Auschwitz proper. The children learned what to expect, depending on their destination. In one laboratory, they knew it was a matter only of routine X rays and blood tests. Other clinics were reserved for more complicated—and painful—experiments. One Mengele lab the twins never saw was his pathology unit, located conveniently on the site of a crematorium. There, an assistant to Mengele toiled quietly, performing autopsies on the bodies of the twins who had died, or been killed, in the course of experiments.

The blood tests were the most basic component of Mengele's program. Virtually all the twins were subjected to daily withdrawals of blood. . . . Blood, often in large quantities, was drawn from twins' fingers and arms, and sometimes both their arms simultaneously. The youngest children, whose arms and hands were very small, suffered the most: Blood was drawn from their necks, a painful and frightening procedure. The blood was then analyzed in a special laboratory located near Birkenau.

Although Mengele was invariably present during the experiments, the tests themselves were often administered by his assistants. Typically, these were Jewish inmates who had been doctors and nurses before the war, and had been spared the gas chamber because of their skills. Most had profound misgivings about their work. But they knew that to betray any hesitation in administering an injection or test, even a very gruesome one, would result in their immediate execution. In spite of their anguishing position, a few managed also to alleviate suffering and helped save some lives. . . .

EVA MOZES:
We were always naked during the experiments.

We were marked, painted, measured, observed. Boys and girls were together. It was all so demeaning. There was no place to hide, no place to go.

They compared every part of our body with that of our twin. The tests would last for hours.

And Mengele was always there, supervising.

SOLOMON MALIK:
Mengele would look at each of the twins and see what interested him the most. We were his guinea pigs. We were his laboratory.

Mengele once put a needle in my arm—only the needle, not the syringe. Blood started spurting out. He calmly placed the blood in test tube.

Then, he gave me a sugar cube. . . .

Nazi Science

The line between science and quackery was not a very fine one at Auschwitz. Mengele's experiments, although ostensibly performed in the name of scientific truth, followed few scientific principles. Mengele would test one twin and not the other. At times, siblings were injected simultaneously as they stood naked side by side. Despite the preferential treatment, the occasional shows of kindness, the children endured unspeakable pain and humiliation.

The eye studies were especially gruesome. In their desire to create a race of perfect Aryans, the Nazis wanted to produce children with lustrous blond hair and blue eyes. Was it possible to genetically engineer such traits? A major focus of Mengele's studies involved changing the color of the twins' hair and eyes. . . .

At times, Mengele's assistants used eye-drops to insert chemicals into the children's eyes;

other times, they used needles.

HEDVAH AND LEAH STERN:

Mengele was trying to change the color of our eyes. One day, we were given eye-drops. Afterwards, we could not see for several days. We thought the Nazis had made us blind.

The strict veil of secrecy imposed over the experiments enabled Mengele to work more effectively. Twins who were subjected to the most grotesque procedures took his secrets to their graves. And those as yet unhurt had only second-hand stories about what was being done. No one at Auschwitz—not the prisoners, not the SS guards, not even other doctors—knew precisely what Mengele was doing with his twins, either while they were alive or after they had died. Even the children who themselves were the subjects of his tests did not know what the objectives of the experiments were. Rumors were rampant, especially when children were taken out in Red Cross trucks, never to be seen again. . . .

The Charmer

The youngest children were not aware of the darker side of the man they affectionately called "Uncle Mengele." They did not know about the surgeries of unspeakable horror. It is not that Mengele confined the more gruesome and painful studies to the older children, but that they were too young to comprehend the sinister experiments. They saw only a cheerful, avuncular doctor who rewarded them with candy if they behaved. But the older twins, and the adults, such as the twins' mothers and Jewish doctors who saw Mengele at work recognized his kindness as a deception—yet another of his perverse experiments, whose aim was to test their mental endurance. The fact that Mengele could behave so nicely even as he inflicted pain, torture, and death made him the most feared man at Auschwitz.

However, in performing his diabolical experiments on twins, Mengele believed he was pursuing high-minded scientific goals. Personal ambition also played its role in propelling Mengele to exceed even Nazi standards of cruelty, so that he stood out from other death-camp doctors. Driven by a need to reach the peak of his pro-

Josef Mengele

fession, he no doubt believed that if he only worked hard enough, performed enough experimental studies, tested a sufficient number of twins, then he would be recognized as the great scientist he thought he was. . . .

ALEX DEKEL:

I have never accepted the fact that Mengele himself believed he was doing serious medical work—not from the slipshod way he went about it. He was only exercising his power.

Mengele ran a butcher shop—major surgeries were performed without anesthesia. Once, I witnessed a stomach operation—Mengele was removing pieces from the stomach, but without any anesthesia.

Another time, it was a heart that was removed, again, without anesthesia. It was horrifying.

Mengele was a doctor who became mad because of the power he was given. Nobody ever questioned him—why did this one die? why did that one perish? The patients did not count.

He professed to do what he did in the name of

science, but it was a madness on his part.

In this sham universe of scientific truths, half-truths, and outright lies, the experiments administered on the children represented a catalog of criminality and cruelty. Blood would be transfused from one twin to the other, and the results duly noted and compared. Bizarre psychological tests, designed to measure endurance, were continually made. For instance, a small child would be placed in isolation, in a small, cagelike room, with or without his twin. The children would be exposed to various stimuli and their reactions recorded. There are twins who recall they were targets of an insidious psychological barrage, but years later were still too traumatized to conjure up the details. And finally, there were the surgeries, the horrible, murderous operations.

Mengele would plunder a twin's body, sometimes removing organs and limbs. He injected the children with lethal germs, including typhus and tuberculosis, to see how quickly they succumbed to the diseases. Many became infected and died. He also attempted to change the sex of some twins. Female twins were sterilized; males were castrated. What was the point of these ghoulish experiments? No one, neither the child-victims nor the adult witnesses, ever really knew. . . .

If Mengele's experiments seemed to each twin to become ever more diabolical, that was only an illusion: The intended objective had always been the death of the children. What the twins who had arrived in the spring and summer of 1944 did not know was that many other groups had preceded them. It was only a matter of time before their turn came.

MOSHE OFFER:

One day, my twin brother, Tibi, was taken away for some special experiments. Dr. Mengele had always been more interested in Tibi. I am not sure why—perhaps because he was the older twin.

Mengele made several operations on Tibi.

One surgery on his spine left my brother paralyzed. He could not walk anymore.

Then they took out his sexual organs.

After the fourth operation, I did not see Tibi anymore.

I cannot tell you how I felt. It is impossible to put into words how I felt.

They had taken away my father, my mother, my two older brothers—and now, my twin.

Selection 7

Why Germans Killed Jews

Daniel Jonah Goldhagen

*In his controversial and best-selling book based on his doctoral dissertation, Daniel Jonah Goldhagen attempts to explain why the Holocaust happened in Germany and why or-*dinary German citizens went along with Hitler's orders to murder hundreds of thousands of innocent Jewish men, women, and children. Contrary to conventional wisdom, he points out that German soldiers were not killed or punished if they refused to participate in the atrocities. He argues that it was the pervasiveness of anti-Semitism in Germany that*

Excerpted from Daniel Jonah Goldhagen, *Hitler's Willing Executioners.* Copyright © 1996 Daniel Jonah Goldhagen. Reprinted with permission from Alfred A. Knopf, a division of Random House, Inc.

prompted Germans to act as they did. Gold-hagen is associate professor of Government and Social Studies at Harvard University and an Associate at the university's Minda de Gunzburg Center for European Studies.

Captain Wolfgang Hoffmann was a zealous executioner of Jews. As the commander of one of the three companies of Police Battalion 101, he and his fellow officers led their men, who were not SS men but ordinary Germans, in the deportation and gruesome slaughter in Poland of tens of thousands of Jewish men, women, and children. Yet this same man, in the midst of his genocidal activities, once stridently disobeyed a superior order that he deemed morally objectionable.

The order commanded that members of his company sign a declaration that had been sent to them. Hoffmann began his written refusal by saying that upon reading it, he had thought that an error had been made, "because it appeared to me a piece of impertinence to demand of a decent German soldier to sign a declaration in which he obligates himself not to steal, not to plunder, and not to buy without paying. . . ." He continued by describing how unnecessary such a demand was, since his men, of proper ideological conviction, were fully aware that such activities were punishable offenses. He also pronounced to his superiors his judgment of his men's character and actions, including, presumably, their slaughtering of Jews. He wrote that his men's adherence to German norms of morality and conduct "derives from their own free will and is not caused by a craving for advantages or fear of punishment." Hoffmann then declared defiantly: "As an officer I regret, however, that I must set my view against that of the battalion commander and am not able to carry out the order, since I feel injured in my sense of honor. I must decline to sign a general declaration."

Hoffmann's letter is astonishing and instructive for a number of reasons. Here is an officer who had already led his men in the genocidal slaughter of tens of thousands of Jews, yet who deemed it an effrontery that anyone might sup-pose that he and his men would steal food from Poles! The genocidal killer's honor was wound-ed, and wounded doubly, for he was both a soldier and a German. His conception of the obligations that Germans owed the "subhuman" Poles must have been immeasurably greater than those owed Jews. Hoffmann also understood his parent institution to be so tolerant that he was willing to refuse a direct order and even to record his brazen insubordination in writing. His judgment of his men—a judgment based, no doubt, on the compass of their activities, including their genocidal ones—was that they acted not out of fear of punishment, but with willing assent; they acted from conviction, according to their inner beliefs. . . .

Explaining the Holocaust is the central intellectual problem for understanding Germany during the Nazi period. All the other problems combined are comparatively simple. How the Nazis came to power, how they suppressed the left, how they revived the economy, how the state was structured and functioned, how they made and waged war are all more or less ordinary, "normal" events, easily enough understood. But the Holocaust and the change in sensibilities that it involved "defies" explanation. There is no comparable event in the twentieth century, indeed in modern European history. Whatever the remaining debates, every other major event of nineteenth- and twentieth-century German history and political development is, in comparison to the Holocaust, transparently clear in its genesis. Explaining how the Holocaust happened is a daunting task empirically and even more so theoretically, so much so that some have argued, in my view erroneously, that it is "inexplicable.". . .

Until now the perpetrators, the most important group of people responsible for the slaughter of European Jewry, excepting the Nazi leadership itself, have received little concerted attention in the literature that describes the events and purports to explain them. Surprisingly, the vast literature on the Holocaust contains little on the people who were its executors. Little is known of who the perpetrators were, the details of their actions, the circumstances of many of their deeds, let alone their motivations. A decent estimate of how many people contributed to the genocide, of how many perpetrators there were, has never been made. . .

Perpetrators

The Holocaust was primarily a German undertaking. Non-Germans were not essential to the perpetration of genocide, and they did not supply the drive and initiative that pushed it forward. To be sure, had the Germans not found European (especially, eastern European) helpers, then the Holocaust would have unfolded somewhat differently, and the Germans would likely not have succeeded in killing as many Jews. Still, this was above all a German enterprise; the decisions, plans, organizational resources, and the majority of its executors were German. Comprehension and explanation of the perpetration of the Holocaust therefore requires an explanation of the *Germans'* drive to kill Jews. Because what can be said about the Germans cannot be said about any other nationality or about all of the other nationalities combined—namely no Germans, no Holocaust—the focus here is appropriately on the German perpetrators. . . .

The Holocaust was the defining aspect of Nazism, but not only of Nazism. It was also the defining feature of German society during its Nazi period. No significant aspect of German society was untouched by anti-Jewish policy; from the economy, to society, to politics, to culture, from cattle farmers, to merchants, to the organization of small towns, to lawyers, doctors, physicists, and professors. No analysis of German society, no understanding or characterization of it, can be made without placing the persecution and extermination of the Jews at its center. The program's first parts, namely the systematic exclusion of Jews from German economic and social life, were carried out in the open, under approving eyes, and with the complicity of virtually all sectors of German society, from the legal, medical, and teaching professions, to the churches, both Catholic and Protestant, to the gamut of economic, social, and cul-

tural groups and associations. Hundreds of thousands of Germans contributed to the genocide and the still larger system of subjugation that was the vast concentration camp system. Despite the regime's half-hearted attempts to keep the genocide beyond the view of most Germans, millions knew of the mass slaughters. Hitler announced many times, emphatically, that the war would end in the extermination of the Jews. The killings met with general understanding, if not approval. No other policy (of similar or greater scope) was carried out with more persistence and zeal, and with fewer difficulties, than the genocide, except perhaps the war itself. The Holocaust defines not only the history of Jews during the middle of the twentieth century but also the history of Germans. While the Holocaust changed Jewry and Jews irrevocably, its commission was possible, I argue, because Germans had *already* been changed. . . .

Germans' antisemitic beliefs about Jews were the central causal agent of the Holocaust. They were the central causal agent not only of Hitler's decision to annihilate European Jewry (which is accepted by many) but also of the perpetrators' willingness to kill and to brutalize Jews. The conclusion of this book is that antisemitism moved many thousands of "ordinary" Germans—and would have moved millions more, had they been appropriately positioned—to slaughter Jews. Not economic hardship, not the coercive means of a totalitarian state, not social psychological pressure, not invariable psychological propensities, but ideas about Jews that were pervasive in Germany, and had been for decades, induced ordinary Germans to kill unarmed, defenseless Jewish men, women, and children by the thousands, systematically and without pity. . . .

For the extermination of the Jews to occur, four principal things were necessary:

1. The Nazis—that is, the leadership, specifically Hitler—had to decide to undertake the extermination.
2. They had to gain control over the Jews, namely over the territory in which they resided.

3. They had to organize the extermination and devote to it sufficient resources.
4. They had to induce a large number of people to carry out the killings. . . .

It is commonly believed that the Germans slaughtered Jews by and large in the gas chambers, and that without gas chambers, modern means of transportation, and efficient bureaucracies, the Germans would have been unable to kill millions of Jews. The belief persists that somehow only technology made horror on this scale possible. "Assembly-line killing" is one of the stock phrases in discussions of the event. It is generally believed that gas chambers, because of their efficiency (which is itself greatly overstated), were a necessary instrument for the genocidal slaughter, and that the Germans chose to construct the gas chambers in the first place because they needed more efficient means of killing the Jews. It has been generally believed by scholars (at least until very recently) and non-scholars alike that the perpetrators were primarily, overwhelmingly SS men, the most devoted and brutal Nazis. It has been a widespread conviction (again until recently) that had a German refused to kill Jews, then he himself would have been killed, sent to a concentration camp, or severely punished. All of these views, views that fundamentally shape people's understanding of the Holocaust, have been held unquestioningly as though they were self-evident truths. They have been virtual articles of faith (derived from sources other than historical inquiry), have substituted for knowledge, and have distorted the way in which this period is understood. . . .

Ordinary Men

One explanation argues for external compulsion: the perpetrators were coerced. They were left, by the threat of punishment, with no choice but to follow orders. After all, they were part of military or police-like institutions, institutions with a strict chain of command, demanding subordinate compliance to orders, which should have punished insubordination severely, perhaps with death. Put a gun to anyone's head, so goes the thinking, and he will shoot others to save himself.

A second explanation conceives of the perpetrators as having been blind followers of orders. A number of proposals have been made for the source or sources of this alleged propensity to obey: Hitler's charisma (the perpetrators were, so to speak, caught in his spell), a general human tendency to obey authority, a peculiarly German reverence for and propensity to obey authority, or a totalitarian society's blunting of the individual's moral sense and its conditioning of him or her to accept all tasks as necessary. So a common proposition exists, namely that people obey authority, with a variety of accounts of why this is so. Obviously, the notion that authority, particularly state authority, tends to elicit obedience merits consideration.

A third explanation holds the perpetrators to have been subject to tremendous social psychological pressure, placed upon each one by his comrades and/or by the expectations that accompany the institutional roles that individuals occupy. It is, so goes the argument, extremely difficult for individuals to resist pressures to conform, pressures which can lead individuals to participate in acts which they on their own would not do, indeed would abhor. . . .

A fourth explanation sees the perpetrators as having been petty bureaucrats, or soulless technocrats, who pursued their self-interest or their technocratic goals and tasks with callous disregard for the victims. . . .

A fifth explanation asserts that because tasks were so fragmented, the perpetrators could not understand what the real nature of their actions was; they could not comprehend that their small assignments were actually part of a global extermination program. . . .

The explanations can be reconceptualized in terms of their accounts of the actors' capacity for volition: The first explanation (namely coercion) says that the killers could not say "no." The second explanation (obedience) and the third (situational pressure) maintain that Germans were psychologically incapable of saying "no." The fourth explanation (self-interest) contends that Germans had sufficient personal incentives to kill in order not to want to say "no."

The fifth explanation (bureaucratic myopia) claims that it never even occurred to the perpetrators that they were engaged in an activity that might make them responsible for saying "no."

Each of these conventional explanations may sound plausible, and some of them obviously contain some truth, so what is wrong with them? . . .

The conventional explanations suffer from two major conceptual failings. They do not sufficiently recognize the extraordinary nature of the deed: the mass killing of people. They *assume* and imply that inducing people to kill human beings is fundamentally no different from getting them to do any other unwanted or distasteful task. Also, none of the conventional explanations deems the *identity* of the victims to have mattered. The conventional explanations imply that the perpetrators would have treated any other group of intended victims in exactly the same way. That the victims were Jews—according to the logic of these explanations—is irrelevant.

I maintain that any explanation that fails to acknowledge the actors' capacity to know and to judge, namely to understand and to have views about the significance and the morality of their actions, that fails to hold the actors' beliefs and values as central, that fails to emphasize the autonomous motivating force of Nazi ideology, particularly its central component of antisemitism, cannot possibly succeed in telling us much about why the perpetrators acted as they did. Any explanation that ignores either the particular nature of the perpetrators' actions—the systematic, large-scale killing and brutalizing of people—or the identity of the victims is inadequate for a host of reasons. All explanations that adopt these positions, as do the conventional explanations, suffer a mirrored, double failure of recognition of the human aspect of the Holocaust: the humanity of the perpetrators, namely their capacity to judge and to choose to act inhumanely, and the humanity of the victims, that what the perpetrators did, they did to these people with their specific identities, and not to animals or things.

My explanation—which is new to the scholarly literature on the perpetrators—is that the perpetrators, "ordinary Germans," were animated by antisemitism, by a particular *type* of antisemitism that led them to conclude that the Jews *ought to die*. The perpetrators' beliefs, their particular brand of antisemitism, though obviously not the sole source, was, I maintain, a most significant and indispensable source of the perpetrators' actions and must be at the center of any explanation of them. Simply put, the perpetrators, having consulted their own convictions and morality and having judged the mass annihilation of Jews to be right, did not *want* to say "no.". . .

Interpreters of this period make a grave error by refusing to believe that people could slaughter whole populations—especially populations that are by any objective evaluation not threatening—out of conviction. Why persist in the belief that "ordinary" people could not possibly sanction, let alone partake in wholesale human slaughter? The historical record, from ancient times to the present, amply testifies to the ease with which people can extinguish the lives of others, and even take joy in their deaths.

No reason exists to believe that modern, western, even Christian man is incapable of holding notions which devalue human life, which call for its extinction, notions similar to those held by peoples of many religious, cultural, and political dispensations throughout history, including the crusaders and the inquisitors, to name but two relevant examples from twentieth-century Christian Europe's forebears. Who doubts that the Argentine or Chilean murderers of people who opposed the recent authoritarian regimes thought that their victims deserved to die? Who doubts that the Tutsis who slaughtered Hutus in Burundi or the Hutus who slaughtered Tutsis in Rwanda, that one Lebanese militia which slaughtered the civilian supporters of another, that the Serbs who have killed Croats or Bosnian Muslims, did so out of conviction in the justice of their actions? Why do we not believe the same for the German perpetrators? . . .

The perpetrators were working within institutions that prescribed roles for them and assigned them specific tasks, yet they individually and collectively had latitude to make choices regarding their actions. Adopting a perspective which acknowledges this requires that their choices, especially the patterns of their choices, be discerned, analyzed, and incorporated into any overall explanation or interpretation. Ideal data would answer the following questions:

What did the perpetrators actually do?

What did they do in excess of what was "necessary"?

What did they refuse to do?

What could they have refused to do?

What would they not have done?

What was the manner in which they carried out their tasks?

How smoothly did the overall operations proceed?

In examining the pattern of the perpetrators' actions . . . two directions beyond the simple act of killing must be explored. First, in their treatment of Jews (and other victims), the Germans subjected them to a wide range of acts other than the lethal blow. It is important to understand the *gamut* of their actions towards Jews. . . . Second, the perpetrators' actions when they were *not* engaged in genocidal activities also shed light on the killing. . . .

Breaking Taboos

It is not the only aspect of the Germans' treatment of the Jews that demands systematic scrutiny and explication. Not only the killing but also *how* the Germans killed must be explained. The "how" frequently provides great insight into the "why." A killer can endeavor to render the deaths of others—whether he thinks the killing is just or unjust—more or less painful, both physically and emotionally. The ways in which Germans, collectively and individually, sought in their actions, or merely considered, to alleviate or intensify their victims' suffering must be accounted for in any explanation. An explanation that can seemingly make sense of Germans putting Jews to death, but not of the manner in which they did it, is a faulty explanation. . . .

We must attempt the difficult enterprise of imagining ourselves in their places, performing their deeds, acting as they did, viewing what they beheld. To do so we must always bear in mind the essential nature of their actions as perpetrators: they were killing defenseless men, women, and children, people who were obviously of no martial threat to them, often emaciated and weak, in unmistakable physical and emotional agony, and sometimes begging for their lives or those of their children. Too many interpreters of this period, particularly when they are psychologizing, discuss the Germans' actions as if they were discussing the commission of mundane acts, as if they need explain little more than how a good man might occasionally shoplift. They lose sight of the fundamentally different, extraordinary, and trying character of these acts. The taboo in many societies, including western ones, against killing defenseless people, against killing children, is great. The psychological mechanisms that permit "good" people to commit minor moral transgressions, or to turn a blind eye even to major ones committed by others, particularly if they are far away, cannot be applied to people's perpetration of genocidal killing, to their slaughter of hundreds of others before their own eyes—without careful consideration of such mechanisms' appropriateness for elucidating such actions.

Explaining this genocidal slaughter necessitates, therefore, that we keep two things always in mind. When writing or reading about killing operations, it is too easy to become insensitive to the numbers on the page. Ten thousand dead in one place, four hundred in another, fifteen in a third. Each of us should pause and consider that ten thousand deaths meant that Germans killed ten thousand individuals—unarmed men, women, and children, the old, the young, the healthy, and the sick—that Germans took a human life ten thousand times. Each of us should ponder what that might have meant for the Germans participating in the slaughter. When a person considers his or her own anguish, abhorrence, or revulsion, his or her own moral outrage at the murder of one person, or of a contemporary "mass murder" of, say, twenty people—whether by a serial killer, or by a semi-automatic-toting sociopath in a fast food outlet—that person gains some perspective on the reality that these Germans confronted. The Jewish victims were not the "statistics" that they appear to us on paper. To the killers whom they faced, the Jews were people who were breathing one moment and lying lifeless, often before them, the next. All of this took place independent of military operations.

The second item to bear in mind, always, is the horror of what the Germans were doing. Anyone in a killing detail who himself shot or who witnessed his comrades shoot Jews was immersed in scenes of unspeakable horror. . . . Blood, bone, and brains were flying about, often landing on the killers, smirching their faces and staining their clothes. Cries and wails of people awaiting their imminent slaughter or consumed in death throes reverberated in German ears. Such scenes—not the antiseptic descriptions that mere reportage of a killing operation presents—constituted the reality for many perpetrators.

Selection 8

How Ordinary Men Became Killers

Christopher R. Browning

In this selection Christopher R. Browning tries to explain how ordinary men became killers. Browning looked specifically at one Nazi unit, Reserve Police Battalion 101, a group of policemen, most of whom were recently drafted family men too old for combat, who were sent to Poland and were involved in the murder of Jews. Their most ghastly action was the murder of fifteen hundred men, women, and children in the village of Józefów. These men were not hard-core Nazis, the stereotypical monsters of the SS. In most cases, they were clerks, salesmen, and blue-collar workers drafted into unpleasant service. If such men could commit atrocities, is it possible to say that anyone could resist the kind of pressure they faced to become murderers? *Young people in the United States face all sorts of peer pressure to take drugs, drink alcohol, steal, and act in other antisocial or illegal ways. Under the right circumstances, could peer pressure also turn Americans into murderers? Browning is a professor of history at Pacific Lutheran University and a contributor to Yad Vashem's multivolume history of the Holocaust.*

Excerpted from Christopher R. Browning, *Ordinary Men: Reserve Police Battalion 101 and the Final Solution in Poland.* Copyright © 1992, 1998 Christopher Browning. Reprinted with permission from HarperCollins Publishers, Inc.

*a*mong the perpetrators [of the Holocaust] of course, orders have traditionally been the most frequently cited explanation for their own behavior. The authoritarian political culture of the Nazi dictatorship savagely intolerant of overt dissent, along with the standard military necessity of obedience to orders and ruthless enforcement of discipline, created a situation in which individuals *had no choice.* Orders were orders, and no one in such a political climate could be expected to disobey them, they insisted. Disobedience surely meant the concentration camp if not immediate execution, possibly for their families as well. The perpetrators had found themselves in a situation of impossible "duress" and therefore could not be held responsible for their actions. Such, at least, is what defendants said in trial after trial in postwar Germany.

There is a general problem with this explanation, however. Quite simply, in the past forty-five years no defense attorney or defendant in any of the hundreds of postwar trials has been able to document a single case in which refusal to obey an order to kill unarmed civilians resulted in the allegedly inevitable dire punishment. The punishment or censure that occasionally did result from such disobedience was never commensurate with the gravity of the crimes the men had been asked to commit.

A variation on the explanation of inescapable orders is "putative duress." Even if the consequences of disobedience would not have been so dire, the men who complied could not have known that at the time. They sincerely thought that they had had no choice when faced with orders to kill. . . .

For small shooting actions, volunteers were requested or shooters were chosen from among those who were known to be willing to kill or who simply did not make the effort to keep their distance when firing squads were being formed. For large actions, those who would not kill were not compelled. Even officers' attempts to force individual nonshooters to kill could be refused. . . .

The testimonies are filled with stories of men who disobeyed standing orders during the ghetto-clearing operations and did not shoot infants or those attempting to hide or escape. Even men who admitted to having taken part in firing squads claimed not to have shot in the confusion and melee of the ghetto clearings or out on patrol when their behavior could not be closely observed. . . .

Were Nazis Brainwashed?

To what degree, then, did the conscious inculcation of Nazi doctrines shape the behavior of the men of Reserve Police Battalion 101? Were they subjected to such a barrage of clever and insidious propaganda that they lost the capacity for independent thought and responsible action? Were devaluation of the Jews and exhortations to kill them central to this indoctrination? The popular term for intense indoctrination and psychological manipulation, emerging from the Korean War experience of some captured American soldiers, is "brainwashing." Were these killers in some general sense "brainwashed"?

Unquestionably, [Heinrich] Himmler set a premium on the ideological indoctrination of members of the SS and the police. They were to be not just efficient soldiers and policemen but ideologically motivated warriors, crusaders against the political and racial enemies of the Third Reich. Indoctrination efforts embraced not only the elite organizations of the SS but also the Order Police, extending even to the lowly reserve police, though the reservists scarcely fit Himmler's notion of the new Nazi racial aristocracy. For instance, membership in the SS required proof of ancestry untainted by Jewish blood through five generations. In contrast, even "first-degree *Mischlinge*" (people with two Jewish grandparents) and their spouses were not banned from service in the reserve police until October 1942; "second-degree *Mischlinge*" (one Jewish grandparent) and their spouses were not banned until April 1943.

In its guidelines for basic training of January 23, 1940, the Order Police Main Office decreed that in addition to physical fitness, use of weapons, and police techniques, all Order Police battalions were to be strengthened in character and ideology. Basic training included a one-month unit on "ideological education." One topic for the first week was "Race as the Basis of Our World View," followed the second week by "Maintaining the Purity of Blood." Beyond basic training, the police battalions, both active and reserve, were to receive continued military and ideological training from their officers. Officers were required to attend one-week workshops that included one hour of ideological instruction for themselves and one hour of practice in the ideological instruction of others. A five-part study plan of January 1941 included the subsections "Understanding of Race as the Basis of Our World View," "The Jewish Question in Germany," and "Maintaining the Purity of German Blood.". . .

Many of the Nazi perpetrators were very young men. They had been raised in a world in which Nazi values were the only "moral norms" they knew. It could be argued that such young men, schooled and formed solely under the conditions of the Nazi dictatorship, simply did not know any better. Killing Jews did not conflict with the value system they had grown up with, and hence indoctrination was much easier. Whatever the merits of such an argument, it clearly does not hold for the predominantly middle-aged men of Reserve Police Battalion 101. They were educated and spent their formative years in the pre-1933 period. Many came from a social milieu that was relatively unreceptive to National Socialism. They knew perfectly well the moral norms of German society before the Nazis. They had earlier standards by which to judge the Nazi policies they were asked to carry out. . . .

In summary, the men of Reserve Police Battalion 101, like the rest of German society, were immersed in a deluge of racist and anti-Semitic propaganda. Furthermore, the Order Police provided for indoctrination both in basic training and as an ongoing practice within each unit. Such incessant propagandizing must have had a considerable effect in reinforcing general notions of Germanic racial superiority and "a certain aversion" toward the Jews. However, much of the indoctrination material was clearly not targeted at older reservists and in some cases was highly inappropriate or irrelevant to them. And material specifically designed to harden the policemen for the personal task of killing Jews is conspicuously absent from the surviving documentation. One would have to be quite convinced of the manipulative powers of indoctrination to believe that any of this material could have deprived the men of Reserve Police Battalion 101 of the capacity for independent thought. Influenced and conditioned in a general way, imbued in particular with a

sense of their own superiority and racial kinship as well as Jewish inferiority and otherness, many of them undoubtedly were; explicitly prepared for the task of killing Jews they most certainly were not.

Going Along to Get Along

A vital factor . . . was conformity to the group. The battalion had orders to kill Jews but each individual did not. Yet 80 to 90 percent of the men proceeded to kill, though almost all of them—at least initially— were horrified and disgusted by what they were doing. To break ranks and step out, to adopt overtly nonconformist behavior, was simply beyond most of the men. It was easier for them to shoot.

Why? First of all, by breaking ranks, non-shooters were leaving the "dirty work" to their comrades. Since the battalion had to shoot even if individuals did not, refusing to shoot constituted refusing one's share of an unpleasant collective obligation. It was in effect an asocial act vis-à-vis one's comrades. Those who did not shoot risked isolation, rejection, and ostracism—a very uncomfortable prospect within the framework of a tight-knit unit stationed abroad among a hostile population, so that the individual had virtually nowhere else to turn for support and social contact.

This threat of isolation was intensified by the fact that stepping out could also have been seen as a form of moral reproach of one's comrades: the nonshooter was potentially indicating that he was "too good" to do such things. Most, though not all, nonshooters intuitively tried to diffuse the criticism of their comrades that was inherent in their actions. They pleaded not that they were "too good" but rather that they were "too weak" to kill.

Such a stance presented no challenge to the esteem of one's comrades, on the contrary, it legitimized and upheld "toughness" as a superior quality. For the anxious individual, it had the added advantage of posing no moral challenge to the murderous policies of the regime, though it did pose another problem, since the difference between being "weak" and being a "coward" was not great. . . .

Insidiously, therefore, most of those who did not shoot only reaffirmed the "macho" values of the majority—according to which it was a positive quality to be "tough" enough to kill unarmed, noncombatant men, women, and children—and tried not to rupture the bonds of comradeship that constituted their social world. Coping with the contradictions imposed by the demands of conscience on the one hand and the norms of the battalion on the other led to many tortured attempts at compromise: not shooting infants on the spot but taking them to the assembly point; not shooting on patrol if no "go-getter" was along who might report such squeamishness; bringing Jews to the shooting site and firing but intentionally missing. Only the very exceptional remained indifferent to taunts of "weakling" from their comrades and could live with the fact that they were considered to be "no man.". . .

The behavior of any human being is, of course, a very complex phenomenon, and the historian who attempts to "explain" it is indulging in a certain arrogance. When nearly 500 men are involved, to undertake any general explanation of their collective behavior is even more hazardous. What, then, is one to conclude? Most of all, one comes away from the story of Reserve Police Battalion 101 with great unease. This story of ordinary men is not the story of all men. The reserve policemen faced choices, and most of them committed terrible deeds. But those who killed cannot be absolved by the notion that anyone in the same situation would have done as they did. For even among them, some refused to kill and others stopped killing. Human responsibility is ultimately an individual matter.

At the same time, however, the collective behavior of Reserve Police Battalion 101 has deeply disturbing implications. There are many societies afflicted by traditions of racism and caught in the siege mentality of war or threat of war. Everywhere society conditions people to respect and defer to authority, and indeed could scarcely function otherwise. Everywhere people seek career advancement. In every modern society, the complexity of life and the resulting bureaucratization and specialization attenuate the sense of personal responsibility of those implementing official policy. Within virtually every social collective, the peer group exerts tremendous pressures on behavior and sets moral norms. If the men of Reserve Police Battalion 101 could become killers under such circumstances, what group of men cannot?

The Ghettos and the Concentration Camps

Chapter 3

Introduction

Jews made up a significant proportion of the population of many cities overrun by the Nazis as they marched across Eastern Europe. Before Hitler decided on the most efficient way to murder thousands of people at once, the Jews of Poland and the German-occupied areas of the Soviet Union were herded into ghettos. The first ghetto was established in 1940, and soon the Jews in places such as Lublin, Cracow, Warsaw, Vilna, and Lodz were isolated.

Tens of thousands of Jews were locked behind walls in small areas that had been home to a fraction of that population before the war. The ghettos were governed by Jewish councils (Judenrat) appointed by the Nazis to maintain order and to apportion food, jobs and most other necessities. The lack of food and sanitation in the ghettos led to starvation and disease. The Jews tried to live as normally as possible, but survival was a daily struggle.

This chapter contains descriptions of life in the ghettos in general and the story of two of the most infamous ghettos, Theresienstadt and Warsaw. The former was a camp near Prague that the Germans used to fool visiting members of the Red Cross. Just before the camp was to be inspected, the Nazis cleaned up the camp and prepared an elaborate charade to convince the visitors the Jews were being treated well. The deception worked and the world was told about the wonderful way the Germans treated the Jews. The Jews were later deported and most met their end in Auschwitz.

Most of the Warsaw ghetto residents also met a similar fate, but, first, a courageous band led an uprising that shocked the world. No more than twelve hundred Jews armed with a handful of pistols, seventeen rifles, and a few Molotov cocktails held out against the overwhelming German opposition for more than a month before the ghetto was liquidated.

Many Jews never made it out of the ghettos, but those who did usually were deported to a concentration camp. The first camp, Dachau, was built in 1933 to house political prisoners. Later, hundreds of camps were built to hold the Jews and other enemies of the Nazis. Six camps were devoted explicitly to murder. The death camps at Chelmno, Treblinka, Sobibor, Belzec, Majdanek, and Auschwitz/Birkenau killed millions of Jews, Gypsies, and others. This chapter also describes life in the concentration camps, what it took to survive, and the operation of the death factories.

Life in the Ghettos

Yehuda Bauer

For most people the first image that comes to mind when the word Holocaust *is mentioned is a concentration camp; however, tens of thousands of Jews died long before they were sent to camps. Millions of Jews living in Eastern Europe and hundreds of thousands in Poland and parts of the Soviet Union were first herded into ghettos. Some ghettos were closed while others were relatively open—at least for a while. Ghetto life might not seem so bad compared to that of the camps; after all, Jews still had some possessions, could live in houses and sleep in regular beds, work (sometimes for pay), and were not subject to the daily rigors and brutalization of camp life. Ghetto life was nevertheless one of squalor, hunger, disease, and despair that grew worse as time passed. Humiliation and brutality became more common, and the constant fear of deportation to an unknown (but probably worse) fate was ever present. This excerpt describes some of the deprivations that the Jews in ghettos faced and the efforts they made—establishing schools, holding religious services, forming orchestras—to retain a measure of normalcy and dignity. Yehuda Bauer is one of the foremost authorities on the Holocaust and the Jona M. Machover Professor of Holocaust Studies and a permanent academic chair of the Institute of Contemporary Jewry at Hebrew University. He has also served as chair of the Vidal Sassoon International Center for the Study of Anti-Semitism.*

The ghettoes provided slave labor for the Nazi war machine. From the first days of German occupation, in addition to slave labor camps, the ghettoes supplied labor for German offices, installations, and workshops. In other instances, Jewish slave labor had no recognizable purpose other than dehumanization. In some locations, wages were not paid; in others a minimal sum of 0.50–0.80 reichsmarks ($1 = 2.50 RM) per day was paid. . . .

In the Warsaw ghetto a new aristocracy arose, an aristocracy of smugglers who frequented expensive cafes and restaurants to obtain food. Ruthless and lacking in social consciousness, the smugglers nevertheless risked their lives to bring in food and other essential products. Without them, the ghettoes would have died out quickly. Formerly wealthy people, in contrast, frequently lost their will to live and joined those begging for food on the streets. . . .

In the Warsaw ghetto, the most serious problem was the tremendous influx of refugees . . . . Of a population of close to 450,000 early in 1941, 150,000 were refugees. Elsewhere in occupied Poland, 470,000 other refugees were crammed into the ghettoes, 230,000 of whom were evicted between April and August 1940

A woman hands change to a young beggar in the Warsaw ghetto. Thousands of Jews succumbed to starvation and disease in the ghetto.

from western and southern Poland.

Driven out of their homes with only small bundles on their backs and thrust into a strange environment, the refugees became dependent on social welfare. The meagre resources of the Judenrat, especially in Warsaw, were incapable of feeding this multitude, and the refugees, consequently, were the first victims of starvation and epidemics. In Warsaw, they lived in cellars, synagogues, former schools and cinemas, often without heat and with many broken windows; sanitary facilities were inadequate or nonexistent. They became candidates for death. When efforts to help themselves failed, thousands of adults and children resorted to the streets to beg for food from Warsaw Jews who were themselves underfed and starving. The typhoid epidemic, which began in late 1940, claimed 43,239 lives in 1941 (out of a population of 420,116 in August 1941) and 22,760 in January–May 1942. These deaths reflect the spread of typhoid and other starvation-induced illnesses. Because not all deaths were reported, the actual figures are probably even higher. The 1941–42 deathrate of 10 percent of the ghetto population began to decline in the spring of 1942, as the typhoid epidemic receded. The weakest had died. As time went on, through the efforts of the illicit workshops selling their produce to Poles and also of the smugglers, the situation at least stabilized. A major proportion of the inhabitants of the ghettoes could have survived had the Nazis not decided otherwise. . . .

The Will to Survive

To foil the Nazi goal of breaking their spirit, ghetto inhabitants formed social welfare, religious, educational, cultural. and political (underground) organizations. In some cases, all activities were underground. Membership was usually voluntary. The groups were usually either independent of, or only partially connected with, the Judenrat. . . .

The Judenrat had to acquiesce, in 1941, to the Nazi demand for disinfection actions, supposedly instituted against the spread of epidemics. Polish and Nazi doctors, accompanied by Jewish police, entered apartments and took away warm bedding and clothing to be disinfected. If not stolen, these items were returned, often ruined and torn. People were marched off to baths where they had to stand naked in the bitter cold of an unheated building in the Polish winter while their clothes were disinfected. They showered in boiling hot water and then, without benefit of towels, put on their damp and ruined clothes. Many became ill; epidemics and death were spread rather than averted by these practices. Disinfection squads operated throughout 1941. . . .

Religious Life

The Nazis forbade all public religious practices, despite their claim that their antisemitism was racial, not religious. Jews dressed in traditional garb, especially bearded Jews and others recognizable as believers, were singled out for especially brutal treatment.

Towards the end of 1939 all male Jews of Rawa were forced to assemble in the town square to cut their beards. Among them was Rabbi Rappaport, the rabbi of Rawa, an old man with a white beard. The rabbi had always been on good terms with the local priest, a German, ever since the German occupation during World War I, and also under Polish rule. The daughter of the rabbi went to the priest and asked him to prevent the cutting of her father's beard. The priest went to the town square to intervene on the rabbi's behalf. After the officer in charge had heard the priest's request, he upbraided him for intervening in favor of a Jew. But as he did not dare to ignore the priest's request, he declared—either the beard will be cut off, or one hundred lashes will be administered. The rabbi preferred the lashes. After a number of strokes, the rabbi fainted, covered in blood. He was brought to a hospital where he lay for two weeks, but his beard remained intact. . . . When they put fire to the synagogue of Sierpec at the end of September, 1939, all the Jewish inhabitants were ordered to assemble around the burning synagogue. From among the crowd a young, brilliant student of the Jewish law, Moshe was his name, emerged and ran into the burning house of worship, into the blazing fire, and took out of the ark two scrolls of the Torah, one in each hand. When he came out, he was met with a hail of bullets at the hands of the evil ones. He fell with the Torah scrolls in his hands, and was burned to ashes with them and the synagogue. May the Lord revenge his soul.

Diarist Chaim Kaplan, a teacher, noted:

Public prayer in these dangerous times is a forbidden act. Anyone caught in this crime is doomed to severe punishment. If you will, it is even sabotage, and anyone engaging in sabotage is subject to execution. But this does not deter us. Jews come to pray in a group in some inside room facing the courtyard, with drawn blinds on the windows. . . . Even for the high holy days, there was no permission for communal worship. I don't know whether the Judenrat made any attempt to obtain it, but if it didn't try it was only because everyone knew in advance that the request would be turned down. Even in the darkest days of our exile we were not tested with this trial. Never before was there a government so evil that it would forbid an entire people to pray. Everything is forbidden to us. The wonder is that we are still alive, and that we do everything. And this is true of public prayer too. . . . Hundreds throughout Warsaw organize services, and do not skip over even the most difficult hymns in the liturgy. There is not even a shortage of sermons. Everything is in accordance with the ancient customs of Israel. . . .

They pick some inside room whose windows look out onto the courtyard, and pour out their supplications before the God of Israel in whispers. This time there are no cantors and choirs, only whispered prayers. But the prayers are heartfelt; it is possible to weep in secret, too, and the gates of tears are not locked.

Although prayer was forbidden in some ghettoes . . . at least 600 *minyanim* [congregants worshipped] in Warsaw alone. In Lódź, public prayer was permitted in 1940. In Riga (Latvia), refugee German Jews were allowed to pray, local Jews were not. In Vilna and Kovno (Lithuania), public prayer was not permitted. In March 1941, Hans Frank, the German governor, permitted religious activity in private homes and in synagogues and prayer houses on the sabbath and holidays. For many people, prayer became more meaningful. Additional liturgy was read, such as prayers for deliverance (e.g., Psalms 22 and 23) and the special prayers written during the Crusades and the persecutions of the Middle Ages when the devout "sanctified the Lord's name" (that is, accepted the martyrdom of death rather than deny the Jewish faith).

Observing the Jewish religious commandments (*mitzvot*) under ghetto conditions was difficult. Keeping the sabbath was impossible because people were forced to labor on that day as well as on festivals and high holy days. Keeping dietary laws (*Kashrut*, the separation of dairy and meat dishes), as well as other commandments, including rules of hygiene, was especially difficult. Starving Jews were prepared to forgo non-kosher meat. In special cases, rabbis permitted the consumption of non-kosher food, because the preservation of life is more important under Jewish law than dietary laws and the sabbath. In Lódź, for instance, rabbis permitted pregnant women to eat non-kosher meat. Jews fasted, especially on the Day of Atonement (Yom Kippur), although their starvation rations forced them to fast on many other days as well. . . .

Education and Cultural Activity

Following the Nazi entry into Poland, and later the USSR, education was forbidden. Newspapers were not permitted and libraries were closed. Under the auspices of Alfred Rosenberg, the official Nazi ideologue, special Nazi units entered the large ghettoes to liquidate Jewish libraries and rob them and other institutions of Jewish cultural treasures. But some treasures were hidden, especially by youth and children, and ghetto libraries were established. Writers continued to write, and painters to paint, and scientists continued their research. The few archives that survive supply ample evidence of a feverish intellectual activity during the ghetto period. The Jewish reverence for education would not be denied.

Orchestras were active in the Vilna and Warsaw ghettoes and elsewhere as well. . . .

Because education was forbidden in Warsaw (in September 1941 the Germans permitted the Judenrat to operate some elementary classes) so-called *complets* sprang up, initiated by teachers or parents for groups of 4 to 8 children. . . . An illegal high school of the Dror Zionist youth movement, which existed between 1940 and the summer of 1942, was supported . . . to prepare youngsters for Polish matriculation exams. Beginning with 3 pupils and 7 teachers, by the spring of 1942 there were 120 pupils and 13 teachers. Scientists and educators earned some slices of bread by teaching math, history, biolo-

gy, philosophy, and literature to half-starved youngsters. Illicit vocational training courses were offered in pharmacology and technical drawing, as well as university-level courses in education, medicine and technical subjects. The school eventually contained elementary grades 4 to 6, all six high-school grades, and two college-level grades. Most pupils belonged to youth movements and were to participate in the Warsaw ghetto rebellion.

In the Lódź ghetto, education was permitted. During 1940 and 1941, 14,000 students attended 2 kindergartens, 34 secular and 6 religious schools, 2 high schools, 2 college-level schools, and 1 trade school (weaving). In Vilna, 2,700 children, aged 7 to 14, attended school.

Yitzhak Rudashevksy, aged 15, who lived in Vilna, wrote:

A boring day. My mood is just like the weather outside. I think to myself. what would happen if we did not go to school, to the club, and did not read books? We would die of dejection inside the ghetto walls.

Historical Documentation

To document Nazi inhumanity and to preserve the history of life in the ghettoes, various secret archives were established. The most important, the Oneg Shabbat of Warsaw, was founded by . . . historian Dr. Emmanuel Ringelblum, who persuaded writers, journalists, economists, social scientists, and rabbis to contribute to the documentation.

In addition to a number of permanent workers, the archive commissioned others to investigate specific topics. Journalists such as Peretz Opoczynski reported on life in the ghetto. The leader of the health organization TOZ, Dr. Israel Milejkowski, organized a group of doctors to study the effects of hunger on the human body. Discovered after the war, their study was published in Warsaw in 1946. Others reported on education, on cultural life, on slave labor camps. Writers and poets gave their works to Ringelblum for safe-keeping. Others reported on the situation in other ghettoes. . . .

In the summer of 1942, most Oneg Shabbat members were deported to their deaths. Ringelblum managed to hide in the non-Jewish part of Warsaw where he continued to write in his diary. His hideout was discovered in March 1944 and he, his family, and the Polish family with whom they lived were murdered. The archive was buried in the ghetto in three milk pails. Two of these were uncovered after the war; one was never found.

Parts of other archives, collected in Bialystok, by Mordechai Tennenbaum, the commander of the underground, and in Vilna, were discovered after the war. Although many of the diaries written during that period were lost, some survived. . . .

Ghettoes in the USSR

Jews in the USSR were living fairly ordinary lives in 1939–41. But their hope that the Germans would not invade Russia or fail to conquer it if they did was shattered with the outbreak of the German-Soviet war on June 22, 1941. On June 24, 1941, Kovno, Lithuania, was captured. . . .

From the morning of June 23 until the evening of June 24 [1941], Kovno was a no-man's-land. Groups of nationalist Lithuanians and armed criminal elements calling themselves partisans and freedom fighters controlled the city. They seized the opportunity to attack Jews, accusing them of handing over Lithuania to the Soviets. They rioted. They robbed and attacked Jews, killing many during the two days of terror. The atrocities initiated when the German army entered Kovno reached a peak on the night of June 25 when whole families in the poverty-stricken district of Slobodka were killed in a house-to-house murder march.

Throughout the first week of occupation Jews were arrested en masse. First taken to jail, they were then removed to the Seventh Fort, one of a series of nineteenth century fortifications surrounding the city. Ten thousand people were kept without food or drink, some of them in the open, others in the cellars of the old fort. Daily, groups of men were taken out and shot not far from the fort. Women were raped and then shot. On July 7 the surviving women were sent back to the town; 6,000 to 7,000 men were buried in large pits that had been dug by Soviet prisoners of war.

Lithuanian extremists, not Nazis, committed the murders. Here and there some Germans took part, but the authorities described the massacre as a quarrel between Lithuanians and Jews. In actual fact, however, Nazi security police pulled the strings that made the Lithuanians dance. . . .

On August 7 Lithuanian partisans jailed 1,200 men. About 200 were later released; the others were taken outside the town and killed. Kovno Jews were ordered to move into the ghetto on August 15. On August 8, 534 Jewish intellectuals—teachers, lawyers, doctors—were taken, supposedly to do some special intellectual work in the city archives. They were transported not to the archives but to the Fourth Fort where they were shot. . . .

After the ghetto gates were closed, systematic murder actions began. On September 26, Jewish residents of one ghetto area were assembled in the square, where those fit for work were separated from those less fit. After two days, the "fit" ones were released; the others, about 1,000 men, women, and children, were transported to the Ninth Fort and murdered. On October 4 the whole so-called small ghetto was liquidated. Those who were artisans or members of artisans' families were released into the large ghetto, the others—1,500—were transported to the Ninth Fort. When the hospital in the small ghetto was burned down, its 60 patients and the doctors and nurses were burned alive.

Three weeks later, on October 27, the Judenrat received an order to assemble inhabitants, without exception, in Democracy Square, for "control." It was clear that a "selection" would be made and that some would die. Some Judenrat members wanted to refuse to convey the German order. But an opinion expressed by Rabbi Shapiro was decisive: "If a Jewish community (may God help it) has been condemned to physical destruction, and there are means of rescuing part of it, the leaders of the community should have courage and assume the responsibility to act and rescue what is possible.". . .

The "selection" was made. The survivors were permitted to return to the ghetto; the others, more than 10,000 people, were escorted under heavy guard to the small ghetto to replace those who had been "selected" in the previous murder action. Next morning the death march proceeded . . . to the Ninth Fort, where huge pits had been prepared. The Germans and Lithuanians forced the Jews toward the pits in small groups and mowed them down with machine guns. The bodies were covered with lime and earth. This massacre was termed the "big action" by surviving Jews. Mass murder then ceased for two and a half years.

The ghetto became a slave labor camp of nearly 17,000 inhabitants, less than half the original number of Kovno Jews. The labor office of the Judenrat was the most important institution in the ghetto. At first, all men between the ages of 14 and 60 were recruited. Later, women were added. Men worked six or seven days a week; the women worked three days at first, then five. By the spring of 1942, most ghetto inhabitants had been assigned specific jobs. Those without a permanent job were ordered to appear at the gate every morning to be assigned a temporary job. The foremen of the ghetto workshops were Jewish, which served as a protection of sorts. Outside the ghetto, the foremen were Germans or Lithuanians. Those who worked outside the ghetto were escorted to work by armed Germans or Lithuanian "partisans." In return for their work, they received as much food as the Nazis decided to provide, but it was not supplied on a regular basis. Often some rations were simply withheld. . . .

A grade school was opened, and a second one followed. . . .

At the end of February 1942, Nazis confiscated all books. Schooling continued, however, until August 1942, when any kind of schooling or instruction was forbidden. Although the two schools were closed, education did not cease. Small groups of children continued to study in various homes. Soon the Judenrat obtained permission to organize a vocational school to train young workers for the workshops. In addition to smithery, carpentry, tinnery, sewing, and so on, basic elementary subjects were taught when the Judenrat extended school hours. A choir, a drama circle, and even a ballet group functioned under the auspices of the vocational school.

In the summer of 1942, the well-known musician Misha Hofmekler asked the Judenrat's permission to form an orchestra. Dr. Elkes was doubtful. An orchestra might be interpreted as an expression of joy, which in the ghetto conditions would be an abomination. Explaining that music satisfied an inner emotional need, Hofmekler got his orchestra. . . . When the chords of the first concert were struck in August 1942, both the performers and the audience cried, tears not only of sorrow but of pride.

Religious observance continued in the Kovno ghetto. Although wearing a beard and sidelocks and showing other outward signs of religious observance were dangerous, many people did so.

A multitude of rabbinical decisions were asked for and given: How should one treat Jews who had been ordered to tear up Torah scrolls and trample on them? Could the clothes of dead Jews be worn? Should those still alive praise God for having been saved?

On August 26, 1941, the Germans closed all prayerhouses. Soon, however, in defiance of the Nazi order, observant Jews reopened illegal prayerhouses to pray and study the Torah.

Theresienstadt: The Model Ghetto

Ruth Elias

*Immediately after the liberation of the con-
centration camps, it was common to hear the
claim that no one knew about the camps. It
was not true. Information about what was
happening in the camps seeped out to the Allies and Western press as early as 1942. In
addition, people living near the camps could
have little doubt about what was going on
when they saw the half-dead prisoners or
black smoke billowing from chimneys accompanied by the smell of burning flesh. In one
place the Nazis organized a tour to enable
people outside Germany to see how wonder-
fully they were treating Jews and other prisoners. The site of this propaganda extrava-
ganza was the Theresienstadt ghetto in
Czechoslovakia. The Red Cross was allowed
to visit once; afterward, it concluded that,
while wartime conditions made all life difficult, life at Theresienstadt was acceptable
and that the Jews were being treated all
right. This memoir by Ruth Elias, one of the
survivors of Theresienstadt, tells a very different story.*

*a*pproximately 55,000 to 60,000 Jews were
crammed into Theresienstadt, where once
there had lived 3,000 civilians and about
10,000 to 13,000 soldiers. To make room for
more Jews . . . Jews were loaded into freight cars
like cattle and shipped to the East. None of us
knew the destination of these transports; no news
about them ever came back to Theresienstadt. . . .

Completely separated and closed off from the
outside world, we still knew nothing about concentration camps, the use of gas, or the extermination of the Jews. All we had were our instincts, which told us that we had to avoid the
transports to the East at all costs. . . .

It was not the SS but the Council of Elders
[the *Judenrat*] that had the monstrous job of determining who would be on these transports. I
still don't understand what criteria they used. . . .
Those chosen for a transport had to surrender
their food-ration cards. You could not exist in
Theresienstadt without one of these cards. With
rations close to the starvation level, no one could
afford to share his food with someone else. If
someone tried to get out of reporting for a transport, he was sure to be caught. Then he'd be put
on the next one. . . .

A Fateful Decision

After fourteen or fifteen days in Theresienstadt I
came down with a high fever caused by a seri-

ous throat infection. Before the discovery of antibiotics, this was a dangerous illness, particularly in the ghetto, where medicines were lacking. I lay on my mattresses on the floor, shaking from the fever. Although the doctor came to see me every day, he had nothing but a few aspirin to give me. Then my family received the dreaded notice that we were to be on the next transport east in three days. The doctor pronounced me unfit to go. The regulations then in force stated that people under the age of twenty-one who were not fit to go could shield their immediate families from the trip to the East. Koni [a Jewish friend who was a ghetto policeman] quickly went to see [Elias's] Father [who was suffering from tuberculosis and was living in the men's barracks] and told him that he wouldn't have to report. However, Father said he might actually be able to breathe better in some other place. When Koni brought this bit of news back to us, we were devastated. Father then sent a message saying that the family must stick together and that I, sick as I was, should also go. A day passed. The doctor cautioned me not to leave. Father sent another message, saying that I might get well on the transport. Only one day was now left in which we could strike our names from the list. Again Koni went to see Father, who stuck to his decision that the family should go east together. We'd all be better off there than in Theresienstadt, he said. After an intense discussion, Koni and I arrived at a simple solution. We would get married immediately. That way I would not be staying behind alone, and Father and the rest of the family could leave on the transport. As a member of the ghetto police, Koni was shielded from the transports and as his wife I would be, too.

Koni brought a rabbi to my bedside. One of the women in the room lent me a wedding ring that she had smuggled into the ghetto by hiding it under her tongue. Like every young girl, I had dreamed of a beautiful, festive wedding in a synagogue, with singing and dancing, a long white dress, and bridesmaids. And so I was terribly disappointed with the ceremony, which lasted only a couple of minutes. The rabbi recited the words of the marriage ritual, and we repeated after him, "Behold you are consecrated onto me with this ring according to the laws of Moses and Israel." Then Koni put the ring on my finger. And that was it.

This would be my last day with my family. I wanted to say good-bye to Father, and sick as I was, I went to see him. Having been assigned to the transport, he was forbidden to leave his barracks, but Koni brought him to the wooden fence. There I told him that I would not be going east with the family, that I had just been married and would stay in Theresienstadt with Koni. Father was silent, but there were tears in his eyes. Did he sense perhaps that these would be our last moments together? Too young to understand, I asked him, "Aren't you happy that I'm married?"

Instead of answering me, Father, who was a Cohen, raised his hands in the traditional gesture and began to recite the familiar words of the priestly blessing while tears flowed down his cheeks. Then he whispered only, "My Rutinko, my Rutinko." It was the last time I saw him. When I think of him, dream about him, or talk about him I always see him standing there at the fence at this, our final meeting. . . .

After my family was deported and I had recovered from my illness I, like all the other ghetto inmates, was required to work. Since there were not enough nurses, I volunteered for a nursing job; it would give me a chance to help others. I was assigned to care for the old and the sick in the hospital for incurables. This hospital was on the ground floor of the Jäger Barracks. There was no heat because there was no coal. There were no beds. The patients—each lay on two mattresses on the floor—were always cold because the single woolen blanket they had been allowed to bring to the ghetto was not enough to keep them warm. Patients received only a meager portion of food that contained very few calories, not enough to keep anyone warm. For washing, only cold water was available. There were scarcely any medicines, but there were lots of lice and bedbugs against which people were defenseless. Many of these incurably sick patients were confined to bed, could scarcely get up, and the nursing staff had the almost impossible task of seeing to it that they were washed, kept clean, and cared for. A dreadful stench hung over the hospital, because many of the patients had no control over their bladders or bowels. Having no clean bedding, they lay in their own filth. When I had night duty and some of them died on my shift, I learned to wrap the corpses in sheets and dispose of them. It was gruesome and strenuous work to transport the corpses down to the cellar that served as a morgue. The next morning I had to report the names and the number of people who had died during the night so that these data could be precisely recorded in the main registry. The Germans insisted on order above all else. I don't know how many patients, crying out with longing for their children, died in my arms. I know only that most of them died deserted and alone, without children or other relatives near them. It was my first encounter with death and despair. . . .

Staying Alive

In the ghetto there were no stores where you could buy things, so you had to filch them. You might have a friend who worked in the woodworking shop, and he would *schleus* [swipe] a nail or a piece of wood for you. In exchange you would give him a potato or a piece of bread that you had *schleused* from the kitchen. And so a lively barter system ensued despite a camp detective unit that was set up to prevent these petty thefts. All we were trying to do was make our miserable lives a little easier, each of us eager to find what we urgently needed. When the soles of my shoes developed holes, I would get them back from the repair shop much faster if I brought a potato for the shoemaker. When the baker had his shoes repaired, he would add an extra piece of bread; someone else would come up with a cigarette. Cigarettes were a highly prized and costly item for which the ghetto's Czech gendarmes demanded unbelievably high prices. Smoking was prohibited in the living quarters, and if an SS man or a *Berushka* [an SS woman] arrived unexpectedly and smelled smoke, he or she would launch an immediate search for cigarettes. Usu-

ally other contraband items were found during these searches. The punishment for this, too, was transport to the East. In spite of the constant danger, the inmates continued with their petty thefts, trying to make life in the ghetto a little more bearable. Actually, it was more than that: An extra bite of bread or an extra potato helped ward off starvation and kept one alive. To filch coal in the winter when the temperature hovered between 5° and 15° F (–10° to –15° C) was to have a little warmth to keep from freezing to death. So, *schleuseu* was not stealing. It was trying to stay alive. It was essential. . . .

Immediately after his arrival, each inmate was assigned a job. Everyone had to work eight hours a day to keep all the facets of the "autonomous" ghetto administration running smoothly. But after work, in our free time, there was a tremendous upsurge of cultural activity. It began with lectures to small groups; some people studied Hebrew; choral groups were formed; there were stage productions; and after the first musical instruments were smuggled in there were concerts. All this had to be done secretly. . . .

First an accordion, then a guitar, a violin, a viola, a cello, and other instruments were brought into the ghetto. One problem was that we had no printed music, but the musicians had memorized the scores, so they played by heart. Trios formed, and it was remarkable and incredible to hear these musicians playing from memory without making mistakes. The first concert I attended took place in an attic. . . .

These few hours of spiritual nourishment helped us temporarily to forget our hunger pains and our misery. We longed for another concert, a lecture, or perhaps a play. The performers viewed this as a revolt against the regime. They were using their instruments and their words as weapons against the Nazi terror.

The Model Ghetto

Later the Council of Elders reached an agreement with the SS that officially allowed the Jews to obtain musical instruments and bring them into the living quarters. The result was an incredibly vital and diverse cultural program during our so-called leisure time in Theresienstadt. Working at night, the musicians drew musical staff lines on paper and wrote down, from memory, the parts for each instrument. During the day each inmate had to perform his assigned tasks, but after work many of us were able to forget our suffering for a few hours. The German authorities encouraged this and later used it to support one of their biggest propaganda lies.

In the fall of 1943, it was announced that the Red Cross was coming to inspect Theresienstadt. The Nazis wanted to show the world what a good life the ghetto Jews were leading. Theresienstadt was beautified—even the streets were washed—and playgrounds were built for the children. The Nazis produced a film called *Der Führer schenkt den Juden eine Stadt* (The Führer Gives the Jews a Town). It showed ghetto performances of plays, concerts, and lectures in halls crowded with well-dressed spectators. It was intended to give the world a picture of Theresienstadt as a model ghetto where Jews lived contented, happy lives. A Red Cross commission arrived in June 1944 (by that time I was no longer there), and right after this visit all the improvements that had been made were torn down and the sad, dreary life of the inmates resumed. After the commission left, virtually everyone who had participated in this staged event—now that they were no longer needed—was designated for transport east.

The Rebel Artists

A group of artists—among them Leo Haas, Fritz "Fritta" Taussig, Otto Ungar, Karel Fleischmann, and others—were ordered to produce paintings for the SS. The Nazis dictated the subject matter. But these artists also initiated a major clandestine and illegal undertaking: They captured life in the ghetto on their canvases. While they were working, lookouts were posted to warn of surprise SS visits. When they finished, the paintings were concealed behind walls and in other hiding places. It was intended that after liberation, these paintings would testify to the realities of life in the ghetto. One day the SS arrived without warning, discovered

some of the paintings, and put all the artists into "the Little Fortress," the Theresienstadt prison. There they were tortured to force them to tell where they had hidden the rest of their paintings. When they refused, two of the artists had their fingers mangled. One by one, they perished in the Little Fortress. Only Leo Haas survived. After his liberation in 1945, many of the paintings and the truth about the fate of the other artists came to light. . . .

Unbearable Pain

Until September 1942, the ghetto was "closed"; that is, one could leave one's living quarters only in groups or with a special pass. But as a ghetto policeman, Koni was able to enter the women's quarters. And so he divided his free time among the Dresden Barracks, where his mother lived, the Sudeten Barracks, where his father was housed, and the Hamburg Barracks, which was my "home." After we had been in the ghetto some six months, this closure was eased somewhat and we were permitted to move about freely on the streets. Women still were forbidden to enter the men's barracks, however. To get around this prohibition, I volunteered for the cleaning detail that scrubbed the wooden floors in the men's barracks. It was the only way I could get to see my father-in-law. Instead of scrubbing the floor, I would quickly wipe it with a damp rag so that I would have more time to spend with him.

Koni's father was a man of great personal dignity, but he was slowly wasting away. He could not cope with the suffering, the meager food, and above all the feeling that he was powerless to take care of his family. It was not long before he became ill and was brought to the infirmary. There he lay in a clean bed, but soon he lost all interest in life, and he no longer wanted to get up. After coming down with much-dreaded pneumonia, he died. Yet another parting. Each one left us a little bit older. Where did we find the strength to bear it all? . . .

There were organized sports in the ghetto. Some of the young men had brought soccer balls with them, and soon soccer clubs were formed.

A league was founded, and matches were arranged. The matches were played in the courtyard of the Dresden Barracks, with the spectators standing pressed up against the balustrade of the arcade, cheering for the players in "their" clubs. There were several of these clubs, and they had names like the Cooks, Expediters, Ghetto Police, Transportation, and so on.

Almost every day women's gymnastics lessons were given in the courtyard of the Hamburg Barracks by a former physical education teacher, and more and more women joined in these sessions to keep fit. It was surprising how many inmates, despite their hunger and privation, participated in the exercises.

All these activities helped us to forget. On Friday evenings we sometimes met in one of the barracks with a group of young Zionists to celebrate Shabbat and light the traditional candles. Our common yearning to go to Palestine brought us together and gave us a chance to affirm our belief in a better tomorrow. . . .

Dreaded News

After almost six months, I began to feel sick and queasy in the mornings. I didn't know what was wrong, and I had no mother to ask for advice. It didn't seem serious enough to see a doctor, but by chance I ran into Dr. Mautner during one of my visits to the Hamburg Barracks. He seemed truly happy to see me again. With professional concern he asked me how I was feeling, and I told him about my problem, adding that I probably had gastroenteritis or some similar infection so common in Theresienstadt. Dr. Mautner looked shocked. "My dear," he said, "you're pregnant. You must do everything possible to terminate this pregnancy."

To whom could we go for help? A recently issued regulation prohibited abortions in the ghetto. We made desperate appeals to one doctor after another, but none wanted to take the risk; if the authorities had found out about a doctor performing an abortion, he would have been on the next transport east. . . .

During this time of despair Koni, his mother, and I received the dreaded slips of paper notifying us that we had been picked for transport to the East. I was two months pregnant and I had no choice but to go. Given my condition, how could I make such a trip? Where would my child first see the light of day? I made another desperate round of all the doctors in the ghetto, begging them to help me. In vain.

In mid-December of 1943, it was very cold in Theresienstadt and probably much colder in the East. How could we get hold of warm winter clothes in the short time before we were scheduled to leave? I was able to swap my winter coat and several rations of bread for a warmer coat with a fur collar. In exchange for bread, we also were able to get warm underwear for Koni and his mother.

And now the time had come. Once again we said farewell to friends and colleagues with whom we had lived and worked. Each of these partings marked the end of an era in our lives, a break with all that had gone before. The question "Will we ever meet again?" was never expressed in so many words, but it was implicit in every kiss, every handshake. many of those who stayed behind smiled in embarrassment, just as I used to when I went to say good-bye to friends who were leaving. The embarrassment stemmed from discomfort: Their friends had to leave, and they did not. I could see it in many of the faces now, and I wanted to console them.

Koni and I had spent our last night in the attic room in a tight embrace. We had each packed a suitcase and a backpack in which there was food that friends had given us for the trip. Officially we each received a loaf of bread from the ghetto authorities. Early the next morning we went to the Jäger Barracks. There our suitcases were taken from us and we surrendered our food-ration cards. Then began the inevitable registration; they had to make sure that everyone who was supposed to leave had reported for the transport. The suitcases were stacked in front of the waiting cattle cars. Koni and I recognized ours in a large pile that had not been loaded. We decided not to go into the cars until we were sure that our suitcases had been put on board. Meanwhile, people whose names were called were chased into the cars by SS troopers shouting, "Hurry up, hurry up!" Then one car after another was closed and locked from the outside. We knew that soon it would be our turn. Watching what was going on through a crack in the window of one of the barracks rooms—something that was strictly forbidden—we saw that our suitcases were still on the platform, and we stuck to our decision not to board without them.

We hid in a closet in a corner of the room. There would be another transport in two or three days and we would leave on it if our suitcases were put aboard. We heard them call, "Everybody out to the loading ramp!" A search of the barracks ensued. SS men repeatedly passed by our hiding place. To this day I am amazed that they didn't find us. We stood absolutely still inside the closet, not moving a muscle, but our hearts were beating wildly. Had they caught us, we would have been given *Sonderbehandlung* (special treatment): an individual transport straight to death. We heard the train whistle and then the chugging as the train departed. It became very quiet. We knew that everyone had left the barracks and the nearby area. We wondered who had been forced to take our places on this transport.

We opened the closet door carefully, made sure no one was around, took our backpacks, and returned to our attic room in the ghetto. . . . We all knew that sooner or later the authorities would find out. Our action was really senseless and rash, since we knew that we couldn't survive in the ghetto without food-ration cards. In addition, detailed records were kept of all the ghetto inmates, and if we were caught it would mean *Weisung* (banishment), a word all of us dreaded even though none of us knew what actually happened to those who were banished. We could no longer move about freely in the ghetto; there was always the danger of being caught. Like hunted animals, we longed for the day when the next transport would leave and we would finally be able to get out of Theresienstadt. That happened three days later. . . .

We told a Jewish clerk that we had been scheduled to leave on the earlier transport and had already handed in our food-ration cards. He sent us to the train without raising any further obstacles. Our suitcases didn't matter anymore. This time we didn't even see them.

Selection 3

The Last Days of the Warsaw Ghetto

Alexander Donat

The popular image of Jews during World War II is that they were passive victims, "sheep led to the slaughter." The reality was that, in most instances, people had little chance to resist. One of the most hopeless cases, however, was also perhaps the most heroic—the Warsaw Ghetto Uprising. The Jewish population, which had been herded into the ghetto and forced to live in desperate conditions with little food and constant danger, man-

aged to smuggle a handful of weapons with which to challenge the might of the powerful German army. This selection tells the story of these Jewish resisters and the gut-wrenching decision many parents faced over how to save their children from almost certain death. Often, parents could not bear to part with them, but in this case a father and mother sent their child away to save him. This is the story of the author, Alexander Donat, a Polish journalist who survived the Warsaw ghetto and is now a writer in the United States.

My wife, Lena, and I thought constantly about saving our little boy. We went over and over the list of the "Aryans" we knew, trying to think which of them might be both willing and able to take him. I began to write letters to our Polish friends, telling them of our situation and begging them to save the life of an innocent child. Needless to say, these letters could not go through the mails: they had to be delivered by messenger. But even if one got hold of someone willing to deliver a letter outside the walls, the recipient was usually reluctant to accept a letter from the ghetto brought by a stranger: there was too much danger of blackmail. So I first had to alert my friends by phone, and tell them to expect a letter from me. To make these calls, I used the phone in the office of the T.O.Z. (one of the Jewish welfare agencies) at 56 Zamenhof Street, which I could get to through secret passages. The phone was in constant use: by people on errands like mine, or by smugglers contacting their confederates about conditions at the gates or arranging to receive parcels to be thrown over the wall. Each call took hours of waiting my turn. And then not everyone I wanted to reach had a phone. I would often call my former partner, Stanislaw Kapko, at his office and have him get a message to someone that he was to come to Kapko's office and await a call from me. Then I would have to call Kapko the next day to find out if the appointment had been made. When I finally spoke to the friend, I had then to persuade him to come and talk to me at the printing shop on Leszno Street. There was no danger for Gentiles in coming to the printing shop because it was located outside the ghetto, and they could always pretend to be out buying Jewish goods. Still, they were not easy to persuade. Some never came, some came and refused my request. Finally one possibility to save Wlodek began to take shape: the Maginskis.

Stefan Maginski had been a member of the group with whom I had fled Warsaw in September 1939 (whence I returned to be with my family). He was a brilliant journalist and a highly cultivated man. I loved him, and he treated me rather as if I were his younger brother. His wife, Maria, a former actress, was both a beauty and a great lady. They had no children.

Mrs. Maginski agreed to meet us in Leszno Street. She spoke of a friend in the country who, for a modest fee, would be willing to take the child. She vouched for the decency and honesty of her friend, and promised us that Wlodek would be well looked after. They themselves could not take him, because they were too old suddenly to appear with a five-year-old child, and they were, besides, working night and day with the Polish resistance. The fee was indeed modest, and happily we could afford it. Sometime earlier I had managed to increase my income by going into partnership with Izak Rubin to smuggle out some of the kerchiefs made from pillowcases in the ghetto. Thus I had the money to pay for Wlodek's care for several months in advance. By some child's instinct for self-preservation, Wlodek did everything in his power to win Mrs. Maginski, and she was much taken with him. She promised to make the necessary preparations. . . .

At the end of March, Mrs. Maginski came once more to Leszno Street—this time to tell us that all the arrangements for Wlodek had been made and we had two weeks in which to prepare him for leaving us.

eeks: in which we tried to memorize
ear-old son to the look and to the
in which I watched approvingly
on's mother taught him to disavow
on with us. "Remember, you have
the ghetto. You are not a Jew. You
Catholic. Your father is a Polish
who was taken prisoner. Your
in the country. Mrs. Maginski is
ria."

s turned out to be only seven
ski unexpectedly returned to
one afternoon, terribly upset.
round had received word that
he ghetto was to take place
ild must be smuggled out the
rning, Lena washed and fed
st time. At eight o'clock we
' marching column, and at
ski came to the shop for him.
, smiling. But just as we were
e clutched his mother and said,
ll never see you again?" "What a
re!" she managed to say. "Just as
ar is over, I am coming to get you."
aginski took Wlodek's hand and
riskly out of the building. Wlodek
beside her, and didn't look back once.
ossed Leszno and turned into Orla, out
t. A Jewish policeman who was a friend
s followed them for a little way on his bi-
. Everyone crowded around to congratulate
Ve had been very lucky, they said. So, in-
i, we had. . . .

The End Is Near

On . . . Sunday (April 18) at 6 o'clock P.M., Polish police surrounded the ghetto. Within an hour
the underground declared a state of emergency.
The fighters were assigned to their posts.
Weapons, ammunition, and food were distributed, along with supplies of potassium cyanide.
By 2 A.M. the next morning (April 19) the Poles
had been joined by Ukrainian, Latvian, and SS
units, who ringed the ghetto walls with patrols
stationed about thirty yards apart.

I had just come on guard duty at our apartment
house when two boys from the Z.O.B. [a Jewish
resistance organization] arrived to order us all to
our shelters. They were about twenty years old,
bare-headed, with rifles in their hands and
grenades stuffed into their belts. It did not take
long to alert everyone; by dawn the ghetto was a
ghost town. I awakened Lena and the others in
our flat; we put on the best clothing we could
find, and took the linen bag we had filled with
lump sugar and biscuits cut up into small squares.
About thirty people gathered in our shelter.

We had only one weapon among us: Izak's revolver. Izak crouched at a peephole near the entrance to the shelter, from which he could see
part of the courtyard. An ingenious network of
tunnels connected us with the "outside" world.
Through a tunnel extended to the front attic of
our house, in turn connected with others, one
could reach a spot just above the corner of Muranowska and Zamenhof Streets. The north side
of the building, which fronted on Niska Street
and the *Umschlagplatz* [this was the transfer
point near the railway line which the mass deportations had made notorious], could be reached
by a special passage that had been drilled
through the carpenter's apartment. This same
passage connected with No. 62 Zamenhof Street,
where a resistance group was preparing to make
its last-ditch stand. On the second floor a hole
had been bored through to one of the lavatories in
No. 42 Muranowska, from which we were put
into connection with every building on the block.

Despite all our elaborate preparations, the
German operation came upon us suddenly
enough to upset all plans—those of the hundreds of people who had prepared to slip out to
the "Aryan" side at the very last moment, and
had documents and lodgings waiting for them,
and, of course Kapko's grand scheme. That
"very last moment" had come, and it was now
too late for anything.

The Uprising

On Monday morning, the Germans marched into
the ghetto through the gate at Gesia and Zamenhof Streets and took up positions in the little
square opposite the *Judenrat* [Jewish council] of-

fices. Convinced that the resistance would not fire on Jews, they sent members of the Jewish police in their front ranks. Our fighters let the Jewish police go by, and barraged the Germans who followed with bullets, hand grenades, and home-made bombs. The intersection of Zamenhof and Mila Streets, where the resistance occupied the buildings on all four corners, became the scene of a real battle. Home-made incendiary bombs, flung from an attic window, hit first one tank and then another. The tanks burst into flames and their trapped crews were burned alive. The troops panicked and scattered in disorder.

I lay on the attic floor with Izak, watching all this going on below. Izak's orders were to cover the withdrawal of our unarmed people should it become necessary for them to leave the shelter; several times I saw him point his gun and then, reluctantly, withdraw it. Below us German officers were trying to urge on their panicked "*Judenhelden*" with pistols and riding crops: the men who had been so powerful and assured when dealing with women and children and old men were now running from the fire of the resistance. Scores of German bodies lay scattered on the pavement.

When Izak and I returned to the others in the shelter to report on what we had seen, people embraced and congratulated one another, laughing and crying. Some began to chant the Psalms, and an old man recited blessings aloud.

(Later we learned from some of the fighters that the first battle of the Warsaw Ghetto resistance had occurred at the corner of Nalewki and Gesia Streets, where a German unit marching into the ghetto had been caught totally off guard and where, after several hours, this first German unit withdrew, leaving behind their dead and wounded. But replacements came, and the fighting continued at this corner off and on all day. The resistance group's meager supply of grenades and bombs finally gave out, and they then had to retreat through the back of the house at 33 Nalewki Street. Before pulling back, they set fire to the warehouse at 31 Nalewki, where the SS stored their Jewish loot. The warehouse continued to smolder and burn until the very end.) . . .

The original battle, the one at Nalewki and Gesia Streets, had not gone so well for us. There had been heavy losses on both sides; but when our boys were forced to retreat from their position, the Germans took over Gesia Street and, with it, the ghetto hospital. The SS first worked its terrible vengeance on the sick, going through ward after ward with bayonets and guns; then they shelled the building and set fire to it. Those patients and staff members who had made it to the shelters died in the fire.

All day Tuesday we watched the glow in the sky that indicated shelling in the vicinity of the Brushmakers. The Brushmakers had its own independent fighting unit, headed by Marek Edelman; and when the Germans opened attack on the district—for only twenty-eight people out of 8,000 responded to the Germans' summons to report for deportation—they walked into a mined boobytrap at the entrance to 6 Walowa Street. Stroop [the Nazi officer in charge of the Warsaw assault] then called for artillery fire on the entire Brushmakers' area. The resistance suffered very heavy losses, and house after house caught fire. Fighting was taken up again in Muranow Square. There the Germans had set up a concentration of tanks, heavy machine guns, and flamethrowers. The resistance, on the other hand, had an underground passage to the "Aryan" side, and throughout the battle was being supplied ammunition by the Polish resistance. Muranow Square was the only Jewish position that did not suffer from an extreme shortage of weapons. In the end, some of the Jewish fighters managed to escape through their passage to the "Aryan" side. . . .

The apartment house across the street [from us] caught fire, and the sparks carried by the wind constituted a real danger to us. In accordance with a plan previously agreed upon, I made my way to the building next door where—amazingly enough—there was still a telephone in working order. I calmly reported the fire to the fire department, and within a few minutes they appeared to put it out. It took some time before the fire department, undoubtedly under German orders, ceased responding to our calls.

Tuesday evening a blood-red glow hung over

the southern end of the ghetto, and here and there throughout the rest of the ghetto a building was burning: in some instances, like that of the warehouse, from a fire set by the resistance, more often from the shelling and occasional air bombardment. That night the grapevine offered sensational news: the uprising had spread from the ghetto to the whole of Warsaw. Organizations like the AK (the Home Army) and the GL (the People's Guard) were joining their Jewish comrades; an unlimited supply of arms was making its way to the ghetto; more important, we heard, the Allies had promised to parachute troops and supplies to us. We would show the bastards yet!

For the first time in two days, we lit the stove and ate cooked potatoes and kasha from our reserve stock. We then went to sleep in our own beds, full of hope for tomorrow.

Hope Is Dashed

But Wednesday was no different from the day before. We could hear the same gunfire and explosions. The fires were spreading. This was the day that Stroop began to close in, using two thousand trained troops, and thirty officers, with tanks, machine guns, and air power. Ammunition was giving out. And our boys were retreating from one position to another. There was no question that we would be defeated—but everyone fought on.

For Stroop the major problem was the tens of thousands of civilian Jews holed up in their shelters. [SS leader Heinrich] Himmler's order had been categorical, but to pull the Jews individually out of their hiding places before destroying the ghetto might take months. The resistance understood this too, and after two days of street fighting, decided to save their ammunition for the defense of the bunkers. Stroop, then, was faced with the challenge of extricating Jews from the ghetto at the risk of a house-to-house skirmish for each and every one of them.

It was a challenge he was equal to. He called in the army engineers and ordered them to set fire to every building. The engineers moved methodically from house to house, drenching the

ground floor with gasoline and setting off explosives in the cellars. The ghetto was to be razed to the ground. . . .

In his report of April 22, 1943, Stroop wrote: "Whole families of Jews, enveloped in flames, leaped out of windows, or slid to the ground on bedsheets tied together. Measure were taken to liquidate these Jews at once."

Then came Easter Sunday. The day was bright, and the citizenry of Warsaw, dressed in their finest, crowded into the churches. I thought, perhaps Wlodek is among them. When the mass was over, the holiday crowds pushed through the streets to catch sight of Warsaw's newest spectacle. . . . Batteries of artillery were set up in Nowiniarska Street, from which the Germans kept up a steady barrage against the ghetto. And everywhere the flame, and the stench of roasting human flesh. The sight was awesome—and exciting. From time to time a living torch would be seen crouched on a window sill and then leaping through the air. Occasionally one such figure caught on some obstruction and hung there. The spectators would shout to the German riflemen, "Hey, look over there . . . no, over there!" As each figure completed its gruesome trajectory, the crowds cheered.

Fighting of a sort was still going on inside the ghetto—scattered and disorganized, but determined. Those people who had been burned out of their shelters were roaming the streets, looking for hiding places. We allowed another ten people into our shelter.

Escape!

It was now the ninth day of the uprising, Tuesday, April 27. Someone who had been sent out to reconnoiter brought us word that the Germans were coming into our street. We heard shots in the courtyard. . . .

"They are setting fire to the staircases and the ground floor apartments," Izak whispered. We could hear nothing, but in half an hour the heat became unbearable and black smoke began to fill the shelter. Our turn had come.

Izak announced that we were to evacuate the shelter. Nearly half our companions refused to budge. They had chosen to use their potassium cyanide, and with a kind of gentle indifference they sat watching the rest of us scurrying around. Below us was an inferno: our only way out was by the roof. There were five of us now, Izak, Lena, I, and two other friends; I never saw what happened to the others. We crossed the roof to the neighboring house, not yet on fire. Then began a tortuous journey through attics, and passages and dugouts and cellars. Our plan was to get as far away from our burning house as possible, and, under cover of night, cross the pavement to the backs of the houses on Mila Street, then down Mila and across Nalewki to a certain house that still had a passageway out of the ghetto.

By late afternoon we were at the middle of the block. At dawn Izak went to scout: we had to cross the street, find a shelter, contact a fighting group. Before he returned, we heard the now-familiar sound of windows breaking and smelled the smoke. The staircases in this building were in worse condition than our own had been. We went to the roof again, and sat, dazed by the fresh air and sunshine, straddling the roof's peak. What were we to do now? The look of death had come over Lena's face and I discov-ered that in the scramble for the roof, the little bag she had been wearing around her neck had slipped loose and was gone. In that bag was our last refuge: cyanide. We had to decide, then, whether to remain on the roof and burn alive or to try to make our way down. One of our friends decided for us: "There is always time to die," he said. We scrambled down through the burning staircase and ran out of the doorway with our hands above our heads. We were led by a wait-ing German officer out into Muranowska Street. A large number of Jews from the surrounding apartment houses were already gathered there. Among them were a few of our neighbors.

One of the SS men kept staring at Lena and asked her her name. She gave him her married name, and he walked away without a word. They had been classmates together at the university.

We were lined up five across, and made our way toward the *Umschlagplatz*. As we passed Niska Street, Lena clutched my hand. A woman, holding a child by the hand, stood screaming at an upper-story window and then threw herself into the street. This was our last sight of the Warsaw Ghetto.

Selection 4

Living and Working in the Camps: The Germans

Tom Segev

Much has been written about the concentration camps and the treatment of Jews, but far less attention has been devoted to the Germans who worked in those camps. It turns out that the camp commandants did not hold high ranks and were generally not held in high esteem. Compared to many other positions, especially of common soldiers fighting an armed enemy, the commandants had good jobs. This selection describes the institution of concentration and death camps and some of the men chosen to run them. Tom Segev is an Israeli author who has written several books related to the history of Israel.

*O*n March 21, 1933, Joseph Kramer read in *Völkischer Beobachter,* the Nazi party's morning newspaper, that on the following day, Wednesday, a concentration camp would open some 9 miles north of Munich. The local police chief told a press conference that the camp, the first of its type, would have space for 5,000 inmates. The buildings in the camp had been a gunpowder factory during World War I. Not far away, at the foot of an old castle, lay a picturesque town called Dachau. The newspapers published the item concerning the opening of the camp inconspicuously. Outside of Germany it evoked only limited interest: *The New York Times* gave the announcement a few lines on front page, but the name of the man who had made the statement was not yet known to American readers in those days at the dawn of the Nazi regime. It was Heinrich Himmler.

Joseph Kramer was an unemployed electrician of 27, and lived in city of Augsburg. He was a member of the Nazi party and had already served for half a year as a volunteer in the SS. The *Völkischer Beobachter* reported that the concentration camp at Dachau had been established as part of the redoubled efforts to wipe out Communist subversion. Kramer was pleased. He hated the Communists. Within two years of reading about the opening of the camp at Dachau, he had joined its staff. He was to serve in concentration camps over a period of more than a decade. During this time, camps were set up all over Europe. They expanded and became more brutal from year to year. Kramer was party to this development from the start and accustomed him-

self to it gradually, step by step, from Dachau to Auschwitz to Bergen-Belsen. When soldiers of the British army entered Bergen-Belsen in 1945, they found 60,000 prisoners, wasting away from hunger and disease, many of them on the edge of insanity. Tens of thousands of bodies were strewn between the barracks; there were signs that some of them had been eaten. "It was not always like this," Joseph Kramer told his captors, and he was right. When he looked back, a short time before he was executed, a few months after the camp was captured, he noted in a letter to his wife, "Yes, we came a long way."

The night before the opening of the camp at Dachau several supporters of the Communist party were led to imprisonment at another abandoned munitions plant, near Oranienburg, nine miles north of Berlin. The Nazi propaganda authorities would in the future allow, from time to time, outside visitors, journalists, and representatives of foreign embassies to tour the site. Werner Schäfer of the "storm troopers" *(Sturmabteilung,* or SA) was there to receive them. He was always careful to emphasize to them that the Oranienburg camp was, in fact, the first concentration camp in Germany. His pride for what, in his words, he had created from scratch and through his own efforts and "pioneering devotion" was so great that he wrote an entire book about his camp; Dachau was not even mentioned.

In those days there was still confusion about internment. No one knew for sure who was responsible for what. Within weeks of Hitler's ascension to power the regular jails were filled to bursting. As the arrests continued, from Berlin to Munich, there was a need for new prison facilities. Before the establishment of the official concentration camps, improvised prisons sprouted up all over Germany, set up by the SA and the *Schutzstaffel* (SS) on their own initiative in abandoned factories, sports fields, and farms, in order to confine—and sometimes obliterate—their enemies. Even before the Nazis took over, brown-skirted hooligans would often kidnap anyone who had crossed them personally—debtors, business competitors, bothersome neighbors, even relatives. These activities were part of the atmos-

Excerpted from Tom Segev, *Soldiers of Evil* (NY: McGraw-Hill 1987). Reprinted with permission from Harris-Elon Agency.

phere of general anarchy which pervaded Germany in the last days of the Weimar Republic. . . .

The Dachau camp served the official law-enforcement agencies from the start, and as such it truly was the first of its kind. With the exception of a short period in which it was closed for construction and renovation, it served continuously as a concentration camp, throughout the Third Reich's twelve years of existence, until it was captured by the U.S. Army some three weeks before Germany surrendered.

When Dachau opened, a few weeks after Nazi rule was established, only a few dozen prisoners were held there. On the eve of its capture by the U.S. Army their number was 50,000. A total of more than 200,000 prisoners from thirty-eight countries passed through the camp, most of them during the war. At least 30,000 of them died there. In six years before the war, concentration camps were also established at Sachsenhausen and Buchenwald in northern Germany, Mauthausen in Austria, Flossenbürg in northern Bavaria, and Ravensbrück (this a women's camp) in northeast Germany. At the outbreak of the war these camps held about 20,000 prisoners; towards its conclusion the number was more than 385,000. Some 975,000 prisoners passed through the six large camps in operation before the war; some 360,000 of them died. The International Red Cross located, after the war, close to 2,000 prison facilities and forced-labor camps. The great majority were set up during the war, in all the areas of the Nazi occupation. Only about twenty were considered major concentration camps; the others all functioned as secondary camps, branches, and labor details.

The Camp System Expands

The first concentration camp established outside Germany opened in May 1940 in Galicia, about 90 miles southeast of Warsaw, not far from a small village known as Oświecim—in German, Auschwitz. The site was originally intended as a transfer camp for Polish citizens on way to concentration camps within the borders of the Reich. With time it became the largest of all the camps. Its original facilities, which served the

Polish artillery forces, were known later as Auschwitz I. They were expanded in October 1941 in the direction of the village Brzezinka or, in German, Birkenau. This part of the camp later became known as Auschwitz II. There, in a farmhouse, the gas chambers for the annihilation of the Jews were installed. In 1942 a special camp was set aside for the chemical concern I. G. Farben, which manufactured synthetic rubber there. This part of the camp, near Monowice, was called Auschwitz III. . . .

The prison facility the Germans had set up in Lublin, 80 miles southeast of Warsaw, was declared a major concentration camp. The last remnants of the Jews who remained in the city were brought there. The camp was later used for the extermination of Jews as well. It is located in one of the city's neighborhoods, Mejdan Tatarski; the inhabitants called it, for short, Majdanek. At the same time that Majdanek became a concentration camp, in April 1943, a camp was established some 50 miles north of Hannover in northern Germany, originally intended for Jews with dual citizenship. The intention had been to exchange them for Germans who had been taken prisoner by the British. The camp is located on the main road connecting two villages, Bergen and Belsen. During the last stages of the war prisoners evacuated from camps in the east were transferred there, just before those camps fell into the hands of the Russians. . . .

About half a year before Germany's surrender one of Buchenwald's subsidiary camps was also added to the list of major concentration camps. That was in November 1944. The place was 40 miles northwest of Buchenwald and was known by the code name of "Dora," the place the V-2 rocket was manufactured. This was the last prison facility to be officially designated a concentration camp.

How Many Prisoners?

It is impossible to be certain how many people were held as prisoners in Nazi concentration camps. The registration records of many camps were destroyed or lost. The numbers of some inmates were given to others after their deaths. But

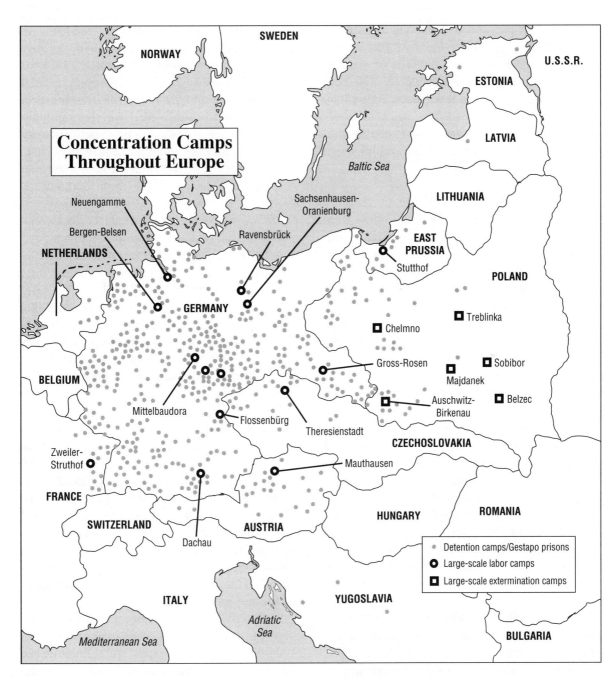

Concentration Camps Throughout Europe

SWEDEN

NORWAY

U.S.S.R.

ESTONIA

LATVIA

Baltic Sea

LITHUANIA

Neuengamme

Sachsenhausen-Oranienburg

Bergen-Belsen

Ravensbrück

EAST PRUSSIA

NETHERLANDS

Stutthof

POLAND

GERMANY

Treblinka

Chelmno

Gross-Rosen

Sobibor

BELGIUM

Majdanek

Mittelbaudora

Auschwitz-Birkenau

Belzec

Flossenbürg

Theresienstadt

Zweiler-Struthof

CZECHOSLOVAKIA

Mauthausen

FRANCE

HUNGARY

ROMANIA

SWITZERLAND

AUSTRIA

Dachau

● Detention camps/Gestapo prisons
◉ Large-scale labor camps
▣ Large-scale extermination camps

ITALY

YUGOSLAVIA

Adriatic Sea

BULGARIA

Mediterranean Sea

there were also prisoners who were listed more than once, as they were transferred from camp to camp. There were some who were never registered. In any case, on January 15, 1945, there were some fourteen camps still functioning, holding close to 700,000 prisoners, among them 200,000 women. During the trial of Oswald Pohl, who headed the camp administration during the war, it was estimated that not less than 10 million people ended up at the camps. According to the same estimate, more than 1 million prisoners died in the concentration camps; in addition, close to 6 million Jewish prisoners were murdered in the six extermination camps. The great majority of the victims died during the war. As defeat approached, the camps in the east were evacuated and the prisoners were forced to endure long marches to other camps in the west.

Thousands died or were killed along the way. At the same time the camps in the west were in total chaos—the overcrowding, the lack of sanitary facilities, the epidemics, the hunger and cold raised the death rate to a level much higher than it had ever been before. When Joseph Kramer wrote before his death that he had gone "a long way" from Dachau to Bergen-Belsen, he spoke from personal experience. . . .

Reeducation

Many of the opponents of the Nazi regime were brought to the concentration camps to be destroyed, but many others were brought in the sincere hope that they would accept the principles of Nazism and become loyal to the government. A correspondent for *The New York Times* allowed to visit Dachau some time after it was opened received the impression that Theodor Eicke, commandant of the camp, and his men were very serious about the educational goals they set for themselves. "They honestly and sincerely believed that their task was pedagogic rather than punitive," the correspondent wrote. "They felt sincerely sorry for the misguided non-Nazis who had not yet found the true faith."

Documents captured after the war confirm the impressions of the correspondent, at least in part. An internal memorandum written at Gestapo headquarters in 1934 stated that the victory of the Nazi movement would not be complete until all its opponents learned to support it—not from fear or for practical reasons, but through complete identification with it. . . .

It is difficult, of course, to believe that the brutal conditions turned any opponents of the Nazi movement into its disciples. At the most they learned to keep quiet during their time as prisoners. In any case, the fact is that tens of thousands of them were, over the years, released, after it was established that they were no longer dangerous to society or to the regime. . . .

The first inmates were, for the most part, opponents of the regime, Communists, Social Democrats, or their supporters. Later, the concentration camps were used to imprison criminals, prostitutes, homosexuals, vagrants, gypsies, clergymen, Jehovah's Witnesses, and pacifists. All were considered by the new regime to be negative elements harmful to society and dangerous to its stability. Not all were considered appropriate for reeducation—many were described as hopeless cases, unable to change their ways or opinions. There were some Jews among these prisoners, but arrests of Jews simply because they were Jews did not begin, for the most part, until after the pogroms which raged all over Germany on the night of November 10, 1938, known as *Kristallnacht*. Most of the prisoners in Nazi concentration camps were not Jews, although Jews were by far the largest number killed in them. . . .

Forced Labor

Vast numbers of prisoners were brought to the camps as forced labor for various factories. In 1938 the SS founded a company for stone quarrying and cutting, Deutsche Erd- und Steinwerke (DEST). The company based its activities on the work of the prisoners at Sachsenhausen and Buchenwald. The wave of mass arrests in Germany during the second half of the thirties was meant, in part, to provide laborers for the SS factories. The camps near the village of Flossenbürg, not far from the Czechoslovakian border, were set up near granite quarries, as part of a program to expand the economic activity of the SS. In time the concentration camps became the foundation of a huge economic empire and a central component of the political influence of the SS. The camps also provided forced labor for military industry.

With time, the camps also served to camouflage various activities that required secrecy. At Sachsenhausen the prisoners were employed in forging passports, stamps, and foreign banknotes for Nazi intelligence. Underground factories in the Dora camp manufactured rockets, and in some camps the prisoners were used for "medical experiments" and "scientific research" in race theory. During the war some POWs were brought to the camps for execution. At one point, close to 2,000 prisoners were even conscripted into a special combat unit and sent to the front, under the command of one Oscar Dirlewanger, an unbalanced embezzler and adventurer and one of Heinrich Himmler's protégés. Extermination facilities were set up at two concentration camps, Auschwitz and Majdanek, which were used from 1942 onward in the liquidation of Jews in the framework of the "Final Solution." (Four other extermination facilities were not officially designated concentration camps.)

The Germans Know the Truth

After the war, many argued that they knew nothing: "All I know about the atrocities of Gross Rosen I learned during the trials against me," said the camp's commandant, Johannes Hassebroeck. That was, of course, a lie. The Nazi regime never knew what would best serve its interests—hiding the truth about the camps or publicizing it. In reality they did both. The power of totalitarian authority is not only the strength of the support it receives from its subjects, but also the power of arbitrariness and fear. For this reason the authorities made sure that all citizens, even if they supported the regime and observed its laws, knew that they could find themselves at any time, and without any reason, on the other side of the electrified fence of one of the concentration camps, and not necessarily after due process.

German newspapers frequently reported the internment of citizens in concentration camps; they did not hide the fact that people were sent to the camps for unlimited terms, sometimes after they had served their full court-mandated sentences in regular jails. Information about what was going on in the camps made its way into Germany through radio broadcasts from across the border. Tens of thousands of prisoners were released, in time, from the camps. Before they were allowed to return home they were forced to promise to keep secret what had happened to them, but there is no reason to believe that they all did. There were judges, lawyers, members of the clergy, social workers, and repairmen who were allowed in to perform various tasks, and suppliers who came to unload merchandise. Many camps employed local civilians on a regular basis, and nearby factories and even farmers sometimes hired prisoners as day laborers. There were also the tens of thousands of staff members who served in the camps. . . .

Rules of Brutality

Preserved among the SS documents are a number of judgments condemning camp guards for brutalizing prisoners in excess of what was permitted. In 1937 Theodor Eicke publicized the case of SS Sergeant Paul Seidler. Seidler, Eicke wrote to his men, beat one of the prisoners at Sachsenhausen "with sadistic cruelty" and was as a result put on trial, demoted to the rank of private, and expelled permanently from the SS. "I am making this incident public so that it can serve as a warning. The camp guards should once more be told the serious results of brutality to inmates. . . . The commandant may impose extremely heavy and serious punishments on troublesome inmates; there is no need to add private initiatives to these. Whenever a guard is illegally brutal to an inmate, he will be expelled from the SS. We will do our best to preserve the good name of the organization.". . .

Two concentration camp commandants, Adam Grünewald and Karl Chmielewski, were tried and found guilty of the deaths of prisoners as a result of brutality in their camps. A total of several hundred staff members of camps were tried for mistreatment of inmates. . . .

The judgments of courts in various countries which tried Nazi crimes after the war contain uncountable testimonies of the blood-curdling atrocities which were an inseparable part of the daily routine in the concentration camps. They involved acts of brutality against individual prisoners or groups of prisoners. They were performed in public, in broad daylight, with the full knowledge of the camp commandants, and often at their initiative and with their active participation, deliberately ignoring the disciplinary regulations. Random brutality, forbidden by the regulations, became the norm in the camps. . . .

Prisoners Are Not All Equal

Towards New Year's Day 1944, Heinrich Himmler ordered that certain prisoners should have their conditions of imprisonment eased. These prisoners were allowed to wear civilian clothes and would be identifiable only by an insignia on their sleeve. Himmler instructed that these prisoners were to be given a special barracks within the camp. From the very start there were "privileged prisoners" among the rest, including some who had made names for themselves in politics, culture, and the media. Among these some were accorded better treatment than others; in contrast, there were those who were tortured and humiliated because of their notoriety. Christian clergy were also often subject to more difficult conditions than were other prisoners. Some prisoners received authority over their comrades, and as such became part of the camp hierarchy, headed by the commandant. At the head of the prisoners stood the "dean of the camp," who served as liaison between the prisoners as a group and the camp command. Alongside him sometimes functioned officials whose area of responsibility was limited to certain facilities, such as the hospital. The dean was responsible for, among other things, the office work in the prisoners' compound, almost all of which was done by the prisoners, as well as for the work of those prisoners who were employed as clerks in the camp headquarters, in the political department, or in the clinic. A prisoner-overseer was in charge of each of the barracks, subordinate to the dean, and under him were prisoner-overseers of each of the rooms in the barracks. A prisoner was appointed *kapo* (which in Italian means "head") over each labor detail. Subordinate to the kapo were assistant overseers and work directors who were also prisoners. Prisoners with such positions in the camp were supplied with special sleeve insignias: black for the dean and the dean's staff; red for the barracks overseers; yellow for the kapo. The entire system was based on two hierarchies which were actually one, said the prosecutor at the Neuengamme trial—from the last of the prisoners to the commandant of the camp.

There were among the prisoners those with authority who greatly mistreated their fellows, sometimes no less than the SS men themselves. . . .

Rules for Murder

Dozens of the standing orders sent to the concentration camp commandants were meant to establish procedures for the execution of prisoners, the cremation of their bodies, and the notification of their relatives. . . . In 1938, the camp commandants were told to send telegrams to the relatives of prisoners who had died, without noting the circumstances of their death. The relatives could notify the camp within twenty-four hours of their desire to see the body before it was cremated. They were required to arrive at the camp within three days. This arrangement was later canceled. In 1942 the camp commandants received instructions not to notify relatives directly of the deaths of prisoners, since these notices, it was said, had caused disquiet among the population. Instead, the commandants were to notify the authority in the prisoner's place of residence that brought about the prisoner's arrest. The local authorities would deliver the death announcement to prisoners' families. At a certain point the camps were freed of the obligation to make notification of the death of Jewish prisoners. Afterwards, this order was also amended: as before, notification was to be made of the death of a Jewish prisoner—if the prisoner's relatives were not Jews. There was no obligation to make notification of the death of a Jewish prisoner to Jewish relatives. . . .

The Death Camps

The first extermination facilities were set up on an experimental basis in the Chelmno camp, in December 1941. After the Wannsee conference, during which the details of the execution of the Final Solution were clarified, facilities for extermination in gas chambers were activated also in the Belzek camp (March 1942), Sobibor (May 1942), and Treblinka (June 1942), all within a radius of 300 kilometers of Warsaw. These camps were in operation for close to a year and a half. They were extermination facilities, not concentration camps they were not used to imprison people, but to murder them. Extermination facilities also operated in Auschwitz and Majdanek. Camps for the liquidation of Jews on a more modest scale operated also near Vilna, Riga, Minsk, Kowno, and Lvov.

"The freight trains," stated the verdict against [Nazi war criminal] Adolf Eichmann, "which carried the Jews earmarked for destruction, arrived at a special platform at the camp, near the extermination facilities. Advance notification was sent by Eichmann's office, which dispatched the trains, and they were marked with special numbers and letters, in order to prevent their confusion with shipments of other prisoners. There was an average of 2000 Jews on each train. After removing the Jews from the trains and counting them—lists of names did not exist—they all passed by two SS doctors who divided those fit for work from those unfit. On the average, 25 percent were found fit. The belongings of the Jews remained on the platform and would be brought afterwards to storage rooms for sorting. Among the unfit for work, the men were separated from the women and children, and they were brought to the closest vacant extermination complex. There they had to strip, in rooms which gave the impression of being delousing facilities. The hesitant were told to hurry so that those after them would not have to wait long, and to pay attention to where they laid their clothes in order to be able to find them after the shower. From there they were brought to the gas chamber, which was disguised as a shower room by the installation of showerheads, pipes, and drains. After they had all entered the door was locked and the Zyklon B gas was dropped from the top, through a special opening. It immediately vaporized and did its work. Death came in from three to fifteen minutes. Thirty minutes afterwards the gas chamber was opened and the bodies were transferred to the crematories, after the women's hair had been cut off and gold teeth removed. There were five crematories in which 10,000 bodies could be burnt every day. The ashes were crumbled into dust and thrown into the Vistula River."

Selection 5

Life in the Camps: The Jews

Yitzhak Arad

The Nazis murdered people in many different, often gruesome ways. The way they treated people while they still were alive was also horrible and led to the deaths of tens of thousands of men, women, and children. Try to imagine being confined in a prison with little or nothing to eat. The temperature outside may be freezing and your clothes are little more than rags. You might not have any shoes or a coat. You have to stand outside at attention for hours and perhaps work at a backbreaking task. If you get hurt or sick, you probably will be killed. If you break a rule by, say, trying to get extra food, you can be severely beaten. The guards might beat you for no reason at all. Is it any wonder so few people survived for more than a few months in the camps? The miracle is that anyone survived. This excerpt describes the daily life of prisoners in the camps. Most of the specifics relate to Treblinka, but they apply to most of the other camps as well. Yitzhak Arad is one of the leading experts on the Holocaust and a former chairman of Yad Vashem.

The routine of the prisoners' daily life began early in the morning, usually at four o'clock. In the summer at this time it was already light, but in the winter it was still pitch dark. [Camp survivor] Rudolf Reder described the start of the day in Belzec:

> At 3:30 in the morning the Askar [Ukrainian] who guarded the barrack during the night knocked on the door and shouted: "Get up! Get up!" Before we could even rise, the bully Schmidt burst in and rushed us out with a whip. We ran out with one shoe in our hand, and sometimes even barefoot. Usually we slept in our clothes and shoes because we had no time to get dressed in the morning. . . . We got up feeling miserable and tired. The same feeling we had gone to sleep with.

As the prisoners got up, the entire area of the Jews' living barracks came alive. The doors of huts were opened from the outside by the Ukrainians and the urination and excrement bowls were taken to the toilets. The huts were cleaned, the blankets were folded, and the prisoners were allowed to leave for their meager breakfast, which was followed by roll call.

During the roll call the prisoners were lined up in several rows in front of the huts. The "barrack elders" reviewed their people and reported the number to the "camp elder." He, in turn, added up the total number of prisoners and submitted his report to the SS man who was reviewing the roll call. These statistics were then reported to the camp commander or his deputy.

After the morning roll call, the prisoners were divided into work groups. The capos [prisoner leaders] escorted the work groups to the work sites and supervised the prisoners throughout the day. Throughout the workday the prisoners were exposed to the harsh treatment of the SS supervisors. Dov Freiberg testified about these cruelties in Sobibor:

> I shall tell the story of one day, an ordinary day, much like any other. That day I worked at cleaning a shed full of belongings and transferring them to the sorting shed. An umbrella had gotten stuck in a roof beam, and the SS man Paul Groth ordered a boy to get it down. The boy climbed up, fell from the roof and was injured. Groth punished him with twenty-five lashes. Groth was pleased with what had happened and called over another German and told him he had found "parachutists" among the Jews. We were ordered to climb up to the roof, one after another. The agile—and I was one of them—succeeded in climbing up without falling. But the majority did not succeed; they fell down, broke legs, were whipped, bitten by [the guard dog] Barry, and shot.

> This game was not enough for Groth. There were many mice around, and each of us was ordered to catch two mice. He selected five prisoners, ordered them to pull down their trousers, and we dropped the mice inside. The people were ordered to remain at attention, but they could not without moving. They were whipped.

> But this was not enough for Groth. He called over a Jew, forced him to drink alcohol until he felt dead. When the work was finished, we were ordered to lay the man on a board, pick him up and slowly march while singing a funeral march.

> This is the description of one ordinary day. And many of them were even worse. . . .

The Workday

The workday usually lasted from six in the morning until six in the evening, with a short break for lunch. At twelve noon the signal for lunch would be given, and the prisoners, work group by work group, led by the capos, were taken in the direction of the kitchen, where they received their meal. Shortly after, the signal for the end of the lunch break was sounded, and the prisoners were returned to their work sites. On

Excerpted from Yitzhak Arad, *Belzec, Sobibor, Treblinka: The Operation Reinhard Death Camps* (IN: Indiana University Press, 1987). Reprinted with permission from the publishers.

A prisoner is supported by fellow inmates during roll call. Prisoners who seemed ill or weak were removed from the formation and killed.

the way to and from work, the prisoners were made to sing, and whoever dared sing without "enthusiasm" was whipped. During periods when there was not much activity going on in the camps, work on Sunday would last only until the afternoon, and the rest of the day would be spent cleaning the living barracks, airing out the blankets, and performing various other cleaning jobs. At six in the evening, the signal for the end of the workday was given, and the prisoners were returned to Roll-Call Square for the evening roll call. This roll call took much longer than the morning roll call and sometimes lasted as much as a few hours. After attendance was taken, the sick or weak-looking prisoners were taken from the ranks, brought to the *Lazarett* [pit], and shot. Reder described a scene of this sort in Belzec:

> Usually the doctor prepared the list of the feeble, or the *Oberzugführer* who was in charge of the prisoners prepared the list of the "transgressors" in order to execute thirty to forty

prisoners. They were taken to the pit and shot. They were replaced by the same number of people, taken from the arriving transport. . . .

Floggings and "Sports"

At the evening roll call, punishment was meted out to those prisoners who had committed some "crime" during the workday. Any small infringement was an excuse for punishing a prisoner: if he did not work fast enough, or energetically enough; if he did not respond properly when an SS man passed him; or if, in a search of his belongings, food, money, a cigarette, or a picture or memento—the only tangible thing left him from his past—was found. Even those prisoners who had already received "treatment" during the workday and who still bore fresh whip lashes on their bodies were given additional "treatment" at the evening roll call.

The punishment at the evening roll call was generally whipping. In Treblinka, at Roll-Call Square, there was a special bench cemented into the ground for this purpose. The prisoner was tied to the bench with straps in a way that his torso rested on the bench while his feet dangled on the floor at a 90-degree angle to his body and his buttocks protruded exactly at the corner of the bench.

In the first months of the camp's existence, they would whip the prisoners while they were dressed. But at one of the whipping sessions it seemed to [SS guard] Kurt Franz, who happened to be present, that there was something suspicious. He ordered the prisoner to take off his pants, and then they saw that the prisoner had stuck a towel in the seat of his pants to soften the blows. From then on the prisoners were ordered to lower their pants before they were strapped to the bench, and the blows were inflicted on the bare skin.

Prisoners were usually given between twenty-five and fifty lashes with a special leather strap. The SS usually did the whipping; sometimes a Ukrainian was given the assignment. Frequently the prisoner had to count the number of lashes out loud, and if he made a mistake, or if he had no more strength to count, they would start over—from the beginning. There were prisoners who, gritting their teeth, took their lashes without a sound; others screamed to high heaven. There were instances of beatings of twelve- or fourteen-year-olds, and their screams shocked and terrified the prisoners standing on the sides. But the SS enjoyed it. As the screams grew louder and louder, Franz and [another guard] Küttner—when they attended the roll call—enjoyed themselves all the more. When the whipping was over, the prisoner's buttocks were a piece of bleeding meat. . . .

Another form of punishment was "sports activities." In Treblinka the prisoners who received punishments of this kind had to run in a circle and alternately drop to the floor and get up, and all the while the SS and the Ukrainians would whip them. The prisoners who had no strength to continue with this "exercise" were taken to the side. The "sports" would continue until all the weak had collapsed and had been removed from the circle of runners. With the completion of the "sports activities," all those who had not been able to go on were taken to the *Lazarett* and put to death. The "activity" itself was a selection in which the strong survived and the weak were finished off. . . .

The whipping, the "sports," and the killing were all part of the routine of the evening roll call. The prisoners had to stand and watch the selections the whipping, and the "sports" until the end. After the orchestra, under the direction of Artur Gold, was established, when the whipping was finished they would play marches and the choir would sing. At the end of the roll call, all the prisoners had to sing the "Treblinka Anthem," and only then was the "Dismissed!" order given. The prisoners finally could return to their quarters. . . .

There was no shower in the area of the living quarters, and the prisoners had no opportunity to wash or shower for months at a time. The limited amount of water that they were rationed was hardly enough to quench their thirst, let alone for washing. . . . Conditions such as these all but invited disease and epidemics.

Food in the Camps

The food that was distributed to the prisoners in the camps was very meager, and it was difficult to live on it for an extended period of time—especially since we are talking about people who were put to work at hard labor for many hours of the day. For breakfast the prisoners received a cup of warm water, which was supposed to be coffee, with 150 to 200 grams of frequently stale bread. For lunch they were given soup with some unpeeled potatoes; sometimes this meal also included horse meat. In the evening they got only coffee.

In Treblinka during the period of almost daily transports, until December 1942, the prisoners were able to help themselves to the food that the transportees had brought with them. In the parcels of those who were taken to the gas chambers were substantial quantities of food, since the deportees thought they were being taken to work camps in the East. The packages usually included bread, potatoes, meat, butter, and other foodstuffs. Although the prisoners were ordered to transfer everything to the camp authorities, the SS became resigned to the fact that some of the large quantity of food that was brought into the camp by the deportees remained for the prisoners. There was therefore never a scarcity of food during the period of the transports, and the prisoners were not hungry. In December, however, as the frequency of the transports subsided, the SS men and Ukrainians took for themselves all the food that was brought into the camp, and the prisoners were forbidden to take any of it. Prisoners caught with a single piece of bread were executed. When the transports for extermination stopped, the Jewish prisoners began starving and had to make do with the meager portions that the Germans distributed. One of the prisoners describes the hunger:

> From day to day our meager rations were reduced. Food was distributed only once a day, in the evening. Every man received six cooked potatoes with the peels still on them. In addition, they distributed a slice of bread which was for the morning and which we were not allowed to eat until then. As we twisted and fumed on the bunks at night, our insides were so empty that we couldn't stop thinking about that slice of bread until we broke off a piece of the bread that tasted like clay and smelled like a sick animal. There were those who gobbled up the entire piece but who were still hungry afterward. What's more, in the morning they could expect harsh punishment as well.

The hunger brought on trade and speculation in food. Money, gold, and other valuables that the prisoners took from the clothes and belongings of the murdered were used to buy food. Trade in food, on a limited scale went on in the camps during the entire time, even when food was relatively plentiful. During those times the prisoners would buy special foods like salami, canned goods, alcoholic drinks, and cigarettes. But when the hunger set in, they bought anything they could get their hands on: bread, potatoes, fat, sugar, and so on. Then the prices

soared: they would have to pay gold rubles for a loaf of bread or tens of dollars for a half pint of vodka. The middlemen in the food trade were the Ukrainian guards: the Jewish prisoners paid, and the Ukrainians brought in food from the villages around Treblinka. . . .

A prisoner who was caught with smuggled food, or with money or valuables that he intended to trade for food, paid with his life. The SS men kept a close watch over the buyers and sellers of food. In testimonies about Treblinka, there are even stories of Jews who for the slightest favors or for additional food would be willing to inform on their friends. Informers of this kind were known to all the prisoners. . . . [Former inmate] Shmuel Wilenberg writes:

> Certain informers were executed by the prisoners. It was done at night when the entire camp was deep in sleep. Four men would approach the informer, throw a blanket over his head, tie a rope to one of the roof beams and hang the accused. In the morning, when the SS men would see the hanging man, they would not be surprised, for it was a frequent sight—many people would commit suicide by hanging or by swallowing poison.

Other testimonies of prisoners in Treblinka contain no mention of the killing of informers.

Despite the efforts of the SS personnel and despite the executions that were carried out, the trade in and smuggling of food in Treblinka never stopped; it continued during the entire period that the camps functioned.

In testimonies from Belzec and Sobibor there is no mention about food smuggling.

Lavatories and *Scheissmeister*

Throughout the day the prisoners were under the careful watch of the SS, the Ukrainians, and the capos. Theirs was a day of perpetual work and motion, and woe to anyone who stopped to rest. Anyone who slowed down would be whipped on the spot or recorded by the capo or the SS man in charge for "treatment" at the evening roll call. The only place the prisoners were able to sit quietly for any amount of time without being watched was in the lavatories. There were only a few toilets in the camps, but the prisoners—and especially the weak and sick among them who continued working only out of fear that if they stopped working they faced certain death—found the only place for a short rest was in the lavatories. In general the Jewish capos were considerate of the sick and looked the other way during their frequent visits and long stays in the lavatories. During the winter that the typhus epidemic spread through Treblinka, the toilets became the main rest area.

In Treblinka, Küttner began noticing the "exaggerated" use of the toilets by the prisoners and, to put a stop to it, he appointed a Jewish supervisor over every toilet; these supervisors were given the title *Scheissmeister* ("shit master"). For their entertainment, the Germans dressed the *Scheissmeister* in a special outfit: the clothes of a rabbi and an eight-cornered cantor's turban. He had to wear a large alarm clock around his neck and carry a whip. He was also ordered to grow a Vandyke beard. He would have to make certain that the prisoners did not stay in the toilet for more than two minutes and that there should be no more than five people in the lavatory at a time. It was the duty of the *Scheissmeister* to chase out those who dallied. A prisoner who did not obey the *Scheissmeister* was registered and his number was submitted to Küttner.

Thus the lavatories, which had been the only place where the prisoners I had found some semblance of peace, turned into yet another place of hardship and torture.

Night in the Camp: A Time of Rest and Reflection

At nine in the evening, the prisoners were locked into their barracks. Shortly thereafter, the lights were turned out and night fell on the camp. In Belzec the lights were turned out half an hour after nightfall, and the prisoners were not even allowed to talk with one another. In Treblinka lights-out was usually at 21:00 and in Sobibor at 22:00.

The night hours in the huts were the only time that the prisoners were able to rest, relax a bit, collect themselves and their thoughts, with no Germans or Ukrainians spying on them Wilenberg describes night in Treblinka:

> We would welcome the night and the few hours of relative quiet that we had for sleeping. Sleep allowed us to forget the harsh life in the camp, dulled our suffering and sometimes transported us to a dreamland where everything was fantasy. But usually nightmares came to haunt us, actually they were the impressions of what we had seen during the day. Because we were suffering from sickness and weakness from hunger and hard labor, into our sleep came all kinds of weird thoughts, extraordinary notions that, combined with the hallucinations that ruled our subconscious, expressed themselves in nightmares and horrible dreams. Sometimes the stillness of night was broken by a sigh or scream; sometimes by the muffled cough of someone suffering from tuberculosis, or someone snoring loudly. Here and there someone would wake up, let out a juicy curse, punch his noisy neighbor, and then fall back to sleep—which was more of a snatched nap. But there were also nights with no sleep, full of work, beatings, and endless running.

. . . In spite of the hell they lived in, which became their daily existence, those who survived continued to go through this routine and, to a certain extent, even got used to it. Dov Freiberg says:

> It is difficult for me to explain what happened to us—how we could continue to live. I remember in the beginning when a transport arrived, we wanted to die. But later, after some time, transports arrived, and we were sitting and eating. Even the suicides stopped, and those who did commit suicide were the newcomers who were not yet used to living in this inferno. All this in spite of the fact that we knew that our end would also be cremation in Camp III. If someone among us looked a little better than the others, we used to tell him jokingly, "You'll burn better because of your fat. . . ."

Daily Life

The conditions under which the prisoners were kept in the camps, the daily selections, the torture and punishment, the hunger and disease, all contributed to the fact that the average time that a Jewish prisoner remained alive in the camps was a few months at most. Only a few survived for longer periods. Those who entered the camp around the time of its establishment and lasted until the final stages of the camp's existence can be counted on one hand.

The constant turnover in the prisoner ranks, the daily executions and replacement with new arrivals from transports that came from different cities and countries retarded the growth of personal contact and deeper ties among the prisoners. That hardly anyone knew anyone else was a deterrent to establishing close relationships. It also protected the prisoners from future emotional hurt in the event of a death of a friend.

Selection 6

Operation Reinhard

Yitzhak Arad

When experts speak out about the Holocaust in terms of how many people were killed, it is easy to see why other mass murders are also described as holocausts. It was not the number of people murdered, however, that made this event different, it was the way the Final Solution was conducted. Thousands were simply taken out and shot, but millions were killed in more diabolical ways. Elaborate precautions were taken, for example, to deceive the victims into believing they were not going to die. The following selection describes the plan, code-named Operation Reinhard, to exterminate the Jews in Nazi-occupied Poland. It involved the construction of death camps at Belzec, Sobibor, and Treblinka. Yitzhak Arad, from Israel's Yad Vashem, an organization that memorializes the Jews who perished in the Holocaust, is one of the leading scholars on the Holocaust.

Soon after the [Einsatzgruppen] task forces had begun their campaign of extermination in the occupied areas of the Soviet Union, the deputy of the Governor General Hans Frank, Secretary of State Dr. Bühler, remarked at the Wannsee Conference:

> that the General Government would welcome it if a start were to be made on the final solution of this question in the General Government, because here transportation does not pose a real problem nor would the deployment of a labor force interfere with the process of this operation. Jews should be removed from the area of the General Government as quickly as possible, because it is here that the Jew represents a serious danger as a carrier of epidemics, and in addition his incessant black marketeering constantly upsets the country's economic structure. Of the approximately 2.5 million Jews in question, the

Excerpted from Yitzhak Arad, "Operation Reinhard," *Yad Vashem Studies*, vol. 16, 1984. Reprinted with permission from Yad Vashem Research.

majority are anyway unfit for work.

. . . The General Government consisted of the districts of Warsaw, Cracow, Lublin, Radom, and Lvov. According to the estimate of the German authorities, they were inhabited by approximately 2,284,000 Jews. A special organization was set up in Lublin to prepare for their extermination. The actual killing was to be carried out in three death camps—Belzec, Sobibor and Treblinka, at the eastern border of the General Government.

The geographical location of the extermination sites also served as a pretext for the claim that the Jews were to be deported to ghettos in the East. Their disappearance could thus be explained in terms of their transportation to labor camps in the huge areas then occupied by the German armed forces in the Soviet Union.

SS-Brigadeführer Otto Globocnik was entrusted with conducting Operation Reinhard—named after Reinhard Heydrich who had been assassinated on May 2, 1942. . . .

The principal tasks of Globocnik and his staff in Operation Reinhard were: the overall planning of the deportations and of the extermination operations; the construction of extermination camps; to coordinate the deportation of Jews from the different administrative districts to the extermination camps; the killing of the Jews in the camps; to secure their belongings and valuables and transfer them to the appropriate German authority. . . .

The first Jews brought to the camps were those from the vicinity. They were used for construction work and also performed various services for the German camp personnel. They were generally skilled workers or craftsmen such as carpenters, blacksmiths, tailors, and shoemakers. As soon as the construction phase was completed, most of them were killed in trial gassings.

When the organized mass gassings began, the camp administration needed more and more workers from amongst the death transports. A few, especially skilled workers, were employed in the extermination camps according to the specific directives of the German and Ukrainian camp leaders. Others had to work in the gas chambers,

removing and incinerating the corpses, and also sorting the clothes and baggage of the victims. In the initial period, in particular, they were kept alive for only a few days or weeks before being killed and replaced by Jews from newly arrived transports. In each of the camps the Jewish labor force consisted of 600 to 1,000 prisoners. At a later stage Jewish prisoners became part of the permanent staff of the camp. While members of the German or Ukrainian camp personnel were occasionally transferred to other camps, once Jewish prisoners had entered a camp they never left it again. . . .

In the second half of December [1941], Christian Wirth was appointed Camp Commandant of Belzec. . . .

Wirth developed his own ideas on the basis of the experience he had gained in the "Euthanasia" program. Thus, in Belzec he decided to supply the fixed gas chamber with gas produced by the internal-combustion engine of a motorcar. Wirth rejected Cyanide B which was later used at Auschwitz. This gas was produced by private firms and its extensive use in Belzec might have aroused suspicion and led to problems of supply. He therefore preferred a system of extermination based on ordinary, universally available gasoline and diesel fuel. . . .

Wirth continued to experiment in his search for the most effective method of handling the transports of Jews, from their arrival at the camp to their extermination and the subsequent removal of the corpses. Everything was arranged in such a way that the victims should remain unaware of their impending doom. The intention was to convey to them the impression that they had arrived at a work or transit camp from which they would be sent on to another camp.

In addition, everything was to proceed at top speed so that the victims would have no chance to grasp what was going on. Their reactions were to be paralyzed to prevent escape attempts or acts of resistance. . . .

Construction of Treblinka began after Belzec and Sobibor were in operation. The experience gained from the installation and the extermination procedures in those two camps was taken into consideration in the planning and building of Treblinka. Thus, it became the most "perfect" extermination camp of Operation Reinhard. . . .

Organized mass extermination began with the deportation of the Jews of Lublin on March 17, 1942. This date marks the actual onset of Operation Reinhard. . . .

> The camp [at Belzec] looked "peaceful." The victims were unable to discern either graves, ditches or gas chambers. They were led to believe that they had arrived at a transit camp. An SS-man strengthened this belief by announcing that they were to undress and go to the baths in order to wash and be disinfected. They were also told that afterwards they would receive clean clothes and be sent on to a work camp.

> Separation of the sexes, undressing, and even the cropping of the women's hair could not but reinforce the impression that they were on their way to the baths. First the men were led into the gas chambers, before they were able to guess what was going on; then it was the turn of the women and children.

The gas chambers resembled baths. A group of young and strong Jews, a few dozen, occasionally even a hundred, was usually selected during the unloading of a transport. Most of them were taken to Camp II. They were forced to drag the corpses from the gas chambers and to carry them to the open ditches. Several prisoners were employed in collecting the victims' clothes and belongings and carrying them to the sorting point. Others had to remove from the train those who had died during the transport and to take those unable to walk to the ditches in Camp II. These Jews were organized into work teams with their own Capos [or leaders]. They did this work for a few days or weeks. Each day some of them were killed and replaced by new arrivals.

SS-man Karl Alfred Schluch, a former "Euthanasia" worker, who spent ca. sixteen months in Belzec from the very beginning, described what else happened to the transports inside the camp:

> The unloading of the freight cars was carried out by a Jewish work commando, headed by a Capo. Two to three members of the German camp personnel supervised it. . . . After the unloading, those Jews able to walk had to make their way to the assembly site. During the unloading the Jews were told that they had come for resettlement but that first they had to be bathed and disinfected. . . . Immediately after this, the Jews were led to the undressing huts. In one hut the men had to undress and in the other the women and children. After they had stripped, the Jews, the men having been separated from the women and children, were led through the tube. . . .

> After the Jews left the undressing hut I had to direct them to the gas chamber. I believe that I eased the way there for the Jews because they must have been convinced by my words or gestures that they really were going to be bathed. After the Jews had entered the gas chambers the doors were securely locked. . . . Thereupon [another SS guard] started the engine with which the gassing was carried out. After 5–7 minutes—and I merely estimate this interval of time—someone looked through a peephole into the gas chamber to ascertain whether death had overtaken them all. Only then were the outside gates opened and the gas chambers aired. . . . After the gas chambers had been aired, a Jewish work commando headed by a Capo, arrived and removed the corpses. . . . The Jews had been very tightly squeezed into the gas chambers. For this reason the corpses did not lie on the floor but were caught this way and that, one bent forward, another one backward, one lay on his side another kneeled, all depending on the space. At least some of the corpses were soiled with feces and urine, others partly with saliva. I could see that the lips and tips of the noses of some of the corpses had taken on a bluish tint. Some had their eyes closed, with others the eyes were turned up. The corpses were pulled out of the chambers and immediately examined by a dentist. The dentist removed rings and extracted gold teeth when there were any. He threw the objects of value obtained in this manner into a cardboard box which stood

there. After this procedure the corpses were thrown into the large graves there.

It is difficult to establish exactly how many of the gas chambers were in operation during the first three months of the mass extermination in Belzec. At times not all three gas chambers functioned because of technical problems or actual defects. Problems also arose with the burial of the victims. When a ditch was filled with corpses, it was covered with a thin layer of soil. As a result of the heat, the decomposition process, and sometimes also because water seeped into the ditches, the bodies swelled up and the thin layer of soil burst open.

Those no longer able to walk were led directly to the ditch where they were shot. Robert Juhrs, an SS-man who started his service in Belzec in the summer of 1942, described how such shootings were conducted: . . .

The Jews in question were taken to the gate by the Jewish work commando and from there conveyed to the ditch by other working Jews. As I recall, there were seven Jews, both men and women, who were laid inside the ditch.

At this point I should like to stress that the victims concerned were those persons who had suffered most severely from the transport. I would say that they were more dead than alive. It is hard to describe the condition of these people after the long journey in the indescribably overcrowded freight cars. I looked upon killing these people in that manner as a kindness and a release.

The first large Jewish community taken to Belzec for extermination came from Lublin. Within four weeks, from March 17 to April 14, close to 30,000 of the 37,000 inhabitants of the ghetto were deported to Belzec. Within the same period of time an additional 18,000–20,000 Jews from the Lublin Bezirk were sent to Belzec.

Polish women are led to their execution. Operation Reinhard, the plan to exterminate Jews in Nazi-occupied Poland, began in 1942.

The first Jewish transport from the Lvov Bezirk came from Zolkiew, a town 50 km. southwest of Belzec. This transport consisted of approximately 700 Jews and reached Belzec on March 25 or 26, 1942. Subsequently, within the two weeks up to April 6, 1942, some 30,000 other Jews from the Lvov Bezirk arrived in Belzec.

After 80,000 Jews had been murdered in a major operation, which lasted about four weeks, the transports were discontinued. . . .

Sobibor Adopts Belzec's Lessons

The extermination installations in Sobibor had been tested in April 1942, and mass exterminations began during the first days of May. [Sorbibor's] Commandant Stangl introduced into his camp the extermination techniques employed in Belzec. . . .

Ada Lichtmann, a survivor from Sobibor, reported how the arrivals were "greeted":

We heard word for word how SS-Oberscharführer Michel, standing on a small table, convincingly calmed the people; he promised them that after the bath they would get back all their possessions, and said that the time had come for Jews to become productive members of society. They would presently all be sent to the Ukraine where they would be able to live and work. The speech inspired confidence and enthusiasm among the people. They applauded spontaneously and occasionally they even danced and sang.

Older people, the sick and invalids, and those unable to walk were told that they would enter an infirmary for medical treatment. In reality, they were taken on carts, pulled by men or horses, into Camp II, straight to the open ditches where they were shot.

During the first weeks the arrivals had to undress in the open square in Camp II. Later, a hut was erected for this purpose. . . . There were signs pointing toward the "Cash Office" and the "Baths." At the "Cash Office" the Jews had to deposit their money and valuables. . . . The victims handed over their money and valuables through the window of this room. They had been warned that those trying to hide something would be shot. When time permitted, the Jews were given numbers as receipts for the items handed over, so as to lull them into a sense of security that afterwards everything would be returned to them. . . .

Frequently, the entire procedure, from the unloading to entry into the gas chambers, was accompanied by beatings and other acts of cruelty on the part of the Germans and the Ukrainians. There was a dog called Barry whom the SS-men had trained to bite Jews upon being called to do so, especially when they were naked. The beatings, Barry's bites, and the shouting and screaming by the guards made the Jews run through the "tube" and of their own accord push on into the "baths"—in the hope of escaping from the hell around them. . . .

Altogether, 61,330 Jews from Lublin Bezirk were taken to Sobibor. Simultaneously, transports arrived with 10,000 Jews from Austria, 6,000 from the Protectorate of Bohemia and Moravia, and part of the 24,378 Slovak Jews who were murdered in this camp by the end of 1942. The first wave of extermination in Sobibor lasted three months, claiming at least 77,000 Jewish victims, excluding those deported from Slovakia. . . .

Treblinka Perfects Killing

The Pole Franciszek Zabecki described the arrival of the deportation train from the Warsaw ghetto:

A small locomotive stood ready in the railroad station to transport the first section of freight cars into the camp. Everything had been planned and prepared in advance. The train consisted of 60 closed freight cars fully loaded with people: young ones, old ones, men and women, children and babies. The car doors were locked from the outside and the air holes covered with barbed wire. On the running boards on both sides and on the roof about a dozen SS-soldiers stood or lay with machine guns at the ready. It was hot and most of the people in the freight cars were deadly exhausted. . . .

As the train approached the extermination camp, the engine blew a prolonged whistle which was the signal for the Ukrainians to man their position in the reception sector and on the roofs of the buildings. One group of SS-men and Ukrainians took up positions on the station platform. As soon as the train was moving along the tracks inside the camp, the gates behind it were closed. The deportees were taken out of the freight cars and conducted through a gate to a fenced-in square inside the camp. At the gate they were separated: men to the right, women and children to the left. A large placard announced in Polish and German:

> Attention Warsaw Jews! You are in a transit camp from which the transport will continue to labor camps. To prevent epidemics, clothing as well as pieces of baggage are to be handed over for disinfection. Gold, money, foreign currency, and jewellery are to be deposited at the "Cash Office" against a receipt. They will be returned later on presentation of the receipt. For physical cleanliness, all arrivals must have a bath before travelling on.

The undressing procedure and the manner in which the victims were led to the gas chambers were almost identical to those described for the Sobibor camp.

During this first phase, from the beginning to the middle of August, 5,000–7,000 Jews arrived every day in Treblinka. Then the pace of the transports increased; there were days on which 10,000–12,000 deportees reached the camp, together with thousands who were already dead and others who were utterly exhausted.

Abraham Goldfarb, who arrived there on August 25, described the scene:

> When we arrived in Treblinka and the Germans opened the freight cars we beheld a horrible sight. The car was full of corpses. The bodies were partly decomposed by chlorine. The stench in the cars made those still alive choke. The Germans ordered everyone to get out; those still able to do so were half dead. Waiting

SS and Ukrainians beat us and shot at us. . . .

> On the way to the gas chambers Germans with dogs stood along the fence on both sides. The dogs had been trained to attack people; they bit the men's genitals and the women's breasts, ripping off pieces of flesh. The Germans hit the people with whips and iron bars to spur them on so that they pressed forward into the "showers" as quickly as possible. The screams of the women could be heard far away, even in the other parts of the camp. The Germans drove the running victims on with shouts of: "Faster, faster, the water will get cold, others still have to go under the showers!" To escape from the blows, the victims ran to the gas chambers as quickly as they could, the stronger ones pushing the weaker aside. At the entrance to the gas chambers stood the two Ukrainians, Ivan Demaniuk and Nikolai, one of them armed with an iron bar, the other with a sword. They drove the people inside with blows. . . . As soon as the gas chambers were full, the Ukrainians closed the doors and started the engine. Some 20-25 minutes later an SS-man or a Ukrainian looked through a window in the door. When they had ascertained that everyone had been asphyxiated, the Jewish prisoners had to open the doors and remove the corpses. Since the chambers were overcrowded and the victims held on to one another, they all stood upright and were like one single block of flesh.

. . . Some 268,000 Jews met their deaths in the first extermination wave in Treblinka, which lasted five weeks—from July 23 to August 28. . . .

The first period of operation in Belzec and Sobibor lasted about three months, in Treblinka five weeks. After this initial phase, those holding key positions in Operation Reinhard decided to introduce "improvements" into the camps so as to increase their extermination capacity. This decision was brought on by [SS leader Heinrich] Himmler's order of July 19, 1942 that all the Jews in the General Government, with a few exceptions, were to be eradicated by the end of that year.

The main problem was finding a way to speed up the extermination procedure, i.e., increasing the absorption capacity of the gas chambers.

Belzec was the first camp in which large gas chambers were built. . . .

These new gas chambers were able to take in 1,500 persons at one and the same time, i.e., a transport of about 15 freight cars. . . .

The most urgent need for an increase in the absorption capacity was felt in Treblinka already in the first months of operation, because the small gas chambers there constantly led to chaos in the extermination process. . . .

The new building comprised 10 gas chambers. . . .

In order to speed up the construction, a group of Jewish masons was brought from Warsaw. . . . A total of 40 Jewish prisoners worked on the gas chambers. Jankiel Wiernik described their feelings:

> The construction of the new building took five weeks. To us it seemed like eternity. The work continued from sunrise to sunset, accompanied by lashes from whips and blows from rifle butts. Woronikow, one of the guards, beat and ill-treated us mercilessly. Every day several workers were murdered. The extent of our physical fatigue was beyond human imagination, but our mental agony was still greater. New transports arrived daily; the deportees were ordered to undress, then they were taken to the three old gas chambers. They were led past the building site. Several of us recognized our children, wives or relatives among the victims. If, in his agony, someone ran to his family, he was shot on the spot. Thus we built the death chambers for ourselves and for our brothers!

Selection 7

Life Changes in One Day

Elie Wiesel

When most Jews arrived at a concentration camp, they had no idea where they were, what was in store for them or what they were supposed to do. When they got off the trains, it was like being awakened from a deep sleep in the middle of the night. Suddenly, they were confronted by soldiers and guns and dogs. They were usually told to leave the meager belongings they had brought from home in the train. Men and women would be separated, tearing apart families. Before they knew what was happening, they'd be marched off, stripped, deloused, heads shaved, and assigned a number that would replace their names as their identity. And these were the lucky ones. The rest were marched from the trains to the gas chambers. All this would happen within minutes or hours. Elie Wiesel was a teenager when he was sent to Auschwitz and later to Buchenwald. He has written perhaps the most powerful works of fiction and nonfiction relating the experience of the Holocaust. One of the world's leading human rights advocates, Wiesel was a founding chairman of the U.S. Holocaust Memorial Council and is a professor at Boston University. In 1986 Wiesel won the Nobel Peace Prize.

*T*he cherished objects we had brought with us thus far were left behind in the train, and with them, at last, our illusions.

Every two yards or so an SS man held his tommy gun trained on us. Hand in hand we followed the crowd.

An SS noncommissioned officer came to meet us, a truncheon in his hand. He gave the order:

"Men to the left! Women to the right!"

Eight words spoken quietly, indifferently, without emotion. Eight short, simple words. Yet that was the moment when I parted from my mother. I had not had time to think, but already I felt the pressure of my father's hand: we were alone. For a part of a second I glimpsed my mother and my sisters moving away to the right. Tzipora held Mother's hand. I saw them disappear into the distance; my mother was stroking my sister's fair hair, as though to protect her, while I walked on with my father and the other men. And I did not know that in that place, at that moment, I was parting from my mother and Tzipora forever. . . .

"Here, kid, how old are you?"

It was one of the prisoners who asked me this. I could not see his face, but his voice was tense and weary.

"I'm not quite fifteen yet."

"No. Eighteen."

"But I'm not," I said. "Fifteen."

"Fool. Listen to what *I* say."

Then he questioned my father, who replied: "Fifty."

The other grew more furious than ever.

"No, not fifty. Forty. Do you understand? Eighteen and forty."

He disappeared into the night shadows. A second man came up, spitting oaths at us.

"What have you come here for, you sons of bitches? What are you doing here, eh?"

Someone dared to answer him.

"What do you think? Do you suppose we've come here on our own pleasure? Do you think we asked to come?"

A little more, and the man would have killed him.

"You shut your trap, you filthy swine, or I'll squash you right now! You'd have done better to have hanged yourselves where you were than come here. Didn't you know what was in store for you at Auschwitz? Haven't you heard about it? In 1944?"

No, we had not heard. No one had told us. He could not believe his ears. His tone of voice became increasingly brutal.

"Do you see that chimney over there? See it? Do you see those flames? (Yes, we did see the flames.) Over there—that's where you're going to be taken. That's your grave over there. Haven't you realized it yet? You dumb bastards, don't you understand anything? You're going to be burned. Frizzled away. Turned into ashes.". . .

I heard murmurs around me.

"We've got to do something. We can't let ourselves be killed. We can't go like beasts to the slaughter. We've got to revolt."

There were a few sturdy young fellows among us. They had knives on them, and they tried to incite the others to throw themselves on the armed guards.

One of the young men cried:

"Let the world learn of the existence of Auschwitz. Let everybody hear about it, while they can still escape. . . ."

But the older ones begged their children not to do anything foolish:

"You must never lose faith, even when the sword hangs over your head. That's the teaching of our sages. . . ."

Selection

The wind of revolt died down. We continued our march toward the square. In the middle stood the notorious Dr. [Josef] Mengele (a typical SS officer: a cruel face, but not devoid of intelligence, and wearing a monocle); a conductor's baton in his hand, he was standing among the other officers. The baton moved unremittingly, sometimes to the right, sometimes to the left.

I was already in front of him:

"How old are you?" he asked, in an attempt at a paternal tone of voice.

"Eighteen." My voice was shaking.

"Are you in good health?"

"Yes."

"What's your occupation?"

Should I say that I was a student?

"Farmer," I heard myself say.

This conversation cannot have lasted more than a few seconds. It had seemed like an eternity to me.

The baton moved to the left. I took half a step forward. I wanted to see first where they were sending my father. If he went to the right, I would go after him.

The baton once again pointed to the left for him too. A weight was lifted from my heart.

Not far from us, flames were leaping up from a ditch, gigantic flames. They were burning something. A lorry drew up at the pit and delivered its load—little children. Babies! Yes, I saw it—saw it with my own eyes . . . those children in the flames. (Is it surprising that I could not sleep after that? Sleep had fled from my eyes.)

So this was where we were going. A little farther on was another and larger ditch for adults.

I pinched my face. Was I still alive? Was I awake? I could not believe it. How could it be possible for them to burn people, children, and for the world to keep silent? No, none of this could be true. It was a nightmare. . . . Soon I should wake with a start, my heart pounding, and find myself back in the bedroom of my childhood, among my books. . . .

My father's voice drew me from my thoughts:

"It's a shame . . . a shame that you couldn't have gone with your mother. . . . I saw several boys of your age going with their mothers. . . ."

His voice was terribly sad. I realized that he did not want to see what they were going to do to me. He did not want to see the burning of his only son.

My forehead was bathed in cold sweat. But I told him that I did not believe that they could burn people in our age, that humanity would never tolerate it. . . .

"Humanity? Humanity is not concerned with us. Today anything is allowed. Anything is possible, even these crematories. . . .

His voice was choking.

"Father," I said, "if that is so, I don't want to wait here. I'm going to run to the electric wire. That would be better than slow agony in the flames."

He did not answer. He was weeping. His body was shaken convulsively. Around us, everyone was weeping. Someone began to recite the Kaddish, the prayer for the dead. I do not know if it has ever happened before, in the long history of the Jews, that people have ever recited the prayer for the dead for themselves. . . .

We continued our march. We were gradually drawing closer to the ditch, from which an infernal heat was rising. Still twenty steps to go. If I wanted to bring about my own death, this was the moment. Our line had now only fifteen paces to cover. I bit my lips so that my father would not hear my teeth chattering. Ten steps still. Eight. Seven. We marched slowly on, as though following a hearse at our own funeral. Four steps more. Three steps. There it was now, right in front of us, the pit and its flames. I gathered all that was left of my strength, so that I could break from the ranks and throw myself upon the barbed wire. In the depths of my heart, I bade farewell to my father, to the whole universe. . . . The moment had come. I was face to face with the Angel of Death. . . .

No. Two steps from the pit we were ordered to turn to the left and made to go into a barracks. . . .

Never shall I forget that night, the first night in camp, which has turned my life into one long night, seven times cursed and seven times sealed. Never shall I forget that smoke. Never shall I forget the little faces of the children, whose bodies I saw turned into wreaths of smoke beneath a silent blue sky.

Never shall I forget those flames which consumed my faith forever.

Never shall I forget that nocturnal silence

which deprived me. for all eternity, of the desire to live. Never shall I forget those moments which murdered my God and my soul and turned my dreams to dust. Never shall I forget these things, even if I am condemned to live as long as God Himself. Never.

Selection 8

Auschwitz: The Death Factory

Ota Kraus and Erich Kulka

It is difficult to believe, looking back with the benefit of hindsight and after having read books and seen movies about the Holocaust, that the Jews did not know what was going to happen when they entered the concentration camps. Some people may have heard rumors, but they would not have believed them. The Nazis took elaborate pains to disguise their intentions—from putting signs over the entrance to camps reading "Arbeit Macht Frei" ("Work Makes One Free") to putting signs on the gas chambers reading "Delousing" and asking the victims to remember the number of the hook on which they place their clothes so they could collect them when they come out of the "shower." You may recall the powerful scene in Schindler's List *when a little girl makes a gesture of slashing her throat as a trainload of prisoners goes by. Victims did not get these hints; in fact, the prisoners in the camps were strictly forbidden from saying so much as a word to new arrivals to ensure that there would be no resistance. This excerpt was written by two political prisoners, Ota Kraus and Erich Kulka, each of whom spent virtually the entire war in concentration camps. Both survived Auschwitz.*

*T*he first mass destruction by gas in Auschwitz [I] took place in the spring of 1942, at the only crematorium then in existence—in Auschwitz I. Before this, gassing had been carried out on some small group of emaciated prisoners, notably Russian prisoners of war.

The Auschwitz crematorium was small. It had one gas chamber for 600-800 people, and six furnaces.

One of the first experiments in mass execution by gas took place when 700 Slovak Jews arrived from Žilina in May, 1942. . . .

In the "confession" which he wrote in Cracow prison in 1947, Rudolf Hoess, former Commandant of Auschwitz, described the first experiments at Auschwitz as follows:

"One day in 1941, when I was on duty, my deputy, Fritsch, carried out a test execution by gas on some prisoners. For this he used hydrocyanic cyclon B which up to then had been used for de-

Excerpted from Ota Kraus and Erich Kulka, *The Death Factory* (London: Pergamon Press, 1966).

stroying insects in the camp. The gassing took place in the cells of Block II. I subsequently went to inspect the results wearing a gas mask. The prisoners, packed tight in the cells, had died immediately when the crystals of cyclon gas were thrown in. A few stifled cries—and all was over.

"This first attempt at exterminating people with gas did not weigh at all heavily on my conscience—perhaps because I was considerably excited by the efficiency of the experiment. I have a more vivid memory of the gassing of 900 Soviet prisoners of war. This took place shortly afterwards in the old crematorium, since the use of Block II would have caused considerable inconvenience and made it necessary to take elaborate security measures.

"As the Russians were getting out of the train, several holes were drilled in the roof of the mortuary at the crematorium. The Russians undressed in the entrance hall and then filed quietly into the mortuary, having been told that they were to be deloused. Once they were inside the room which they filled completely, the doors were bolted behind them and the gas was turned on through the holes in the roof. I do not know how long they took dying but they made quite a din for some time. As the gas was fed in, some of the prisoners shouted 'gas,' which was followed by prolonged shouting and a furious battering on the door. But the door held. After some hours the mortuary was opened up and aired.

"This was the first time I had seen so large a pile of gassed bodies. I had expected death by gas to be bad enough, but this made me feel ill. I was overcome by a feeling of horror. . . . All the same I have to state quite frankly that I was quite satisfied with the gassing of this convoy because we had soon to begin with the mass extermination of the Jews, and up to that day neither [Final Solution architect Adolf] Eichmann nor I had had any clear idea how to set about the task of mass executions. We knew that some kind of gas had to be used, but we were not sure which gas or how to use it. Thanks to this experiment we had found both the gas and the method of use.". . .

People were brought in lorries [to Birkenau].

As they were unloaded they found themselves surrounded by a close cordon of SS guards, armed with automatic rifles, hand grenades and machine guns. The guards also had trained dogs.

The victims were ordered to enter the undressing-rooms in groups, women and children in one, men in the other. They were told that they were in a work camp and must have a bath and be disinfected as a precaution against infection.

Next they were ordered to undress to the skin and to arrange their clothes and other belongings tidily. They had to hand in their valuables but were promised that they would get them back. After this the SS drove them into the gas chambers. If any of them saw through the trick and offered resistance, the SS beat them with sticks, whips and rifle-butts.

As soon as a gas chamber was full—up to 150 people were crammed into a space of 21 square yards—the SS banged the doors, screwed up the bars, and fed in the poison through the window in the wall. The window was then hermetically sealed, and for some minutes shouting and groaning could be heard.

After about half an hour the SS opened the rear doors. It was a ghastly sight. Naked women and children were convulsed into the most horrible attitudes, their skin lacerated, their fists clenched and their limbs bleeding from biting each other in their pain. The victims died standing up, for they were so wedged together that they could not fall.

The *Sonderkommando* (special work squad) then set to work throwing the corpses into deep pits prepared in the vicinity. The rooms were quickly cleaned out, whitewashed and sprayed with eau de Cologne (brought in ample quantities by the victims themselves, especially the women). The next convoy must know nothing of the terrible tragedy which had been enacted there but a moment before and now awaited them.

The process of gassing, clearing away the corpses and cleaning the rooms lasted about an hour; a convoy of from two to three thousand people was thus destroyed and cleared away within a few hours.

After a few months, although the corpses

*Human remains are visible inside these furnaces, where
the bodies of gassed Holocaust victims were burned.*

were covered with chlorine, lime and earth, an intolerable stench began to hang around the entire neighbourhood. Deadly bacteria were found in springs and wells, and there was a severe danger of epidemics.

To meet this problem, the *Sonderkommando* was increased in size. Day and night, working in two shifts, the prisoners in the squad dug up decaying corpses, took them away on narrow-gauge trucks and burnt them in heaps in the immediate vicinity. The work of exhuming and burning 50,000 corpses lasted almost till December, 1942. After this experience the Nazis stopped burying their victims and cremated them instead.

Such were the emergency methods used for destroying people at Birkenau in the early days.

They continued in use until February, 1943, when the crematoria were completed and brought into use—first Crematorium I, and then the others. . . .

The four cremations together had eight gas chambers with a capacity of 8000 people; there were forty-six furnaces all told, each capable of burning at least three bodies in 20 minutes. . . .

When the furnaces were unable to cope with the number of bodies—a frequent occurrence—the corpses were burnt by the thousand on great heaps. . . .

Direct from Train to Gas Chamber

Until June, 1944, trains to Auschwitz stopped for "classification" at a special ramp, invisible both from the camp itself and the immediate vicinity. A train would consist of from fifty to eighty cattle trucks. As soon as it arrived at the ramp, it was surrounded by a close cordon of SS guards with their dogs. Personnel from the "Canada" Disposal Squad opened up the trucks, and with much yelling and shouting the people were driven out of them in a state of utter confusion.

The first duty of the "Canada" Squad at the station was to unload the newcomers' luggage as quickly as possible and take everything away from them except their handbags. The people were told that their baggage would be returned to them in the camp. If any person tried to object, his luggage was taken off him by force.

The "Canada" Squad were forbidden, under pain of death by shooting, to speak to the new arrivals, and the SS guards watched to see that this order was obeyed.

As the men got out of the trucks, they were separated from the women and children. Then an SS doctor and SS officer, after a superficial examination of each man, would show by a jerk of the thumb whether they were to go to the right or left—life or death.

Children were assigned to death, and women who did not want to be separated from their children went with them. Of the remaining women only those from sixteen to thirty who were young and healthy were selected for the camp; the rest were sent to the gas chambers. Of the men some 15 to 20% were classified as fit for work.

People destined for the gas chambers were loaded on to waiting lorries. Those classified as fit for work had to walk to the camps on foot, but before they left they were given the option of going on the lorries, if they thought they could not walk—which meant death in the gas chambers. . . .

The "Canada" Disposal Squad

The "Canada" Disposal Squad consisted exclusively of Jews, both; men and women, though its leaders, also prisoners, were German men and women from the Reich. . . .

Members of the "Canada" squad . . . sabotaged their work wherever possible. The parcels and suitcases brought by the new arrivals were thrown into their blocks in fantastic disarray, and once the blocks were full up the goods were deposited outside. Often the various classified items, such as blankets, underwear, feather-beds, footwear, medicines and other goods, lay about in the rain for weeks on end until they were soaked through and utterly useless. The place was like a huge open-air jumble sale with silk underwear, eau de Cologne, expensive soap, furs, shoes, cigarette lighters, knives, ladies' handbags.

A special detachment from the squad ripped up clothes, tore shoes apart, and searched the various ointments, toothpastes and face-creams for any precious items that might be hidden there, such as gold, diamonds or foreign currency. Some members of the squad deliberately destroyed everything they could lay their hands on, tearing up dollar bills and other bank-notes, breaking watches, and so on. . . .

When they finished work, the "Canadians" were closely searched and often had to strip naked. They were again checked at the entrance to the camp. Nevertheless they still found ways and means of smuggling things into the camp.

"Canada" played an extremely important role in the camp. It was the source from which the prisoners obtained the wherewithal to make their life to some degree bearable. When an escape was being planned, "Canada" supplied money, clothing, compasses, field-glasses, wigs and identity cards. Cameras were also obtained in this way, and some members of a secret organization actually succeeded in taking photos of people being "selected" for the gas chamber. These photos were among the documentary material which we subsequently sent out from the camp through the partisans in the neighbourhood.

On the other hand, many prisoners met their death as a result of their contact with "Canada," for all persons caught carrying forbidden goods, especially valuables, were viciously punished.

Selection 9

Treblinka

Jean-François Steiner

One characteristic of the Holocaust that distinguishes it from other instances of genocide is the scientific, technological approach the Nazis applied to murder. They killed many of their victims in old-fashioned ways like shooting, stabbing, and hanging, but they also devoted a great deal of time and energy to devising new methods of killing that would be more efficient. And they were never satisfied with their efforts; they always sought to find a better way. This excerpt taken from the book Treblinka, *written by Jean-François Steiner, is not an easy one to read, but it is included to illustrate German determination and ingenuity when it came to extermination. The scene is Treblinka, a death camp in Poland.*

The sky darkened as [concentration camp inmates] Djielo and Adolf got closer to Camp Number Two. The smell, which from Camp Number One was only a vague scent, bitter and slightly sickening, became stifling. Unconsciously they breathed less and less deeply. Slowly they began to hear the sound of a motor in two alternating tones: a slow regular hum which periodically became a more violent sound, gasping and deafening. As they came still nearer they discovered behind these mechanical noises a loud roar like the sound of a forest fire. The heavy door of solid wood opened as in a dream. They took one step, then another, and stopped suddenly, ready to faint.

Nothing that they had seen up to then could be compared with the hell which they suddenly discovered before their eyes. To the left yawned an immense ditch and moving around it were three excavators, mechanical giants which jerkily plunged their long jointed arms to the bottom of the pestilential pit and lifted them more slowly, loaded with dismembered bodies. The bodies seemed to lean forward as if to escape or to dangle their heads like drowned men. Each long steel arm ended in a monstrous set of jaws which closed gradually as they rose, inexorably eliminating anything that was too long, severing heads, torsos, and limbs, which fell heavily into the ditch. After that the mechanical arm would describe a wide circle, pause, shudder, and brutally open its jaws, hurling to the ground its cargo of damned.

A few dozen yards away, immense bonfires roared. As the flames reached them, the faces of the dead suddenly came back to life. They twisted and grimaced as if contorted by unbearable pain. The liquid fat and lymph that suddenly exuded covered their faces with a kind of sweat that further reinforced the impression of life and intense suffering. Under the effect of the heat the belly of a pregnant woman burst like an overripe fruit, expelling the fetus, which went up in flames.

THE GHETTOS AND THE CONCENTRATION CAMPS 157

Between the ditches and the fire a race of slaves scurried.

Djielo and Adolf let themselves be led wordlessly to the barracks, which rose at the other end of the big yard. The head *kapo* [prisoner in charge of other prisoners], Singer, greeted them with these words:

"Welcome to hell. Here the work is hard, but the food is adequate. You will receive new clothing every two weeks and your linen will be washed every week."...

What the early days of Camp Number Two were like, no one remembers. The prisoners had become animals, wild animals. All day, while they were busy carrying the bodies, they were beaten; not just occasionally, but without interruption. In the evening they fought among themselves for food, and at night for a place to sleep. The slightest word was a pretext for bloody brawls, which always resulted in several deaths. You had to choose between food and sleep. Anyone who took time to eat had to give up the idea of sleeping for lack of room, and anyone who wanted to sleep had to run to the barracks as soon as work was done. When there was enough room for everyone in the barracks, the fight for survival limited itself to food.

Beacons of Faith

Two [Treblinka inmates] played a leading role in the moral rehabilitation of the prisoners. First, Pinhas Alter, the fanatical Hasid and friend of Berliner, and later Dr. Zimmermann, *kapo* of the "dentists." Pinhas Alter, whose physical stamina matched his moral strength, spent his nights taking down the bodies of hanged men and separating brawlers. Alone, inspired by an extraordinary faith and a fierce love for God and for life, he slept only a few hours in the morning when the prisoners, prostrate with fatigue, had fallen every which way on the floor. Before falling asleep too, he would pray at length, praising the Lord for the interest He showed in His people, thanking Him for the ordeals with which He tormented them, assuring Him that His wrath was even dearer to him than His kindness. Pinhas Alter died of exhaus-

tion at the beginning of the typhus epidemic.

Dr. Zimmerman, who carried on his work, resembled him in nothing except determination. The son of a family of poor artisans, he had worked his way through medical school to become one of the most celebrated doctors in Warsaw. In the presence of doctors, even Jewish ones, the Technicians [Nazis] felt a kind of uneasy respect. Dr. Zimmerman took advantage of this respect to obtain more tolerable living conditions for the prisoners. Meanwhile, for long hours in the evening he urged them not to despair and to pull themselves together. He forced them to bathe when they had finished work and to clean their shoes, which were covered with shreds of skin, blood and rotted flesh, before re-entering the barracks. At his suggestion the Germans appointed a barracks guard whose job it was to see that these regulations were followed. . . .

In Camp Number Two, however, the living conditions and morale were such that a dream world was created among the prisoners. When they were not working, the prisoners met in groups in the barracks and talked about their former lives. All claimed that they had been millionaires and that they had lived in marvelous apartments. Every day they would add new details about a cure at Baden-Baden, their hunting preserves, or their property on the Baltic. It was an inexhaustible mirage. They loved other people's lies as much as their own, and by a kind of tacit agreement it was forbidden to question a single detail. One day Moshe, a former cab driver, almost got knocked down for shouting during one of these sessions, "All millionaires, but where the hell are the poor people of Warsaw?"

There was another evidence of this need for the dream, this need for hope in this apocalyptic world. Every time the prisoners gathered to drink contraband vodka, before bringing the mouth of the bottle to their lips they would each repeat the wish that all Jews have made at the end of the Passover ceremony since the destruction of the Temple: "Next year in Jerusalem." This wish, which is at the same time an oath of loyalty and an act of faith, was their way of affirming their absurd and desperate hope, their will to live, their denial of death. . . .

Treblinka Is Swallowed Up

Life was following its deadly course when [SS leader Heinrich] Himmler arrived. He came to sign Treblinka's death sentence. The Germans wanted to wipe away all traces before closing shop. A few days later the earth opened.

But it is one thing to kill and another to burn, as [Nazi overseer] Lalka would learn from humiliating experience. The soil of Treblinka contained seven hundred thousand bodies, or an approximate weight of thirty-five thousand tons and a volume of ninety thousand cubic yards. Thirty-five thousand tons is the weight of a battleship. Ninety thousand cubic yards represents a square tower nearly three thousand feet high and ten yards across. The task was gigantic, superhuman; the problem apparently insoluble. With an output of one thousand bodies per day, which seems at first glance a good rate, you would have to allow seven hundred days, or almost two years, without stopping a single day; provided, moreover, there was not a single convoy more to process. The future was dim, not to say hopeless, and anyone but a Technician would have given up from the start. Lalka, however, set courageously to work. The orders of the supreme leader of the Technicians were not questioned, even if they seemed impossible to execute.

He began by having one ditch opened. The bodies appeared, arranged in an orderly fashion, head to foot, and emitting a pestilential odor on which [Nazi overseer] Kiwe, stopping his nose, commented, unconsciously parodying a remark made by a king of France: "They smell even worse dead than alive." It was not in the best taste, but it relaxed the atmosphere.

Lalka then had several dozen quarts of gasoline poured on the bodies and gave the order to light the fire. A huge flame burst forth with a roar and a thick curl of black smoke began to rise. Rolling back on itself it fell, engulfing the spectators. The fire rumbled for a long time in the artificial haze of its smoke, then began to die down more and more rapidly. The smoke whitened and thinned, revealing the frozen forms of the spectators. Suddenly the fire went out, releasing a last sluggish curl of smoke. The S.S. approached anxiously. The bodies were still there, barely singed by the blaze. One, two, three more experiments were made, with just as poor results. . . .

Lalka's fertile brain had conceived another method. Arriving at the yard at dawn, he had the excavators dig a very wide and shallow ditch to the middle of which the prisoners carried one hundred bodies, forming a pile as tall as it was wide. After the gasoline was poured and the prayer said, the pile was ignited in its turn. Flames, smoke, haze, anticipation, hope: the fire subsided, the smoke lifted, the bodies were still there. They were a little more burnt than they had been the day before, but the failure was apparent, as Lalka admitted to himself.

In the days that followed the experiment was repeated by varying the shape of the piles, the quantity of gasoline, and the position of the fire, but the results were just as disappointing. At the end of a week some hundred bodies could be regarded as completely burned and even then it had taken several hundred quarts of gasoline to arrive at this result. By rapid calculation Lalka estimated the number of years necessary to finish the job at one hundred and forty. Even for the Thousand Year Reich, it was a long time. . . .

The Specialist

Blond and slight, with a gentle face and a retiring manner, he arrived one fine morning with his little suitcase at the gates of the kingdom of death. His name was Herbert Floss, and he was a specialist in the cremation of bodies. Self-educated, he had perfected his art in the little local camps to which the vagaries of fortune had brought him one after the other. . . .

According to his investigations—and judging from the results, they were very thorough—the old bodies burned better than the new ones, the fat ones better than the thin ones, the women better than the men, and the children not as well as the women but better than the men. It was evident that the ideal body was the old body of a fat woman. Floss had these put aside. Then he had the men and children sorted too. When a thousand bodies had been dug up and sorted in this way, he proceeded to the loading, with the good fuel underneath and the bad above. He refused gasoline and sent for wood. His demonstration was going to be perfect. The wood was arranged under the grill of the pyre in little piles which resembled camp fires. The moment of truth had come. He was solemnly handed a box of matches. He bent down, lit the first fire, then the others, and as the wood began to catch fire he walked back with his odd gait to the group of officials who were waiting a little way away.

The mounting flames began to lick at the bodies, gently at first, then with a steady force like the flame of a blow torch. Everyone held his breath, the Germans anxious and impatient, the prisoners dismayed and terrified. Only Floss seemed relaxed; very sure of himself, he was muttering abstractedly, "*Tadellos, tadellos. . . .*" The bodies burst into flames. Suddenly the flames shot up, releasing a cloud of smoke, a deep roar arose, the faces of the dead twisted with pain and the flesh crackled. The spectacle had an infernal quality and even the S.S. men remained petrified for a few moments, contemplating the marvel. Floss beamed. This fire was the finest day of his life. . . .

The experiment had been conclusive. Now they had to translate it from the experimental to the industrial realm. Herbert Floss attacked the problem. . . .

As a first innovation, the excavators would extract the bodies and set them in a pile outside the ditch, where the prisoners would find and transport them to the fires at a ratio of two prisoners per body. This was the first stage. Then Floss noticed that it was difficult for the three excavators to put their loads in the same place and that the prisoners were crowded for room. He divided the prisoners into three teams, each of which served one machine: progress. But a bottleneck occurred at the fire. The number of fires was increased to three: progress. New problem: below a certain level the bodies extracted were dismembered and the prisoners transported them in pieces, a leg under one arm

and a torso under the other. As a result they transported many less. Herbert re-enlisted the litters that had been used to carry the bodies from the gas chambers to the ditches: progress. But it happened that limbs fell off along the way during the transfer, which was done at a run. The litters were modified, the canvas was replaced by crates: progress. Then it was remarked that the rails were sagging under the effect of the heat. New supporting pillars were constructed within the enclosure: progress.

The output was now two thousand bodies per day. One evening at roll call Floss made a speech.

"Today we burned two thousand bodies. This is good, but we must not stop here. We will set ourselves an objective and devote all our efforts to reaching it. Tomorrow we will do three thousand, the day after tomorrow four thousand, then five thousand, then six thousand, and so on until ten thousand. Every day we will force ourselves to increase the output by one thousand units. I count on you to help me."

A good-natured little man incapable of hurting a flea, sounding like the head of a factory to his workers, Herbert Floss then had each prisoner given an extra ration of bread.

The improvements continued. . . . Since the prisoners were losing time loading and unloading their litters, the crews were again divided into three: a crew of loaders, another of carriers, and a third of burners, which acquired the name of fire commando: progress. But the ten-thousand figure had still not been reached. The pyres were loaded during the day and lit in the evening. They now covered a distance of over fifty yards. It was possible to extend them even further, but the fueling had reached a plateau. It was at this level that the bottleneck was occurring. Floss discovered a further improvement. When the carriers reached the piles of bodies they stopped and rested while their litters were being loaded. This represented an enormous loss of time. To offset this disadvantage the excavators were ordered to lay their bodies not in a compact pile but in the form of an arc. The loaders were arranged along this arc and the carriers were instructed to walk along the line of the loaders. Herbert Floss had rediscovered the principle of the assembly line. The loaders were no longer responsible for one crate, but instead they threw a piece of a body into each crate that filed by.

It was at this point that the prisoners reacted. Three prisoners were responsible for counting the bodies. Their comrades, feeling that they were about to die of exhaustion, asked them to make The Artist happy and give him his ten thousand bodies. The next day Floss was informed that the goal of ten thousand bodies had been reached. He insisted on thanking the prisoners for their zeal in the work.

One day an excavator ran out of gasoline. The driver rushed out to get a can and the prisoners seized the opportunity to catch their breath. Just then Floss arrived. The prisoners, knowing that he did not hit them, were not too afraid of him, and explained that the excavator had broken down and that they were waiting for it to be fixed.

"How long will it take?" asked Floss.

"Three or four minutes," they answered at random.

"Four minutes? You have just enough time to make one haul with the next excavator."

"For one haul," they replied, "we will lose more time going back and forth than we will waiting."

To which Floss replied, "One haul for the principle, to prove to yourselves that you aren't good for nothing. We'll call it the Haul of Honor."

Herbert Floss was mad.

Selection 10

Jews as Slaves

Benjamin Ferencz

Though Hitler was determined to exterminate every last Jew, some of his minions believed this goal could be temporarily delayed in the case of those Jews healthy enough to work. Because most German workers were in the military fighting, the country's industry was desperately short of employees and concentration camps offered a large, readily available supply. Of course, these Jewish workers were not paid or given any rights associated with employment. On the contrary, *many of the jobs, such as carrying heavy bags of cement, were meant to kill them. Many Jews do owe their lives to the fact that working allowed them to "escape" concentration camp life. Still, thousands died, and German industrialists from such well-known companies as BMW and Mercedes-Benz were content to use whatever labor they could get. Throughout 1999, lawyers representing these slave laborers pursued claims against the German government and the companies that employed them. This selection offers an overview of the system of slave labor created by the Nazis. Benjamin Ferencz practices law in New York City.*

y 1942 the drain on German manpower became so acute and the need for armaments so great that second thoughts had to be given to the wholesale slaughter of the Jews which was taking place. In February [SS leader Heinrich] Himmler presented to Hitler and to the newly appointed minister for armaments and munitions, Albert Speer, a proposal which would enable him to build armaments plants inside the concentration camps and put able-bodied inmates to work on armaments production. Propaganda Minister [Joseph] Goebbels recorded in his diary for March 27, 1942: "The Jews in the General Government are now being evacuated eastward. The procedure is a pretty barbaric one . . . not much will remain of the Jews. On the whole it can be said that about 60% of them will have to be liquidated whereas only about 40% can be used for forced labor." Goebbels underestimated the number which would be murdered outright. At least two out of three went straight to the gas chambers. With the growing awareness that available manpower would have to be preserved came the need for a reorganization of the SS Main Office. A new department was created, the *Wirtschafts und Verwaltungshauptamt* (Economic and Administrative Main Office), WVHA, to deal with economic problems. Oswald Pohl, who had joined the party in 1926 and had risen to the rank of *Obergruppenführer*—a lieutenant general of the SS—was to be the man in charge of the new Main Office. . . . By the end of April Pohl was able to report to Himmler with pride that he had completely reorganized the existing concentration camps "for the mobilization of all prisoners who are fit for work." At the same time all the camp commanders were told that "this employment must be in the true meaning of the word, exhaustive, in order to obtain the greatest measure of performance."

Thus a compromise was reached between the ideological demands that the inferior race of Jews be eliminated and the economic demands for productive labor. The solution was to spare those who could work, as long as they could work, and kill all the others. . . .

Forty thousand Jews from occupied France, forty thousand from Holland, and ten thousand from Belgium were scheduled to be shipped to Auschwitz in special trainloads of one thousand per day. Priority was to be given to those who were capable of work. . . .

Worked to Death

On September 14, 1942, the minister of justice, Dr. Georg Thierack, who had just taken office the preceding August and who had been specifically authorized by Hitler "to deviate from existing law," met with Propaganda Minister Goebbels to consider further action to eliminate so-called "antisocial" elements. Goebbels said that "Jews and gypsies should be exterminated unconditionally." As for Poles and Czechs, and even Germans who had been sentenced to long prison terms, "the idea of exterminating them by labor is the best." Four days later, at Himmler's invitation, Thierack met with him to discuss the same subject. It was agreed that the "asocial elements," which included Jews and gypsies, were to be delivered to Himmler for the purpose of *Vernichtung durch Arbeit*—to be worked to death (literally, "to be destroyed through work"). . . .

By the end of 1942 Himmler received a secret report that about four million Jews had been eliminated from greater Germany and other European countries. Close to 200,000 Jews were in forced labor. On November 26, 1942, Fritz Sauckel, Plenipotentiary for Labor Allocation, in agreement with Himmler and Göring, ordered that even those German Jews who were engaged in essential war production were to be deported and exchanged for Poles, who were to be shipped into the Reich without their families and trained to replace the Jews." "We will strive," said Himmler, "to substitute Poles for these Jewish workers. . . . Of course . . . the Jews shall some day disappear in accordance with the Führer's wishes."

There can be little doubt from the quoted official records of such Nazi leaders as Göring, Goebbels, Himmler, Sauckel, Thierack, Streckenbach, and countless others that the Jews were earmarked for outright extermination or for a slower death through exhausting labor for the

German war machine. The ultimate goal was racial purity for Germany. The SS sought complete control of Jewish labor as part of the process of eventual annihilation of Jewry in accordance with the Nazi ideology.

Armaments minister Speer's principal responsibility was to increase armaments production. He was skeptical about the effectiveness of Himmler's plan to manufacture munitions and arms inside the concentration camps. The Army High Command was also dubious about the advisability of Himmler's acquiring an independent capacity to produce arms. In discussing the problem with Hitler in September 1942, Speer argued that Himmler's plan was not feasible. The requisite new machinery could not be supplied and there would not be enough space available in the camps for mass production of the wide variety of war-related equipment and supplies. Speer noted that these obstacles did not exist if armaments production continued in the hands of private companies, which were already being scattered outside the cities to avoid the hazards of Allied air attacks. Speer proposed that production could be increased by putting double shifts to work and this would not require any new machines nor any new space. He felt that concentration camp (KZ) inmates could be used on both shifts. Since Speer anticipated that Himmler might take a dim view of allowing "his" prisoners to be used outside the concentration camps, Speer suggested that Hitler offer Himmler a "sweetener" in the form of three to five percent of all of the weapons or munitions which the inmates would produce. Hitler agreed. Under that agreement, 35,000 inmates were made available for use by the Armaments Ministry. Over 250,000 concentration camp inmates were requisitioned directly from the Main Office of the SS by private German firms which by-passed Speer's ministry.

From around the beginning of 1942 until the summer of 1944, when Allied bombing was effectively destroying German productive capacity, the demand for manpower from any source was overwhelming. No German company had to be coerced into taking labor. On the contrary, the firms had to use all their influence and persuasion to get all the help they felt they needed. The private companies were to pour millions of marks into the coffers of the SS for the privilege of using the camp inmates. An elaborate accounting system was set up to be sure that the companies paid the SS for every hour of skilled or unskilled labor and that deductions for the food provided by the companies did not exceed the maximum allowed. The inmates of course received nothing. They remained under the general control of the SS but under the immediate supervision of the companies that used them. The companies were required to see to it that adequate security arrangements, such as auxiliary guards and barbed wire enclosures, eliminated all possibility of escape.

The long and unproductive march of the inmates from the main camp at Auschwitz II soon inspired the Farben directors to have a camp annex built adjacent to the Buna construction site. By October 1942 inmates from the main camp were transported to the new barracks at Monowitz. Four hundred persons were crowded into a "block" intended for 162. Each wooden bunk, padded only with a thin layer of filthy straw, was shared by three inmates. Dysentery and diarrhea added to the misery. Farben also controlled the nearby coal mines known as Furstengrube and Janina, where Polish workers and later POWs, illegally employed in violation of the Hague Conventions, were replaced by concentration camp inmates in 1943.

The conditions of work for the foreign laborers, the POWs, and the concentration camp inmates were reported by reliable witnesses after the war. It was well-known to all that the inmates were literally being worked to death. They were forced to run while unloading heavy cement bags weighing one hundred pounds. "If a prisoner collapsed at work," reported a British POW to the court at Nuremberg, "he was kicked and beaten in order to determine if he was still alive." Another testified that the inmates "were all starving to death. . . . If the German civilians saw us giving the soup (an inedible watery brew) to the inmates, they would kick it over." Inmates were forced to trot like dogs behind the bicycles of their amused German masters. Drinking water was contaminated, clothing was sparse, and the food totally inadequate. Many died of freezing or starvation. The conditions for all the forced laborers were terrible, but by far the worst were the conditions of the Jews. Five times as many Jews were crowded into the barracks as the number of ethnic German workers. Said another British soldier. "Of all the persons working at IG Auschwitz, the Jewish inmates had the worst time of it." "The German civilians often threatened the inmates that they would be gassed and turned into soap." "They looked on killing Jews as killing vermin." The I.G. Farben directors who visited the camp regularly and received all the reports were later to testify in their defense at Nuremberg that they never noticed anything was wrong, and besides, they were only carrying out orders and doing what was "necessary."

In fact the death rate was too high even for Himmler. With more than half the prisoners dying, it was impossible to keep up the inmates' working capacity. Hundreds of new forced labor camps appeared throughout Germany and the occupied territories. Hundreds of thousands of Jews and prisoners of all nationalities were put to work at the mercy of their masters while awaiting deportation or death. As part of the incredible pattern of deception, the entrance gates of Auschwitz and other camps were spanned by the inscription in large metal letters: *Arbeit Macht Frei*—"Work Will Make You Free.". . .

The names of other prominent German firms appeared regularly to the SS records. Each company using labor from each camp was given a secret code number which the camp commanders were directed to use on all correspondence relating to that company. These included the aircraft companies like Messerschmidt, Junkers, and Heinkel, automobile companies like BMW (Bavarian Motor Works) and Daimler-Benz, munitions companies like Dynamit Nobel and Rheinmetall, and the electrical companies, Siemens, AEG (Allgemeine Elektricitats-Gesellschaft), and Telefunken.

Many construction companies turned to the nearby camps for labor, and names like Moll, Holzmann, and Hugo Schneider A.G. (HASAG) were frequent customers of the concentration camps. So too were the mining companies like BRABAG (Braunkohle-Benzin A.G.). The Organization Todt, the armed forces, and of course the WVHA itself created its own corporations to employ about 10 percent of the concentration camp inmates for work in the mines and quarries to produce the stone for the highways and edifices of the Reich as well as the equipment and clothing for the SS. In February 1944 Göring offered Himmler a squadron of planes if Himmler would provide the aircraft industry with the maximum possible number of concentration camp inmates. German aircraft production was beginning to have to move underground, and the prisoners were particularly well suited for the work, which was so arduous that even Speer later described it as "barbarous.". . .

In April 1944 Hitler ordered Himmler to deliver 100,000 Jews to help build the new underground aircraft factories. . . .

Despite the shortage of labor, most of those who came down the loading ramp at Auschwitz from the ghettos and cities of occupied Europe went straight to the gas chambers. In only forty-six days, 250,000 to 300,000 Hungarian Jews who were considered unfit for work were put to death in the five gas chambers of Auschwitz by the Zyklon B gas crystals, which could suffocate 60,000 men, women, or children in a twenty-four-hour period. Commander [Rudolf] Höss explained: "We execute about 400,000 Hungarian Jews alone at Auschwitz in the summer of 1944." The crematoria could not keep up with the flow of dead bodies. Those who were young and appeared to be healthy, including thousands of Hungarian girls, were spared to be used by German companies. The SS invited the armaments industry to come, look over the stock, and take them away. It was recommended that they be picked up "in batches of 500." Krupp lost no time in putting in a bid.

Auschwitz and its forty-two branch camps

held 144,000 slaves available for work. Although no more than 10,000 persons were ever employed at the Buna plant at any one time, it was reported that during the three years of its operations, over 30,000 people perished while working there for I.G. Farben.

Selection 11

From One Hell to Another

Ernest W. Michel

Many Jews were imprisoned in more than one concentration camp. They were lucky in the sense that this meant they had lived long enough to move to a new prison. Ernest W. Michel spent 674 days in Auschwitz and survived. That was the good news. The bad news was that when the camp was evacuated, he was sent to a subcamp of Buchenwald called Berga, where he was forced to do backbreaking work in underground tunnels to help the Nazis build an armament factory. There he encountered American prisoners of war who had been sent to work beside the political prisoners. As the Allies approached, the Nazis evacuated the camp and began to march their prisoners away from the advancing armies. Michel managed to escape along the way. His parents perished in the camps, and he has the lasting reminder of his time in Auschwitz tattooed on the inside of his arm. He devoted the remainder of his life to helping the Jewish people and raising money for Israel and the broader Jewish community as an official of the United Jewish Appeal. He also kept a promise he made to organize a worldwide reunion of Holocaust survivors.

"It can't last much longer. The Americans have penetrated the German border. From there to Cologne isn't very far. Once they cross the Rhine they'll break through. It's only a matter of time."

As 1944 came to a close, this was the main theme, the only theme, in Auschwitz. You could feel it. It wasn't going to last much longer. The important thing was to stay alive. If the rumors were true, Germany, sooner or later, would have to capitulate. It would be suicidal for the Germans to keep fighting. We had to hold out.

The news from the Eastern Front was that the Russians had reached Warsaw, then Tarnow. One rumor was that the Red army had captured Lublin and was moving West. How long would it be before they reached Krakow and then Oswiecim-Auschwitz? How long before they get here?

Here we were, the remnants of the millions who had come in on the trains to Birkenau. We were the survivors, 40,000–50,000 of us, in the three camps called Auschwitz.

What would the SS do with us? Would they let the Russians march in without a fight? What would happen? Would they let the Russians see the murder factory, the gas chambers, the crematoria, the emaciated corpses?

None of us, even the most optimistic, believed that the SS leadership would simply give up and turn us over to the Russians. So what would they do? Kill us all? forty to fifty thousand of us? Why not? They'd done it before.

Come on, you Russians. Come fast, while there is still some hope. Free us! Liberate us! Can't you hear our silent prayers? Come! Soon!

Those were our thoughts, hopes, and prayers during those cold, bitter winter days and nights. December turned to January. It was 1945. It was five years and four months since my arrest in Mannheim.

One of the men who frequently went to Birkenau said the gassing had stopped. We heard that the gas chambers and crematoria were dynamited by the Germans. That made sense. The selections, too, came to a halt. The flow of bodies stopped. The transports from the KB to Birkenau stopped. The trains also, finally stopped coming.

More new rumors.

"The SS plans to move us to Germany before the Russians get here!"

"Impossible!"

"How can they ship forty to fifty thousand prisoners on trains to the West? There aren't enough cattle cars. Even if they shove eighty of us into each car, they'd need over six hundred cars!"

That's how it went. The rumor mill was going full blast. Every day, every hour. We worked halfheartedly. Even the SS men became less vicious. There were fewer beatings, and the killings stopped. . . .

On January 15, a new rumor swept the camp. The Russians had broken through and were on their way to liberate Auschwitz. Later that night, the rumor was confirmed. . . .

At noon one day, all the barracks commanders were ordered to meet at the Appellplatz [place for roll call]. . . . "Something big is happening," Heinz Lipman, our Blockaelteste [barracks elder] told us. . . . He walked off.

In less than half an hour he was back. We met him in the hallway, desperate to hear what he had to say.

"We're all being evacuated. We leave tomorrow or the day after."

"How?"

"On foot."

"On foot?!" We looked at each other with disbelief.

"That's the order."

"Where to?"

"They won't say.". . .

At 1:00 p.m., the first of the inmates of Auschwitz-Buna shuffled through the gate. We each were given two pounds of bread. That was all. We were told it had to last for five days. No other food would be distributed. With the SS guards gone, chaos reigned. Anyone who could, stormed the kitchen to take whatever food was there. Others raced to the clothing storage to grab coats, caps, shoes—anything they could get their hands on. We needed to keep warm for the march. . . .

The departure took longer than the Nazis anticipated. All three camps were being evacuated at once. This meant 40,000 to 50,000 inmates began the march that day. Barracks group after barracks group, marched out the gate. We were among the last. . . .

We left the hospital compound for the last time. I remembered the first time I came through those gates and how lucky I was to survive for the last 22 months. . . .

How many bodies did I carry during those months? Thousands. . . . They came from all the corners of Europe and spoke different languages. They were individuals, each one once part of a family and having a future. Then they became numbers, tattoo marks on an arm. Who would remember their names? . . .

Late in the afternoon of Thursday, January 18, 1945, I marched through that gate for the last time.

I had lived through 674 days in a man-made hell.

Six hundred seventy-four endless days and nights.

Six hundred seventy-four nights in the abyss. And so the march began.

Marching to and from Hell

"Keep going! Pull yourself together!"

"It can't be much farther to the rest stop."

"If you give up now, you're dead!"

A column of prisoners marches from Dachau on April 29, 1945.

Tired and weak, we encouraged each other to keep going. Honzo, Felix and I stuck together. We were a team with one goal—survival.

We marched for 15 hours straight, without rest. Those who couldn't keep up littered the roadside—living corpses. Earlier, the Nazis shot stragglers. Now, even they were too weary to care. They simply left them to fall onto the ground where they would certainly freeze to death in the snow. Some prisoners feigned exhaustion and dropped. They probably hoped to meet up with Polish partisans in the area.

When the SS guards showed signs of fatigue, they climbed onto carts drawn by inmates. We dragged ourselves through villages and along main roads. We made a ghoulish panorama—tens of thousands of prisoners in striped prison suits, guarded by the SS, dragging themselves trailing through snow and ice. It took hours for our columns to pass. The Polish men and women along the way stared at the spectacle, but rarely said a word. They looked at us without pity and just shook their heads.

Prisoners began collapsing in droves. They lay helpless in the snow, unable to continue.

Thousands were dying from exposure. . . .

We spent the first night in a huge brick factory, crowding together to keep warm. The second night we were in Gleiwitz, where, rumors lead it, we would be boarding trains to Germany. By day three, we were out of bread.

We reached the train station just outside the city and we were crammed into open cattle cars. The last time I was herded into one was almost two years before, when we left [my hometown of] Paderborn for Auschwitz.

The train ride took five days and nights. (On the second day some bread was thrown into the car. Lack of water was a major problem, but the snow saved us. Our ranks shrank as dead bodies were tossed out of the car. We'd lost half of those who began the march, almost 20,000 people.

The SS had a very simple disposal system. They ordered us to stack the corpses in the first car. Then they filled the second car. Those still able to move were transferred to boxcars with those of us who were still alive. The Nazis obviously didn't want to discard the bodies in the villages, so we all rode together, the living and the dead.

Something amazing happened on the way. It happened near Prague. As the open train and its skeletal passengers passed by a factory, we were recognized by the workers, undoubtedly because of our striped prison clothing. Within moments they bombarded us with anything useful they could get their hands on. Sandwiches, sausages, shirts, hats—whatever they could find was as thrown into the open cars and quickly grabbed by those of us who were lucky. It was a rare outbreak of spontaneous compassion from people who didn't have much and reached out to those who had nothing.

Thank you, Czechs. We've never forgotten you.

Welcome to Buchenwald

It was a bitter, glittering day. Eight days had passed since Auschwitz. We marched into KZ [concentration camp] Buchenwald, through the gate inscribed, "Right or Wrong—My Country." Directly underneath were the words, "To Each His Own."

The camp was jammed beyond capacity, and new transports arrived continuously.

Buchenwald was in the heart of Germany, located near Weimar, the cite of Goethe. It was being used as the dumping ground for prisoners from camps in danger of being overrun by the Allies.

That night, we were put in Barracks 58, in the so-called "small camp." A thousand of us were trying to find a place to sleep in a barracks designed to hold no more than 300. I don't know which was worse, the hunger, the dirt, the fatigue or the lice. It was quite a combination. There were no blankets, no mattresses, not even straw. All we had were barren wood planks. The three of us decided to take turns so we could all get some sleep.

There were major differences between Auschwitz and Buchenwald. First of all, there was absolutely nothing to do. We stood around all day, waiting for one of two meals: a breakfast of sawdust bread in the morning and thin soup at night. The death *Kommando* made rounds through the barracks each morning to collect the bodies. There were no washing facilities. Toilets were filthy and disease-laden. Many who survived the march died.

The second major difference was the way we were treated by those in charge of the barracks. Most were old-time prisoners. There were no beatings, no unnecessary harassment. Their attitude was to maintain the status quo and not increase the distress factor.

There was one more thing. Twice each day, loudspeakers in the barracks would broadcast the latest official German news. And despite the fact that they continued to claim victory as they reported the heroic battles of the German armies, the cities they named made it clear that the Allied armies were slowly, but surely, advancing on all fronts.

We could hardly wait for the newscasts. They gave us the incentive to hang on. Without them, Felix, Honzo and I would not have had the courage to fight to stay alive. I later learned what happened to those we left behind in Buna. Auschwitz was liberated by the Russian army on January 23. The inmates who survived the five days between when we left and the Russians arrived, were cared for by Russian doctors. I met some of the survivors after the war.

Meanwhile I continued to wonder what would happen to us. . . .

One day, I witnessed cannibalism. Some of the barely alive prisoners were eating the flesh of those newly dead. It was a horror and is still etched in my mind. . . .

March 1945: The Move to Berga

One morning, the Blockaelteste read names off his transport list. Honzo and I were to be sent to another camp, two hours away. Felix wasn't listed, so we begged the kapo to allow Felix to join us and he agreed. The three of us, with 40 other prisoners, were loaded into a truck and transported to the sub-camp Berga, which held 1,500 prisoners. Here, for the first time, we encountered American POWs [prisoners of war].

We were put to work digging tunnels for underground munitions factories. The Americans were working right next to us, forced to do the same hard work. We observed their leather shoes and their wrist watches. We had seen neither in years.

When I tried to speak to them in German, some, to my total surprise, replied in Yiddish. They were Jews—American Jews! American Jewish prisoners of war! . . .

The SS guards were nervous. They knew that it was only a matter of time until the war was over. Their demeanor showed it. They were less brutal, perhaps because they hoped to buy some "protection insurance" by behaving almost civilly towards us. The sound of the battles raging west of us seemed to come ever closer, and they heard the guns as clearly as we did.

"Any day now. Let's hold out. Let's not do anything to provoke the guards," we kept repeating to each other.

Once again, our hopes for liberation were shattered. The SS announced it would evacuate the entire camp. The date was April 11. We were told to take along one blanket and our tin bowls. We assembled early in the morning and began another march. . . .

Roosevelt Is Dead

Early next morning, we were hit with a surprise announcement when we lined up.

"Achtung! I have important news." The SS officer, using his mega-phone, stood on a large rock at the edge of the forest. "The American warmonger, President Roosevelt, is dead!"

It was another one of those moments that remain with me, etched in space and time. I remember Honzo's expression, the dazed look in his eyes, his mouth open, his hand reaching out to me. "It can't be! Not Roosevelt!"

Ever since I could remember, in my early days at school, the American President, Franklin D. Roosevelt in a wheelchair, was a symbol of everything we hoped for and did not have—freedom, stability, democracy, and full acceptance as Jews. We knew Roosevelt opposed Hitler and choreographed America's entrance into the war, the creation of the Allied Forces and, finally, the landing in Europe on 'D' Day in June, 1944. The

only other person whose name mattered as much to us was that of General Dwight D. Eisenhower, the commander of the Allied Forces.

The survivors stirred restlessly.

"Listen!" the officer shouted. "This is the turning point of the war! Germany will throw the Allies back! The Fuehrer will succeed. And now, form your rows. March!"

In shock, we regrouped and the march continued. The march to nowhere. On the third night, after watching a random incident, the three of us decided to try to escape.

Several men were pulled from the transport, taken to a clearing and, in full view of all of us, were summarily executed. The pretext, according to the SS officer's warning, was that they had tried to steal some food from a farm during the night.

"Let this be a warning to all of you!" he yelled after the men had been shot. "We will not permit this. You are still camp inmates. My responsibility is to deliver all of you, and I mean all of you, to our destination. We expect to be there in a few days."

Making a Run for It

I don't remember which of the three of us first uttered the word escape. We tried to weigh our chances carefully. How could we do it? When could we do it? Should we organize a mass escape and take the chance of a large number of us being killed?

Should we try to overwhelm the SS men? We quickly discarded that idea. The SS were positioned so that there was always a backup with machine gun at the ready. Any attempt to overpower them would result in a blood bath with few survivors.

Honzo closed the discussion, whispering quietly as we curled up in our thin blankets out in the woods. "Look, I didn't survive three years of concentration camps, hunger, murder, dirt, and lice to get shot within the sound of the Allied armies. They'll be here in a matter of weeks, maybe days. Mass escape is out of the question."

He was right. "We must think of a better way. Think about it and give me some ideas." It took a long time to fall asleep. Escape. How?. . .

Late in the afternoon of April 18, just as it was getting dark, the three of us slowly walked a few steps into the woods, and pulled down our pants as if we were following a call of nature. We weren't the only ones. Others were doing the same thing. The difference was that we kept going, slowly sneaking deeper and deeper into the woods. . . .

My heart pounded so loudly, I thought I could hear it. I was scarcely able to breathe. Honzo was 30 feet to my left; Felix was ahead of me, about the same distance to my right. We moved further into the woods, putting a considerable distance between ourselves and the group. Faintly, we heard the Nazis order the columns to march. We ran through the trees. I looked around and couldn't see anyone but Honzo and Felix.

Totally out of breath, I fell in the middle of the forest, tears streaming down my cheeks.

I was free. Free! Free!

Selection 12

The Boys Who Survived

Martin Gilbert

If you try to imagine what you would have done had you been a Jew in Europe when the Nazis were in power, your choices were limited. The chances of survival depended on where you were, how you acted, your age, the shape you were in, and many variables beyond your control. Sometimes everything depended on luck. Realize also that you have the advantage of hindsight. You know what happened to the Jews, but hard as it may be to believe now, most people at the time had no idea what would happen to them. This excerpt comes from a book about 732 young people who survived the horrors of the labor camps. Author Martin Gilbert is Winston Churchill's official biographer, a leading expert on the Holocaust and one of the foremost historians of our time.

*T*he only Jews who were not deported from the ghettos to the death camps were those who had been selected for slave labour. Mostly this selection was done at the moment of deportation. . . .

This was the slave labour camp at Skarzysko-Kamienna, an armaments factory in the centre of the Radom district. Divided into three sections, known as Werk A, B and C, it was run throughout the war by a German company based in Leipzig, Hugo Schneider Aktiengesellschaft, known as HASAG. The general manager of the works was an SS colonel. By May 1942 there were five thousand Jewish slave labourers in the factory. After the German defeat at Stalingrad at the end of 1942, the number of Jews sent to the camp increased dramatically as munitions production became a priority. The treatment of the Jewish slave labourers at Skarzysko-Kamienna made it one of the most notorious camps of all. The total number of Jews who were sent there has been estimated at between 25,000 and 30,000; the number who died has been estimated at between 18,000 and 23,000—more than two-thirds of the total inmates—killed by the guards or dying from exhaustion and starvation. . . .

Every slave labour camp had its own panoply of horrors. Mangy boys have terrible memories of Skarzysko-Kamienna. 'There are many incidents which I remember,' Moishe Nurtman later wrote, 'but the most memorable one was when a German was walking by, and a girl said something, and he just shot her.' Moishe Nurtman also recalled an episode when he was taken outside the camp. 'I remember one time when I went into the town, escorted by Jewish police. We were approached by a Ukrainian, and he said I should not be escorted, because I was not allowed to buy bread, because a Jew had no rights. He took me into another room. There the Ukrainians put two revolvers at my head. They hit me and took my money and bread. And they pulled the trigger, but it was not loaded. It really gave me a tremendous shock. Those Ukrainians were real animals.'

Sam Freiman also recalled the horrors of Skarzysko-Kamienna. 'I remember when I first came to Skarzysko camp,' he wrote, 'I was put on thread machines and lots of oil was spraying on me. All my clothing got soaked with oil, and from that I got sores on my body which festered. After a while I was transferred to a capstan machine and was supposed to produce a hundred rounds of two-centimetre bullets an hour. In one hour at the beginning I could not produce that amount. One of the German overseers, with a kapo, took me into the office, put me over a chair, and the two of them started to beat me. By the time they were finished I could not move. When I walked out of the office I remember I walked like a duck.

'When I was beaten up so much I felt very low in spirit and degraded, and became very ill. Every day the Germans used to pick out some Jews to be taken to the woods and shot. When I was selected to be taken to the woods there was one overseer—his name was Liedig—he used to shoot Jews himself. He used to come out at Appel and boast that he could not eat his breakfast because he had not shot any Jews. But he al-ways used to rescue me. He always shouted to me, "Kleiner, zurück an die Maschine" ("Little one, go back to the machine"). One day two prisoners ran away. The Germans caught them, brought them back to camp, and ordered a roll-call. Everybody was brought out of barracks, and the two escapees were executed. I lost three uncles, my mother's brothers, in that camp. The Germans hanged them. They had taken some leather from the machines.'. . .

Chaskiel Rosenblum also recalled the problems of survival at Skarzysko-Kamienna. 'From time to time there were "selections" during the soup time. The skinnier ones—called "Musulmen", i.e. walking ghosts—were sent on a truck: this meant death by shooting. On one of these occasions I was sent on the truck. My father ran to the Polish foreman and told him: "My son is on the truck". The foreman went to the Germans in charge and said: "I need him, he is in charge of the breaking machine". They let me get off the truck: for them, one Jew or another was the same. They took the truck full of Jews to the forest, made them dig their own graves, and shot them. A few hours later, the truck came back with the clothing and the shoes. We started to fight about who got what. I cannot admit what animals we were. But we were.

'At one Appel, we were standing in the line, and a German said that he needed a Jew who could speak German to be a foreman. They promised he would have a double portion of bread and soup. I pushed my father to step forward, since he spoke German perfectly. But he kicked my ankle, and this kick still aches. I did no more, and, at the barracks, he told me that all those people who were foremen and beat Jews would have to pay for it one day, since they would be accused of collaboration. He preferred not to smoke and not to have an extra piece of bread, he preferred to remain one of the inmates.

'Four months later, my father died. I think he couldn't go on living. He had lost everything, and he hoped that I would make it. He couldn't stand his own misery looking at me. nor his own misery having lost all his family. Before he passed away, he told me that I would survive and go to Bolivia to meet my uncle. I think he gave up his life, leaving room for me to live.

'Before those who were in charge of taking away the dead came to take my father away, I stripped off his trousers and sold them for a piece of bread. I was hungry. They had made animals out of us: we had no feelings. . . .

'Life went on by myself. Two brothers slept above my bunk. They worked outside the factory. They were the rich ones. They had a "general store": bread, cigarettes, rolls. They smuggled all the goods from the town of Skarzysko into the barracks. They were big money movers, and were envied by all the inmates of the barracks, including me. One night I sat on my bunk and put my hand on their bunk. A pair of trousers was hanging there. I put my hands in the pocket and grabbed a handful of money wrapped in paper. I went out of the barrack, dug a hole and hid it. The following morning they woke up shouting that they had been robbed. Of course I kept my mouth shut. From then on, I had an extra portion of bread every day for quite a time. This helped me to survive.'

Kopel Kendall's memories of Skarzysko-Kamienna are similarly vivid after more than a century. He was fourteen years old. . . .

'We heard rumours in the camp of people being gassed and put in crematoria. I myself could not understand why, or believe it. Every so often there were selections, when we would be lined up, partially clothed, and then have to pass by tables with SS men sitting looking at us. Their finger would point in either direction. I got away with it twice, but the third time my number came up. The following morning when my number was called out I didn't respond. Luckily for me I got away with it. The rest were taken away and never seen again.

'Typhoid was rampant in the camp by now and thousands were dying every day. I contracted it, twelve days' high fever and on the thirteenth day you either lived or died. The lady who looked after the so-called hospital barrack hid me every time they came to take the sick and dead away to be disposed of. I lost all my hair and had to learn to walk again. (I feel that in my second life I came back like a gorilla smothered in hair). The longer I stayed in the camp the more streetwise I became. I was promoted to a sweeper, a higher status that gave me time to help deliver the soup and therefore scrounge round the kitchen where I found a few scraps.'. . .

Alec Ward also recalled, fifty years later, some of the 'outstanding incidents' at Skarzysko-Kamienna, writing of 'the hangings of prisoners, the selections, the dead bodies lying at the barbed-wire fences early in the morning—'of Jewish prisoners who had tried desperately to escape during the night and were shot. The painful hunger and malnutrition. The beatings: The man who cried every time he saw me—as I reminded him of his young son who had perished at the hands of the Nazis.'

On one, occasion, the Germans took Alec Ward and his friend Chaim Ickowicz to the place where prisoners were frequently executed, and made them dig a communal grave. 'They lined up the prisoners taken from the sick-bay and shot them, and they fell into the grave. We were forced to cover the half-dead bodies with earth. In most cases they shot the gravediggers as well. We were very lucky.'

The worst of the work at Skarzysko-Kamienna was making mines. 'The mines were made from picric acid,' Alec Ward recalled, 'and the prisoners only lived for three months doing that work, as the powder affected their lungs. It was a sheer miracle that I survived that length of time there. I put it down to being young, strong and extremely lucky. Before the war, workers carrying out this type of dangerous work drank a large amount of milk and worked short hours. We worked twelve-hourly shifts with half an hour break. There was no milk.

'The hours between two and five in the morning were torturous. One could not keep one's eyes open, but one had to, otherwise the German overseer would beat you over the head. Our skin turned yellow at that work and it was not until six months after I left the camp that my skin returned to the normal colour.'. . .

Alec Ward, who was then fifteen, also recalled the time when he was 'so very weak and despondent, and could not walk up the two steps leading into our hut, and a miracle happened which saved my life. I was queuing up for my ration of soup when a girl asked me who I was. When I told her, she informed me that she was my late Uncle Yidl's lover and that they were planning to marry when my uncle was shot by the invading German troops in Laskarzew where they lived. That angel of a girl—her name was Henia—did some knitting for the Polish Christian women who came into the factories to work as paid workers, and they gave her some food occasionally, some of which she passed on to me. It was not long after meeting Henia that I began to negotiate the two steps into the hut normally. As far as I know, she did not survive the war, but should I ever meet her again I would be prepared to give my all to her for saving my life.'. . .

Another cruel aspect of that 'deadly hell' at Skarzysko-Kamienna was a call one day for volunteers to go to Palestine. When some men volunteered, hoping against hope that this was one of the much-talked about exchanges of Jews in German-occupied Poland for German civilians in British-Mandated Palestine, the German overseer picked others, who had not put their hands up, for this miraculous journey. On the following day Salek Orenstein was one of those ordered for a special work duty. 'We had no idea what to expect,' he recalled. 'When we reached the appointed place, we found heaps and heaps of clothing: shoes, underwear, caps, spectacles, anything that you can possibly conceive a man or woman wearing. None of us could understand the meaning of it. But this was not the time to ponder. We were given sacks and told to stuff these items of clothing inside them. Then the whole lot was taken away to a warehouse for searching, in case any precious items had been concealed in the hems of garments or secreted in the heels of shoes. As I worked, I could see stains of blood around in blotches on the grass, the ground. It puzzled me, but I carried on.

'Later that day, the regular Polish machine-operators arrived at the factory. A standard feature of the place was that these workers came in from their nearby villages each day to instruct us on how to operate the machinery. They had been employed by the Polish government before the war. The Germans relied on them to continue its smooth running. The news they brought us that morning was of quite a different nature. "You know what happened to the Jews?" they told us. "They had to undress and they were driven naked to the railway station and packed into cattle wagons." All sorts of different theories began circulating; it was said that the naked people on those trains had been caught trying to escape and were shot dead. I did not know what to make of these conflicting reports.' The Jews who had been told they were going to Palestine had in fact been sent by train to Treblinka, and murdered there on arrival. . . .

Every slave labour camp had its catalogue of horrors. Sam Laskier, who had been born in Warsaw, was one of those who experienced the slave labour camp at Blizyn. He was just fifteen years old. 'We worked in a quarry,' he later wrote. 'The rations were so meagre there was never a moment when we were not hungry—starving. Work was extremely hard, and our Ukrainian guards were very brutal. One day I was pulling a small wagon filled with quarried stone up an incline when a guard accused me of leaning on the wagon, not pulling it. He pulled me into a nearby field and repeatedly ordered me to fall into the mud and get up. I became so exhausted I begged him to shoot me. He just hit me with his rifle butt and forced me back to work.

'One German in Blizyn would pick on well-built Jewish prisoners. He would beat them to death with a leather whip which had a metal tip. Many prisoners, including my cousin Avram Klaiman, died of typhus and they were buried in the nearby forest.'

As each boy recounts his or her story, elements emerge that are common to all, especially the hunger and the fear. Yet in every story there is also something not seen elsewhere, a unique aspect of the torment of the six million, and of the survival of the hundred thousand. The case of fourteen-year-old Harry Balsam in the slave labour camp at Plaszow, just outside Cracow, is one which stands out in its extraordinary mixture of chance and luck. 'We arrived in Plaszow after a night's journey in cattle trucks,' he recalled. 'When we arrived we had to give up everything we had brought with us. The SS guards were waiting for us and told us to throw any jewellery and money we had on to a pile. They said if anyone was trying to hide anything they would shoot them, but people don't give up their belongings so easily. Most people started throwing their money and jewellery on to the pile when suddenly they took one person and searched him. They found that he still had some money hidden on him and shot him on the spot.

'I happened to be very near and when I saw that, it frightened me and I pulled everything out of my pockets and slung it on the pile and passed by. On that particular day they must have shot seven or eight people. Then we were assembled for roll-call and we were standing in line waiting for the commandant to arrive, he had to decide what to do with us. We stood waiting for about three or four hours, it was fairly cold as I remember, and we were told by the guards that we would have to stand and wait until the commandant came.

'After a while we saw him coming and everybody got scared including the Jewish police who were already in the camp as even they didn't know what their fate would be. When he arrived he looked us up and down. There were three hundred of us. He was marching backwards and forwards and suddenly he realised that there were quite a number of small boys in the group. He started screaming and shouting and said that when he asked for people to be sent to the camp he didn't ask for little boys but for men who could be put to work. He shouted that all the boys must separate from the men. We did this and stood in columns of five.

'Naturally we were all shivering with fear and were shuffling our feet. I was one of the smallest and got pushed to the side where the commandant was standing. I turned round and said. "Can you stop pushing me?" and as I said it he called me out, and I thought. "Oh yes, this is my lot, my luck has run out now, all because I opened my big mouth." As he called me over, I

started begging that I had done nothing and that I had only told them to stand still. He didn't listen and said, "Will you please follow me?" I thought to myself, this is it, I'm about to be shot.

'I followed him into an office where two Jewish prisoners were working, one, a girl, the other a boy. The girl, I can remember now, was a pretty young girl of about eighteen and the boy must have also been eighteen or nineteen. He was dictating something to the girl, who was working on the typewriter. The commandant, Josef Müller, took me into the office and said, "Sit down here." I didn't know what it was all about, but he said that I would become his shoeshine boy.' Through this quirk of fate, Harry Balsam was to survive as Josef Müller's servant and errand boy. . . .

Also at Plaszow was Moshe Rosenberg, originally from Cracow, who reached his sixteenth birthday in February 1944. He was being whipped one day by guards for daring to take a rest while road-building. After twenty-five lashes the whipping unexpectedly stopped. He looked up and saw the German factory-owner Oscar Schindler. 'I'll take care of this one,' Schindler told the guards, and proceeded to drag the young man to a nearby stable. 'Loud enough for the Germans to hear,' Moshe Rosenberg recalled, 'he shouted, "What's this shit?" Then he threw some food wrapped in paper and walked out. It was his way of smuggling food to the Jews. Without him stepping in, the guards would have beaten me until I was dead.'

A few months later, while he was working in Schindler's factory making grenades, Moshe Rosenberg, exhausted by the night shift and drained by the intense heat of the machines, sat down for a moment. It was already almost morning. At that very moment Schindler came in to the factory, followed by the notorious commandant, Amon Goeth. Schindler saw the young man first, 'raced ahead of Goeth, grabbed my jacket and slapped my face, shouting, "Get back to work!" It was an act. Schindler never hit anyone or raised his voice. If Goeth had found me sitting down he would have shot me on the spot.'. . .

After thirteen months in Biezanow the slave

labourers there were moved to a camp that had been built by the SS on the site of a Jewish cemetery in Cracow. It was called Jeruzolimska, the Jerusalem Camp. Compared with Biezanow, Zisha Schwimmer recalled, 'this was hell. Every day the SS rounded up Jews, marched them under guard to a pit, and shot them. We were there for six weeks. It seemed an eternity. We never thought we would come out of this camp alive. . . .

'Warta was a very big labour camp. It had an ammunition factory attached to it. It was the only labour camp I have been in that had women as well. When we first came there it was small, with only a couple of barracks. More and more barracks were being built, and more and more transports of Jews arrived, including women. There were about three barracks of women. No men were allowed inside the women's barracks, for obvious reasons. In spite of this, there were some women who became pregnant. If any man was found by the Germans inside a women's barrack, he would be taken to the assembly yard in front of the barracks. Everybody was called out on the orders of the commandant to witness his execution by shooting. His body was left in the yard until the next morning as a warning to others.

'The sleeping bunks were stretched from one end of the barracks to the other. With three rows, bottom, middle and top. People just slept next to each other with hardly any room to move. There were no washing facilities. The only way you could wash yourself was by using some of the black tea ration we were given. However, this labour camp was heaven after Jeruzolimska. Although life was bad, and we were not safe, we felt safer than there. We worked in the ammunition factory attached to the camp, assembling bullets into boxes. You had to work fast, but as long as you did your job they did not bother you.'. . .

A few days after the deportation from Kozienice, the Jews working at Szyczki were given permission by their Polish overseer to conduct the Kol Nidrei evening service, with which Yom Kippur—the Day of Atonement—begins. 'As a result,' Moniek Goldberg recalled, 'some people figured that nothing would happen if they didn't report to work the next day. I was still ob-servant at the time and wanted to stay in. There was a man, Moishe Zowoliner, whom my father had known very well, and he had written to him to ask him to look after me. He made me go to work that morning. When we returned to the barracks in the evening the SS from Radom were there. We were all marched to a clearing in the forest nearby. Those who had stayed in were already there. They had dug a ditch and upon our arrival they were all massacred, and we were ordered to fill the ditch with dirt. That was the first massacre I witnessed—on Yom Kippur 1942. I was fourteen years old.'. . .

Every boy recalls at least one episode when he came close to death. This happened to Moniek Goldberg on the day before Christmas 1943. An Ethnic German Volksdeutsche in the camp—'he must have been drunk—for no reason whatsoever began beating me with a rubber hose. I had been beaten before but this time I reacted. First, I tried to avoid the blows—to no avail. So, I turned round and swung my pail at him, hit his head, and split it open. The supervisor called the guards and they took me to the main gate. I was made to do exercises for hours. The Ukrainians had their amusement.

'Every workplace had a German director. When the director for the generating plant was informed, he came to the guardhouse and struck me across the face with a riding crop. He told me that I was to be hanged as a punishment. As it happened, when one of the cooks heard about my altercation she got in touch with the German lady who was in charge of the kitchen. She was an old lady who walked with a cane. Once the director had declared my sentence she approached him and protested. She said that I belonged to her. Having seen me in the kitchen so often she must have believed this to be the case. She went on to say that I could be punished but not hanged. She must have been well connected to the main director, Brandt, because she won the tussle. I was given twenty-five lashes and lived to tell the story. In retrospect, it was a foolish act taken by an impetuous young boy. I had forfeited my life and was saved by a most improbable fluke.'

Selection 13

What It Took to Survive

Kitty Hart

Inmates in concentration camps—at least those who were not immediately murdered— were cold, hungry, exhausted, sick, depressed, and abused. Sometimes the body was not strong enough to withstand the agony and no amount of determination could prevent death. In other cases, the will was not strong enough and a person gave up and eventually died. Those who survived usually were physically strong enough to hold on until liberation and had the resolve to live. Luck also played a vital role, and so did the ability to organize camp necessities. Organization *was the term prisoners used for obtaining clothes, food, cigarettes, and other things—through trade or theft—that could mean the difference between life or death. Prisoners often did what they had to do, even when it was as distasteful as taking the clothes from the dead. Still, many retained a moral compass that allowed them to distinguish between right and wrong. Thus, for example, while it was considered permissible to take from the dead, who had no use for their possessions anymore, stealing from the living was tantamount to murder. This excerpt from Kitty Hart's memoir describes her survival skills at Auschwitz. Hart returned to Auschwitz in 1978 with her son, David, and filmed what became the interna-tionally acclaimed television documentary,* Return to Auschwitz.

The girl tattooing my mother's arm had talked quietly to her as she did so. . . . She was surprised that anyone of my mother's age had been allowed into this part of the camp instead of going "over there." She nodded towards the window.

"What *is* over there?" I asked.

"You'll find out soon enough."

But the girl promised in an undertone that she would try to help my mother as far as possible. It might be possible to fix her up with work indoors, but not right away: nothing could be done during the six weeks of quarantine. "I don't know if you'll last out those six weeks. The average life of a prisoner here is about three weeks.". . .

I noticed some girls peering at us from behind one of the other blocks. After a while a few made their way across to us, and one spoke to me.

"You want to buy a scarf?"

The rag she was holding out would be just the thing to cover my bald, cold head.

"What do you want for it?" I asked.

"Two pieces of bread or one of sausage."

I told her we'd had no rations at all so far, and asked how she had managed to get the scarf.

"I organized it, of course."

This was my first encounter with the most important word in the Auschwitz language: "organization" was the key to survival. It meant to steal, buy, exchange, get hold of. Whatever you wanted, you had to have something to barter for it. Some people spent every waking minute "organizing": stealing from their fellow prisoners, bribing others, swapping a crust of bread for a can of water, a crumpled sheet of notepaper for a more comfortable corner of a bunk. . . .

On that first night I fought for a place in the *koje* [bunks near the heater]. As a newcomer to a block holding over 800 women, I stood no chance of getting on to the top layer. I squeezed in somehow on the outside of a lower bunk, which meant I had to cling to the edge if I was not to be pushed off. Neither the stinking straw mattress nor the single threadbare blanket reached to where I lay. We were all wet through from the steady rain outside, but none of us dared to undress.

My immediate neighbour was a gipsy who whispered to me that she had got here just two weeks ahead of us. She sounded very strained and feeble, but in the gloom she brought her face close to mine and said:

"I see great strength in your eyes, child. Let me have your palm, and I'll see what it has to say." She bent closely over it. "Yes, I can see you *will* come out of here. How, I don't know, but you will be one of the few to see freedom again. Remember, you must never lose your will to live. Fight for your life, or you'll be finished very quickly."

My first day in Auschwitz was over.

Borrowing from the Dead

At about four in the morning we were awakened by the deafening shrill of whistles. It was still dark and for a few seconds I hadn't the faintest idea where I was. My cold, damp clothes clung to my skin. Then I recognized the voice of the *Blockälteste* [block elder] screaming at us to get up. I rolled off the bunk and turned to shake the gipsy. There was no response. She was stone cold and must have died hours before; and I had been lying pressed against her body. . . .

I searched her and found several rations of bread hidden away. I hesitated for a moment; then helped myself to the bread and to her shirt, which was less rough than my ex-army garment

and could be worn underneath without showing. This was the first time I had ever taken from the dead. It wouldn't be the last. . . .

The roll-call last night had taught me one thing—when the rows formed up it was best to fight your way into the middle. In there you stood less chance of being casually whipped or clubbed by the *Blockälteste* and her subordinates, or by the S.S. supervisor as she checked the final count with her stick. Those in the front row and at the sides got the worst of it. There was a lot to learn, and survival depended on it.

During the quarantine period you were at everyone's mercy. For six weeks you were on the slave market. Locked out of the hut after roll-call, you spent the day on that grassless meadow until someone came hunting victims for a work party. Ten, twenty, one hundred might be needed to dig trenches or pits, to lay roads or work on the railway line. You tried to hide behind the block, or run round the buildings. They kept chasing you with their whips, and would not rest until the requisite number had been rounded up. Then, once the party had been marched off, screamed at and beaten most of the way, you could relax . . . until the next raid.

It was during these six weeks that many of the *Zugänge* [newcomers] died, usually from shock. Large numbers of them from foreign countries had been literally seized in their homes, transported in appalling conditions to this distant camp, and thrown into the horror of it without warning. Mother and I had gone through what you might call an apprenticeship, on the run, in the ghetto, and in prison. Nothing could ever again take us entirely by surprise. We were hardened by now. But not so the dazed, stricken Jews of remoter lands. They went down like flies, dying of shock, dysentery, or typhus, which always raged through the camp. It was particularly bad for those who arrived in winter from warmer climates: Greek girls brought from the warmth of their own country into the middle of a Polish winter stood no chance in this marshy and misty lowland. . . .

Promotion

Promotion was much easier if you could prove yourself a bully and a willing murderer along Nazi lines. Most of the great complex of Auschwitz and Birkenau camps was in fact run by the prisoners themselves, and it was hideous to see how readily one of your own people would turn against you in return for a few privileges and the chance of a few more months of life. Some were as proud of their armbands, which denoted their status, as of a military decoration, and appeared genuinely touched when they got a word of commendation from an S.S. officer. They set themselves to making careers within the camp, and were very conscious of their status.

The vast majority of prisoners were under supervision all the time, but not always by the people you expected. Nobody was to be trusted: anyone could be a thief, a murderer, a traitor, a spy. Everywhere, all the time, prisoners were to be found aping our oppressors. Every block had its *Blockälteste,* herself a prisoner, and above her was the leading prisoner or *Lagerälteste*. Every work party had its *Kapo* (from the Italian *Capo,* or head), quite possibly a fellow Pole and Jew, who showed her admiration for German discipline by whipping and kicking you. She in turn was fawned on by her *Unterkapo* and *Vorarbeiter,* or leading worker, who could expect promotion if they were assiduous enough in beating up their fellow inmates. Other trustees included the camp police, made up exclusively of Reich German criminals, who were even prouder of their status: no matter what his criminal record, a Reich German was obviously superior to the lesser races, who deserved all they got.

Anybody might attack you and beat you up, and indeed it was expected of the prisoner officials. You had to be on the lookout the whole time. Every minute of the day you had to be on your guard, thinking "I must get over there . . . mustn't stay here. . . ." You had to sense from which direction trouble was coming, and make sure you weren't on the scene when it arrived. That was the key to survival: to be somewhere else . . . to be *invisible*. . . .

As a counter to such self-seeking treachery little "families" formed within a block: three or four friends would stick together and organize things together. One acquired some bread, another found a handkerchief or a pencil and some scraps of paper, another a mug of water. Members of a group helped each other and defied the rest. Outside the family there had to be bribery; within there was love and mutual help. . . .

The daily ration of food, even if you got it in full, was far less than half what an ordinary human being needs just to exist, without doing a stroke of even the lightest manual labour. To be on *Aussenarbeit* [outside work], breaking stones, laying roads or railway track, was to invite early death, especially in winter. . . .

We were divided up into work parties of about 200 and marched out to the sound of the band. . . .

For miles we marched. An hour, two hours. . . .

When we stopped, we thought we would have a brief rest after that painful tramp in our clogs, but at one side of the road was a heap of huge stones and these had to be carried to a spot much further on, where another work detail was breaking them up for road-building. I stared. Lifting any one of them would be beyond me, let alone carrying distance. . . .

I looked for the smallest. But they were all enormous. With an effort I got one up into my arms and tottered away with it. After three trips, I was finished. My back felt as if it was breaking and I had a pain in my stomach. Not the ache of a twisted muscle, but the sickening wrench of diarrhoea. My guts were going to drop out. And they did—or at any rate, a filthy mess ran down my legs. That was another of the things you had to get used to if you worked so many hours a day and were beaten up so often. And beaten up I was. As soon as I faltered, an S.S. woman with a dog came racing towards me. . . .

Her whip lashed the edge of my cheek. She kicked me in the back as I went down, and there was a pain through my wrist as her Alsatian dog sank its teeth into me. A stinking old lemon— yes, already I was probably that. A few more days of this, and I wasn't sure I'd live to be very much older.

Yet I did live. I worked on *Aussenarbeit* for weeks on end, whipped and kicked by the women and bitten by the savagely trained dogs. Hunger gave us all stomach cramps; the food made us ill. But it was essential not to lose the will to go on: giving up was the first step to self-destruction.

Organize to Survive

There were girls in our block who worked in a potato field. I decided to try my luck, dodge one work party and attach myself to another, and smuggle in with the farm contingent. It worked. Digging potatoes was not so arduous, and the first day I was able to smuggle two potatoes back into camp, one under each armpit. Now, if only I could organize myself a coat, the floppier the better, it would be possible to carry even more potatoes in the hem and up the sleeves. To manage this I didn't eat any of the potatoes for a while, brought lots of them in, and then at last exchanged them for a ragged old coat. I now had the means for bringing in larger quantities all at one go.

Cooking was something else which had to be organized. Wood had to be found to light a fire in the stove, and water in which to cook the potatoes. With all the restrictions and so many treacherous prowlers ready to betray you, it was only possible to make the attempt after dark when all was quiet. Even then there was a risk. But a few of the other girls brought in some carrots, and we started a fire and so managed the occasional feast of half-cooked vegetables. . . .

Life in Auschwitz was a matter of organizing, of grabbing the bare necessities wherever you could find them. But we would never let ourselves be demoralized into cheating the living. If we took anything, it must be from the dead. People today may flinch from such an idea. But what use had the dead for their clothes or their pitiful rations? . . . To rob the living, or the half-living, was to speed them on their way to death. To organize the relics of the dead was to acquire material which helped keep the living alive, and keep the half-living breathing, with just enough strength maybe to survive until the gates opened on to a freer, sweeter world outside. . . .

Being Invisible

I had already grasped the value of being invisible. Not being around when the hunters came. Having an unidentifiable face. There were thousands and thousands of women in the various sections of the camp, and even the *Kapos* were unable to tell one from another. With shaven heads, ravaged faces and ill-fitting garments, everybody looked so much alike. That was part of the Nazi plan, after all: to reduce all of us to impersonal, downtrodden nothingness. Even a *Blockälteste* could have up to 1,000 women in her hut, and the continually shifting population made it impossible for her to pick out any individual unless there had been some breach of regulations and she needed a scapegoat. As long as numbers tallied, nobody cared about faces.

It was strictly forbidden to move from one block to another. Social calls were not encouraged in Auschwitz. Friends disappeared, and you had no way of looking for them or saying goodbye. If you had been parted from a sister, cousin or friend, you stayed parted. Yet people did dodge between blocks and make contact. It was dangerous, but then everything in that place was dangerous. You could be beaten to death if caught; but you could be beaten to death for almost anything, so it was up to you to decide which risks to avoid and which to take. . . .

I had noticed that a large number of girls in the block next to ours worked on a special *Kommando* distinguished by red scarves. After inquiry I found they worked at the Siemens factory which had been built outside Auschwitz to make the most of slave labour. They were divided into a day shift and a night shift, which meant that there would be prisoners allowed to sleep inside during the day, unlike most of the other blocks. Now I knew what I had to do.

My first step was to organize similar clothes. Their striped dresses were noticeably different from the sort I had been issued with, and I didn't possess a red scarf. So it was back to my old contacts in the potato fields. Once I had smuggled enough produce into the camp, the dress and scarf were soon forthcoming. Then one morning I hung about as the night shift came off duty, slipped into their ranks as they collected their rations and went on with them through the doorway of the block. Nobody spotted me. They were all too exhausted, thinking only of a few bites to eat and then some hours of sleep. I wriggled with the others into the *koje* and settled down, then got back to my own block for the evening *Zählappell* [roll call] and the distribution of our bread ration before going to bed for the night. In this way I managed double rations, lots of sleep, and no work to wear me out. Above all I was not exposed to the random beatings of *Kapos* or S.S. guards. . . .

Don't Give Up

The men or women who gave up soonest were not always the ones you might have predicted. It had nothing to do with social background, intellect, or even religious belief. You might think an intellectual ought to have been able to cope better than a bewildered peasant, but it was often the other way round. The well-educated man, in good health and with a clear mind when he was thrown into the camp, tried to find some rational, philosophical way of coping with the incredible situation; and just because it was so foul and incredible, his mind cracked and surrendered. Those of us who had been gradually conditioned to what lay in store, and who kept our eyes fixed only on our fundamental day-to-day existence, were hardier. Insensitive, if you like. Sensitivity was something you had to stow away for the duration. . . .

Cleanliness Is Next To . . .

In a sudden surge of "cleanliness is next to godliness" enthusiasm, the authorities next decreed the construction of washrooms. Months had gone by since I had last washed in water—we all made do with our undrinkable tea—and the prospect was delightful. But the *Waschraum* [washroom], which had real taps, produced only trickles of marshy water, there were hundreds of women to those few taps, and ordinary prisoners stood precious little chance of getting to them. You needed an armband and a stick to be sure of your place in the queue. Some girls washed in

their own urine, having read in some magazine in the distant past that it was good for the complexion. And it was supposed to be a disinfectant.

My own skin had become a mixture of dark grey and red. It was quite impossible to kill all the lice that overran every inch of human skin, forming crusts, especially on the scalp. As with many other things in those cramped conditions, you became obsessed by them. You tried to cope with your own fleas and lice, and took a sort of family pride in them at the same time as hating them. Other people's lice were even more hateful, particularly when they tried to shift over on to you. They dug under the skin, and it was impossible to get them out; impossible, too, to keep from scratching, yet that was the worst thing you could do, for when the skin was broken it soon became infected. My whole body was blotched with scabs and boils, especially on my legs, which oozed pus. After a while I ceased to notice that they hurt; I squeezed them out regularly, but they wouldn't heal, and the holes they left got bigger and bigger.

We were rotting to a slow death. . . . It was impossible to keep the body clean, yet if you failed you were hastening your own death. To have *Krätze* (scabies) or any other obvious infection meant you would be hauled to one side during medical inspection—or selection, as it was called. . . .

Every one of the women had to strip and parade naked in front of [S.S. doctor Josef] Mengele. In his immaculate white gloves he stood there pointing sometimes to the right, sometimes to the left. Anyone with spots on her body, or anyone whose slumping and shuffling denoted a *Muselmann* [prisoner on the brink of death], was directed to the right. That meant death. On the left you were allowed to rot a little longer. Out of 400 girls parading before him that day, Mengele chose 320 to die. . . .

Keeping Silent

Another of the insane, obscene things in the camp was that you were not supposed to know about the gassing or burning. Everybody knew really, yet nobody dared mention it. In a fit of

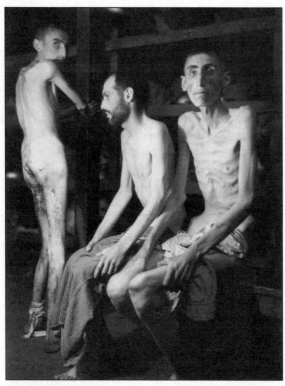

Camp inmates who were not immediately killed endured starvation, beatings, overwork, and disease.

Every day if you were out of doors you could see trains near the main entrance, where the railway line now reached, tipping out hundreds and hundreds of people. There would be almost unbroken columns of women and children, and sometimes older men and boys, plodding along towards the crematoria. Each group left its luggage behind on the platform, and from those belongings came most of the "organized" luxuries and extra food in the camp.

With each incoming transport and each internal selection from the camp blocks there would be a build-up of that glow in the sky, and the sickly burning smell would drift across the whole area. Still you were not supposed to refer to it. The S.S. wanted no panic and no stampeding mobs: keep everything tidy, steady and methodical, please.

You didn't want to believe, anyway. Least of all could you accept that it would ever happen to you personally. Perhaps something awful was being done to other people, but you were better off not knowing, or at any rate not being quite sure. I don't think any of the women I knew, even those who were dragged away screaming, ever really accepted the truth of what was waiting for them until they were face to face with it.

Even the Germans had an innocuous way of referring to the matter in their records. "Selection for special treatment" was the phrase. It sounds almost inviting: as if they were offering a treat rather than "treatment." If they had their reasons for pretending even to themselves, then it was only by presence that the rest of us could hope to stay sane. And maybe stay alive long enough to get out one day and tell the whole world the truth, that what was special about it was that its chief aim was the extermination of the entire Jewish race.

rage some S.S. woman might threaten and wave her arm meaningly towards the distant buildings and chimneys, and the interminable selections of women to be dragged away and never returned could mean only one thing. Yet at other times even a trusted *Kapo* who had been overheard talking about extermination chambers would herself be shot, beaten to death on the spot, or taken away to be gassed. The same thing would happen immediately to any prisoner of lower standing who even mentioned the subject: you were gassed as punishment for having dared to suggest that any gassing whatsoever was going on!

Victims

Chapter 4

Introduction

Jews were the primary targets of Hitler's genocidal policies, but they were not the only ones. Gypsies (also called Roma), homosexuals, and Jehovah's Witnesses also became subject to persecution. Even American citizens—Jews and a few non-Jews—were among those who died in concentration camps.

Surviving the camps, and the war in general, depended very much on factors beyond anyone's control, such as age, gender, and health. Young children and the elderly, for example, had little chance because they were usually killed immediately. Women also tended to be less likely to survive because they could not always withstand the hard labor in the camps. Older teens had better odds because they would sometimes be used for forced labor. The treatment by the guards, the freezing weather, and the back-breaking work also took its toll on everyone, but anyone in poor health stood little prospect of living long in the camps. Even a strong, healthy person could catch a cold or some other illness and would have difficulty recovering given the lack of medical care or nourishing food.

The selections in this chapter offer a few examples of what happened to Jews and non-Jews during the war.

Selection 1

Children and the Holocaust

U.S. Holocaust Memorial Museum

It is not fair to try to distinguish among the victims of the Holocaust, and yet it is impossible not to feel especially sad and angered by the senseless slaughter of children. No one knows how many were killed for sure, but the number is unquestionably in the millions. The horror of what was done to children is too great to go into detail. Why was it necessary to kill infants? What possible threat did they pose to the Third Reich? In Hitler's mind, any Jew was a parasite, the carrier of disease, the source of impurity. To exempt children from the Final Solution would have been to allow Jews to have a future. When Hitler said he planned to exterminate the Jews, he meant every last one. We know that the Jewish people—and the entire world— lost many great musicians, artists, philosophers, and doctors during the Holocaust. How many of the children would have grown up to become Albert Einsteins, Leonard Bernsteins, Henry Kissingers, or Marc Chagalls? How many would have married and had children who would have grown up and made the world a better place? How many children would have become loving husbands, wives, fathers, and mothers? Many articles in this encyclopedia deal with decisions people made during the Holocaust. Children had no choice. This article from the U.S. Holocaust Memorial Museum briefly describes the fate of Jewish children during World War II.

*F*ull statistics for the tragic fate of children who died during the Holocaust will never be known. Some estimates range as high as 1.5 million murdered children. This figure includes more than 1.2 million Jewish children, tens of thousands of Gypsy children and thousands of institutionalized handicapped children who were murdered under Nazi rule in Germany and occupied Europe.

Although children were seldom the targets of Nazi violence because they were children, they were persecuted along with their families for racial, religious, or political reasons. Children are not a single unified group because of the enormous and complex variations in their situations and ages. It is important to separate the distinct needs of three different age groups: (1) infants and toddlers up to age 6; (2) young children ages 7 to 12; and (3) adolescents from 13 to 18 years old. Their respective chances for survival and their ability to perform physical labor varied enormously by age. Chances of survival were somewhat higher for older children, since they could potentially be assigned to forced labor in concentration camps and ghettos.

The Jews were a special target of Nazi ideology and policies, which ultimately resulted in the Holocaust, the systematic, state sponsored murder of almost 6 million European Jews. From the very first, Jews and their children suffered at the hands of the Nazis, and thus the world of Jewish children was rapidly restricted

Reprinted from the United States Holocaust Memorial Museum, "Children of the Holocaust," an online article found at www.ushmm.org/education/children.html. Reprinted with permission from the United States Holocaust Memorial Museum.

as soon as the Nazis came to power in Germany in January 1933. Before 1939, German Jewish children were trapped in a no man's land between the alternatives of an increasingly hostile German milieu and the insecure and often unreachable world of potential safety through emigration, the latter was linked to the fate of their families. After 1935, close friends suddenly avoided the company of their Jewish classmates, sometimes becoming hostile, unfriendly, and even spiteful. Letters from German children to the editors of the Nazi tabloid *Der Stürmer* reveal a shameful potpourri of stupidity and fanaticism against their Jewish classmates. There were additional humiliations confronting Jewish and Gypsy children in German classrooms with the oppressive teaching and humiliating tenets of racial biology that humiliated them and designated them as racially inferior. As a result, education as a form of resistance was developed in German Jewish schools after 1933 and provided both background and experience for the later clandestine schools created in the ghettos and concentration camps after 1939.

One of the first laws that affected Jewish students was the "Law against Overcrowding in German schools and universities" of 25 April 1933 that restricted the number of Jewish children in schools, not to exceed 1.5 percent of the total number of students. Jewish children of war veterans and those with a non-Jewish parent were initially exempted. Many schools placed Jewish students on vacation in April 1933, a temporary expedient while awaiting legislative developments. These decrees escalated in intensity and shortly after the November 1938 pogrom ("Kristallnacht"/ Crystal Night). On 15 November 1938, German Jewish children were prohibited from attending German schools. This same measure also excluded Gypsy children from German schools. The segregated Jewish schools existed under steadily deteriorating conditions and increased Nazi pressure until 1942; they were finally closed on 7 July 1942, after the first wave of deportations of German Jews to the East had been completed. After 1938, Gypsy children fell through the social net and their schooling was not of serious concern to Nazi authorities.

First in Germany and later in occupied Europe, the Jewish communal experiences of persecution and pauperization affected children. The world of childhood and adolescence, usually a time of testing and experimentation, became inverted into a world of shrinking horizons and vulnerabilities after 1933. German Jewish children were systematically driven from the wider German milieu, creating a community under beleaguered isolation. They could no longer belong to the same clubs and social organizations as Aryan children, they were banned from using public recreational facilities and playgrounds, and were instead vulnerable to the traumas of loss and separation from their homes and familiar milieus. A few thousand German and Austrian Jewish children were able to escape the Nazi net, since they were sent abroad in "Kindertransports" to the Netherlands, Great Britain, Palestine, and the United States before 1939.

With the onset of war, Jewish children in occupied Poland and later throughout Europe were confined with their families in overcrowded ghettos and transit camps, exposed to malnutrition, disease, exposure, and early death.

Euthanasia

Gypsy and handicapped children were similarly categorized in Nazi Germany and occupied Europe by race and biology. The Nazi quest for a biologically homogeneous society already in July 1933 included the Law to Prevent Offspring with Hereditary Defects. In ever escalating legislation, mentally and physically handicapped children were vulnerable to sterilization prior to 1939 and to murder in the so-called euthanasia program after 1939. Eugenic and racial measures also extended to the small number (ca. 600) of German mulatto children (the offspring of German women and African French colonial troops occupying the Rhineland in the 1920s). These Afro-German children were registered by the Gestapo and Interior Ministry in 1937 and they were all brutally sterilized in German university hospitals that same year.

The methods of children's euthanasia were developed between February and May 1939. First, the physicians and Nazi officials registered their potential victims. Thus, registration forms, called *Meldebogen,* collected data from midwifes and physicians reporting all infants born with specific medical conditions. The first killings of children in special wards by overdoses of poison and medicaments already occurred in October 1939. Recalcitrant parents who attempted to remove their children from the killing wards were rarely able to succeed. With fathers already absent as soldiers, mothers who disagreed were often assigned to contractual labor, thereby necessitating the commitment of handicapped children in state institutions. The killing of disabled children marked the beginning of the euthanasia program and continued throughout the war. Children's euthanasia was central, because children represented posterity and the Nazi physicians considered the elimination of those they considered diseased and deformed as essential to their aim of racial purification. Although it is impossible to calculate the number of children killed in these special children's wards during World War II, the best estimate is that at least 5,000 German and Austrian children were killed in these programs.

Survivors

Nazi persecution, arrests, and deportations were directed against all members of Jewish families, as well as many Gypsy families, without concern for age. Inevitably the children were among the prisoners at highest risk. Homeless, often orphaned, they had frequently witnessed the murder of parents, siblings, and relatives. They faced starvation, illness, brutal labor, and other indignities until they were consigned to the gas chambers. In relationship to adult prisoners, their chances for survival were usually smaller although their flexibility and adaptability to radically changed circumstances could sometimes increase the odds in their favor. That these Jewish children survived at all and also created diaries, poems, and drawings in virtually all ghettos and concentration camps is truly remarkable.

*Jewish children in Birkenau after the camp was liberated. Very
few children survived the ghettos and concentration camps.*

After 1939, there are four basic patterns that can describe the fate of both Jewish and non-Jewish children in occupied Europe: (1) those killed immediately on arrival in concentration camps and killing centers; (2) those killed shortly after birth (for example, the 870 infants born in the Ravensbrück concentration camp, largely to Jewish and Gypsy women, between 1943 and 1945); (3) those few born in ghettos and camps and surviving, such as the three year old Stefan Georg Zweig born in the Cracow ghetto and carried in a specially prepared rucksack through the concentration camp at Plaszow to Buchenwald in 1944, where he was hidden and protected by German communist prisoners; and (4) those children, usually above the age of 10, utilized as prisoners, laborers, and subjects for Nazi medical experiments. Thus, of the 15,000 children imprisoned in the Theresienstadt ghetto, only about 1,100 survived.

Children sometimes also survived in hiding and also participated in the resistance (as runners, messengers, smugglers). There is no comprehensive study about the fate of children in Nazi Germany and occupied Europe, since the story has been told in an episodic fashion as part of the fate of Jews in each country affected.

A Child in the Convent

Jane Marks

Once Jews realized the danger posed by the Nazis, they would go to great lengths to save themselves and, especially, their children. Many Jews hid their identities and pretended to be non-Jews. Some went so far as to convert or hide in monasteries. This excerpt is the story of Renee Roth-Hano, whose family fled to Paris in 1940 and decided to send her and her sisters to a convent. Roth-Hano explains the conflict she felt as a Jew pretending to be a Catholic and the experience of hiding from the Germans. Jane Marks is a writer who has written a family therapy column for Parents *magazine and specializes in problems of children and families. Roth-Hano's story is just one of those of the hidden children she interviewed.*

 enee Roth-Hano, a psychiatric social worker and author, is tall, expressive, and friendly. . . .

"I was born in Mulhouse in 1931. Germany, moving fast after France lost the war, annexed Alsace, where we lived. A few days later, we were expelled. We took refuge in Paris, but it wasn't any real sanctuary. Fourteen major anti-Semitic decrees were passed between 1940, when we arrived in Paris, and 1942, when we

had to go into hiding. The one that bothered me most was the one that said I had to wear the Star of David. I was ten years old. I had always been a very inquisitive, outgoing kid, but wearing the star was like the final straw, the most damaging of all; it made me feel ashamed. I became very withdrawn.

"Six weeks later fourteen thousand Jews were arrested in a roundup. A secret maid's room was found for my parents to hide in. Meanwhile my two sisters and I were sent off to a convent called 'La Chaumière,' or 'The Cottage,' in Flers, a small town in Normandy. I resented the fact that my parents hadn't found another way to hide us. I knew that friends of ours and even relatives had managed to stay together as a family. I really felt abandoned, but I couldn't say so. As the eldest in the family, I understood that it was my job to maintain the family honor and take care of my two little sisters, Denise and Lily. It was a stiff-upper-lip kind of thing: I felt cornered and very burdened, but I had to make the best of it.

"Ours was not the usual kind of hiding: We were not in an attic or underground; we were in plain sight. What we were hiding was our Jewishness. We no longer wore the Star of David. We were passing for Catholics—and steeping ourselves in the Catholic religion. We learned catechism and we breathed the religion every day. Actually I found it comforting. My Jewishness had not been very firmly entrenched. Yes, we'd gone to temple for the holidays, and I hadn't liked the fact that women had to be separate from the men, which meant I couldn't stay with my father. So that was the only real feeling I had about my Jewishness.

"That was why I'd felt so incensed by the decrees, which were telling me, 'You are a Jew,' even though I didn't feel like a Jew and hadn't been raised as one. Still I had some scruples: I tried not to cross myself often or go in the front door, because if I did, I would have to genuflect. What I loved most was the singing. It made me feel like I belonged, which I needed desperately then. We sang hymns every evening, and I loved that. It wasn't so much God—I didn't believe in God. He was lousy to the Jews! But if you cannot pray to him, who can you pray to? At least when I was singing, there was hope coming from my heart. It was a way of begging God to listen. And as our voices harmonized, I didn't feel so alone or scared.

"On the whole the nuns were very good to us. Sister Pannelay, the Mother Superior, was very strict. One day she scolded my sister and me because my sister was massaging my legs. She was doing it only because I was freezing, but Sister Pannelay saw it as something sexual. She fiercely told us, 'Don't ever do that again!' I felt hurt, embarrassed, and misunderstood. It was only in later years that I could think of Sister Pannelay with real gratitude, understanding that it was she who had taken us into the convent—and saved our lives!

"There was another nun, Sister Madeleine, who was extra nice. We were often hungry, but we children were not supposed to ask for extra food. Sometimes Sister Madeleine would scream to summon my sisters and me to the kitchen. She made it sound as if she were scolding us. Once we were safely out of sight of the others, she would give us special treats, such as eggs. She was wonderful. A couple of times she baked cakes and sent them to my parents!

"Still, I felt sad and frightened. I mostly kept to myself, afraid to make any real friends among the other children, who had no idea that I was Jewish. I didn't want to blow my cover. . . .

"During that time at the convent we had very little contact with my parents. Letters had to be perfunctory because all mail was censored. My father looked and sounded too obviously Jewish to risk going anywhere. But he wouldn't even write to us because he was ashamed of his written French. My mother wrote, but during the two years she only came to visit us once. That visit was a disaster for me. She found lice in my hair and cut it all off. I cried so! I wished she hadn't come. I was twelve years old at that time and had a crush on a boy named Marcel. I was so mortified that he would see me looking ugly without my hair. I tried to hide, but he saw me. He was so sweet! He said, 'I really like that haircut.'

Baptism of Fire

"Soon after that I was baptized. The Germans were now in the town, and baptism was meant to make me more like the other children and consequently safer. But I was filled with fear. I thought, Once you're baptized, that's it. I had guilty visions of flying up to heaven without my parents. I was in anguish, but I couldn't tell anyone. I had terrible anxiety attacks, and once I was found sleepwalking in the graveyard. Then I got sick with jaundice for sixty days. I was sure I would die.

"Fortunately I recovered. The nuns said it was a miracle. I felt grateful. Three weeks later the Allied troops landed. It was late afternoon. The nun tried to shoo me outside to play with the other children, but I was worried. I wanted to stay near the kitchen to hear the news on the radio. All during supper I was frightened. Afterward I looked outside and I saw this formation of planes come in—like a flock of birds! Then I saw the planes stop, and the bombs fall. I saw it happening! I started to scream: '*Au secours*! Help!' Then the bombing grew more intense. We were bombed for three solid days. Again I thought I was going to die. On D-Day, June 6th, I made a vow: 'God, if you get me out of this one, I promise to become a nun.' From that moment on I was totally committed.

"Shortly after D-Day the police came to the convent to tell us to go and hide in the country. It seemed that the convent was near an ammunition depot targeted by the English. The nuns told us to run and get a change of clothing and a blanket and come right back. Then we left. We hiked six miles to the farm of a lady named Madame Huet, who supplied milk to the convent. There all thirty of us children and the nuns joined a great many other local people, who were also taking refuge. It was something! We had lice, fleas, and worms. . . .

"At first we'd had rations of food, but then we hit bottom. There was nothing left. We didn't even have water. There was a pump, but it was full of rust. German soldiers, who were on the run from the British, would come out of the woods and try to steal the few potatoes still growing, but Madame Huet faced them down, telling them they should be ashamed of themselves for stealing food from children. Toward the end we were so weak, we didn't get up in the morning. Sympathetic, the nuns told us, 'Stay where you are.'

"Finally the war was over. Relieved, we all trekked back to the convent. A real shock awaited us. The entire town was destroyed. Only one wall of the convent and the statue of the Virgin Mary were still standing, nothing else! . . .

To Be or Not to Be a Jew

"Soon after that my sisters and I were reunited with our parents. But even though the war was over and I no longer needed to hide my Jewishness, I felt ashamed of being a Jew. For years I told people I was Catholic. Even as I turned eighteen, I lived in terror that they would find out the truth and ridicule me. It was painful keeping that secret; it was always a barrier in my mind that prevented me from getting close to anyone. I felt so conflicted! I had not forgotten my earlier vow to become a nun. For five years I walked around thinking, I don't want to be a nun, but feeling that I was compelled to make good on my promise. Then one day the calling left—and I felt totally empty and depressed, like I had no belief in anything. I didn't know where

I belonged either.

"When I was nineteen, I came to the United States by chance, as a governess. One day something amazing happened. I was at Macy's in the early spring—I thought in terms of Easter. There were two ladies at the cosmetics counter, one actually hollering to the other, 'How was your seder last night?' I froze. I thought, 'Wait! You can't talk about a seder here, in public!' I gasped. But nobody minded. I said to myself, 'My God, it's wonderful! Nobody's even ashamed.' The two women went on talking like it was no big thing. I felt something inside me breaking free.

"Since then the process of reaccepting myself has continued. I became a psychiatric social worker. Maybe that was my way of being a nun after all! I found I could relate well to anybody feeling oppressed, and I could help them with real understanding. . . .

My sister, Lily, who lives in France, doesn't consider herself Jewish, nor do her kids. One of them actually makes anti-Semitic comments, and she doesn't stop him. Recently she said to me, 'For many French people it's still a calamity to marry a Jew.' I've tried to tell her, 'It's okay to be a Jew—to be anything you are.' But she doesn't know what I'm talking about.

"In the last decade my healing and happiness have grown deeper. I married an accountant named John. . . . I also wrote an autobiographical children's book, *Touch Wood: A Girlhood in Occupied France*. . . . In November 1991 the town of Flers held a special event to honor me. There was a dinner, and they presented me with a medal. . . .

"Now I feel so close to the people of Flers. I'm a special citizen of the town. I almost feel like when I die, I want to be buried there. It's so healing at this point in my life to learn that I can be completely honest and open about myself and still be liked. How strange—and also wonderful—to find that I'm rewarded for the very thing that I had once been made to feel so very much ashamed of!"

Selection 3

Coming of Age in Auschwitz

Livia E. Bitton Jackson

This excerpt gives a survivor's detailed account of what it was like to be a woman in a concentration camp. It is immediately evident that women had to contend with humiliations, degradations, and physical changes that men did not. For example, it was not as traumatic for men to have their heads shaved. For women, it altered their appearance to the extent that they were virtually unrecognizable even to their families. Men lost weight and often became walking skeletons, yet the psychological impact was not the same as it was for women, who stopped looking like women. Livia E. Bitton Jackson was only thirteen when the Germans deported the Jews from her Hungarian town. She was sent to Auschwitz, Plaszow, and Dachau before being liberated. Her aunt was gassed at Auschwitz and her father died in Bergen-Belsen two days before the camp was liberated. Her mother and brother survived.

Sometime during the fourth night, the train comes to a halt. We are suddenly awakened by the noise of sliding doors thrown open and cold night air rushing into the wagon. . . .

Excerpted from Livia E. Bitton Jackson, "Coming of Age," in editors Carol Rittner and John Roth, *Different Voices—Women and the Holocaust.* Copyright © 1993 Paragon House. Reprinted with permission from Livia E. Bitton Jackson.

A rough voice [shouts orders at us]. A figure clad in a striped uniform. Standing in the wide open doorway, his back illuminated by an eerie, diffused light, the man looks like a creature from another planet. . . .

Two or three other striped figures leap into the wagon and begin shoving the drowsy men, women, and children out into the cold night.

A huge sign catches my eye: AUSCHWITZ.

The pain in my stomach sends a violent wave of nausea up my gullet.

The night is chilly and damp. An other-worldly glow lights up tall watchtowers, high wire fences, an endless row of cattle cars, SS men, their dogs, a mass of people pouring out of the wagons. . . .

Metal buttons glisten on SS uniforms.

"My things! I left everything in the wagon!"

"On line! Everyone stand on line! By fives! Men over there! Women and children over here!"

"The diapers! I forgot the diapers in the wagon!" Young Mrs. Lunger starts for the wagon at a run, a child in each hand. Little Frumet is crying but Yingele is fast asleep on her shoulder. The man in the striped suit holds her back. "You won't need any diapers."

"But I do. Both children are in diapers. I brought a large bundle of diapers along. Let me get them, please . . . please!"

"You are not allowed to go back to the wagon.

Stay on line right here! Where you are going, you won't need any diapers."

Mrs. Lunger's beautiful brown eyes open wide with astonishment. Uncomprehending, she hesitantly joins the others on the line. I stand behind her and her mother-in-law and the two Lunger girls. Lunger *bácsi* is on the other side of the tracks. Mommy and Szerén *néni* and I make only three. Two more women are shoved alongside us to make it five. My brother is hustled farther, on the other side of the tracks. He tries to say good-bye to us and trips on the wire flanking the tracks. Daddy's new gray hat rolls off his head. He reaches to pick it up. An SS man kicks him in the back sending him tumbling on the tracks. Mother gasps. Szerén *néni* cries a shriek and grasps Mommy's arm. I hold my mouth: A spasm of nausea hurls a charge of vomit up my throat. . . .

The column of women, children, infants begins to move. Dogs snarl, SS men scream orders, children cry, women weep good-byes to departing men, and I struggle with my convulsing stomach. And I march on. Behind the lovely young Mrs. Lunger with her two little children on her arms and the oldest one hanging on to her skirt. Behind Mrs. Bonyhádi and her Tommi and Suzie docilely marching in the line before them. Next to me Mommy is silently supporting Aunt Szerén by the shoulder. I march and the sights and sounds of Auschwitz only dimly penetrate my consciousness. Daylight is slowly skirting the clouds, and it turns suddenly very cold. We left our coats in the wagons. We were ordered to leave our belongings behind. Everything. We will get them later, they told us. How will they find what belongs to whom? There was such wild confusion at the tram. Perhaps they will sort things out. The Germans must have a system. Leave it to them. The famous German order.

The marching column comes to a sudden halt.

An officer in gray SS uniform stares facing the lines of women and children. Dogs straining on short leashes held by SS soldiers flank him on both sides. He stops each line and regroups them. Some to his right and some to his left. Then he orders each group to march on. I tremble as I stand before him. He looks at me with a soft look in friendly eyes.

"*Goldene Haar!*" he exclaims as he takes one of my long braids into his hand. I am not certain I heard it right Did he say "golden hair" about my braids?

"*Bist du Jüdin?*" Are you Jewish?

The question startles me. "Yes, I am Jewish."

"*Wie alt bist du?*" How old are you?

"I am thirteen."

"You are tall for your age. Is this your mother?" He touches Mommy lightly on the shoulder: "You go with your mother." With his riding stick he parts Szeren *néni* from my mother's embrace and gently shoves Mommy and me to the group moving to the right.

"Go, and remember, from now on you are sixteen."

Szerén *néni*'s eyes fill with terror. She runs to Mommy and grabs her arm.

"Don't leave me, Lórika! Don't leave me!"

Mother embraces her fragile, older sister and turns to the SS officer, her voice a shrieking plea:

"This is my sister, *Herr Offizier*, let me go with her! She is not feeling well. She needs me."

"You go with your daughter. She needs you more. March on! *Los!*" With an impatient move of his right hand he shoves Mother toward me. Then he glares angrily at my aunt: "Move on! *Los!* You go that way!" His stick points menacingly to the left.

Aunt Szerén, a forlorn, slight figure against the marching multitude, the huge German shepherd dogs, the husky SS men. A savage certainty slashes my bruised insides. I will never again see my darling aunt! I give an insane shriek: "Szerén *néni!* Szerén *néni!* I'll never see you again!"

A wild fear floods her large hazel eyes. She stretches out her arms to reach me. An SS soldier gives her a brutal thrust, hurling her into the line marching to the left. She turns again, mute fear lending her added fragility. She moves on.

The road to the left leads to the gas chambers. . . .

A New Life

Our march to the right slows to a halt. A tall, metal gate looms darkly ahead. Above it huge

metal letters arch like a sinister crown:
ARBEIT MACHT FREI!

Work sets you free! Perhaps Mommy was right. We will work. And be treated like human beings. Fed and clothed. But "*frei*"? Free? What do they mean by that? Will they really let us move about freely if we work? Where?

The immense portals of the gate open and we march through them into an enclosure with tall wire fences. Several rows of wire. Plain wire fence flanked by barbed wire.

It's growing lighter rapidly. And colder. I wonder when we will get our things. I need my coat. The eerie light of the watchtowers grows dimmer. Rows of barracks, long, flat buildings, on both sides of the black pebble-strewn road enclosed in barbed wire. It's a road without an end. It stretches far into the fog. And we march.

Motorcycles. SS officers. Dogs. . . .

It's cold. We march on.

Groups of people linger about the barracks on the other side of the fence. Are they men or women? Their heads are shorn but they wear gray, dresslike cloaks. They run to the fence as we pass. They stare at us. Blank stares. They must be insane. This must be an asylum for the mentally ill. Poor souls.

The road ends. Our silent, rapid march ends. By fives we file through the entrance of a long, flat gray building. . . .

The buxom SS woman begins to swing her whip above the heads, and the other SS soldiers in the room, as if on cue, begin cracking their whips, snapping into faces. A sharp pain slashes at my left cheekbone. I feel a firm welt rise across my face. . . . "*Sich auskleiden! Alles herunter!*" Get undressed, everybody! Take off everything! "*Los!*"

The room is swarming with SS men. Get undressed, here? In front of the men? No one moves.

"Didn't you hear? Take off your clothes. All your clothes!"

I feel the slap of a whip on my shoulders and meet a young SS soldier's glaring eyes.

"Hurry! Strip fast. You will be shot. Those having any clothes on in five minutes will be shot!"

I look at Mommy. She nods. Let's get undressed. I stare directly ahead as I take off my clothes. I am afraid. By not looking at anyone I hope no one will see me. I have never seen my mother in the nude. How awful it must be for her. I hesitate before removing my bra. My breasts are two growing buds, taut and sensitive. I can't have anyone see them. I decide to leave my bra on.

Just then a shot rings out. The charge is ear-shattering. Some women begin to scream. Others weep. I quickly take my bra off.

It is chilly and frightening. Clothes lie in mounds on the cement floor. We are herded, over a thousand, shivering, humiliated nude bodies, into the next hall, even chillier. More foreboding. It is darker here. Barer.

"*Los! Schneller, blöde Lumpen!*" Faster. Move faster, idiotic whores.

The Loss of Individuality

We are lined up and several husky girls in gray cloaks begin shaving our hair—on our heads, under the arms, and on the pubic area. My long, thick braids remain braided and while the shaving machine shears my scalp, the hair remains hanging, tugging at the roots. The pain of the heavy braid tugging mercilessly at the yet unshaven roots brings tears to my eyes. I pray for the shaving to be done quickly. As my blonde tresses lie in a large heap on the ground, the indifferent hair butcher remarks: "A heap of gold." In a shudder I remember the scene at the selection—the SS officer's admiration of my "golden hair," the separation from Aunt Szerén. Where is she now? Is her hair shorn off and is she stripped of her clothes, too? Is she very frightened? Poor, darling, Szerén *néni*. If my hair were shorn before the selection, we would be together with her now. We would not have been separated. It's because of my blonde hair that Mommy and I were sent to the other side. Poor darling. If only we could have stayed together!

The haircut has a startling effect on every woman's appearance. Individuals become a mass of bodies. Height, stoutness, or slimness: There is no distinguishing factor—it is the absence of hair which transformed individual women into like bodies. Age and other personal differences melt away. Facial expressions disappear. Instead, a blank, senseless stare emerges on a thousand faces of one naked, unappealing body. In a matter of minutes even the physical aspect of our numbers seems reduced—there is less of a substance to our dimensions. We become a monolithic mass. Inconsequential.

From *blöde Lumpen*, "idiotic whores," we became *blöde Schweine*, "idiotic swine." Easier to despise. And the epithet changed only occasionally to *blöde Hunde*, "idiotic dogs." Easier to handle.

The shaving had a curious effect. A burden was lifted. The burden of individuality. Of associations. Of identity. Of the recent past. Girls who have continually wept at separation from parents, sisters and brothers now began to giggle at the strange appearance of their friends. Some shriek with laughter. Others begin calling out names of friends to see if they can recognize them shorn and stripped. When response to names comes forth from completely transformed bodies, recognition is loud, hysterical. Wild, noisy embraces. Shrieking, screaming disbelief. Some girls bury their faces in their palms and howl, rolling on the ground.

"*Was ist los?*" What's the matter? A few swings of the SS whip restores order.

I look for Mommy. I find her easily. The haircut has not changed her. I have been used to seeing her in kerchiefs, every bit of hair carefully tucked away. Avoiding a glance at her body, I marvel at the beauty of her face. With all accessories gone her perfect features are even more striking. Her high forehead, large blue eyes, classic nose, shapely lips and elegant cheekbones are more evident than ever.

She does not recognize me as I stand before her. Then a sudden smile of recognition: "Elli! It's you. You look just like Bubi. Strange, I have never seen the resemblance before. What a boyish face! They cut off your beautiful braids. . . ."

"It's nothing. Hair can grow."

"With the will of God."

We are herded en masse into the next hall. Clutching a cake of claylike object handed to me

at the door, the nude mass of bodies crushing about me, I shriek with sudden shock as a cold torrent gushes unexpectedly from openings in the ceiling. In a few minutes it is over, and once again we are rushed into another room. Gray dresses are handed to us and we are urged with shouts of *Los!* and *blöde Schweine* to pull them over wet, shivering bodies. Everyone has to pick a pair of shoes from an enormous shoe pile. "*Los! Los!*"

As we emerge, still wet, in gray sacks, with clean-shaven heads, from the other end of the building and line up, by now relatively quickly, in rows of five, the idea strikes me. The people we saw as we entered the camp, the shaved, gray-cloaked group which ran to stare at us through the barbed-wire fence, they were us! We look exactly like them. Same bodies, same dresses, same blank stares. We, too, look like an insane horde—soulless, misshapen figures. . . .

The *Zehlappel* lasts almost three hours. This word, meaning "roll call," became the dread and the life style of Auschwitz. Twice daily we would be lined up with lightning speed by fives in order to be counted. Lined up at 3 A.M. We would stand three or four hours until the official SS staff showed up to count our heads. In the evening it lasted from five to nine. The lineup had to be accomplished in seconds in order to stand endless hours awaiting the roll call, *Zehlappel*.

It was inconceivable to me that the mad rush inside the showers would culminate in an endless wait outside. We bodies in a single loose cotton robe exposed to the chill morning, traumatized bodies hurled out to the cold wind to stand in a senseless, long wait.

The smartly stepping German staff appears briskly. With the tip of a stick lightly touching the head of the first girl in every row of five, we are counted and officially initiated into the camp. We become members of an exclusive club. Inmates of Auschwitz. . . .

Life Changes

Three weeks pass and I do not menstruate. Neither does anyone else. With amazement we all realize that menstruation ceased in the camps. The first week after our arrival there were many menstruant women, even in the wagon on our way to Plaszow there were several girls who bled profusely. Then, menstruation ceased abruptly. There is bromide in our food, we are told by old-timers. Bromide is supposed to sterilize women. The Germans are experimenting with mass sterilization.

The information causes panic among the inmates and at first many refuse to eat the cooked food, determined to survive on the bread ration alone. Soon hunger wins, and the food is consumed as before. The whole sterilization story may be just a rumor anyway.

I am secretly grateful for the bromide. Avoiding the fear, pain and embarrassment of menstruation is worth any sacrifice to me at the moment.

But the topic does not die. Married women keep wondering about the bromide in their food again and again. Will they bear children again? What will their husbands say when they find out? Perhaps less of the food will cause less of a damage. Some try to eat less and the conflict is painful. Rejection of a means of survival for the sake of a dubious gain.

No one can help. Rumors have no way of being checked. The old-timers, mostly Polish Jews who have been in the camps for over two years, bitterly resent us, Hungarian Jews. They are bitter about the fact that we arrived only recently. We lived in the security and comfort of our homes for the past two years while they were exposed to the torture of the camps. "You went to the theaters and resorts in Hungary, while our families were shot and burned, and we suffered in the camps," they would say to us. Then they would dramatize the dangers of the camp. They would tell us to forget our families, we will never see them again. Whoever was separated from us was promptly killed. They hinted darkly at the gas chambers and crematoriums. They told of torture of children. Of medical experiments. They told us we were fortunate our children were killed by gas and then burned. Their children were shot and often tortured or burned alive. Years ago there were no gas chambers, only crematoriums, and whole families were burned in them alive.

When I first heard some of these things I could not sleep. Everyone of us believed they were untrue and told to us by the Polish Jews in order to torture us, to avenge our "soft life." But I wondered. I sensed an ominous, horrible ring of truth to their words. . . .

Every night I used to cry myself to sleep. In the morning Mommy would say it is all nonsense. Of course, they are all lies. Incredible, cruel lies. The Polish Jews knew we were ignorant about the camps and were trying to frighten us. Everyone knew the things they said were lies. So was the rumor about bromide in the food. We stopped menstruating because we are near starvation. We lost weight and our organs are too weak to function properly. Look what happened to our breasts.

Mommy was right in that. The breasts began to sag at first and then became virtual hanging sacks. Some very fat ladies had the most ridiculously hanging empty sacks, like long, narrow, stretched-out empty balloons weighed down by a single marble in each, reaching almost to the navel. Then the empty sacks became shorter. Eventually the skin, too, was absorbed and the breasts disappeared completely. We were all like men. Flat. In time the bones began to protrude and shrunken skin lay taut on every pointed bulge.

It is true. Even our stomachs slowed down in time. Hunger became less nagging, and the fullness of the stomach after the evening meal—less satisfying. The women stopped "cooking up" imaginary meals during work, and talk about food became less frequent.

Even talk about our families lessens. We think about them less frequently. We think less and talk less in general.

There remains only our daily routine—the *Zehlappel*, the work commandos, the evening meal. Dodging the more difficult commandos and making every effort to get into lighter ones.

In time we discover that there are less cruel *Kapos* [prisoners in charge of other inmates], easier work, a longer lunch period. There are *Arbeitführers* [work supervisors] who actually talk to you in polite tones, and get two cauldrons of food instead of one for their commando. There are ways to avoid the worst *Kapos* and to be picked by the nicer ones. In time we learn the game of the camp. This game is the stuff of our life. Beyond it things start to matter less and less.

The stone commando is the worst. We are lined up in a chain reaching the top of a steep hill. From the bottom of the hill large rocks have to be passed through the chain up to the top. The rocks are heavy and the *Kapo* of the stone commando, the most tyrannical. He murdered his father and would boast about it when administering some especially cruel punishment. He demands that the stones be passed quickly. If a stone is dropped, it hurtles against the women below. Work on the stone chain is the dread of the camp.

When Mother and I are picked up for the stone commando, she would order me to pass only the smaller stones, and the larger ones she would pass to the girl beyond me, skipping me. This would be dreadful. Mother would have to lean forward with the heavy rock, balancing it precariously, while the girl above me would have to lean down to receive it from her hand, causing additional burden to her. I would then insist on passing the large rocks and Mother would angrily ignore me. This caused me so much hurt and anxiety that my dread of the stone commando turned into perpetual nightmare. But Mother would not yield. She did not understand that it is easier to bear the heavy stones than her indulgence at the expense of her effort and that of another woman.

There are days when we managed to move a huge hill of rocks to the top of the mountain, and the following day we are ordered to move it down again to the foot of the mountain. With the same speed. . . .

One of the commandos is digging up graves in the nearby Krakow Jewish cemetery. It is being turned into a new concentration camp, an extension to the ground we are leveling for construction. Work in this commando is easier because the large monuments afford shade and hiding places for occasional rest. To me, however, this is the most difficult work. Sometimes you dig up small bones and skulls. The bones of children. Of infants. Despite lowered sensitivity, I am still pained by handling these bones. Despite a lack of contemplative powers, I think about the skeletons long after I am supposed to sleep.

Once I was picked for the cleaning commando, the favorite of commandos. It is a small commando in charge of cleaning the barracks of the Germans. We are given pails and washcloths and told to scrub the floors in about fifty barracks. At noon we are given scraps from the meals of the German soldiers. This makes it into a dream commando. But that day it was Tish'a B'Av, and I was fasting. With tears of regret I gave my lunch to another girl. This is my destiny. Two thousand years ago, the Romans picked the day when I was to taste real food to destroy the Temple in Jerusalem.

One hot day in July our lunch is interrupted by the arrival of large-covered trucks rolling into the square. We have been working in *Planierung* [digging and leveling] right above the camp and have our lunch on the shady slope directly opposite the center square of the camp. Men and women in civilian clothes descend from the trucks and are herded into the command barrack. They are well-dressed and have an air of independence about them. Like people. Not like camp inmates.

One of the men makes a defiant gesture as an SS man shoves him forward with the point of his gun. The civilian, a man in a light gray trench coat, turns and shoves the German soldier. A shot is heard and the civilian collapses. Then he stands up and begins to run. Another shot. He tumbles. A third shot levels him prone on the ground. He begins to crawl, drawing a line of red in the dust. The SS soldier goes wild. He discharges a barrage of bullets into the crawling figure, then starts kicking him uncontrollably. The others are herded into the barrack of the SS command and the single figure remains lying in the dust in the center of the square, a pool of blood ever widening about him.

We go on eating. There is no time to pause: This is Jacko's commando and the lunch hour is short.

Anne Frank's Last Words

Anne Frank

Anne Frank was born in 1929 in Frankfurt am Main, Germany. When Hitler came to power, Anne's parents, Edith and Otto Frank, decided to flee to the Netherlands in 1933. Anne was four years old. Her childhood was safe and carefree until 1940, when Germany occupied the country and began to institute anti-Jewish regulations. Beginning in 1942, Jews began to receive notices to report for the "work" camp Westerbork. It was virtually impossible to escape Holland, and the penalty for refusing to report was death, so most Jews did so. Those who did not, had to find a place to hide. On July 6, 1942, the Franks hid in the annex of the building that housed Otto's business. For two years they were cut off from the outside world, having to face hunger, boredom, the pressure of living in a confined space, and the fear of being caught. On August 4, 1944, the security police discovered the annex, and Anne Frank and the seven others in hiding were arrested and sent to a series of concentration camps. Only her father survived the camps. After the war, he decided to publish the diary Anne kept for the two years they spent in the attic. The following excerpt is the last entry in the diary, written three days before she was arrested.

*D*ear Kitty [the name given to her diary],
"Little bundle of contradictions." That's how I ended my last letter and that's how I'm going to begin this one. "A little bundle of contradictions," can you tell me exactly what it is? What does contradiction mean? Like so many words, it can mean two things; contradiction from without and contradiction from within.

The first is the ordinary "not giving in easily; always knowing best, getting in the last word," *enfin*, all, the unpleasant qualities for which I'm renowned. The second nobody knows about, that's my own secret.

I've already told you before that I have, as it were, a dual personality. One half embodies my exuberant cheerfulness, making fun of everything, my high-spiritedness, and above all, the way I take everything lightly. This includes not taking offense at a flirtation, a kiss, an embrace, a dirty joke. This side is usually lying in wait and pushes away the other, which is much better, deeper, and purer. You must realize that no one knows Anne's better side and that's why most people find me so insufferable.

Certainly, I'm a giddy clown for one afternoon, but then everyone's had enough of me for another month. Really, it's just the same as a love film is for deep-thinking people simply a diversion, amusing just for once, something which is soon forgotten, not bad, but certainly not good. I loathe having to tell you this, but why shouldn't I, if I know it's true anyway? My

Anne Frank

lighter superficial side will always be too quick for the deeper side of me and that's why it will always win. You can't imagine how often I've already tried to push this Anne away, to cripple her, to hide her, because after all, she's only half of what's called Anne: but it doesn't work and I know, too, why it doesn't work.

I'm awfully scared that everyone who knows me as I always am will discover that I have another side, a finer and better side. I'm afraid they'll laugh at me, think I'm ridiculous and sentimental, not take me seriously. I'm used to not being taken seriously but it's only the "light-hearted" Anne that's used to it and can bear it; the "deeper" Anne is too frail for it. Sometimes, if I really compel the good Anne to take the stage for a quarter of an hour, she simply shrivels up as soon as she has to speak, and lets Anne number one take over, and before, I realize it, she has disappeared.

Therefore, the nice Anne is never present in company, has not appeared one single time so far, but almost always predominates when we're alone: I know exactly how I'd like to be; how I am too . . . inside. But, alas, I'm only like that for myself. And perhaps that's why, no, I'm sure it's the reason why I say I've got a happy nature within and why other people think I've got a happy nature without. I am guided by the pure Anne within, but outside I'm nothing but a frolicsome little goat who's broken loose.

As I've already said, I never utter my real feelings about anything and that's how I've acquired the name of chaser-after-boys, flirt, know-all, reader of love stories. The cheerful Anne laughs about it, gives cheeky answers, shrugs her shoulders indifferently, behaves as if she doesn't care, but, oh dearie me, the quiet Anne's reactions are just the opposite. If I'm to be quite honest, then I must admit that it does hurt me; that I try terribly hard to change myself; but that I'm always fighting against a more powerful enemy.

A voice sobs within me: "There you are, that's what's become of you: you're uncharitable, you look supercilious and peevish, people dislike you and all because you won't listen to the advice given you by your own better half." Oh, I would like to listen, but it doesn't work; if I'm quiet and serious, everyone thinks it's a new comedy and then I have to get out of it by turning it into a joke, not to mention my own family, who are sure to think I'm ill, make me swallow pills for headaches and nerves, feel my neck and my head to see whether I'm running a temperature, ask if I'm constipated and criticize me for being in a bad mood. I can't keep that up: if I'm watched to that extent, I start by getting snappy, then unhappy, and finally I twist my heart round again, so that the bad is on the outside and the good is on the inside and keep on trying to find a way of becoming what I would so like to be, and what I could be, if . . . there weren't any other people living in the world.

Yours, Anne

Selection 5

The Diary of Mary Berg

Mary Berg

The diary of Anne Frank is famous. Anne's story has been made into a successful stage play and movie. Less well known is the story of another teenager who kept a diary during the war. Fortunately, her story has a happier ending. This young woman was an American living in Poland, and she kept a diary chronicling the horrors Jews suffered in the Warsaw ghetto. Her name was Mary Berg. In July 1942 the Bergs were told that all foreigners who had their papers in order would be exchanged for Germans held by the Allies. Mary's family, along with the other foreigners, were then put in Pawiak prison. In January 1943 the Germans decided to release all of the Americans. More than a year later, the Bergs were allowed to go to the United States, nearly three and a half years after being sent to the ghetto. This brief excerpt from Berg's diary covers the summer of 1942, when she was in prison.

President Adam Czerniakow has committed suicide. He did it last night, on July 23. He could not bear his terrible burden. According to the rumors that have reached us here, he took his tragic step when the Germans demanded that the contingents of deportees be increased. He saw no other way out

Excerpted from Mary Berg, *Warsaw Ghetto* (NY: L.B. Fischer, 1945).

than to leave this horrible world. His closest collaborators, who saw him shortly before his death, say that he displayed great courage and energy until the last moment.

The community has elected a new president to replace Czerniakow. He is old Lichtenbaum, whose son, Engineer Lichtenbaum, is the director of the Construction Office of the community. . . .

August, 1942

Behind the Pawiak [prison] gate we are experiencing all the terror that is abroad in the ghetto. For the last few nights we have been unable to sleep. The noise of the shooting, the cries of despair, are driving us crazy. I have to summon all my strength to write these notes. I have lost count of the days, and I do not know what day it is. But what does it matter? We are here as on a little island amidst an ocean of blood. The whole ghetto is drowning in blood. We literally see fresh human blood, we can smell it. Does the outside world know anything about it? Why does no one come to our aid? I cannot go on living; my strength is exhausted. How long are we going to be kept here to witness all this?

A few days ago, a group of neutrals was taken out of the Pawiak. Apparently the Germans were unable to use them for exchange. I saw from my window several trucks filled with people, and I tried to distinguish familiar faces among them. Some time later, the prison guard came panting to us, and told us that the Jewish citizens of neutral European countries had just been taken to the *Umschlagplatz* [collection point] to be deported.

So our turn may come soon, too. I hope it will be very soon. This waiting is worse than death. . . .

Work Means Life?

The Germans have blockaded entire streets in the ghetto. Since the 10,000 people a day they are now demanding have failed to report, the Nazis are using force. Every day they besiege another street, closing all the exits. They enter the apartments, and check the labor cards. Those who do not possess the necessary documents or who, according to the Germans' estimate, are unqualified for work, are taken away at once. Those who try to resist are shot on the spot.

Just now, while I am writing this, such a blockade is taking place on Nowolipie Street, only two blocks from our prison. It has been going on for two days now. The street is completely closed; only the Jewish policemen are allowed to use it.

The wives and children of the men employed in the German factories in the ghetto are officially exempt from deportation, but this exemption is effective only on paper. In actual fact, a husband returning home from work often finds that his whole family has been taken away. He runs in despair to Stawki Street to find his kin, but instead of being able to rescue them he himself is often pushed into one of the cattle cars.

The German factories in the ghetto now work twelve hours a day, with only one hour's rest. The workers receive a quart of watery soup and a quarter of a pound of bread a day. But despite their hunger and slavery, these workers are among the luckiest in the ghetto, for their jobs protect them from deportation. . . .

Good-Bye Children

Dr. Janusz Korczak's children's home is empty now. A few days ago we all stood at the window and watched the Germans surround the houses. Rows of children, holding each other by their little hands, began to walk out of the doorway. There were tiny tots of two or three years among them, while the oldest ones were perhaps thirteen. Each child carried a little bundle in his hand. All of them wore white aprons. They walked in ranks of two, calm, and even smiling. They had not the slightest foreboding of their fate. At the end of the procession marched Dr. Korczak, who saw to it that the children did not walk on the sidewalk. Now and then, with fatherly solicitude, he stroked a child on the head or arm, and straightened out the ranks. . . . They went in the direction of Gesia Street, to the cemetery. At the cemetery all the children were shot. We were also told by our informants that Dr. Korczak was forced to witness the executions, and that he himself was shot afterward.

Thus died one of the purest and noblest men who ever lived. He was the pride of the ghetto. His children's home gave us courage, and all of us gladly gave part of our own scanty means to support the model home organized by this great idealist. He devoted all his life, all his creative work as an educator and writer, to the poor children of Warsaw. Even at the last moment he refused to be separated from them. . . .

The "Lucky" Prisoners

Our family of internees in the Pawiak now numbers sixty-four persons. . . .

We are allowed to go out in the prison yard only once a day. We walk for an hour between the laundry and our building. . . .

Last night was horrible. It was stuffier than ever. We lay naked on our straw bags. The atmosphere was so thick that it could almost be cut with a knife. Through the window a patch of blue sky and a few stars could be seen. Not the slightest noise came from the street. None of us could sleep.

At about eleven o'clock we suddenly heard the heavy screech of a lock opening, and two persons left by one of the prison gates. The heavy steps of soldierly boots could be clearly distinguished from the small steps of a woman. The steps came gradually closer to our windows. Then we heard a woman's tearful voice and several words pronounced in a German-Yiddish accent. . . . But suddenly these words were drowned by the sound of revolver shots. The first shot resounded high in the air near our window, the second was lower, and the third level with the pavement, as though the soldier were firing at the unfortunate woman as she lay on the ground. Then we heard muffled noises, which might have been kicks, and then, finally, there was silence. . . .

The shootings and the cries coming from the streets are slowly driving us mad. The nights are horrible. Last night nearly forty persons were shot under our windows. All of them were men. The slaughter lasted for two hours or more. The murderers finished off their victims with kicks and with blows with the butts of their guns. . . .

Roundups

September 19, 1942

My mother lies on her mattress all day long; she is so starved that she cannot move. Ann [Mary's sister] is like a shadow, and my father is terribly thin, just skin and bones. I seem to bear the hunger better than the others. I just grit my teeth when the gnawing feeling in my stomach begins. At night I begin to wait for the next morning, when we are given our four ounces of bread and the bitter water that is called coffee. Then I wait for lunch at noon, when we are brought our first soup, a dish of hot water with a few grains of kasha. Then again I wait impatiently for the evening, when we get our second dish of hot water with a potato or a beet. The days are endless, and the nights even more so, and full of nightmares The shootings continue, hundreds of people are perishing daily. The ghetto is drenched in blood. People are constantly marching along Dzielna Street toward the *Umschlagplatz* on Stawki Street. No job or occupation is a complete protection any longer. Recently even the families of those employed have been deported, mostly the women and children.

A few weeks ago the Nazis began to round up the wives and children of the men working at Toebens and Schultz. Those who are not working are ruthlessly dragged away. Parents now take their children with them to their work, or hide them in some hole. . . .

September 20, 1942

There have been fewer shootings today. Resistance is subsiding. . . .

Engineer Lichtenbaum asked Mrs. W. whether she had been told by any of the prison officials what the Nazis were planning to do in the Warsaw ghetto. How absurd for him, a high community official, to ask us what is going to happen to the survivors in the ghetto! Is there still any doubt after what has happened before our very eyes? But everyone asks everyone else, hoping to hear a hopeful word.

According to Lichtenbaum and [his friend] First, more than 200,000 Jews have been deported, and more than 10,000 have been killed. Thus nearly 200,000 people still remain.

The underground movement has become more active than ever. Death sentences were carried out not only against the Nazis, Ukrainians, and Lithuanians who murdered the population during the bloody days, but also against the few Jews who allowed themselves to be used as Nazi tools during the massacre. Colonel Szerynski and several community officials are now on the black list. They know it, and dare not appear on the streets without armed bodyguards.

The Germans for their part are liquidating all the collaborators whom they can no longer use. They shoot them without ceremony, and their bodies are often found on the streets. . . .

The massacres have aroused the underground leaders to greater resistance. The illegal papers are multiplying and some of them reach us even here in the Pawiak. They are full of good reports from the battle fronts. The Allies are victorious in Egypt, and the Russians are pushing the enemy back at Moscow. The sheets explain the meaning of the deportations and tell of the fate of the deported Jews. The population is summoned to resist with weapons in their hands, and warned against defeatist moods, and against the idea that we are completely helpless before the Nazis. "Let us die like men and not like sheep," ends one proclamation in a paper called *To Arms!*

The situation improved somewhat in the last days of August, and some began to take an optimistic view of the future. But this was only the lull before the storm. On September 3 and 4 the Germans began to blockade the workshops organized by the community. Elite Guards, accompanied by Lithuanians and Ukrainians, entered the shops, and took several dozen people out of each, alleging that they needed skilled workers. These workers, numbering more than a thousand, were led away to Stawki Street and deported to the Treblinki camp.

Now it is generally known that most of the deportees are sent to Treblinki, where they are killed with the help of machines with which the Germans are experimenting for war purposes. But no one knows any details.

Selection 6

Distinctions Among Prisoners

Ruediger Lautmann

All concentration camp inmates were not created equal. Prisoners were given different badges to indicate different categories, such as political, criminal, antisocial, homosexual, Jewish, and Jehovah's Witness. The elderly and the young were also treated differently. This excerpt focuses on differences in the way gay prisoners were treated, especially compared with political prisoners and Jehovah's Witnesses. Ruediger Lautmann has written extensively on the treatment of gays in Nazi Germany.

*T*he concentration camp was one weapon in the campaign to bring state and society into conformity with fascism. If physical extermination formed the most frightful instrument of that policy, it was not the only one. A range of attempts were made to isolate people

Excerpted from Ruediger Lautmann, "Gay Prisoners in Concentration Camps as Compared with Jehovah's Witnesses and Political Prisoners," in editor Michael Berenbaum, *A Mosaic of Victims: Non-Jews Persecuted and Murdered by the Nazis* (NY: New York University Press, 1990). Reprinted with permission from New York University Press.

and to use fear to inhibit "undesirable" behavior. Whatever the reasons for imprisonment, all incarcerations were the result of Nazi ideology and posed a danger to the prisoner's life. The categories of prisoners differed from one another in how they were selected and treated. Those groups whom the Nazis deemed inimical but not racially undesirable were not completely rounded up, but taken only in random samples. They also fared differently within the camps. Homosexuals, political prisoners, and Jehovah's Witnesses are among the groups who were sent to the concentration camps for reeducation. They were supposed to renounce their particular orientation. . . .

Democratic freedom makes pluralism possible. In democracies, deviations from the norm concern not only criminality but also sexuality, ethnicity, religion, and attitudes toward work. The Nazi system was concerned with deviations in all these areas. It classified political, sexual, religious, and working-attitude deviations in separate categories. In all probability, the Hitlerian state required these definitions of the enemy and was, in its own terms, correct in its choice of these groups. Within a society, minority and separationist groups represent a seedbed of possible revolt. Homosexuality has always and everywhere existed. Hitler considered homosexuality as a predisposition that could not be changed. It was assumed that a homosexual orientation could not be eliminated, that only its manifestations could be blocked. Thus, the pink triangle worn by the homosexual in the concentration camp represented the Nazis' intention to reeducate him. Severe measures were in fact intended only as behavioristic conditioning: a way to cause unlearning through aversion.

No credence was placed in a simple change of opinion by homosexuals, such as was granted to Jehovah's Witnesses, who were not taken entirely seriously, or even to political prisoners. Two categories were seen among homosexuals: the constitutionally hard-boiled homosexual and the occasional offender. Since in neither case was the Aryan status of the homosexual in doubt, all could remain alive. If necessary, homosexuals were to be castrated, but they were permitted to continue to work. As a matter of policy, extermination was therefore restrained. In practice there were other contrary impulses on the part of the SS, and those who wore the pink triangle met an unusually harsh fate. The social controls directed at homosexuals within the camp represented a continuation and an intensification of social controls imposed by society at large. . . .

Social Controls

The concentration camp was an extreme instance of social control. It mixed ordinary and singular characteristics of social regulation. For example, it was and is "normal" to categorize and stigmatize people; it is "singular" to ascribe total uselessness to a certain group. It is "normal" to organize the life of an inmate; it is "singular" to view the life of a prisoner as being of almost no value. It is "normal" to devalue homosexual activities and to impose certain disadvantages on those who engage in them; it is "singular" to impose this devaluation by physical force and without constitutional procedures. It is "normal" (up to the present day) to stigmatize homosexuals; it is "singular" to attempt to eliminate homosexual life-styles and to destroy the subculture completely by organizing police raids.

The closer a prisoner's category was to the heart of Nazi ideology, the more dangerous his circumstances in the camp. Furthermore, the more repressively a group was controlled in society, the harder the fate of its members within the camp. Increasing the number of those sentenced, and imposing stricter rules in the military and party organizations, was followed by an increased death rate in the camp. The more marginal the social position of a group, the more marginal their position was within the camp.

The prisoners with the pink triangle had certainly shown "precamp" qualities of survival, but they did not get a chance to apply these qualities in the camp. Because their subculture and organizations outside had been wantonly destroyed, no group solidarity developed inside the camp. Since outside the concentration camp homosexuals were regarded as effete, they were given no tasks of self-administration inside the camps. Since every contact outside was regarded as suspicious, homosexuals did not even dare to speak to one another inside (as numerous survivors have reported in interviews). Since homosexuals were generally regarded as worthless, their fellow prisoners had a lower regard for them. Thus, few accounts of the pink triangles exist, and those that do exist have a spiteful flavor.

Differences Between Prisoner Categories

To regard the prisoners according to their categories means distinguishing between major and minor sufferings. Is that permissible? We could even ask: Is social science still possible after Auschwitz? Nevertheless, various developments have virtually given a positive answer to these questions. After 1945 differences in the fate of different groups of prisoners have been recognized by differences in compensation. Research, too, has given varying degrees of attention to the different groups of victims. The color of the assigned triangle (i.e., the prisoner category) was the basis for a collective fate. . . .

The individual pink-triangle prisoner was likely to live for only a short time in the camp and then to disappear from the scene. After four months, one in four had left; after a year, one in two. It was otherwise for the Jehovah Witnesses and politicals: after a year four out of five and two out of three, respectively, were still in the camp. This thinning out is due to deaths: three out of four deaths among the homosexuals occurred within the first year after their committal. In comparison with the red and violet triangles, the pink triangle seems to signify a category of less value. The destinies of Jews and homosexuals within the camp approximate each other. In the concentration camp, both groups found themselves at the bottom of the current hierarchy below the non-Jewish racially defined groups of prisoners.

The collective devaluation of the wearers of certain triangles supports the idea of a connection between internal camp treatment of the marginal groups and the sociostructural control they were subjected to in society at large. With regard to the homosexuals, there were many reports of how the SS deliberately treated them brutally and how the other prisoners looked down upon them. This contrasts with reports stating that Jehovah's Witnesses were admired outside the camp or that politicals were full of respect for one another's activities. . . .

There is a tendency of the literature to associate the pink triangle with the criminal green. The few surviving pink-triangle wearers were treated similarly by state and society after 1945, when cautious attempts toward compensation were finally and definitely rejected. Interviews with such survivors revealed that for many years they never told anyone they had been in a concentration camp. The extreme devaluation was accepted as a self-evaluation. Gay interest groups arose again only in the 1950s, and the movement as a whole took until the 1970s to return to the position it had held in 1932. Noticeably often, ex-wearers of the pink triangle report that they subsequently got married.

Selection 7

The Persecution of Jehovah's Witnesses

Watchtower Bible and Tract Society

Out of a German population of 65 million, only about 20,000 were Jehovah's Witnesses; nevertheless, the group was viewed as a

Excerpted from Watchtower Bible and Tract Society, "The Evils of Nazism Exposed," *Awake!* August 22, 1995. Reprinted with permission from the Watchtower Bible and Tract Society.

threat to the Nazis because of its civil disobedience. They refused to join the army, say "Heil Hitler," or participate in other mandated activities. The Witnesses believed the Nazis represented the devil and must be defeated. Despite Nazi efforts to stop them from doing so, the group continued to hold prayer meet-

ings and distribute their literature throughout the war. Thousands were sent to concentration camps and those who remained free lost their jobs and were denied their civil rights. What was extraordinary about the Witnesses was that they could have gained their freedom from the camps at any time by recanting their faith, but few ever did. This article is taken from the website of the Watchtower Bible and Tract Society, the legal organization of the Jehovah's Witnesses.

In the 1920's, as Germany struggled to recover from its defeat in World War I, Jehovah's Witnesses were busy distributing tremendous amounts of Bible literature. Not only did this offer comfort and hope to the German people but it alerted them to the rising power of militarism. . . .

The *Golden Age* and *Consolation* magazines often drew attention to the militaristic stirrings in Germany. . . .

On the eve of Hitler's taking power, *The Golden Age* of January 4, 1933, said: "There looms forth the menacing promontory of the National Socialist movement. It seems incredulous that a political party so insignificant in its origin, so heterodox in its policies, can, in the space of a few years, develop into proportions that overshadow the structure of a national government. Yet Adolf Hitler and his national socialist party (the Nazis) have accomplished this rare feat."

An Appeal for Understanding

Hitler became prime minister of Germany on January 30, 1933, and a couple of months later, on April 4, 1933, the Magdeburg branch office of Jehovah's Witnesses was seized. However, the order was rescinded on April 28, 1933, and the property was returned. What would happen next?

In spite of the evident hostility of the Hitler regime, Jehovah's Witnesses organized a convention in Berlin, Germany, on June 25, 1933. Some 7,000 persons assembled. The Witnesses publicly made their intentions clear: "Our organization is not political in any sense. We only in-

sist on teaching the Word of Jehovah God to the people, and that without hindrance."

Thus Jehovah's Witnesses made a good-faith effort to state their case. What were the consequences? . . .

Immediately after the Berlin convention concluded, the Nazis again seized the branch office at Magdeburg, on June 28, 1933. They broke up Witness meetings and made arrests. Soon Witnesses began to be dismissed from their jobs. They suffered raids on their homes, beatings, and arrests. By early 1934 the Nazis had seized from the Witnesses 65 tons of Bible literature and had burned it outside Magdeburg.

Witnesses Condemn Hitler

Despite these initial attacks, Jehovah's Witnesses stood their ground and publicly denounced the oppression and injustice. The November 1, 1933, issue of [the Witness publication] *The Watchtower* featured the article "Fear Them Not." It was prepared especially for the German Witnesses, exhorting them to take courage in the face of mounting pressure.

On February 9, 1934, J. F. Rutherford, the president of the Watchtower Society, sent a letter of protest to Hitler stating: "You may successfully resist any and all men, but you cannot successfully resist Jehovah God. . . . In the name of Jehovah God and His anointed King, Christ Jesus, I demand that you give order to all officials and servants of your government that Jehovah's witnesses in Germany be permitted to peaceably assemble and without hindrance worship God."

Rutherford set March 24, 1934, as the deadline. He said that if by that time relief did not come to the German Witnesses, the facts about the persecution would be published throughout Germany and the rest of the world. The Nazis answered Rutherford's demand with stepped-up abuses, sending many of Jehovah's Witnesses to the concentration camps that had recently been set up. Thus, they were among the first inmates of these camps. . . .

On October 7, 1934, all congregations of Jehovah's Witnesses in Germany assembled to hear a letter read that was being sent to the officials of the Hitler government. It said: "There is a direct conflict between your law and God's law. . . . Therefore this is to advise you that at any cost we will obey God's commandments, will meet together for the study of His Word, and will worship and serve Him as He has commanded."

On the same day, Jehovah's Witnesses in 49 other countries met in special assembly and sent the following telegram to Hitler: "Your ill-treatment of Jehovah's witnesses shocks all good people of earth and dishonors God's name. Refrain from further persecuting Jehovah's witnesses; otherwise God will destroy you and your national party."

The Nazis responded almost immediately by stepping up their persecution. Hitler himself screamed: "This brood will be exterminated in Germany!" But as opposition intensified, the determination of the Witnesses stiffened correspondingly.

In 1935, *The Golden Age* exposed the Inquisitionlike torture methods of the Nazi regime and its spy system. It also revealed that it was the aim of the Hitler Youth organization to purge Germany's youths of their belief in God. The following year a nationwide Gestapo campaign resulted in the arrests of thousands of Witnesses. Soon after, on December 12, 1936, the Witnesses answered with their own campaign, blanketing Germany with tens of thousands of copies of a resolution protesting the persecution of Jehovah's Witnesses. . . .

Jehovah's Witnesses were among the first targets of Nazi abuse, but they also loudly decried atrocities against Jews, Poles, the handicapped, and others. . . .

Witnesses Exposed Existence of Camps

Although Auschwitz, Buchenwald, Dachau, and Sachsenhausen were names unknown to most people until after World War II, they were well known to readers of *The Golden Age* and *Consolation*. The reports of Jehovah's Witnesses, smuggled out of the camps at great risk and publicized in Watch Tower literature, exposed the murderous intent of the Third Reich.

In 1933, *The Golden Age* carried the first of many reports of the existence of concentration camps in Germany. In 1938, Jehovah's Witnesses published the book *Crusade Against Christianity,* in French, German, and Polish. It carefully documented the vicious Nazi attacks on the Witnesses and included diagrams of the Sachsenhausen and Esterwegen concentration camps.

Nobel prize winner Dr. Thomas Mann wrote: "I have read your book and its terrible documentation with deepest emotion. I cannot describe the mixed feeling of abhorrence and loathing which has filled my heart while perusing these records of human degradation and abominable cruelty. . . . To keep quiet would serve only the moral indifference of the world . . . *You have done your duty in publishing this book* and bringing these facts to light."—Italics ours. . . .

Horrors of Camps Exposed

Although the public was largely unaware of the existence of the concentration camps until 1945, detailed descriptions of them appeared often in Watch Tower publications in the 1930's. In 1937, for example, *Consolation* told of experiments with poison gas at Dachau. By 1940, Witness publications had named 20 different camps and had reported on their unspeakable conditions.

Why were Jehovah's Witnesses so well acquainted with the concentration camps? When World War II started in 1939, there were already 6,000 Witnesses confined in camps and prisons. German historian Detlef Garbe estimates that the Witnesses constituted at that time between 5 and 10 percent of the total camp population!

At a seminar on the Witnesses and the Holocaust, Garbe stated: "Of the 25,000 persons who admitted to being Jehovah's Witnesses at the beginning of the Third Reich, about 10,000 were imprisoned for any length of time. Of these, over 2,000 were admitted to concentration camps. This means that the Jehovah's Witnesses were, with the exception of the Jews, the worst persecuted by the SS of all the religious based groups."

In June 1940, *Consolation* said: "There were

3,500,000 Jews in Poland when Germany began its Blitzkrieg . . . , and if reports which reach the Western world are correct their destruction seems well under way." In 1943, *Consolation* noted: "Whole nations like the Greeks, Poles and Serbs are being exterminated systematically." By 1946, *The Golden Age* and *Consolation* had identified 60 different prison and concentration camps. . . .

Nazis Frustrated by Witnesses

Although the Nazis tried to stem the flow of Watch Tower literature, a Berlin official admitted: "It is hard to find the secret places in Germany where the Bible Students' literature is still being printed; no one carries names or addresses and no one betrays another."

Despite their frantic efforts, the Gestapo were never able to capture more than half the total number of Witnesses in Germany at any given time. Imagine the frustration of the elaborate Nazi spy system—it could not round up and silence this tiny army or stop the flow of literature. The literature found its way to the streets and even penetrated the barbed-wire fences of the concentration camps! . . .

A Jew who survived the Buchenwald concentration camp explained: "There I met the *Bibelforscher*. They constantly testified to their beliefs. In fact, nothing would stop them speaking about their God. They were very helpful to other prisoners. When the pogrom sent a mass influx of Jews to the camp on November 10, 1938, the *'Jehovah's schwein'*, as the guards termed them, went round with a bread ration to the aged and famished Jews, going without food themselves for up to four days."

Similarly, a Jewish woman imprisoned in the Lichtenburg camp said of the Witnesses: "They were a brave people, who bore their fate patiently. Though the gentile prisoners were forbidden to talk to us, these women never observed this regulation. They prayed for us as if we belonged to their family, and begged us to hold out.". . .

Jehovah's Witnesses were a small, peaceable enclave within the Nazi realm. Yet, they waged and won a battle in their own way—a battle for the right to worship their God, a battle to love their neighbor, and a battle to tell the truth.

Selection 8

Gypsies in the Holocaust

Yitzhak Arad, Vera Laska, and Helen Fein

One group systematically killed by the Nazis in the same way as the Jews were the Roma, or Gypsies. The Gypsies originated in India and adopted a wandering lifestyle in the late

Excerpted from Yitzhak Arad, *Belzec, Sobibor, Treblinka—The Operation Reinhard Death Camps* (Bloomington: Indiana University Press, 1987); Vera Laska, ed., *Women in the Resistance and in the Holocaust: Voices of Eyewitnesses* (Westport, CT: Greenwood Press, 1983); and Helen Fein, *Accounting for Genocide: Victims and Survivors of the Holocaust* (NY: The Free Press, 1979).

Middle Ages. The Nazis viewed the Gypsies as threats to the purity of Aryan blood. They were sent to slave labor and death camps and murdered by the Einsatzgruppen. *No one knows how many Gypsies were murdered, but the figure is probably in the hundreds of thousands, with perhaps as many as half of the European Gypsy population being murdered. This article consists of a series of ex-*

cerpts culled by the author of a webpage on the treatment of the Gypsies.

"For Nazi Germany the Gypsies became a racist dilemma. The Gypsies were Aryans, but in the Nazi mind there were contradictions between what they regarded as the superiority of the Aryan race and their image of the Gypsies. . . .

At a conference held in Berlin on January 30, 1940, a decision was taken to expel 30,000 Gypsies from Germany to the territories of occupied Poland. . . .

The reports of the *SS Einsatzgruppen* [special task forces] which operated in the occupied territories of the Soviet Union mention the murder of thousands of Gypsies along with the massive extermination of the Jews in these areas.

The deportations and executions of the Gypsies came under [SS leader Heinrich] Himmler's authority. On December 16, 1942, Himmler issued an order to send all Gypsies to the concentration camps, with a few exceptions. . . .

The deported Gypsies were sent to Auschwitz-Birkenau, where a special Gypsy camp was erected. Over 20,000 Gypsies from Germany and some other parts of Europe were sent to this camp, and most of them were gassed there. . . .

[One prisoner] described the arrival of the largest Gypsy group brought to Treblinka, in the spring of 1943:

> One day, while I was working near the gate, I noticed the Germans and Ukrainians making special preparations. . . . Meanwhile the gate opened, and about 1,000 Gypsies were brought in (this was the third transport of Gypsies). About 200 of them were men, and the rest women and children. . . . All the Gypsies were taken to the gas chambers and then burned. . . .

Gypsies from the General Government [Poland] who were not sent to Auschwitz and to the Operation Reinhard camps were shot on the spot by the local police or gendarmes. In the eastern region of the Cracow district, in the counties of Sanok, Jaslo, and Rzeszow, close to 1,000 Gypsies were shot. . . ." [Excerpted from Yitzhak Arad. *Belzec, Sobibor, Treblinka—The Operation Reinhard Death Camps.* Bloomington: Indiana University Press, 1987, pp. 150–153.] . . .

Treated Like Jews

"Like the Jews, Gypsies were singled out by the Nazis for racial persecution and annihilation. They were 'nonpersons,' of 'foreign blood,' 'labor-shy,' and as such were termed asocials. To a degree, they shared the fate of the Jews in their ghettos, in the extermination camps, before firing squads, as medical guinea pigs, and being injected with lethal substances.

Ironically, the German writer Johann Christof Wagenseil claimed in 1697 that Gypsies stemmed from German Jews. A more contemporary Nazi theorist believed that the Gypsy cannot, by reason of his inner and outer makeup (*Konstruktion*), be a useful member of the human community.

The Nuremberg Laws of 1935 aimed at the Jews were soon amended to include the Gypsies. In 1937, they were classified as asocials, second-class citizens, subject to concentration camp imprisonment. As early as 1936, some had been sent to camps. After 1939, Gypsies from Germany and from the German-occupied territories were shipped by the thousands first to Jewish ghettos in Poland at Warsaw, Lublin, Kielce, Rabka, Zary, Siedlce and others. It is not known how many were killed by the Einsatzgruppen charged with speedy extermination by shooting. For the sake of efficiency Gypsies were also shot naked, facing their pre-dug graves. According to the Nazi experts, shooting Jews was easier, they stood still, 'while the Gypsies cry out, howl, and move constantly, even when they are already standing on the shooting ground. Some of them even jumped into the ditch before the volley and pretended to be dead.' The first to go were the German Gypsies; 30,000 were deported East in three waves in 1939, 1941 and 1943. Those married to Germans were exempted but were sterilized, as were their children after the age of twelve.

Just how were the Gypsies of Europe 'expedited'? Adolf Eichmann, chief strategist of these diabolical logistics, supplied the answer in a telegram from Vienna to the Gestapo:

> Regarding transport of Gypsies be informed that on Friday, October 20, 1939, the first transport of Jews will depart Vienna. To this transport 34 cars of Gypsies are to be attached. Subsequent trains will depart from Vienna, Mahrisch-Ostrau and Katowice [Poland]. The simplest method is to attach some carloads of Gypsies to each transport. Because these transports must follow schedule, a smooth execution of this matter is expected. Concerning a start in the Altreich [Germany proper] be informed that this will be coming in 34 weeks. Eichmann.

Open season was declared on the Gypsies, too. For a while Himmler wished to exempt two tribes and 'only' sterilize them, but by 1942 he signed the decree for all Gypsies to be shipped to Auschwitz. There they were subjected to all that Auschwitz meant, including the medical experiments, before they were exterminated.

Guinea Pigs

Gypsies perished in Dachau, Mauthausen, Ravensbrück and other camps. At Sachsenhausen they were subjected to special experiments that were to prove scientifically that their blood was different from that of the Germans. The doctors in charge of this 'research' were the same ones who had practiced previously on black prisoners of war. Yet, for 'racial reasons' they were found unsuitable for sea water experiments. Gypsies were often accused of atrocities committed by others; they were blamed, for instance, for the looting of gold teeth from a hundred dead Jews abandoned on a Rumanian road.

Gypsy women were forced to become guinea pigs in the hands of Nazi physicians. Among others they were sterilized as 'unworthy of human reproduction' (*fortpflanzungsunwuerdig*), only to be ultimately annihilated as not worthy of living. . . . At that, the Gypsies were the luckier ones; in Bulgaria, Greece, Denmark and Finland they were spared.

For a while there was a Gypsy Family Camp in Auschwitz, but on August 6, 1944, it was liquidated. Some men and women were shipped to German factories as slave labor; the rest, about 3,000 women, children and old people, were gassed.

No precise statistics exist about the extermination of European Gypsies. Some estimates place the number between 500,000 and 600,000, most of them gassed in Auschwitz. Others indicated a more conservative 200,000 Gypsy victims of the Holocaust. " [Extracted from Vera Laska, ed., *Women in the Resistance and in the Holocaust: The Voices of Eyewitnesses.* Westport, CT: Greenwood, 1983.] . . .

No More German Gypsies

"Despite a 1937 law excluding Gypsies from army service, many served in the armed forces until demobilized by special orders between

A Gypsy mother and child interned at a transit camp in Austria about 1940.

1940 and 1942. Gypsy children were also dismissed from schools beginning in March 1941. Thus, those who were nominally free and not yet concentrated were stripped systematically of the status of citizens and segregated. The legal status of Gypsies and Jews, determined irrevocably by the agreement between Justice Minister [Georg] Thierack and SS Reichsfuehrer Himmler on 18 September 1942, removing both groups from the jurisdiction of any German court, confirmed their fate. Thierack wrote, 'I envisage transferring all criminal proceedings concerning [these people] to Himmler. I do this because I realize that the courts can only feebly contribute to the extermination of these people.'

The Citizenship Law of 1943 omitted any mention of Gypsies since they were not expected to exist much longer. Himmler decreed the transport of Gypsies to Auschwitz on 16 December 1942, but he did not authorize their extermination until 1944. Most died there and in other camps of starvation, diseases, and torture from abuse as live experimental subjects. By the end of the war, 15,000 of the 20,000 Gypsies who had been in Germany in 1939 had died." [Excerpted from Helen Fein, *Accounting for Genocide: Victims and Survivors of the Holocaust.* New York: Free, 1979.]

Selection 9

Homosexuals in the Holocaust

James Steakley

Though the "Final Solution" was directed primarily at the Jews, Hitler also sought to rid the world of other groups he considered inferior, defective, or degenerate. This was why the other groups who were given special treatment were the disabled, Gypsies, and homosexuals. It is perhaps not surprising that Aryan "Supermen" would be offended by the gay lifestyle, but it was only the diabolical Nazi regime that would move from offense to extermination. Like Jews, gays had their own badges, pink triangles, which made them easy targets of concentration camp inmates and guards who wanted to further abuse them. Today, the symbol is used by gay activists. This article by James Steakley briefly describes the persecution of homosexuals in the Third Reich.

*a*fter roll call on the evening of June 20, 1942, an order was suddenly given: "All prisoners with the pink triangle will remain standing at attention!" We stood on the desolate, broad square, and from somewhere a warm summer breeze carried the sweet fragrance of resin and wood from the regions of freedom; but we couldn't taste it, because our

Excerpted from James Steakley, "Homosexuals and the Third Reich," *The Body Politic*, Issue 11, January/February 1974. Reprinted with permission from the author.

throats were hot and dry from fear. Then the guardhouse door of the command tower opened, and an SS officer and some of his lackeys strode toward us. Our detail commander barked: "Three hundred criminal deviants, present as ordered!" We were registered, and then it was revealed to us that in accordance with an order from the Reichsfuhrung SS, our category was to be isolated in an intensified-penalty company, and we would be transferred as a unit to the Klinker Brickworks the next morning. The Klinker factory! We shuddered, for the human death mill was more than feared. . . .

Thousands, perhaps as many as ten thousand homosexuals were interned in Nazi concentration camps. They were consigned to the lowest position in the camp hierarchy, and subjected to abuse by both guards and fellow prisoners; most of them perished. . . .

The words at the beginning of this article were written by one concentration camp survivor, L.D. Classen von Neudegg, who published some of his recollections in a German homophile magazine in the Fifties. Here are a few more excerpts from his account of the treatment of homosexuals in the concentration camp at Sachsenhausen:

> We had been here for almost two months, but it seemed like endless years to us. When we were "transferred" here, we had numbered around three hundred men. Whips were used more frequently each morning, when we were forced down into the clay pits under the wailing of the camp sirens. "Only fifty are still alive," whispered the man next to me. "Stay in the middle—then you won't get hit so much."
>
> . . . (The escapees) had been brought back. "Homo" was scrawled scornfully across their clothing for their last walk through the camp. To increase their thirst, they were forced to eat oversalted food, and then they were placed on the block and whipped. Afterwards, drums were hung around their necks, which they had to beat while shouting, "Hurrah, we're back!" The three men were hanged. . . .

Dr. Neudegg's recollections are confirmed in many details by the memoirs of Rudolf Hoss, adjunct and commander of the concentration camps at Sachsenhausen and, later, Auschwitz. Neudegg's account is something of a rarity: the few homosexuals who managed to survive internment have tended to hide the fact, largely because homosexuality continued to be a crime in postwar West Germany. This is also the reason why homosexuals have been denied any compensation by the otherwise munificent West German government.

The number of homosexuals who died in Nazi concentration camps is unknown and likely to remain so. Although statistics are available on the number of men brought to trial on charges of "lewd and unnatural behaviour," many more were sent to camps without the benefit of a trial. Moreover, many homosexuals were summarily executed by firing squads; this was particularly the case with gays in the military—which encompassed nearly every able-bodied man during the final years of the war. Finally, many concentration camps systematically destroyed all their records when it became apparent that German defeat was imminent. . . .

Political Expediency

The beginning of the Nazi terror against homosexuals was marked by the murder of Ernst Rohm on June 30, 1934: "the Night of the Long Knives." Rohm was the man who, in 1919, first made Hitler aware of his own political potential, and the two were close friends for fifteen years. During that time, Rohm rose to SA Chief of Staff, transforming the Brownshirt militia from a handful of hardened goons and embittered ex-soldiers into an effective fighting force five hundred thousand strong, the instrument of Nazi terror. Hitler needed Rohm's military skill and could rely on his personal loyalty, but he was ultimately a pragmatist. As part of a compromise with the *Reichwehr* (regular army) leadership, whose support he needed to become Führer, Hitler allowed Goering and Himmler to murder Rohm along with dozens of Rohm's loyal officers.

For public relations purposes, and especially

to quell the outrage felt throughout the ranks of the SA, Hitler justified his blatant power play by pointing to Rohm's homosexuality. Hitler, of course, had known of Rohm's homosexuality since 1919, and it became public knowledge in 1925, when Rohm appeared in court to charge a hustler with theft. All this while the Nazi Party had a virulently anti-gay policy, and many Nazis protested that Rohm was discrediting the entire Party and should be purged. Hitler, however, was quite willing to cover up for him for years until he stood in the way of larger plans. . . .

The Nazi Party came to power in 1933, and a year later Rohm was dead. . . . [When] offered a gun and the opportunity to shoot himself, Rohm retorted angrily: "Let Hitler do his own dirty work.". . .

Hitler had good reason to be concerned about the reputation of Nazi organizations, most of which were based on strict segregation of the sexes. Hitler Youth, for example, was disparagingly referred to as Homo Youth throughout the Third Reich, a characterization which the Nazi leadership vainly struggled to eliminate. Indeed, most of the handful of publications on homosexuality which appeared during the Fascist regime were devoted to new and rather bizarre methods of "detection" and "prevention."

Rudolf Diels, the founder of the Gestapo, recorded some of Hitler's personal thoughts on the subject: "He lectured me on the role of homosexuality in history and politics. It had destroyed ancient Greece, he said. Once rife, it extended its contagious effects like an ineluctable law of nature to the best and most manly of characters, eliminating from the reproductive process precisely those men on whose offspring a nation depended. The immediate result of the vice was, however, that unnatural passion swiftly became dominant in public affairs if it were allowed to spread unchecked.". . .

Legislating Morality

The tone had been set by the Rohm putsch, and on its first anniversary—June 28, 1935, the campaign against homosexuality was escalated by the introduction of the "Law for the Protection of German Blood and German Honour." Until 1935, the only punishable offence had been anal intercourse; under the new Paragraph 175a, ten possible "acts" were punishable, including a kiss, an embrace, even homosexual fantasies! One man, for instance, was successfully prosecuted on the grounds that he had observed a couple making love in a park and watched only the man. . . .

Once Paragraph 175a was in effect, the annual number of convictions on charges of homosexuality leaped to about ten times the number in the pre-Nazi period. The law was so loosely formulated that it could be—and was—applied against heterosexuals whom the Nazis wanted to eliminate. The most notorious example of an individual convicted on trumped-up charges was General Werner von Fritsch, Army Chief of Staff; and the law was also used repeatedly against members of the Catholic clergy. But the law was undoubtedly used primarily against gay people, and the court system was aided in the witch-hunt by the entire German populace, which was encouraged to scrutinize the behaviour of neighbours and to denounce suspects to the Gestapo. The number of men convicted of homosexuality during the Nazi period totaled around fifty thousand. . . .

The Gestapo was the agent of the next escalation of the campaign against homosexuality. Ex-chicken farmer Heinrich Himmler, Reichsfuhrer SS and head of the Gestapo, richly deserves a reputation as the most fanatically homophobic member of the Nazi leadership. In 1936, he gave a speech on the subject of homosexuality and described the murder of Ernst Rohm (which he had engineered) in these terms: "Two years ago . . . when it became necessary, we did not scruple to strike this plague with death, even within our own ranks." Himmler closed with these words: "Just as we today have gone back to the ancient Germanic view on the question of marriage mixing different races, so too in our judgment of homosexuality—a symptom of degeneracy which could destroy our race—we must return to the guiding Nordic principle: extermination of degenerates.". . .

Into the Camps

Himmler personally favoured the immediate "extermination of degenerates," but he was empowered to order the summary execution only of homosexuals discovered within his own bureaucratic domain. Civilian offenders were merely required to serve out their prison sentences (although second offenders were subject to castration).

In 1936, Himmler found a way around this obstacle. Following release from prison, all "enemies of the state"—including homosexuals—were to be taken into protective custody and detained indefinitely. "Protective custody" (*Schutzhaft*) was an euphemism for concentration camp internment. Himmler gave special orders that homosexuals be placed in Level Three camps—the human death mills described by Neudegg. These camps were reserved for Jews and homosexuals. . . .

The chances for survival in a Level Three camp were low indeed. Homosexuals were distinguished from other prisoners by a pink triangle, worn on the left side of the jacket and on the right pant leg. There was no possibility of "passing" for straight, and the presence of "marked men" in the all-male camp population evoked the same reaction as in contemporary prisons: gays were brutally assaulted and sexually abused. . . .

"During the first weeks of my imprisonment," wrote one survivor, "I often thought I was the only available target on whom everyone was free to vent his aggressions. Things improved when I was assigned to a labour detail that worked outside the camp at Metz, because everything took place in public view. I was made

clerk of the labour detail, which meant that I worked all day and then looked after the records at the guardhouse between midnight and 2 a.m. Because of this 'overtime' I was allowed seconds at lunch—if any food was left over. This is the fact to which I probably owe my survival. . . . I saw quite a number of pink triangles. I don't know how they were eventually killed. . . . One day they were simply gone.". . .

The ruthlessness of the Nazis culminated in actions so perversely vindictive as to be almost incomprehensible. Six youths arrested for stealing coal at a railroad station were taken into protective custody and duly placed in a concentration camp. Shocked that such innocent boys were forced to sleep in a barracks also occupied by pink triangles, the SS guards chose what to them must have seemed the lesser of two evils: they took the youths aside and gave them fatal injections of morphine. Morality was saved. . . .

The institutionalized homophobia of the Third Reich must also be seen in terms of the sexual revolution that had taken place in Germany during the preceding decades. The German gay movement had existed for thirty-six years before it (and all other progressive forces) was smashed. The Nazis carried out a "conservative revolution" which restored law and order together with nineteenth-century sexism. A system of ranking women according to the number of their offspring was devised by Minister of the Interior Wilhelm Frick, who demanded that homosexuals "be hunted down mercilessly, for their vice can only lead to the demise of the German people."

Women and the Holocaust

Carol Rittner and John K. Roth

The Nazis murdered Jewish men, women, and children. Age or sex did not matter, only religion. Hitler wanted to exterminate all Jews. Still, men, women, and children were not treated exactly the same. For example, a key to survival, at least in the short run, was often the ability to work. Someone who was too old or too young to work had no value and was more likely to be murdered sooner than later. The authors of this excerpt argue that women also were treated differently, in part because they were the source of Jewish life, which Hitler wanted to extinguish. Though statistics relating to the Holocaust are difficult to determine, they suggest that more women than men may have been murdered by the Nazis. Carol Rittner was the founding director of the Elie Wiesel Foundation for Humanity and, more recently, the executive director of Mercyworks International. John K. Roth is the Russel K. Pitzer Professor of Philosophy at Claremont McKenna College.

*O*ne result of the Shoah [Holocaust] was that millions of women, the vast majority of them Jewish, perished during its devastation. . . .

The racism of Nazi ideology ultimately im-

plied that the existence of Jewish women constituted a deadly obstacle to the racial purity and cultural superiority that Germany "deserved." What follows . . . will suggest and show that the Holocaust's killing operations, especially where the Jews were concerned, made explicit distinctions between men and women. As [Holocaust scholar] Joan Ringelheim has argued . . . the Holocaust's deportation and death lists often included gender identification. Women and men were segregated in concentration and death camps. Traditional attitudes among German Nazis partly account for such separations, and early on they treated Jewish women more benignly than Jewish men, but once World War II began in 1939 and the "Final Solution" was fully under way in 1942, Jewish women were increasingly at risk.

In wartime elderly Jewish women were useless to the Nazis, and they were sentenced to death by starvation, disease, shooting, or gas. Of more troubling concern to Nazi Germany were Jewish women of child-bearing age. On one hand, their work for the Third Reich could be productive. On the other, their menace was especially acute because they could produce Jewish children. Hitler's war against the Jews was determined to prevent that outcome.

Any consistent Nazi plan had to target Jewish women specifically as women, for they were the only ones who would finally be able to ensure the continuity of Jewish life. Indeed, although the statistical data about the Holocaust will never be exact, there is sound evidence that the odds for surviving the Holocaust were worse for Jewish women than for Jewish men. For even though Jewish men often perished before and probably at a faster rate than Jewish women until 1942, the loss of life overall during the Holocaust was apparently greater for Jewish women than for Jewish men. At Auschwitz, for example, the Jewish women selected for labor were mainly in their late teens and early twenties and without children. Auschwitz selection policy kept children, usually those under fourteen, with their mothers. Along with older women, those mothers were typically dispatched to the gas chambers on arrival. At the end of the war, more men than women could be found among the total of Jewish survivors, and more of the men were older, too. In sum, to use Ringelheim's telling phrase, the Holocaust put Jewish women in "double jeopardy." In less extreme ways, the same point could be made about the thousands of non-Jewish women who also found themselves trapped in the Holocaust's web because they were suspect politically or identified as belonging to other groups—Slavs, for example, or Gypsies—that the Nazi racial hierarchy classified as inferior. . . .

No calculus of cruelty should be used to make the insidious wholesale judgment that what happened to one gender during the Holocaust was worse than what happened to the other or that one gender's reflections and memories are clearer or more truthful and important than the other's. Similar experiences are not identical, however, and in the Shoah differences between men and women made a significant difference. As [literary scholar] Myrna Goldenberg aptly sums up the situation, the hell may have been the same for women and men during the Holocaust, but the horrors were different.

Why Focus on Women?

How did women respond to their circumstances during the Holocaust? What was most important to women who had to live under conditions of deprivation, humiliation, terror, and death? Were there gender-related resources that women drew upon to sustain hope as well as life in the ghettos and camps? What particular vulnerabilities exposed them to extraordinary suffering and death? Does the study of women and the Holocaust highlight new or at least different questions that we should be asking—not just about women but about every human being who had to endure the Holocaust's darkness? The history of the Holocaust is incomplete without responses to such questions, and they have not received the attention they deserve. Not everyone, however, welcomes the emphasis on women. . . . For example, Joan Ringelheim reports dissent by interpreters such as Helen Fagin and Cynthia Ozick. Focusing on the particularity of women's experiences, they have argued, involves two dangers: (1) It may denigrate the Holocaust's significance by turning the Shoah merely into an example of sexism. (2) It may detract from the much more fundamental fact that, as Ozick once put it, "the Holocaust happened to victims who were not seen as men, women, or children but *as Jews."*

The counterargument, however, is more compelling. Precisely because the Nazis targeted Jews and others in racial terms, they had to see those victims in their male and female particularity. Far from reducing the Shoah to an example of sexism, emphasis on what happened to women reveals what otherwise would remain hidden: a fuller picture of the unprecedented and unrelenting killing that the "Final Solution's" antisemitism and racism entailed. . . .

The Life of a Jewish Poet

Gertrud Chodziesner was born in Berlin on December 10, 1894. Descended from Jewish merchants who had once lived in the Polish town of Chodziez (Kolmar, as the Germans called it) she would grow up in comfortable Berlin surroundings before adopting Kolmar as her pen name. . . .

Gertrud Kolmar was growing up as an introverted, solitary girl who filled her life with history and nature, languages and writing. During World War I, while Hitler served in the trenches of the German army, she worked as an interpreter and a postal censor. But by the time Hitler, stunned by Germany's capitulation, was recovering at the war's end from a poison-gas attack his army unit had experienced, some of her poems were in print. . . .

In the summer of 1923, not long before Hitler's November attempt in Munich to bring down the government of the Weimar Republic he despised, the Chodziesner family moved from Berlin to a rural suburb named Finkenkrug. . . .

In 1933, there were about 566,000 Jews in Germany—a little over half of them women. Most were highly assimilated. The German census of 1939 would show that figure shrinking to a little over 200,000—nearly 60 percent of them women. Single Jewish men had the best chances to emigrate. As a result, more German-Jewish women than men would be deported and killed in the "Final Solution." Gertrud Kolmar, like so many of her Jewish sisters and brothers, did not—indeed, probably could not—imagine, let alone prepare for, what was coming. . . .

Camps for Women

An early women's camp functioned at Moringen from October 1933 to March 1938. Meanwhile [SS leader Heinrich] Himmler and his associates consolidated SS control over all the camps, expanding them and systematizing their procedures. Run more along Dachau's lines, a second women's concentration camp opened in March 1938 at Lichtenburg, a former men's camp that became available when its inmates and SS guard units were transferred to Buchenwald, which had started operations in 1937. The Lichtenburg camp closed in May 1939, when a permanent installation for women opened at Ravensbrück. This camp stood about fifty miles north of Berlin, near the railway station at Fürstenberg.

Built on reclaimed swamp land, Ravensbrück was designed to hold about 15,000 prisoners. By 1944 it held 42,000 from twenty-three nations. On average about 15 percent of the camp population was Jewish. Along with Gypsies, who numbered about 5.5 percent of the prisoner population, the Jewish women were segregated from and treated more harshly than the other inmates. The camp was a forced-labor installation; it focused on textile work, including the produc-

tion of SS uniforms. Ravensbrück also provided training for many of the 3,000 women who eventually served as administrators and guards at other camps, Auschwitz among them. Maria Mandel, who became SS Chief Supervisor at the women's camp in Auschwitz, got training at Ravensbrück. So did Irma Griese, one of the most notorious female guards at Auschwitz.

Ravensbrück would not be liberated until late April 1945. When the Soviet forces arrived, they found only 3,500 sick women still in the camp. Records in the Ravensbrück archives showed, however, that during the camp's overall existence a total of 132,000 women and children had been imprisoned there. The fact that children could be found in Ravensbrück should not be overlooked. Some arrived with their mothers. Others were born there—863 of them between 1943 and 1945. Lacking adequate food and health care, nearly all of them died there, too. In a pattern that would be widely replicated, the Nazi targeting at Ravensbrück could keep women and children together. But where Jews and other "inferior" lives were at stake, the mother-child relationship was ultimately one the Nazis were determined to destroy. Nothing about the "Final Solution" was more definite than that.

Early on, the mortality rate at Ravensbrück had been comparatively low, but after 1941 it worsened. Eventually death claimed 92,000 of Ravensbrück's total prisoner population. That number included some 32,000 who had been gassed in the camp's final months when the Germans evacuated to Ravensbrück prisoners from camps in the East made vulnerable as the Red Army forced Germany's retreat. In the end, no other concentration camp in Germany had such a high percentage of murdered prisoners.

Gertrud Kolmar spent no time in Moringen, Lichtenburg, or Ravensbrück. She was neither a socialist or a communist, a political or religious dissident, nor a prostitute or criminal, nor had she violated any of Nazi Germany's race-defilement laws—all misdeeds sufficient to put a woman in such places. Of course, her Jewish identity could cause misfortune, too, but before 1939, as [historian] Sybil Milton points out,

"Jewish women were incarcerated in the jails and concentration camps of Nazi Germany . . . *only if* they belonged to one of the other affected categories." In addition, at least until World War II began with Germany's invasion of Poland on September 1, 1939, the Nazis' anti-Jewish policies aimed more at forced emigration than at incarceration or death. Instrumental in creating a climate of terror that would persuade Jews to leave Germany, certainly incarceration and death did occur, and thus Jewish women were always among the victims of the women's camps on German soil. Nevertheless, prior to 1939 and the outbreak of war, Kolmar's situation was similar to that of many German Jewish women. Living inside a vise that was closing, she experienced pariah status, but that condition was still moderated by "normal social inhibitions" that restrained Nazi violence toward Jewish women. . . .

Meanwhile, poetry occupied Gertrud Kolmar. So did the study of Hebrew, which she began in early April. With increasing seriousness and intensity, she began to write in a different voice, as she explains in a letter dated November 24, 1940, only a few days after the Warsaw ghetto had been sealed: "I have just recently learned what a Hebrew poem should *not* be, and how I should not write, and feel now that I will soon know how I *must* write. This poem that does not yet exist . . . is already forming within me. Perhaps it will take months or years . . . but it will see the light. . . . Perhaps because of this I have written nothing more in German recently." Unfortunately, Kolmar did not have months and years—at least not many of them—and no trace of her Hebrew poetry remains. . . .

The Vise Tightens

Orders sent from [Reichsmarschall] Hermann Göring's Berlin office on July 31, 1941, charged [security police chief] Reinhard Heydrich with responsibility to plan the "final solution of the Jewish question."

Unlike the circumstances in many other European countries controlled by Germany, ghettos were not established in Germany. But the German

Jews were increasingly crowded together, and so, a few weeks before Göring sent his "Final Solution" order to Heydrich, Kolmar and her father had been herded along with other Jews into closer Berlin quarters. She had also been ordered to report for factory labor. Three months later—in October—the deportation of German Jews eastward to ghettos in Poland, Lithuania, and Latvia began. If those ghettos were not always death traps themselves, they became staging areas for further deportations to camps that were.

For a time Gertrud Kolmar was spared. She continued her factory labor and was still able to get mail to her sister in Switzerland. She reports, for instance, her "romance" with a young medical student she met at the factory in Charlottenburg where they worked, and on March 5, 1942, she speaks about her efforts, against disheartening odds, to keep writing: "When I have made even a little progress with it," she says, referring to a story she had started, "and feel that what I have done is good and beautiful, then at times I am very happy.". . .

Gertrud Kolmar was still alive at the end of 1942. She may have sensed, however, that her days were numbered. One of her last letters—dated December 15, 1942—speaks about her sense of fate. It reflects the disposition of the Roman Stoics she admired: "Even though I do not know what [my fate] will be, I have accepted it in advance, I have given myself up to it, and know that it will not crush me, will not find me too small."

In February 1943, the Germans made a special drive to deport the last Jews from Berlin, even those who worked in war-essential industries. The last letter from Gertrud Kolmar is dated February 20–21. She was most likely caught in the roundup of Jewish workers that occurred a few days later. Camp records indicate that from late February until mid-March 1943, numerous transports brought several thousand Jews from Berlin to Auschwitz-Birkenau. Most of the women and children were gassed on arrival. The circumstances of Gertrud Kolmar's death are uncertain, but she probably was among those who were immediately killed. Berlin was declared *judenfrei* [free of jews] in June. The liquidation of German Jewry was officially completed in July. . . .

Auschwitz was liberated by the Red Army on January 27, 1945. Those troops found about 7,000 sick and exhausted prisoners—4,000 of them women. A much larger number, however, had been evacuated by the Nazis on January 17–18. The last roll call had included 31,894 prisoners—16,577 of them women. Most of these prisoners were force-marched westward until they dropped or arrived at camps where the Germans still planned to extract labor from them. In April most of the remaining camps were liberated by the Allies. Nazi Germany surrendered in early May, but even then the Holocaust did not end. Death continued to take its Jewish toll in the camps for "displaced persons." Other Jews lost their lives trying to enter Palestine clandestinely. All who survived had to cope with what Holocaust survivor Ida Fink so aptly calls "the ruins of memory.". . .

Consider a few things more. On the night of May 24, 1944, a transport of 3,500 Hungarian Jews departed the Carpathian city of Berehovo for Auschwitz-Birkenau. Arriving two days later, this transport rolled directly through the camp's gates, taking advantage of a special spur added to the rail network earlier that spring. The ensuing "selection" left the new arrivals just steps away from the barracks where some of them would live or from the gas chambers where most of them, especially the women and children, would die.

The handling of the Berehovo transport was routine—with one major exception. Usually photography was strictly forbidden at Auschwitz, but on this occasion, two SS cameramen were on the ramp where the cattle cars unloaded. They took nearly two hundred pictures of the Jews from Berehovo, documenting the selection process thoroughly. . . .

Lili Jacob, eighteen, was one of those selected to work. After being quarantined for several weeks, her left arm was tattooed with number A-10862 on July 25, 1944. The eldest of six children and the only daughter, she would be the sole survivor of her family. In December 1944,

she was evacuated from Auschwitz-Birkenau and sent to Dora, a missile plant located underground near Nordhausen, Germany. Gravely ill from typhus and malnutrition as that labor camp was being liberated in April 1945, Jacob was carried into a recently vacated SS barrack by some fellow prisoners. There she not only began to recover but also discovered a brown clothbound album containing photographs. To her amazement, she recognized people in them. She recognized the place where the photographs had been taken, too. Lili Jacob possessed what has come to be known as *The Auschwitz Album,* the series of pictures taken by the SS cameramen who recorded the Auschwitz arrival and decimation of the Berehovo transport she had been on a year before.

Thanks to Lili Jacob Meier, knowledge about the Holocaust, including awareness about women has been enhanced. The same can be said of Danuta Czech. Born in Poland in 1922, she was an active member of the resistance during World War II. In 1955, she joined the research staff at the Auschwitz archives and eventually became head of the scientific research department. Her *Auschwitz Chronicle, 1939–1945,* translated from Polish into English in 1990, is a vast, painstakingly assembled record of what happened in the camp day by day. The detail of its overwhelming 855 pages is possible because the Germans kept extensive records at Auschwitz. Beginning in the summer of 1944, they began to cover their tracks by erasing the incriminating evidence of their crimes, but there was more evidence than could be destroyed: original German documents, resistance-movement reports, testimony by former prisoners, trial records, even diaries unearthed from the ground where members of the *Sonderkommandos,* the doomed labor squads who operated the crematoriums, had buried them.

Czech's calendar makes a special effort to include the names of Auschwitz prisoners. "Not numbers," she contends, "but only real, specific human beings can touch the feelings and imagination of other human beings." The *Chronicle,* she rightly adds, "is not only a framework for research into the camp's history and the fate of the prisoners and an aid for criminal investigations, it is an epitaph, a memorial book for those who suffered and struggled in Auschwitz-Birkenau and its auxiliary camps, for those who did not survive Auschwitz, who died nameless—I am thinking especially of those who were killed in the gas chambers immediately after their arrival, without even being registered."

The *Chronicle*'s entries are filled with references to women. For example, its record for January 6, 1945, names four Jewish female prisoners—Ella Gärtner, Roza Robota, Regina Safir, and Estera Wajsblum—who were hanged publicly on that date in the women's camp at Auschwitz-Birkenau. They had been caught after resisting their fate by helping to smuggle explosives to other prisoners who sabotaged Auschwitz-Birkenau's Crematorium IV during the *Sonderkommando* revolt that occurred on October 7, 1944.

The four of them epitomize the valor of women who resisted the "Final Solution" in ghettos, partisan groups, and camps. The same can be said of a condemned Polish woman who figures in Czech's leap-year entry for February 29, 1944. In Birkenau's Crematorium IV, Czech reports,

> A young woman steps forward from among the condemned and says, facing the SS men, that all those present are clear about the fact that they are about to die in the famous Auschwitz gas chambers and burn in the crematorium, but that the times in which these crimes can be committed in secret were now past. Today the entire world knows what is going on in Auschwitz, and for every person murdered here the Germans will have to pay dearly. Finally, she says she leaves this world convinced that an end to these crimes is not far away. While entering the crematorium the condemned sing "Poland is not yet lost" and "To the Barricades."

That woman had a name. If she knew it, no doubt Danuta Czech would have included it, but probably no one knows that woman's name anymore. Yet the *Auschwitz Chronicle* contains her voice, and, like the photos in Lili Meier's *Auschwitz Album,* what it tells bears remembering because no one should assume that what went on in Auschwitz will never happen again.

Selection 11

The Abandonment of Americans in Hitler's Camps

Mitchell G. Bard

For many Americans, the Holocaust is an event that took place a long time ago, in a faraway place, to strangers. Few people are aware that tens of thousands of American citizens were also in Europe during World War II and that many of them were Jews. Though the numbers are comparatively small, perhaps a few thousand at most, American citizens, including non-Jews, were victims of Nazi oppression. Little is known about what happened to these Americans because the numbers were few and researchers have focused on the bigger picture. The U.S. government has also played a role, however, concealing information during and after the war about the fate of its own citizens. This selection documents what the U.S. government did, and mostly did not do, to help Americans endangered by the Nazi occupation of Europe. Mitchell G. Bard, the editor of this encyclopedia, is a political scientist and one of the nation's leading experts on Middle East affairs. This chapter was taken from the first book to highlight these forgotten victims of the war.

*a*mericans *were* killed in concentration camps. American Jews were subject to the same anti-Semitic regulations and dangers as any other Jews who came under the control of the Nazis. Non-Jews did not face the same peril; however, thousands were sent to internment camps.

Hundreds, perhaps thousands of lives could have been saved had the United States government taken action to rescue people claiming American citizenship. Often it did just the opposite, creating obstacles that impeded Americans from obtaining the necessary documents to escape from the Nazis.

The [Franklin D.] Roosevelt Administration knew Americans were trapped behind enemy lines. In 1939, more than 80,000 American citizens were believed to be living abroad. That year, the State Department established a little-known "Special Division" for handling matters related to the whereabouts and welfare of Americans abroad, including civilian internees and POWs [prisoners of war]—evidence that the

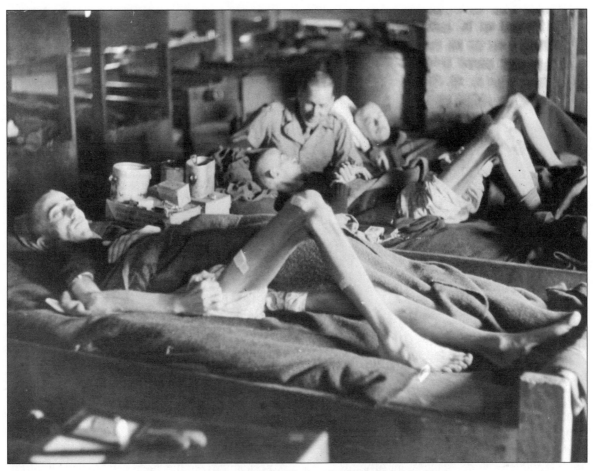

*The emaciated bodies of American POWs held by the Nazis
testify to the brutal conditions captured soldiers faced.*

United States anticipated the problems that would later arise. . . .

On November 25, 1939, Assistant Secretary of State George Messersmith wrote that Americans in danger zones were given the opportunity to return home but for business or private reasons did not do so. State Department officials held that citizens who chose to live abroad without any apparent intention of returning to the United States could not expect their government to feel any obligation to protect them. An even deeper prejudice lay behind this viewpoint: the belief that citizens returning from abroad would become "welfare" cases. "Their real status," Messersmith wrote, "does not differ very much from that of the many thousands of unfortunate persons deserving of our sympathy, and having

no claim to American citizenship, who would desire to come to this country in order to escape from danger zones or for other reasons and who seek immigration visas and passport visas to that end." The attitude that would condemn hundreds of Americans to death was expressed in the same letter:

> This government considers that by reason of having already met this particular responsibility, no situation should arise, even if conditions should become more aggravated in certain places, that would warrant it in providing further special facilities to enable Americans to return to this country.

The State Department was not sympathetic to Americans who were caught in the Nazi net. Although it acknowledged the U.S. obligation "to facilitate in every way possible the return" of U.S. nationals during an emergency "from places where danger may exist," State also maintained that Americans who failed to take advantage of the opportunity for repatriation did so knowing the risks involved. The Department sent five ships in 1939 and four more in 1940 to bring home United States citizens from the European war zone, and they returned with space available. "It therefore seems safe to draw the conclusion," a Special Division policy paper written four years later says, "that those United States nationals who remained in threatened areas did so, for the most part, voluntarily, and with full realization of the occupational risks they were taking."

Thus, U.S. officials took the position that Americans who, in their eyes, missed the boat home were on their own. But this view was to have tragic consequences. Few people in places like France could imagine in 1939 or 1940 what would happen two or three years later. In the case of Americans especially, the thought that they, U.S. citizens, would not be protected must have seemed unimaginable. In fact, it *was* unimaginable to State Department officials.

At the beginning of 1941, for example, Secretary of State Cordell Hull said the Department had learned anti-Jewish laws were being imposed in France, but he expected Americans to be exempted. A couple of months later, the U.S. Ambassador to France informed Hull he was mistaken. The Germans said that measures taken against Jews "do not admit of any exceptions and must be applied to all persons residing in France, regardless of their nationality." Despite being specifically told Americans would not be exempted from the anti-Jewish decrees, Hull still said he expected this to happen in a subsequent message to his Chargé [subordinate diplomat] in Germany. . . .

American Jews were perhaps in the greatest peril in Hungary. At the end of January 1941, the Hungarian authorities began to impose new measures on Jews, including depriving them of their real estate. The U.S. government could

have taken action at this point. Hull did instruct the U.S. minister in Hungary to help Americans but not to make any financial commitments. Herbert Pell responded that the probability was small that Americans in Hungary or Yugoslavia would get visas without the United States exerting pressure on Germany.

By the summer of 1941, it had become extremely difficult for Americans in the occupied territories to travel and communicate; they needed special permits to leave and those were rarely given. The situation was exacerbated when German consular offices in the United States were ordered closed by July 10, 1941, and the Germans retaliated by closing U.S. offices in Germany and the occupied territories. All American business was subsequently conducted by the Swiss Legation. . . .

Even after being informed of the seriousness of the plight of Jews in Rumania, Hull's response was bureaucratic. When an American is molested because of race or religion, he said, "you should exercise your discretion in the matter of extending unofficial good offices to him with a view to discontinuance of the molestation. . . . Person whose status as native-born American citizen has been established should in present situation be given protection and if necessary issued passports limited to short periods. Necessity for deviation from policy followed in normal times required out of humanitarian considerations."

The reluctance to assist Jews in Rumania was evident in a statement by Cavendish Cannon of the State Department's Division of European Affairs, who objected to a proposal two years later to move 300,000 Jews out of Rumania to Syria or Palestine. He said, "Endorsement of such a plan [was] likely to bring about new pressure for an asylum in the western hemisphere" and that, because atrocities were also underway in Hungary, "a migration of Rumanian Jews would therefore open the question of similar treatment for Jews in Hungary and, by extension, all countries where there has been intense persecution." The view that rescuing Jews somehow posed a danger to the Allies or would "take the burden or the curse off Hitler" was held by several State Department officials (and was a particularly prevalent feeling in the British Foreign Office).

Fear of Spies

This was not the only excuse used to make life difficult for both Americans and non-Americans trying to escape from Europe. At the beginning of 1941, Breckinridge Long, the head of the Special Division, had told Roosevelt that consuls had been instructed to be "as liberal as the law allows" and to expedite action, but because of reports of Nazi agents pretending to be refugees, "it has been considered essential in the national interest to scrutinize all applications carefully." In another letter to the President, Long said he was proposing new regulations for travel to and from the United States for all persons, *including* U.S. citizens, because the laxity of the current law allowed subversives to enter the United States.

There is no record of Roosevelt objecting to Long's proposals. The fact that the President could have made a difference, however, was apparent early in the war when Roosevelt sent a list of 200 names to the State Department in January 1940 with instructions that they be given emergency visas. Despite repeated requests to take similar action to bypass State Department obstacles, the President refused throughout the war to intervene.

U.S. officials were subsequently reluctant to make exchanges because of the fear that Americans who were repatriated might be spies. "As Americans received in the recent exchange were found to include some Nazi agents, we might very well expect to receive many subversive agents among aliens who have long been exposed to Nazi methods of indoctrination," wrote James Keeley, assistant chief of the Special Division. "It would be almost an impossible task to separate the bona fide from the male fide in such a conglomerate assemblage of people as would in the circumstances seek to come to the United States."

In fact, the FBI reported consistently throughout the war that enemy espionage and sabotage efforts were unsuccessful. The possibility of enemy infiltration existed, but it was more likely that Americans returning from occupied territories would be valuable intelligence resources. For example, a group of American correspondents exchanged for Axis nationals in the United States in mid-1942 relayed the news to American officials that hundreds of thousands of Jews had been killed.

Besides fear of Nazi sympathizers infiltrating, the State Department adopted the policy that it could not save any one group if it could not save everyone. "If we once open our doors to one class of refugee," Keeley wrote in December 1942, "we must expect on the basis of our experience in extending relief in occupied territories, that all other sufferers from Nazi (including Japanese) oppression (the Belgians, Dutch, Poles, Greeks, Yugoslavs, Norwegians, Czechs, Chinese, et cetera) will likewise wish to avail themselves of our hospitality. . . . Even the most optimistic dispenser of largess could scarcely expect us to become an unrestricted haven of refuge for all suffering peoples. Furthermore, to accede to the request of one group, while refusing similar refuge to other oppressed peoples, might well give rise to bad feeling and engender disunity among the happy family of the United Nations."

The general sentiment in the State Department and the White House was that the Nazi discrimination of Jews should not be highlighted, nor should Jews be given special consideration. As Long said in a letter to Rep. Emanuel Celler, Jewish refugees were being taken in "not as Jews but as human beings in distress who have had our very deep sympathy." He added that "all questions which may affect individual groups are subservient" to the objective of defeating Hitler. In an ironic choice of words, he concluded: *"The final solution can be more speedily and more easily arrived at if the special interests of any group can be merged in the common interest to support the war"* (emphasis added).

All of this concern referred to saving fewer than 2,000 Americans in German internment camps in 1942, not the millions of European Jews whose lives were threatened. And despite the small number of Americans, the State Department cast doubt on the authenticity of those claiming United States citizenship. This was perhaps necessary to justify lumping Americans in with everyone else. . . .

The Danger Grows

On January 20, 1942, Reinhard Heydrich held a conference at Wannsee where be outlined the "Final Solution." In the following months, deportations to the death camp at Chelmno were eliminating the Jews of western Poland. Gas chambers were being built at Belzec and Sobibor and were soon in daily operation. The first deportations to Auschwitz were in March.

The situation in Europe had deteriorated to the point where the State Department finally recognized the danger to American citizens and made some effort to help. By this time, however, the United States was at war with Germany and its options were constrained. Going to war, in itself, was the most dramatic measure the government could take to save people from Hitler, but in the time it would take to achieve an Allied victory, thousands of Americans were imperiled. On March 19, Undersecretary [Summer] Welles gave his Department the following instruction:

> It is essential to get all Americans out of enemy and enemy-occupied territory in Europe who wish to leave and negotiations necessary to attain that end are to be immediately initiated.

The problem, Special Division's Joseph Green noted, was the absence of any means of informing Americans in Axis territory of the opportunity for repatriation. Green suggested that the Passport Division provide a list of passports issued in Europe during 1941, as well as a list of Americans whose passports were validated in 1940 or 1941 for continued stay in Europe, so the Department could check for Americans in Europe who might be entitled to repatriation. Long argued it was impracticable to search lists of thousands of passports. He left it to Swiss officials in charge of American affairs to identify U.S. citizens but refused to permit the Swiss to have access to American files, which, Green said, was contrary to the usual practice. Even a limited search would have provided a list of Americans in Europe, but the records were never checked. Thus, the Undersecretary's orders to be proactive were subverted and the burden was placed on U.S. citizens to contact American officials or their representatives and request assistance.

The State Department correspondence indicates, moreover, the opportunity for repatriation would not have been open to all American citizens even if they had been found. In fact, officials planned to decide whom they wanted to allow to return to the United States. Americans in Germany awaiting repatriation, Long said in June 1942, "ought to be examined and *only those we want* should be accepted" (emphasis in the original).

Long's attitude reflected the public opposition to immigration that was prevalent at the time. Having just come out of the Great Depression, David Wyman noted, Americans were concerned about unemployment. They were also xenophobic and anti-Semitic. The irony, of course, was that Long was not referring to hundreds of thousands of European Jews; he was speaking about *Americans* who were being treated like foreigners because they had chosen to live abroad. . . .

Americans Are Jailed

One of the earliest reports of Americans being arrested came in a letter from the Swiss Consulate in Amsterdam dated January 26, 1942. The report said that approximately 18–25 American men were arrested in Holland immediately after the German declaration of war. All were in a police prison. Several months later, a telegram from Secretary of State Hull to the American Interests office in Norway said that 200 Americans had been arrested there. A representative of the American Red Cross subsequently wrote to the Secretary of the American Legation in Bern that 30–40 Americans, mostly merchant seamen, had been interned in Norway and then transferred to Germany.

In March 1942, the State Department learned that "only 236" Americans in territory occupied by German troops, including Poland, have been "provisionally arrested for police and safety reasons.". . . A memo written by Joseph Green, however, said 5,111 Americans were interned then in Germany, of whom 1,191 had passports.

The Germans assured the United States that American civilians would be treated like POWs according to the Convention of July 24, 1929. When the Nazis began arresting more Americans in Berlin and the Eastern territories, they claimed their actions were a response to similar measures taken by the United States with respect to German citizens. Hull admitted that individuals were arrested on national security grounds but denied interning Germans on any mass scale "had occurred or was contemplated."

While logistical excuses were given for the failure to help Americans in Hungary, people in Slovakia were abandoned primarily for political reasons. In 1942, the State Department determined it was impossible to assist 35 American Jews threatened with deportation from Slovakia and another 70 Americans seeking repatriation. The Department refused to help them because it believed Slovak authorities were trying to use the Americans to pressure the United States to recognize Slovakia.

Once the decision was made not to aid Americans, the State Department was forced to cover up its failure to act out of fear of public reaction. The Special Division's Joseph Green admitted that *"if the Axis propaganda mill should give publicity to the proposed ill treatment of American citizens of Jewish race in Slovakia there may be considerable criticism of the Department by Jewish circles in the United States* (emphasis added)." This is perhaps the clearest statement that the State Department was aware of the seriousness of the plight of Jews in Eastern Europe, was sensitive to public opinion and still was unwilling to act.

When U.S. officials learned in January 1943 that American Jews residing in Germany were subject to the same regulations applied to German Jews, they warned that U.S. policy toward Germans interned in the States might be reconsidered if Americans were discriminated against. But that is all the United States did—hardly enough to persuade Germany that America was seriously concerned about the treatment of its citizens. . . .

Americans Are Interned

As late as September 1944, more than 30,000 Americans were in Europe. Hull reported that approximately 500 Americans were in Hungary and needed protection. In fact, 800 were in Budapest alone.

Most American citizens who were arrested were imprisoned in internment camps. There were more than a dozen such camps including Compiegne (northeast of Paris), Vittel (southern France), Laufen (upper Bavaria), Liebenau (near Stuttgart), Tittmoning (branch camp of Laufen), Tost (at Tost in Silesia) and Biberach (east of Munich). In 1942-44, these camps held more than two thousand Americans.

Some Americans spent years in such camps. . . .

Though they placed severe restrictions on the inmates' freedom, the internment camps were in no way like concentration camps. . . .

U.S. Citizens in Concentration Camps

Little publicity was given to the plight of Americans in internment camps. Even less attention was paid to whether Americans were in concentration camps. When the issue was raised, the government denied any Americans were in the camps and, in fact, officials investigating reports of U.S. citizens in concentration camps came back with negative answers. But the U.S. government did know at least some Americans were in concentration camps. For example, the State Department had reliable information that about 200 people claiming U.S. citizenship were in Bergen-Belsen in July 1944. . . .

This was a rare instance where the public was informed American civilians were held by the Nazis, albeit without much fanfare. A November 17, 1944, Associated Press (AP) dispatch that appeared the next day in the *New York Herald Tribune* had the headline: "Nazis Hold 200 Claiming to Be Citizens of U.S." The State Department told AP it was trying to learn the names of the Americans and arrange for them to be transferred to an internment camp. The story ended with a request that anyone having information that American citizens were being held at Belsen provide it to the Department. The story did not contain any description of Bergen-Belsen. No further information about the fate of these Americans could be found. . . .

Most Americans who survived the concentration camps never made their stories public. Consequently, the evidence of their presence in them is often unclear or restricted to a single reference in a memoir or unrelated report. For example:

- Moscow radio quoted an American civilian who had been in the concentration camp at Bunzlau, Germany.
- In May 1944, the American Legation learned that Marcel Cadet, "allegedly" an American, was in Buchenwald. The Germans responded that Cadet was a French citizen and therefore considered the matter closed.
- Martin Gilbert said 17 U.S.-born people were deported to Auschwitz, at least 10 of whom were American citizens. But he does not footnote the information.
- According to the Jewish Historical Institute in Poland, five Americans were in the Auschwitz camp hospital on March 7,1945: Julius Schiller (age 57), Vittoris Benbossa (age 21), Albert Wenger (age 46), Friedrich Lewinson (age 46) and Franz Striefel (age 29).
- The State Museum of Auschwitz found references to a number of Americans who spent time in the concentration camp. Ralph de Leon was transferred from Auschwitz to Buchenwald on May 15, 1944. Wilhelm Pasternak was transferred to Dachau on October 27, 1944. Johann Kokoszynki, a New Yorker, was listed in a book about prisoners in Block 11 of Auschwitz. The Museum also listed the five men cited by the Jewish Historical Institute in Poland as having been among 700 people liberated from Auschwitz on January 27, 1945.

- The Museum also had copies of two reports written by Albert Wenger, an American lawyer and economist who was in Vienna when Hitler declared war. Wenger said he was arrested on February 24, 1943, by the Gestapo for sheltering a Jewish woman and was deported to Auschwitz. In January 1944, two New Yorkers, Herbert Kohn and Burger Mayers, were killed in the gas chambers. He said he could cite other cases but could not remember the victims' names.
- In the files of the prisoners of the Police Prison in the Small Fortress in Terezin, one American is listed. According to *Terezin Ghetto 1945,* a book published by the Czechoslovakian Ministry of Protection of Labour and Social Welfare, 17 American citizens were among the more than 30,000

Dachau prisoners stand at attention. A few Americans were among the inmates found when Dachau was liberated.

prisoners liberated from Ghetto Terezin on May 21, 1945. In all likelihood, these people were not Jewish.

- According to death certificates, no Americans died in Dachau. Polish sources reported, however, that 11 Americans were in the camp on April 26, 1945. The OSS Section of the Seventh Army found a total of 31,432 internees when the camp was liberated April 29, 1945. Six of the total were Americans. A document listing the nationalities of the prisoners in April 1945 indicates 10 Americans were in Dachau.

- An American citizen named Charles Negrin, who claimed he was a former employee of the American Consul in Budapest before the war, said he was imprisoned in Mauthausen from 1939 until its liberation.

- According to Evelyn Le Chene, eight Americans, four of whom were Jews, were among the 63,000 prisoners in Mauthausen on May 1, 1945. . . .

How many American Jews could have been saved had the United States taken steps to protect its citizens? Obviously, it is impossible to say. As noted earlier, the records of people claiming American citizenship are incomplete, but the State Department acknowledged more than 30,000 American civilians were still in Europe in 1944. If only a tiny fraction of these had been Jews, the State Department failure to act would have been that much more inexcusable. Would it have been so difficult to help those few people, especially given the information available by the time of Hitler's extermination campaign?

Even when the Germans wanted to exchange Americans, the United States frequently demonstrated an unwillingness to act on its citizens' behalf. In early 1943 for example, the German government believed the U.S. had agreed to exchange Germans in the United States for Americans in Germany. The Nazis said that the United States government would determine how long Americans would be interned in Germany. The State Department's response was that the United States "does not deem it in the public interest to reply to the German government" and therefore "Ameri-

cans must continue to remain under German control." To show how many people might have been affected, a year earlier, nearly 2,500 Americans had been on a list to be considered for exchange. Ultimately, several exchanges were made to repatriate Americans held in Germany and Germans held in the United States, but thousands of people remained trapped in Europe.

At the very least, U.S. officials could have shown flexibility and leniency in the evaluation of claims of American citizenship. Instead, the Department adhered to a strict policy that required claimants to prove their citizenship. Simultaneously, the Department adopted an equally inflexible policy to obstruct Americans from obtaining the necessary documentation, prohibiting the transfer from the United States to enemy territory of any documents, including those that could substantiate claims to American nationality. On top of this, bureaucrats in the Department were fighting turf battles over who would authenticate citizenship.

The absurdity of this position was to place the burden on the Jew in Nazi hands, as occurred when the government demanded proof of citizenship from a man held in Auschwitz. Many Jews may not have had legitimate claims, but the State Department knew that rejecting applicants effectively condemned them, initially to persecution and later to death.

State modified its policy somewhat in 1944. It still would not send documents to enemy territory but said it "is always prepared to protect American interests in enemy territory by furnishing information concerning the American nationality of the American nationals involved." The government also took steps to protect its employees. Secretary of War Henry Stimson assigned military ranks to diplomats, trying to insure they would be treated as POWs if they were captured.

Throughout the war, two major obstacles to the rescue of European Jewry were xenophobia and anti-Semitism. Had the news of Americans being mistreated been publicized, however, greater public sympathy might have been aroused for saving Jews, bombing the concentration camps and relaxing immigration quotas.

Selection 12

A Jewish GI in Hell

William J. Shapiro

Approximately six hundred thousand Jews served in the U.S. armed forces. The U.S. military increased the probability of captured Jews being identified by stamping their dog tags with an "H" for Hebrew, ostensibly so they would get the proper burial. When a Jewish GI was taken prisoner, he never knew what to expect. Most were aware that Soviet Jewish prisoners of war (POWs) were murdered, so many Jews hid their dog tags or swapped them with non-Jews. Generally, Jewish soldiers were not treated differently, but there were exceptions. The special treatment they received ranged from various types of discrimination to physical abuse. Handfuls of American POWs were sent to concentration camps, including Dachau, Sachsenhausen, Flossenbürg, Buchenwald, and Mauthausen. One of the most dramatic cases involved the segregation of Jewish prisoners of war at the Stalag 9B prisoner of war camp and their deportation to the Berga concentration camp. An American Jewish medic who survived had kept the memories of his experience buried for more than fifty years. Here, he tells part of his story. William J. Shapiro is a retired physician in Florida.

Excerpted from William J. Shapiro, "A Medic Recalls the Horrors of Berga," an online article found at www.us-israel.org/jsource/ Holocaust/Shapiro.html. Reprinted with permission from the author.

I was transferred out of Stalag 9B on February 8, 1945, in a group of 350 men. My entire barracks was emptied and we were joined by men from other barracks. About 80 of us were Jewish, others included the so-called troublemakers or undesirables of the camp and there were men arbitrarily selected because their names sounded Jewish. I did not know that we were designated to be a work force, called Arbeitskommando in German, until we arrived in Berga. We were told that we were being transferred to another POW camp. . . .

Berga am Elster— Arbeitskommando 625

I believe it was five days later, on February 13, 1945, we arrived in Berga am Elster, located in Thuringian province of Germany. . . .

We were marched up a long road to our camp, which was essentially two one story barracks made of wood with tar paper covering. There were barred, small windows high on the walls and there was a center doorway. Through the doorway into a corridor, at the end was the latrine consisting of a cold water tap on a sink and a central bucket. Each side of the corridor was a room with triple decked bunks. There were straw mats for bedding and nothing else. Outside the barracks was a field in which we would line up at least twice daily to be counted. . . .

In Berga, the Guards were much older men, maybe 60 years of age, many with obvious physical disabilities which probably deferred them for more active duty in the German army. They were members of the Volksturm, the civilian guard, and for the most part they were nonthreatening. There was no use of dogs to guard us and accompany us when we left the camp area. I have no recall of the first officer in charge of us. I do remember the person who had most control over us. He was Unterofficier, Erwin Metz, a noncommissioned officer, a Sergeant in the National Guard. He took his orders from SS. Lt. Hacke, the head man who directed the Schwalbe V project, a joint undertaking by [Heinrich] Himmler's SS and an industrial complex. In effect, he was in charge of the slave-tunnel project to construct underground armaments factories. Lt. Hacke was in charge of all the various slave laborers—political, Russian POWs and now a particular group of American POWs.

Metz was a heavy set man in his late forties or early fifties, wore glasses, had a pointed nose, about 6 feet tall and weighed about 200 pounds. He had a distinctive voice that you knew who was talking when you heard it. Recently, I have heard that other POWs described it as a "Donald Duck" voice. Unquestionably, in Berga and on the Death March, his cruel, indifferent, oppressive and deliberate actions caused the deaths of many of the POWs and added to our indescribable sufferings. . . .

The longer that we stayed at Berga, the more and more did the men manifest all the sicknesses of deprivation, starvation and exhaustion. It followed that many men appeared at morning sick call, deathly ill and unable to go to work in the tunnels. Metz instituted his personal appearance at morning sick call for the men. It was his determination alone that decided whether these very sick men could remain in their barracks or must go to the slave tunnel work. It occurred often for all of us to note that the men that he forced back to work at morning sick call were found dead in their beds the following morning. . . . It was some 50 years after the fact, I learned that a trial of these beasts had occurred. The subsequent outcome of this trial, the insignificant applied sentences for their evil deeds, and the amnesty granted to them by parties not even remotely involved in the crimes, were expressions of the most egregiously disgusting and disgraceful injustice for the victims—the American POWs under their control for 11 weeks in 1945. Simply put—these beasts got away with murder.

Shortly after arrival we were assigned our individual work details. You were selected for a particular job by the Arbeitskommandoführer, Metz. There were nine Medics in the group and we were assigned to the food detail and to remain in the barracks to attend the sick men. The remainder of our group were to become slave laborers, working in two 12 hour shifts every day of the week for 40 days straight. They worked in slave tunnels, not unlike numerous other tunnels in different sites in Germany where underground armament factories were being constructed. I was selected for the food detail and to work in the dispensary. My International Red Cross card identified me as a Medic. It was the most important factor in the selection of my particular work detail and it was the ultimate factor in my survival.

Unquestionably, the type of assigned work detail impacted heavily upon the chances of survival in Berga and subsequently on the death march. The slave-tunnel work resulted in the exposure to strenuous, dangerous and exhausting labor in very cold, wet and slate dust-covered environment for 12 hours daily. This work was to continue without respite for 40 straight days. On Easter Sunday, in late March, a day's holiday was declared. . . . There was daily exposure to and occurrences of injuries. However minor these injuries might be, the end result was a major insult to the starved and debilitated men. A POW's particular work detail was proportional to the exhaustion he would suffer—the heavier the work load, the more exhaustion. At times, men in the various 17 tunnels had different job assignments so that some men fared better than others. But all were debilitated by starvation and exposed to various communicable diseases common in crowded, lice and vermin infested barracks. In a short period of time, the effects were disastrous.

The Food Detail

My food detail consisted of eight men who assembled every morning about 4:00 A.M. . . . At that time of the year, it was very dark, cold, damp, and often the blowing winds of February and March made our trek on snow, ice or slush very treacherous and difficult. I was miserably cold and unbelievably uncomfortable, suffering in silence, but not a whisper of a complaint because I knew the alternative in the tunnels.

We pushed a large, four wheel wagon similar to a small hay wagon. . . . On the flat bed were three very large "Marmite" cans or containers of the size used by Company mess sergeants to feed large groups of men. . . . The distance from our barracks to the Concentration camp annex was about a mile or perhaps a mile and a half. . . . Our food was made and provided to us by adolescent political prisoners at the concentration camp annex. In the morning, presumably after washing our containers, they would fill them with hot ersatz (hot coffee-like fluid). Sometimes, we also received our bread rations in loaves of bread, occasionally included were long sausages. . . . In the evening, we would get that universal political prisoner soup made of turnip heads with the greens attached, a variety of greens that looked like weeds, and sometimes it contained pieces of rotted potatoes. Other times there was a detail sent into town for bread rations and then occasionally marmalade would be added to the ration. In general, I recall that a loaf of bread was to be divided by 6–8 men. This was performed in the barracks with the men who bunked near you and after the soup was finished. We used to rotate the cutting of the bread or the sausage among us so we could be sure of fairness. . . . That was our daily food ration until the end of March when we received our only Red Cross parcel to be divided among four men. . . .

I had never witnessed a public hanging nor let alone ever seen a hanging other than in photographs. In the concentration camp, I saw many hangings in the courtyard not far from the entrance gate, near our kitchen waiting area. At different times, as we waited for our rations, I saw two, three, or four persons, some emaciated, others not emaciated, all in the same pajamas, hanging from a rope from a broad beam supported at each end by angled beams of wood. It was there! In front of us! Out in the open! The area was cleared of any buildings and we came to accept this as part of the camp's physical appearance. I had no idea of the why, what or who of these public hangings. But every time that I saw a hanging, I was frightened, lost, felt defenseless, and intimidated. . . .

The Work Details

The German Volksturm guards recognized that pushing the three full Marmite cans up the hill was a heavy chore, particularly on frozen ground or in wet cold rain. On very harsh blustery days, they would assign 10 men to the food detail. Adding more men to the detail was an opportunity in which we were able to assist some of our buddies in their escape from the camp. We would try to confuse the guards by telling them that we only had eight men on the detail at the start but, in fact, we were 10 men. We would move about changing positions on the wagon to confuse the guards into believing that there were eight of us. During the darkness of the morning, beyond the lights of our camp, they would slip away from the detail. Several men escaped the camp this way.

Three men, the former Man of Confidence of Stalag 9B, Hans Kasten and his two German-speaking assistants, escaped in the first week at Berga. They were captured, spent the rest of the war in a punishment Stalag, but they survived.

I know that we used this trick twice with Morton Goldstein. I had met him in Stalag 9B and he was a garrulous, bombastic man who could not be confined and certainly could not do the work in the tunnels. His first escape ended in recapture and extra duty, and he was forced to stand out in the cold for a long time. About the third week in March, on our trip in the morning to pick up breakfast, Goldstein and another POW joined us and then took off. Goldstein was recaptured and was shot in the back of the head by Sgt. Metz. At the War Crime Trial of Metz, who was charged with killing an

American prisoner, he claimed that Goldstein was attempting to run away after he was captured. Goldstein was brought back to camp by some other Medics. Metz would not allow a burial for one week. His body laid on a stretcher between two barracks as a warning to others who would attempt escape. . . .

The men assigned to work in the tunnels were divided into two shifts, working 12 hour periods, seven days per week. They received no food nor drink while they were in the tunnels. They were marched to the tunnel area about a mile from our barracks by our guards. In the slave tunnels they were under the command of the same work gang bosses and civilian engineers as the slave political prisoners from the concentration camp annex. Their work was identical to the political prisoners but at a different shift time.

This was an SS/Military work complex called Schwalbe V, under the immediate direction of an SS Lt. Hacke, that utilized slave labor political prisoners controlled by Himmler's SS troopers to build underground armament factories. . . .

The slave work consisted of excavating rocks and dirt by hand and shovel after it was loosened by explosives laid by the German engineers. The men hand loaded rocks onto or shoveled slate fragments and dirt onto flatbed cars similar to coal cars. They hand pushed the cars on its track to an area where the rocks could be dumped into the Elster river. They worked with primitive drills, old mining machines and often the men were utilized in place of machine power or horse power to move heavy objects. Accidents and beatings with rubber hoses were common. Slate dust was choking and ever present. . . . Even after this torture there was a further delay of the much deserved rest because they had to stand in line for the evening count of the prisoners. These repetitive, disruptive, inane counts made the suffering more harsh. Finally, the meager rations of a bowl of rotted potato or turnip top green soup and a slice of hard, grainy black bread was distributed. . . .

There was little comfort at night. In our locked barracks, the cold, wet, wintry weather continued to rack our bodies. The barracks was heated by a pot belly stove in the middle of the room. However, the wood allotment was very small and heat could be generated for a couple of hours. Many of us would heat some water obtained from the sink in the latrine. It rarely ever came to a boil for sterilizing the water, but it was hot. I was dressed in everything that I owned. I used my overcoat for a combination pillow and blanket in addition to the German-issued thin blanket. When I got partially undressed to wash myself, I had to ask a buddy to pay close attention to my belongings since theft was rampant. Washing my body was rare but washing my hands was often. I did not shave nor did I ever have a haircut. Some men did have scissors and would offer a haircut for a cigarette. . . .

There was very little interactive talk—period. The men were all consumed in caring for themselves. They were half-starved, exhausted, had different types of wounds, illnesses and pains which involved them with their respective misery. They sat on or lay on their bunks tending to their own needs. There was cold water for washing but many men were not interested in washing at any time. They appeared totally detached from their surroundings, did not talk to others and functioned in isolation. They would only react to the presence of food or commands by the guards. Food would activate them into a frenzy but after the distribution of the food, they would go off, climb onto their bunks and disassociate themselves from the other men. . . .

"Doctor" Metz

Every morning, there was a dread about returning to the tunnel. Men would line up for sick call in the very early morning to avoid going to work. Most had legitimate reasons of sickness or injury to be excused from work. I recall that there were many men who could not get out of bed and had to be assisted to sick call. The slave tunnel work and starvation had profound effects, so large numbers of men reported to sick call. Sergeant Metz took over as the judge who would determine the seriousness of a soldiers' sickness and his ability to work. He attended sick call every morning and his determining exam was to look at the soldier's tongue. I do not know what criteria in the appearance of the tongue made the decision for rest in barracks or return to work. This barbaric and capricious diagnostic test was incorrect many, many times. After sending the man to work, he would do his shift in the tunnels and then we would find him dead in his bunk the next morning. . . . After being in Berga for about two weeks, the men had numerous diseases such as dysentery, dehydration, advanced emaciation, large ulcers on feet and hands, leg edema, pneumonia and probably tuberculosis. About you in every direction—the man below your bunk, next to your bunk, across the room, in the latrine—were exhibiting some ailment. Impending death was all about me. . . .

A fair estimate was that about 50 former very able-bodied and healthy men died or succumbed to severe illness in just seven weeks. . . .

About the last week in March, we were moved to barracks situated alongside of the concentration camp annex. . . . The work detail of the men was significantly changed. They no longer had to work in the tunnels. There were several different jobs but all were above ground, away from the slate dust and cold damp air of the tunnels. Some had to take a train to a rail yard where they moved sections of track or track bed material. Others worked near the tunnels and pushed the tram carts which came out of the tunnel onto a turntable and dumped the excavated material into the Elster river. The work was strenuous but the weather was warming and the breathing was easier. Even the shifts were changed to a more favorable time during the day. My job was less tiring, there was no hill to climb and a minimal amount of pulling and pushing was necessary to get our wagon over the bridge near the entrance of the concentration camp. . . .

Further Torment

In the middle of March, we saw a truck delivering Red Cross parcels to our camp. . . .

At a line up for the evening count of the prisoners, Sergeant Metz made a proclamation that no parcels will be distributed until the men cleansed themselves, shaved and appeared orderly. What a brutal blow! More torment! How devastating and incredibly cruel to expect starved, sick, low functioning and half-crazed men to comply with this order. A delay in the distribution was in effect a new order to further punish us. Make us suffer in order to achieve complete dominion over us. Make us beg and twist the demands a little tighter. It was almost impossible to even modestly perform to the order. Men could not even walk about because of foot sores, dazed from hunger, exhaustion and completely focused on getting to that food in the parcel. Few had the necessary razor or even an old used blade to shave, there was no soap and no cloth or old paper to use as toweling to dry off the cold water for washing. So you froze until your body heat dried your body after the wash up. We had no other uniforms and we all wore the same clothes since the day that we were captured. How could you look orderly dressed when you were in rags with stained fecal smelling pieces of uniform? We were craving for the packages, fantasizing about its contents, and directed our wishes and hopes that the parcels would forever quell our hunger pains. . . .

Eventually he allowed the distribution of one Red Cross box to be divided among four men. This was welcomed by us at that time. However, I know that he kept many boxes intended for our use and gave them to the 25 guards and many others. . . .

I strongly believe that the willful cruel delay in the distribution of the packages for about 7–10 days was an important factor in the subsequent death of many more men at Berga and on the march to nowhere (Death March). The parcels contained meat products, milk, vitamins, many forms of carbohydrates—all of which would have served to replenish the depleted liver and muscle—basic needs for life. Each delayed day led to further depletion in a body already severely compromised. Metz' actions in withholding the needed nourishment deprived some men of the chance to rebuild their body storage of fats, protein and energy carbohydrates for the forced march of the next three weeks. Again, his actions revealed the demonic nature of the man. . . .

A Very Long March into Hell

On April 6, 1945, we were ordered to evacuate the barracks and started a road march from one city to another in a southeasterly direction, supposedly, to get to Bavaria. This was a Death March, so properly termed by the thousands of Jews from across Europe who were forced to walk for endless days, starved, beaten, prodded and arbitrarily shot. The march was to nowhere in particular, often deliberately made longer, circuitous, hazardous, maintained for 10–12 hours each day with minimal food and water—all designed to promote death. In some ways it was comparable to the overcrowded boxcar transports of Jews taken on long journeys, exposed to the elements of freezing cold or hot baking sun while tightly sealed, starved and without water. Again, all this was designed to bring about death of Jews from "natural" causes. None of us American prisoners who started that march in April 1945 had any idea as to what was expected of us or where we were going. No one had any idea of how destructive this march, per se, would be to our group of debilitated soldiers. It was simply walking, no strenuous work in the tunnels, no lifting heavy rail ties, no moving of rail track for 12 hours daily. This was a walk at a slow pace, interrupted by a break every hour and one half in order to defecate, urinate or just sit down along the gutters of the road. Simple! Yes, simple except that we were debilitated, maimed, sick and emaciated. We were totally unprepared for the horrors that we would encounter—the profound despair, the inability to continue to make another step forward, the discovery of dead buddies each morning and the wanton, gross murder along the roads. The guards told us that we were marching to the next town. Every day, that was the same response to our questions as to where next. The answer was always to the next town.

Metz was ordered to take all of the Americans onto the road, even the sick and disabled. He commandeered a horse drawn wagon for several of the men who were extremely sick if not moribund and for some of the guards' luggage.

After eight weeks in Berga, only 280 out of 350 men started on this march, 25 men died, 25 men were hospitalized and about 20 men who escaped had an unknown fate. We walked along each side of the road at a slow pace, strung out for a long distance and alongside of us were our elderly Volksturm guards. . . .

I do not recall what happened at every night stop in our march but I do remember the route from Berga to Greiz, to Hof and then south to Cham, a distance of about 200 kilometers (120 miles). At each stop, we slept mostly in hay lofts or on the open ground in fields. We would get our bread ration at night and some soup. I had some of my food from the Red Cross package which I nibbled a small piece slowly each night. On the road, some of the German civilians were passing out turnips, potatoes and some men even got bread and other foodstuffs. The civilians were not hostile to us, perhaps, they also knew that Allied forces were not very far away. We could hear the artillery fire in the distance but we had no idea as to where they were, how close, whether they were Americans or Russians, or any sense of direction. . . .

I did fairly well for the first three days of the march until we got to Hof, our third stop. On the previous nights in the other two towns, there were reports of two or three deaths. The men walked all day, held out until night and they would die in their sleep. When we arrived in Hof about 10 men died. It was only about 50 miles to Hof but the walking became unbearable. . . .

We were there on April 12, the day that [President Franklin D.] Roosevelt died. . . . I remember that we all began to cry and this, superimposed upon our existing anguish brought us to hopeless despair. After all this suffering, I thought that there was no hope, no chance for liberation. . . .

As we approached a steep hill, I saw the most gruesome, cruel, barbarous, inhumane acts that I have ever seen in my entire life even to this day. As we climbed the hill in the road ahead of us and caught up to where we had seen the political prisoners in the distance, we saw on each side of the road hundreds of dead Jews. Most of them were in the kneeling position, many on their side in a fetal position and all were dead by obvious gun shots behind the head. Many heads were blown open by the force of the shot and the brains were splattered about. It was ghastly. It was indescribably frightening. It was unspeakable. It was so shocking to look at the very recent awesome destruction of human beings, presumably because they could not continue the march up the inclined road. . . .

It was unbelievably frightening to me and I am sure to my buddies walking up the hill. What was in store for us? Is this the manner in which it will all end? . . . After all the suffering that these Jews had encountered, so close to freedom, their inability to climb the hill resulted in instant death. I was engulfed by the same persistent thought of what if I cannot continue—this is what happens if you do not continue. I was exhausted and just dragged along, fearful of stopping until we were told that it was time for a break. I became an automaton. As we continued to walk through them and past them we came to another group of political prisoners in similar positions. As we ascended the steeper part of the hill, there were more and more victims. You became immune to the sight, you expected it, it was walking into a hell. The "trees" lining the sides of the road to hell were dead Jews. . . .

Liberation—April 23, 1945

Liberation was near the town of Cham. I believe that I was in that twilight zone before death that I have observed in some men in Berga. I do not believe that I was sick with any disease except severe weight loss, intermittent diarrhea, exhaustion and lice infestation. We were billeted in a hayloft and a large tank rolled in front of the barn. I thought that it was a German panzer. I saw the white star on the side of the tank and then some men started to shout that they are Americans. It was after some time, about ten minutes, that I realized that I was liberated. My mind was blank and I was not functioning. I walked out of the barn, it was a bright sunny day. I saw many tanks roll by, soldiers were hanging over the turrets and throwing food and chocolate D ration bars at us. I picked one up and had great difficulty opening the package. A jeep pulled up and told me to get in. I remember sitting alongside of the driver, mumbling and trying to chew on the chocolate bar. I do not recall any extended conversation. He knew that I was in the 28th Infantry Division by the shoulder patch on my field jacket. I knew that he was part of the 11th Armored Division and this was part of [George] Patton's Third Army. I did not cry, nor shout, nor jump or run about as some of the others did.

Selection 13

The Jews of One Small Polish Town Disappear

Eva Hoffman

Virtually the entire Jewish population of Poland, three million men, women, and children, were murdered by the Nazis and their accomplices. It is difficult to grasp the magnitude of this figure or to comprehend it in human rather than statistical terms. By looking at what happened to one small Polish town and a few individuals from that town, the horror becomes more real. In this passage, Eva Hoffman recounts the life and death of the Jews of Brańsk. Here we have a microcosm of the Holocaust, Jews murdered in horrible ways, others who managed to escape with the aid of righteous non-Jews, and a handful of Jews who resisted and became partisans fighting the Germans. Hoffman was born in Poland. She is an author and former editor of the New York Times Book Review.

In each of my conversations with the farmers of Brańsk, the inevitable question falls: What do you remember from that time—from the war? The robust peasant who has expressed relief at the absence of Jews in Brańsk says he remembers all kinds of things. . . .

And did he know what happened to the Jews here? Ah yes, he answers eagerly, his eyes twinkling. All kinds of things happened. One time during the German occupation, on a morning after a night of shooting, there were many Jewish bodies in the street. The Germans had piled all the bodies in one place and, as he was passing on his cart, they ordered him to haul the corpses to a mass grave.

"Well, if that's what they say, you can't do anything," he remembers. "So I said, 'But sir, for so many bodies, I need someone to help.'" Then, with someone's assistance, he took the bodies to the other side of the river and threw them into a big open grave. Many of them had their clothes ripped at the seams, because the Germans were looking for gold.

"Well, we did what we had to, and we turned back."

"And that was it?" I ask.

"That was it. We went home—but through the river. Because you can imagine the state the cart was in."

No sentiment, no softening of the horrid tale, no pity or regret. . . . To him, by now, it is just a story. But I sense something more than neutral distance, and as he goes on, the farmer peels away layers of hostility toward the Jews, and deep resentments. He recalls the Jews who, at the beginning of the war, welcomed the Soviet army that had invaded from the east. Some of them were rewarded with a small measure of very temporary power, and undoubtedly on occasion flaunted it. "The Jews treated the Poles very odiously under the Soviets," the farmer says. "I met my friend Shmulko once, in his new uniform and with his gun, and said, 'Shmulko, how are you?' And Shmulko showed me his backside and said, 'Sniff it.'

"Yes, yes," the farmer assures me when I look at him dubiously, "that's how it was."

Possibly. But was Shmulko's gesture an act of gratuitous vulgarity, an abuse of his short-lived and rather pathetic privilege? Or was it a repayment, a petty if nasty revenge, for insults addressed to him in the past? Was the farmer, harboring even now a rankling belief in Jewish exploitation, one of those who stood in front of Jewish stores, preventing customers from going in? Surely, he would have approved of the boycotts.

Impossible to know, impossible to unravel the coils of conflict, injustices, and injuries that had preceded the moment when the farmer's Jewish acquaintance turned away from him so unceremoniously. As he reaches further back in his memory, the farmer reveals more strands of preconceptions and fragments of stereotypes. In times of peace, such prejudices might simmer in his breast, creating perhaps an air of cockiness or aggression about him at the market, but not wreaking any enormous harm. But in times of war? . . .

What of others like him? I can imagine how, with the incitements of Nazi rhetoric ringing in his ears, with the imagery of anti-Semitic posters before his eyes, with the repeated warnings that helping Jews was punishable by death, and with the orders, shouted in German, to turn Jews in to the authorities or else; with the sight, above all, of Jews being publicly hounded, humiliated, killed—how, with all that, a farmer might turn his murky notions and muddy aversions into the clear knowledge that, as far as Jews were concerned, anything was permitted, anything at all. I can see such a man, in such a time, slipping into the kind of darkness in which

a fatal betrayal might be perpetrated, or a murder committed, quite casually, in the light of day.

One Who Helped

In the evening, I go with Zbyszek to meet a person of quite a different ilk: one of those who helped. She is Janina Woińska, a small, elderly woman with a heart-shaped face and a sweet, mild manner. She is a retired pharmacist, and was already working at the pharmacy when the war started, although she had moved to Brańsk only shortly before. She has reasons to remember that time very clearly. Her brother was taken to Auschwitz, and then to Buchenwald, as a member of the Polish resistance. She was a young woman then, in her early twenties, but she marshaled all her resources to help him. She raised a big sum of money in a scheme to get him out which did not succeed; she mailed packages to him at Buchenwald. She still marvels that in a carton of 120 eggs she sent him, only four arrived broken.

Almost by accident, she found herself helping others as well. When the ghetto was established in Brańsk in 1941, the pharmacy building sat in the middle of it, fenced off arbitrarily from the designated Jewish area. She could see from her window what was going on in the ghetto, and at first it was not horrifying. People could easily sneak in and out; Poles went in to trade food, and Jews smuggled goods to and from Bialystok. But then, in November 1942, everything changed. One night early that month, someone jumped over the ghetto fence and ran into the pharmacy. It was Lejb Shapiro, the pharmacy's prewar owner. He told Woińska that the ghetto was surrounded, and nobody knew what was going to happen. He wanted to hide with his wife, his two sons, and his brother's fiancee in the basement of the pharmacy. Woińska, and two other women living in the building, decided that this was a suicidal plan: the pharmacy was right in the ghetto, and frequented by Germans and Poles. Instead, it was agreed that the Shapiros should go to another building, close by but outside the ghetto area. There, Woińska made a hiding place behind piles of lumber. Together with the two other women, she brought the fugitives food for the next few days.

"Did you know what the danger was?" I ask. "Maybe not palpably," she answers. "I was so naive." The penalty for a deed like hers was death—but perhaps she could not allow herself to know this with full clarity when she took her risk, any more than a person trying to survive can afford to feel the imminence of death.

Her sense of danger was sharpened, however, after a close call with the Gestapo, who came to the pharmacy a few days later and ordered a search. By that time, with the help of a young priest, the Shapiros had gone on to another, safer place outside Brańsk. The Gestapo found their suitcases, left behind in the pharmacy's attic. "Someone has been here," one of the Germans said. "How can I vouch that someone has or has not been here?" Woińska responded.

"I spoke logically," she now says, "although I was very afraid. You should see the Gestapo man. He had those high boots, and he didn't talk—he shouted." As it happened, the whole "aristocracy" of Brańsk had gathered in the pharmacy, including a doctor, a priest, and a teacher. They all knew about the hiding place. No one said a word.

During the search, another Gestapo man started hitting a peasant quite viciously. He wasn't one of the truly brutal Gestapo men—he was Brańsk's "good German," and tried to spare Jews from the worst—but he had to react. He ordered the pharmacy cordoned off more securely from the ghetto.

"It's a miracle we survived," Woińska says. This must have been brought home to her all too vividly by the sights and sounds she witnessed on the days and nights following the Shapiros' appearance: screams, shots, people falling dead in the streets. The ghetto was being liquidated. At night she could make out silhouettes of people trying to escape through the pharmacy's courtyard. Once she watched as two Poles ("this is a shameful thing to talk about," she says) pointed out to the Gestapo a hole in the fence through which people could flee. One afternoon she saw people being herded onto horse-drawn

carts, which were to take them on their deadly journey to Treblinka. . . .

Janina Woińska was an inadvertent witness, forced to look at terrible things that, in a way, had nothing to do with her—although, by accident of proximity, they implicated her in life-and-death choices. Almost inadvertently, she made the decision to help save lives rather than turn away.

But why? Why did she act as she did, briefly and impulsively perhaps, but in disregard of her own safety? "A human being is a human being," she answers. "I was helping human beings."

That must have been true, because in the abstract she was hardly a philo-Semite. Before the war, she had a close Jewish friend at school, but as for Jews in general, her views are hardly pure. She thinks they "had money in their hands, and exploited others' dependence on them.". . . "Eighty percent of the professions were in Jewish hands," she says with considerable exaggeration, but undoubtedly repeating inflated propaganda figures. "Students were fighting for their places.". . .

"But how did you feel," I ask again, "when the Shapiros came to ask for help?" I want to plumb the mystery of motive. "When a person needs help, you have to help them," Woińska says. "Those are our feelings. Anyway, that's our faith as well, that you help those in need." Signs of Catholic piety are displayed in her apartment: religious pictures on the walls, a photograph of herself with the pope.

The young priest who arranged for the Shapiros' second hiding place, and who escorted them on their short but hazardous journey, was Vicar Józef Chwalko. His superior, Rector Boleslaw Czarkowski, reiterated in his sermons that "one must help people" who were in need. A priestly word, a priestly example, carried enormous moral authority in a congregation such as Brańsk's—perhaps enough weight to tip the scales of conscience for people like Woińska. As I keep probing her memories and reasons, she says that somewhere inside her was the thought that someone else might one day help her brother. Perhaps through her altruistic gestures she was propitiating fate, making sure she was not tipping the scales of justice, or of mercy, to the wrong side.

Invasion

In the dawn hours of September 1, 1939, the loud drone of airplanes was heard over Brańsk. At nine o'clock that day, a radio announcement informed the town's inhabitants that the Germans had marched into Poland. The news aroused rage and disbelief in everyone, but the Jewish population knew it had more reasons to be afraid. Rumors of the Nazis' anti-Semitic policies in Germany had probably seemed disquieting, but remote. Now the knowledge of German attitudes contributed to the feeling of general terror. . . .

On September 14, German tanks rolled into Brańsk. Anti-Jewish policies went immediately into effect, and three hundred people were herded into a church and shipped to Germany. On the twenty-third, the Germans set the Old Synagogue on fire, pushing the caretaker and his family into the burning building. . . .

When the order to create a ghetto was given in the fall of 1941, . . . about 2,400 people, among them Jews from the nearby villages, were herded into the two ghettos. The Poles living within these areas were relocated.

I try to imagine: families loading their belongings onto carts, the hasty leave-takings, the moment of indecision about whether to lock the house; most realized this would be a futile gesture. And the fear, the constriction of heart and nerves, the sense of unknown fatality hanging over it all. The journey to the ghetto wasn't long, but it involved the crossing of an irrevocable line. The Jews were now placed on the "other side," symbolically beyond the pale of society or solidarity. More than that, posters in the town warned the Poles that the penalty for helping Jews, taking food to them, or sheltering them was death. Acts of compassion were being criminalized, made nearly unaffordable.

In the ghetto, overcrowding led to a high rate of disease and mortality. Food was severely rationed. A boot factory was opened, and Jews had to supply the labor. Yet at first a kind of life, and a kind of coping, could go on. . . . The ghettos were not yet closed off, although their inmates weren't allowed to leave their houses without good reason. Still, the absence of a physical barrier made movement on the sly fairly easy. Smuggling into and out of the ghetto was widespread. Occasionally, whole cows were brought in and slaughtered in the proper way; before Passover, matzo was made in secret. Amazingly, some people managed to spend whole days outside, working in Polish homes as cobblers, tailors, domestics. . . .

Jews in the Brańsk Ghetto

In the summer of 1942, the two ghettos were consolidated into one area, and the main ghetto was enclosed by a twelve-foot-high fence. . . .

The closing of the ghetto had one temporarily positive side effect: people could now walk freely on the ghetto's streets and exchange speculations, news, griefs. The news—sometimes hard to distinguish from rumor—was somber. People were beginning to learn of the roundups and deportations from other towns. They had heard about the construction of Treblinka, but were as yet unsure what it was intended for. . . .

On the night of November 1, 1942, a warning came from Bialystok: the Brańsk ghetto was going to be liquidated the next day. Despair and pandemonium followed. Some people tried to escape before the action was carried out, others ran to hiding places in the ghetto, having prepared for this eventuality.

In the dawn hours of November 2, the roundups started. The Germans, as they had done in other towns, brought in special units of Lithuanian and Ukrainian guards to aid them. Poles were not forced to participate in these brutal procedures, perhaps because they were considered too anti-German or too unruly, or because they lacked the mettle for the job. Despite the sinister cordon surrounding the ghetto, a large number of people broke through the fence or fled through underground openings. Some were wounded or killed before they got out. Several hundred people escaped to the nearby forests or looked for shelter in farmers' houses.

A few found refuge; others were turned away by Poles terrified by the murderous atmosphere and by the threat—reiterated constantly over loud-speakers—of execution for helping Jews. In the next few days, many people returned to the ghetto, not knowing what else to do.

On November 6, the Gestapo gave the order to assemble in the center of the ghetto. At that point, people knew what was in store for them. . . .

In the next three days, two thousand people were transported to Bielsk and then to Treblinka. On November 10 several hours after arriving at the concentration camp, they were all murdered in the gas chambers.

In the chaos of the ghetto's liquidation, there seemed to be a range of responses from the Polish population. There were examples of monstrous cruelty, such as a Polish policeman who gratuitously shot and killed Jewish children. Others delivered Jews to the Gestapo. In the village of Oleksin, the mayor, named Józef Adamczuk, forced some of the inhabitants to join a search for Jews, whose presence in the surrounding forests had become known. He was the cause of fourteen deaths. (In 1948, a Polish court gave him a life sentence, which was later commuted to ten years.)

But insofar as one can judge from scattered stories and memories, among the populace the impulse of ordinary compassion was still alive. In an incident described in the Yizkor Book, when a Gestapo officer caught several Jews trying to escape from the ghetto, a group of Poles, summoned by the distressing cries, gathered round and pleaded for their release. . . .

No Escape

In the following days, placards appeared declaring Brańsk to be *Judenfrei*. Nevertheless, the Nazis in their bureaucratic efficiency, realized that a sizable number had managed to escape their net. The actual figures are difficult to pin down; Zbyszek estimates that between 200 and 350 people were unaccounted for. In any case, the Nazis announced a hunt for the hidden Jews. The Catholic priest, to his credit, preached a sermon in which he told people to "wash their hands" of such murderous activity, and enjoined them to help those in need. . . .

There was still one major hiding place left in the ghetto, a bunker with about thirty people huddled inside. It was destroyed when a woman inadvertently started a fire while cooking. As the people emerged from the burning enclosure and tried to flee, they were shot by the Nazis. . . . Twenty-three of the people were killed, and buried by Christians in the Jewish cemetery.

This was the end of the Brańsk ghetto, and of the Jewish community. From then on, there were only remnants, human atoms scattered in the forests and in Polish houses. For them, there were two ways to survive: through solitary ingenuity or through attempts to join with others in similar danger.

People knew that an old woman in Brańsk had been killed by the Nazis for sheltering Jews. Another Polish family narrowly escaped death when their property was burned down by the Germans, and remained in hiding for the rest of the war. Another person was sent to a concentration camp for offering minimal help. Yet others were sent to labor camps, including a man who was punished when a young Jewish boy was found to be huddling, without the man's knowledge, in his field. In what was perhaps the most shocking incident to the local populace, in July 1943 a priest named Henryk Opiatowski, who was a member of the Home Army, was executed for helping Jews and Soviet deserters from labor camps. . . .

The End of Jewish Life

For Brańsk the war did not end in 1944, or even in 1945. The Soviet army remained in the town until January 1945. . . .

After the Jewish survivors emerged from their hiding places, they congregated in one house in Brańsk. There were sixty-four of them, although seventy-six survived altogether. They were painfully aware of the utter devastation of their community and their way of life. They were desolated; this was the first time they took the measure of their losses. They still did not feel secure in their hometown. They could see that Polish peasants, who had occupied Jewish homes, were afraid that the former owners would try to reclaim their properties and belongings. They were aware of the atmosphere of lawlessness and disarray. In March 1945, two young Jewish women who were taking sewing lessons from a Polish seamstress were murdered for unknown reasons. The seamstress was killed as well. At that point, the cluster of survivors decided to move to Bialystok. In 1947, a Jewish man who had come to the Brańsk market was shot dead in the middle of the day. It is rumored that he had stolen some money, and this was the lawless revenge. But from then on, no Jewish person came to Brańsk for a long time.

By 1948, most of the remaining Jews of Brańsk had emigrated to the United States and to Israel. Jack puts his reasons for leaving Poland succinctly: "How could I stay in a place where the land was soaked in blood?"

Selection 14

Holocaust Photographs: Documenting the Horror

E. Harry James Cargas

The number of books written on the Holocaust now must number in the thousands. On the Internet, dozens of sites are devoted to the subject. How many pages of text have attempted to describe, define, and explain this single event? Perhaps millions. And yet much of what one needs to know can be gleaned simply by looking at photographs. In this brief selection, E. Harry James Cargas tells us a great deal about the Holocaust by contemplating the meaning of four photographs. Cargas chaired the Department of Literature and Language and taught religion at Webster College. He also served as a member of the President's Commission on the Holocaust.

Such care is being taken to hang this woman properly. Look at the expressions of each of these men. They are paying such close attention to every last detail. They perform rather artistically for the photographer here, each relating so intently to a particular aspect of the unholy task literally *at hand*! Note how well dressed the men are. The executioner on the left wears trousers that have been carefully creased. (This was long before the invention of permanent press.) And how about the man working from above, with tie and hat. When he left home, did his neighbors think he was heading for the office? Did he ask his wife, "What's for dinner tonight?" thinking that today's work would not interfere with a hearty appetite?

But we cannot consider only the killers. Our eyes are continually brought back to the woman who is soon to die. She seems hardly to pose a

*Two men prepare to hang a woman while
an earlier victim appears draped at right.*

the cause of this victim's condition might be to dishonor him. But we may wonder if he survived the moment. His pain seems too complete, so overwhelming that this may have been the final expression of his life. Jewish psychiatrists who themselves had concentration camp experiences have written about how some (of the few) who survived the death camps were able to do so. Bruno Bettelheim suggests that certain men and women took on the personalities of their aggressors in order to get through alive. Leo Eitinger, after having analyzed many patients who, like himself, barely outlived Auschwitz and other camps, feels that one almost indispensable element to the survival of many was having a close relative sharing the atrocious experiences. Those who lost their entire families or who were sep-

threat. She looks like my grandmother, is undoubtedly somebody's grandmother. What is she thinking? Is she praying? How frightened is this woman? Does she hope for some miracle to save her, or does she despair because she knows that a tremendous human slaughter is taking place, that she is only a single unit in an overwhelming event that will number 50,000,000 units? She may be almost at peace; somehow the camera suggests this. How many has she seen hanged before her? The corpse on the right suggests that there may have been several. How long will she be able to maintain a certain dignity, before the bulk of her body, in opposition to her neck, will force her to attempt to flail her legs and arms in one futile gesture toward life? Did she know the shrouded victim? Was it her husband or a child of hers? Did she die quickly?

However we define Hope, we see here a man who has none. His anguish is not superficial; it has penetrated his soul. To speculate on

*A photo captures the agony of a
dying man in liberated Bergen-Belsen.*

arated from them in a kind of absolute way did not have this opportunity. Viktor Frankl, the founder of logotheraphy, a psychiatric approach based on hope—the hope of being reunited with a loved one, of completing a particular project—saw this as being important to a relatively large number of survivors. But the man in this photograph seems to have none of these. His posture is hardly that of one who is aggressive in any form. Furthermore, here he seems so alone that abandonment by family, friends, even God, appears to be reflected in his cry. And it is despair, not hope, which is reflected in his face, a despair that may have come from a realization that he is a creature suspended on earth, with ties to no one, no thing. Nor are we taking into account any physical pain this person is suffering. How cold is he? How long has it been since he has eaten? Is disease ravaging his body the way it

did nearly all who lived for any length of time in the death camps? In a culture saturated with the false emotions of Hollywood, television soap operas, advertisers, self-pitiers and sycophants in general, can we long contemplate the true emotion of this miserable, miserable human being? We must.

How old is the little boy in this photograph? Perhaps seven. But his eyes contain centuries. What a pitiful incongruity. Innocence, by its very nature, does not encompass experience. But then this photograph is of a situation that is not consistent with nature. The Holocaust was, by every civilized measure, antinatural. The boy intuits this. Something is horribly topsy-turvy, terribly frightening. A man is holding a weapon on him, during this roundup of Jews in Warsaw. For what reason? No reason could ever be invented to justify what is happening in this scene, and the real cause is

Jews are rounded up during the Warsaw Ghetto Uprising of 1943. This photo was used after the war to convict the soldier pointing the gun at the boy.

ludicrous in the root sense of that word. This boy is being taken to his death because he has been judged a danger to European equilibrium. He is a Jew. That is crime enough in some people's minds. And while we could focus our attention exclusively on him in this picture, there are others who need to be considered. For instance, the child with his hands raised isn't even the youngest Pole in the group. Just above his right shoulder we see another who is about four or five years old. Another threat, another Christ-killer to some. A second boy to the left of center, looking off to his right, also exhibits in his eyes a terror no child should know. Eyes, in fact, can be considered a theme, if we dare to be academic about this setting. The camera's eye must be considered. It *must* be. Who has dared to take this photograph? For what purpose? Why memorialize this sin? What is the intended audience? Who will enjoy viewing this? Clearly this picture could *not* have been made without official permission. The victims were not snapping shutters. No, the persecutors were. Note that no eyes of the prisoners are looking at the camera. Those eyes are concentrated on something other than publicity. There is one, however, who is looking directly into the lens: the guard who has his gun directed at the little boy up front. We may take it that he is posing for this photographer. Why? Is he proud of what he is doing? Is he pleased to be carrying out his government's policy concerning Jews? Did he request a copy of the photo to show his friends and family? I have heard that after this photograph became famous, this guard was found as a civilian. I do not know the accuracy of this, but if true, he really has seen *himself* in this situation. How does he feel about it? Does he ever wonder if God's eye has recorded the same event? Does he have some thoughts about Judgment Day? What else did he do in the war that is memorable?

This was a face. It is grotesque, reminding us of novelist Flannery O'Connor's reply to a question about the bizarre situations and characters she rendered to present her theological

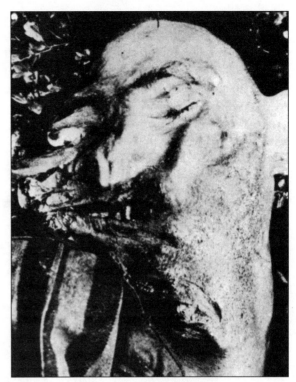

*The face of a man bludgeoned
to death with a hammer.*

viewpoint. She insisted that to the hard of hearing you have to shout. The photograph here is a response to those who would hail war as a noble effort, or worse, who would deny that the Holocaust ever really happened. Since over forty books in Europe and the United States have been published denying the actuality of Nazi tortures, let the authors study this picture. This man was beaten to death with a hammer. Who was he? When he was nursing in his mother's arms, what hopes did she have for him when he reached maturity? Did she dream that he would become a medical doctor who might perform heroic acts of healing? Perhaps she hoped that her baby would become a rabbi and attend the spirit rather than the body. Possibly the boy would be trained as a scientist, become a good family man. He may have been a father. It is not impossible that a son of his saw him being bludgeoned to death. Surely the mother could not have dared to imagine her son's cruel end; he has become, for the world, only a victim, his face and head bones crushed because some guard was somehow irritated with him. And what of the guard? Was he mad or sane in the way the world ordinarily judges? When he finished his human massacre, was he able to look upon his effort or did it disgust him? Did he brag about his heroics or was he as ashamed of himself as we are of him now? This was a face, the face of a man who lived and dreamed and died a ghastly death. We cannot look at this face—and yet we dare not avert our eyes lest . . .

Selection 15

The Shame of Surviving

Primo Levi

Everyone has had difficulties in their lives, and these hardships are often difficult to put behind us. Even when a person succeeds in moving on from a bad experience, the memory of it may overwhelm him or her unexpectedly. For Holocaust survivors, memories are even more difficult to overcome. One prisoner of war who spent time at Buchenwald said that for forty years he would shave in the morning and see bodies in the mirror. Part of the torture of these memories is the question many survivors ask: Why did I survive? While most felt happy and lucky to be alive, almost all felt some guilt over surviving and shame in failing to have done more to alter their fate and that of others. This excerpt by Holocaust survivor Primo Levi gives a sense of the feelings of survivors.

I now reread the passage from my own book, *The Reawakening*, which was published in Italy only in 1963, although I had written these words as early as 1947. In it is

Excerpted from Primo Levi, "Shame," in *The Drowned and the Saved*, edited by Raymond Rosenthal. English translation copyright © 1988 Simon & Schuster. Reprinted with permission from Simon & Schuster.

a description of the first Russian soldiers facing our Lager [camp] packed with corpses and dying prisoners.

> They did not greet us, nor smile; they seemed oppressed, not only by pity but also by a confused restraint which sealed their mouths, and kept their eyes fastened on the funereal scene. It was the same shame which we knew so well, which submerged us after the selections, and every time we had to witness or undergo an outrage: the shame that the Germans never knew, the shame which the just man experiences when confronted by a crime committed by another, and he feels remorse because of its existence, because of its having been irrevocably introduced into the world of existing things, and because his will has proven nonexistent or feeble and was incapable of putting up a good defense.

I do not think that there is anything I need erase or correct, but there is something I must add. That many (including me) experienced "shame," that is, a feeling of guilt during the imprisonment and afterward, is an ascertained fact confirmed by numerous testimonies. It may seem absurd, but it is a fact. . . .

Around May 1944 our almost innocuous

Kapo [prisoner in charge of other prisoners] was replaced, and the newcomer proved to be a fearsome individual. All Kapos gave beatings; this was an obvious part of their duties, their more or less accepted language. After all, it was the only language that everyone in that perpetual Babel could truly understand. In its various nuances it was understood as an incitement to work, a warning or punishment, and in the hierarchy of suffering it had a low rank. Now, the new Kapo gave his beatings in a different way, in a convulsive, malicious, perverse way: on the nose, the shin, the genitals. He beat to hurt, to cause suffering and humiliation. Not even, as with many others, out of blind racial hatred, but with the obvious intention of inflicting pain, indiscriminately, and without pretext, on all his subjects. Probably he was a mental case, but clearly under those condi-

tions the indulgence that we today consider obligatory toward such sick people would have been out of place. I spoke about it with a colleague, a Jewish Croatian Communist: What should we do? How to protect ourselves? How to act collectively? He gave me a strange smile and simply said: "You'll see, he won't last long." In fact, the beater vanished within a week. But years later, during a meeting of survivors, I found out that some political prisoners attached to the Work Office inside the camp had the terrifying power of switching the registration numbers on the lists of prisoners destined to be gassed. Anyone who had the ability and will to act in this way, to oppose in this or other ways the machine of the Lager, was beyond the reach of "shame"—or at least the shame of which I am speaking, because perhaps he experiences something else. . . .

Concentration camp survivors in Ebensee, Austria. Guilt often accompanied the survivors' feelings of relief and joy.

We had lived for months and years at an animal level. Our days had been encumbered from dawn to dusk by hunger, fatigue, cold, and fear, and any space for reflection, reasoning, experiencing emotions was wiped out. We endured filth, promiscuity, and destitution, suffering much less than we would have suffered from such things in normal life, because our moral yardstick had changed. Furthermore, all of us had stolen: in the kitchen, the factory, the camp, in short, "from the others," from the opposing side, but it was theft nevertheless. Some (few) had fallen so low as to steal bread from their own companions. We had not only forgotten our country and our culture, but also our family, our past, the future we had imagined for ourselves, because, like animals, we were confined to the present moment. Only at rare intervals did we come out of this condition of leveling, during the very few Sundays of rest, the fleeting minutes before falling asleep, or the fury of the air raids, but these were painful moments precisely because they gave us the opportunity to measure our diminishment from the outside.

I believe that it was precisely this turning to look back at the "perilous water" that gave rise to so many suicides after (sometimes immediately after) Liberation. It was in any case a critical moment which coincided with a flood of rethinking and depression. By contrast, all historians of the Lager—and also of the Soviet camps—agree in pointing out that cases of suicide *during* imprisonment were rare. Several explanations of this fact have been put forward; for my part I offer three, which are not mutually exclusive.

First of all, suicide is an act of man and not of the animal. It is a meditated act, a noninstinctive, unnatural choice, and in the Lager there were few opportunities to choose: people lived precisely like enslaved animals that sometimes let themselves die but do not kill themselves.

Secondly, "there were other things to think about," as the saying goes. The day was dense: one had to think about satisfying hunger, in some way elude fatigue and cold, avoid the blows. Precisely because of the constant imminence of death there was no time to concentrate on the idea of death. [Italian novelist Italo] Svevo's remark in *Confessions of Zeno* when he ruthlessly describes his father's agony, has the rawness of truth: "When one is dying, one is much too busy to think about death. All one's organism is devoted to breathing."

Thirdly, in the majority of cases, suicide is born from a feeling of guilt that no punishment has attenuated; now, the harshness of imprisonment was perceived as punishment, and the feeling of guilt (if there is punishment, there must have been guilt) was relegated to the background, only to re-emerge after the Liberation. In other words, there was no need to punish oneself by suicide because of a (true or presumed) guilt: one was already expiating it by one's daily suffering.

What guilt? When all was over, the awareness emerged that we had not done anything, or not enough, against the system into which we had been absorbed. About the failed resistance in the Lagers, or, more accurately, in some Lagers, too much has been said, too superficially above all by people who had altogether different crimes to account for. Anyone who made the attempt knows that there existed situations, collective or personal, in which active resistance was possible, and others much more frequent, in which it was not. It is known that, especially in 1941, millions of Soviet military prisoners fell into German hands. They were young, generally well nourished and robust; they had military and political training, and often they formed organic units with soldiers with the rank of corporal and up, noncommissioned officers, and officers. They hated the Germans who had invaded their country, and yet they rarely resisted. Malnutrition, despoilment, and other physical discomforts, which it is so easy and economically advantageous to provoke and at which the Nazis were masters, are rapidly destructive and paralyze before destroying, all the more so when they are preceded by years of segregation, humiliation, maltreatment, forced migration, laceration of family ties, rupture of contact with the rest of the world—that is to say, the situation of the bulk of the prisoners who had landed in

Auschwitz after the introductory hell of the ghettos or the collection camps.

Therefore, on a rational plane, there should not have been much to be ashamed of, but shame persisted nevertheless, especially for the few bright examples of those who had the strength and possibility to resist. I spoke about this in the chapter "The Last" in *Survival in Auschwitz,* where I described the public hanging of a resistor before a terrified and apathetic crowd of prisoners. This is a thought that then just barely grazed us, but that returned "afterward": you too could have, you certainly should have. And this is a judgment that the survivor believes he sees in the eyes of those (especially the young) who listen to his stories and judge with facile hindsight, or who perhaps feel cruelly repelled. Consciously or not, he feels accused and judged, compelled to justify and defend himself.

I Come First

More realistic is self-accusation, or the accusation of having failed in terms of human solidarity. Few survivors feel guilty about having deliberately damaged, robbed, or beaten a companion. Those who did so (the Kapos, but not only they) block out the memory. By contrast, however, almost everybody feels guilty of having omitted to offer help. The presence at your side of a weaker—or less cunning, or older, or too young—companion, hounding you with his demands for help or with his simple presence, in itself an entreaty, is a constant in the life of the Lager. The demand for solidarity, for a human word, advice, even just a listening ear, was permanent and universal but rarely satisfied. There was no time, space, privacy, patience, strength; most often, the person to whom the request was addressed found himself in his turn in a state of need, entitled to comfort.

I remember with a certain relief that I once tried to give courage (at a moment when I felt I had some) to an eighteen-year-old Italian who had just arrived, who was floundering in the bottomless despair of his first days in camp. I forget what I told him, certainly words of hope, perhaps a few lies, acceptable to a "new arrival," expressed with the authority of my twenty-five years and my three months of seniority; at any rate, I made him the gift of a momentary attention. But I also remember, with disquiet, that much more often I shrugged my shoulders impatiently at other requests, and this precisely when I had been in camp for almost a year and so had accumulated a good store of experience: but I had also deeply assimilated the principal rule of the place, which made it mandatory that you take care of yourself first of all. I never found this rule expressed with as much frankness as in *Prisoners of Fear* by Ella Lingen-Reiner (where, however, the woman doctor, regardless of her own statement, proved to be generous and brave and saved many lives): "How was I able to survive in Auschwitz? My principle is: I come first, second, and third. Then nothing, then again I; and then all the others."

In August of 1944 it was very hot in Auschwitz. A torrid, tropical wind lifted clouds of dust from the buildings wrecked by the air raids, dried the sweat on our skin, and thickened the blood in our veins. My squad had been sent into a cellar to clear out the plaster rubble, and we all suffered from thirst: a new suffering, which was added to, indeed, multiplied by the old one of hunger. There was no drinkable water in the camp or often on the work site; in those days there was often no water in the wash trough either, undrinkable but good enough to freshen up and clean off the dust. As a rule, the evening soup and the ersatz coffee distributed around ten o'clock were abundantly sufficient to quench our thirst, but now they were no longer enough and thirst tormented us. Thirst is more imperative than hunger: hunger obeys the nerves, grants remission, can be temporarily obliterated by an emotion, a pain, a fear (we had realized this during our journey by train from Italy); not so with thirst, which does not give respite. Hunger exhausts, thirst enrages; in those days it accompanied us day and night: by day, on the work site, whose order (our enemy, but nevertheless order, a place of logic and certainty) was transformed into a chaos of shattered constructions; by night, in the hut without ventilation, as we gasped the air breathed a hundred times before.

The corner of the cellar that had been assigned to me by the Kapo and where I was to remove the rubble was next to a large room filled with chemical equipment in the process of being installed but already damaged by the bombs. Along the vertical wall ran a two-inch pipe, which ended in a spigot just above the floor. A water pipe? I took a chance and tried to open it. I was alone, nobody saw me. It was blocked, but using a stone for a hammer I managed to shift it a few millimeters. A few drops came out, they had no odor, I caught them on my fingers: it really seemed water, I had no receptacle, and the drops came out slowly, without pressure: the pipe must be only half full, perhaps less. I stretched out on the floor with my mouth under the spigot, not trying to open it further: it was water made tepid by the sun, insipid, perhaps distilled or the result of condensation; at any rate, a delight.

How much water can a two-inch pipe one or two meters high contain? A liter, perhaps not even that. I could have drunk all of it immediately; that would have been the safest way. Or save a bit for the next day. Or share half of it with Alberto. Or reveal the secret to the whole squad. I chose the third path, that of selfishness extended to the person closest to you, which in distant times a friend of mine appropriately called us-ism. We drank all the water, in small, avaricious gulps, changing places under the spigot, just the two of us. On the sly. But on the march back to camp at my side I found Daniele, all gray with cement dust, his lips cracked and his eyes feverish, and I felt guilty. I exchanged a look with Alberto; we understood each other immediately and hoped nobody had seen us. But Daniele had caught a glimpse of us in that strange position, supine near the wall among the rubble, and had suspected something, and then had guessed. He curtly told me so many months later, in Byelorussia after the Liberation: Why the two of you and not I? It was the "civilian" moral code surfacing again. The same according to which I the free man of today perceive as horrifying the death sentence of the sadistic Kapo decided upon and executed without appeal,

silently, with the stroke of an eraser. Is this belated shame justified or not? I was not able to decide then and I am not able to decide even now, but shame there was and is concrete, heavy, perennial. Daniele is dead now, but in our meetings as survivors, fraternal, affectionate, the veil of that act of omission, that unshared glass of water, stood between us, transparent, not expressed, but perceptible and "costly.". . .

Survival of the "Good"?

After my return from imprisonment I was visited by a friend older than myself, mild and intransigent, the cultivator of a personal religion, which, however, always seemed to me severe and serious. He was glad to find me alive and basically unhurt, perhaps matured and fortified, certainly enriched. He told me that my having survived could not be the work of chance, of an accumulation of fortunate circumstances (as I did then and still do maintain) but rather of Providence. . . .

Such an opinion seemed monstrous to me. It pained me as when one touches an exposed nerve, and kindled the doubt I spoke of before: I might be alive in the place of another, at the expense of another; I might have usurped, that is, in fact, killed. The "saved" of the Lager were not the best, those predestined to do good, the bearers of a message: what I had seen and lived through proved the exact contrary. Preferably the worst survived, the selfish, the violent, the insensitive, the collaborators of the "gray zone," the spies. It was not a certain rule (there were none, nor are there certain rules in human matters), but it was nevertheless a rule. I felt innocent, yes, but enrolled among the saved and therefore in permanent search of a justification in my own eyes and those of others. The worst survived, that is, the fittest; the best all died.

Chaim died, a watchmaker from Krakow, a pious Jew who despite the language difficulties made an effort to understand and be understood, and explained to me, the foreigner, the essential rules for survival during the first crucial days of captivity; Szabo died, the taciturn Hungarian peasant who was almost two meters tall and so was the hungriest of all, and yet, as long as he had the strength, did not hesitate to help his weaker companions to pull and push; and Robert, a professor at the Sorbonne who spread courage and trust all around him, spoke five languages, wore himself out recording everything in his prodigious memory, and had he lived would have answered the questions which I do not know how to answer; and Baruch died, a longshoreman from Livomo, immediately, on the first day, because he had answered the first punch he had received with punches and was massacred by three Kapos in coalition. These, and innumerable others, died not despite their valor but because of it.

My religious friend had told me that I survived so that I could bear witness. I have done so, as best I could, and I also could not have done so; and I am still doing so, whenever the opportunity presents itself; but the thought that this testifying of mine could by itself gain for me the privilege of surviving and living for many years without serious problems troubles me because I cannot see any proportion between the privilege and its outcome. . . .

And there is another, vaster shame, the shame of the world. It has been memorably pronounced by John Donne, and quoted innumerable times, pertinently or not, that "no man is an island," and that every bell tolls for everyone. And yet there are those who, faced by the crime of others or their own, turn their backs so as not to see it and not feel touched by it. This is what the majority of Germans did during the twelve Hitlerian years, deluding themselves that not seeing was a way of not knowing, and that not knowing relieved them of their share of complicity or connivance.

Selection 16

Could You Forgive a Murderer?

Simon Wiesenthal

It is impossible to appreciate what it must have been like to live under the Nazis. Still, you cannot escape the questions: What would you have done? If you were a German, would you have refused orders to kill innocent civilians? Could Nazi indoctrination have turned you into a killer the way it did so many ordinary Germans? If you were a Jew, would you have had the foresight to leave Germany before it was too late? Simon Wiesenthal pointedly asks the reader of his memoir to confront the dilemma he did: Should a Nazi who confessed his crimes on his deathbed and begged for absolution so he could die in peace be forgiven? This excerpt reveals what one Nazi told him and what Wiesenthal did. Simon Wiesenthal was imprisoned in several ghettos and concentra-

tion camps. After the war he founded the Jewish Historical Documentation Center, now based in Vienna, with the aim of identifying and locating Nazi war criminals. He is the world's best-known Nazi hunter, and his center takes credit for bringing more than one thousand criminals to justice.

rom the bed I heard a weak, broken voice exclaim: "Please come nearer, I can't speak loudly."

Now I could see the figure in the bed far more clearly. White, bloodless hands on the counterpane, head completely bandaged with openings only for mouth, nose, and ears. . . .

I did not know who this wounded man was, but obviously he was a German.

Hesitatingly, I sat down on the edge of the bed. The sick man, perceiving this, said softly: "Please come a little nearer, to talk loudly is exhausting."

I obeyed. His almost bloodless hand groped for mine as he tried to raise himself slightly in the bed.

My bewilderment was intense. I did not know whether this unreal scene was actuality or dream. Here was I in the ragged clothes of a concentration camp prisoner in the room of the former Dean of Lemberg High School—now a military hospital—in a sickroom which must be in reality a death chamber. . . .

"I have not much longer to live," whispered the sick man in a barely audible voice. "I know the end is near.". . .

I was unmoved by his words. The way I had been forced to exist in the prison camps had destroyed in me any feeling or fear about death. . . .

"I know," muttered the sick man, "that at this moment thousands of men are dying. Death is everywhere. It is neither infrequent nor extraordinary. I am resigned to dying soon, but before that I want to talk about an experience which is torturing me. Otherwise I cannot die in peace.". . .

"I heard from one of the sisters [nuns] that there were Jewish prisoners working in the courtyard. Previously she had brought me a letter from my mother. . . . She read it out to me

and then went away. I have been here for three months. Then I came to a decision. After thinking it over for a long time. . . .

"When the sister came back I asked her to help me. I wanted her to fetch a Jewish prisoner to me, but I warned she must be careful, that nobody must see her. . . .

The Confession

"My name is Karl. . . . I joined the SS as a volunteer. Of course—when you hear the word SS. . . ."

He stopped. His throat seemed to be dry and he tried hard to swallow a lump in it. . . .

"I must tell you something dreadful. . . . Something inhuman. It happened a year ago . . . has a year already gone by?" These last words he spoke almost to himself.

"Yes, it is a year," he continued, "a year since the crime I committed. I have to talk to someone about it, perhaps that will help."

Then his hand grasped mine. His fingers clutched mine tightly, as though he sensed I was trying unconsciously to withdraw my hand when I heard the word "crime." Whence had he derived the strength? Or was it that I was so weak that I could not take my hand away?

"I must tell you of this horrible deed—tell you because . . . you are a Jew."

Could there be some kind of horror unknown to us?

All the atrocities and tortures that a sick brain can invent are familiar to me. I have felt them on my own body and I have seen them happen in the camp. Any story that this sick man had to tell couldn't surpass the horror stories which my comrades in the camp exchanged with each other at night. . . .

"I was not born a murderer, . . ." he wheezed.

He breathed heavily and was silent.

"I come from Stuttgart and I am now twenty-one. That is too soon to die. I have had very little out of life."

Of course it is too soon to die I thought. But did the Nazis ask whether our children whom they were about to gas had ever had anything out of life? Did they ask whether it was too soon for them to die? Certainly nobody had ever asked me the question.

As if he had guessed my mental reaction he said: "I know what you are thinking and I understand. But may I not still say that I am too young . . . ?"

Then in a burst of calm coherency he went on: "My father, who was manager of a factory, was a convinced Social Democrat. After 1933 he got into difficulties, but that happened to many. My mother brought me up as a Catholic, I was actually a server in the church and a special favorite of our priest who hoped I would one day study theology. But it turned out differently; I joined the Hitler Youth, and that of course was the end of the Church for me. My mother was very sad, but finally stopped reproaching me. I was her only child. My father never uttered a word on the subject. . . .

"He was afraid lest I should talk in the Hitler Youth about what I had heard at home. . . . Our leader demanded that we should champion our cause everywhere. . . . Even at home. . . . He told us that if we heard anyone abuse it we must report to him. There were many who did so, but not I. My parents nevertheless were afraid and they stopped talking when I was near. Their mistrust annoyed me, but, unfortunately, there was no time for reflection in those days. . . .

"When the war broke out I volunteered, naturally in the SS. . . . My mother wept when I left. As I closed the door behind me I heard my father say: 'They are taking our son away from us. No good will come of it.'

"His words made me indignant. I wanted to go back and argue with him. I wanted to tell him that he simply did not understand modern times. But I let it be, so as not to make my departure worse for all of us by an ugly scene.

"Those words were the last I ever heard my father speak. . . .

"We were first sent to a training camp at an army base where we listened feverishly to the radio messages about the Polish campaign. We devoured the reports in the newspapers and dreaded that our services might not after all be needed. I was longing for experience, to see the world, to be able to recount my adventures." . . .

And now I began to ask myself why a Jew must listen to the confession of a dying Nazi soldier. If he had really rediscovered his faith in Christianity, then a priest should have been sent for, a priest who could help him die in peace. If I were dying to whom should I make my confession if indeed I had anything to confess? And anyway I would not have as much time as this man had. My end would be violent, as had happened to millions before me. Perhaps it would be an unexpected surprise, perhaps I would have no time to prepare for the bullet. He was still talking about his youth as if he were reading aloud and the only effect was that it made me think of my youth too. But it was so far away that it seemed unreal. It seemed as if I had always been in prison camps, as though I were born merely to be maltreated by beasts in human shape who wanted to work off their frustrations and racial hatreds on defenseless victims. Remembrance of time past only made me feel weak, and I badly needed to remain strong, for only the strong in these dire times had a hope of survival. I still clung to the belief that the world one day would revenge itself on these brutes—in spite of their victories, their jubilation at the battles they had won, and their boundless arrogance. The day would surely come when the Nazis would hang their heads as the Jews did now. . . .

All my instincts were against continuing to listen to this deathbed disavowal. I wanted to get away. . . . I would stay, although I wanted to go. Quietly he continued talking:

"Last spring we saw that something was afoot. We were told time after time we must be prepared for great doings. Each of us must show himself a man. . . . He must be tough. There was no place for humanitarian nonsense. The Führer needed real men. That made a great impression on us at the time.

"When the war with Russia began, we listened over the radio to a speech by [Heinrich] Himmler before we marched out. He spoke of the final victory of the Führer's mission. . . . On smoking out subhumans. . . . We were given piles of literature about the Jews and the Bolsheviks, we devoured the [anti-Semitic newspaper the] 'Sturmer,' and many cut caricatures from it and pinned them above our beds. But that was not the sort of thing I cared for. . . . In the evenings, in the canteen we grew heated with beer and talk about Germany's future. As in Poland, the war with Russia would be a lightning campaign, thanks to the genius of our leader. Our frontiers would be pushed further and further eastward. The German people needed room to live."

For a moment he stopped as though exhausted.

"You can see for yourself on what sort of career my life was launched."

He was sorry for himself. His words were bitter and resigned. . . .

"At the end of June we joined a unit of storm troops and were taken to the front in trucks. . . .

Encountering Jews

"One hot summer day we came to Dnepropetrovsk. . . .

"In a large square we got out and looked around us. On the other side of the square there was a group of people under close guard. I assumed they were civilians who were to be taken out of the town, in which fighting was still going on. And then the word ran through our group like wildfire: 'They're Jews.'. . . In my young life I had never seen many Jews. No doubt there had formerly been some, but for the most part they had emigrated when Hitler came to power. The few who remained simply disappeared later. It was said they had been sent to the Ghetto. Then they were forgotten. My mother sometimes mentioned our family doctor, who was a Jew and for whom she mourned deeply. She carefully preserved all his prescriptions, for she had complete trust in his medical knowledge. But one day the chemist told her that she must get her medicines prescribed by a different doctor, he was not allowed to make up the prescriptions of a Jewish doctor. My mother was furious but my father just looked at me and held his tongue.

"I need not tell you what the newspapers said about the Jews. Later in Poland I saw Jews who were quite different from ours in Stuttgart. At the army base at Debicka some Jews were still

working and I often gave them something to eat. But I stopped when the platoon leader caught me doing it. The Jews had to clean out our quarters and I often deliberately left behind on the table some food which I knew they would find.

"Otherwise all I knew about the Jews was what came out of the loudspeaker or what was given us to read. We were told they were the cause of all our misfortunes. . . . They were trying to get on top of us, they were the cause of war, poverty, hunger, unemployment. . . ."

I noticed that the dying man had a warm undertone in his voice as he spoke about the Jews. I had never heard such a tone in the voice of an SS man. Was he better than the others—or did the voices of SS men change when they were dying?

"An order was given," he continued, "and we marched toward the huddled mass of Jews. There were a hundred and fifty of them or perhaps two hundred, including many children who stared at us with anxious eyes. A few were quietly crying. There were infants in their mothers' arms, but hardly any young men, mostly women and graybeards.

"As we approached I could see the expression in their eyes—fear, indescribable fear . . . apparently they knew what was awaiting them. . . .

"A truck arrived with cans of petrol which we unloaded and took into a house. The strong men among the Jews were ordered to carry the cans to the upper stories. They obeyed—apathetically, without a will of their own, like automatons.

"Then we began to drive the Jews into the house. A sergeant with a whip in his hand helped any of the Jews who were not quick enough. There was a hail of curses and kicks. The house was not very large, it had only three stories. I would not have believed it possible to crowd them all into it. But after a few minutes there was no Jew left on the street."

He was silent and my heart started to beat violently. I could well imagine the scene. It was all too familiar. I might have been among those who were forced into that house with the petrol cans. I could feel how they must have pressed against each other; I could hear their frantic cries as they realized what was to be done to them.

The dying Nazi went on: "Then another truck came up full of more Jews and they too were crammed into the house with the others. Then the door was locked and a machine gun was posted opposite."

I knew how this story would end. My own country had been occupied by the Germans for over a year and we had heard of similar happenings in Bialystok, Brody, and Gródek. The method was always the same. He could spare me the rest of his gruesome account.

So I stood up ready to leave but he pleaded with me: "Please stay. I must tell you the rest."

I really do not know what kept me. But there was something in his voice that prevented me from obeying my instinct to end the interview. Perhaps I wanted to hear from his own mouth, in his own words, the full horror of the Nazis' inhumanity.

"When we were told that everything was ready, we went back a few yards, and then received the command to remove safety pins from hand grenades and throw them through the windows of the house. Detonations followed one after another. . . . My God!"

Now he was silent, and he raised himself slightly from the bed: his whole body was shivering.

But he continued: "We heard screams and saw the flames eat their way from floor to floor. . . . We had our rifles ready to shoot down anyone who tried to escape from that blazing hell. . . .

"The screams from the house were horrible. Dense smoke poured out and choked us. . . ."

His hand felt damp. He was so shattered by his recollection that he broke into a sweat and I loosened my hand from his grip. But at once he groped for it again and held it tight.

"Please, please," he stammered, "don't go away, I have more to say."

I no longer had any doubts as to the ending. I saw that he was summoning his strength for one last effort to tell me the rest of the story to its bitter end.

". . . Behind the windows of the second floor, I saw a man with a small child in his arms. His clothes were alight. By his side stood a woman, doubtless the mother of the child. With his free

hand the man covered the child's eyes . . . then he jumped into the street. Seconds later the mother followed. Then from the other windows fell burning bodies. . . . We shot. . . . Oh God!"

The dying man held his hand in front of his bandaged eyes as if he wanted to banish the picture from his mind.

"I don't know how many tried to jump out of the windows but that one family I shall never forget—least of all the child. It had black hair and dark eyes. . . ."

He fell silent, completely exhausted. . . .

"I can see the child and his father and his mother," he went on.

He groaned and his breath came gasping from his lungs.

"Perhaps they were already dead when they struck the pavement. It was frightful. Screams mixed with volleys of shots. The volleys were probably intended to drown the shrieks, I can never forget—it haunts me. I have had plenty of time to think, but yet perhaps not enough. . . .

"Shortly afterwards we moved on. On the way we were told that the massacre of the Jews was in revenge for the Russian time bombs which had cost us about thirty men. We had killed three hundred Jews in exchange. Nobody asked what the murdered Jews had to do with the Russian time bombs.

"In the evening there was a ration of brandy. Brandy helps one forget. . . . Over the radio came reports from the front, the numbers of torpedoed ships, of prisoners taken, or planes shot down, and the area of the newly conquered territories. . . . It was getting dark. . . .

"Fired by the brandy we sat down and began to sing. I too sang. Today I ask myself how I could have done that. Perhaps I wanted to anesthetize myself. For a time I was successful. The events seemed to recede further and further away. But during the night they came back. . . .

"The pains in my body are terrible, but worse still is my conscience. It never ceases to remind me of the burning house and the family that jumped from the window."

He lapsed into silence, seeking for words. He wants something from me, I thought, for I could not imagine that he had brought me here merely as an audience.

"When I was still a boy I believed with my mind and soul in God and in the commandments of the Church. Then everything was easier. If I still had that faith I am sure death would not be so hard.

"I cannot die . . . without coming clean. This must be my confession. But what sort of confession is this? A letter without an answer. . . ."

No doubt he was referring to my silence. But what could I say? Here was a dying man—a murderer who did not want to be a murderer but who had been made into a murderer by a murderous ideology. He was confessing his crime to a man who perhaps tomorrow must die at the hands of these same murderers. In his confession there was true repentance, even though he did not admit it in so many words. Nor was it necessary, for the way he spoke and the fact that he spoke to *me* was a proof of his repentance.

"Believe me, I would be ready to suffer worse and longer pains if by that means I could bring back the dead, at Dnepropetrovsk. Many young Germans of my age die daily on the battlefields. They have fought against an armed enemy and have fallen in the fight, but I . . . I am left here with my guilt. In the last hours of my life you are with me. I do not know who you are, I only know that you are a Jew and that is enough."

I said nothing. The truth was that on his battlefield he had also "fought" against defenseless men, women, children, and the aged. I could imagine them enveloped in flames jumping from the windows to certain death.

He sat up and put his hands together as if to pray.

"I want to die in peace, and so I need. . . ."

I saw that he could not get the words past his lips. But I was in no mood to help him. I kept silent.

"I know that what I have told you is terrible. In the long nights while I have been waiting for death, time and time again I have longed to talk about it to a Jew and beg forgiveness from him. Only I didn't know whether there were any Jews left. . . .

"I know that what I am asking is almost too much for you but without your answer I cannot die in peace."

Now, there was an uncanny silence in the room. I looked through the window. The front of the buildings opposite was flooded with sunshine. The sun was high in the heavens. They was only a small triangular shadow in the courtyard.

What a contrast between the glorious sunshine outside and the shadow of this bestial age here in the death chamber! Here lay a man in bed who wished to die in peace—but he could not, because the memory of his terrible crime gave him no rest. And by him sat a man also doomed to die—but who did not want to die because he yearned to see the end of all the horror that blighted the world.

Two men who had never known each other had been brought together for a few hours by Fate. One asks the other for help. But the other was

Simon Wiesenthal

himself helpless and able to do nothing for him.

I stood up and looked in his direction, at his folded hands. Between them there seemed to rest a sunflower.

At last I made up my mind and without a word I left the room. . . .

Well, I kept silent when a young Nazi, on his deathbed, begged me to be his confessor. . . . And how many bystanders kept silent as they watched Jewish men, women, and children being led to the slaughterhouses of Europe?

There are many kinds of silence. Indeed it can be more eloquent than words, and it can be interpreted in many ways.

Was my silence at the bedside of the dying Nazi right or wrong? This is a profound moral question that challenges the conscience of the reader of this episode, just as it once challenged my heart and my mind. There are those who can appreciate my dilemma, and so endorse my attitude, and there are others who will be ready to condemn me for refusing to ease the last moment of a repentant murderer.

The crux of the matter is, of course, the question of forgiveness. Forgetting is something that time alone takes care of, but forgiveness is an act of volition, and only the sufferer is qualified to make the decision.

You, who have just read this sad and tragic episode in my life, can mentally change places with me and ask yourself the crucial question, "What would I have done?"

Selection 17

Judging the Victims

Michael R. Marrus

When researchers began to study the Holocaust in the early 1960s, they did not have access to all of the information available today. It is not surprising, therefore, that some conclusions reached then have been challenged over the last forty years. One example is the often stated notion that Jews went to their deaths like sheep to the slaughter. In fact, one of the most prominent historians of the Holocaust, Raul Hilberg, someone whose work is cited in this volume, suggested that Jews were largely passive victims. This article examines Hilberg's thesis and how the evidence unearthed since he first expressed this idea has led to a more complete understanding of Jewish reactions to their tormentors. Michael R. Marrus is a history professor at the University of Toronto and the author of several books on Jewish history.

Excerpted from Michael R. Marrus, *The Holocaust in History.* Copyright © 1987 Michael R. Marrus. Reprinted with permission from the author.

There are few more durable generalizations about the history of the Holocaust than the characterization of Jewish passivity in the face of mortal threat. "The Jews," it has often been said "went to their deaths like sheep to the slaughter." While the Nazis certainly commented in this sense at the time and subsequently, this most famous of analogies, with its overtones of biblical sacrifice, came in the first instance from the Jews themselves as a call to arms and a refusal to acquiesce in German policies. At the beginning of 1942, young Zionists in the ghetto of Vilna issued a manifesto in Hebrew and Yiddish, composed by Abba Kovner and entitled "Let Us Not Be Led Like Sheep to the Slaughter," that helped spark the formation of a united front of resistance. A year later, in Warsaw, in an effort to goad their hesitant or resigned compatriots to a suicidal revolt, the mainstream Jewish Fighting Organization issued a proclamation: "Jewish masses, the hour is drawing near. You must be prepared to resist, not to give yourselves up to slaughter like sheep." Another manifesto, attributed to the right-wing Jewish Military Union, declared: "Know that deliverance is not to be found in going to your death impassively, like sheep to the slaughter." And again, the Warsaw ghetto diary of Emmanuel Ringelblum contains this anguished entry for 15 October 1942, after the massive deportations of that year: "Why didn't we resist when they began to resettle 300,000 Jews from Warsaw? Why did we allow ourselves to be led like sheep to the slaughter?"

Raul Hilberg argued powerfully for this assessment in his magisterial *Destruction of the European Jews,* which first appeared in 1961. Only a few pages of Hilberg's work concerned Jewish reactions, but these lines were undoubtedly the most controversial and passionately contested. They were also the product of firm conviction, for almost a quarter of a century later his contention reappears without change or modification in the new and definitive edition. Hilberg is unsparing in his critique of Jewish passivity. "The reaction pattern of the Jews is characterized by almost complete lack of resistance," he writes. "The Jews attempted to tame the Germans as one would attempt to tame a wild beast. They avoided 'provocations' and complied instantly with decrees and orders. They hoped somehow that the German drive would spend itself." At times, in efforts to curry favor with the oppressor or simply to prevent unnecessary suffering, Jews even moved ahead of the Germans, in what the author calls "anticipatory compliance." Hilberg sees this pattern,

moreover, not only in the behavior of Jewish leaders, but in the responses of the masses as well. The death camps, he notes, were thinly guarded—by as few as four thousand men. Everything depended upon the Jews moving along an assembly line, the product of which was murder. For the most part, the Jews were incapable of acting otherwise. Outbreaks did happen, he acknowledges, but these were almost always "local occurrences that transpired at the last moment." How does he explain this reaction? Hilberg assumes that this response was peculiarly Jewish and can be traced to "a 2,000-year old experience." Throughout their long period of exile, "the Jews had always been a minority, always in danger, but had learned that they could avert or survive destruction by placating and appeasing their enemies." Having responded in this manner for so many centuries, the Jews could not act otherwise when confronted by Nazism. "A 2,000-year-old lesson could not be unlearned; the Jews could not make the switch. They were helpless."...

East European Ghettos

Discussion of the Jewish leadership moved to a new plane with the publication in 1972 of Isaiah Trunk's *Judenrat,* devoted to the study of the Jewish councils set up by the Nazis in occupied eastern Europe.... At the very least, one must conclude from his exposition that there was a variety of Jewish responses. Beyond this, Trunk emphasized that the Jews were *forced* to establish the councils, that individuals were *forced* to serve on them, and that the councils were *forced* to provide services for the Germans. The ghettos' widely detested Jewish police, who often participated in the "resettlements" of Jews for deportation, were subjected to the most cruel forms of blackmail to induce them to do so. Almost invariably they were told that only through such actions could they and their families be spared a similar fate. While in retrospect it seems plain that the *Judenräte* did assist the Nazis, at the time most of their members felt they had little choice.... Trunk noted that some councils supported resistance activities—some violent, and some not—and that others opposed them; some ran corrupt and class-ridden ghettos, and others strove for equality. One might, of course still make harsh judgments on the basis of this evidence; interestingly, Trunk's survey of the attitudes of survivors suggests that with the passage of time their own evaluations of the Jewish councils were increasingly positive.

What to Do

The increasing recourse to Jewish sources has by no means guaranteed a sympathetic view of ghetto leadership. Hilberg found confirmation of his views in the diary of the head of the Warsaw *Judenrat,* Adam Czerniakow, published in English in 1979. An industrial engineer and Polish patriot, Czerniakow was an assimilationist Jew active in communal affairs, named by the mayor of Warsaw to lead the Jewish community in that city after its previous chairman fled. When the Germans arrived, Czerniakow was summoned to Gestapo headquarters and told to organize a Jewish council. Czerniakow, Hilberg notes, "was a caretaker, not so much of a community, as of its countless afflictions, and his entire official life was much less a singular daily effort to save a people than a whole series of efforts to save people every day." He constantly intervened with the German authorities to obtain concessions, alleviate shortages, and suspend the most cruel of regulations. His daily notes portray Czerniakow as a courageous man of little vision, crushed by the terrible burdens he faced, and unable to break out of his imposed task. In the end, when faced in the summer of 1942 with the Nazis' demands for deportees, he swallowed cyanide and killed himself. For Hilberg, leaders like Czerniakow became "psychological captives of the perpetrator," lulled into a state of "institutional subservience." Almost always his efforts were stamped with failure. His diary "gives voice to an overwhelming sense of powerlessness and futility."

Others, however, see nobility in the engineer turned community leader, who sacrificed himself for what he believed to be a historic task. They see Czerniakow as struggling valiantly to maintain Jewish communal existence—no mean achievement in the face of escalating German pressures and demands. They stress his evasive responses to the authorities, his exploitation of differences among the Germans, his constant playing for time. Of course, such strategies may not fit our heroic model and may not have been the wisest in the long run. So it appears in hindsight. Yet at the time of Czerniakow's suicide, . . . even the Jewish underground hesitated, was unsure of the best path to follow, and was uncertain about the ghetto's fate. . . .

Rather than buckling under the Nazis' pressures, Chaim Rumkowski in Lodz and Jacob Gens in Vilna developed intensely authoritarian styles of leadership, coming to believe that they alone could save a portion of the ghetto inmates. In both cases the Germans gave reason to believe that a productive ghetto might be saved. Both leaders negotiated to save lives in exchange for Jewish labor. Prying loose favors from an implacable foe, both of these men riveted upon the bargaining process. Lives indeed hung on their every move. Both developed illusions about their own achievements, inflated their own self-image to megalomanaical proportions, and developed regal styles of personal rule. Rumkowski rode about the ghetto in a horse-drawn carriage, issued banknotes with his portrait, and was known as King Chaim. While less flamboyant, Gens too assumed dictatorial authority and ruled as Jacob the First. Opinion on these leaders differs, even today. To some the outstanding fact about such *Judenrat* chiefs is their arrogant, single-minded, ruthless style of rule. From the leader's standpoint, however, things looked different. Attacked from every quarter at once, increasingly isolated at the top, facing impossible demands, they often felt that they were the only hope for a squabbling, bitterly divided Jewish community. Both leaders, one should add, understood the charges of collaboration that were made against them at the time and declared their willingness to face courts of honor after the war. Both argued that theirs was the only way to save Jews and confidently expected postwar vindication for what they did.

And neither survived to face such judgment. . . .

There are literally scores of ghetto leaders, and it is important to remember that the Germans tolerated only those who satisfied or appeared to satisfy their demands. The others usually did not last long. *Judenrat* leaders were subjected to beatings, direct intimidation, and threats to their families; some were simply shot. Among those who did the Germans' work, it should be added, there were virtually none who "collaborated" in the sense of identifying with wider Nazi aims—such as are found in every occupied society in Europe. Some Jews opposed the formation of the *Judenräte,* and sometimes the Germans simply dragooned Jewish representatives on their own. Once in place, leaders faced the excruciating dilemmas of "collective responsibility": in reprisal for opposition, or even recalcitrance in the executions of their demands, the Germans kidnapped for forced labor or simply massacred ghetto inmates. It is hardly surprising then that those leaders who remained at their posts demonstrated "compliance" with Nazi orders and called for "order" within the ghetto. Beneath the surface, at times, there was other activity. Trunk notes the ambivalence of certain *Judenrat* chiefs: "They were afraid that resistance activities might hinder their carefully contrived strategies to gain time and postpone the liquidation of their ghettos for as long as possible. On the other hand, they favored the idea of physical resistance when the end came." In Bialystok, Efraim Barash maintained links with the Jewish resistance, but insisted that any uprising be delayed until just before liberation by the Red Army. In the end, no such opportunity presented itself, the rebels tried to break out of the ghetto, and Barash himself was deported to a death camp. . . .

Central and West European Jewry

Research on the Jewish leadership in other countries has similarly undermined some of the sweeping generalizations of Jewish passivity. In particular, investigations of German Jewry suggest a far more persistent and resourceful response to persecution—albeit with the most meager of resources—than traditional stereotypes would allow. Studies of Jewish emigration from the Reich, for example, are hardly consistent with the idea of a community burying its head in the sand. One out of ten of the approximately 525,000 people in Germany identifying in some way with the Jewish religion left the country immediately after the Nazis took power, and close to 150,000 emigrated before Kristallnacht, in November 1938. This was roughly one-fourth of the total population deemed "non-Aryan" by the Nazis. Thereafter, under increasingly heavy pressure, another 150,000 left. Undoubtedly more would have done so if they had been permitted access to countries in western Europe and America, and to Palestine. And virtually no one, not even the most experienced Zionist leaders, those who one might think would be especially prescient on the need for mass evacuation from Europe, looked to a complete termination of the Jewish presence in Germany in the immediate future. From the standpoint of emigration, then, the notion of German Jews blindly deluding themselves under Hitler seems hardly tenable. . . .

The Camps

From the Nazis' administrative accounts, we are able to place the hundreds of concentration camps within the framework of the Third Reich and to differentiate the special role of the handful of death camps—those that were mainly or exclusively devoted to murder. It is important to see these grotesque creations as part of a vast system, holding more than 600,000 inmates of every nationality by 1943 and 1944. This growth coincided with the radicalization of the regime and notably the increasing importance of the SS, under Heinrich Himmler. At the end of 1938 the system held about 30,000 prisoners, with a large turnover as inmates were released after a period of intimidation. With the outbreak of war, the concentration camp network vastly expanded. Thereafter, the rates of violence, maltreatment, and mortality soared. It is not certain how many ultimately passed through the camps. . . .

According to most authorities, the entire camp structure underwent significant changes in 1942, as the German war effort bogged down and the demand for labor increased. Gradually, the camps were seen as pools of forced labor in addition to being part of the terror apparatus of the regime. During this period the camps came under the authority of the Main Office for Economy and Administration of the SS (Wirtschafts-und Verwaltungs Hauptamt, or WVHA), and several industrial giants of the German economy made arrangements with the SS to exploit the prisoners' labor. At the same time, however, killing became a distinct function of the system. On orders from Berlin, several camps took over part of the murderous operations that were proceeding with such destructive force in former Soviet territories. In the autumn of 1941, the first experiments with the deadly Zyklon B gas were undertaken at Auschwitz, using Soviet prisoners of war. Shortly after, gassings occurred at Chelmno, near Lodz in western Poland. Systematic killings on a similar model followed at Belzec, Sobibor, and Treblinka in 1942. That spring, with Operation Reinhard, murder operations targeted the *Generalgouvernement* of Poland. In the summer, deportations from western Europe reached Auschwitz, which became the principal killing center in 1943. According to Hilberg, up to 3 million Jews died in camps of various kinds, most of whom perished in the principal death camps in Poland. In addition, however, several hundred thousand were worked to death or otherwise died of maltreatment in dozens of satellite camps in Germany or eastern Europe, or in major centers such as Mauthausen, in Austria. . . .

Following the patterns they established every-where, the Nazis preferred whenever possible to have others bear the burden of control and management: they empowered camp elders, clerks, block leaders, and so forth to supervise the inmates and assume primary responsibility for the routines of daily life. Kapos, as they were called, directed the laborers and were themselves controlled by a small group of SS who remained in the background. The general impression is of a highly stratified system, in which the Nazis encouraged division and widespread corruption, broadly referred to in camp jargon as "organization." Jews remained at the bottom of this system—ruled by other categories of prisoners (usually non-Jewish Germans or criminals) and encouraged to prey upon their fellows to scrape together the means and conditions of subsistence. . . .

Within the camps, the Nazis set out deliberately to dehumanize their victims, to break down their autonomy and turn them into "docile masses from which no individual or group act of resistance could arise." When they succeeded, the result was the often-observed phenomenon known by camp jargon as *Muselmänner,* taken from an alleged Muslim belief in fatalism— "people who were so deprived of affect, self esteem, and every form of stimulation, so totally exhausted, both physically and emotionally, that they had given the environment total power over them." More than one survivor has claimed that the *Muselmänner* formed, as Primo Levi says, "the backbone of the camp," the great majority of the prisoners. . . .

Survival depended overwhelmingly on being liberated from the outside and on extraordinary good luck. Relatively speaking, there was very little that prisoners could do to affect their fate.

Resistance

Chapter 5

n discussions of the Holocaust, it is common to hear the phrase, "the Jews went to the gas chambers like sheep to slaughter." It simply isn't true. In most cases the Jews did not know what they were facing. It may seem inconceivable now, but the Nazis had so successfully disguised their actions that most of their victims were unaware that they were about to be murdered. Killings often took place suddenly, with little or no warning. People who thought they were being transported to work camps were suddenly herded off trains in the middle of the night or early morning after suffering without food or sleep for hours or days. The Germans gave them no time to think or to acclimate to their surroundings. And even if they had a hint of their fate, they could do little or nothing when surrounded by dogs and heavily armed guards.

Still, many examples of resistance have been recorded. In addition to the Warsaw Ghetto uprising discussed in the last chapter, Jews fought against the Nazis with partisan groups. At several concentration camps, groups of prisoners fought against all odds. Prisoners attacked the guards at Treblinka, for example, and two hundred escaped. A group of inmates blew up one of the crematoria at Birkenau. In the most dramatic revolt, a Soviet Jewish prisoner led a daring escape at Sobibor during which the guards were overpowered and three hundred inmates fled the camp into the forest.

This chapter describes several of the instances of Jewish resistance. In Primo Levi's interesting memoir we also get insight into the reasons more Jews did not revolt. Also in this chapter is the story of The White Rose, one of the few groups that dared to challenge Hitler's rule within Germany.

Selection 1

The White Rose

Jacob G. Hornberger

The Nazi machine was extremely effective in muzzling dissent. Children were taught in school to turn in their parents for speaking against the Führer. Informers were every-

Reprinted from Jacob G. Hornberger, "The White Rose," an online article found at www.fff.org. Originally published by The Future Freedom Foundation in Fairfax, VA. Reprinted with permission from the author.

where. Suspicious behavior or words could land a person in a concentration camp. Despite the danger, some Germans did have the courage to denounce Hitler and to protest against the Nazi actions. Unfortunately, the Nazis had little difficulty rooting out these "subversives" and eliminating them. One of the more celebrated examples of resistance was The White Rose, a group started by two German teenagers who hoped to arouse the public to rebel against the Nazis. This essay by Jacob G. Hornberger, founder and president of The Future of Freedom Foundation, highlights the efforts of these extraordinary young people.

Hans and Sophie Scholl were German teenagers in the 1930s. Like other young Germans, they enthusiastically joined the Hitler Youth. They believed that Adolf Hitler was leading Germany and the German people back to greatness.

Their parents were not so enthusiastic. Their father, Robert Scholl, told his children that Hitler and the Nazis were leading Germany down a road of destruction. Later, in 1942, he would serve time in a Nazi prison for telling his secretary: "The war! It is already lost. This Hitler is God's scourge on mankind, and if the war doesn't end soon the Russians will be sitting in Berlin." Gradually, Hans and Sophie began realizing that their father was right. They concluded that, in the name of freedom and the greater good of the German nation, Hitler and the Nazis were enslaving and destroying the German people.

They also knew that open dissent was impossible in Nazi Germany, especially after the start of World War II. Most Germans took the traditional position, that once war breaks out, it is the duty of the citizen to support the troops by supporting the government. But Hans and Sophie Scholl believed differently. They believed that it was the duty of a citizen, even in times of war, to stand up against an evil regime, especially when it is sending hundreds of thousands of its citizens to their deaths.

The Scholl siblings began sharing their feelings with a few of their friends, Christoph Probst, Alexander Schmorell, Willi Graf, as well as with Kurt Huber, their psychology and philosophy professor.

One day in 1942, copies of a leaflet entitled "The White Rose" suddenly appeared at the University of Munich. The leaflet contained an anonymous essay that said that the Nazi system had slowly imprisoned the German people and was now destroying them. The Nazi regime had turned evil. It was time, the essay said, for Germans to rise up and resist the tyranny of their own government. At the bottom of the essay, the following request appeared: "Please make as

Sophie Scholl bids farewell to her brother Hans (second from right) and friends, including fellow White Rose member Alexander Schmorell (right), as they leave for the Russian front on July 23, 1942.

many copies of this leaflet as you can and distribute them."

The leaflet caused a tremendous stir among the student body. It was the first time that internal dissent against the Nazi regime had surfaced in Germany. The essay had been secretly written and distributed by Hans Scholl and his friends.

Another leaflet appeared soon afterward. And then another. And another. Ultimately, there were six leaflets published and distributed by Hans and Sophie Scholl and their friends, four under the title "The White Rose" and two under the title "Leaflets of the Resistance." Their publication took place periodically between 1942 and 1943, interrupted for a few months when Hans and his friends were temporarily sent to the Eastern Front to fight against the Russians.

The members of The White Rose, of course, had to act cautiously. The Nazi regime maintained an iron grip over German society. Internal dissent was quickly and efficiently smashed by the Gestapo. Hans and Sophie Scholl and their friends knew what would happen to them if they were caught.

People began receiving copies of the leaflets in the mail. Students at the University of Hamburg began copying and distributing them. Copies began turning up in different parts of Germany and Austria. . . . The members of The White Rose did not limit themselves to leaflets. Graffiti began appearing in large letters on streets and buildings all over Munich: "Down with Hitler! . . . Hitler the Mass Murderer!" and "Freihart! . . . Freihart! . . . Freedom! . . . Freedom!"

The Gestapo was driven into a frenzy. It knew that the authors were having to procure large quantities of paper, envelopes, and postage. It knew that they were using a duplicating machine. But despite the Gestapo's best efforts, it was unable to catch the perpetrators.

The Nazis Nip the Rose in the Bud

One day, February 18, 1943, Hans' and Sophie's luck ran out. They were caught leaving pamphlets at the University of Munich and were arrested. A search disclosed evidence of Christoph Probst's participation, and he too was soon arrested. The three of them were indicted for treason.

On February 22, four days after their arrest, their trial began. The presiding judge, Roland Freisler, chief justice of the People's Court of the Greater German Reich, had been sent from Berlin. [Richard] Hansen writes [in *A Noble Treason*]:

He conducted the trial as if the future of the Reich were indeed at stake. He roared denunciations of the accused as if he were not the judge but the prosecutor. He behaved alternately like an actor ranting through an overwritten role in an implausible melodrama and a Grand Inquisitor calling down eternal damnation on the heads of the three irredeemable heretics before him. . . . No witnesses were called, since the defendants had admitted everything. The proceedings consisted almost entirely of Roland Freisler's denunciation and abuse, punctuated from time to time by half-hearted offerings from the court-appointed defense attorneys, one of whom summed up his case with the observation, "I can only say fiat justitia. Let justice be done." By which he meant: Let the accused get what they deserve.

Freisler and the other accusers could not understand what had happened to these German youths. After all, they all came from nice German families. They all had attended German schools. They had been members of the Hitler Youth. How could they have turned out to be traitors? What had so twisted and warped their minds?

Sophie Scholl shocked everyone in the courtroom when she remarked to Freisler: "Somebody, after all, had to make a start. What we wrote and said is also believed by many others. They just don't dare to express themselves as we did." Later in the proceedings, she said to him: "You know the war is lost. Why don't you have the courage to face it?"

In the middle of the trial, Robert and Magdalene Scholl tried to enter the courtroom. Magdalene said to the guard: "But I'm the mother of two of the accused." The guard responded: "You should have brought them up better." Robert Scholl forced his way into the courtroom and told the court that he was there to defend his children. He was seized and forcibly escorted outside. The entire courtroom heard him shout: "One day there will be another kind of justice! One day they will go down in history!"

Robert Freisler pronounced his judgment on the three defendants: Guilty of treason. Their sentence: Death.

They were escorted back to Stadelheim prison, where the guards permitted Hans and Sophie to have one last visit with their parents. Hans met with them first, and then Sophie. Hansen writes:

> His eyes were clear and steady and he showed no sign of dejection or despair. He thanked his parents again for the love and warmth they had given him and he asked them to convey his affection and regard to a number of friends, whom he named. Here, for a moment, tears threatened, and he turned away to spare his parents the pain of seeing them. Facing them again, his shoulders were back and he smiled. . . .

Then a woman prison guard brought in Sophie. . . . Her mother tentatively offered her some candy, which Hans had declined. "Gladly," said Sophie, taking it. "After all, I haven't had any lunch!" She, too, looked somehow smaller, as if drawn together, but her face was clear and her smile was fresh and unforced, with something in it that her parents read as triumph. "Sophie, Sophie," her mother murmured, as if to herself. "To think you'll never be coming through the door again!" Sophie's smile was gentle. "Ah, Mother," she said. "Those few little years. . . ." Sophie Scholl looked at her parents and was strong in her pride and certainty. "We took everything upon ourselves," she said. "What we did will cause waves.". . . She left them, her parents, Robert and Magdalene Scholl, with her face still lit by the smile they loved so well and would never see again. She was perfectly composed as she was led away. Robert Mohr [a Gestapo official], who had come out to the prison on business of his own, saw her in her cell immediately afterwards, and she was crying. It was the first time Robert Mohr had seen her in tears, and she apologized. "I have just said goodbye to my parents," she said. "You understand. . . ." She had not cried before her parents.

For them she had smiled.

No relatives visited Christoph Probst. His wife, who had just had their third child, was in the hospital. Neither she nor any members of his family even knew that he was on trial or that he had been sentenced to death. While his faith in God had always been deep and unwavering, he had never committed to a certain faith. On the eve of his death, a Catholic priest admitted him into the church. . . . "Now," he said, "my death will be easy and joyful."

> That afternoon, the prison guards permitted Hans, Sophie, and Christoph to have one last visit together. Sophie was then led to the guillotine. One observer described her as she walked to her death: "Without turning a hair, without flinching." Christoph Probst was next. Hans Scholl was last; just before he was beheaded, Hans cried out: "Long live freedom!"

Unfortunately, they were not the last to die. The Gestapo's investigation was relentless. Later tried and executed were Alex Schmorell (age 25), Willi Graf (age 25), and Kurt Huber (age 49). Students at the University of Hamburg were either executed or sent to concentration camps.

Today, every German knows the story of The White Rose. A square at the University of Munich is named after Hans and Sophie Scholl. And there are streets, squares, and schools all over Germany named for the members of The White Rose. The German movie *The White Rose* is now found in video stores in Germany and the United States. Richard Hansen sums up the story of The White Rose:

In the vogue words of the time, the Scholls and their friends represented the "other" Germany, the land of poets and thinkers, in contrast to the Germany that was reverting to barbarism and trying to take the world with it. What they were and what they did would have been "other" in any society at any time. What they did transcended the easy division of good-German/bad-German and lifted them above the nationalism of time-bound events. Their actions made them enduring symbols of the struggle, universal and timeless, for the freedom of the human spirit wherever and whenever it is threatened.

Selection 2

Warsaw Jews Shock the Nazis

Israel Gutman

One reason that more Jews did not put up resistance against the Nazis is that for a long time they did not know they were to be exterminated. When they did learn the truth, and had the means, the Jews often did fight back. Perhaps the most dramatic case occurred in the Warsaw ghetto, where tens of thousands of Polish Jews were isolated. By 1943 it became clear to most Jews in the ghetto that the Germans were planning to murder them all. The younger Jews especially, who were not responsible for wives, husbands, or children, decided to make a stand. With great resourcefulness they managed to obtain handfuls of guns and to make their own crude weapons. Despite the overwhelming superiority of the German forces, a small group of Jews decided they would fight. They harbored no illusions about the outcome; they knew they would die, but they still believed it was better to be killed defending themselves than to be murdered. This excerpt describes the motivation of the ghetto fighters and how they prepared for the uprising that stunned the world. Israel Gutman survived the uprising and lives in Israel, where he teaches mod-

ern Jewish history at Hebrew University and directs the research center at Yad Vashem, Israel's national Holocaust museum.

The second expulsion, or "action," against the Jews of the Warsaw ghetto began on Monday, January 18, 1943, and lasted four days. It was not entirely unexpected. Those Jews who remained from the mass expulsion could no longer delude themselves. They knew that they were not to enjoy a prolonged or stable existence. The Germans would soon end the ghetto.

Information about the deportations and the complete liquidation of ghettos throughout Poland continued to come in from far and wide. Rumors concerning actions that were soon to take place in Warsaw spread rapidly throughout the ghetto. On Monday, January 11, Abraham Levin recorded in his diary:

Our mood is very gloomy and depressed. News which reached us from various places indicates that the Germans intend to finish off the Jews completely. They will not leave a single Jew alive. This was the fate of Radomsko, and other places. This news is unbearably depressing. We fear that the new "action" here within our midst will be the last for all of us.

. . . Units of the Jewish Fighting Organization

and the remaining Jews in general began to prepare themselves to maintain a permanent state of
readiness. Groups of workers and skilled artisans were taken out of the workshops to unknown destinations. Every report of movements
by the German police on the Polish side of Warsaw, or a suspicious German move near the
gates of the central ghetto, only intensified the
nervousness. Mondays were the days that had to
be watched, for this was the day on which the
expulsions usually began or were renewed.

Nevertheless, the expulsion on Monday, January 18, was something of a surprise. . . .

At 6:00 A.M. the expulsions began. Armed
Germans and Ukrainians, who were certain that
it would be an easy job, tried to repeat the system
they had used in the previous expulsion: they
called out for Jews to come out of their houses
and concentrate in the courtyards. But they soon
learned that the ruse would not work. Jews were
not prepared to obey their orders as in the past,
and many work places were unoccupied.

The expulsion started in the central ghetto. . . .

Among those who turned up for work that
day were members of the Judenrat, and some of
them were also taken to the transports together
with their families.

Some pursuers managed to surprise inhabitants of the houses and lay their hands on workers. Most of the people of the ghetto, however,
escaped to hiding places that they had prepared
in advance. Some were in improvised corners of
their cellars, in attics, and in rooms disguised by
cupboards or wooden walls. . . .

The surprise German move against the ghetto
had prevented the national committee from
meeting and discussing whether the time was
ripe for resistance action. Armed companies
could not coordinate their steps. So they sprang
into action independently.

The first shot was fired by Arieh Wilner when
the pursuers penetrated a dwelling of members
of the Jewish Fighting Organization . . . ; the
first battle in the ghetto was led by Mordecai
Anielewicz. His plan was a simple one. Anielewicz chose a dozen fighters with pistols and
stood prepared for the struggle. The fighters

were to join the lines going to the *Umschlagplatz* [collection point], and at a certain point on
the way and at a given signal, they were to burst
out of the lines and attack the German guards
escorting the queue.

Thus, members of the group entered the long
line of hundreds concentrated on Mila Street,
and at the corner of Zamenhof and Niska, near
the transports, the signal was given and the battle began. Each Jewish fighter assaulted the
nearest German. Even on a one-to-one basis,
this was not a battle between equals. The Jews
were armed with a few pistols and limited ammunition, while the Germans had semiautomat-
ic rifles and ample ammunition.

The Jews had the momentary advantage of
surprise and exploited it fully. After a few minutes, the Germans recovered from the shock of
being attacked, and the initial forces were soon
augmented by reserves. Most of the Jewish
fighters fell in battle.

The battle was a decisive one. The hundreds
of Jews who had been standing in the lines dispersed; the Germans saw that they were facing
Jewish resistance, and the first Germans fell in
the streets of the ghetto. At the same time, the
Jews drew encouragement from the dust of the
battle, and many ghetto dwellers adopted whatever means of passive resistance possible in the
circumstances—that is, not to obey the German
orders, to hide, and to evade deportation. . . .

Another group led by Yitzhak Zuckerman defended themselves from a house in Zamenhof
Street. They had entrenched themselves in an
apartment, and when the Germans entered to
search, the fighters opened fire. . . .

January 18 marked a turning point in the existence of the Jewish Fighting Organization. The
Germans had anticipated a smooth and simple
process, but they encountered opposition and
paid for it with casualties. For the first time, the
Jew was no longer seen as a submissive victim.

Moreover, from that day onward, the Germans refrained from searching the dwellings
and from climbing up to attics and down to cellars. The ease with which they had taken Jews
was a thing of the past, and as they witnessed, to

their amazement, one could lose one's life not only on the battlefield at the front but also in the narrow lanes of the Warsaw ghetto.

One cannot wholly understand the change that took place in the Jewish public's attitude without appreciating the impression made by the events of January 1943. Jews were no longer passive; they could fight back. Yitzhak Zuckerman concluded that "the revolt in January is what made possible the April rebellion." Without the initiative taken in January, the subsequent widespread revolt three months later would not have occurred. The mute acceptance of their fate and the sense of hopelessness that accompanied the mass expulsions in the summer of 1942 gave way to more defiant attitudes. Evading the Germans proved possible. . . .

The second expulsion, the January action, was over in four days. From the second day, the Germans were obliged to invest enormous effort in catching the Jews. They succeeded only in catching the sick and the feeble, or those they happened upon accidentally. During those four days, some 5,000–6,500 people were taken from the ghetto or murdered. . . .

On the last day, there was mass slaughter. In a hail of bullets the Nazis murdered a thousand Jews in the streets of the ghetto in apparent retaliation for the fact that the ghetto was no longer silent and submissive. SS Senior Colonel Ferdinand von Sammern-Frankenegg, police commandant of the Warsaw district, evidently did not report to his superiors on the dead and wounded among his soldiers resulting from the resistance in the Warsaw ghetto.

There is no precise information on the German casualties during the January resistance. The Poles spoke of dozens, but this is certainly an exaggeration. At any rate, ambulances were heard racing in and out of the ghetto. One can assume that on the eve of the last action in April von Sammern did not dare to enlighten his superiors as to the true situation in the ghetto and was not eager to reveal the events of January and the existence of the armed Jewish force in the area under his supervision. The mere fact that the Jews were capable of fighting and that the

Jewish people could be considered an active enemy rather than a subhuman group ready for extermination was perhaps beyond the Nazis' comprehension.

Notwithstanding the mass murders and the thousands hunted down in January, the Jews assumed that the Germans were deflected from carrying out their plans and forced to stop the action midway. Jewish resistance, they felt, had led to the failure of the mass expulsion and the withdrawal of German troops from the ghetto. This perception was also shared by the members of the military forces of the Polish underground. Neither Jews nor Poles had any reliable information stemming from German or other sources. The Jews responded to what was happening around them, and thus they assumed that the second expulsion would be total. After the Germans managed to uproot some 300,000 people in one concentrated sweep, it followed that during the second round they would complete the process by removing all the Jews of Warsaw. . . .

The Jews assumed that the resistance had revealed the Achilles' heel of the German military machine. They also believed that the Germans had been forced to recruit considerable forces for this action. From the German point of view, an outburst of street fighting could incite the Poles, who were thought to be waiting to get into the fray, and news of the resistance in Warsaw could not be hidden from the rest of the world, and would attract attention to their plight.

The Germans determined that the mass slaughter would continue as long as it proceeded smoothly. But when confronted by Jewish resistance, the Germans were halted. Filled with renewed confidence, the fighters mistakenly thought that the Nazis might stop the annihilation of the remaining Jews altogether.

The Poles were amazed at this manifestation of Jewish resistance, and the Polish underground press contained considerable praise for the Jews. . . .

A Lost Cause?

At the beginning of the first action, the resistance had appeared to many—including the "reasonable" circles of the underground—as a dangerous game that might hasten the deaths of those who could be rescued. Now, ironically, after a few months the resistance was viewed as a means of saving the remainder of the Jews. Thus, those who resisted were no longer seen as adventurous fighters who endangered the rest of the public but as faithful pathfinders whose bravery was the only possible response to an insoluble and utterly lost situation.

Only in Warsaw did the Uprising enjoy widespread mass support. In other ghettos where Jewish underground organizations had been active, such as Vilna and Bialystok, the masses had not taken to the idea of fighting and did not join the fighters during their uprisings. Many were impressed by the young people who were prepared to enter the fray, knowing that this battle could be their last and could end in utter disaster and death. Naturally, this manner of fighting—in which all those who participate are prepared to die fighting—attracted only the remarkable few, mostly young people who were responsible for neither their parents nor their children. Parents with children consistently clung to any solution or glimmer of hope, and when in the end they were without hope, they accepted their fate. In Warsaw, in the time between the first mass expulsions and the final destruction of the ghetto, the resolve of the fighters and the distrust of other ghetto residents hardened. The Jewish masses saw no grounds for hope except through fighting. Even if their perceptions were misleading, many were provoked to strong-willed actions. . . .

On February 16, [SS leader Heinrich] Himmler sent an order to [Wilhelm] Krüger [the head of the SS and police in Kraków] from his field headquarters which stated:

> For reasons of security, I am ordering you to destroy the Warsaw ghetto after transferring the concentration camp from there. At the same time, all building parts and materials of any kind which can still be used are to be preserved.
>
> The destruction of the ghetto and the transfer of the concentration camp is essential, otherwise we shall not succeed in getting Warsaw

into a calm state and as long as the ghetto is standing, it will be impossible to wipe out the crime. A general plan for the destruction of the ghetto should be submitted to me, and in any case, we must arrive at the stage in which the residential area, which exists at present for 500,000 sub-humans [Untermenschen], and which had never been suitable for the Germans, will disappear from the face of the area, and the city of Warsaw, with its million inhabitants, which has always been a center of agitation and rebellion, should be reduced in size.

In the not quite three months between the January and April expulsions, when the remaining Jews of Warsaw were to be uprooted and the ghetto erased from the face of the earth, preparations were well under way for the approaching resistance and final struggle—the Warsaw Ghetto Uprising. . . .

Preparing for the Uprising

Almost every remaining Jew in Warsaw participated in the construction of shelters and hiding places and in the preparation of equipment for survival in hiding. The shelters were readied in cellars and tunnels beneath the courtyards of buildings. The more secure were specially built for hiding, on the assumption that the enemy would find plans for all the houses and could then follow the outlines of existing cellars to find them.

The work of digging and preparing the bunkers was mainly done at night, mostly in rotation by the people who were to share the bunker. The earth that had been dug out was buried in the ordinary cellars, in order not to leave any trace of the work. Those individuals who formed a group to construct a bunker were obliged to pay a large sum of money to equip it adequately to be used as a hiding place. The work was done cleverly and with a great deal of thought. Wooden bunks were installed, sanitary arrangements made, and considerable attention was given to the stocking of foodstuffs. Smuggling provided for foods that would last.

A good bunker linked up with the central

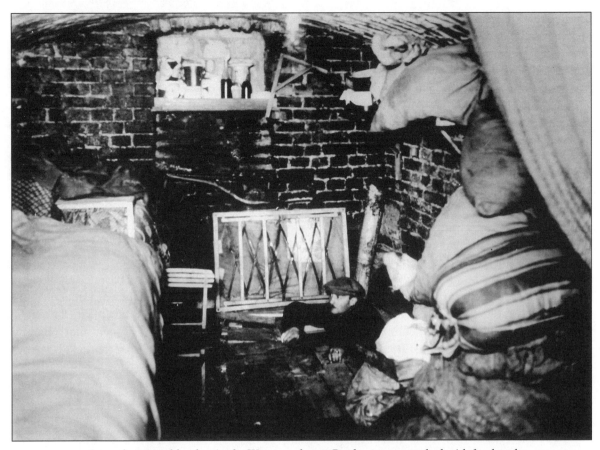

An underground bunker in the Warsaw ghetto. Bunkers were stocked with food and medical supplies, and some had access to water, electricity, and tunnels out of the ghetto.

water supply system of the city, which passed under the ghetto and ensured the flow of fresh water. This applied to electricity as well. The organizers of the installation and occupation of the bunkers were very keen on having a medical doctor among them and on obtaining a supply of medicines. The best bunkers were not only well equipped but also had a camouflaged source of air. Exceptional bunkers also attached to a tunnel leading out of the ghetto or to the vacant area between the no man's land and the inhabited ghettos. Much thought was needed to plan the disguised entrances to the bunkers, which had to be completely invisible from the outside. Some professionals took part in their planning and construction, and frequently experts were hired for the purpose. Every bunker had its guiding group to ensure its efficient operation. . . .

Between January and April 1943, the Jewish Fighting Organization was unified; the hierarchy of personnel and the strategic plans were laid down for the inevitable struggle. The period between the two expulsions was one of marked change and preparation for the last battle. The organization did not delude itself that its resistance would prompt the Nazis to give up the idea of wiping out the ghetto and to leave them alone; instead, the imminent annihilation required swift preparations since it was the enemy who would determine the date of the battle. . . .

The ghetto was divided into three sections: the central ghetto, the large workshop area, and the brushmakers' area. The central ghetto was the primary focus of the organization, and its headquarters, led by Mordecai Anielewicz, was entrenched there. The commander of the local force, which consisted of nine fighting squads dispersed throughout the area, was Israel Kanal.

In the workshop area, eight squads were led by Yitzhak Zuckerman, and in the brushmakers' area, five squads were under the command of Marek Edelman.

During the organization's formation, a strategic plan was developed that proved to be of great importance during the armed conflict. The members had no military experience and lacked understanding or knowledge of fighting methods, least of all military maneuvers in urban surroundings. Having no alternative, they had to base their strategy on a thorough knowledge of the area and on their recent experience. From the events of January, they knew that the organization could not engage in hand-to-hand battles in the streets or squares of the ghetto, as these would be decided by the crushing force of the Germans. In January this technique had worked, and changed the mood and stand of the ghetto, but in a calculated struggle over a period of time, different methods were required, including the deployment of forces in many places which could exploit the area and the element of surprise. . . .

Positions were chosen from which to open fire, overlooking the crossroads through which Ger-

man forces would pass to enter the ghetto. The weakest aspect of the plan was the lack of arms. In fact, after the events of January, many Jews sought to join the group but were refused due to the shortage of weapons. But by the beginning of April, every fighter in the fighting squads was armed with a revolver. In the interim the Jewish Fighting Organization [ZOB] "cleaned house." There were two fields of activity: the punishment and the execution of people in the ghetto who had collaborated with the Germans to the detriment of the Jews or had helped the Germans to carry out the expulsion. Emanuel Ringelblum named thirteen who were shot.

The ZOB did not prepare for withdrawal, and hence the strategy lacked a basic component of an ordinary battle plan. This was not accidental. Fighters planned to fight and fall in the streets and the neighborhoods. At their first meeting, according to Henryk Wolinski, "Jurek," or Arieh Wilner, the fighting organization's emissary, said, "We do not wish to save our lives. None of us will come out of this alive. We want to save the honor of mankind."

Selection 3

Against All Odds: The Jewish Resistance

Abram L. Sachar

The question "How could the Germans slaughter 6 million Jews?" is sometimes turned on its head and rephrased: "How could 6 million Jews allow themselves to be murdered?" But, whole nations with large armies, such as France, Belgium, and Poland, could not do anything to prevent the Nazis from overwhelming them. How can anyone believe for a second that unarmed Jews, including the elderly, women, and children, could have fought back and saved themselves? The remarkable thing is that many did resist. In fact, amazingly, a small number of poorly armed Jews put up a longer fight against the Nazis in the Warsaw ghetto than the Polish army did in defending against the invasion of the country. This excerpt provides a few examples of the heroic resistance efforts of Jews in some of the countries occupied by the Germans. Abram L. Sachar was the founding president of Brandeis University.

*F*or some years after World War II, the emphasis in evaluating the Holocaust was on the magnitude of its toll and the callousness with which it was achieved. The photographs that came to light at war's end, those taken clandestinely by correspondents and onlookers, and those taken by the Nazis themselves, all too frequently depicted groups of broken people shuffling along under the supervision of smartly uniformed guards. Inevitably the combination of statistics and repeated visual images induced a haunting question: How could six million Jews permit themselves to be led meekly to their slaughter? Would there not have been some dignity in their death if it came in resistance, rather than through execution or induced starvation and disease? The murdered became the defendants. . . .

I asked Arie Eliav, himself a survivor, who captained a ship bearing illegal immigrants to Palestine and later became a Labor party Minister of Agriculture in Israel, to comment on the alleged lack of resistance after the murderous objectives of the Nazis were no longer in doubt. Eliav suggested that the wrong question was being asked. The wonder was, he said, not that there had been so little resistance, but that there had been so much. Eliav noted that, placed in the setting of the almost impregnable Nazi power, any resistance at all by the Jews

was itself a miracle of daring. Hitler's sweep through most of Europe in less than a year demonstrated the immense force of German arms. When reprisals were ordered by the Nazis, there was no distinction between the resisters and the resigned. In the prison camps there were millions of non-Jews, nearly all of whom yielded helplessly to their fate. France surrendered in the Blitzkrieg without a major battle. The Baltic and Balkan states submitted with scarcely any defense or defiance. Their peoples were deported for slave labor, many of them never to return, and when they were herded into the trucks and trains there was little resistance from them. Some of the Jewish survivors of the death camps, placed on the defensive, asked the critics of their submission where *they* were during the Nazi dominion. Since they had not been called upon to share the ordeal of the victims, what had they done to earn the right to pontificate?

Yet there *was* resistance, and the Jews were most often in the forefront. . . . The indispensable need, of course, was arms. As soon as some of the Jews, even in the camps themselves, obtained possession of a weapon, however pathetically inadequate—a rifle, a knife, an ax, a sewer cover, a homemade bomb—they used it and often took Nazis with them to death. . . .

In Germany itself anti-Nazi attempts at dissent, much less resistance, were invariably crushed. Between 1933 and 1944 the courts meted out more than 32,000 death sentences for purported treason. In 1944 the young aristocrat Count [Claus] von Stauffenberg, General [Erwin] Rommel, and other highly placed army officers plotted to eliminate Hitler, hoping thereby to negotiate better than unconditional surrender terms from the onrushing Allies. The conspiracy ended in a merciless purge. . . . Hitler had the films of the executions shown to his aides, compelling them to sit through the ordeal. Thoroughly cowed, German resistance had no organized structure and there were no partisan groups. How then could Jews, their economic and social strength already drained, manage any significant resistance against Nazi power? . . .

Polish Resistance

There was Niuta Teitelbaum, "Little Wanda with the braids," born of a pious Lodz Hasidic family, a twenty-four-year-old who looked sixteen. Wearing traditional Polish costume, a flowered kerchief on her head, she became a valuable courier for the Jewish underground. On one occasion she charmed her way past sentinels and guards into the offices of Gestapo officials. She whispered "Private business," to the guards, who winked and let her by. Once in the presence of her target she drew her revolver, shot the SS chief, and left as calmly as she had entered. It was a simple act but its audacity electrified the ghetto.

Wanda's daring took other forms. She helped to organize women's detachments in the Warsaw Ghetto underground, acting as an instructor in many cells. She was involved in missions that blew up trains, bombed German clubs and other gathering points, and blasted artillery emplacements. One who served with her said in wonderment, "No one could lead Jews out of the ghetto, or smuggle hand grenades and weapons in, past the guards, as did Niuta." She survived the spring of 1943 when the Warsaw Ghetto was razed, but was captured in July. Unsuccessful in her attempt to take poison to circumvent the ordeal of torture, she managed to get a message out that nothing her captors inflicted would compel her to betray her comrades. She kept her vow. When the war was won, Niuta/Wanda was posthumously awarded the Grunwald Cross, the highest battle decoration of the new Polish government.

Such acts, however dramatic, could have little effect in slowing down the deportations. Gradually the ghettos were emptied and usually razed. Only one hope to save Polish Jewry remained, a revolt by the Poles themselves. . . .

By April 1943, so many Jews had been deported that there were only 65,000 left in Warsaw. The younger militants decided to wait no longer. They were the last of the three and one-half million who had once comprised the largest Jewish community in Europe.

The Warsaw Ghetto uprising of 1943 was the first mass open rebellion on the continent against the Nazis, except for the resistance of the Yugoslav guerillas under [Josip] Tito. Leadership in the uprising was supplied by Mordecai Anielewicz, who emerged from the ranks of the left-wing Zionist movement. In 1942, Mordecai, all of twenty-three, helped coordinate the covert fighting units under the rubric of the Jewish Combat Organization, usually referred to by the initials of its Polish name, ZOB. . . .

He watched in frenzied dismay as his people were shipped out in a steady stream to the extermination camps, and told the historian Emmanuel Ringelblum that three precious years had been "wasted" in educational and cultural activities. The able-bodied in the ghetto should have been given training in the use of arms for a self-respecting defense. When [SS leader Heinrich] Himmler himself visited the ghetto in January 1943, Anielewicz knew that the final liquidation was about to begin. He marshaled twenty-two combat units of about thirty members each, and assigned them to strategic locations in the ghetto. The planning had to be undertaken against the strenuous opposition of the Nazi-appointed Judenrat, the ghetto's governing council, whose leadership was terrified by the possible punitive consequences of defiant strategy.

What Anielewicz anticipated in January came to pass at midnight on April 19, when a strong contingent of Nazi troops backed by Ukrainian and Lithuanian collaborators, more heavily armed than usual, marched into the ghetto. Earlier, the defenders had dug a deep hole under the entry street, filling it with explosives. As a German column passed over the cache, the charge was blown, and some of the troops were killed and wounded. Further casualties resulted from a simultaneous volley of machine gun fire, hand grenades, and Molotov cocktails. A second considerably reinforced German contingent moved in. It too was routed. The Polish underground radio station, SWIT, announced that the Warsaw Ghetto had been transformed into a miniature Stalingrad. The defenders, Polish and Jewish flags flying above them, dodged from house to house, from rooms to bunkers, from cellars to sewers. They suffered heavy losses but there was exultation that Jewish casualties were exacting a toll. Anielewicz fell in mid-May in a bunker in the command headquarters. He had sent a farewell note to one of his comrades who was attempting to obtain arms in the Polish sections of the city: "We bid you farewell, you on the 'outside.'. . . The greatest wish of my life has come true. Jewish resistance and vengeance have been transformed into acts."

The Nazi timetable called for the ghetto to be subdued in a matter of hours, at the most a day or two. But resistance went on for more than a month, against several thousand Nazis, who were reinforced with flamethrowers, tanks, and planes. As ammunition ran out among the defenders, iron bars torn from the area ways of houses and even stout pieces of furniture became weapons. The resisters made use of boiling water. They sprayed the stairs of their hideouts with gasoline and oil, setting fire to them when the enemy came seeking them. Himmler sent an angry message to Jurgen von Stroop, who had been given the assignment for the Warsaw Ghetto liquidation. "The round-ups in the Warsaw Ghetto," he wrote, "must be carried out with relentless determination and in as ruthless a manner as possible. The tougher the attack the better. Recent events show just how dangerous these Jews really are." Von Stroop was compelled to order the leveling of the ghetto, house by house if necessary. It was necessary. The ghetto defenders fought for every foot of space, even into the sewers that had to be blasted to flush out the desperate remnants. On May 16, von Stroop issued a bulletin: "The former Jewish quarter no longer exists. . . . The *Grossaktion* is terminated." As a final vindictive measure and, by von Stroop's lights, a cautionary message to all the Jews of Poland and Europe, he ordered the Great Synagogue dynamited. Yet despite von Stroop's triumphant announcement, the resistance continued for at least another four months. . . .

Twenty thousand people died, but as Anielewicz had noted, they took a humiliating toll from the fully armed Nazis. The Polish government-in-exile in London announced, with understandable exaggeration, that 1,200 Germans had been killed and many military factories and ammunition dumps had been destroyed. But the signal for the Polish underground to join in the fighting was still withheld.

The news of the uprising received international coverage and helped to create a new image of Jewish militancy among the Allies. It had taken the Germans longer to subdue the Warsaw Ghetto than to overrun Poland itself or to bring surrender from the French. . . .

In Bialystok, an important textile manufacturing center, lived 35,000 Jews; they had priority on the early death list of the Nazis. Here resistance was organized by Mordecai Tenenboim-Tamarov who, in his twenties, already had an impressive record of defiance in some of the other ghettos, notably Grodno. . . .

Mordecai obtained occasional arms by paying extortionate prices to Polish peasants, scavengers who had stripped the weapons from the dead on the Russian-German battlefields of 1941 and 1942. Some arms were also stolen from the German barracks. But his most effective assistance came from an anti-Nazi German, Otto Busse, who was the director of a German factory in the city. Busse had been smuggling food and medical supplies into the besieged ghetto and providing homes for Jews who took refuge in the Aryan sections of the city.

In the Bialystock ghetto, some few crude weapons had been manufactured—hand grenades, bottles filled with vitriol, axes, knives, scythes. "The ghetto was a mess of blood soaked pillows, shattered buildings, personal possessions, lying sodden in the mud, bodies crumpled on every doorstep." With all his preparations, Mordecai's forces could do little more than offer hopeless resistance. Nevertheless, it took the Nazis four days of bitter fighting, supported by tanks and armored cars, to subdue Tenenboim's little force. He was among the last to go, a suicide, to avoid falling into Nazi hands. Before his death, he appealed to the ghetto fighters to leave nothing of value for the enemy. "When you leave your house, set fire to it. Set fire to the factories, demolish them. Do not let our assassins be our beneficiaries as well." He urged those who opted for flight to join the forest guerillas, and not leave any equipment behind, no matter how much it handicapped movement.

The combatants followed his last wishes. They exacted a toll of SS troops and damaged some valuable industrial workshop equipment. Reuben Ainsztein, one of the historians of the resistance in eastern Europe, writes: "Had only one load in ten of the arms brought by the RAF [Britain's Royal Air Force] aircraft for the Polish underground reached them, the fighters of the Bialystok ghetto would have made their murderers pay a fairer price for the lives they attempted to defend."

Such actions inflicted casualties and losses, but they could not of course prevail against the overwhelming German might. By the end of August 1943, all that was left of one of the great historic settlements were six girls who had escaped detection by posing as Aryans, and a few survivors whom they guided out of the doomed city to join the Partisans in the woods. . . .

No account of the resistance in Minsk would be complete without mentioning some of the children who were couriers to and from the forest hideouts. Two young boys, Banko and David, and a blond moppet, Sima, became legend. Blue-eyed Sima, her parents murdered in a pogrom, was, at twelve, already a veteran in facing death and dodging it. "Don't worry," she told the ghetto leaders, "the Fritzies will not take me alive." Armed with a pistol whose size challenged her little body, she would squirm her way under the barbed-wire fence of the ghetto to deliver small caches of arms to the Partisans in the forest. She then sneaked back into the ghetto by way of the cemetery. Sima lived to march with other decorated Partisans in the Minsk victory parade after the Nazis were driven out. She was fourteen years old.

Banko and David, both thirteen, three times a week guided Jews out of the ghetto to appointed rendezvous with Partisans in the forest. Banko still had his mother; David was an orphan. They were inseparable, although it was David who gave the commands. The children sounded for all the world like grizzled campaigners of some forgotten war. Young David would proclaim be-

fore each sortie: "I hope all will go well, and in a few hours from now you will be free people without yellow badges." For several months the children led hundreds of people, some of them doctors, out of the ghetto, David at the head of the file, Banko guarding the rear. Banko stayed with his mother each time he stole back to the ghetto. He won approval to include her on one of his sorties. "But remember," he told her, "ours is a combat detachment. You'll have to stand guard and hold a rifle. But we'll be together in a detachment in a dugout."

The Germans, in retreat from Russia in August 1943, decided to take full revenge on what was left of the Minsk ghetto and on the Partisans in the forest hideouts. Their "heroic victory" over Minsk took fifteen days and a full-scale front-line operation. Every house in the ghetto, every clump of trees, every cave they could smoke out, was systematically destroyed. Banko was taken and burned alive. David wept with his elders as the charred body . . . was buried after the Germans passed by. . . .

Vilna became the prime example of the tragedy that set in when the Nazis manipulated the captive Judenrat to regulate the affairs of the community. They appointed Jacob Gens, a former Lithuanian Army officer, as liaison with the Jewish community. Gens was constantly forced into the Solomonic dilemma of either obeying the Nazis or sacrificing his entire Jewish community. As police chief, it was he who had to select the Jews to make up the quotas for deportation. Under threat, he was required to name the hiding places of resistance groups. Four rabbis, pleading with him to refuse, quoted the response given by the medieval sage Maimonides: "And should the idolaters say to them: 'Deliver unto us one of you and we shall kill him, or we shall kill all of you!' let them all be killed rather than deliver a single Jewish soul." Gens's response, invariably, was "better for the few to die than to have the catastrophe swallow up the entire community." This was the *cri de coeur* [passionate outcry] of many Jewish leaders in Europe, who were compelled to perform the odious work of selection, breaking down the communal will even as the victims died. Finally the Nazis demanded the surrender of Itzik Wittenberg, head of Vilna's underground. He had been hunted unremittingly, but, with the help of loyal comrades, always managed to escape. The Nazis made the whole community hostage, declaring that, unless Gens produced Wittenberg, the ghetto would be razed and its inhabitants liquidated. Gens begged Wittenberg to give himself up to save the thousands who would otherwise die. Wittenberg emerged from his hideout and was executed immediately. "In order that certain Jews should live, I was obliged to lead others to their death," Gens claimed. "In order that some Jews should be able to leave the ghetto with clear consciences, I was obliged to wallow in filth and act without conscience." Ironically, most Jews in the hostage community were killed anyway. . . .

Gens was killed by the Gestapo when he had served the Nazi purpose. The Nazis enjoyed no greater triumphs than when, in this way, they set the Jews against each other. After Israel won its independent status and brought into its midst the surviving remnants of the Holocaust, one of the issues that split the country was judgment on the actions of Judenrat leaders who had been obliged to make the life-and-death decisions in the ghettos. The wounds inflicted by the Nazis in shifting such responsibility to appointed Jewish leaders left deep scars in the political and social life of Israel that were never fully healed. . . .

The French Jewish Resistance

Since the Jews had been singled out for special malevolence, it was hardly surprising that they were well represented in the French Resistance. They comprised less than 1 percent of the French population but many times this proportion in the ranks of the freedom fighters. . . .

Then there was a young Polish émigré, Abraham Lissner, who had lived in Palestine, fought against [dictator Francisco] Franco's forces in Spain, and, when the Fascists triumphed there, fled to France. . . . His men ambushed and attacked marching German brigades in the open Paris streets, hurled hand grenades through the windows of German billets, cut off both ends of a boulevard and fired from rooftops on the trapped German troops until their columns were cut to pieces. . . . Lissner's contingent assassinated Wehrmacht General Abt and Karl Ritter, assistant to the Gauleiter for France. They raided arsenals and cached precious stores of arms in remote places. Lissner's diary also noted that between March and November 1943, in Paris alone, nineteen hotels were set on fire, along with thirteen warehouses and twenty-three military bases. German planes were blown up and two million liters of gasoline destroyed. More than 150 collaborators and double agents were "removed.". . .

The Hungarian Ruse

There had been little significant anti-Nazi resistance in Budapest, or even in Hungary, either by its Jews or by the general population. . . .

Hungary had strong Zionist groups that had grown in size and influence as the situation darkened for its Jews. They had no arms; no sympathy from the general population, nor even from their own people; and no lines of communication with underground groups. One of those who refused to accept his fate supinely said, "We have to be both the fighters and the weapons." But while those who opted for resistance admitted that they did not expect any positive results from defiance, they insisted that even if there was no hope of personal survival, the message must be sent to the world, and to their own people, that death with dignity carried renewed life within it.

The stratagems to which the Zionists resorted often seemed quixotic, yet their very inconceivability caught the Nazis off guard. The president of Mizrachi, the Hungarian Orthodox Zionist group, owed his life and ultimate freedom to their audacity. He was awakened one night by the banging on his door and the shouted command, "Jew Frankel, open up!" A Nazi squad burst into his room, beat him up, and dragged him out to what he thought must be the site of his murder. Instead, hustled to a bunker in a remote part of the city, Frankel discovered that the "Nazis" in fact were disguised comrades from the young Zionists. They had learned from members who had infiltrated the Nazi inner councils that Frankel was listed for execution. They came for him in the guise of the executioners, beating him in the presence of the concierge to lend credibility to their disguise. . . .

Nothing perhaps better summarizes the role of the resistance efforts by isolated groups of Jews in Europe than the fate of twenty-three-year-old Hannah Senesch, the Hungarian-born young woman who volunteered for parachute duty behind the Nazi lines in the Balkans and was caught and shot when betrayed by collaborators in the Partisan ranks. Hannah was born in 1921 into an affluent, highly cultured Jewish family in Budapest. At eighteen, in 1939, when girls of Hannah's background would ordinarily be involved in university life, Hannah was jubilant that she had obtained a certificate to emigrate to Palestine and rejoiced further when her brother decided to go with her. Her widowed mother was aghast at their choice, for the Senesch family's friends were thoroughly assimilated Hungarians to whom Palestine was an alien aberration.

Hannah had developed talent as a poet, but she welcomed the laborious agricultural work of her kibbutz in Caesarea and the military discipline that had become an essential part of it. Palestinian Jews had been volunteering to fight the Axis by the side of the British, and Hannah hoped that she too could qualify to join such volunteers. She listened to her comrades discuss the usefulness of developing a parachute corps to drop behind enemy lines in the Balkans for intelligence and rescue missions. The Ploesti oil fields in Rumania, for example, had been repeatedly bombed, and many British and American airmen had been shot down and were either imprisoned or were lost in the forests of Transylvania. Parachutists could reach these downed Allied airmen and perhaps guide them across frontiers to Adriatic ports. Too, in 1943 there were still about a million and a quarter Jews alive in Hungary, Slovakia, Rumania, and Bulgaria. The Palestinians could be enormously valuable in aiding these people, for many were Balkan-bred and they knew the terrain and the languages of the regions. . . .

The British did not need to be persuaded that parachute infiltrators in conquered territory could be invaluable; they were already experts in this type of warfare. But they showed as little enthusiasm for a special corps of Palestinian Jews as they had when [president of the Jewish Agency for Palestine Chaim] Weizmann and [Zionist and labor leader David] Ben Gurion broached the idea to them early in the war that Jewish Brigades should be assigned to the most dangerous fronts in Europe. No one doubted the courage and resourcefulness of such recruits; but would they not inevitably create problems after the war was over, exactly because they would be so well trained? It was inevitable that fighting would break out in Palestine between the Arabs and the Jews, and the British would simply be compounding their problems of mediation if they had such veterans to challenge their decisions. The Jewish militants were persistent, however, and by the end of 1943, as the war reached its climax, they finally wore down the objections of the British command. The enlistment of the special parachute corps began at once. Hannah was among the first to volunteer and she was enlisted as one of thirty-two men and women who were sent off to Cairo in January 1944 to begin their training.

After several months she was flown with two men to Slovenia and dropped among the Tito Partisans. There were many narrow escapes as they made their way more than two hundred miles through German-controlled territory across the border into Hungary, where her small party arrived in early June 1944. But her mission came to naught as one of the Partisan guides proved to be an informer. She was betrayed, as were several others who had taken different routes. Only seven of the original team survived.

Hannah was brought to a Budapest prison to be tortured into revealing the details of her mission. She had carried radio apparatus with her and her captors were eager to learn the British code signals, what communications she was receiving, and from whom. When she defied torture, the Nazis arrested her mother, who had no idea her daughter was not in Tel Aviv, and the two women had a few brief opportunities to talk. Hannah had been told by the police that unless she revealed her mission and exposed the location of its participants, her mother would be killed. Hannah gasped out why she must remain loyal to her pledge. A week later, the distraught mother, once the darling of her cultured middle-class family, set out before the permitted time to visit Hannah in prison. That same morning, Hannah had been offered commutation of her death sentence if she confessed to her crime of spying and pleaded for mercy. She had responded: "I ask no mercy from hangmen." Her mother was sitting in an office in the prison when a shot rang out from the nearby courtyard. Hannah Senesch, aged twenty-three, who had also refused to be blindfolded, had just been executed.

A few days later the Russians were in Budapest. Mme Senesch lived to escape and join her son in Israel. By then her daughter had become a legend of heroism and dedication. Her likeness in military uniform, young and radiant, was in the homes of every village and town in Palestine. And the poem that Hannah had written before her execution had become the best known and most beloved in Israel:

Blessed is the match that is consumed in kindling flame.
Blessed is the flame that burns in the secret fastnesses of the heart.
Blessed is the heart with strength to stop its beating for honor's sake.
Blessed is the match that is consumed in kindling flame.

Selection 4

Revolt and Revulsion

Primo Levi

Why didn't more Jews revolt? It is possible to list lots of reasons: exhaustion and illness, lack of weapons, overwhelming odds, and fear. Another factor was resignation, an acceptance of the inability to change the situation, and submission after months and years of humiliation. In heroic tales, one person may rally others to his or her side to fight against tyrants, even when the odds are impossible. During the Holocaust, such heroes rarely emerged. This brief excerpt offers an example of how the prisoners at Auschwitz reacted to the brave act of defiance of a man who apparently contributed to one remarkable act of resistance. Primo Levi was an Italian-born chemist who was deported to Auschwitz in 1944. He survived and wrote about his experience in a series of memoirs and became a respected author. He died in 1987.

*O*nce again the music from the band, the ceremony of *"Mützen ab,"* hats smartly off in front of the SS; once more *Arbeit Macht Frei* ["Work Brings Freedom"], and the announcement of the Kapo: *"Kommando 98,* *zwei and sechzig Häftlinge, Stärke stimmt,"* sixty-two prisoners, number correct. But the column has not broken up, they have made a march as far as the roll-call square. Is there to be a roll-call? It is not a roll-call. We have seen the crude glare of the searchlight and the well-known profile of the gallows.

For more than an hour the squads continued to return, with the hard clatter of their wooden shoes on the frozen snow. When all the Kommandos had returned, the band suddenly stopped and a raucous German voice ordered silence. Another German voice rose up in the sudden quiet, and spoke for a long time angrily into the dark and hostile air. Finally the condemned man was brought out into the blaze of the searchlight.

All this pomp and ruthless ceremony are not new to us. I have already watched thirteen hangings since I entered the camp; but on the other occasions they were for ordinary crimes, thefts from the kitchen, sabotage, attempts to escape. Today it is different.

Last month one of the crematoriums at Birkenau had been blown up. None of us knows (and perhaps no one will ever know) exactly how the exploit was carried out: there was talk of the *Sonderkommando*, the Special Kommando attached to the gas chambers and the ovens, which is itself periodically exterminated, and which is kept scrupulously segregated from the rest of the camp. The fact remains that a few hundred men at Birkenau, helpless and exhausted slaves like ourselves, had found in themselves the strength to act, to mature the fruits of their hatred.

The man who is to die in front of us today in some way took part in the revolt. They said he had contacts with the rebels of Birkenau, that he carried arms into our camp, that he was plotting a simultaneous mutiny among us. He is to die today before our very eyes: and perhaps the Germans do not understand that this solitary death, this man's death which has been reserved for him, will bring him glory, not infamy.

At the end of the German's speech, which nobody understood, the raucous voice of before again rose up: *"Habt ihr verstanden?"* Have you understood?

Who answered *"Jawohl"*? Everybody and nobody: it was as if our cursed resignation took body by itself, as if it turned into a collective voice above our heads. But everybody heard the cry of the doomed man, it pierced through the old thick barriers of inertia and submissiveness, it struck the living core of man in each of us:

"Kamaraden; ich bin der Letz!" (Comrades, I am the last one!)

I wish I could say that from the midst of us, an abject flock, a voice rose, a murmur, a sign of assent. But nothing happened. We remained standing, bent and grey, our heads dropped, and we did not uncover our heads until the German ordered us to do so. The trapdoor opened, the body wriggled horribly; the band began playing again and we were once more lined up and filed past the quivering body of the dying man.

At the foot of the gallows, the SS watch us pass with indifferent eyes: their work is finished, and well finished. The Russians can come now: there are no longer any strong men among us, the last one is now hanging above our heads, and as for the others, a few halters had been enough. The Russians can come now: they will only find us, the slaves, the worn-out, worthy of the unarmed death which awaits us.

To destroy a man is difficult, almost as difficult as to create one: it has not been easy, nor quick, but you Germans have succeeded. Here we are, docile under your gaze; from our side you have nothing more to fear; no acts of violence, no words of defiance, not even a look of judgement.

Alberto and I went back to the hut, and we could not look each other in the face. That man must have been tough, he must have been made of another metal than us if this condition of ours, which has broken us, could not bend him.

Because we also are broken, conquered: even if we know how to adapt ourselves, even if we have finally learnt how to find our food and to resist the fatigue and cold, even if we return home.

We lifted the *menaschka* on to the bunk and divided it, we satisfied the daily ragings of hunger, and now we are oppressed by shame.

A Jewish Partisan

Shalom Yoran

Jews had few options once the Nazis con-quered most of Europe. By the time the Ger-mans took over a country, it was usually too late to immigrate to another country. If a Jew did not leave, the combination of the army, SS, Gestapo, and informers was likely to find them and deport them to a concentration camp. Handfuls of Jews did escape the Nazi dragnet and managed to live in the forests and fight with non-Jewish partisans engaging in hit-and-run sabotage operations. Shalom Yoran was one of these Jewish partisans. This excerpt describes his involvement in blowing up German trains. Yoran made his way across Europe after the war and eventually smuggled himself into Palestine. He became an officer in the newly formed air force of Is-rael and later played a major role in the de-velopment of Israel's aircraft industry. He is now the chairman of a commercial aircraft company in the United States.

*T*he plan was to come close to the tracks early in the night, observe the move-ment of the enemy patrols, and lay the mines that same night. There were two sets of tracks and each group was responsible for blow-ing up one set. . . .

When it became dark on the second day, all was quiet and we continued to move toward the tracks. There were enemy bunkers strewn all along the way, and their patrols moved constant-ly. Also, the areas which were closer and more accessible to the tracks were cleared of obsta-cles and planted with mines. After a brief dis-cussion with our guides, we decided to approach the tracks from an open field close to one of the bunkers. It seemed to be the place from which an approach would be least expected.

We set off again, cautiously crouching, our weapons ready, careful not to make a noise. We stopped on a small hill, hidden by a few trees, and looked around. There was an open field sloping down to the tracks. Lying down, mo-tionless, we began to observe the surroundings and plan our move. Our guides refused to go fur-ther, and we agreed that they should await our return at that spot.

Planes flew overhead constantly. From afar we could see fire and we heard echoes of distant bomb explosions, probably around Vilna. We watched patrols passing and timed them. Trains rarely moved at night, but the patrols guarded the tracks anyway.

I was excited, in anticipation of blowing up German trains. It would again fulfill my person-al vow of revenge and be yet another contribu-tion in the fight against the enemy.

The second group was about a third of a mile away from us. At exactly 1 A.M. Sergeant Usi-akov signaled and we began to move toward the tracks. Crawling confidently behind him, I could clearly see the tracks down the hill. When we reached the bottom we saw that the tracks were on an embankment, which we had to climb.

We reached the tracks. Usiakov and his helper began to prepare to lay the mines, while I continued to crawl along the tracks, away from them, for another thirty yards. My job was to protect the two men while they were laying the mines. Someone else was protecting them from the other side of the tracks. We were supposed to fight off any approaching enemy, and thus enable the rest of our group to retreat. I saw Markh and another partisan dragging a heavy machine gun, which they set up at the bottom of the embankment to protect both groups from another direction.

With my automatic rifle cocked, I looked ahead along the tracks. Glancing back, I saw the two men digging frantically under the tracks. My fear dissipated and I keenly observed what was happening around me. Occasionally I placed my ear on the tracks to check for the vibration of an oncoming train.

At one point, it seemed to me that I could hear something. I tensed. I put my ear to the track, and sure enough, I heard something but didn't know what. I waited for a minute and put my ear to the track again. Now I was certain. The vibration was stronger; a train was definitely approaching. I lifted myself a bit and gave the prearranged hand signal. But the two men continued laying the mine. I wasn't sure they had seen my signal, and by now I could clearly hear the train. I signaled again and again, but they were still working. Each second dragged on eternally for me. By now I was sure the men heard the train too. I saw the outline of the locomotive. The men went on working. Desperate, I surveyed the situation. Ahead of us, open fields. The night wasn't very dark. The train was about five hundred yards in front of me. If the mine exploded under the train, I would be blown up with it. Or else, if the guards on board saw me fleeing, I would be a very easy target for them.

The train began to slow down; the locomotive was now about two hundred yards from me. I looked back and saw Usiakov and the second guy jump off the tracks and run away into the open fields. They were not carrying the mine. Relieved that I could leave my post, I also jumped off the tracks and rolled down the embankment. I picked myself up and ran as fast as I could. I was trying to run back up the hill to hide behind it, but the ground was soft and my feet sank into the dirt at every step. I still had to cover about a hundred yards to the top of the hill, so I dragged myself along. I was short of breath, and my knees buckled. Ahead of me I caught a glimpse of Markh, desperately running, bent under a load of ammunition from the machine gun. Behind me I saw the train approaching the point where the mine had been placed. There was another fifty yards to the top of the hill, but my body gave up. I hugged the ground, covered my head with my arms and waited for the big explosion. Nothing happened.

I heard the train slowing down. I lifted my head a bit and saw the locomotive standing just about where the mine was supposed to be. Then it slowly moved on, past the danger point, and began to pick up speed. Still nothing happened. Later, we assumed that the driver of the locomotive had seen some shadows or movement which aroused his suspicion and caused him to slow down and move cautiously. When he saw that all was quiet, he had continued on his way.

I got up and ran back to the top of the hill, where I met the rest of my group. It turned out that the mines had been laid under the tracks, but at the last minute the detonator was removed because the men saw that there was no time for us to take cover. If the train had blown up we all would have been killed.

Finishing the Job

As soon as it was safe, we returned to the track to finish the job. We reconnected the detonator and replaced the whitewashed pebbles as they were before, so that the patrols would not detect that anything had been tampered with. The detonator had been set under the rail of one of the tracks, and was now adjusted so that the weight of people or even an empty car would not set it off. It needed the weight of a locomotive or a heavily loaded boxcar to explode it. We planned it this way, because the Germans often pushed an empty train car ahead of the locomotive, so that if it exploded, the locomotive and the train were not damaged, and the tracks could be quickly repaired.

As soon as we finished, both groups retreated, satisfied that the first part of our mission was accomplished.

We decided to go up a hill one or two miles beyond the village, from where we could watch the tracks. . . .

It was about six o'clock, and in the early morning light we saw a train approaching. From the distance we were uncertain just where the mines were. Someone said he thought the train had passed the spot already, but an instant later there was a tremendous blast and the locomotive took off into the air and fell into the ditch, dragging along a string of cars, which piled on top of each other. From a distance they looked like toys. There was something surreal about the whole scene.

We hugged each other in excitement. About half an hour later another explosion tore the air. We couldn't actually see a train coming from the opposite direction, but we assumed that the second group's mines exploded another train.

We left the spot as quickly as we could and went deeper into the woods. . . .

We went to our contact and received his report stating that a train from Vilna was blown up at 6 A.M., and the locomotive with thirty cars was destroyed. The train was carrying ammunition and military equipment. At 6:30 A.M. another train, coming from Lida, exploded and another locomotive with thirty-five cars full of military equipment was also destroyed. Many soldiers on the trains were killed and wounded—the exact numbers were unknown. . . .

One More Time

We waited for a night that was cloudy and dark, and then set out in a different direction. . . .

We decided to place our mines in a spot about half a mile from the train station, where we thought no one would expect us. Each group would place their mine on a different track, not far from each other. This would cover trains coming from both directions. . . .

We were so close to the station that we could hear people talking, doors slamming, and patrols passing. We lay there until way past midnight, until there was not a sound anywhere.

We then crawled up to the tracks. This time I was one of the two men whose job it was to lay the mine. I strapped my weapon on my back so that my hands were free to carry the mine to the tracks. I put down the mine and carefully started collecting the pebbles, which were painted white, and set them aside. The mine had to be placed under the inner track, midway between two railroad ties, so that the blown-up train would be thrown out into the ditch. With our bayonets we dug a hole under the track, collecting the dirt into rain capes which were spread alongside. I checked to see whether the hole was deep enough for the dynamite. No, I needed to dig more. I dug and dug, covered in sweat. Again I checked, and this time the size was right. I carefully placed the mine in the pit, and pushed the detonator into the hole on top. Then I screwed on a special mechanism for blowing up trains—a fine steel shaft with a flat adjustable head, which I placed directly under the rail.

Next came the most critical part. I adjusted the head to almost touch the rail, but left enough space to run a match under it. In that way only a heavy weight like the locomotive would bend the rail enough to press the shaft, which would detonate the bomb. Very, very carefully we began to cover the mine and to fill in the hole with the dirt which we had dug out, leaving the shaft above ground. It was visible only if one bent to look under the rail. I constantly reminded myself not to accidentally hit the plunger. When the ground was level, the final detail was to replace the white stones. Everything looked untouched.

Dragging away the soil that remained in the cape, we began the crawl back to where our heavy machine gun was positioned, and met up with both groups. . . .

We were back at the village of Mosti by daybreak, but we couldn't resist seeing a train exploding again. We went back up the hill and watched and waited.

It was a beautiful summer morning. The sun was just out. I looked down at the station, trying to figure out just where I had placed the mine. I saw a train leaving the station. It looked so small, like a matchbox. It gathered speed and approached the danger point. I held my breath. Another ten yards, another five. Will it explode? At that instant I saw a pillar of flame rising into the sky, and the train was thrown into the air, writhing like a tortured snake before it fell into the ditch. And then I heard the boom. It blasted the windows in the village. Then all I could see

of the train was smoke and fire.

Later, we found out that the train was full of German soldiers. Thirty cars were destroyed, several hundred Germans were killed and hundreds more wounded. Another train from Vilna, coming to evacuate the wounded and bring reinforcements, was also blown up by the mine laid down on the other side.

I needed to see the destruction and the havoc that I personally helped create. Seeing the wreckage I felt that, in the only way I could, I was fulfilling my aim to fight the German war machine and take revenge.

Selection 6

Life in the Lublin Forest

Isaiah Trunk

The Jews who evaded the Nazis usually were on their own or in very small groups and had to rely on their ingenuity and luck. For most people, the sole concern was staying alive, and that usually meant hiding. Some Jews, however, chose a more dangerous course, seeking out the Nazis and their collaborators and attacking them. The Jews who were involved in these activities usually escaped into the forests and joined the efforts of the partisans. In this account, however, a Jew who escaped into the forest in Poland started his own small resistance operation and, at least temporarily, fed and protected Jews hiding from the Nazis. Isaiah Trunk is a noted au- *thor and the chief archivist of the YIVO Institute for Jewish Research.*

G. Born in Lublin in 1912; lived there. Recorded by Icek Shmulewitz in New York in January 1955. The witness describes the events in Lublin after the outbreak of the war; his experiences in the Piaski Ghetto, near Lublin, until the liquidation of the ghetto. He was able to escape through a bunker and continues at this point.

I came out of the bunker all alone—it was the dead of night. I jumped over a wall, but a Polish policeman saw me. He yelled for me to stop but I kept on running. He fired a couple of times but missed. Running wildly, I rushed down the next street and found myself back inside the ghetto. It wasn't completely by accident—I was desperate for a drink of water and couldn't have kept run-

Excerpted from Isaiah Trunk, *Jewish Responses to Nazi Persecution*, (NY: Stein and Day, 1979).

ning without it. As soon as I started drinking from the ghetto well, a group of Polish policemen rushed at me. I ran out of the ghetto again, with the policemen after me, but they couldn't catch up.

I stumbled and ran through the fields all night long, not knowing where I was headed. . . . I passed many peasant huts along the way. I drank from cattle troughs to quench my thirst. When I drank my fill, I got up to run, but soon I was overcome with exhaustion. I crept into a peasant's shed and lay down on the hay to rest. But then a dog ran up and started howling, so I had to keep running. I walked and ran all night long, till at daybreak, I reached the Skrzynice Forest near Lublin. This was in the fall of 1942. . . .

Right at the edge of the forest, I saw a woman jump up from the fields and dash in between the trees. I caught up to her. All I said to her was, "*Amkho*?" The woman answered, yes, she's a Jewish daughter. She told me that deeper in the forest, her two small children lay hidden together with other Jewish women—some of them old—and their children. Altogether, this group of women and children numbered twelve people.

The woman was from Lublin and she told me that during the deportation from the Lublin Ghetto, she and her two children and the other women with their children escaped into the forest from the ghetto. Polish peasants confronted them in the woods, but they took pity on the women and children and let them live. She said she was on her way from the village where she'd gotten hold of two bottles of water—she had a small kettle in the woods and wanted to boil the water for the children. As we were finishing talking, we came upon the spot in the woods where the Jewish women and children were hiding. Before me was a horrible sight:

The women and children lay stretched out on the ground, bundled up in rags. The small children cried terribly and a fire had started in the underbrush and was spreading all around them. . . . [After the fire was put out] and I asked them how they had managed to keep alive, they told me that every evening, they were visited by a good-hearted Jewish youth from Lódź, Yulek

Rozenshtayn, who was taken out of the *Lodzer* Ghetto with other Jews in 1940, but had escaped from his transport. He stayed in the woods somewhere and the peasants thought he was Christian. For two years, this young man worked as a caretaker for the forest warden. In the end, the warden found out he was a Jew and got rid of him. The women told me he visits them every evening and brings them beets, potatoes, and other things to eat. I waited for him, and that same evening, I met Yulek Rozenshtayn.

We became friends right away. He told me he sometimes still went to see the warden for whom he'd worked, and the warden gives him bread. Yulek Rozenshtayn told me he couldn't stay in the area long, because the peasants make raids in the woods to capture Jews in hiding, and strip them of everything they own. The peasants also beat the Jews up—sometimes, to death. This young man told me a peasant woman lived near the forest with her children—her husband was taken away for forced labor to Germany. At night, Yulek Rozenshtayn comes in through her yard and sleeps in the cellar, and the peasant woman doesn't know a thing about it. During the day, of course, he roams through the woods.

Yulek brought me down to the woman's cellar. We stayed there and talked our situation over. In the morning, I took up potatoes from the cellar and brought them to the women and children in the woods. While we were standing around the campsite fire, baking potatoes, a Pole and a Russian, both armed with rifles, attacked us. They stripped off my boots and suit and then left. This Pole had been exiled from Poznań and the Russian was a Soviet soldier who escaped from a German camp. Both of them hunted the woods for Jews, and when they found them, they robbed them of everything they had.

Yulek and I returned to the peasant woman and she gave me some wooden clogs to wear. Then we took two shovels and an axe from the woman and went off to dig a bunker in the forest for the women and children, who had to lie on the sodden ground. It took us several days to finish the bunker. We padded it with straw and burlap, the children and their mothers went down inside and baked and ate potatoes there. Now they had some means of security.

A reward of a quarter-kilo of sugar was offered by the Germans to any Pole who revealed the hideout of a Jew. During the night, while I lay in the woman's cellar with my friend Yulek, a mob of peasants stormed into the woods, dragged the Jewish women and children from the bunker, and took them off to the Germans. . . .

Going on Offense

We decided to get guns to protect ourselves, since we were always in danger of falling into the hands of the Poles. We decided to ask the peasant woman in whose cellar we used to sleep, about guns. . . .

The woman told us to climb down through a trapdoor—there was a pit down there covered by a boulder where her husband had buried something when the Polish soldiers were demobilized.

My friend and I got down in the pit the woman spoke of, we started digging, and found a rifle there, manufactured at the Radom munitions works. We also found a revolver with bullets down there. The rifle and revolver were very rusted. The woman gave us paraffin and rags, we went off to the woods, and for a whole day, we polished the rusted guns. We loaded the rifle and revolver with the bullets and crossed into another part of the woods.

My friend and I headed in a completely new direction. During the night, we stole into a peasant's yard. When the peasants saw we were armed, they gave us bread and other kinds of food and we went back to the woods. This was in the Chmiel Forest. While we were there, we heard volleys of shots from the Skrzynice woods. At night, we returned to the peasant woman who lived near the Skrzynice Forest to find out what the shooting was about. She told us the warden informed the Germans there were partisans in the woods—meaning us—that we had attacked him and taken his rifle. Later, Germans and Poles came into the woods with their dogs. The dogs started sniffing out the Jews hiding in the forest and the Germans shot them. There were many Jews who were safely hidden

in the depths of the forest, but they panicked because of the dogs and the soldiers and abandoned their shelters. They ran for the fields where the Germans shot them all. But many Jews didn't leave the forest. They stayed inside their hideouts. After the Germans had finished in the forest, they went after the Jews hiding in the villages.

My friend and I went to the Skrzynice Forest to find the Jews in hiding the peasant woman had told us about. Walking through the forest, we saw smoke in the distance—some small fire was burning—and we crept up quietly. When we got to the clearing, we saw Jewish families I had known in Lublin, Głusk, and *shtetlekh* [little Jewish villages] near Lublin, gathered in a circle. They were baking potatoes over the fire, and as we came near, they told us there had been a raid in the woods yesterday—the shooting we'd heard—but they hadn't given up their hiding place, lying flat all day, and because of this, had saved themselves from the Germans and the Polish peasants. . . .

Becoming Partisans

The group of people also told us there was a young Jew wandering around the forest, who kept to himself. He was called Heniek—he was from Lublin—and had belonged to the Polish partisans, but the Poles robbed him of everything, so he left them and came to these woods.

As my friend and I were standing and talking like this to the group in the forest, the young man appeared out of nowhere. He recognized me from Lublin and told me it was true—he'd been with a Polish partisan unit. He wore a cross around his neck—he said he had a good Polish accent, the Poles couldn't tell he was a Jew. Heniek soon realized, though, that whenever Jews joined the partisan unit to which he belonged, they were taken on only to be shot the same night. He was scared they would find out he was a Jew and shoot him, too. So he left the Polish partisan unit and came to the small town of Osmolice. In Osmolice, he went up to a peasant for bread, but the peasant recognized him from the partisans and knew he'd run away from them.

The peasant found out he was a Jew and dragged him off to the Germans. At night, he escaped through a window and came back to the forest. The young man told me he was afraid to stay with the other Jews in the forest because they talk loudly and yell among themselves, so he keeps his distance from them.

Then I told him my friend and I were armed and we also had a gun for him if he decided to join us. I suggested the three of us take our guns and search around for food to bring back to the Jews hiding in the forest, and later, we would decide what to do next. The young man took the rifle and left for the village that night with me and my friend. The peasant watchmen who stood guard in the village during the night took aim to shoot at us, but when we said we were partisans, they held their fire. The peasants gave us bread, potatoes, and butter, and we took these back to the forest where our people were hiding. Later, we told the peasant watchmen to inform the village chieftain there were partisans in the woods, and not to arm any more peasants in the village at night against Jews looking for food, and to stop handing us over to the Germans. We went back to our group in the forest, and now had a supply of food for a few days.

They told us there were other Jews hiding in the forest, but they were scattered all over, and one didn't know where the other was. Snow started falling, and this was bad, because we left tracks in the fields and villages when we went to get hay for our bunker. That same day, the forest warden came to us and asked that we leave the area because the Germans were tracking us by our footprints. . . .

We knew we had to get arms at any cost if we were going to form a partisan unit which could resist the Germans. At night, the three of us went to the peasant Skulski looking for guns we heard he'd hidden. We threatened him and told him we knew about the hidden guns he denied having. We told him if he didn't give us the guns, we'd take his wife and children from the hut, shoot him, and burn everything down. The peasant still refused to give us the guns.

Then the three of us took bundles of straw into the hut and set them on fire. His wife cried and begged Skulski to give us the guns, but he kept denying he knew anything about them. . . .

Then the [village] chieftain took us aside and told us Skulski had robbed and murdered countless Jews who were in hiding—that is, when he didn't have the Germans do it. When I heard this, I lost control completely. I told my two friends to take the peasant's wife and children away, and for the chieftain to get them somewhere to stay. The house burned, and my friend raised his gun and shot Skulski dead.

After we shot him and the house was all in flames, the peasant's wife told us to climb down to the foundation where we'd find the guns. . . . We then found two rifles and a full crate of ammunition. We carried this back to the forest where our people were. We told the chieftain to inform the peasants in the village that if partisans came, they should surrender their guns, and if anyone informed or retaliated against the Jews in hiding, we'd put the whole countryside to the torch. . . .

Nowhere to Run

In the spring of 1943, the five of us [they were now joined by two other Jews] armed ourselves and went to the Skrzynice Forest again, to see if there were any Jews still alive. We roamed through the woods all day until we finally reached a spot where a group of Jews—young men and women—were sitting around a small fire. When they saw us coming up with our guns, they rushed toward us, crying from great excitement and emotion. They said there was an integrated partisan group in the woods—meaning us—who'd killed a peasant and terrorized all the other peasants in the region to stop marauding the Jews in hiding. We five armed Jews again went into the village and brought back bread and potatoes for the young Jews hiding in the woods. . . .

The five of us returned to the woods near Pieczkow and the other people stayed on in the Skrzynice Forest. We met Jews who were hiding in the Pieczkow woods, but we brought them to the Skrzynice Forest so all the Jews would be together. All in all, there were twenty-six of us in the forest: men, women, and the two small children, a brother and sister, Srul and Faygaleh B—. These two are grown now, and live with their parents in the Bronx. In the beginning, everyone hid in one small pit in the ground which was covered over. Later, we dug a large bunker farther back in the woods, where we could all stay together comfortably. . . .

One morning—it was a Sunday—some peasants came to collect firewood near where we were. They spotted us, and the next day, Germans were here. We had all left the bunker by chance and were roaming around different parts of the woods. Only Itche Klayman of Głusk stayed behind in the bunker. There was something wrong with his foot and he couldn't walk. The Germans broke into the bunker and shot Klayman. The rest of us took up new positions deeper in the woods. We started shooting back and the Germans retreated from the forest. We all came together again afterwards, and moved to another part of the forest. Soon, the Germans had us surrounded and fired at us from all sides. During the exchange, they shot Fishl Spivak's wife, Yosl Aynshtayn, and a young woman named Masheh. The rest of us escaped still deeper into the woods.

We got together at night, and decided to regroup in the woods near Mentow. The Germans ordered the Poles to cover up the Jews who were shot with earth and leaves, right where they'd fallen. A few days later, we returned to this spot, dug up the mounds where the dead Jews lay, and buried them in four separate graves, one next to the other. At the head of each grave, we placed boards, and inscribed the name of the person who'd fallen, their place of origin, and that they'd fallen in battle against the Nazis.

Selection 7

Escape from Sobibor

Yitzhak Arad

It was difficult for anyone to resist the guards at a concentration camp. Still, examples of resistance in different camps can be found. Sometimes it was on an individual level, someone refusing to give in to despair. In one case a group of Jews blew up a crematorium and many Jews roamed the forests with the partisans. One of the most dramatic cases, and the only one involving a mass escape from a concentration camp, was the uprising at Sobibor. In that instance, a Soviet prisoner of war helped organize an underground within the camp that carried out a daring escape. Roughly three hundred prisoners got away and, amazingly, about two hundred prisoners were never recaptured. This excerpt describes the uprising. Yitzhak Arad is one of the leading experts on the Holocaust and a former chairman of Yad Vashem.

Excerpted from Yitzhak Arad, *Belzec, Sobibor, Treblinka: The Operation Reinhard Death Camps* (Bloomington: Indiana University Press, 1987). Reprinted with permission from the publishers.

 ctober 14 was a clear, sunny autumn day. It began as any routine day—with the morning roll call and the prisoners dispersing to their workplaces. The atmosphere was tense, however. Many felt that something unusual was going on that day. A sharp eye would have noticed that some of the prisoners had put on their best clothes and boots. Those who were privy to the secret of the impending uprising removed money and valuables from their hiding places in the hope that this would increase their chances for survival once they were outside the camp. The Underground Committee even directed the members of the Underground to remove any valuables in the workshops or warehouses and distribute them among the trustworthy prisoners. . . .

The quiet liquidation of the SS staff in the camp started around 15:30. . . . [Underground Committee member] Feldhendler, who was in charge of the operation in Camp II, had based his plan on the greed of the SS men for goods in the warehouse where the property of the victims was sorted and prepared for transport. The SS men frequently visited these storerooms and selected clothes and valuables for themselves or for their families. They asked prisoners who worked there to find them special items and to call them when something of value turned up.

According to Feldhendler's plan, [fellow Underground member Boris] Tsibulsky and his team would take up their hidden positions inside the storeroom and then the SS men would be invited, one by one, by one of the *putzers* to try on a new leather coat.

The first SS man invited into the storeroom was *Unterscharführer* Josef Wulf. He did not suspect a thing. When he entered the storeroom, everything looked normal. There were some prisoners piling the clothes in bins. One of them approached Wulf with a coat, another prisoner stood behind him to help him into it. At that moment, Tsibulsky and another prisoner of war stepped out of their hiding place behind a bin and cracked Wulf's head with their axes. Wulf fell without a sound. The dead body was dragged into a bin and covered with clothes. The blood on the floor was covered with sand. Wulf's pistol was taken by Tsibulsky.

The die was cast, the first SS man had been killed—the Underground had crossed the point of no return. . . .

The operation in Camp I started as planned at four o'clock. Exactly at that time the deputy commander of the camp, *Untersturmführer* Niemann, rode his mare into Camp I and reined up in front of the bakery. He dismounted, left the horse to one of the prisoners, and entered the tailor shop. There Josef, the head of the tailor shop and a member of the Underground Committee, brought him his new uniform and began to take the fitting. At that moment, Shubayev approached from behind and hit Niemann on the head with an axe. Niemann died on the spot. His body was dragged into the back room and stuffed under a bunk, and the bloodstains on the floor were wiped away and covered. The presence of Niemann's horse close to the tailor shop for longer than the time needed for a uniform measurement could arouse suspicion, so one of the Underground members took it to the stables. . . .

The liquidation of the SS men was gaining momentum. *Oberscharführer* Goettinger, who was in charge of Camp III, came into the shoemaker's shop. Jakub, the head of the shop and a member of the Underground Committee, handed him a pair of boots and asked him to try them on. . . . Arkady Vaispapir approached from behind and smashed Goettinger's head with an axe.

The next task imposed on Feldhendler was to cut the telephone wires leading from the administration building to outside the camp and to disconnect the electricity of the camp. This was carried out by Schwartz, an electrician from Czechoslovakia. . . .

For about an hour and a half, from 15:30 to 17:00, the uprising action had been carried out according to plan. Most of the SS men had been liquidated, among them three key persons: Niemann, the acting commander of the camp; Greischutz, the commander of the Ukrainian guard; and Goettinger, the commander of Camp III. The prisoners had armed themselves with pistols taken from the killed SS men and the rifles brought by [Underground Committee member Shlomo] Szmajzner. . . .

At five o'clock in the afternoon, as the time for

the evening roll call approached, [uprising commander Alexander] Pechersky faced a dilemma: whether to wait for Frenzel, the last remaining SS man who could organize the Ukrainians for an action against the prisoners and an immediate pursuit after their escape or to go ahead with the plan, leaving Frenzel alive. By that time it was difficult to keep the prisoners quiet as the tension was so high. Most of them already knew about the killings, and at any moment the Underground could lose control over the events. . . .

Pechersky described what happened in Camp I after the signal for roll call was given:

People came streaming from all sides. We had previously selected seventy men, nearly all of them Soviet prisoners of war, whose task it was to attack the armory. That was why they were in the forefront of the column. But all the others, who had only suspected that something was being arranged but didn't know when and how, now found out at the last minute. They began to push and jostle forward, fearing they might be left behind. In this disorderly fashion we reached the gate of Camp I.

A squad commander, a German from Near-Volga, approached us. "Hey, you sons-of-bitches," he shouted, "didn't you hear the whistle? So why are you pushing like a bunch of cattle? Get in line, three in a row!"

As though in response to a command, several hatchets suddenly appeared from under coats and came down on his head. . . .

According to the plan, a group of prisoners under the command of Nachum Plotnicky and Alexey Vaitsen were supposed to penetrate the armory and take control of the arms there. . . .

Mordechai Goldfarb, who was with the attacking group, described what was happening in the armory: "Four of us ran to the armory. . . . There was an SS man. . . . He wanted to shoot at us, but Boris threw sand into his eyes, we jumped at him and killed him. We grabbed some rifles and ran to the fence.". . .

At that point, the "quiet" part of the uprising came to an end. The killing of the *Volksdeutsche*,

a squad commander of the Ukrainians, which took place in the open, close to the gate of Camp I, was spotted by the guards. When the attack on the armory was carried out, in addition to the SS man Werner Dubois, who was badly wounded, there were some Ukrainians present. Automatic fire from a watchtower and some other directions was opened on the prisoners running toward the camp's main gate. *Scharführer* Frenzel, who until then had not been seen, came out from a barrack close to the main gate and opened automatic fire on the escaping prisoners. The prisoners who had run through the gate killed the Ukrainian guard posted there, but further escape through the camp's main gate was cut off by the fire of Frenzel and some guards. The prisoners ran toward the fences and minefields. Pechersky and the other leaders of the uprising had lost all control over the events and the mass of prisoners, who were running in all directions. This was around 17:15.

With the escape through the main gate cut off by gunfire, the prisoners who were still in Camp I, which constituted the majority, ran toward the fences and minefields, south and southwest of the camp. The prisoners who were first to cross the minefields were killed or wounded. They remained lying in the field, just behind the fences. Those who followed them had clear passage through the minefields, because the mines had blown up with the first wave of escapees. Ada Lichtman wrote:

Suddenly we heard shots. In the beginning only a few shots, and then it turned into heavy shooting, including machine-gun fire. We heard shouting, and I could see a group of prisoners running with axes, knives, scissors, cutting the fences and crossing them. Mines started to explode. Riot and confusion prevailed, everything was thundering around. The doors of the workshop were opened, and everyone rushed through. . . . We ran out of the workshop. All around were the bodies of the killed and wounded. Near the armory were some of our boys with weapons. Some of them were exchanging fire with the Ukrainians, others were running toward the gate or through the fences. My coat was caught on the fence. I took off the coat, freed myself and ran further behind the fences into the minefield. A mine exploded nearby, and I could see a body being lifted into the air and then falling down. I did not recognize who it was. Many were shot on the fences. Behind the mines was a ditch, luckily without water. With the help of two other women, I crossed the ditch and reached the forest.

. . . When the shooting started it was already dusk. At least two SS men, Frenzel and Bauer, and about a dozen Ukrainians who were on guard duty opened fire from machine guns, rifles, and pistols on the escaping prisoners. The most dangerous gunfire was from the two watchtowers in the southern corners of the camp. From these towers the Ukrainians had full control of gunfire on Camp I, on the Forward Camp, and on the southern fences and camp's gate—all the places through which the prisoners tried to escape. Those Underground members who were armed returned fire, trying to silence the guards on the watchtowers and cover the escape of the prisoners. Pechersky described the situation at this stage:

The guards on the watchtower opened intensive machine-gun fire on the escaping prisoners. The guards who were at and between the barbed-wire fences joined them. Yanek the carpenter aimed and shot at the guards on the watchtower. The machine gun fell silent. The locksmith Henrick used the captured submachine gun to silence the gunner from the second watchtower. But this machine gun continued to fire incessantly. The remaining SS men tried with automatic fire to cut off the way of the crowd of prisoners. . . . The main body of the prisoners turned toward the fences of Camp I. Some ran directly over to the minefields. According to the plan, stones and planks had to be thrown on the mines to explode them, but in the confusion nobody did it. Many found their death there, but they paved the way to freedom for the prisoners who followed them. A special group started to cut the fences close to the house where the comman-

der of the camp lived. . . . When I passed by this house, I saw Frenzel crouching behind another house and shooting with a submachine gun. I shot at him twice with my pistol but missed him. I did not stop. A large group of prisoners under the command of Leitman tried to cross the barbed-wire fences close to the main gate. The guard on the watchtower aimed his fire on Leitman's group. I was one of the last to leave the camp.

. . . The first stage of the uprising—the quiet liquidation of the majority of the SS staff in the camp, among them the commanding officers—had been accomplished successfully. The only exception was Frenzel. However, the second stage of the uprising, the "ordinary" roll call and march toward the gate, was not carried out according to plan. A combination of events—among them the survival of Frenzel, the killing of the *Volksdeutsche* Kaiser near the gate of Camp I, which was seen by the Ukrainian guards, and the unexpected return to the camp of [SS guard] Erich Bauer—contributed to the fact that the second stage of the plan was carried out only in part. And although the leaders of the uprising had taken into account such a development and had formulated an alternative escape route through the fences and minefields, this alternative was not planned in detail. It remained more of a general idea than a true plan of action. Therefore, when the shooting began and the majority of prisoners began running in their confusion in all directions, the Underground leadership lost control. Still, over half of the prisoners, about 300 out of the 600 who were in the main camp, succeeded in the evening twilight in crossing the fences and minefields and escaping into the forests. . . .

The killing of eleven SS men and two or three Ukrainians and *Volksdeutsche* guards, in addition to several wounded, produced turmoil among the German authorities in the General Government and was reported to the highest authorities in Berlin. It was a rare—and perhaps the only—case where prisoners, Jews or non-Jews, had revolted and had succeeded in a single action in liquidating such a large number of SS men.

A group of high-ranking SS officials headed by SS *Gruppenführer* Jacob Sporrenberg . . . arrived in Sobibor on the afternoon of October 15. . . . Sporrenberg ordered the execution of all the remaining Jewish prisoners in the camp. There were at least 150 of them.

There were also prisoners in Camp III who had known nothing about the uprising until the shooting broke out. These prisoners were also killed. . . . This execution was the immediate response and revenge of the Nazi authorities to the killing of the SS men and Ukrainians. . . .

The fact that the searches and pursuit only started on the morning of October 15 gave the prisoners the entire night for an undisturbed head start. During the breakout from the camp, people ran in any direction they could in the hope of reaching the nearest forest and getting as far away as possible from Sobibor. After covering some distance from the camp, the individual escapees and small groups merged into larger groups, some of them numbering dozens of prisoners. But the prisoners were not familiar with the surrounding area of Sobibor, nor did they know in which direction to run. In some cases, after running the whole night, in the morning they discovered that they had run in a circle and were still very close to the camp. . . .

Pechersky's departure [to lead a smaller prisoner group] raised fear and resentment among the remaining fifty prisoners. He and his men, all from the Minsk transport, took with them most of the group's weapons and the rest were left with one rifle; they felt themselves forsaken and leaderless. Tovia Blatt, who was with this group, claims that Pechersky did not even tell them he was leaving, but that he said he was going to reconnoiter the area and would soon return. Some other testimonies of survivors confirm Blatt's version.

The fate of the remaining Jews after Pechersky and his group left is related by Shlomo Alster, a Polish Jew:

Sasha's people left us and went away. We remained without a leader. What could we do? Without arms and without a man to lead us. Together with us were French, Dutch, and Czechoslovakian Jews. They could not find their way without knowing the language and the surroundings. Like us, they also divided themselves into small groups. They went out to the road, which was full of SS men, and all of them were caught alive. Also the local people caught them one by one and brought them to Sobibor, where they were liquidated. None of them survived.

We, the Polish Jews, remained a small group. What should we do? To stay in the forest was dangerous, because either the Germans or the local people would catch us. We had to get away from this place, and from Sobibor—as far as possible. But this was not so simple—where could we go? I was hungry, my clothes were torn to pieces. I decided to go back to my native town, to Chelm, maybe there I could find some chance of survival. I couldn't see any other alternative.

. . . Pechersky and his group succeeded in crossing the Bug River on the night of October 19/20, and three days later they met Soviet partisans in the area of Brest-Litovsk and joined up with them.

Feldhendler and a group of prisoners succeeded in hiding in the forest during the days when the German forces combed the whole area. Some other groups from among the Polish Jews also succeeded in avoiding the search units. . . .

Of about 300 Jews who escaped from Sobibor, 100 were caught and shot during the four days that followed the uprising. All the others survived the pursuit action. . . .

A few more of the escaping prisoners were caught during October 19–21.

In view of the large German forces that were involved in the combing operations, which were even supported by airplanes, the search could not have been considered a success. Only one-third of the fleeing prisoners were caught. The rest escaped.

The Rescuers

Chapter 6

Introduction

*T*he Yad Vashem Holocaust Memorial Museum in Israel honors people who risked their own lives to save others during World War II. These individuals are given the title of "Righteous Persons." Most of the civilians in the territories occupied by the Germans were either perpetrators or bystanders, but more than 17,000 people (nearly one-third in Poland) did have the courage to rescue those in need.

More stories of courage have come to light in recent years. Some rescuers have become famous, such as Raoul Wallenberg, the Swedish aristocrat who rescued as many as 100,000 Jews from Hungary, and Oskar Schindler, whose list saved more than a thousand Jews and who was immortalized in Steven Spielberg's Oscar-winning film, *Schindler's List*. Many rescuers are less well known, such as Portuguese diplomat Aristides de Sousa Mendes and Japanese diplomat Chiune Sugihara, who provided thousands of visas to help Jews escape. In a couple of instances, whole towns helped save Jews. The story of one of these, Le Chambon, is included here.

Without being in the same position it is difficult to know what we would do given the same circumstances. Certainly, we all hope to have the courage to be rescuers. The selections in this chapter offer insights into why some people did and some did not become saviors.

Selection 1

Oskar Schindler

Southern Institute for Education and Research

Thousands of people have been recognized for their efforts to rescue Jews during World War II, but only a handful of names are familiar. One that went unnoticed until his story was dramatized on film was Oskar Schindler. In interviews, Steven Spielberg has often spoken about how it took years before he was able to make the film Schindler's List *and, after doing so, it changed his life. The profit he earned from the film was directed to the Shoah Foundation, which he dedicated to gathering 50,000 testimonies by Holocaust survivors and making them available to the public so everyone can hear what happened from those who lived to talk about it. One reason Schindler's story is so compelling is that he was not a pure, untainted hero. On the contrary, he was selfish, arrogant, a drunk, and a womanizer. He profited handsomely from the war and openly caroused with some of the most vicious Nazis. This same man also became determined to save the Jews in his employ and his list, as they say in the film, was life. This excerpt comes from a teaching guide for the film created by the Southern Institute for Education and Research at Tulane University.*

O skar Schindler was born on April 28, 1908, in Zwittau, an industrial city in the Austro-Hungarian Empire. He was baptized in the Catholic church. Today the city of Schindler's birth is Zvitava in the province of Moravia of the Czech Republic.

At the beginning of the 16th century, the Schindler family emigrated to Zwittau from Vienna, the capital of the Austrian (Habsburg) Empire. The region, heavily populated by Germans, became known as the Sudetenland, after the nearby Sudeten Mountains.

Schindler's father, Hans, was the owner of a factory which produced farm machinery, and Oskar and his sister, Elfriede, were raised in privileged circumstances, a fact of considerable importance.

The typical young man in the regimented Austro-Hungarian Empire had to follow societal rules if he expected to land a job after his schooling. But Oskar Schindler was not typical. He was guaranteed a position with the family business—whether or not he complied with societal rules. This economic security gave Schindler patrician self-assurance and, perhaps, a willingness to flaunt the rules he believed did not apply to him. In a word, Schindler's privileged upbringing allowed him to be different.

Schindler's mother, Louisa, who he adored, was a deeply religious women, forever "redolent of incense" from her frequent visits to the Catholic church. His father, Hans, preferred sipping cognac in the local coffee house to attending services at the Catholic church, a preference he bequeathed to his son, who spoke little of God. The extent of the elder Schindler's political involvement seems to have been lighting a candle each year to honor the birth of the Austro-Hungarian Kaiser (or Emperor) Franz Josef , beloved by the Jews of his empire.

As Austrians living amidst a subject people (the Czechs), the Schindler family ranked high among the social and economic elite of Zwittau. Schindler's early life was pleasant, at least from the material point of view. His father gave him an extravagant birthday gift; a powerful motorcycle. The teenage Schindler entered several racing contests. He was adventuresome, reckless, and a daredevil. A tall young man with charm and good looks, he was a womanizer of the first order, even after he married Emilie Schindler in 1927.

Emilie was educated in a Catholic convent, and, like Schindler's mother, she was deeply religious. She and Schindler met in 1927 when he made a sales trip to her father's farm. At the time Schindler was selling electric motors for the family business. . . .

After a six week courtship, the two were married. At a young age, Schindler was long accustomed to getting what he wanted. Emilie's father refused to give Schindler the traditional dowry, a bitter point with the son-in-law. The marriage became rocky after a short while, as Schindler resumed his drinking and womanizing.

Oskar Schindler and Emilie did not have children, but Schindler had two children outside of the marriage.

If Schindler's youth had been one of privileges, the privileges did not include a warm and loving relationship between his parents. In 1935, the Schindler factory went bankrupt due to the worldwide depression triggered by Wall Street's collapse in 1929. Just as economic disaster struck the family business, Schindler's father abandoned his wife. Schindler's mother died not long after his father left home.

The family business in ruins, Schindler became a salesman for another machinery company, a job that took him to nearby Poland. Though raised in privileged circumstances, young Oskar had made little of his life. He was known as a delightful personality, but not a seri-

Excerpted from the Southern Institute for Education and Research, *Schindler's List Teaching Guide*, found online at www.tulane.edu/~so-inst/slindex.html. Reprinted with permission from the Southern Institute for Education and Research.

ous person. The thought of work made him tired. He slept late, had a roving eye for beautiful women, and could not decline a drink. . . .

Hitler promised to restore the Reich to its former glory. He pledged to end unemployment and usher in a new era of economic prosperity and security. He vowed to destroy the communists. And he offered a scapegoat for Germany's problems: The Jews. It was a rare Sudeten German who did not respond to Hitler's message.

Schindler's wife, Emilie, was one of them. She despised the Nazis from the start. According to Keneally, she believed "simply that the man (Hitler) would be punished for making himself God." Schindler's father also despised the Nazis, but because he sensed that they would lose the war Hitler intended to launch. . . .

The Munich Conference

On September 30, 1938, Hitler signed the Munich Pact with representatives of England and France, which forced Czechoslovakia to cede the German populated Sudetenland to Nazi Germany. The two Western democracies, which had been allies of democratic Czechoslovakia, sought to "appease" Hitler's ambitions by abandoning the Central European nation. British Prime Minister Neville Chamberlain described this as "peace in our time, peace with honor." Ultimately, appeasement failed, and the term "Munich" has come to symbolize betrayal.

When the German army occupied the Sudetenland, the local German populace greeted it rapturously. The Czechs and the Jews of the region, however, were less enthusiastic. Almost immediately they were expelled and their property confiscated. The Nazi Aktion was conducted with characteristic brutality, and Schindler, according to Keneally, was repulsed by the Nazis' behavior.

But moral indignation did not interfere with opportunity. After all, he quickly joined the Nazi Party and began wearing the Nazi swastika on his lapel. In the late autumn of 1938, Schindler joined the Abwehr (German military intelligence). Schindler was an ideal operative, a bon-vivant who could strike up a conversation with anyone,

preferably in a bar. He travelled frequently to Poland on business and returned with information about Poland's military preparedness. It is noteworthy that Schindler's Abwehr membership excused him from active military service.

In the early morning hours of September 1, 1939, the Second World War began with the German attack on Poland. The Poles, valiant but disorganized, their army utterly antiquated, were quickly overwhelmed by the German tactics of "blitzkreig" or "lightning war.". . .

On September 6, 1939, German armored forces captured the southern Polish city of Krakow, the ancient seat of Polish kings. Shortly thereafter the Nazis established in Krakow their government for Nazi-occupied Poland, known as the General-Government. Hans Frank, Hitler's longtime lawyer, became Reichsfuehrer of the General-Government and immediately issued a decree for the "voluntary departure" of all but the "economically indispensable" Jews. He could not abide the thought of Germans breathing the same air as Jews.

In the wake of the German army, Oskar Schindler arrived in Krakow. A Sudeten-German businessman, a member of the Nazi Party, and a failure in life, Schindler was determined to reverse his fortunes in Nazi-occupied Poland.

He was thirty-one years old.

Schindler Sees an Opportunity

During the Second World War, private businessmen like Oskar Schindler operated factories in Nazi-occupied Poland, exploiting both Polish labor and Jewish slave labor for the benefit of both the German war machine and (not coincidentally) the factory owners.

Arriving in Krakow during the first week of the Second World War, Schindler quickly won the friendship of key officers in both the SS (Nazi elite) and the Wehrmacht (German army). He won their friendship by his unusually personable manner and by his seemingly inexhaustible supply of desired goods: cognac, cigars, coffee, and women. Most of these items Schindler obtained from the thriving black market in Krakow.

True to his roots in the old Habsburg Empire, Schindler knew how to make a bribe seem like an act of friendship. His friends in high places would assure Schindler a steady flow of army contracts. Now Schindler had to locate a factory to produce the desired goods.

For this he turned to the Jews.

The Polish Jews

When the Second World War began in 1939, three and a half million Jews lived in Poland, fully ten percent of the population. Krakow was home to 56,000 Jews, a size equal to that of the entire Jewish population of Italy. The majority of the Polish Jews were utterly impoverished, as were the Poles. But the relatively few wealthy Jews, and the omnipresent Jewish store on the corner, gave rise to the generalization that the Jews were "rich." At the same time, however, the Jews were identified with communism, although most of the Polish Jews were Orthodox and far removed from the atheist world of communism.

Under the fairly benevolent rule of the Austrians before the First World War, Krakow had developed a reputation as a "liberal" city. The Jews were allowed to pursue their lives with more freedom than in the Russian and Prussian (German) controlled regions of Poland. The Krakow Jews were mostly middle class and had lived in Krakow since the early 14th century. They began speaking Polish (as opposed to Yiddish or Hebrew) in the early 19th century. In 1867, Emperor Franz Josef ascended the throne in Vienna, and the Jews were permitted to live outside the ghetto for the first time. The local Polish and German middle classes bitterly protested this relative freedom given to their economic competitors. . . .

In November 1939, one month into the brutal occupation that would last five years, the Nazis issued a decree demanding that all Jews over the age of nine wear a blue and white armband emblazoned with the Star of David. Thus, the first step in the destruction of the Jews had been taken.

In Poland, the Nazis quickly expropriated Jewish businesses. Through a process termed "Aryanization," Jewish property was sold to "Aryans" (i.e., Germans) for a considerably reduced price. The Jews, of course, had no right to protest this virtual confiscation.

In this manner, Schindler located a formerly Jewish-owned factory on the outskirts of Krakow, which, after retooling, would produce enamel pots and pans and, later, in 1941, munitions. Through the good graces of his high ranking friends and with the usual bribes, Schindler won lucrative contracts to supply his kitchenware to the German army.

The name of Schindler's factory was Deutsche Email Fabrik, or Emalia. . . .

Schindler's Accountant

Having found a Jewish factory, Schindler next located the capital necessary to purchase it and to get operations underway. His key contact was a Jewish accountant, Itzhak Stern. . . .

According to Stern's postwar recollection, he immediately recognized that Schindler was that rare item in Nazi-occupied Poland: The "good" German. When Schindler commented that it must be hard to be a priest during times like these, when life did not have "the value of a pack of cigarettes," Stern seized the moment to recite the Talmudic verse: "He who saves one life, it is as if he has saved the entire world." Schindler replied, "Of course, of course."

Keneally writes, "Itzhak, rightly or wrongly, always believed that it was at that moment that he had dropped the right seed in the furrow."

The influence of Itzhak Stern is of decisive importance in understanding Schindler's evolution from war-profiteer to rescuer of Jews. When Stern was buried in 1969, Schindler stood at the graveside, crying like a child.

Stern was the first person to inform Schindler that Jewish slave labor cost less than Polish labor. Schindler, with an eye towards a profit, recognized the advantage of Jewish labor. Thus began his relationship with the Jews. He would be Herr Direktor, they would be his employees. He would always have a kind word for them. In the end, he would save many of them from annihilation.

The first indication that Schindler was of a different breed came on December 3, 1939. He whispered less than ambiguous words into Stern's ear: "Tomorrow, it's going to start. Jozefa and Izaaka Streets are going to know all about it." Talk like this was highly dangerous. Coming from a German, it was bewildering.

Jozefa and Izaaka Streets were located in Kazimierz, the Jewish quarter. Here, the SS staged a terror-filled Aktion or "strike" the next day, beating, humiliating, robbing, and killing Jews in a seemingly haphazard manner.

Schindler had taken a first step, however tenuous, towards rescue.

War-Profiteer

To get the ball rolling, Stern introduced Schindler to a group of wealthy Krakow Jews. These Jews had managed to retain their wealth despite the Nazis' best efforts to seize it. With few options, these Jews invested their capital in Schindler's factory, but with the provision that they would work in the factory and, apparently, be spared the uncertain future (which, in the film, Schindler bluntly and indeed cruelly cites in order to strengthen his bargaining position).

Schindler, who arrived in Krakow with little more than his natural panache and the swastika on his lapel, had acquired a Jewish factory, Jewish capital, Jewish labor, and Jewish expertise, all with very little if any personal investment. . . .

Schindler was the quintessential war-profiteer. Initially, he was able to overlook the dehumanized condition of the Jews under Nazi rule. He was interested in profit, and he was not above exploiting the Jews to this end.

Spielberg's film focuses on Schindler's evolving relationship with the Jews. A central theme emerges: In the pursuit of profit, Schindler becomes dependent on the Jews for their expertise—particularly, it seems, on Itzhak Stern—and as he becomes dependent upon the Jews, Schindler begins to know them as human beings. They appear to be quite different from the Nazi propaganda's depiction of Jews as "vermin" and as "rats." Schindler has a financial investment in his Jewish workers, but at the same time he develops an investment in them as human beings.

Twenty years after the war, with the benefit of hindsight, Schindler explained his rescue of Jews this way: "I knew the people who worked for me. When you know people, you have to behave towards them like human beings."

On another occasion, Schindler described his behavior differently: "There was no choice. If you saw a dog going to be crushed under a car, wouldn't you help him?"

The Krakow Ghetto

On March 3, 1941, the Nazis established a Jewish ghetto—an area into which Jews were segregated—in Podgorze, a suburb of Krakow across the Vistula River. A wall was constructed to enclose the ghetto, and the Jews watched ominously as the wall was shaped in the form of Jewish grave stones. The ghetto comprised three hundred and twenty apartment buildings into which a Jewish population of about seventeen thousand was crammed. The rest of the Jews in Krakow had already been expelled to the neighboring countryside. The overcrowding in the ghetto was severe, as families were forced to live together in cramped apartments. This contributed significantly to Jewish demoralization, a key German tactic.

Fearing for the safety of the Jews, Stern implored Schindler to hire more Jewish workers. Schindler agreed.

When the Jewish workers arrived at his factory, Schindler told them, much to their astonishment: "You'll be safe working here. If you work here, then you'll live through the war.". . .

The Child in Red

In June 1942, Schindler inadvertently witnessed an Aktion in the Krakow ghetto. The Aktionen were Nazi "strikes" on the ghetto to round up Jews for deportation to the death camps. They were meticulously planned and usually the Nazis were assisted by their foreign collaborators (Ukrainian, Lithuanian, Latvian, Estonian) and by local collaborators (Polish "blue" police and Jewish ghetto police).

At the time, Schindler and his mistress were out for a pleasant horseback ride on a hilltop when the macabre Aktion opened directly below them. Astonished by the Nazi ferocity, Schindler's eye was drawn to a little girl clad in red who, alone, stood out from the mass of Jews being herded to the trains and to their death. . . .

Many years later, with a certitude perhaps bolstered by distance, Schindler looked back on this Aktion and said, "Beyond this day, no thinking person could fail to see what would happen. I was now resolved to do everything in my power to defeat the system."

"Essential Workers"

The Jews who were deemed "essential workers" for the German war effort, including the Jews who worked for Schindler, were temporarily spared deportation.

In the early years of the Second World War, the Germans waged a fierce debate among themselves regarding the fate of the "essential worker"—Jews. Hitler and the hard-core Nazis wanted to destroy all of the Jews, but the less ideological Nazis, with many German businessmen as their allies, argued that it was impractical to murder a people whose labor was absolutely essential to the war effort (and to their own profits).

Ironically, there were some SS officers who also chimed in on behalf of the "essential-workers." If all of the Jews were destroyed and the camps liquidated, the SS rightly feared they would have nothing to do in occupied-Poland and would be sent to fight on the Russian Front. Much to the relief of the German industrialists, the SS, and, not least, the Jews, Hitler begrudgingly agreed to spare the Jewish "essential workers," but only for the time being. As SS leader Heinrich Himmler noted in September 1942, "One day even these Jews must disappear, in accordance with the Fuehrer's wish."

On March 13, 1943, at the time of the final "liquidation" of the Krakow ghetto, the Jewish "essential workers" in Krakow were sent to the labor camp at Plaszow. It was constructed just outside of Krakow on the grounds of two uprooted Jewish cemeteries. Jewish tombstones were used as pavement slabs by the Germans. . . .

On June 2, 1942, the first deportation, or "re-settlement," from the Krakow ghetto began. The Germans planted the rumor that the ghetto was too crowded and the Jews not fit for labor had to be removed. It seemed a plausible explanation. The ghetto was overcrowded. . . .

During the first deportation from Krakow, seven thousand Jews were sent by train to the Belzec death camp in eastern Poland. In this early stage of the destruction process, the Jews had no idea what awaited them.

On October 28, 1942, the Nazis struck the Krakow ghetto a second time. . . . The Nazis informed the ghetto that only "essential workers" would be spared deportation. . . .

Like the June deportations, the Nazis removed seven thousand Jews from the ghetto. . . .

In a 1994 interview, Emilie Schindler said, "At first we knew nothing about the Jews. Eventually everyone in Krakow knew that they were killing Jews. My God, how could we not know?". . .

The final "liquidation" of the Krakow ghetto occurred on March 13, 1943. . . . The last of the Krakow Jews were either deported to Auschwitz-Birkenau or, if deemed "essential workers," they were sent to the Plaszow labor camp outside of Krakow.

The Germans tried to prevent Jewish parents from smuggling their children to Plaszow, but nonetheless three hundred children reached the camp. . . .

The Schindlerjuden who were living in a sub-camp at Schindler's enamel factory were allowed to remain there . . . for the time-being. Schindler had doubtless resorted to the usual means of bribery to prevent the "liquidation" of his camp. . . .

Amon Goeth

The SS officer Amon Goeth (pronounced Gert) commanded the Plaszow labor camp. He had orchestrated the final "liquidation" of the Krakow ghetto as well as the ghettoes in several provincial towns, including nearby Tarnow. Goeth had additional experience at three death camps in eastern Poland, Belzec, Sobibor, and Treblinka. . . .

"I knew Goeth," said Anna Duklauer Perl, a Jewish survivor. "One day he hung a friend of mine just because he had once been rich. He was the devil.". . .

Initially, the Schindlerjuden were allowed to live in a sub-camp at Schindler's factory. In August 1944 they were forced to move to the Plaszow labor camp. According to Keneally, Schindler befriended Goeth for the purpose of protecting his workers and keeping his profits rolling in. After all, the murder of the Jews meant the end of his thriving business. The exact nature of the Schindler-Goeth relationship is unknown, but it is not implausible that Schindler and Goeth were friends. Schindler enjoyed friendly relations with the top SS and Gestapo people in Krakow. He spent virtually all of his time in the company of murderers.

After the war, when Schindler was visiting some of the Schindlerjuden in Israel, a journalist asked, "How do you explain the fact that you knew all the senior SS men in the Krakow region and had regular dealings with them?" Schindler answered evasively with characteristic wit : "At that stage in history, it was rather difficult to discuss the fate of Jews with the chief rabbi of Jerusalem."

A great many of the Nazis were susceptible to bribery, Goeth among them. Feathering his nest, Schindler plied Goeth with money and the usual variety of black market goods. The SS arrested Goeth in September 1944, charging him with theft of Jewish property (which 'belonged to' the Reich and should have been forwarded to Berlin). After the war, on September 13, 1945, Goeth was hung by Polish authorities at the site of the former camp at Plaszow. He died unrepentant. . . .

The "List"

As the Soviet armies advanced from the east towards Poland, Hitler ordered the extermination of the hitherto protected "essential worker." In effect, Hitler decided that it was more important for the Jews to be destroyed than it was for the essential war factories to continue operating. The war against the Jews took precedent over that against the Allies.

In the summer of 1944, trains deporting the Hungarian Jews to Auschwitz received right-of-

Oskar Schindler

way over war transports to the Russian front. Indeed, Auschwitz's most lethal period was during the last months of the war when the German army was retreating on all fronts and Allied bombs were daily falling on the Reich.

Once the tide had changed, the Nazis tried to destroy the evidence of their killing. At death camps like Belzec, Treblinka, and Sobibor, the Nazis ordered commandos of Jewish slaves to unearth the thousands upon thousands of bodies that had been buried. The bodies were burned in huge bonfires. . . .

On September 4, 1944, as the Eastern Front crumbled and the Soviet Red Army approached Krakow, the Nazis closed the Jewish camp at Schindler's factory. The Schindlerjuden were sent to Plaszow. On October 15, 1944, Plaszow itself was "liquidated." It was at this point that Schindler established his "list." Hitherto, Schindler's actions on behalf of Jews had been subtle and the result of self-interest. In the autumn of 1944, that changed.

Determined to save his Jewish workers from

extermination, Schindler bribed Goeth to send the Schindlerjuden to a new factory that Schindler planned to establish at Brunnlitz in Czechoslovakia, near his hometown of Zwittau. The site was directly over the Sudeten mountains from Auschwitz-Birkenau.

To strengthen his argument, Schindler insisted that his Schindlerjuden were needed to build the "secret weapons" that Hitler had promised would win the war. It was a clever argument; many Germans held out the hope that the Fuehrer would produce yet another miracle.

Schindler's "list" comprised the names of the Jewish workers who were ostensibly needed to operate Schindler's "war essential" factory. It was, in essence, a list of those who would live and, by exclusion, those who would not. The Nazis reduced life to a brutal equation: I want to live; hence, you must die.

Auschwitz-Birkenau

The Schindlerjuden were transported by train from Krakow to the new factory in Czechoslovakia, but three hundred Jewish women were mistakenly routed to the death camp at Auschwitz-Birkenau. The rescue of these Jewish women has never been satisfactorily explained. After the war, in 1949, Schindler and Stern told a journalist that the women had been sent to Gross-Rosen, a concentration camp in eastern Germany. In his book, Keneally acknowledges that the entire affair is clouded with uncertainty.

To effect the rescue, Schindler had resorted to bribery. It is not unreasonable to suspect that Schindler dealt with Nazi officials who, recognizing that the war was coming to an end, were determined to fatten their wallets prior to escaping to South America. The Nazi criminals who were so efficient at killing an unarmed people were also remarkably efficient in making good their post-war escape, an escape financed by the wealth of those they had murdered.

In any event, Schindler did rescue these women from a Nazi camp, a fact to which many of the women have testified. That "was something nobody else did," said Johnathan Dresner, a Tel Aviv dentist, whose mother was among the rescued.

Brunnlitz

The Jews who arrived at Schindler's new factory at Brunnlitz numbered over a thousand. Schindler also rescued an estimated 85 Jews who had been sent from Auschwitz-Birkenau to a nearby Nazi labor camp at Golleschau. The Jews were put to work at the factory producing munitions, but it is said that Schindler sabotaged the production line so that little of any value ever left the factory.

The main problem at Brunnlitz was food. The neighboring German community was not in the least bit interested in a Jewish labor camp in the vicinity and were loath to share what little food was available with the despised Jews.

It is in Brunnlitz that the role of Emilie Schindler became paramount. "It was so little that they [the Nazis] gave the people to eat," Emilie Schindler said in a 1993 interview. "To everyone, not just the Jews. No matter who they were. For everyone it was very little." Emilie recalled that within ten days the Jews had consumed their monthly allotment of food. For the next twenty days, they had nothing to eat but "air."

Emilie Schindler worked indefatigably to secure food for the Brunnlitz camp. Emilie insists that there was much more to Oskar Schindler than the altruist depicted in the book and movie. She says that Oskar Schindler, who abandoned her after the war, procured no food for the camp. "I don't recognize it when he lies. You know, when he says that he brought the food? No, nothing did he bring! All the food, I brought! . . . All the food that the Jews ate, that the Germans ate, that the SS ate, I brought. Not him. He brought nothing."

The War Is Over

On May 8, 1945, the war in Europe ended. Schindler gathered his Jews before him. One of them, Murray Pantirer, recalled the words of Herr Direktor: "He said, 'Meine Kinder (my children), you are saved. Germany has lost the war."

A day later, the 1,200 Schindlerjuden were liberated by a lone Russian officer on horseback, the vanguard of the Soviet Red Army. The officer, who was Jewish, said, "I don't know where you ought to go. Don't go east —that much I can tell you. But don't go west either. They don't like us anywhere."

Two thirds of European Jewry had been exterminated, and the few words spoken by a Russian officer summarized the Jewish lesson of the Second World War. Upon those words the nation of Israel was founded.

Before he and Emilie fled west in the direction of American forces (dressed in prison garb, under the "protection" of eight Schindlerjuden, and with a letter in Hebrew testifying to his lifesaving actions), Schindler received a gift from his grateful Jews: A ring made from gold fillings extracted from one of the grateful Jews. The ring was inscribed with the Talmudic verse: "He who saves one life, it is as if he saved the entire world."

The fate of the gold ring symbolized Schindler's frailties and contradictions that rendered his heroism even more perplexing. Several years after the war, a Schindlerjuden asked him what he had done with the gold ring? "Schnapps," Schindler replied, referring to the liquor which he had gotten in exchange for the gold ring. . . .

Schindler After the Second World War

Not unlike before the war, Oskar Schindler's postwar life was characterized by a notable lack of achievement. In fact, Schindler was a failure in everything he attempted. Immediately after the war, he tried to produce a film. The effort failed. In 1949, the Jewish Distribution Committee ("Joint") made Schindler an ex gratia payment of $15,000 in appreciation of his wartime efforts. In addition, Schindler received one hundred thousand marks from the West German government as indemnification for his property confiscated by the communists in the east.

With this tidy sum (and with his wife Emilie, his mistress, and half a dozen Schindlerjuden families), Schindler emigrated to Argentina, the destination of many former Nazis. There he purchased a farm and tried his hand at raising chickens and nutria, the latter a small animal whose fur was deemed a luxury item. The effort failed. Nutria fur did not become popular, and, in any event, Schindler squandered his money.

What did he spend it on? "Idiocies," said his wife. When Emilie was asked what Schindler did for a living, she replied, "Schindler doesn't do anything. He just runs around with young women in luxury hotels and spends money."

By 1957, a bankrupt Schindler and his wife lived in a house outside of Buenos Aires provided by the Jewish organization B'nai B'rith.

In 1958, Schindler left Argentina for West Germany. He never returned, abandoning both his wife and mistress. The two became close friends.

"The first thing he did was sell his return ticket," Emilie said. She was left in very difficult straits and lost the farm when she was unable to pay the mortgage. Emilie then raised dairy cows on a small plot of rented land.

With additional money given to him by "Joint" and by grateful Jews, Schindler tried to establish a cement factory. It failed. Explaining this series of financial debacles, Keneally has written that Schindler had "a low tolerance for routine."

In the late 1950's, Schindler lived in a cheap apartment overlooking the train station in Frankfurt, West Germany. It was hardly an enviable setting for the man accustomed to a beautiful woman on the arm of one of his tailored suits. Schindler's life had turned a full circle since his glory days in Krakow when he boasted to his wife that he had 350 employees in contrast to his father who in his heyday had only 50.

Schindler's subsistence was now based on gifts from the grateful Jews he saved, and his spirits reflected the reversal of fortune. Poldek Pfefferberg, urging the Schindlerjuden to donate at least a day's earnings per year to their savior, described Schindler's mental state as one of "discouragement, loneliness, disillusion."

One of the Schindlerjuden, Mosche Bejski, the forger of Nazi documents who later became an Israeli supreme court justice, said, "If we sent him three thousand to four thousand dollars, he spent it in two or three weeks. Then he phoned to say he didn't have a penny."

In 1961, a group of Schindlerjuden invited Schindler to Israel for a visit. This was the year that Adolf Eichmann, the SS officer who organized the deportation of Jews to the death camps, was tried in Jerusalem. One of the witnesses against Eichmann was a German civilian engineer named Herman Grabbe. He had rescued Jews in Ukraine. . . .

During the Eichmann trial, Grabbe's testimony highlighted the existence of the non-Jews who had risked their lives to rescue Jews, a subject that hitherto had enjoyed little publicity. In turn, the contrast between Eichmann and Schindler, who was then vacationing in Israel, was noted by the Israeli press, and an effort began to honor Schindler as a Righteous Gentile.

The honor came on his birthday in 1962. Yad Vashem bestowed upon Schindler the medal inscribed with the Talmudic verse (in Hebrew and French): "He who saves one life, it is as if he saves the entire world." In addition, Schindler was invited to plant a carob tree (with a plaque bearing his name) on the Avenue of the Righteous at Yad Vashem.

The surviving Schindlerjuden turned out in great number to honor their wartime savior, but, as with Herman Grabbe, reaction in West Germany was not exactly cordial.

As with many Righteous Gentiles after the war, Schindler was ostracized by many of his countrymen precisely because he had saved Jews. His postwar testimony against Nazi war criminals compounded the hatred many Germans had for him. Schindler was hissed at on the streets of Frankfurt. Stones were thrown at him. "Too bad you didn't burn with the Jews!" a group of workmen shouted. In 1963, Schindler punched a factory worker who called him "a Jew kisser." Schindler was dragged into a local court, given a lecture by the judge, and ordered to pay damages. "I would kill myself," Schindler wrote to one of the Schindlerjuden, "if it wouldn't give them so much satisfaction."

The Last Years

Each spring, from 1961 to his death in 1974, the Schindlerjuden invited Schindler to Israel. His Jewish friends paid his expenses. Usually accompanied by a mistress, Schindler invariably slept late, never arising before eleven in the morning. Each day he "held court" with friends at a street-side cafe in Tel Aviv.

On April 28th of each year, the Schindlerjuden gathered to celebrate Schindler's birthday. He always waited until everybody was seated before he made a grand entrance "like a prime minister," as a Schindlerjuden recalled. "He loved children. He saw all the children and grandchildren of those he had rescued as his own family."

Today, the descendents of the 1,200 Schindlerjuden number 6,000.

Schindler, whose raspy voice and ruddy face were the marks of a drunkard, followed his pleasures to the grave. He died of liver failure on October 9, 1974, at age sixty-six. At his side was a mistress, this time the wife of his doctor.

"One of the church's least observant sons," Keneally writes, was buried at the Catholic cemetery in Jerusalem. Five hundred Schindlerjuden stood at his grave, paying last respects to the enigmatic man to whom they owed their lives.

Selection 2

Jan Karski: Eyewitness to the Holocaust

E. Thomas Wood and Stanislaw M. Jankowski

Today we expect the media to inform us of anything newsworthy, especially if it is a catastrophe involving life and death. During World War II, surprisingly little information was published in the press, and what was printed was often buried in a way that raised doubts about the credibility of the information. Reporters had little access to Nazi-controlled territories, except what Hitler permitted for his own propaganda purposes. The other people who knew what was happening to the Jews were either unable to speak or chose not to. The victims had virtually no chance to tell the world what was happening to them, the Nazis wanted to keep it a secret, and the bystanders preferred to remain silent. Well, most of them did. One who could not stand by was Jan Karski, a Polish Catholic involved in the Polish underground who was persuaded to make a covert visit to the Warsaw ghetto and a camp where Jews were held before being transported to the Belzec extermination camp. The horrors Karski witnessed were beyond his imagination, and he was entrusted with the job of relaying information about what was happen-

ing in Poland, and specifically what he had seen, to British officials and Jewish leaders in hopes of stimulating an Allied response to the Final Solution. This excerpt describes how Karski got into the ghetto and camp and some of what he saw. E. Thomas Wood is a reporter for the Tennessean, *and Stanislaw M. Jankowski is a journalist and historian who is considered a leading authority on the Polish underground.*

The Jewish resistance movement was in an embryonic state as the liquidation of the Warsaw Ghetto began in July 1942, although efforts to organize it had been under way for some time. The brutal German sweeps settled a debate that had preoccupied the Ghetto's Jewish leaders in previous months. Some wanted to take up active resistance against Hitler's henchmen, in whatever desperate form might be possible. Others counseled against resistance, arguing that any such action would not only be doomed to failure but would also provoke the Germans to abuse the Ghetto's residents even more savagely. The dispute had split the Jews roughly along prewar political lines. Left-wing Zionist youth groups and the socialist Bund movement, among others, gravitated toward confrontation, while many prewar members of the Right Labor Zionist and General

Zionist parties held positions in the German-directed Ghetto administration and took an accommodationist stand.

Only one group of Ghetto dwellers had any meaningful weaponry. The Jewish Military Union had been formed soon after the German occupation of Warsaw. . . .

On July 28, 1942, as the first wave of mass deportations was under way, left-wing militant youths and other factions in the Ghetto proclaimed the establishment of a resistance cell that was to become the Jewish Fighting Organization. Despite political differences, this movement and the Jewish Military Union cooperated to some extent. Completely lacking in weapons, however, this movement could accomplish little during the peak deportation period of late July, August, and early September 1942.

The nascent Jewish underground had several representatives beyond the ghetto walls in Warsaw. These were generally individuals whose physical features did not identify them as Jews; they entered and exited the Ghetto through secret passageways. There was Arie Wilner, a militant leader from the leftist Hashomer Hatzair youth group. There was Adolf Berman, a prominent Zionist figure before the war. There was Menachem Kirschenbaum, one of the very few General Zionists to take part in underground activity. And there was Leon Feiner, probably the most important Jewish leader outside the Ghetto. A lawyer and labor leader whose activities had landed him in a Polish prison before the war, Feiner had returned to Warsaw from Russia in 1941 to head the socialist Bund movement in occupied Poland. "With his distinguished gray hair and whiskers, ruddy complexion, erect carriage, and general air of good health and refinement," Jan would later write, Feiner "passed easily as a Polish 'nobleman.'"

Through sewers and other secret passages, Feiner and others entered and exited the Ghetto regularly. The Bureau of Information and Propaganda, in turn, maintained contact with these Jewish leaders, gathering information on conditions in the Ghetto and the relentless progress of the extermination campaign. Beginning in September 1942, the BIP also relayed urgent requests for weaponry from the Jews to the Home Army's high command. The questions of how responsive the military movement was to these pleas, what it could have possibly done to help the Jews of Warsaw, and why it didn't do more have been subjects of often-bitter debate between Poles and Jews since the end of the war. The Home Army did provide some guns and ammunition before and during the ghetto uprising of April and May 1943. . . .

A Catholic Takes an Interest

At twilight on a late-August evening, huddled over a single candle in a bombed-out house, two Jews and a Polish Catholic conversed in excited whispers about the ruin of European Jewry. The Catholic was Jan. He had learned through underground channels that Jewish leaders wanted to see him. . . . As usual, he did not know the true identities of the men he was encountering. He knew only that one represented the Bund and the other was a Zionist, and that the leaders were emphasizing the solidarity of disparate Jewish factions by meeting jointly with him. . . .

Karski wrote two years later:

> It was an evening of nightmare, but with a painful, oppressive kind of reality that no nightmare ever had. . . . I sat in an old, rickety armchair as if I had been pinned there, barely able to utter a word. . . . [Feiner and the Zionist] paced the floor violently, their shadows dancing weirdly in the dim light. . . . It was as though they were unable even to think of their dying people and remain seated.

. . . Before the discussion of Nazi atrocities had gone far, the Zionist burst into tears.

"What's the good of talking?" he sobbed, head in hands. "What reason do I have to go on living? I ought to go to the Germans and tell them who I am." Nobody could ever understand the horrors that had befallen the Jews, moaned the Zionist.

Jan sat perfectly still.

Feiner laid a calming hand on his colleague's shoulder. As the Zionist apologized for his outburst and tried to regain his composure, Feiner recited a catalogue of Nazi-inspired horrors to Jan. "You Poles are also suffering," said Feiner. "But after the war, Poland will be restored. Your wounds will slowly heal. By then, however, Polish Jewry will no longer exist. Hitler will lose this war, but he will win the war he has declared against the Polish Jews."

There was no power in Poland that could help the masses of Jews now facing imminent destruction, Feiner continued. Neither the Polish nor the Jewish underground movements could offer more than marginal assistance. Therefore, the responsibility for at least making some effort to help lay with the governments of the nations allied against Germany. "Let not a single leader of the United Nations be able to say that they did not know that we were being murdered in Poland and could not be helped except from the outside," declared the Bund leader. History, he added, would hold them responsible if they failed to act.

Feiner and the Zionist then laid out a series of demands to be carried to various parties in the West. Jan was to seek out certain Jewish leaders in London and relay the following demands, which were then to be presented to Allied leaders:

First: There was to be a public declaration by the Allies that prevention of the physical extermination of the Jews would henceforth be among the official war aims of the coalition fighting Hitler. The two Jews insisted that this goal should be incorporated into the overall strategy for the conduct of the war.

Second: Allied propaganda was to inform the German nation of Hitler's crimes through radio, air-dropped leaflets, and any other available means. The names of German officials taking part in the genocide and the methods of murder being employed should be widely circulated, so that the German populace could not claim ignorance about what was being perpetrated in its name.

Third: The Allies should appeal publicly to the German people to bring pressure to bear on Hitler's regime so that the slaughter would stop.

Fourth: The Allies were to declare that if the genocide continued and the German masses did not rise up to stop it, they would be considered collectively responsible for it.

Fifth: In the event that none of the other steps effected a halt in the extermination program, the Allies were to carry out reprisals in two forms: through the bombing of selected sites of cultural importance in Germany, and through the execution of Germans in Allied hands who still professed loyalty to Hitler after learning of his crimes.

When Feiner and the Zionist reached the point about retaliation against Nazi sympathizers, Jan spoke up. "Gentlemen, it is impossible," he said. "It is against international law. I know the British. They will not do it. It is hopeless. It weakens your case."

"No!" spat the Zionist in a hoarse whisper. "Say it! We don't know what is realistic or not realistic. We are dying here! Say it!"

Jan nodded, promising to carry the message faithfully. Later, as he predicted, this demand fell on deaf ears in London.

In addition to the demands Jan was to present to Jewish and Allied leaders, the two spokesmen in the ruined house also set out appeals to other persons. They asked Jan to tell the figurehead president of Poland, Władysław Raczkiewicz, about the fate of the country's Jews. They suggested that Raczkiewicz approach Pope Pius XII and ask the prelate to use all means at his disposal, including excommunication, in an effort to dissuade Nazi officials from carrying out the liquidations. The Jews also sent word to Prime Minister Sikorski, requesting that he issue an order to the population of his occupied nation urging Poles to render assistance to Jews in hiding. Polish blackmailers should be sentenced to death by the underground's justice system, argued the Jews. Polish authorities later agreed, and a decree published in March 1943 vowed punishment for any Pole who attempted extortion against imperiled Jews. The underground eventually executed several Poles who had blackmailed Jews.

Feiner and the other Jewish leader went on to appeal for whatever material assistance could be provided. Jan was instructed to tell Allied leaders that they could help some Jews to escape by providing hard currency for bribes and blank passports, which might allow Jews to be included in exchanges of Allied and Axis nationals. The free world would have to grant asylum to Jews who somehow escaped the cauldron of Hitler's empire—an indulgence that the western governments had been slow to grant in the past. And living provisions for Jews in hiding were direly needed. Jan was to urge Allied governments and Jewish organizations to provide such aid, explaining that it could be dropped into Poland by the RAF [British Royal Air Force] flights that were already delivering supplies to the Polish underground. The movement could then convey money and materials to their intended recipients through its efficient clandestine channels.

All hopes for succor of any kind hinged on making nations beyond Hitler's reach comprehend what was happening to Europe's Jews. Understanding this fact, and knowing that the Jews had no official advocate for their cause in Allied councils, Feiner desperately exhorted the Polish Catholic huddled with him to convince Jewish leaders in London of the situation's gravity. "Let the Jewish people do something that will force the other world to believe us," hissed Feiner. "We are all dying here; let them die too." The Bund leader said the Jews of Britain and America should go on a hunger strike, blockading the offices of Allied leaders, dying a slow death, if that was what it took to "shake the conscience of the world."

Finally, the Zionist, Feiner, and Karski came to the end of their long discussion. All three were physically drained. Feiner raised one last point. "Witold," he said, "I know the English. When you describe to them what is happening to the Jews, they will probably not believe you." If Karski went to London and simply repeated what he had heard from two overwrought Jewish leaders, the result would be no different than the results of Feiner's earlier efforts to spread

the news—for he had sent telegrams and detailed written reports to London before. No, Witold would need to present more tangible evidence. He would need to see the Nazi extermination machine in operation. He would need to be a witness.

It could be arranged, if Jan would agree to go along. Jan agreed.

Seeing Death Firsthand

Between August 20 and 25, 1942, the wave of terror in the Warsaw Ghetto briefly abated; the German murder network was busy clearing the Jews from several outlying towns. In an area already shrunken to a fraction of its former population, the Ghetto's remaining inhabitants were momentarily free to go about the business of living and dying—mostly dying, of starvation, disease, and suicide—relatively unmolested. The tenuous social order that had been enforced by the Nazi-directed Jewish administration of the Ghetto had dissolved by this time. It was a convenient by-product of the chaos that nobody was likely to notice a stranger on the Ghetto's streets.

In the guise of ordinary Poles, Karski and Feiner entered an apartment building at number 6 Muranowska Street, on the "Aryan side" of the ghetto wall. A janitor who went by the name "Staszek" greeted them and guided them to the cellar. Awaiting them there was a twenty-two-year-old member of the Jewish Military Union, "Dudek" Landau. He knew little about this Pole's mission to the Ghetto; his commander had told him only that a very important man was coming to visit and that it would be his responsibility to guard the secret tunnel by which the guest would enter. A squad of Jewish children under the command of the Jewish Military Union had excavated the tunnel, digging from the cellar of a building on one side of Muranowska (which was divided lengthwise by the wall) to the basement on the other side of the street. Landau led Karski and Feiner through the earthen passageway, which extended nearly forty yards at a height of no more than four feet. The men crawled through the cramped darkness in silence, aside from the curse Karski muttered when his head hit a pipe.

When they reached the opposite side, a member of the Jewish Fighting Organization took over from Landau as escort. Feiner and Karski donned ragged clothes adorned with the Star of David. Thus disguised, the men crept out of the building into the daylight.

Jan Karski

The first thing that amazed Jan as he and Feiner emerged in the Ghetto was the utter transformation the Bund leader had undergone. Moments before, he had played the part of the jaunty, self-assured Polish magnate. Now he was a bent, sickly, pitiful old Jew, just another victim awaiting his fate. Jan tried to project the same appearance, stooping in his threadbare suit, cap pulled down over his eyes. During a second meeting, Feiner and the Zionist leader had assured him that a trip to the Ghetto involved a minimum of risk. Jan hoped they were right.

Karski and Feiner shuffled down the street with the Jewish underground member at their side. This had never been a posh area; that was

why the Germans made it a ghetto. The buildings were older and smaller, the streets narrower than in most of the rest of Warsaw. The Germans had ordered the street signs to be printed in elaborate Hebrew characters. As in the rest of the city, there were demolished homes on every block—but none of the makeshift rebuilding efforts visible in the rest of Warsaw were in evidence here. The streets were packed with humanity and its remnants. "There was hardly a square yard of empty space," Karski recalled. "As we picked our way across the mud and rubble, the shadows of what had once been men or women flitted by us in pursuit of someone or something, their eyes blazing with some insane hunger or greed." The cries of the mad and the hungry echoed through the streets, mingled with the voices of residents offering to barter scraps of clothing for morsels of food.

Jan identified the stench just as he discerned the unclothed corpses. Strewn in the gutters were the bodies of the old and young, all as naked in death as they had been in birth.

"What does it mean?" Jan asked under his breath.

"When a Jew dies," Feiner calmly replied, "the family removes his clothing and throws his body in the street. Otherwise they would have to pay a burial tax to the Germans. Besides, this saves clothing."

The visitors reached the Plac Muranowski, a square at the northeast corner of the Ghetto that had once been a park. Mothers crowded the benches, nursing emaciated infants. Stunted children filled the area, some sitting listlessly, others cavorting in the dirt.

"They are playing, you see." Jan thought he heard Feiner's voice break with emotion. "Life goes on. They play before they die."

"These children are not playing," responded Jan. "They only make believe it is play."

On the streets, Feiner relentlessly pointed out every macabre example of the zone's bestial conditions. Over and over the men would come upon human forms crumpled against the sides of buildings, their catatonic stares fixed on nothing, only a slight rustling beneath their rags betraying the fact that they were still breathing. At each instance, Feiner would stop for a moment. "Remember this," he said, over and over. "Remember this."

As the tour continued, a commotion ensued on a side street. People were fleeing. Suddenly, Feiner and the other Jew grabbed Jan by the arms and hustled him into an apartment building: "Hurry!" Feiner growled at the confused Pole. "You must see this.". . .

Jan could see two adolescent boys dressed in the crisp uniforms of the Hitlerjugend—the Hitler Youth, the cadet corps of the Third Reich.

"Look at it! Look at it!" Feiner hissed in Karski's ear. "They are here for the hunt."

The boys stood in a deserted street, broad smiles on their faces, their blond hair glistening in the sunlight. One had drawn a pistol. His eyes canvassed the surrounding buildings. The other said something that made him laugh. Then the first boy raised his gun and fired. Jan heard the tinkling of broken glass and a moan of pain from an adjoining building.

The boy who fired the shot let out a victorious whoop. His fellow "warrior" congratulated him. It was another successful *Judenjag*—another "Jew hunt." The Hitler Youth turned and strolled serenely away.

Jan remained crouched by the window, still frozen in horror, long after the boys left. Then, noticing a hand on his shoulder, he turned to find the woman who lived in the apartment standing behind him. "You came to see us? It won't do any good," she said. "Go back, run away. Don't torture yourself anymore. Go, go."

Jan insisted on leaving immediately. With Feiner and the underground's escort, he returned to the building on Muranowska Street. "Dudek" Landau was waiting in the cellar. Within minutes, the visitors had passed once again into the world of the living, beyond the Ghetto.

"You didn't see everything," Feiner said, in parting. Karski nodded, offering to return for another visit if necessary.

Two days later, Jan and a different guide repeated the Ghetto tour. This time they spent three hours within the walls. As Karski met with Jewish underground leaders in an apartment, listening to their pleas for help from the outside world, he was offered a glass of water and a slice of bread—a parody of hospitality amid the savagery of a prison city. Jan's reaction was the talk of the Jewish underground for days: He gently pushed the bread away from his place at the table. Everyone understood. Jan did not need to say that he could not, in good conscience, accept even a morsel that might otherwise feed the starving. . . .

A Look at the Final Solution

The courier would have to see even more if he was to bear witness effectively to the world. . . . Doing so would involve a much more dangerous fact-finding mission than the Ghetto tours. But Karski agreed without hesitation to carry out the unprecedented mission: to walk into a Nazi death camp of his own free will.

A few days after his second trip to the Ghetto, Jan arrived at a rendezvous point outside Warsaw's central train station. The Jewish underground was to furnish a guide who would get him to the site of the camp. . . .

The Jewish guide took Jan to a hardware store and handed him over to its proprietor, a member of the Polish underground. As planned, Jan found the uniform of a Nazi-affiliated Ukrainian militiaman (bribed to take the day off) awaiting him at the store. Not long after Jan finished donning the uniform, another Ukrainian guard appeared at the store, having also accepted a bribe to take this curious Pole through the camp. . . .

Before long, Jan could hear an otherworldly keening from the direction in which he was headed. As Jan drew nearer, he thought he detected the stench of burning flesh. Emerging into a clearing, he approached the camp from a slight rise. He could see a barbed-wire fence about twelve feet in height, camouflaged with branches stripped from the surrounding trees. The fence enclosed a sizeable area. A walled wooden ramp extended from the camp to the nearby railroad track. Within the enclosure were a few small sheds or barracks. Several gates were cut into the fence. At one of them, Jan's Ukrainian escort lazily saluted two of his German masters. They casually gestured for the men to enter.

Spread out before Jan was a broad, open space. To Jan, it seemed to be completely covered by "a dense, pulsating, throbbing, noisy human mass" of "starved, stinking, gesticulating, insane" Jews. Of all ages and both genders, some in various states of undress, the captives sat and lay on the ground. Like the stupefied figures slumped along the Ghetto's streets, many of these victims appeared to be in shock. Here and there in the vast crowd—there must have been thousands—a guard was beating or kicking a Jew. . . .

Behind the mass of humanity stood a long line of boxcars rolled onto the rail siding. Jan could see some of his Ukrainian "colleagues" lining the cars with a thick layer of white powder, as the guard had told him they would. It was quicklime, calcium oxide. Jan made his way along the fence, taking up the position indicated by the guard.

At a signal from a German officer, several of the Ukrainians formed a cordon around the Jews on the ground and began herding them toward the boxcars. Jan stood by the fence and observed the procedure, carefully keeping his distance from the "other" Ukrainians. The guards moved steadily forward against the chaotic mass of flesh, striking out with clubs and rifle butts to force the victims toward the ramp leading to the boxcar doors, shooting and bayoneting any too weak or traumatized to move.

The low moan of misery that emanated from the crowd on the ground gave way first to shrieks of pure panic as the Jews stumbled up the ramp, then to echoing wails of agony as they were packed into the boxcars and felt the quicklime burning their skin and lungs. The guards fired at random into the crowd on the ramp, hurling the dead and wounded into the car to land on the heads of those already packed in. When no more bodies could be crammed into a car, a Ukrainian slammed its iron doors shut, crushing any protruding limbs.

Jan watched the Nazis fill several boxcars in this manner. He estimated that thousands of human beings were being packed into the cars.

He visualized the fate awaiting them, these creatures who had endured not only ghetto life but also the hideous trip to this way station, followed by days of brutal confinement here—only to meet such an end. . . .

Later in life, Karski would be asked frequently to bear witness to the scenes he encountered at the Ghetto and the camp. Sometimes he would attempt to do so. More often, he would refuse to go into detail, instead conveying his experience in a simple sentence: "I saw terrible things.". . .

Karski Holds the Key

Back in the Polish capital, Jan tried to focus on the journey ahead. By the beginning of September 1942, preparations for the political substance of his trip were nearing completion. . . . Another month would elapse, however, before Jan could depart for London—a month of frustration for Jan, whose mission had taken on a previously unimaginable significance. With each passing day, he realized, thousands more would die. But organizing a courier's passage across occupied Europe took time. . . .

The Home Army's Bureau of Information and Propaganda, with its contingent of Jews and intellectuals sympathetic to the Jewish cause, had meanwhile begun assembling written information on the Jewish crisis for Jan to carry. The bureau was charged with producing a roll of microfilm that would contain all the documentary material to be carried by the envoy. . . .

Also included in the material to be microfilmed was a late arrival, an eloquent protest from Zofia Kossak's Front for the Rebirth of Poland (FOP). . . . Its text made clear that Jan had told Kossak everything he had seen:

In the Warsaw Ghetto, behind the wall that cuts it off from the world, several hundred thousand of the condemned are awaiting death. The hope of rescue does not exist for them; no help is coming from anywhere. Assassins speed through the streets, shooting anyone who dares to leave his house. They also shoot anyone who stands at the window. Unburied bodies are strewn about the streets.

The protest went on to summarize the progress of deportations in the Ghetto. Then it described what happened to the deportees:

> At the ramps, boxcars are waiting. The hangmen push up to 150 of the condemned into each one. A thick layer of lime and chlorine is spread on the floors, with water poured over it. The boxcar's doors are sealed. Sometimes the train leaves as soon as it is loaded; sometimes it sits on the track—perhaps for a couple of days—but it doesn't matter to anyone anymore. Of the people packed so tightly that the dead cannot fall and continue to stand shoulder-to-shoulder with living, of the people slowly dying in the fumes of lime and chlorine, deprived of air or even a drop of water, none will live. Wherever, whenever the death trains arrive, they will contain nothing but corpses. . . .

We do not want to be like Pilate. We have no means of actively opposing the German murders; we cannot overcome them or save anybody. But we *protest*, from the bottom of our hearts, which are filled with compassion, loathing, and horror. That protest is demanded of us by God—God, who has forbidden us to kill. It is demanded by the Christian conscience. Every creature calling itself a man has the right to the love of his neighbor. The blood of the helpless calls to the heavens for vengeance. Whoever among us does not support this protest is not a Catholic.

. . . All this material was to be shrunken to fit on a tiny roll of film. That film would then be stuffed into a hollow house key, which would then be welded shut. All Jan had to do was carry it across Hitler's empire.

Selection 3

Raoul Wallenberg: The Missing Hero

David Metzler

When discussing those individuals who stood up and went above and beyond the call of duty and humanity to save people during the war, the name that first comes to mind is Raoul Wallenberg, the Swedish diplomat who courageously provided documents that allowed perhaps as many as 100,000 Jews to escape the Nazis. This Swedish diplomat, in his early thirties at the time, used whatever methods he could, from bribery to extortion, to help those threatened with deportation from Hungary. He literally invented a protective pass and then convinced the Germans to accept it. What should be a triumphant story of a great hero actually ends more tragically with the disappearance of Wallenberg after the war and the uncertainty of whether he died in a Soviet prison or by some miracle remains alive. Wallenberg's actions earned him recognition from

Excerpted from David Metzler, "Who Raoul Wallenberg Was," an online article found at www.raoul-wallenberg.com. Reprinted with permission from the author.

Yad Vashem, the Israeli Holocaust museum, as a "righteous person," and the street on which the U.S. Holocaust Memorial Museum was constructed was named in his honor.

During the spring [of] 1944 the world had awoken and realized what Hitler's "Final Solution" meant. In May 1944 the first authentic eyewitness report reached the western world of what happened in the extermination camp Auschwitz. It came from two Jews who managed to escape the German gas chambers.

Hitler's plans for total extermination of the Jews of Europe became known. In Hungary, which had joined Germany in the war against the Soviet Union in 1941, there still lived an estimated 700,000 Jews at the beginning of 1944.

When the Germans lost the battle of Stalingrad [in] 1943, Hungary wanted to follow Italy's example and demand a separate peace. Hitler then called the Hungarian head of state Miklós Horthy and demanded continued solidarity with Germany. When Horthy refused to meet the demands, Hitler invaded Hungary on March 19th 1944. Soon after that the deportations of Jews started. The destination was Auschwitz-Birkenau in southern Poland, and a certain death.

The Germans started deporting the Jews from the countryside, but the Jewish citizens of Budapest knew that their hour of fate was also soon to come. In their desperation they sought help from the embassies of the neutral countries, where provisional passes were issued for Jews with special connections to these countries.

The Royal Swedish Legation in Budapest succeeded in negotiating with the Germans that the bearers of these protective passes would be treated as Swedish citizens and exempt from wearing the yellow star of David on their chest. It was Per Anger . . . a young diplomat at the legation in Budapest, who initiated the first of these Swedish protective passes. . . .

In a short period of time the Swedish Legation issued 700 passes, a drop in the ocean compared to the enormous amount of Jews being threatened. The legation requested immediate staff reinforcements from the Ministry of Foreign Affairs in Stockholm.

In Sweden at the same time the World Jewish Congress had a meeting in Stockholm. The most important issue was organizing a rescue operation for the Hungarian Jews.

In 1944 the USA established the War Refugee Board (WRB), an organization with the purpose of saving Jews from Nazi persecution. The WRB soon realized that serious attempts were being made from the Swedish side to rescue the Jewish population in Hungary. The WRB's representative in Stockholm called a committee with prominent Swedish Jews to discuss suitable persons to lead a mission in Budapest for an extensive rescue operation. Among the participants was Raoul Wallenberg's business partner Koloman Lauer, chosen as an expert on Hungary.

The first choice was Folke Bernadotte, chairman of the Swedish Red Cross and relative to the Swedish King. After Bernadotte was disapproved by the Hungarian government, Koloman Lauer suggested that his business partner Raoul Wallenberg should be asked. Lauer emphasized that Wallenberg had made many trips to Hungary while working for their joint company. Raoul was considered too young and seemed inexperienced, but Lauer was persistent. Raoul was the right man according to him—a quick thinker, energetic, brave and compassionate. And he had a famous name.

Soon everybody had approved Wallenberg. At the end of June 1944 he was appointed first secretary at the Royal Swedish Legation in Budapest with the mission to start a rescue operation for the Jews. Raoul was very excited to go to Hungary, but first he wrote a memo to the Swedish Ministry of Foreign Affairs. He was determined not to get caught in the protocol and paperwork bureaucracy of diplomacy. He demanded full authorization to deal with whom he wanted without having to contact the ambassador first. He also wanted to have the right to send diplomatic couriers beyond the usual channels.

The memo was so unusual that it was sent all the way to prime minister Per Albin Hansson, who consulted the King before he announced that the demands had been approved. . . .

Wallenberg's Rescue Operation

When Raoul Wallenberg arrived in Budapest by July 1944, it was late. Under the leadership of Adolf Eichmann the Germans had already sent away more than 400,000 Jewish men, women, and children. They had been deported on 148 freight trains between the 14th of May and the 8th of July. When Wallenberg came to Budapest there were only about 230,000 Jews left.

The German SS officer Adolf Eichmann was now preparing a plan that in one day would exterminate the whole Jewish population in Budapest. In a report to Berlin he said that "the technical details will take a few days."

If this plan had been put into action Raoul Wallenberg's mission would have been meaningless. Then the "Jewish issue" would have been "permanently solved" for . . . Hungary. The Hungarian head of state Miklós Horthy . . . meanwhile received a letter from King Gustaf V of Sweden (1858–1950) on June 30th with an appeal that the deportations would stop. The telegram read: *"Having received word of the extraordinarily harsh methods your government has applied against the Jewish population of Hungary, I permit myself to turn to Your Highness personally, to beg in the name of humanity, that you take measures to save those who still remain to be saved of the unfortunate people. This plea has been evoked by my long-standing feelings of friendship for your country and my sincere concern for Hungary's good name and reputation in the community of nations."* On July 12th Horthy replied as follows: *"I have received the telegraphic appeal sent me by Your Majesty. With feelings of the deepest understanding, I ask Your Majesty to be persuaded that I am doing everything that, in the present situation, lies in my power to ensure that the principles of humanity and justice are respected. I esteem to a high degree the feelings of friendship for my country that animate Your Majesty and I ask that Your Majesty preserve these feelings toward the Hungarian people in these times of severe trial."* The Germans' deportations were canceled, one train with 1,600 Jews was stopped at the border and sent back to Budapest.

Oddly enough the German authorities approved the cancellation of the deportations. The explanation may have been that Heinrich Himmler, one of the top Nazi officials during this time played a high level game for peace. He thought he could negotiate a separate peace with the western allies and might have thought he'd stand a better chance if the pressure on the Jews was decreased. Adolf Eichmann could do nothing but wait.

At this time minister Carl Ivan Danielsson was head of the Swedish Legation. His closest man was secretary Per Anger. Raoul Wallenberg now headed the department responsible for helping the Jews. . . .

Raoul Wallenberg did not use traditional diplomacy. He more or less shocked the diplomats at the Swedish Legation with his unconventional methods. Everything from bribes to extortion threats was used with success. But when the rest of the staff of the legation saw Wallenberg's results he quickly got their unreserved support.

Raoul Wallenberg's first task was to design a Swedish protective pass to help the Jews against the Germans and Hungarians. He had previous experience that both the German and Hungarian authorities were weak for flashy symbols. He therefore had the passes printed in yellow and blue with the coat of arms of the Three Crowns of Sweden in the middle, and added the appropriate stamps and signatures on it. Of course Wallenberg's protective passes had no value whatsoever according to international laws, but it provoked respect. To begin with Wallenberg only had permission to issue 1,500 passes. Quickly though he managed to negotiate another 1,000, and through promises and empty threats to the Hungarian foreign ministry he eventually managed to raise the quota to 4,500 protective passes.

In reality Wallenberg managed to issue more than three times as many protective passes. He controlled a staff of several hundred co-workers. They were all Jews and thanks to their work with Wallenberg they didn't have to wear the degrading yellow star.

In August 1944 the Hungarian head of state

Raoul Wallenberg

Horthy fired his pro-German prime minister Sztójay and let general Lakatos succeed him. The situation for the Jews improved considerably. Through diplomatic pressuring, mediated and emphasized by Raoul Wallenberg, the responsibility to "solve the Jewish issue in Hungary" was taken away from Adolf Eichmann.

Now Wallenberg thought his department at the legation could be dismantled and that he himself could return back to Sweden. He expected the invading and winning troops of the Soviet Union to soon take over Budapest.

[On] October 15th the head of state Miklós Horthy declared that he wanted peace with the Soviets. But his radio speech had barely been broadcast until the German troops took command. Horthy was overthrown immediately and replaced by the leader of the Hungarian Nazis, Ferenc Szálasi. He was the leader of the Arrow Cross organization, who was just as feared as the German Nazis for their cruel methods against the Jewish population. Adolf Eichmann returned and received free hands to continue the terror against the Jews.

Raoul Wallenberg kept on fighting in spite of the ruling powers of evil and appeared often as an unwelcome witness to the atrocities. In many cases he managed to save Jews from the clutches of the Nazis with his firm action and courage as his only weapon.

Now Raoul started to build his "Swedish houses." It was some 30 houses in the Pest part of the city where the Jews could seek refuge. A Swedish flag hung in front of the door and Wallenberg declared the house Swedish territory. The population of the "Swedish houses" soon rose to 15,000.

The other neutral legations in Budapest started to follow Wallenberg's example and issued protective passes. A number of diplomats from other countries were inspired to open their own "protective houses" for Jewish refugees.

Toward the end of the war, when the situation was totally desperate, Wallenberg issued a simplified form of his protective pass, one copied page with his signature alone. In the existing chaos even that worked.

The newly instated Hungarian Nazi government immediately let it be notified that with the change of power the protective passes were no longer valid. Meanwhile Wallenberg managed to befriend himself with the Baroness Elizabeth "Liesel" Kemény. She was the wife of the new Hungarian foreign minister, Baron Gabor Kemény, and with her cooperation the passes were made valid again.

During this time Eichmann started his brutal "death marches." He went through with his promised deportation plan by having large numbers of Jews leave Hungary by foot. The first march started November 20th 1944, and the conditions along the 200 kilometer long road between Budapest and the Austrian border were so horrendous that even the Nazis themselves complained.

The marching Jews could be counted in the thousands along never-ending rows of starving and tortured people. Raoul Wallenberg was in place all the time to hand out protective passes, food and medicine. He threatened and he bribed, until he managed to free those with Swedish passes.

When Eichmann's killers transported the Jews in full trains Wallenberg intensified his rescue efforts. He even climbed the train wagons standing on the tracks, ran along the wagon roofs, and stuck bunches of protective passes down to the people inside. The German soldiers were ordered to open fire, but were so impressed by Wallenberg's courage that they deliberately aimed too high. Wallenberg could jump down unharmed and demand that the Jews with passes should leave the train together with him.

Raoul Wallenberg's department at the Swedish Legation grew constantly and finally kept 340 persons busy. Also in their building lived another 700 persons. . . .

Toward the end of 1944 Wallenberg moved over the river Danube from Buda to Pest where the two Jewish ghettos were situated. The minimal level of law and order that once existed was now gone. The Arrow Cross, police and German war machine shared the power.

Wallenberg searched desperately for suitable people to bribe, and found a very powerful ally in Pa'l Szalay, a high ranking officer in the police force and an Arrow Cross member. (After the war Szalay was the only Arrow Cross member that wasn't executed. He was set free instead in recognition for his cooperation with Wallenberg.)

The second week of January 1945 Raoul Wallenberg found out that Eichmann planned a total massacre in the largest ghetto. The only one who could stop it was general August Schmidthuber who was commander in chief for the German troops in Hungary.

Wallenberg's ally Szalay was sent to deliver a note to Schmidthuber explaining that Raoul Wallenberg would make sure that the general would be held personally responsible for the massacre and that he would be hanged as a war criminal after the war. The massacre was stopped in the last minute thanks to Wallenberg's action.

Two days later the Russians arrived and found 97,000 Jews alive in Budapest's two Jewish ghettos. In total 120,000 Jews survived the Nazi extermination in Hungary.

According to Per Anger, Wallenberg's friend and colleague, Wallenberg must be honored with saving at least 100,000 Jews.

What Happened to Wallenberg?

On January 13th 1945 an advancing Soviet troop saw a man standing and waiting for them in front of a house with a large Swedish flag above the door. In fluent Russian Raoul Wallenberg explained to a surprised Russian sergeant that he was Swedish chargé d'affaires for those of the Russian liberated parts of Hungary. Wallenberg requested, and was given permission to visit the Soviet military headquarters in the city of Debrecen east of Budapest.

On his way out of the capital on January 17th—with a Russian escort—Wallenberg and his driver stopped at the "Swedish houses" to say good-bye to his friends. To one of his colleagues, Dr. Ernö Petö, Wallenberg said that he wasn't sure if he was going to be the Russians' guest or their prisoner. Raoul Wallenberg thought he'd be back within eight days—but he has been missing since then.

If Raoul Wallenberg is alive or not is uncertain. The Russians proclaim that he died in Russian captivity on July 17th 1947. A number of testimonies indicate though that he was alive and that he still could be alive. . . .

The Russians probably believed that Wallenberg had another reason for his rescue efforts. They probably suspected him to be an American spy too. Most certainly they were skeptical [of] Raoul Wallenberg's contact with the Germans also.

Raoul Wallenberg and his driver Vilmos Langfelder never returned from Debrecen. According to reliable testimonies they were arrested and sent to Moscow. They were arrested by NKVD, an organization that later changed its name to KGB. Wallenberg and Langfelder were placed in separate cells in the Lubjanka prison

. . . according to eye witnesses. . . .

It would take some time though until authorities in Stockholm got concerned over Raoul Wallenberg's disappearance. In a letter to the Swedish ambassador in Moscow, the Russian vice foreign minister Dekanosov declared that "the Russian military authorities had taken measures and steps to protect Wallenberg and his belongings."

The Swedes of course expected Raoul Wallenberg to come home soon. When nothing happened, Raoul's mother, Maj von Dardel, contacted the Russian ambassador in Stockholm, Aleksandra Kollontaj, who explained that she could be calm, since her son was well kept in Russia. To the Swedish foreign minister Christian Günthers wife, Aleksandra Kollontaj said at the same time that it would be best for Wallenberg if the Swedish government wouldn't stir things up. . . .

On March 8th 1945 the Soviet controlled Hungarian radio announced that Raoul Wallenberg had been murdered on his way to Debrecen, probably by Hungarian Nazis or Gestapo agents. This created a certain passiveness with the Swedish government. Foreign minister Östen Undén and Sweden's ambassador in the Soviet Union presumed that Wallenberg was dead. In most places however, the radio message wasn't taken seriously. . . .

[On] February 6th 1957 the Russians announced that they had made extensive investigations and found a document most likely to be regarding Raoul Wallenberg. In the hand written document it was stated that "the for you familiar prisoner Wallenberg passed away this night in his cell." The document was dated July 17th 1947 and signed Smoltsov, head of the Lubjanka prison's infirmary. The document was addressed to Viktor Abakumov, the minister for state security in the Soviet Union.

The Russians regretted in their letter to the Swedes that Smoltsov deceased in May 1953, and that Abakumov had been executed in connection with cleansing within the security police. The Swedes were very distrustful towards this declaration, but the Russians have till this day stuck to the same statement.

Testimonies from different prisoners who had been in Russian jails after January 1945 tell. in contradiction to the Russian information, that Raoul Wallenberg was imprisoned during the whole 1950's. . . .

Is Raoul Wallenberg alive today? During the 1980's the interest for Wallenberg grew around the world. [In] 1981 he became an honorary citizen of the United States of America, 1985 in Canada, and 1986 in Israel, and all over the world a large opinion that still think he's alive, demand that he'd be released from his Russian captivity. . . .

In 1989 the Wallenberg family went to Moscow to receive the "suddenly located" passport and personal possessions of Raoul. They saw the official paperwork for his 1946 arrest and were given an official apology, along with the same old story that he had died at age 35. In spite of a large number of secret documents opened after the fall of the Soviet Union in 1991, Raoul Wallenberg's fate remains a mystery.

Wallenberg's Right Arm: Per Anger

Arthur Stocki

Raoul Wallenberg is perhaps the most famous rescuer of World War II, but he was by no means alone. In fact, before Wallenberg arrived in Budapest, a Swedish diplomat named Per Anger was already taking steps to help save Jews from being deported from Hungary, such as issuing travel documents similar to the ones given to Swedes who lost their passports. After Wallenberg arrived, Anger aided his efforts and directly saved people when Wallenberg was not available to personally intervene. This profile comes from Arthur Stocki, who wrote it for the Per Anger website.

Per Johan Valentin Anger was born December 7th, 1913, in Gothenburg, Sweden. He studied law at the University of Stockholm, and then later at the University of Uppsala. After he graduated in November 1939, the same day as war broke out between the Soviet Union and Finland, Per Anger was drafted to the army. Shortly thereafter the Ministry of Foreign Affairs offered him a trainee position at the Swedish legation in Berlin, Germany. Per Anger finished his army service in January 1940, and

Reprinted from Arthur Stocki, "Per Anger: The History of a Swedish Hero," an online article found at www.raoul-wallenberg.com/per-anger/history.html. Reprinted with permission from the author.

by the end of that month he arrived in Berlin. This is where his diplomatic career began.

Berlin 1940–1941

Per Anger was young and inexperienced when he arrived in Berlin in January 1940. World War II had been going on for almost five months at this time. He was placed in the trade department and worked on trade between Sweden and Germany. He has told about how he up close witnessed the large masses' fascination over Hitler and his propaganda. Probably the most dramatic experience of his time in Berlin was when the Swedish legation had received reliable information from underground movements regarding the Nazi-German attack on Norway and Denmark. There was uncertainty if Sweden was included in the plan. Per Anger was now responsible to send the coded telegram to Stockholm. That night he couldn't sleep due to his thought that he might have made a mistake when he sent the cipher, so that the Foreign Department couldn't interpret it—then one would be able to read in future history books about how "Sweden because of the Swedish attaché Per Anger in Berlin were taken by surprise by a German invasion army!"

Thankfully the message got through as it should though, but the Foreign Department in Sweden didn't believe these statements and did not inform its neighboring countries. A few days later the legation desperately sent a new message to the Foreign Department with information from an even more reliable source. Now it was taken seriously, and Norway was warned. The Norwegian foreign minister Kut called for the German military attaché and asked him straightforward if this information was accurate. He of course denied everything. The following day that same officer took control over entire Oslo. In June 1941 Anger returned to Stockholm and became an official Swedish diplomat. Between that time and until March 1942 he worked at the Foreign Department's trade section on the relations between Sweden and Hungary. The work mostly concerned the import of Hungarian food provisions in exchange for Swedish steel.

The Legation in Budapest

On June 12th, 1942, Per Anger was appointed second secretary at the Swedish legation in Budapest, Hungary. On November 26th that same year he entered his duties there. The Swedish legation in Budapest was a very small unit at that time. The equivalent to ambassador was Minister Carl Ivan Danielsson, and thereafter Per Anger in the order of precedence. Formally he was the second secretary, but in protocol he acted as first secretary. Further the legation consisted of Dénes von Mezey who was in charge of administration, Harry Wester who was the military attaché, Margareta Bauer and Birgit Brulin who were secretaries, and finally the Swedish Red Cross representative in Budapest, Valdemar Langlet. Per Anger's main work was still Swedish-Hungarian trade. The years from his arrival in Budapest till the German occupation in 1944, Anger has described as relatively harmonious. There was no shortage of food, the restaurants were open, and the Gypsies played music in the restaurants, like before the war. The Jews were discriminated [against] and didn't have the same rights as others, but their situation was not difficult like it would become after the German invasion.

The Holocaust

In his book, Per Anger describes how reports of liquidation in gas chambers in Poland, one way or another, already in 1942, had reached Budapest.

On March 19, 1944, Germany invaded Hungary. After the German invasion the situation changed drastically. Per Anger witnessed the Nazis' persecutions and how their "final solution" plans were put in motion. He was shocked the first day when suddenly every fourth person on the street was wearing a yellow Star of David—the humiliation, and knowledge of how low humanity could sink.

In an interview for the magazine "Vi" Per Anger [said]:

> First then everything was revealed. Mainly by stories from people who managed to escape. We sent home reports of extermination camps, sketches of the gas chambers in Auschwitz . . . // . . . We became witnesses to what we didn't think was possible: a systematic extermination of people.

The Rescue Operation Begins

In an interview with Dr. Paul Levine, Per Anger speaks about the first days after the occupation:

> The first days we couldn't do so much. I mean, we didn't know what was going to happen. We understood that now would be a hard time for the Jewish population and it (the persecutions) started just a few days later. So then we were forced to mobilize our powers. From that moment everything that had to do with trade with Sweden or other routine errands were of course put aside, and we concentrated . . . the whole legation concentrated on one thing. To save . . . try to save human lives.

Jews with relatives or business associates in Sweden started to line up in front of the Swedish legation to ask for help. Per Anger came up with the idea to issue provisional passports. The passport was in fact a kind of travel document which was given to Swedish citizens abroad who had lost their real passports. Minister Danielsson gave his approval for them, but said that Per Anger would take responsibility for them. Afterwards the Swedish Foreign Department also came to approve the passports. Dénes von Mezey managed through his contacts with the Hungarian authorities to negotiate that the bearer of such a passport would be respected as a Swedish citizen, and that this person would need to wear the yellow star of David. This way internment and deportation would be avoided.

Per Anger also came up with the idea to issue special certificates to the many Jews who had applied for Swedish citizenship. More than 700 provisional passports and certificates were issued at first, and the rumor started to spread among the Jews of Budapest. The documents completely lacked any form of legality in international law.

Raoul Wallenberg's Arrival in Budapest

The Swedish legation acted on behalf of seven countries in Hungary at this time. Simultaneously the stream of people seeking help from the Swedes increased. This brought about the legation's request for reinforcements. At the same time negotiations were taking place between the American War Refugee Board, the Swedish Foreign Department and the World Jewish Congress regarding sending a person to Hungary with a mission to lead the rescue of Hungary's Jews.

It was Raoul Wallenberg who was appointed to be this person. He was given the status of legation secretary in Budapest and arrived there July 9, 1944.

Wallenberg looked at the old documents and then presented the idea of a new document he thought would be more effective; the protective passes—Schutzpasse. Wallenberg was well aware of how flashy papers printed in color with signatures, seals and stamps impressed the Germans. The result was a document printed in yellow and blue with the "Tre Kronor"—three crowns from the Swedish state symbol—and the signature of the Minister. Once again, these documents had no legal support whatsoever, but Germans as well as Hungarians came to respect them.

In August 1944, Per Anger traveled to Stockholm to request even more reinforcements for the legation. The new people came to be the attaché Lars Berg, the administrator Göte Carlsson, and the Swedish "Save The Children" representative Asta Nilsson. Consul Yngve Ekmark was also tied to the legation and organized storage and distribution of food, medicine and clothing for the rescue operation.

At the Train Station

In an interview with the Los Angeles Times, Per Anger was asked if he ever partook in the direct rescue of Jews. He answered that he sometimes received calls from Wallenberg who asked him to go to the train station to save people from the deportations when he was hindered to do it himself. This is how Anger described one of those situations:

> When Wallenberg one day was somewhere else, I went to a station from where a train with Jews was about to depart. There was no time to be diplomatic with the Germans. I explained that a terrible mistake had been done because they apparently were on their way to deport Jews with Swedish protective passes. If they weren't released immediately I would see to it that Veesenmayer was notified. The German train commander didn't dare risking being reported to the feared Veesenmayer. I went in to the wagons to call for names, but only found two Jews with protective passes. With the help of the present Hungarian police officer, Batizfalvy, who in secrecy worked in cooperation with Raoul Wallenberg and me, I succeeded, in defiance of the SS commander's order, to leave the station with 150 Jews towards freedom, 148 of them without protective passes.

Along the Death Marches

On November 10, 1944, the Russians and Americans bombed the Hungarian railroads and made train deportations to Auschwitz impossible. Adolf Eichmann then suggests to let the Jews in Budapest march 180 kilometers by foot to the Hungarian-Austrian border station at Hegyeshalom. Possession of protective passes didn't help this time. Per Anger describes in his book how "thousands of people were taken as they walked and stood."

Raoul Wallenberg, Per Anger, and the legations of other neutral countries reacted quickly. In his book Anger describes one of their car trips along the death marches:

> One of the first days in December 1944 Wallenberg and I took a car ride along the road the Jews [were] marching on. We passed these crowds of miserable people, more dead than alive. With gray faces they staggered forward under chops and hits from the soldier's rifles. The road was lined by dead bodies. We had our car filled with food that we managed to distribute in spite of prohibitions, but it didn't last very long. At Hegyeshalom we saw how the ones who arrived were handed over to a German SS commando under Eichmann, who counted them like cattle. '489—correct' ('vierhundertneunundachtzig—stimmt gut!'). The Hungarian officer received a receipt that everything was in order.

> Before this handing over we managed to save some hundreds of Jews. Some had Swedish protective passes, others were gotten out by pure bluffing. Wallenberg didn't give up and made renewed journeys when he in similar ways managed to reunite some additional Jews with Budapest.

The death marches to Hegyeshalom ended on December 10, 1944. At that time 37,000 Jews had been put on march from Budapest—27,000 arrived at the border station.

The Soviets Arrive, and the War Ends

When the Soviet troops seriously got closer to Budapest, the Swedish legation was offered to leave the country by the Foreign Department due to the large risks. In spite of bombs and grenades falling over their heads, and that their lives were threatened by the Arrow Cross, everyone remained in Budapest, except one of the women who was persuaded to go home. They knew that if they'd leave the country their protégés wouldn't stand a chance and all rescue work would have been in vain. There was no other guarantee for their safety.

From now on and till the Soviet army's entry in Budapest, one lived in constant threat for life. Life was spent more under ground now in shelters, than above. Dispersed over different places in the city the Swedes quickly lost contact with each other. After the Russians' entry everyone found each other again though, except for Raoul Wallenberg.

The last time Per Anger met Wallenberg was January 10, 1945. He had then asked Wallenberg to cancel his operation and stay in the Buda-side of the city, otherwise his life would be in great danger. Wallenberg refused to interrupt his work. On January 17, 1945, Raoul Wallenberg was taken away by the Russians and his destiny is a mystery till this day.

The members of the Swedish legation were put in Soviet "custody" over some period, until order of their return home came from Moscow. [On] April 18, 1945, the Swedish legation from Budapest arrived in Stockholm. This ended the "Budapest adventure" for secretary Per Anger.

The war was over, but now Per Anger's search for Wallenberg started. He has been one of the foreground figures in this search throughout the years, and he has also helped spread information about Wallenberg's deeds all over the world. . . .

In 1989, as an example of Ambassador Anger's efforts, he urged the German Chancellor Helmut Kohl to intervene in the Wallenberg affair. Holding an extension phone, Anger listened as Kohl called Mikhail Gorbachev and pleaded *let that old man go.* The Russian had no answer, says Anger, who then went to Moscow to appeal personally to the Soviet leader: *"He showed no interest"* and *"implied that he had no control over the KGB."*

Per Anger has received several awards throughout the years. He was awarded as a "Righteous Among the Nations" by the State of Israel and Yad Vashem in 1982, an award given to gentiles who with danger for their own lives rescued Jews during World War 2. He has a tree planted in his honor in "The Avenue of the Righteous" in Jerusalem. In November 1995 he was honored with the Hungarian Republic's order of merit which was handed to him by the Hungarian president Arpád Göncz. In September 1996 he was honored by the Jewish Council of Sweden. . . .

Per Anger is still alive and well, living half of the year in Sweden and the other half in France.

Selection 5

Varian Fry: An American Hero

Elizabeth Kessin Berman

Research on the Holocaust has found that thousands of people acted in a variety of heroic ways to save Jews and others targeted by Hitler for extermination. In fact, Yad Vashem, the Israeli research institution and museum of the Holocaust, has recognized more than 17,000 people from thirty-four countries as "righteous among the nations." Only one American has this distinction, Varian Fry. He was a young magazine editor who traveled to Marseilles after Germany had overrun France in the summer of 1940. As the representative of a private relief agency, he offered aid and advice to refugees threatened with extradition to Nazi Germany under Article 19 of the Franco-German armistice, the "Surrender on Demand" clause. Fry spent thirteen months working secretly with a small number of associates and helped more than 1,500 people escape from France. Far from being considered a hero at the time, however, Fry was recalled to the United States. He wrote a memoir of his experience in 1945 that was largely forgotten until the U.S. Holocaust Memorial Museum renewed interest in Fry's work with a special exhibition. It is difficult to capture the excitement, danger, and importance of his work by excerpting sections of the memoir, so, instead, the following selection comes from the Afterword written by the curator of the Holocaust Museum exhibit, Elizabeth Kessin Berman, which offers an overview of Fry's work.

Varian Mackey Fry was born on October 15, 1907, and grew up in Ridgewood, New Jersey. He attended several prep schools, including Hotchkiss in Connecticut. At Harvard, he chose the prestigious but austere concentration, Classics. By tradition, his classical education would have sent him directly into the foreign service, a world requiring knowledge of history and culture, and excellence in languages. Harvard also nurtured his literary interests. As an undergraduate, he, together with his classmate, Lincoln Kirstein, was a founding editor of the journal *Hound & Horn*, an innovative and creative quarterly containing prose, poetry, and critical essays. One summer he set out on a tour of Europe, visiting major museums and surveying remote classical sites in Greece.

Fry's exposure to Europe's contemporary scene, as well as to its past heritage, influenced him. After graduation he returned to New York and began studies at Columbia University in the field of international affairs and journalism. By 1935, he established himself as a writer, succeeding the respected Quincy Howe as editor for *The Living Age,* a well-established monthly magazine that reprinted articles and stories from the foreign press. Three years later, he was appointed editor of Headline Books, an educational series of the Foreign Policy Association. He wrote position papers and policy pamphlets, intended by this educational "think tank" to influence American foreign policy in Europe and the Far East.

His travel to Germany in 1935, on behalf of *The Living Age,* made him an eyewitness to the brutal acts of Hitler's anti-Jewish policies. Fry returned to write his first news report describing a pogrom he had witnessed on the streets of Berlin. Shortly thereafter, he met Karl Frank (a.k.a. Paul Hagen), a young leader of Germany's ousted Social Democratic party. Taken by Frank's ardent and persuasive ideas, Fry agreed to help raise funds in the United States to support the anti-Hitler resistance activities of some of Frank's colleagues in Czechoslovakia. Eventually, Frank founded the American Friends of German Freedom, with the influential educators Dr. Frank Kingdon (then president of the University of Newark) and Reinhold Niebuhr (head of Union Theological Seminary, New York) as its principal spokespersons.

Fry's involvement with the American Friends of German Freedom intensified when Germany began to extend control over Europe. In June 1940, Fry was instrumental in organizing a luncheon held to raise funds to support the emigration of the young Social Democrats (the very ones Fry names in *Surrender on Demand* as his first clients at the Hotel Splendide). At the luncheon, held three days after France's capitulation to Germany on June 22, 1940, guests such as Erica Mann, daughter of Thomas Mann, argued that writers, artists, and intellectuals who op-

posed Hitler through their works were also threatened by Article XIX, the so-called "surrender on demand" clause of the Franco-German Armistice. On that day the Emergency Rescue Committee was formed.

In the weeks following the luncheon, the new committee solicited names of endangered intellectual and political refugees from a wide spectrum of prominent leaders in the United States. The German writer Thomas Mann and the French theologian Jacques Maritain joined with other celebrated academic and political exiles to draw up lists of persons caught up, as Fry put it, "in the most gigantic man-trap in history." Max Ascoli provided the names of at-risk anti-fascist Italians; Czech leader Jan Masaryk provided names of stateless Czechs; Alvarez del Vayo and Joseph Buttinger compiled names of Spanish and Austrian anti-Nazis, respectively. Other cultural and academic figures, including Alvin Johnson of the New School for Social Research and Alfred H. Barr, Jr., of the Museum of Modern Art, also sent in names of persons thought to be on the Nazis' "blacklist." These names were sent to the State Department for consideration of special emergency visitors visas. When no one came forward to go to France to help these individuals, Fry volunteered. He expected to contact each one, probably in relaxed, social circumstances, and hand out the money collected. He also assumed that it would be a routine matter to inquire about their individual visa cases at the American Consulate. Fry took a brief leave of absence from his post at the Foreign Policy Association. He suspected that it would take just three weeks to contact the few hundred people on the committee's lists. . . .

Fry persisted without assured funding and lacking home support, because he believed that all refugees who opposed Hitler, regardless of their political or intellectual status, were at risk of the "surrender on demand" clause. . . .

> At the end of January [1941] many of the refugees discovered they could get exit visas. I don't know for certain what the explanation of the sudden change of policy was, but from what I learned later, it seems it meant that the

Gestapo and the other secret-police organizations had completed the task of going over the lists of the political and intellectual refugees in France and decided which of them they wanted and which they would allow to slip through their net. . . . [N]ow we could openly engage in what had all along been our *raison d'etre*—emigration.

In stressing emigration rather than simply handing out relief, as the Red Cross and other relief organizations were doing, Fry saved thousands of persons who would have been interned. Even as he tried to determine who was "blacklisted," for political and cultural reasons, Fry regarded with much concern the increase in anti-Jewish statutes appearing in Vichy France. The first was issued in October 1940, a little more than a month after his arrival in Marseille. Fry wrote of the fate of his most famous Jewish client, the artist Marc Chagall, who was apprehended in late spring, as an example of the application of the anti-Jewish laws. Fry learned that Chagall was arrested not because he was known by the authorities as an esteemed painter whose art had been declared "degenerate," but because he was Jewish. . . .

Fry Is Recalled

His wife, Eileen Hughes Fry . . . launched an aggressive appeal among a prestigious circle of American intellectual figures. They sent a barrage of telegrams and letters to top State Department personnel, pleading for the extension of Fry's work on behalf of refugees. In France, Fry sought support for his mission, engaging leading French cultural and intellectual figures who did not choose to emigrate, including André Malraux, André Gide and Henri Matisse. Ultimately, this effort was unable to help him. The United States Government finally prevailed. The brief letter Eleanor Roosevelt wrote to Eileen Fry on May 13, 1941, accurately describes the situation:

Dear Mrs. Fry:

Miss Thompson gave me your message and I am sorry to say that there is nothing I can do for your husband.

I think he will have to come home because he has done things which the government does not feel it can stand behind. I am sure they will issue him a passport to come home even though it means that someone else will have to be sent to take over the work which he is doing.

Very sincerely yours,
Eleanor Roosevelt
[Varian Fry Papers, Rare Book and Manuscript Library, Columbia University]

Even with his expulsion, disgraceful and undignified as it was, Fry made efforts to contrive ways for refugees to escape. . . .

While Fry was in France, the Emergency Rescue Committee had actively organized exclusive fund-raising dinners, auctions, and lectures. But they failed to gather money to support the wide-ranging rescue effort Fry had championed. The Emergency Rescue Committee found that it could raise money for the likes of Franz Werfel, Lion Feuchtwanger, Konrad Heiden, and Marc Chagall. However, finding public funds for uncelebrated refugees, such as those who sought Fry's aid in Marseille, was difficult indeed. The paperwork required by the United States was overwhelming for the Emergency Rescue Committee's limited staff. . . .

Fry kept no diary while in France; he was compulsive about destroying lists and papers. . . . Fry's cover organization, the Marseille-based *Centre Américain de Secours,* had codes for keeping financial documents and cables. As Fry had always feared censorship and confiscation, he never recorded specific underground operations. . . .

One Person Made a Difference

Despite the array of hurdles—and they were formidable—Fry managed to set in motion an extraordinary rescue effort, rare during World War II. The results were remarkable. Though Fry never took time to count actual cases, he and his coworkers estimate that he was able to offer aid to some 4,000 people. Of these, between 1,200 to 1,800 persons found their way to safety, clandestinely or legally, as a result of his direct efforts. Fry himself claims that he reviewed the cases of 15,000 persons, an astounding number, considering the minimal support and financial backing he had at his disposal and also considering the slow process of issuing visas that the United States consuls had adopted after the fall of France in June 1940.

What Fry did, given his position and his prior experiences, was indeed scandalous, adventurous, and, in the end, blatantly courageous. Fry's escapade was a rare episode of civilian valor worthy of attention, particularly at that time in history. While not a soldier or political leader (Fry was turned down by his draft board due to a history of duodenal ulcers), he did what was completely extraordinary for an American civilian. He engaged black-marketers, organized a network of smugglers, rescued British soldiers from Occupied France, reported on internment camps, set up routes, and arranged illegal escapes across the mountains. All this he did with the aid and collaboration of inexperienced relief workers, wealthy socialites, American students, and with the refugees themselves.

His contributions to the cultural and intellectual climate in New York were hardly less significant than his spontaneous acts of valor. New York was well on its way to becoming the world's center of the modern art world, now that Marcel Duchamp, André Breton, André Masson, and Max Ernst were exhibiting there, publishing their journals and gathering younger American artists to them. The writers to whom Fry had especially tended—Franz Werfel, Heinrich Mann, and Lion Feuchtwanger—were comfortably settled in Los Angeles at the time of the Golden Age of American cinema. Other writers in New York such as Konrad Heiden, Hans Sahl, Walter Mehring, Ivan Heilbut, Arthur Koestler, Hans Habe, Hans Natonek, Leo Lania, and Hertha Pauli, were trying

to establish themselves. Exiled academics were seeking appointments to faculties in the United States, including scientists such as Nobel Prize–winning physicist Otto Meyerhof, and social philosopher Hannah Arendt. Fry's contributions, measured by any scale, are concrete. . . .

Fry's abiding narrative teaches that one person's actions did have consequences during an unprecedented assault on humanity and its culture. It is fitting that Fry, an unsung American who accomplished so much, and who is now recognized as the only American to have saved Jews during the Holocaust by Israel's Yad Vashem, was the subject of the inaugural special exhibition of America's national memorial to victims of the Holocaust. The United States Holocaust Memorial Museum's exhibition, AS-SIGNMENT: RESCUE, *The Story of Varian Fry and the Emergency Rescue Committee,* stresses, as Fry did in *Surrender on Demand,* that one person is able to run against the tide of public opinion and inhumane governmental policy. In his letter to Eileen, days after his expulsion, Fry admits that, despite his role in saving thousands of persons, it was the triumph over his own hesitations that made his story exceptional:

I have had an adventure—there is no other but this good Victorian word—of which I never dreamed. I have learned to live with people and to work with them. I have developed or discovered within me powers of resourcefulness, of imagination, and of courage which I never before knew I possessed. And I have fought a fight against enormous odds, of which, in spite of the final defeat, I think I can always be proud.

Barcelona, September 7, 1941
[Varian Fry Papers, Rare Book and Manuscript Library, Columbia University]

Aristides de Sousa Mendes: Opening the Gate to Freedom

Maria Júlia Cirurgião and Michael D. Hull

One of the few avenues for Jews and others to escape the Nazis early in the war was through Portugal. If those fleeing could reach the country, they could find ships to safe havens. One problem for the refugees, however, was crossing Spain to get there. To do that it was necessary to have documents that would allow entry to Spain and later Portugal. The Portuguese Premier was more concerned with the danger of his country being dragged into the war than saving refugees and he ordered his diplomats not to issue any visas without approval from Lisbon. One man, Aristides de Sousa Mendes, chose to ignore these orders and in so doing saved thousands of lives. He was the right person in the right place at the right time, but his heroic efforts were punished rather than applauded by his superiors. The remarkable story of another of the less celebrated rescuers is told in this article written by Maria Júlia Cirurgião and Michael D. Hull.

Excerpted from Maria Júlia Cirurgião and Michael D. Hull, "Aristides de Sousa Mendes: Angel Against the Blitzkrieg," *Lay Witness*, October 1998. Reprinted with permission from Catholics United for the Faith, Inc.

 brutal new mode of warfare spread fear across Western Europe in the spring of 1940: *blitzkrieg.*

The theory of lightning war—armored thrusts with aerial support—had been developed in the 1930s by British strategists led by Capt. Basil Liddel Hart. But, although they had invented the tank, the British never fully exploited the use of armor as a striking weapon.

Across the English Channel, the concept was readily adopted in Adolf Hitler's Germany, where Field Marshal Heinz Guderian developed and perfected panzer warfare. Unleashed on Poland in September 1939, blitzkrieg crushed the gallant Polish Army in 28 days and, as one author put it, "the death rattle of a people could be heard around the world."

Now, in the bright spring of 1940, blitzkrieg was loosed again. Early that May, fast-moving German armor and infantry columns rumbled into Belgium and Holland and, bypassing the vaunted Maginot Line, mushroomed into France. The River Meuse was crossed at Sedan on May 14, and the Nazi spearheads fanned out across France. Outgunned, outmaneuvered, bewildered, and dispirited, the French Army reeled southward before the German juggernaut.

Panic and confusion reigned across France, and the muddy roads were jammed with refugees fleeing southwestward toward the Pyrenees. Hundreds of thousands of French joined the long columns of Belgians, Dutch, Poles, and Jews, a straggling mass of humanity with only one aim: to keep moving, away from the Germans.

French writers have called the multitude that crammed the roads of France for hundreds of miles "le peuple du désastre" ("the people of the disaster"). By some accounts, they numbered in the millions.

They used everything that could move—cars, trucks, farm wagons, and pushcarts laden with belongings. Men, women, and children wept and shouted. When their means of transportation eventually broke down, or simply ran out of gasoline, they were abandoned. There was no fuel to be found.

Terrified and dazed from weariness, hunger, and thirst, the refugees continued on foot. Few had much money, and few knew where they were going. They trudged along, pinning vague hopes on the southwestern port of Bordeaux. Beyond lay the Pyrenees, and neutral Spain and Portugal. . . .

Latent anti-Jewish sentiment, rekindled by Nazi propaganda, mounted in Bordeaux, making it a hotbed of despair for the most helpless. Sea passage, at suddenly skyrocketing prices, was promptly booked up by the wealthy. Escape by land was possible only through neutral Spain and Portugal. From Lisbon, passage to countries beyond Europe was obtainable. A Portuguese transit visa was necessary to exit France, though, for at the same time Spain permitted no refugee to enter her territory who could not present one.

Generalissimo Francisco Franco, mindful of the blood debt he owed Hitler for assistance to his fascist cause during his country's civil war, was determined to keep Spanish soil rigorously closed off to the pitiful multitude fleeing the oppression of Nazism. The policy did double duty: It showed support for the Führer, and kept unwanted settlers out of his still unsettled Spain, where widespread hunger and consequent ill-health plagued the population. Bread was scarce and already severely rationed.

And thus, in Bordeaux, thousands of desperate refugees stormed the well-appointed Portuguese Consulate at *14 Quai Louis XVIII*, each hoping to gain the all-important Portuguese transit visa before the German Army arrived. They did not know the person in charge of the consulate, only that someone in the building now held their earthly fates in his hands. Hope for a signature and consular stamp that would allow them to pass through Spain and enter the little country with a long coastline and seaports kept thousands rooted to the pavement day and night, in an ever-widening circle around a building that had become unapproachable.

Consul-General Aristides de Sousa Mendes was in charge of the Portuguese Consulate in Bordeaux, in 1940. His colleagues esteemed him an able and dedicated career diplomat. When history catapulted him overnight to the position of custodian of human lives hanging in

Consul-General Aristides de Sousa Mendes

the balance, he proved that he was far more.

For the hope that the refugees pinned on the consul as Consul of Portugal in Bordeaux was quite ill-founded. The consul served Portugal's Premier António de Oliveira Salazar, on whose mind weighed heavy concerns. But the plight of those displaced by the blitzkrieg was not one of these.

The policy of strict neutrality Salazar had formally adopted from the outbreak of the war placed him in the unenviable position of having to juggle two suddenly antagonistic claims on his country's loyalty. England could invoke the Anglo-Portuguese Alliance—the world's longest-standing diplomatic union dating back to the 1386 Treaty of Windsor—to demand concessions in service of her cause. Closer to home, Salazar was also bound to Spain's Generalissimo by the March 1939 Treaty of Friendship and Nonaggression (or *Pacto Ibérico*). . . .

As he saw it, were Franco to join the Axis powers, Portugal would be inexorably annexed into some kind of Germanized grander Spain. . . .

Defying Orders

On Nov. 11, 1939, Salazar issued a directive forbidding his diplomats in Europe from granting transit visas to certain categories of people without express permission from Lisbon. The categories included "Jews expelled from the countries of their nationality or those from whence they issue," and "stateless persons," plus "all those who cannot freely return to the countries whence they come.". . .

On May 17, 1940, Salazar gave the lock another turn: *"Under no circumstances"* was any visa to be granted, unless previously authorized by Lisbon on a case-by-case basis. In practical terms, the new orders from Lisbon meant that the calamities beyond the Pyrenees were to remain beyond the Pyrenees. Portugal was to steer clear of any show of unfriendliness toward Germany, or Spain.

And so, the wretched multitudes around *14 Quai Louis XVIII* were looking for their salvation from someone whose authority had been virtually suspended. As a diplomat, Consul-General

Sousa Mendes had nothing to offer them. What happened next is the little-known story of a man who rose above all personal considerations and did the diplomatically unthinkable: He rebelled against service orders and used his office to overturn them, on behalf of humanity.

First in Bordeaux, then in Bayonne and in the streets of Hendaye near the Spanish border, Aristides de Sousa Mendes indiscriminately issued transit visas for entry into Portugal to an astounding 30,000 refugees, beating the Nazis to their lives. By sheer magnitude of daring and weight of numbers, Sousa Mendes effectively opened up a refugee escape route where none had existed. It would remain through the war and be used by an estimated million refugees. He paved that route with all he had: his good name, position, income, health, friends, and the future of his loved ones.

"I recognize as an act of God that such a man as this was at the right place at the right time," Moise Elias of New York would write 26 years later to the Yad Vashem Holocaust Remembrance Authority. Elias was, with his wife, among the fortunate who, in 1940, happened upon "The Angel of Bordeaux," as Sousa Mendes has been called. By best estimates, 10,000 of the men, women, and children he saved were Jews, who would have ended up in German labor or death camps.

But Sousa Mendes' conscience pitted him against Salazar. Although a mild version of his tyrannical contemporaries, Salazar nonetheless tolerated no disobedience. Both the hero and his humanitarian feat were officially repudiated. For decades, no mention of Sousa Mendes was allowed in the country where he spent the rest of his days as an outcast. The ostracism extended to his family, inflicting suffering on his wife and children. . . .

Standing with God

Salazar's orders restraining his diplomats from granting entry into Portugal to victims of armed invasion were read by his consul-general in Bordeaux with profound revulsion. He found the denial of refuge to the helpless morally objectionable, and the specific targeting of Jews legally objectionable for violating Portuguese constitutional guarantees of non-discrimination on the basis of religious belief, for purposes of granting asylum. For this Christian family man and seasoned diplomat, the inviolability of values held sacred in peacetime remained sacred in war.

Within days of the new orders, Sousa Mendes was taken to task for having granted a visa to a Viennese refugee, Professor Arnold Wiznitzer. Called to task by his superiors, Sousa Mendes answered:

He informed me that, were he unable to leave France that very day, he would be interned in a concentration [read, *detention*] camp, leaving his wife and minor son stranded. I considered it a duty of elementary humanity to prevent such an extremity.

The infraction was only the first. By April 1940, he had violated regulations often enough to earn a stern official reprimand. The Portuguese border patrol, an arm of the PVDE, kept watch for his transgressions and reported them to his superiors. . . .

Too prudent a father to disregard service orders heedlessly, Sousa Mendes fired off hundreds of telegrams to Lisbon, assisted by his 20-year-old son Pedro Nuno. Each telegram had to be written in code, detailing the individual visa requests. Pedro Nuno carried the stacks to the telegraph office, and ensured that they were expedited.

From Lisbon there was mostly silence.

By the second week of June, with talk of an impending Franco-German armistice in the air, tensions increased and law officers had to be posted in and around the consulate. Aristides and Angelina had opened their home to as many of the neediest as the walls could hold. Angelina cared for them. . . .

More and more, as the silence from Lisbon continued, Aristides and Angelina were living the disaster with the victims. Twice, the consul cabled his superiors requesting authority to deal with the emergency. He was tersely referred to the directives that were already in place. He had his orders, and only Lisbon could approve visas. All told, Sousa Mendes was to remain marooned

amidst thousands of the "shipwrecked"—his word to describe the refugees—and he was to accommodate the Nazis, who were virtually at the door.

On June 12, Franco changed Spain's status from "neutral" to a more menacing "non-belligerent." Salazar depended on Teotónio Pereira, his ambassador in Madrid, to keep a finger on Franco's pulse. The Germanophile envoy opposed any change in policy regarding refugees, and warned that sheltering "the scum of the democratic regimes" would bode ill for Portugal in the eyes of Spain.

Too Much Pressure

The effect that Lisbon's unremitting silence had upon Sousa Mendes was recorded in an extant account by his student nephew, César, the son of his twin. César Mendes Jr. had left Paris where he attended the university and taken refuge in Bordeaux. He wrote:

All the rooms in the consulate building were full of people. They slept on chairs, on the floor, on the rugs. Even the consul's offices were crowded, with dozens of refugees who were exhausted, dead tired, because they had waited days and nights on the street, on the stairways, and finally in the offices.

They could not take care of their needs, they did not eat or drink for fear of losing their places in the lines, which happened nevertheless and caused some disturbances. My uncle fell ill, and had to take to his bed. . . . He got up, impelled by a "divine power"—these were his own words—and gave orders to grant visas to everybody.

The three days of Aristides's confinement, June 14, 15, and 16, bear precious witness to Angelina's valor. She became the rock, bearing up under the pressure and sustaining her husband as he lay prostrate, rent by anguish. One son, Sebastian, later heard the father speak of a night spent entirely in prayer, together with his wife. It was during those three days that his father's hair turned white, wrote Sebastian.

What is certain is that on June 17, Aristides

de Sousa Mendes was a man free of all diplomatic constraints, who worked thereafter exclusively to rescue refugees by the thousands, and who could not be intimidated.

The work started immediately. It was an assembly-line operation. Passports were gathered in stacks and in bags. One person stamped them, others filled in the required wording, and the consul signed them. To save time, he often abbreviated his signature to simply "Mendes." No fees were collected, and no entries made in the consular registry. . . . To the countless numbers who had no documents, visas stamped on pieces of paper were handed out.

The work continued all through June 17 until well past midnight, and hardly a dent was made on the crowds: Marshal Henri Pétain's radio address, that day, which left no doubt that an armistice between France and Germany would be signed, on Germany's terms, had brought new waves to the *Quai Louis XVIII.*

The marathon recommenced on the 18th. That day, Henry Count Degenfeld entered the consulate with 19 passports for the imperial family of Austria. Otto of Habsburg's name was at the top of Hitler's blacklist. The count was told to return later that night. The woes of the Habsburgs weighed no heavier on Sousa Mendes than those of the people who had waited days and nights.

After 10 p.m., the count returned and received visas for the Archduke of Austria and his entire household. Then, the archduke went himself to the consulate and obtained a large quantity of visas, stamped on paper, for Austrian refugees in hiding.

Otto of Habsburg and his retinue crossed Spain undisturbed, and entered Portugal on June 20. Not long after, the archduke was informed by Salazar that Hitler had demanded his extradition. The demand would be refused, the Portuguese ruler told him, but hinted that his safety was precarious. The Habsburgs departed for the United States. . . .

Although he did not use force, Salazar did recall his stray consul, on June 24, by way of telegram. Sousa Mendes made full use of his freedom of movement. He remained in France

until July 8, and spent himself in saving the endangered. He had initiated an exodus, and as long as his name and his consular stamp could compel the Spanish border patrol to let refugees through, he would not stop.

The thousands of visas emitted by Sousa Mendes were honored at Irún, on the Spanish border, because the consular stamp made them an official request from one country to another. The *Pacto Ibérico* provided for such niceties between the two nations. But passage through Spain was one way only, with no stops; on that point the Spanish were adamant. As the trains of refugees pulled in at Vilar Formoso, on the Spain-Portugal border, the PVDE raged. The Spanish replied that if they had honored the visas out of courtesy, the Portuguese certainly were bound by them. And the refugees were allowed in.

Sousa Mendes' stand was a *fait accompli* to which Salazar and his political police had to bow. A mechanism had been set in motion: once the refugees crossed the bridge at Hendaye-Irún and were granted passage through Spain, there was no return. Sousa Mendes had forced open an escape route for many.

"It was indeed my objective to save all those persons, whose affliction was beyond describing," he declared later to his government, in a handwritten statement extending to several pages. "The imperatives of my conscience . . . never ceased to guide me in the performance of my duties, with perfect knowledge of my responsibilities," he affirmed.

In Bordeaux, the consulate continued to be besieged through June 19. That night, German planes bombed the city. Panic-stricken, the crowds decamped and ran blindly for Bayonne and Hendaye, closer to the Spanish border. Sousa Mendes left his wife and sons in Bordeaux, and followed the terror-driven refugees.

He made his way through the perilously congested road to Bayonne, where he found the small Portuguese consulate encircled by some 5,000 persons, with another 20,000 lined up along the streets. The consular staffers were effectively caged in, and had devised a passageway for themselves through the roof. As for visas to the distraught, the orders from Lisbon were being faithfully obeyed.

Normal service rules gave Sousa Mendes jurisdiction over the Bayonne consulate. He promptly assumed control: visas to everyone. Reassuring his caged-in subordinate, Consul Machado, that he assumed all responsibility, Sousa Mendes recruited all available hands and duplicated in Bayonne the Bordeaux "visa assembly line." Over the next 48 hours, thousands heard their names called out and were handed the precious, life-giving signature and consular stamp.

Meanwhile, Consul Machado felt obliged to wire Lisbon and report the breach of norms. For good measure, he also telephoned Ambassador Pereira in Madrid. Pereira had no jurisdiction over consulates in France. All the same, he prepared to travel to the frontier and see for himself. It was a trip that would prove fatal to many.

On the afternoon of June 22, Sousa Mendes left Bayonne for Hendaye. France had submitted to the armistice terms dictated by Germany, and the panic of those on the run reached new and explosive levels. They took to the road in a mad frenzy, pushing for the Spanish border. Sousa Mendes wanted to be there.

From Lisbon, two cablegrams were expedited that day, one to Bordeaux the other to Bayonne, instructing Sousa Mendes to stop. But he did not receive either one. By now he was in the streets of Hendaye, handing out large numbers of visas. At this stage, many of the "visas" were odd scraps of paper, variously worded to the effect that the bearers had the right to enter Portugal, and would Spain kindly grant them passage through her territory. The unorthodox documents kept the great exodus moving. . . .

The Door Is Shut

As the afternoon of June 23 drew to a close, Portugal's highest envoy to Spain, Ambassador Pereira, arrived at Irún to survey the anomaly, and took great offense at what he saw. He wrote:

> I came across Consul Aristides Mendes and asked him to explain to me such an extraordinary behavior. . . . From all that I heard, and

from his greatly unkempt appearance, my impression was of a disturbed man, not in his right mind. . . . Mr. Aristides Mendes' behavior suggested such derangement that, as I proceeded on the spot to inform the Spanish authorities of my decision to declare null and void the visas granted by the Consul of Bordeaux to those who were still in France, I had no qualms in stating that I was certain that the consul in question had lost the use of his faculties.

> . . . As the war wore on, many of Europe's persecuted passed through Spain and Portugal to freedom. As to those whom Pereira cut short, their numbers and fates are unknowable. The AP news agency related, the following day, that some 10,000 persons were trying to cross over into Spain, but that authorities no longer recognized certain Portuguese visas. . . .

Much of Sousa Mendes' work among the refugees has been lost to history, but it is known that he began to lead groups to an obscure border post where the guard knew nothing of Teotónio Pereira, and that he did not leave the streets of Hendaye until June 26, when the Germans moved into Bayonne. Returning to Bordeaux, he found Salazar's cablegram, dated June 24: He had been relieved of his post and was ordered to leave France.

Sousa Mendes did not rush. Wehrmacht units started occupying Bordeaux on June 27, and Hendaye the following day. Many thousands were now definitively trapped. He had more work to do. Portuguese passports could prevent deportation to concentration camps, so he began to issue them discreetly. Many were spared by this action, but it did not go unreported for long. He was again censured by Lisbon, and ordered again to leave France.

Sousa Mendes left Bordeaux on July 8.

From Hero to Outcast

The return of the solitary hero of Southwestern France posed a dilemma for Premier Salazar. He named a disciplinary council to define charges against the errant consul and determine penalties. But defining charges was not easy. Cities and towns were filled with refugees from many countries, openly voicing gratitude to the regime that had facilitated their rescue in the nick of time. The consul's disobedience had brought the government much good press. A *Life* magazine spread on July 29, 1940, dubbed Salazar "the greatest Portuguese since Henry the Navigator.". . .

To his credit, Salazar did not again close the country's borders against war refugees. Nor did he ever forgive Sousa Mendes for having forced his hand. He refused to see again his ex-consul of Bordeaux, or to communicate with him in any way. After an acceptable amount of paper shuffling, the disciplinary council determined Sousa Mendes' case one of "professional incapacity." He was rendered contemptible, and officially shunned. The voluminous case files were closed, classified, and locked up.

For Aristides de Sousa Mendes, now a disgraced non-person, the rest of his days would be one long Calvary. He tried many times to obtain a proper hearing, but met a wall of silence. His twin, César, attempted to intervene on his behalf, and found himself suspended from his own post for five years.

Unable to return to employment or be retired, Sousa Mendes and his family were in effect consigned to starve. The education of the younger children had to be cut short, and the older ones could not find jobs. In Salazar's Portugal, all ears were deaf to those shunned by the autocratic ruler. The family began to take meals, along with refugees, at a Lisbon soup kitchen run by the Hebrew Immigrant Aid Society (HIAS).

Occasionally, Sousa Mendes was summoned for a supposed interview with Salazar. He would be kept waiting in the vestibule all day, and then dismissed. Former colleagues ignored his greetings. He was closely watched and interrogated by the PVDE. Active files were also kept on his older children.

The financial hardship and protracted humiliation took a toll. Weeks before the end of the war, Sousa Mendes suffered a stroke which left him partially paralyzed. The children stood by him, as did Angelina, but her own health did not hold for long.

The brave and noble-hearted wife of Aristides de Sousa Mendes had assuaged great pain as streams of suffering humanity invaded her life and her Bordeaux home in those terrible post-blitzkrieg weeks of 1940. But Angelina lacked the strength to see her husband through his punishment. She suffered a cerebral hemorrhage in 1948, and never regained consciousness. . . . Angelina died, at 60. . . .

Sousa Mendes survived his wife by six years. He hoped that some day his good name would be restored by his government, but it did not happen.

With the help of the HIAS, the traumatized Sousa Mendes children emigrated, one by one, to seek lives in Belgium, Africa, Canada, and the United States.

A destitute outcast in his own country, Aristides de Sousa Mendes died on April 3, 1954. . . .

Next to the half-ruined house stands a memorial: a 40-foot monument to Christ the King, attesting to the spirit of a man who told his government "I would stand with God against man, rather than with man against God." Sousa Mendes had the monument erected, at nearly ruinous personal expense in 1933. . . .

Historians have estimated that one million refugees fled from Nazism through Portugal during World War II. The precedent was forcibly created in 1940 by Aristides de Sousa Mendes, who paid in suffering for his deed.

Selection 7

Chiune and Yukiko Sugihara: Japanese Saviors

Eric Saul

The Japanese were allies of Hitler and the enemies of the United States in World War II. They committed many atrocities against U.S. soldiers during the war in the Pacific. Though one can find evidence of anti-Semitism (and other forms of racism) in Japanese society, the Japanese did not participate in any way in the Final Solution. One may argue that this was partly because few, if any, Jews lived in Japan or the areas under its control, but it is more likely that the Japanese did not share Hitler's obsession with the Jews or his interest in exterminating them. In fact, one Japanese diplomat was responsible for rescuing more Jews than perhaps anyone except Raoul Wallenberg. Chiune Sugihara and his wife, Yukiko, were the right people in the right place at the right time. Sugihara defied his superiors, sacrificing his career for the sake of others. Eric Saul's little-known but remarkable story is told in the following excerpt from "Visas for Life: The Remarkable Story of Chiune and Yukiko Sugihara."

Excerpted from Eric Saul, "Visas for Life: The Remarkable Story of Chiune & Yukiko Sugihara," an online article found at www.us-israel. org/jsource/Holocaust/sugihara.html. Reprinted with permission from the author.

In March 1939, Japanese Consul-General Chiune Sugihara was sent to Kaunas to open a consulate service. Kaunas was the temporary capital of Lithuania at the time and was strategically situated between Germany and the Soviet Union. After Hitler's invasion of Poland on September 1, 1939, Britain and France declared war on Germany. Chiune Sugihara had barely settled down in his new post when Nazi armies invaded Poland and a wave of Jewish refugees streamed into Lithuania. They brought with them chilling tales of German atrocities against the Jewish population. They escaped from Poland without possessions or money, and the local Jewish population did their utmost to help with money, clothing and shelter.

Before the war, the population of Kaunas consisted of 120,000 inhabitants, one fourth of which were Jews. Lithuania, at the time, had been an enclave of peace and prosperity for Jews. Most Lithuanian Jews did not fully realize or believe the extent of the Nazi Holocaust that was being perpetrated against the Jews in Poland. The Jewish refugees tried to explain that they were being murdered by the tens of thousands. No one could quite believe them. The Lithuanian Jews continued living normal lives. Things began to change for the very worst on June 15, 1940, when the Soviets invaded Lithuania. It was now too late for the Lithuanian Jews to leave for the East. Ironically, the Soviets would allow Polish Jews to continue to emigrate out of Lithuania through the Soviet Union if they could obtain certain travel documents.

By 1940, most of Western Europe had been conquered by the Nazis, with Britain standing alone. The rest of the free world, with very few exceptions, barred the immigration of Jewish refugees from Poland or anywhere in Nazi-occupied Europe.

Against this terrible backdrop, the Japanese Consul Chiune Sugihara suddenly became the linchpin in a desperate plan for survival. The fate of thousands of families depended on his humanity. The Germans were rapidly advancing east. In July 1940, the Soviet authorities instructed all foreign embassies to leave Kaunas. Almost all left immediately, but Chiune Sugihara requested and received a 20-day extension.

Except for Mr. Jan Zwartendijk, the acting Dutch consul, Chiune Sugihara was now the only foreign consul left in Lithuanania's capital city. They had much work to do.

The Dutch Connection

Now into summer, time was running out for the refugees. Hitler rapidly tightened his net around Eastern Europe. It was then that some of the Polish refugees came up with a plan that offered one last chance for freedom. They discovered that two Dutch colonial islands, Curacao and Dutch Guiana (now known as Suriname), situated in the Caribbean, did not require formal entrance visas. Furthermore, the honorary Dutch consul, Jan Zwartendijk, told them he had gotten permission to stamp their passports with entrance permits.

There remained one major obstacle. To get to these islands, the refugees needed to pass through the Soviet Union. The Soviet consul, who was sympathetic to the plight of the refugees, agreed to let them pass on one condition: In addition to the Dutch entrance permit, they would also have to obtain a transit visa from the Japanese, as they would have to pass through Japan on their way to the Dutch islands.

Sugihara's Choice

On a summer morning in late July 1940, Consul Sempo Sugihara and his family awakened to a crowd of Polish Jewish refugees gathered outside the consulate. Desperate to flee the approaching Nazis, the refugees knew that their only path lay to the east. If Consul Sugihara would grant them Japanese transit visas, they could obtain Soviet exit visas and race to possible freedom. Sempo Sugihara was moved by their plight, but he did not have the authority to issue hundreds of visas without permission from the Foreign Ministry in Tokyo.

Jews wait to receive Japanese transit visas during World War II.

Chiune Sugihara wired his government three times for permission to issue visas to the Jewish refugees. Three times he was denied. The Japanese Consul in Tokyo wired:

CONCERNING TRANSIT VISAS REQUESTED PREVIOUSLY STOP ADVISE ABSOLUTELY NOT TO BE ISSUED ANY TRAVELER NOT HOLDING FIRM END VISA WITH GUARANTEED DEPARTURE EX JAPAN STOP NO EXCEPTIONS STOP NO FURTHER INQUIRIES EXPECTED STOP

(SIGNED) K TANAKA FOREIGN MINISTRY TOKYO

[None of the Jews who had applied for visas to Sugihara had met these legal requirements. Sugihara decided to issue the visas anyway.]

Visas for Life

After repeatedly receiving negative responses from Tokyo, the Consul discussed the situation with his wife and children. Sugihara had a difficult decision to make. He was a man who was brought up in the strict and traditional discipline of the Japanese. He was a career diplomat, who suddenly had to make a very difficult choice. On one hand, he was bound by the traditional obedience he had been taught all his life. On the other hand, he was a samurai who had been told to help those who were in need. He knew that if he defied the orders of his superiors, he might be fired and disgraced, and would probably never work for the Japanese government again. This would result in extreme financial hardship for his family in the future.

Chiune and his wife Yukiko even feared for their lives and the lives of their children, but in the end, could only follow their consciences. The visas would be signed.

For 29 days, from July 31 to August 28, 1940, Mr. and Mrs. Sugihara sat for endless hours writing and signing visas by hand. Hour after hour, day after day, for these four weeks, they wrote and signed visas. They wrote over 300 visas a day, which would normally be one month's worth of work for the consul. Yukiko also helped him register these visas. At the end of the day, she would massage his fatigued hands. He did not even stop to eat. His wife supplied him with sandwiches. Sugihara chose not to lose a minute because people were standing in line in front of his consulate day and night for these visas. When some began climbing the compound wall, he came out to calm them down and assure them that he would do his best to help them all. Hundreds of applicants became thousands as he worked to grant as many visas as possible before being forced to close the consulate and leave Lithuania. Consul Sugihara continued issuing documents from his train window until the moment the train departed Kovno for Berlin on September 1, 1940. And as the train pulled out of the station, Sugihara gave the consul visa stamp to a refugee who was able to use it to save even more Jews.

After receiving their visas, the refugees lost no time in getting on trains that took them to Moscow, and then by trans-Siberian railroad to Vladivostok. From there, most of them continued to Kobe, Japan. They were allowed to stay in Kobe for several months, and were then sent to Shanghai, China. Thousands of Polish Jews with Sugihara visas survived in safety under the benign protection of the Japanese government in Shanghai. As many as six thousand refugees made their way to Japan, China and other countries in the following months. They had escaped the Holocaust. Through a strange twist of history, they owed their lives to a Japanese man and his family. They had become Sugihara Survivors.

Despite his disobedience, his government found Sugihara's vast skills useful for the remainder of the war. But in 1945, the Japanese government unceremoniously dismissed Chiune Sugihara from the diplomatic service. His career as a diplomat was shattered. [He always felt that he was dismissed for his actions in helping to save Jews in Lithuania. He was told by the foreign ministry it was because of that "incident in Lithuania."] He had to start his life over. Once a rising star in the Japanese foreign service, Chiune Sugihara could at first only find work as a part-time translator and interpreter. For the last two decades of his life, he worked as a manager for an export company with business in Moscow. This was his fate because he dared to save thousands of human beings from certain death.

The Miracle of Chanukah 1939

The makings of a hero are many and complex, but Sugihara's fateful decision to risk his career may have been influenced by a simple act of kindness from an 11-year-old boy. He lived with his family in Lithuania, and his name was Zalke Jenkins (Solly Ganor).

Solly Ganor was the son of a menshevik refugee from the Russian revolution in the early 1920s. After the Russian revolution the family moved to Kaunas, Lithuania. The family prospered for years before World War II in textile import and export. Young Solly Ganor, concerned about Polish Jews entering Kaunas, gave most of his allowance and savings to the Jewish refugee boards. Having given away all of his money, he went to his aunt Annushka's gourmet food shop in Kaunas. He went there to borrow a Lithuania lit (Lithuanian dollar) to see the latest Laurel and Hardy movie. In his aunt's store he met Japanese Consul Chiune Sugihara. Consul Sugihara overheard the conversation and gave young Solly two shiny lit. Impulsively, the young boy invited the Consul with the kind eyes to his family celebration of the first night of Chanukah 1939.

The surprised and delighted Consul gratefully accepted the young boy's offer, and he and his wife Yukiko attended their first Jewish Chanukah celebration.

Mr. Sugihara commented on the closeness of the Jewish families and how it reminded him of his family, and of similar Japanese festivals. Fifty-four years later, Mrs. Sugihara remembers with delight the cakes and cookies and desserts offered to them during this Jewish festival of lights.

Solly Ganor and his father were soon friends with the Consul-General and they conversed in Russian. Later Solly Ganor and his father witnessed Consul Sugihara in his office calling the Russian officials to get permission to issue visas across the Russian borders. Solly Ganor and his father later received Sugihara visas but were unable to use them because they were Soviet citizens.

Most of the Ganor family were murdered in the Holocaust. Solly's sister Fanny and Aunt Annushka survived the war. Aunt Annushka returned to Lithuania and died in 1969. Fanny married Sam Skutelsky from Riga and eventually settled in the United States. Their son Robert, Solly's only living nephew, now lives in Boulder, Colorado.

Solly and his father spent over two years in the Kaunas ghetto before being deported to the Landsberg-Kaufering outer camps of Dachau in late 1944. They survived the war and moved to Israel. The older Ganor died peacefully in Tel Aviv in 1966.

Ironically, in May 1945, Solly Ganor was liberated by Japanese American soldiers of the 522nd Field Artillery Battalion, men who had been interned in their own country.

Sempo Sugihara

To Solly, the Japanese face has come to symbolize kindness and liberation.

Who Was Chiune Sugihara?

For the last half century people have asked, "Who was Chiune Sugihara?"

They have also asked, "Why did he risk his career, his family fortune, and the lives of his family to issue visas to Jewish refugees in Lithuania?" These are not easy questions to answer, and there may be no single set of answers that will satisfy our curiosity or inquiry.

Chiune (Sempo) Sugihara always did things his own way. He was born on January 1, 1900. He graduated from high school with top marks and his father insisted that he become a medical doctor. But Chiune's dream was to study literature and live abroad. Sugihara attended Tokyo's prestigious Waseda University to study English. He paid for his own education with part-time work as a longshoreman and tutor.

One day he saw an item in the classified ads.

The Foreign Ministry was seeking people who wished to study abroad and might be interested in a diplomatic career. He passed the difficult entrance exam and was sent to the Japanese language institute in Harbin, China. He studied Russian and graduated with honors. He also converted to Greek Orthodox Christianity. The cosmopolitan nature of Harbin, China, opened his eyes to how diverse and interesting the world was.

He then served with the Japanese-controlled government in Manchuria, in northeastern China. He was later promoted to Vice Minister of the Foreign Affairs Department. He was soon in line to be the Minister of Foreign Affairs in Manchuria.

While in Manchuria he negotiated the purchase of the Russian-owned Manchurian railroad system by the Japanese. This saved the Japanese government millions of dollars, and infuriated the Russians.

Sugihara was disturbed by his government's policy and the cruel treatment of the Chinese by the Japanese government. He resigned his post in protest in 1934.

In 1938 Sugihara was posted to the Japanese diplomatic office in Helsinki, Finland. With World War II looming on the horizon, the Japanese government sent Sugihara to Lithuania to open a one-man consulate in 1939. There he would report on Soviet and German war plans. Six months later, war broke out and the Soviet Union annexed Lithuania. The Soviets ordered all consulates to be closed. It was in this context that Sugihara was confronted with the requests of thousands of Polish Jews fleeing German-occupied Poland.

Sugihara, the Man

Sugihara's personal history and temperament may contain the key to why he defied his government's orders and issued the visas. Sugihara favored his mother's personality. He thought of himself as kind and nurturing and artistic. He was interested in foreign ideas, religion, philosophy and language. He wanted to travel the world and see everything there was, and experience the world. He had a strong sense of the value of all human life. His language skills show that he was always interested in learning more about other peoples.

Sugihara was a humble and understated man. He was self-sacrificing, self-effacing and had a very good sense of humor. Yukiko, his wife, said he found it very difficult to discipline the children when they misbehaved. He never lost his temper.

Sugihara was also raised in the strict Japanese code of ethics of a turn-of-the-century samurai family. The cardinal virtues of this society were *oya koko* (love of the family), *kodomo no tamene* (for the sake of the children), having *gidi* and *on* (duty and responsibility, or obligation to repay a debt), *gaman* (withholding of emotions on the surface), *gambate* (internal strength and resourcefulness), and *haji no kakete* (don't bring shame on the family). These virtues were strongly inculcated by Chiune's middle-class rural samurai family.

It took enormous courage for Sugihara to defy the order of his father to become a doctor, and instead follow his own academic path. It took courage to leave Japan and study overseas. It took a very modern liberal Japanese man to marry a Caucasian woman (his first wife; Yukiko was his second wife) and convert to Christianity. It took even more courage to openly oppose the Japanese military policies of expansion in the 1930s.

Thus Sempo Sugihara was no ordinary Japanese man and may have been no ordinary man. At the time that he and his wife Yukiko thought of the plight of the Jewish refugees, he was haunted by the words of an old samurai maxim: "Even a hunter cannot kill a bird which flies to him for refuge."

A Final Tribute: Righteous Among the Nations

Today, more than 50 years after those 29 fateful days in July and August of 1940, there may be more than 40,000 who owe their lives to Chiune and Yukiko Sugihara. Two generations have come after the original Sugihara survivors, all owing their existence to one modest man and his family. After the war, Mr. Sugihara never mentioned or spoke to anyone about his extraordinary deeds. It was not until 1969 that Sugihara was found by a man he had helped save, Mr. Yehoshua Nishri. Soon, hundreds of others whom he had saved came forward and testified to the Yad Vashem (Holocaust Memorial) in Israel about his lifesaving acts of courage. After gathering testimonies from all over the world, Yad Vashem realized the enormity of this man's self-sacrifice in saving Jews. And so it came to pass that in 1985 he received Israel's highest honor. He was recognized as "Righteous Among the Nations" by the Yad Vashem Martyrs Remembrance Authority in Jerusalem.

By then an old man near death, he was too ill to travel to Israel. His wife and son received the honor on his behalf. Further, a tree was planted in his name at Yad Vashem, and a park in Jerusalem was named in his honor.

Forty-five years after he signed the visas, Chiune was asked why he did it. He liked to give two reasons: "They were human beings and they needed help," he said. "I'm glad I found the strength to make the decision to give it to them." Sugihara was a religious man and believed in a universal God of all people. He was fond of saying, "I may have to disobey my government, but if I don't I would be disobeying God."

Consul Chiune Sugihara, age 86, died on July 31, 1986. Mrs. Yukiko Sugihara had her 83rd birthday on December 17, 1996. She now lives in Kamakura City, Japan.

Selection 8

Le Chambon: The Town with a Conscience

Susan Zuccotti

A number of individuals risked their lives to save Jews. One case of rescue, however, involved not just a handful of people scattered about an occupied country but an entire town that acted as one to protect the Jews who lived there and any who came seeking refuge. This was the French town of Le Chambon-sur-Lignon. Could every town have acted as this one did and, by doing so, prevented the Holocaust? Certainly not. The Nazis would have burned other places to the ground if need be to root out the Jews. This did not happen to Le Chambon in part because of its location. This excerpt describes this and some other unique features that allowed the town to be a haven. Still, it would have taken only one person to betray the entire town. What was it about these people that kept them united in their rescue effort? Susan Zuccotti, who teaches modern European history at Barnard College and Columbia University, offers an explanation for the behavior of this righteous town.

"Roughly fifty kilometers from Puy-en-Velay and about forty kilometers from Saint-Étienne, there is a little town, Le Chambon-sur-Lignon, the tiny capital of the plateau of the same name, an ancient Protestant village. There you can still find the caves where the Protestants gathered to practice their religion as well as to escape the king's dragoons." Thus begins Joseph Bass's postwar report on a remote village on a pine-studded plateau, about 960 meters above sea level, in the Massif Central west of Valence and the Rhône River. Léon Poliakov, who helped Bass hide Jews there, later described the department of Haute-Loire where Le Chambon is located as "one of the poorest and wildest regions of the Cévennes." Its Protestant inhabitants, he added, "distrust all authority, listening only to their conscience—or their pastors."

Long before Bass and Poliakov arrived there, hundreds of Jewish and non-Jewish refugees had already found their way to Le Chambon. Some had wandered into town as early as the winter of 1940–41. Most came independently at first, advised by friends or casual acquaintances of an isolated village of about 1,000 people, reputedly sympathetic. Newcomers found shelter with village families or with the roughly 2,000 peasants, most of them also Protestant, in the surrounding countryside. Others took rooms in one of more than a dozen hotels and boardinghouses in this popular summer resort area of pine forests, clear streams, and bracing air. Most were trying to escape internment, and most, needless to say, were not legally registered.

During the late spring and early summer of 1942, many foreign Jews and non-Jews released from internment camps to the care of charitable agencies also came to Le Chambon. Local institutions to care for them multiplied, openly and legally. Madeleine Barot and other young Protestant social workers of the CIMADE established a family residence at the Hôtel Coteau Fleuri, outside of town. Quakers, with help from Le Chambon's Pastor André Trocmé, funded a boardinghouse for young children. Older students joined two farmschools operated by the Secours suisse, or moved into residences of the École Cévenol, a private Protestant secondary school slightly north of the village. Still others were welcomed at the École des roches in the village itself.

In August 1942, French police rounding up recent Jewish immigrants in the unoccupied zone did not overlook Le Chambon. They arrived in the village with three empty buses, demanding that Pastor Trocmé provide a list of resident Jews. Trocmé not only claimed ignorance, somewhat truthfully, of names and addresses but promptly sent his Protestant Boy Scouts to even the most distant farms to warn Jews to hide. Other local residents had undoubtedly already seen the approach of the police up the valley, along a road visible for miles from the plateau. Then and later, that visibility was one secret to security in Le Chambon. Police searched the region for two or three days and returned regularly for several weeks. They apparently netted only one victim, an Austrian who was later released because he was only half-Jewish.

Jews literally poured into Le Chambon after August 1942. By this point, their presence was totally unofficial. They came with the Service André—Bass later reported that the pastor never hesitated to help him—and with OSE and other clandestine networks. Some stayed in Le Chambon only long enough to find a guide to Switzerland, but many remained, hidden with families or in boardinghouses or schools. They kept coming until, as Poliakov observed, "in some hamlets, there was not a single farm which did not shelter a Jewish family." Roughly 5,000 Jews are estimated to have been hidden among the 3,000 native residents, all of whom knew about the refugees.

In his memoirs, Poliakov describes with touching detail his arrival at a local hotel with a group of Jewish children in 1943:

Frightened, they hovered in a corner of the room. The first peasant couple enters: "We will take a little girl between eight and twelve years old," explains the woman. Little Myriam is called: "Will you go with this aunt and uncle?" Shy and frightened, Myriam does not answer. They muffle her up in blankets and carry her to the sleigh; she leaves for the farm where she will live a healthy and simple life with her temporary parents until the end of the war. . . . In a flash, all the children were similarly housed, under the benevolent eye of Pastor Trocmé.

A Man of Conscience

Who was this pastor whose name appears in every account of Le Chambon-sur-Lignon during the war? Born in Saint-Quentin in Picardy in northern France in 1901, André Trocmé studied at the Union Theological Seminary in New York City, where he met his future wife, Italian-born Magda Grilli, in 1925. A pacifist and conscientious objector, Trocmé made no secret of his beliefs after his arrival in Le Chambon in 1934. Indeed, he and Pastor Édouard Theis, the director of the École Cévenol, were equally frank after 1940 about their dislike of the Vichy regime and the racial laws. Trocmé often spoke from the pulpit about the evils of racial persecution; Theis taught the same principles at the École Cévenol. On August 15, 1942, during a visit to the village by the Vichy youth minister, Georges Lamirand, and the departmental prefect and subprefect, several older students at the school presented the officials with a letter protesting the July 16 roundup in Paris and expressing local support of the Jews.

Trocmé, Theis, and Roger Darcissac, the director of the public school in Le Chambon, were arrested by French police in February 1943 and held for a month. At the end of the year, the two pastors went into hiding. During that period, Theis served as a guide for CIMADE, escorting refugees to Switzerland. Magda Trocmé continued her husband's work during his absence; one scholar has judged that she was at least as important as he in saving lives. Mildred Theis kept the École Cévenol open and continued to shelter refugees. The two women had many aides. Bass remembered pastors named Poivre, Leenhardt, Jeannet, Curtet, Betrix, Vienney, and Besson from surrounding hamlets, as well as the Trocmés' good friend Simone Mairesse. Municipal officials also cooperated, if only by looking the other way. And the people of the plateau, often influenced by their outspoken pastors but guided as well by their own sense of justice, continued to protect their Jewish guests until the Liberation. Of them, Bass wrote after the war, "The conduct of the Protestant pastors and men of action of the plateau of Le Chambon deserves to be told to Jews throughout the entire world."

Why Here?

In considering the rescue of Jews in Le Chambon, two questions arise: why was the local population so sympathetic, and why was it so successful? To answer the first, Madeleine Barot stresses the special status of Protestants in France as a minority persecuted by Catholics. Protestants in Le Chambon still told tales of persecution around their hearths on cold winter nights and visited caves where their ancestors had hidden. The memory of persecution made them suspicious of authority, sympathetic to other minorities, and comfortable with clandestine life. In addition, many French Protestants were skeptical about the Vichy regime, in part because authoritarianism often bodes ill for minorities, but especially because . . . "[Marshall Philippe] Pétain dedicated France to the Virgin, and made it an intensely Catholic state." Finally, Christian anti-Semitism notwithstanding, Bible-reading Protestants of the type living around Le Chambon sometimes articulate a special affinity for the Jews, based on a shared reverence for the Old Testament and a common acceptance of God's special compact with his chosen people.

These various factors certainly did not apply to all French Protestants. Many, especially those of the assimilated and highly educated urban classes who were more removed from their historical and cultural roots, were favorably inclined toward the Vichy regime for the same economic and social reasons as their Catholic neighbors, and held the same variety of attitudes toward Jews. But Protestants around Le Chambon cherished their historic memory. That love, combined with the sturdy individualism and independence of mountain people and the leadership of a group of exceptional pastors, made Le Chambon an equally exceptional place.

But why were the rescuers of Le Chambon so successful? Admittedly, even they had their tragedies and their victims. In the spring of 1943, the Gestapo raided the École des roches, seizing many students along with their dedicated director, Daniel Trocmé, Pastor Trocmé's second cousin. Nearly all, including Daniel, died in deportation. But the Germans did not return and thus failed as miserably as the French police to find most of the Jews they knew were there. Why?

Geographic factors were important. The isolation of the area was made even more extreme by the closing of access roads in winter. Any movement on those same approach roads could be seen from the plateau. Thick forests were good for hiding. The Gestapo and the French Milice, busy elsewhere, were reluctant or perhaps afraid to enter a hostile area that, however dedicated by its pastors to nonviolence, was surrounded by armed Resistance fighters. Why stir up a sleeping hornets' nest? French police and gendarmes not only shared that reluctance but were also affected by local sympathies for refugees.

Two witnesses tell amusing stories. Madeleine Barot later declared of her own experience, "When the *gendarmes* in Tence received an order for an arrest, they made a habit of dragging themselves along the road very visibly, of calling a halt at the café before tackling the steep ascent to the Coteau, announcing loudly that they were about to arrest some of those 'dirty Jews.'" Poliakov confirms the description, explaining that when the gendarmes received an arrest order, "they went to the [local] Hotel May and ordered a glass of wine: comfortably seated at their table, they took their papers from their satchels and spelled out 'Goldberg . . . it's about someone named Jacques Goldberg.' Unnecessary to add that when they arrived at Goldberg's domicile half an hour later, the latter was long gone." Poliakov adds that when a more serious danger approached in the form of the Gestapo or the Milice, a telephone call of warning usually preceded them from the valley.

Barot's and Poliakov's accounts both allude to the most important factor in the rescue success rate in Le Chambon—the determination of local residents to protect their guests. The people of Le Chambon lived in a state of constant alertness, with a warning system prepared. Their solidarity also made it difficult for potential informers to act. To whom could they safely leak information? Municipal authorities sympathized with the majority, as did, it appeared, many of the police. Even local censors of mail were likely to prevent a denunciation. In such a situation, a careless informer might even put himself in danger. In addition, it was psychologically more difficult for a solitary anti-Semite or opportunist to express his bile in a region where he was bucking an obvious majority. He could not so easily convince himself that he was acting as a "good and loyal Frenchman." And in any part of France—where so many individual arrests of Jews by preoccupied and understaffed local Gestapo units were prompted by denunciations—the reluctance of informers was decisive.

Selection 9

Polish Rescuers

Nechama Tec

One of the most difficult places for Jews to survive was Poland. In fact, almost the entire Jewish community, roughly 3 million people, were murdered by the Nazis. Between imprisoning the Jews in ghettos and deporting them to concentration and death camps, it was nearly impossible to escape. Still, Poland had by far the largest number of non-Jews who risked their lives to save their Jewish neighbors. Yad Vashem has recognized more than five thousand Poles as "Righteous Persons," and that number undoubtedly underestimates the total. As this excerpt illustrates, Poles sometimes became rescuers by accident, and other times they went out of their way to help. It was always difficult and dangerous. Nechama Tec is a sociology professor at the University of Connecticut.

*W*hen I met Hela Horska in 1978 in Warsaw she was widowed and lived alone under modest circumstances. This was in sharp contrast to her prewar and wartime position as a nurse and wife of a prominent Polish doctor. During the war she and her husband protected fourteen Jews for over two years. How did this aid come about?

The Horskis lived close to a Jewish section of

Excerpted from Nechama Tec, *When Light Pierced the Darkness.* Copyright © 1986 Oxford University Press, Inc. Reprinted with permission from Oxford University Press, Inc.

a small town. Dr. Horski was a busy physician. During the war, he was assisted by his wife. After the establishment of the ghetto, the Horskis were approached by a Jewish woman patient who begged them to employ her thirteen-year-old son David Rodman. The mother feared that the boy's delicate health would not withstand the strenuous work the Nazis demanded of him. Feeling sorry for the mother, Hela secured permission from the authorities to employ young David, arguing that her work with her husband did not leave enough time for her children and house chores. Soon the boy became an asset because of his winning personality and his hard work. Eventually he won the hearts of the entire family, including the children. Once David had become a valued member of their household, it seemed natural for his employers to want to shield him from danger. Whenever they heard about moves against Jews they warned him and hid him in their house. Eventually David felt secure enough to ask that this privilege be extended to other members of his family. Each time there was to be a deportation in the ghetto a few of his relatives would come and hide, until their number grew to fourteen. During the final liquidation of the ghetto, David's entire family remained in the Horski household. The Rodmans asked for a week's stay, and the Horskis agreed to keep them. David and his relatives expected to be smuggled into Hungary, where at that time the Jews still lived in relative safety. A week passed, but the

Hungarian trip did not materialize. The Rodmans had no place to go, and the Horskis did not have the heart to send them away. Weeks turned into months, and eventually into two years, and then the end of the war.

Different, and yet similar, is Emil [Adam] Jablonski's story. During the war Adam shared a one-room apartment with his wife and mother-in-law. He made a modest living as an administrator of a building. His protection of a Jewish friend, a lawyer, started as follows: *It was 1942, the gates of the building were locked, the curfew was on. I heard a hesitant knock at the door. When I looked, there was Kazik, dirty, unshaven, and sad. I rushed to cover the window so that no one would see him from the outside. Then I asked him in. He told me that the Polish woman with whom he had been staying had sent him away. He had gone to a few friends, but they had all refused to keep him. He assured me that he did not want to endanger me, he had an address to which he would go the next day. He hoped to find permanent shelter there.*

We let him take a bath, fed him, and made him a bed. Because he looked Jewish, he could go out only in the dark when people could not see him well. For his safety I decided to accompany him to the new address. When we reached the place the owner of the apartment, too scared to even talk to us, emphatically refused to shelter him. He had another lead that he followed up and that also resulted in a definite refusal. He had no more addresses. He had nowhere to go.

What could I do? I took him back to my house. I discussed it with my wife. She agreed with me that we could not let him go and die. We decided to keep him until we could find someone with a less exposed place than ours. In the meantime we moved a closet away from the wall, and placed his bed there. And this was where he stayed for over two years. . . .

A Warning Saves Lives

How a seemingly simple act of warning could have far-reaching consequences is illustrated by Bolesław Twardy's experience. Already in 1940, Bolesław had illegally transported Jewish friends from Lódź to Warsaw. This act was soon followed by Bolesław's warning to an entire Jewish community about an impending disaster. How did this happen?

One day a school friend of mine (a Pole) told me that the ghetto Brzeźiny was going to be liquidated. This was a small town that made a living only from tailoring: they made suits for sale in Africa. . . . I wanted to warn them. I went in a carriage pretending at the gate that I was carrying food. I knew, because I worked for the secret service in the underground, that at a certain hour a carriage moved into the ghetto with food. . . . I had friends there. I warned them about the impending liquidation and they simply ran away. Only those that did not want to fight for their life remained, old people, sick, those who were afraid. . . .

A Daring Escort

A single act of escorting someone to a new place was relatively brief; yet such acts often led to dangerous, unexpected complications. This is illustrated by Tomasz Jursky's experience, who as an underground worker had frequently smuggled Jews out of the Warsaw ghetto. When, on April 18, 1943, Tomasz approached the ghetto to bring two Jews to his father's house, he found the entire area surrounded by guards and the opening he usually used for slipping in and out blocked. Young and adventurous, Tomasz was not about to give up. Instead, he sneaked into an adjacent house and waited for a favorable moment. Just before the curfew he succeeded in entering the ghetto. Inside a creeping tension seemed to envelop him. Something was going to happen, it was in the air. Whatever it was, it created an overall fear and anxiety.

Many ghetto inmates knew Tomasz. Some were convinced that he was a Jew who lived on the Christian side, pretending to be a Pole. On that night his friends urged him to move out. Those he came for had already left.

But the late hour prevented Tomasz from leaving, and he decided to stay overnight. The next day was April 19, 1943, the start of the Warsaw ghetto uprising. As yet, the fighting had not spilled into Tomasz's part of the ghetto. All routes of escape, however, seemed sealed. As he searched for a way out, Tomasz met two young Jews who, like he, were eager to leave. The three promised to cooperate. Eventually the two young men managed to bribe a policeman who stood guard while Tomasz and his two companions climbed over the ghetto stone wall and into the Christian world. The fate of those left behind belongs to history; only a handful survived. . . .

Hiding Jews

Poles who hid Jews were faced with more burdens than those who simply had passing Jews share their homes. Building an appropriate hiding place that would withstand the scrutiny of unexpected Nazi raids was a major concern. Feeding the fugitives was another important requirement. Throughout the German occupation, food was scarce. Only those who were officially registered were entitled to special rationing cards. Food on the black market was expensive, but available. The majority of both Polish rescuers and survivors report giving and receiving food.

The cost, however, was not the only burden involved in feeding illegal Jews. Buying and carrying large quantities of food could be dangerous if noticed by the wrong people.

Stefa Krakowska, who hid fourteen Jews, shared the food shopping with her father. They each bought in faraway places where they were unknown and also tried to shop at different times of the day. Varying the hours reduced the chance of neighbors seeing them carrying large quantities of provisions.

Those who hid large numbers of Jews frequently devised ingenious ways of purchasing and getting food into their homes, the most common of which involved rotating the shopping places, hours, and people who did the buying.

Another ever-present potential hazard related to the fugitives' health.

How does one call a doctor for someone who does not exist? Worse still, how does one bury a body that isn't there? More often than not, those in need of medical care did not know about the existence of the special underground units that offered medical aid to fugitives. The presence of such units remained a well-guarded secret both from the authorities and from most of those dependent on such aid.

The rescuers and the rescued were each aware about the disastrous turn that a fugitive's serious illness could take. And when, as inevitably happened, people became sick, neither the rescuers nor the other fugitives could avoid sharing the suffering.

David Rodman is still haunted by such memories.

Moving to a different time and place, imagine a barn in a Polish village with a small attic with a low ceiling. The attic has no toilet facilities, no water, no light. A square opening with a steep ladder leaning against it serves as the entrance and as the main pathway for air. The only other way through which air reaches the area is a small window on the side of the barn, close to the roof. Both of these openings make for poor ventilation. The attic was built as an extra storage room. Most of the time it is empty. In the summer the heat beats mercilessly upon its thin roof making the inside unbearably hot.

In the past no one was affected or worried about the poor ventilation or heat. The war changed all this. Fourteen Jews, ranging in age from three-and-a-half to sixty are brought into these cramped quarters by an old Pole who wants to save them. The straw scattered on the ground serves as their beds. A single pail becomes their toilet. Most nights their protector comes to take care of them. He brings them water, bread, and potatoes. It is not easy to feed fourteen people. It is dangerous. Here in the village people are suspicious of one another, the neighbors are inquisitive. Some nights seem especially threatening. The old man is afraid. At such times the Jews have to do without food and water. They wait.

Washing is out of the question, as is the changing of clothes. Dirt, lice, and different kinds of vermin, no one can even identify, become their constant companions. Names of the vermin don't matter. What matters is that fourteen human beings are defenseless, and at the mercy of these small and yet terrifying intruders that crawl all over them and bite. Their skin becomes infected and full of sores. Reduced to this pitiful condition some of the fugitives seriously consider giving up. Instead, they make a superhuman effort not to complain, especially not in the presence of the Pole, their savior. After all, they are among the lucky ones. They ought to be grateful. The alternative is death. As they wait and wait they cannot even decide which season is less desirable, bitter winter or the oppressive summer.

This is the summer. The vermin are viciously active. Water is in short supply. The stench coming from a variety of directions is strong and nauseating. Now one more problem is added. Someone is sick. Medical attention is out of reach. No one knows what is wrong with the "old woman." She lies on her infested dirty straw, unable to move. She is too weak to defend herself against the crawling, invading pests. They take advantage of her. They are merciless. Her face is red. Her fever must be high. Her lips are parched. She does not ask for water. There is none. She does not ask for anything. Only her distorted features tell that she is in agony. Her eyes speak, not her lips. Her eyes are conscious and knowing. Those eyes see the approaching end.

Only from time to time, she makes an effort and moves her lips. And it is then that those around her hear again and again the same whispered words: *Oh my God, my body may bring disaster to you, what will you do with my body. How will you manage. . .?* The patient died. At night, secretly and in stages, they buried her dismembered body in the garden. . . .

Ignoring Danger

At times even when faced with grave dangers some helpers chose to continue their protection. The reactions of Jan Rybak, the peasant who saved Pola Stein, illustrates this choice.

One winter night the Nazis moved into the village looking for Russian partisans. As they searched one house and then another, news about their raid spread throughout the village. The Steins and their protector knew that it was only a question of time before the Nazis would pay

them a visit as well. They also knew that the attic, which up until now had served as a hiding place and protected Pola and her father from inquisitive neighbors, was unsafe. It was unrealistic even to hope that the Nazis would not discover the place. Therefore, together, they decided that Pola and her father should move to the nearby forest, and return after the raid. Father and daughter dressed warmly against the winter night and were ready to go. Outside a blizzard raged, making furious and terrifying noises.

Eight years old, Pola was afraid of the dark, the cold, and the forest. She was aware of what was happening and clung to her father's coat for protection. She tried to act bravely, but when the time came to hug the Rybaks goodbye, hot tears made their way down her cheeks, slowly and silently. Through misty eyes she noticed with surprise that Jan, their strong and independent host, was also crying, openly and without embarrassment. Then, almost in defiance, he reached for her hand, then to his wife he said: *They were so long with us, if we have to die we will die together. The child will freeze in this snow!* They stayed and the Nazis never came to their farm. . . .

A Matter of Time

Just how time could make a difference between life and death is illustrated by Franek Dworski's experience. During the war Franek, his wife, and little daughter shared their modest house with many who had to hide from the Nazis. Most frequently their illegal guests were Jewish; at times they were Polish underground fighters. For those who turned to him, Franek performed all kinds of services. To some he offered food and shelter, for others he arranged false documents, for some he found employment, some he would escort from place to place. There was hardly a task Franek would have considered too difficult or unworthy of his attention.

On a particular fall evening, about half an hour before curfew, a strong wind, mixed with an equally strong rain, created a strange and threatening backdrop. In sharp contrast to the outdoor fury, the Dworskis' household was peaceful. At that point only two Jews who were passing as Christians shared their home. Both had false papers and both were officially employed, which meant that during a raid they did not have to hide.

On that evening as all of them were gathered around the table for their customary dinner of potatoes and dark bread, they heard a hesitant tap at the window. The same tap was repeated at the door. No one was either surprised or frightened, because people often came there for help. The tap itself was too uncertain, too gentle, too apologetic to suggest that it was anyone who intended to harm them. In any case, those present had relatively little to fear.

Indeed, the opened door admitted three harmless-looking beings: a man, a woman, and a girl not more than seven. The trio hesitated before entering and once inside stood, uncertain, huddled together, while the water from their soaked-through clothes formed puddles on the floor around them. They appeared exhausted, sad, and resigned. The child's red cheeks, shiny eyes, and unfocused look betrayed a high fever. At first speechless, they were soon encouraged by Franek's warm smile and welcoming greetings. They had been directed here by one of Franek's friends and explained that they would like to rest for one night only because a place was waiting for them in the country. Since they had no documents, they felt that it would be safer to reach their new shelter in daylight. They added that they had been forced to leave their present home in a hurry because they had been denounced.

Without hesitation the Dworskis agreed to let them stay. Right away their clothes were set out to dry. They were fed and told that they could sleep in the attic. Franek also explained that since their house was safe, there was no point in the three rushing off. On the contrary, they could rest here for a few days, at least until the child felt better. After that Franek would personally bring them to their new place. Grateful, the strangers went to bed.

At dawn violent knocking shook the entire house. Then heavy boots began to kick the door. Holding on to her daughter, Mrs. Dworski admitted five Gestapo. They pushed her roughly aside and spread swiftly around the ground floor. As they began to search they asked: "Where is the Jewish family? Where are you hiding them?" Clearly someone had tipped them off.

Then, without glancing at those present, the Nazis climbed the ladder to the attic. Left behind, the rest remained immobile and silent, avoiding each other's eyes.

Franek Dworski recalled: *Here were my wife and daughter, clinging to each other, both pale as if the blood had decided to leave their faces. I felt sorry for them—actually I personally had no regrets, only a wave of sadness for my wife and child came over me. This was it. Then I felt nothing. I still felt nothing when, obviously angry and disappointed, the Gestapo came down from the attic.*

What had happened? The Jewish family had sneaked out earlier, leaving the place in perfect order. The Dworskis later found an unsigned note under the mattress thanking them for the warm hospitality and explaining that they were leaving because they did not want to endanger the entire household.

Had the Dworskis refused to accept this Jewish family, these fugitives might have died. On the other hand, had this family stayed a few more hours this could have led to the death of eight people. Much could have happened in a brief span of time.

The Christian Thing to Do

Eric Silver

The people who saved Jews during the Holo-caust are given special recognition. They are rewarded for doing what was right and moral. Why? Because so few people at the time were willing to do so. It took courage to be a rescuer because the consequences of being discovered by the Nazis were severe. Punishment could range from arrest to exe-cution, and in some cases, it was not just the individual rescuer but a whole town that might be held responsible. Someone contem-plating taking a Jew in also had to worry about his or her neighbors. They, too, were scared or, in many instances, sympathetic to the Nazi agenda and prepared to betray their friends. It is particularly remarkable, there-fore, that the entire population in a handful of towns cooperated in sheltering Jews. One of those towns was Andonno, Italy. In this ex-cerpt, Eric Silver tells the story of a group of Italians, led by the village priest, who helped save the lives of a family of Jews fleeing Hitler. Silver is an Israeli journalist who has written for a number of major newspapers and has published several books.

n better times, young Albert Szajdholc felt, he might have enjoyed Christmas Eve in Andonno. The pitched roofs of the tiny

Alpine village, about 6,000 feet above the Italian Riviera, were thick with snow. But in December 1943, all he and his family of Jewish refugees could think of, hiding from the German army in a two-storey outbuilding hugging a side wall of the Catholic church, was keeping warm. Albert, his parents and two younger sisters had little fire-wood and still less to eat. They sat wrapped in blankets, huddling as close to the hearth as pos-sible. Their staple food was wild chestnuts, which grew in abundance on the mountainside. Sometimes they ate them raw, sometimes roast-ed, sometimes boiled for variety. Gradually, they had sold what few possessions they had kept in three years of running—his mother's gold ear-rings, gold from a broken denture—to supple-ment their diet. After trekking over the Alps from France three months earlier, the Szajdholcs had lived rough above Andonno, sleeping in shep-herds' huts, or in the open. As winter set in, the village priest, Father Antonio Borsotto, offered them shelter in a sparsely furnished room beside the church, although the Germans were constant-ly searching Andonno and neighbouring villages for partisans and other fugitives. If they found any trace, they burned, looted and murdered. The priest, a stern, solemn-faced man in his early thirties, was aware of the risk he was taking. So were his flock. There were no secrets in Andon-no. Another Jewish family—a woman, her son and daughter—was already being sheltered by a local teacher.

It was just before midnight on Christmas Eve.

. . . Forty years later, Albert still remembered the bitter cold and the dark sky alive with stars.

"We returned to the hearth and stared at the tiny flame as we reminisced about our own festive celebration of Hanukkah before the war. I closed my eyes and I could see my father lighting our beautiful silver *menorah* [candelabrum]. I could almost hear the sizzling of the traditional potato cakes being fried. . . . I shivered and returned to the not so pleasant present. We sat in a well of silence, each of us drawn into our dreams, when we heard someone rapping at the door. It was well past midnight and we looked at each other, a bit apprehensively. I opened the door a crack. Before me stood a wizened old woman, wrapped in a shawl. She handed me a package of cheese and then whispered a hoarse 'Buon Natale,' a Merry Christmas. Stunned by her gift, we thanked her profusely. She seemed embarrassed by our gratitude and hurried away. Minutes later, there was another knock on the door. I opened it again, and this time a villager offered me a basket of firewood, wishing us 'Buon Natale.' And then another woman came and brought us some bread. The villagers continued coming throughout the night, bringing us their gifts of food, clothing and wood. Poor people sharing with us from their own meagre resources. We were overcome. What had made them share with us, outsiders from a different country, believers in a different religion, strangers in their midst?"

The next morning broke bright and crisp. Christmas Day and the village was still and the world seemed at peace. Albert walked down the single, narrow street with its close-packed, flaking stucco houses. He met Giacomo Rosso, the local barber, wished him "Buon Natale" and then told him what had happened the night before. The barber put his hand on the nineteen-year-old Jew's shoulder and explained with a smile:

"In church last night, Father Borsotto told the story of the birth of our Saviour and the gifts brought to him by the Magi, as he does every Christmas. As usual he described how the Holy Family were lodged in a stable in Bethlehem, alone and friendless. And then how the Magi came with gifts for the Christ child. Father Bor-

sotto then said, 'Just as our Saviour couldn't find any lodging and was born in a manger, alone and rejected, so are Jews today alone and rejected. We have two Jewish families in our midst this Christmas and they too are alone, hungry, hunted for no reason except for being Jews.' Father Borsotto then told us we could now be the Magi and bring gifts to the Jewish families in Andonno."

Albert raced back to tell his parents. His father said, "We are fortunate to be in Andonno, among good Christians." He sent Albert to thank Father Borsotto. "My son," answered the priest, his eyes filling with tears, "you don't have to thank me. It was the Christian thing to do."

A Close Call

Although born in Warsaw, Albert had grown up in Brussels, where his father manufactured leather handbags. When the Germans invaded Belgium in 1940, the family fled with other Jews to southern France, hoping to escape to neutral Spain or Portugal. In Bayonne, the last town before the border, a hostile Polish consul refused to update their old passports. They were Jews, he said, not Poles. Without valid travel documents, they could not cross the Pyrenees. Instead, they took shelter in the village of St Martin Vesubie, above Nice, which was under Italian occupation. Benito Mussolini was Hitler's ally, but not his confederate in the extermination of European Jewry. He promulgated laws discriminating against Jews, but did not kill them.

When Mussolini signed an armistice with the Allies in September 1943, Albert and his family followed the Italian army back across the Alps to the spa of Valdieri. To their dismay, they found the Germans in control. Italy's war was not yet over. Along with other Jewish refugees, the Szajdholcs were ordered to assemble to be inspected for contraband. Few took this explanation at face value, but many complied, believing that they were bound for Paris. In fact, their destination was the Drancy deportation camp, en route to Auschwitz. Albert's father, Shlomo, was not deceived. He instructed his family to slip away and walk up the mountain. "Don't stop, or turn around, not even if somebody calls to you," he said. "Stop only if you hear shooting.". . .

Risky Business

As autumn turned to winter, a freezing wind pierced the wooden slats of the Szajdholcs' mountain refuge. Snow was in the air, and they knew that they could not stay up there much longer. Albert's brother, Alter, nearly two years his senior, had already left with his young wife, Sidi, to find lodgings in Valdieri. Albert and his seventeen-year-old sister, Mariette, went down to Andonno to seek help from Father Borsotto. The priest began by reminding them that it was extremely dangerous to shelter soldiers, partisans or anyone else on the run from the Wehrmacht. "The Germans have warned us that if they find partisans or even abandoned army uniforms in a village, they will burn down the house and maybe even worse," he frowned. They were not bluffing. A week after Christmas, a German truck filled with soldiers was attacked by partisans in Boves, a nearby village. They killed several soldiers before retreating into the mountains. The Germans retaliated by destroying the entire village. The priest was burned alive in his locked church.

In Andonno, Father Borsotto shook his head and paused for a moment, then told Albert and Mariette, "I know it's impossible for you to stay in the mountains through the winter. I will try to help you." That was how the Szajdholc family came to be in the room beside the church on Christmas Eve. Father Borsotto handed Albert the key and advised them to move in at night. "The villagers, of course, will know that you are in the room," he added. "That doesn't concern me. I am only concerned about strangers who might come by. Please tell your family to be very cautious.". . .

The refugees' idyllic Christmas proved to be no more than an interlude. Andonno was off the main road, but the Germans were coming too often for comfort. The Szajdholcs heard on the grapevine that Hungary, an ally of Hitler's, was issuing travel documents to Jews. Albert's sister-in-law, Sidi, volunteered to go to Rome with her mother and see the Hungarian consul. Their family came from Czechoslovakia, formerly part of the Austro-Hungarian Empire, and spoke Hungarian. While they were away, Albert's brother Alter rejoined the Szajdholcs in Andonno. A few days later, Mariette was sent to the nearest town with a neighbour's daughter, Marianna Giordano, to buy suitcases. They were preparing to move on, but soon after Mariette had left the family heard the clatter of gunfire in the mountains. A very agitated Father Borsotto pounded on their door. "You must leave the village immediately," he urged. "The Germans are attacking the partisans. If they find you here, they'll burn down the village.". . .

A New Refuge

Luckily, the Jewish family found a hut that had somehow been overlooked by the bombers. Despite the risk of another raid, they had no choice but to take shelter there. It was icy cold, but they did not dare light a fire for fear of drawing attention to themselves. All they could do was sit huddled together shivering. Towards evening they saw Mariette hurrying up the mountain. She and Marianna had heard the shooting, but had stayed in town until it was over. Marianna's parents, Usebio and Anna Giordano, were worried about the Szajdholc family. They knew it was impossible to stay overnight in the mountains without shelter, so they had sent Mariette to tell them to come back after nightfall. They would leave their barn door unlocked, but the Jews would have to return to the mountains by daybreak.

The first thing Albert did was to go back to the room beside the church to pick up some of their belongings. It was only then that he discovered how close a call it had been. German soldiers had ransacked the room. Clothes were scattered everywhere. Albert's father had left behind his *tefillin*, the leather straps and boxes which observant Jews bind on their arms and foreheads every day during morning prayers. Evidently, the Germans had not known what they were. If they had realized that Jews had been hiding there, they would surely have burned the house and the church, and perhaps even executed Father Borsotto.

The Giordanos kept a grocery store in the village. They had two daughters, Marianna and Anna, who had often played with the Jewish girls. Like everyone else in Andonno, they now knew how ruthless the Germans could be. Many of their neighbours in Boves had been killed during the search operation. The village had been surrounded and anyone trying to escape had been shot. Yet regardless of the danger, the Giordanos left the barn door open every night. . . .

"Every night, when we came in from the freezing cold, a pot of soup awaited us [Albert remembered]. Thanks to their compassion and generosity, we slept in the straw, warmed by the body heat of the animals. In the mornings, Sig-

nora Giordano prepared fresh straw for us. One day, while we were shivering in the snow up above, we were startled to see an old woman, swathed in black, making her way laboriously up the mountain. She was carrying a pot of hot soup for us. We could never find the words to thank these good simple people."

By the spring of 1944, Andonno's conspiracy of goodness came to an end. Sidi returned from Rome with Hungarian papers for the entire family. She had managed to convince the consul that the Polish-Belgian Szajdholcs were Hungarians. Albert became Alex Vamos from Budapest. The family went by train to Florence, then to Rome, where they stayed until the liberation. After the war, they settled in New York.

Selection 11

The War Refugee Board

Arthur D. Morse

As many of the articles in this volume have documented, the Allies in general, and the United States in particular, were not particularly interested in rescuing Jews. It was not until the beginning of 1944 that President Franklin D. Roosevelt created an organization, the War Refugee Board (WRB), to aid the targets of Hitler's extermination campaign. Despite the late start, the WRB did succeed in helping many people, but it was always fighting against the State Department and bureaucrats from other government agencies who opposed its work. This excerpt comes from

one of the earliest investigations of what the U.S. government did and did not do during the Holocaust. It was written by the late Arthur D. Morse, a journalist, television producer, and award-winning documentarian.

Excerpted from Arthur D. Morse, *While Six Million Died.* Copyright © 1967, 1968 Arthur D. Morse. Published by The Overlook Press, 1 Overlook Drive, Woodstock, NY 12498. Reprinted with permission from The Overlook Press.

*F*ranklin D. Roosevelt announced the formation of the War Refugee Board on January 22, 1944. Three days later a cable drafted by [treasury official] John Pehle was sent over the signature of [Secretary of State] Cordell Hull to all United States embassies, consulates and other diplomatic missions. It ordered that "action be taken to forestall the plot of the Nazis to exterminate the Jews and other persecuted minorities in Europe."

The practice of suppressing unpleasant information had ended. The message specified that "communication facilities should be made freely available to . . . private agencies for all appropriate messages for carrying out the policy of this Government.". . .

The objective of the board's Washington staff, which never exceeded thirty, was to develop positive, new American programs to aid the victims of Nazism while pressing the Allies and neutrals to take forceful diplomatic action in their behalf. Crucial to the success of the board would be the performance of its field representatives assigned to U.S. embassies in the neutral nations of Europe: Turkey, Portugal, Switzerland, Spain and Sweden. Pehle envisioned them increasing the flow of refugees to the neutrals, who would then funnel them to safety in North Africa, Palestine, and North and South America. The departure of refugees from the neutrals during this lifesaving cycle would also make room for new arrivals from Nazi-occupied territories. . . .

Breaking the Logjam

The strategic significance of neutral Turkey lay in its accessibility to refugees from Nazi-controlled Hungary, Rumania and Bulgaria. Once in Turkey, they could, theoretically, be moved by rail or sea to Palestine. But a bureaucratic minefield lay between the refugees and their objectives.

Hungarian Jews were denied permission by Rumanian authorities to travel through that country en route to Turkey. In their turn, the Bulgarians forbade transit papers to escaping Rumanian Jews who also sought to reach Istanbul. As if these were not sufficient barriers, the Turkish regulations allowed the entry of only nine families a week en route to Palestine from the three Nazi satellites.

The Jews who had run this formidable gauntlet would find themselves in Istanbul facing further hazard and delay. Immigrants to Palestine required certificates issued by British authorities and it took nine weeks to get them, assuming that nothing derogatory was discovered about the applicant. Even then the immigrant could not depart for his promised land. Turkish bureaucracy imposed an additional six- to eight-

week delay for exit visas.

Within days after the formation of the War Refugee Board, Ira Hirschmann reported to the U.S. embassy in Ankara. With strong support from the American ambassador, Laurence Steinhardt, he soon broke the bottleneck. First, Hirschmann persuaded Kemel Aziz Payman, the Turkish official who had delayed the visas, to streamline his languid procedures, and he impressed British officials with his mandate from the President of the United States. As a consequence, the fifteen- to seventeen-week lag in the issuance of British and Turkish documents was slashed to a maximum of three weeks. Hirschmann also found good use for the funds contributed by the Joint Distribution Committee. Working closely with representatives of the Jewish Agency for Palestine, who were operating covertly in Istanbul, Hirschmann fed these funds to the Black Sea captains, whose antiquated ships began ferrying Jews from Constanza in Rumania to Istanbul. The money was also used to obtain transit visas for travel through the Nazi satellites. Between April and August 1944, four thousand Jews were evacuated from the Balkans. From Turkey the refugees were transported by train to Syria, thence to Palestine.

Hirschmann and Ambassador Steinhardt arranged for their transportation and also assisted in obtaining the British permits for Palestine. Ironically, these had become available because only forty-three thousand of the seventy-five thousand Jews permitted to enter Palestine under the terms of the British White Paper of 1939 had managed to evade the Nazis. The British had therefore extended the deadline for immigration.

Hirschmann also brought order to the chaos created by the presence of representatives of competing Jewish organizations in Istanbul. He co-ordinated their efforts with Christian rescue groups and unified the approach to temperamental and often venal Turkish officials.

Leaning on Neutrals

In Washington the War Refugee Board was now bringing continuous pressure against the Axis satellites, reminding them that their mistreatment of the Jews would be remembered after the war. John Pehle and his colleagues fired off hard-hitting messages to the Axis powers via the neutrals, threatening retribution. This irritated the formalists at the State Department, who warned that these undiplomatic messages were placing the neutrals in an uncomfortable position. Nevertheless, they were delivered with good effect. In particular they struck terror in the Rumanian officials who had banished the Jews to Transnistria.

Ira Hirschmann in Ankara exploited this Rumanian fear. He had learned that Alexandre Cretzianu, the Rumanian minister to Turkey, did not share the Antonescu regime's anti-Semitic views, and he had armed himself with a letter from a former Rumanian ambassador to the United States. The letter urged Cretzianu to co-operate with Hirschmann and stressed the American determination to punish war criminals.

Through Gilbert Simond, a delegate of the International Red Cross, he arranged a meeting with Cretzianu at Simond's home. Prior to the establishment of the War Refugee Board, such a confrontation would have violated the law prohibiting dealings with enemy nationals. This regulation had been waived for representatives of the board, and Hirschmann's ability to "deal with the enemy" markedly enhanced his effectiveness.

At the start of their talk Hirschmann pointed out that a terrible fate awaited those of Cretzianu's countrymen who were adjudged war criminals. Then he demanded that the minister request his government to empty the Transnistrian concentration camps and return the Jews to their homes. By this date only 48,000 had survived of the 185,000 who had been deported and this helpless remnant lay in the path of the retreating German army. A massacre was in-

A pro-Nazi demonstration in Sofia, Bulgaria. Despite being under German control, Bulgaria eventually cancelled its anti-Semitic laws.

evitable and Hirschmann also informed the minister that the United States would hold the Rumanian government responsible. It did not take long to convince Cretzianu that he would share the fate of the other Rumanian officials, so he immediately agreed to recommend that the camps be evacuated and the Jews protected. In return Hirschmann promised to obtain four U.S. visas for the Cretzianu family. . . .

Hirschmann had met with Cretzianu on March 13. On March 17 the American embassy in Ankara was notified that the Rumanians had begun the transfer of Jews from the Transnistrian camps, and on March 20 Gilbert Simond relayed a message from the Red Cross in Bucharest that the safe return of the forty-eight thousand Jews had been completed.

Hirschmann also persuaded the Rumanians to issue transit visas, which enabled several thousand otherwise doomed Hungarian Jews to board rescue ships in Rumania for eventual sanctuary in Palestine. Thus the activities of one man, representing the United States government in Turkey, backed by concerned men in Washington and supported by a sympathetic ambassador, saved more than fifty thousand lives.

Bulgaria Reverses Course

The tireless Hirschmann . . . used similar techniques to pressure the Bulgarian government into revoking its anti-Semitic laws, which had been patterned after the Nuremberg legislation. Some twelve thousand "foreign" Jews had been deported from Thrace and Macedonia in 1943, and the forty-five thousand who remained within Bulgaria were living under a constant threat when Hirschmann made his first contact with the "enemy." Now his adversary was Nicholas Bala-banoff, the Bulgarian minister to Turkey. Like Cretzianu, Balabanoff promised that he would urge his government to moderate its policies. . . .

While Hirschmann threatened Balabanoff in Ankara, Pehle in Washington synchronized the overall offensive against the Bulgarians. Simultaneously, War Refugee Board representatives in other neutral capitals repeated the same theme to the local Bulgarian diplomats.

Early in August, Hirschmann and Balabanoff met again. . . . Hirschmann pressed the Bulgarian for a written statement affirming his government's intentions.

The following day, somewhat to Hirschmann's surprise, the letter arrived. Once again it was sympathetic and asserted that "arbitrary methods" would not be used against the Jews. Once again, however, it failed to guarantee a revocation of the discriminatory laws. Hirschmann now put in writing the advantages to the Bulgarian government if it abrogated the legislation. Taking a cue from his last conversation with Minister Balabanoff, he wrote: "Why send refugees in lost groups to strange lands if, as the Minister of their country asserts, they will gradually find themselves back in the position of respect and responsibility where they were before the war?" The letter was passed to the Sofia government by the daughter of a Bulgarian major general. It was one of several persuasive appeals. On August 30 the Bulgarian Cabinet announced that the laws would be revoked. This constituted the first cancellation of anti-Jewish legislation by any Axis country. It was particularly noteworthy because the United States and Bulgaria were still technically at war and the action represented direct defiance of Germany by one of its satellites.

The Complete History of

Aftermath

Chapter 7

By 1942, if not earlier, the Allies were well aware of the Nazi extermination campaign. It still came as a tremendous shock, especially to soldiers in the field, when the concentration camps were discovered and liberated. Even those who had knowledge of the Nazis' actions were unprepared for what they found in the camps. No one who has seen photographs or newsreels from the camps can forget the haunting images of corpses piled like wood, the charred remains of bodies in crematoria, and the walking skeletons who somehow survived. This chapter includes remembrances from some of the men who were the first to encounter the camps and those whom they found.

Once the war was over, the Allies had to decide on how to punish the people who had perpetrated what came to be called "crimes against humanity." The decision was not an easy one, and many officials simply favored executing the leading Nazis. In the end, thousands were put on trial, with the highest surviving officials tried at once at Nuremberg. Many Nazis escaped thanks to organizations like Odessa, which helped them evade capture and disappear into other countries, often under new identities. A few of these men, most notably Adolf Eichmann, were hunted down and brought to justice. Several selections here discuss the pursuit and trial of war criminals and raise interesting parallels to the treatment of those now accused of war crimes in places like the Balkans and Cambodia.

Selection 1

Americans Encounter the Camps

Harry Herder Jr.

Try to imagine what it would be like to be eighteen and fighting in a war, seeing men maimed and killed all around you. The blood, the fear, the noise, the smells. It is difficult to imagine what it must be like. Perhaps the closest most of us can get to understanding war is to watch a movie like Saving Private Ryan. *Despite all they saw and experienced in battle, none of the Americans were prepared for what they would find when they stumbled on the concentration camps. In most cases, soldiers were on patrol or advancing toward an objective when they ran into barbed wire enclosures. What they found within those fences would haunt many of them for the rest of their lives. One of the men who had this experience was Harry Herder, Jr. He was eighteen when his company accidentally liberated Buchenwald. This is an excerpt of his recollection of that experience. Herder later fought in Korea, where he lost a leg to an enemy land mine.*

O ver fifty years ago, I went through a set of experiences that I have never been able to shake from my mind. They subside in my mind, and, then, in the spring always, some small trigger will set them off and I will be immersed in these experiences once more. . . .

This all happened to a group of us on April 11, 1945. The things we found then were grotesque enough without knowing some of the other things we did learn later. . . . What I do remember is that we eventually drove up some gentle valley where there were trees on either side of us, when we made a sharp left turn, so sharp that those of us on the tops of the vehicles were grabbing things to keep from falling off. By the time we had regained our balance, there it was: a great high barbed wire fence at least ten feet high. Between us and the fence and running parallel to the fence was a dirt road, with high guard towers every fifty yards or so. Beyond the fence were two more layers of barbed wire fence not quite as tall. There seemed to be about five yards between those fences. The barbed wire in those fences was laced in a fine mesh, so finely meshed no one was going to get through it. Our tanks slowed down, but they did not stop; they blew straight at and through the barbed wire. . . .

None of us—well, none of us in the lower ranks—knew what it was we were up to or where we were, but we were fully expecting a fire fight with German troops, whose camp we had just stormed and taken, and we thought they would be angry at us. It turned out there were no German troops present.

Slowly, as we formed up, a ragged group of human beings started to creep out of and from between the buildings in front of us. As we watched these men, the number and the different types of buildings came to my attention. From them came these human beings, timidly, slowly, deliberately showing their hands, all in a sort of uniform, or bits and pieces of a uniform, made from horribly coarse cloth with stripes running vertically. The stripes alternating a dull gray with a dark blue. Some of those human beings wore pants made of the material, some had shirt/jackets, and some had hats. Some only had one piece of the uniform, others had two, many had all three parts. They came out of the buildings and just stood there. . . .

Contact with the Survivors

Hesitatingly we inched closer to that strange group as they also started inching closer to us. Some of them spoke English, and asked, "Are you American?" We said we were, and the reaction of the whole mass was immediate: simultaneously on their faces were relaxation, ease, joy, and they all began chattering to us in a babble of tongues that we couldn't answer—but we could, and did, point the muzzles of our weapons at the ground, making it obvious these weapons were not "at the ready".

It was then that the smell of the place started to get to me. Our noses, rebelling against the surroundings they were constantly subjected to were not functioning anywhere near normally. But now there was a new odor, thick and hanging, and it assaulted the senses. . . .

Sergeant Blowers told us that some of the prisoners spoke English. Then he got even quieter, looked at the ground for a moment, raised his eyes, and looking over our heads, began very softly, so softly we could barely hear him. He told us that this is what was called a "concentration camp", that we were about to see things we were in no way prepared for. He told us to look, to look as long as our stomachs lasted, and then to get out of there for a walk in the woods. I had never known Sergeant Blowers to be like this.

Excerpted from Harry Herder Jr., "The Liberation of Buchenwald," an online article found at www2.3dresearch.com/~june/Vincent/Camps/HerderEng.html.

The man had seen everything I could imagine could be seen, and this place was having this effect on him. I didn't understand. I didn't know what a concentration camp was, or could be, but I was about to learn.

Bill, Tim, and I started off through the trees, down the hill to the front gate which was only a couple of hundred yards away. The gate was a rectangular hole through the solid face of the building over which was office space and a hallway. High up above the opening for the gate was a heavy wooden beam with words carved into it in German script, Arbeit Macht Frei. In a clumsy way I attempted to translate the inscription to Bill and Tim as, "Work will make you free". The three of us headed through the gate, through the twenty or thirty feet to the other side of the building. We were slightly apprehensive of what we might see. Our antennae were up. We had been teased by bits of information, and we wanted to know more. The lane we were walking on bent to the right as we cleared the building. We had barely made the turn, and there it was. In front of us a good bit, but plainly visible.

Contact with the Dead

The bodies of human beings were stacked like cord wood. All of them dead. All of them stripped. The inspection I made of the pile was not very close, but the corpses seemed to be all male. The bottom layer of the bodies had a north/south orientation, the next layer went east/west, and they continued alternating. The stack was about five feet high, maybe a little more; I could see over the top. They extended down the hill, only a slight hill, for fifty to seventy-five feet. Human bodies neatly stacked, naked, ready for disposal. The arms and legs were neatly arranged, but an occasional limb dangled oddly. The bodies we could see were all face up. There was an aisle, then another stack, and another aisle, and more stacks. The Lord only knows how many there were.

Just looking at these bodies made one believe they had been starved to death. They appeared to be skin covering bones and nothing more. The eyes on some were closed, on others open. Bill,

Tim, and I grew very quiet. I think my only comment was, "Jesus Christ."

I have since seen the movie made about Buchenwald. The stack of bodies is vividly displayed in the movie, just as I saw it the first day, but it is not the same. In no way is it the same. The black and white film did not depict the dirty gray-green color of those bodies, and, what it could not possibly capture was the odor, the smell, the stink. . . .

A group of guys from the company noticed us and said, "Wait till you see in there."

They pointed to a long building which was about two stories high, and butted up tightly to the chimney. It had two barn-like doors on either end of the building we were looking at, and the doors were standing open. We turned and walked back to the building where we found others from our company, along with some of the prisoners milling around in the space between the bodies and the building. We moved gently through those people, through the doors and felt the warmth immediately. Not far from the doors, and parallel to the front of the building, there was a brick wall, solid to the top of the building. In the wall were small openings fitted with iron doors. Those doors were a little more than two feet wide and about two and a half feet high; the tops of the doors had curved shapes much like the entrances to churches. Those iron doors were in sets, three high. There must have been more than ten of those sets, extending down that brick wall. Most of the doors were closed, but down near the middle a few stood open. Heavy metal trays had been pulled out of those openings, and on those trays were partially burned bodies. On one tray was a skull partially burned through, with a hole in the top; other trays held partially disintegrated arms and legs. It appeared that those trays could hold three bodies at a time. And the odor, my God, the odor.

I had enough. I couldn't take it any more. I left the building with Bill and Tim close behind me. As we passed through the door someone from the company said, "the crematorium." Until then I had no idea what a crematorium was.

It dawned on me much later—the number of

bodies which could be burned at one time, three bodies to a tray, at least thirty trays—and the Germans still couldn't keep up. The bodies on the stacks outside were growing at a faster rate than they could be burned. It was difficult to imagine what must have been going on.

Later that evening, sitting on the front steps of the barracks with a group of people from the company, Sergeant Blowers among us, the three of us started to pick up the parts of the story we had missed because we were on guard at the towers. All of the German guards had packed up and moved out about three hours before our arrival. There were bits and pieces of personal gear still left around the barracks, but not much.

We saw neither hide nor hair of those German guards. When the Germans left, the crematorium was still going full blast, burning up a storm, the chimney belching out that black smoke. Our First Sergeant, Sergeant Blowers, our Company Commander, and the Leader of the TD group found the source of the fuel, and played around with one thing and another until they figured out how to turn the damned thing off. . . .

Dying Conditions

The prisoners came up and surrounded us. . . .

They were jabbering, and we wanted to listen, to understand, but there seemed to be no way we could. After some moments we figured out they

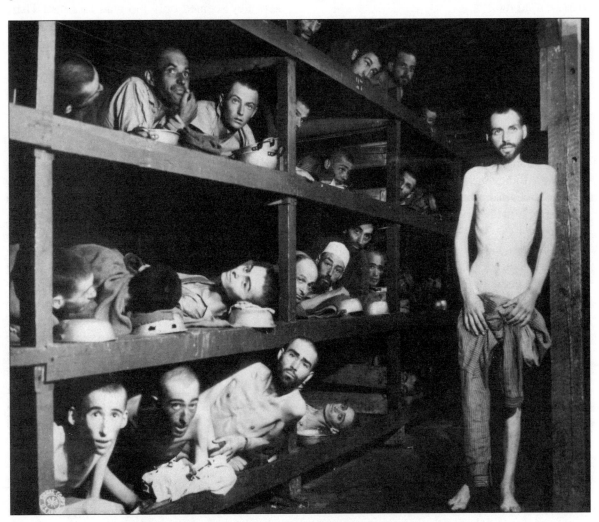

Buchenwald inmates lie in their bunks. American troops who liberated the camp found many of the survivors were close to death themselves.

wanted our cigarettes. In no time we were out of them—they just disappeared. We had nothing else with us they really wanted, but they stuck with us and guided us to another set of buildings, which had the look of large barns with wide doors in the middle of the front. Entering the first of these we found we were entering their home. There were stacks of bunks five or six high, crowded together with very little room between a bunk and the one above it. (It was my thought that one would have a rough time merely rolling over.) The bunks were much too short even for short people. The lower bunks served as rungs of a ladder to the upper ones. How many hundreds of people slept in this one building was beyond me. . . .

Just inside the door were people on the lower bunks so close to death they didn't have the strength to rise. They were, literally, skeletons covered with skin—nothing more than that—there appeared to be no substance to them. . . .

The Commandant's Wife

Sergeant Blowers told us some things about the Commandant of Buchenwald and his wife. We could see their house down the hill through the leafless trees from our seats on the front steps. Blowers painted a picture of truly despicable human beings. The wife, Ilse Koch, favored jodhpurs, boots, and a riding crop. He told us this story about her: Once, she ordered all of the Jewish prisoners in the camp stripped and lined up; she then marched down the rows of them, and, as she saw a tattoo she liked, she would touch that tattoo with her riding crop; the guards would take the man away immediately to the camp hospital where the doctors would remove the patch of skin with the tattoo, have it tanned, and patch it together with others to make lamp shades. There were three of those lamp shades—the history books say there were two, but there were three. One of them disappeared shortly after we arrived. This may give you a glimmer of an idea of what Ilse Koch was like—and her husband—and the camp "doctors."

We learned that only a very few Jews remained at Buchenwald, most of them in terrible physical shape. The Jews who had been healthy, to any degree, had been marched away from the camp weeks before. No one knew why they had been taken away, or where they had been taken. Originally, in the camp, the Jews and the non-Jews were largely separated and given different food rations and different jobs to do. Treatment of the prisoners varied also, depending on ethnic origin. There were a few women prisoners, but we wouldn't see them for a time as they had been taken immediately to the field hospital to be checked over and cleaned up. Those who were able began working with the American nurses or helping out in the kitchen. They gave the impression they no longer felt like slave laborers; in fact, they seemed only too glad to assist. There were children prisoners, some of them born in the camp. The females had been forced into prostitution often (though not the Jews). . . .

The next morning while we were sipping coffee after breakfast, a great commotion broke out down at the gate. We wandered off in that direction, coffee cups in hand. A bright and shiny jeep came through the gate, with this fellow standing in front of the passenger seat, holding onto the windshield. His helmet was gleaming and elaborately decorated, his uniform spic and span, his pistol highly polished and oddly shaped, and, by God, there he was: it was George Patton himself touring this place. From time to time the jeep would stop and he would ask questions. In front of the crematorium the jeep stopped, he alighted and walked inside. He was out of sight for some minutes, appearing again with a very stiff back. Into the jeep and he was all over the place in just a few minutes. He passed us on the way out—and damn he looked mad—about as mad as I had ever seen anyone look. I would not have wanted to cross that man right then. The jeep sped back out the gate and on down the road and George just sat. . . .

Discovering Chocolate

I heard a tiny voice. . . . There, right in the middle of the hole in the fence, looking up, calling me, was this very small person. I waved my arm at him letting him know that it was all right to come on through the fence, to come up the tower. He did so immediately. . . .

He was young, very small, and he spoke no English. He was dressed in bits and pieces of everything, ragged at best, and very dirty. He chattered up a storm and I could not understand one word. First, I got him to slow down the talk, then I tried to speak to him, but he could not understand a word I said. We were at a temporary stalemate. We started again from scratch, both of us deciding that names were the proper things with which to start, so we traded names. I no longer remember the name he taught me, and I wish so badly, so often, I could. Our conversation started with nouns, naming things, and progressed to simple verbs, actions, and we were busy with that. As we progressed I reached over into my field jacket to pull things out of the pocket to name. I came across a chocolate bar and taught him the word "candy". He repeated it, and I corrected him. He repeated it again, and he had the pronunciation close. I tore the wrapper off the chocolate bar and showed him the candy. He was mystified. It meant nothing to him. He had no idea what it was or what he was to do with it. I broke off a corner and put it in my mouth and chewed it. I broke off another corner and handed it to him and he mimicked my actions. His eyes opened wide. It struck me that he had never tasted chocolate. It was tough to imagine, but there it was. He took the rest of the candy bar slowly, piece by piece, chewed it, savored it. It took him a little while but he finished the candy bar, looking at me with wonderment the whole time. While he was eating the bar, I searched around for the old wrapper, found the word "chocolate " on it, pointed to the word, and pronounced the word "chocolate". He worked on the correct pronunciation. I am sure that was the first candy the little fellow had ever had. He had no idea what candy was until then. . . .

It seemed that Patton had become so angry at what he had seen in the camp that he scooted into the nearest major town, Weimar, broke the mayor of the town out, and told him he wanted every citizen up the next morning, ready to march to through [sic] Buchenwald so as to see what the German people were responsible for. The engineers were not to bury the dead until after the grand tour by the German townspeople.

We heard stories that night from two professors who had been non-Jewish prisoners at Buchenwald for over four years. They were intelligent. They had seen and were aware of everything that had happened at the camp. We asked them questions and we were given answers. . . .

Horror Stories

One story: The German army had been losing men on the Russian front because they were freezing to death. Some had been still alive when brought to the field hospitals, but had died in spite of the best efforts of the German doctors. Those field hospitals had requested some research on how to revive human beings who were very nearly frozen to death, but were still alive. The research had been done at Buchenwald. Groups of Jewish men had been taken outside on winter nights, stripped, and sprayed with a mist of water until they were nearly dead. They were then trundled into the hospital, and every effort was made to revive them. Every effort failed. The ungrateful Jewish prisoners just went ahead and died, in spite of the best efforts of German medicine at the time. Finally, some bright medical type thought there might be a kind of animal heat that would revive them. They took one more group out, freezing them until they were nearly dead, brought them back into the hospital, and put them into bed with naked women. Their animal desires would revive them, or so the theory went. It goes without saying the experiment failed—again. The still ungrateful prisoners simply continued to die.

Another story: There had been a factory a couple of kilometers down the railroad line from Buchenwald that was manufacturing something that was in demand by the German government. It was not clear to me what the plant had been making, but, in any event, it was the place where most of the political prisoners worked. Some Jewish prisoners worked there too, but they were only trusted with the menial jobs. One particular night our bombers flew over the camp to the factory, which they pulverized. They leveled it completely. Everyone working there was killed, but that didn't seem to matter to the two professors; not one bomb had missed the factory, not one bomb had fallen inside Buchenwald. The two professors thought that was remarkable—to be able to bomb with such precision. To listen to them was to get the feeling they believed it was a blessing to die in a bombing raid rather than in other circumstances at Buchenwald. The dead were better off, and the factory was out of business also. . . .

Another story (to me the most gruesome): German doctors at the camp were doing research on some human diseases. Groups of Jewish prisoners would be selected (which must have been some kind of an admission they were human beings) and inoculated with the diseases. They would then be observed, and all of their reactions charted until death occurred. A postmortem of the body would be done, and those organs affected by the disease would be preserved and stored. The doctors would then move onto another disease, repeating the process. A building in the camp, near the hospital, held all of those preserved specimens. The two prisoners told us of the building and its location, how we could find it in the morning if we were so inclined. In that building were rooms devoted to each of the organs: a kidney room, a liver room, a heart room, etc. . . .

The next morning we did a check on the building, and there they were. Rooms full of bottles of organs, all neatly and voluminously labeled. We turned and walked away. I had had enough. Any prisoner could tell me anything he wished from now on, and I would believe. That building was enough. . . .

German Civilians Tour Buchenwald

I noticed a lot of action up in the camp. Something important was happening there. People were scurrying about, and most of the prisoners were headed toward the gate. I was too far down the hill to discern the nature of what was going on, but I was betting it was the people from Weimar touring the camp after being marched out from the city. It turned out to be a good guess.

An interpreter met them at the gate, marched them around, and, according to the word I heard later, carefully explained in great detail what had been going on in the camp. In fact all the interpreter would have needed would have been a few words and a pointed finger. The evidence was all there; the massive pile of bodies still stacked, just as they were when we first found them; the doors in the crematorium now all open, and more of the trays pulled out with their contents visible. The German people were seeing what had been going on in that place all of those years. Now we could bury the bodies.

After the tour had been administered, the group headed back out of the gate and back down the road to Weimar. There was a large patrol of our troops marching them, some on either side of the road. As they were moving back to Weimar, not even out of sight of the camp, a number of Germans in the group found something to laugh about. The commander of the American troops heard them and became livid with anger. He turned them around and marched them, then and there, back through the camp again. This time they went through much more slowly. By the time they returned to the camp the bodies in the stacks were already being loaded on to trucks to be carried away to the mass grave. This time, on the march home to Weimar, there was no laughter. The next day we heard that after returning to their town, the mayor of Weimar and his wife both committed suicide.

A Witness to Revenge

The ovens were soon cleaned out, and the bodies were almost all gone, being buried over the top of the hill where the engineers had dug a monstrous trench. The Buchenwald prisoners had found one of their German guards in a nearby village dressed in civilian clothes, and they had him now in a cell in one of the buildings and were interrogating him. . . .

Back inside the cell the former Buchenwald prisoners, and their current prisoner presented a riveting scene: The hands of the German were untied, and, in them was placed a stout piece of rope. He was being given instructions, and, as we watched, it wasn't long before I and the people who had come with me realized he was being told how to tie a noose in the rope. The German guard was corrected three or four times, and had to undo some of his work to re-do it correctly. When he was finished, he had a very proper hangman's noose, thirteen turns of the rope and all. A table was brought to the center of the room and placed under a very strong looking electrical fixture. The guard was assisted on to the table and instructed to fix the rope to the light fixture. Finishing that he was told to put all of his weight on the rope and lift his feet. The fixture held. The guard was told to place the noose over his head, around his neck, and to draw the noose fairly snug. Then he was told to place his hands behind his back and his wrists were tied together. The table was moved until he barely stood on its edge. He couldn't see that—his eyes were unhooded and open, but the noose kept him from looking down. He was talked to some more and then he jumped. He was caught before all of his weight was on the rope, and they set him back on the table. The next time he stepped gently off the end, and the table was quickly slid away from him and out of his reach, and he dangled there. He slowly strangled. His face went through a variety of colors before he hung still. . . .

I walked through the crowd, out the door, through the gate, on up to the barracks, and I didn't say a word. The others with me didn't speak either. It was murder; there can be no doubt of that. The Buchenwald prisoners never touched the rope after it was placed in the German's hands. They did not tie the noose, nor did they fix it to the ceiling. They did not place the rope around the man's neck. They did not pull the table out from under him. In one sense, they had not committed murder; rather, the German had committed suicide. A sophist could rationalize that one I suspect.

That was not what was bothering me, however. I had the ability and the means to stop the whole thing, and I did not. Neither did my com-

panions. Here we were—five or six of us—fully armed with semi-automatic rifles, and we did not make the Buchenwald prisoners stop. We let them continue. In one way, we sanctioned the event. Ever since that day I have been convincing myself that I understood why the Buchenwald prisoners did what they did. I had witnessed their agonies. I had wondered how human beings could treat other human beings as the prisoners at Buchenwald had been treated. I felt I knew why the prisoners of Buchenwald did what they did—so I did not stop them.

I have become some kind of a sophist for myself now. I could have stopped the whole action, and I did not. I have had that under my hat for the past forty-six years. Now I have written it. I have acknowledged it. Maybe it will go away. There are so many things from that week I wish would go away, things I wish could be scrubbed from my memory. When we returned to the barracks we did not tell anyone what we had witnessed. . . .

I wondered. . . . Suppose my ancestors had not come to the United States; suppose they had stayed in Germany, and, through some fluke, the two people who had become my mother and father had met, and I had been born a German citizen. What would I be like? Would I be like the people who had instituted and guarded a place like Buchenwald? Could I have been that? Would I have been in the German army? The answer to the last question is obvious—certainly I would have been in the German army. But what kind of work would I have done? I hoped that I would not have been like most of the Germans I had seen. I could have accepted a likeness to some members of the German army whom we had fought, but there were many I would have been uncomfortable with. Much of what I had seen ran counter to everything my mother had brought me up believing. This whole situation would have appalled her. I have never ever told her, or my father either, most of these stories about Buchenwald. I did not feel it necessary. They knew early on that I had been there. . . .

I was nineteen, Bill and Tim were eighteen—chronologically anyway. We had aged years in a few short hours.

The Liberation of Buchenwald

Robert Abzug

Even the people who were aware of the atrocities committed by the Nazis during the war were unprepared for what they saw when the concentration camps were liberated. The first ones into the camps were usually soldiers who had seen their share of horrors during the fighting, but were still shocked by what they found: piles of corpses, some charred from the crematoria, warehouses full of shoes, glasses, and clothes, and walking skeletons who had somehow survived. This selection describes some of what the liberators of Buchenwald saw when they entered the camp in April 1945. One of the striking passages to note regards something that no book or film can capture, the odors associated with war and death. Robert Abzug is a historian who teaches at the University of Texas.

It is said that often Goethe would leave his Weimar residence and, on a fine spring or summer day, ascend into the beech forest north of the city to commune with nature and write poetry. One spring day Percy Knauth took off on his motorcycle and headed up a hilly road to the same woods, but for a different reason. It

was 1938, and Knauth was a young American reporter investigating rumors of torture, exhausting physical labor, and the breaking of minds and wills—all at a new prison camp named Buchenwald. Those who had been released from Buchenwald were too fearful to confirm the stories, and the camp's SS officers who wandered down to Weimar for women and wine didn't talk about their work. Nonetheless within a year of its opening in 1937, Buchenwald had become a lurid legend to rival Dachau. So Knauth thought he would nose around the perimeter of the camp. He kept his distance in this "forbidden" territory, always fearful that a guard might stop him or, worse still, that a bullet might prevent him from delivering the lame excuse that he had somehow gotten lost. He managed to see an occasional stretch of barbed-wire and the silhouette of a distant watchtower, and once he peered down into a deep quarry at the edge of the forest, on whose far side he saw a small crowd of prisoners in striped uniforms. That was all.

Seven years and a war later, Knauth returned, this time to report on the camp's liberation. "Buchenwald is beyond all comprehension," he observed on that occasion. "You just can't understand it, even when you've seen it.". . .

The Nazis built Buchenwald as a camp for political prisoners (mostly German Communists and Social Democrats), certain classes of incorrigible criminals, and—as the government stepped up its anti-Semitic campaign in 1937–38—for Jews. The site they chose had as its centerpiece the so-called Goethe oak, a tree stump that marked the poet's favorite spot in the woods. This stroke of Nazi black humor had behind it a more sinister purpose: the hidden, forbidding woods so close to Weimar provided a perfect setting for a camp that must remain a mystery yet be ever present in the minds of those who contemplated opposition to the regime.

Whatever Buchenwald's gruesome reputation before the war, the gross butchery of Nazi death squads in Poland and Russia and, by 1941, the creation of the Polish extermination camps put a new light on Buchenwald's torture and slow death. It acquired the reputation of being a "mild" camp. Its population leveled off at more or less 15,000, and the SS somewhat routinized life at Buchenwald through the use of a network of prison trustees. At first this invisible government was dominated by the "greens," non-political and often sadistic criminals whose prison garb sported a green triangle. There resulted a fearful and violent order in the camp, one that made death from overwork and malnutrition (not to mention violent punishment and medical experiments) commonplace. Still the camp's primary purpose was not systematic extermination. That constituted the meaning of mild.

This relatively stable system began to disintegrate in 1942 and continued to do so through to the end of the war. The basic pressure was population. Buchenwald became a center for supply of slave labor in war industries, and filled its labor pool with prisoners from France and Belgium and ever-increasing shipments of evacuees from the death and labor camps in the East. The perimeters of the old camp became tent cities to hold new arrivals; subcamps began to extend out into the Harz Mountains; and health and sanitary conditions for most prisoners deteriorated from their already minimal levels. Especially awful was the new "Little Camp, a section of crude barracks earmaked for Jews, Gypsies. and those sick and exhausted prisoners from the main camp who had outlived their usefulness. . . .

Commandants Come and Go

Karl Koch had been Buchenwald's first commandant. From the beginning he had sought ways of filling his own pockets by selling the property taken from camp prisoners and by running a black market in food and material meant for camp. Such behavior ran counter to the SS ideal of orderly corporate plunder, but Koch bribed a sufficient number of his fellow officers to avoid prosecution. However, local Thuringian officials made enough complaints about the commandant's non-payment of taxes to force the SS to transfer Koch to Majdanek in 1942. He so ill-managed that camp that he was tried and convicted by an SS court and executed for his crimes.

Meanwhile, in all this upheaval, the new commandant Hermann Pister allowed a German Communist prisoner group, some of them original inmates of the camp, to wrest power from the "greens." The Communist prisoners reduced the amount of black marketeering and other common corruption, cut down the amount of wanton sadism on the part of prisoner trustees (or Kapos), and made plans for the ultimate takeover of the camp in case of Nazi defeat. But in other ways the Communists merely shifted the ground of corruption to the assignment of work details, food, medical care, and ultimately life. From their takeover until the end of the war, favored treatment was often received on the basis of political loyalties. The Nazis, for their part, gained from the Communist regime a more predictable work force and a greater sense of order.

By 1945 the camp had grown to a population approaching fifty thousand and had become, by its own standards at least, a society of extremes: a relatively favored group of German Communist, German, and Western European prisoners at the top; Jews, Gypsies, Eastern Europeans, and other disfavored elements in the "Little Camp" at the bottom. . . .

American advances put new pressure on the camp in late March and early April 1945, and a strange drama began to be enacted with Commandant Pister at the center. Berlin had ordered Pister to evacuate, kill, or otherwise get rid of the prisoner population. Pister was of two minds about the order. He was no humanitarian and normally followed orders, but he saw the handwriting on the wall and hoped to present himself to the Americans as a relatively benign presence. To follow Himmler's drastic orders would hardly help support such an image. One of the various underground prisoner organizations, playing on this pragmatic side of Pister, forged a communiqué from the American forces that promised leniency if he handed over the camp and its population in good shape. Meanwhile the Communist underground, having more direct control of the everyday life of the camp, planned ways of resisting the evacuation orders.

Pister attempted to steer a middle course. Between April 3 and April 10 more than 20,000 inmates, half of them Jews, were transported out of the camp. Most of them died on their way to Flossenburg, Dachau, and Theresienstadt. The transports might have claimed twice that number had the Communist-led prisoner committee and other groups not engaged in delaying tactics and outright refusal to follow orders. Pister, for his part, allowed the prisoners to resist without the usual terrible reprisals. Indeed, by April 10 Pister and most of the SS had fled, leaving a skeleton guard to resist the rapidly advancing Americans.

Communist prisoners and Allied underground groups had, over the preceding year, built up a small cache of arms stolen from the SS or painstakingly built from parts smuggled by prisoners working in the nearby armaments plant. They readied themselves for revolt. On the morning of April 11 the prisoners could already hear small-arms fire in the vicinity of the camp, and at one in the afternoon the lead tanks of the Fourth Armored Division could be seen from the heights of the camp. There is much controversy as to what happened next. Communist tradition has it that, with SS guards still in the towers, the prisoners arose, overpowered the Nazis and liberated themselves. Other accounts emphasize that by the afternoon most of the SS were gone; it was at that point, they say, that the prisoner rebels revealed their arms and paraded them with no real enemy in sight. In other words, they rose up in arms when there was no one to shoot and with only the possible motive of taking control of the camp before the Americans arrived. Which, in either case, is what they did.

Liberation by the Americans

The first Americans at Buchenwald, in fact, came upon it by accident. At about noon on April 11, Combat Team 9 of the 9th Armored Infantry Battalion, Sixth Armored Division, took the nearby town of Hottelstedt. There they captured fifteen SS troops and lined them up to be sent to the rear. Suddenly about fifty Russian prisoners emerged from the woods and attempted to seize the SS. They were ordered to desist, did so, but pointed out that these Germans had been guards at Buchenwald concentration camp, just to the south and east. Going to Buchenwald would have been a detour for the Combat Team, whose mission was to drive east toward Ettersberg, but Captain Robert Bennett did send four of his men with some Russians as their guide to investigate the camp. They arrived about an hour after the "revolt" had occurred. Entering through a hole cut in the fence into the main upper camp, the prisoners cheered joyfully and hoisted one of the Americans, Captain Frederic Keffer, on their shoulders, tossed him in the air repeatedly, and only stopped when a somewhat jarred Keffer asked them to put him down. Keffer and his men distributed what rations and cigarettes they had and notified headquarters about the existence and location of the camp. They then left, having seen only the better part of the camp and a hint of what was to come—the prisoners had already pinned some of the captured SS to the ground with stakes.

Later in the day and in the ensuing week, members of the Fourth Armored Division and 80th Infantry took over administration and rehabilitation at Buchenwald. . . . The Americans were met by reasonably healthy looking, armed prisoners ready to help administer distribution of food, clothing, and medical care. . . . Survivors hunted the woods for escaped SS and searched among the liberated prisoners themselves for Nazis who had traded their uniforms for concentration camp stripes. In all, liberated prisoners killed almost eighty ex-guards and camp functionaries in the days following the liberation, sometimes with the aid and encouragement of Americans.

> [It] almost killed me: one of the inmates of the camp when we got up close to two Nazi SS types, kicked the corpse. And that just expressed hatred more vividly than anything you could possibly imagine.—Kenneth Bowers, 19th Tactical Air Command.

Fred Mercer of XX Corps remembered one instance where a German soldier attempted to surrender to the Americans, but was intercepted by a prisoner with a four-foot wood log: "He just stood there and beat him to death. He had to—of course, we didn't bother him."

The Smell of Death

Of course all around these displays of rage and revenge lay Buchenwald's vast fields of human misery and death. Even in the upper camp there was the crematorium with its half-burned bodies still in place; piles of corpses left unburned because the coal supply ran out; and the emaciated survivors of that part of the camp known for its relatively good treatment. . . .

> My first impression of it was the odor. The stench of it was all over the place and there were a bunch of very bewildered, lost individuals who came to me pathetically at the door in their unkempt uniforms to see what we were doing and what was going to be done about them. They were staying at the camp even though their guards and staff had fled because they didn't know where to go or what to do. They had heard news that the Americans had taken over that area and they were waiting for somebody to turn their lives back straight again and they were just lost souls at that time.
>
> Well, my feeling was that this was the most shattering experience of my life.—John Glustrom, 333rd Engineers.

Then there was the Little Camp. At liberation its population was made up of Jews, Gypsies, worn-out laborers, and evacuees from other camps. Most of the 700 children at Buchenwald were in the Little Camp, including a three-year-old child. Both prisoners and barracks offered a somber contrast to the big camp. As opposed to the solid buildings of the main compound, the structures in the Little Camp were dismal barns, each with three to five tiers of wide shelves running the length of the building. On some of the shelves were rudimentary mattresses of rotting straw, covered with vermin. In the center, between the barracks ran an open concrete ditch that gave off an indescribably horrible stench—it was the sole latrine.

The buildings only hinted at the condition of the prisoners. Barracks meant for 450 housed 1000 to 1200 inhabitants. The shelves were stacked with the living, the near dead, and in some cases the truly dead. Even after liberation, every day twenty to twenty-five prisoners in each Little Camp block died.

These prisoners were held in such contempt by both the Nazis and the prisoner leadership of the main camp that even days after the liberation the barbed wire gate to the compound was still locked, and the most sadistic of the Kapos still ruled in each barracks. When on April 12 a massive ceremony of freedom was held on the main square of the camp, the prisoners of the Little Camp rotted in their barracks.

Soon after the liberation of Buchenwald two American psychological warfare observers, a civilian Egon Fleck and 1st Lieutenant Edward A. Tenenbaum, entered the *Kleines Lager* as part of their extensive survey of conditions at Buchenwald. "Even now," they wrote in a secret report, "a trip through the Little Camp is like a nightmare.". . .

The Face of Death

Percy Knauth made sure to see the Little Camp. He was accompanied by a Czech surgeon who had been a prisoner at the time of liberation, and who continued to live among his fellow survivors and aid them as he could. Knauth peered into the surgeon's own dark barracks, and was told that 1500 men lived inside. "It was a long, dim room full of murmurs and movements of figures in all kinds of clothes," Knauth wrote, "from the striped uniform to just a sack draped over bony shoulders."

As Knauth's eyes became accustomed to the darkness, he could see a rag-tag tangle of men "emaciated beyond all imagination or description." Their legs and arms were sticks with "huge bulging joints," and their loins were fouled by their own excrement. "Their eyes were sunk so deep that they looked blind," he remembered. "If they moved at all, it was with a crawling slowness that made them look like huge, lethargic spiders. Many just lay in their bunks as if dead." Knauth, in response to a request for food, pulled a chocolate bar out of his pocket. "The spidery men in the dimness galvanized into sudden motion," he wrote. "A dozen hands reached for the chocolate bar, clutching wildly. The filthy bodies pressed around me, pushed me, nearly knocked me down. I fought for sanity and kept repeating: '*Moment, moment!*'" One man finally reached the chocolate, but no sooner had he grasped it than others pounced on him. "I saw the chocolate in several filthy hands, brown melted gobs of it," Knauth remembered. "—then it was gone.". . .

Knauth and others soon found they could function only by repressing all emotion, however unwillingly. "Numbly, I saw death now," Knauth wrote of his Buchenwald visit, "and before I left the camp that evening I saw it reduced to such ordinariness that it left me feeling nothing, not even sickness at my stomach." For Margaret Bourke-White, whose stunning photographs of Buchenwald opened the eyes of the American public as few other individual photographers had been able to, the camera itself became her shield from the reality she was recording, from the "white horror" in front of her. "People often ask me how it is possible to photograph such atrocities," she later noted in her autobiography. "I have to work with a veil over my mind. In photographing the murder camps, the protective veil was so tightly drawn that I hardly knew what I had taken until I saw prints of my own photographs."

There were dangers, however, in this natural defense against horror. In some cases Americans ignored the Little Camp prisoners in favor of the healthier ones, in part simply to get away from them. Fleck and Tenenbaum warned that this might be a problem. "They are brutalized, unpleasant to look on," they wrote of the worst cases. "It is easy to adopt the Nazi theory that they are subhuman, for many have in fact been deprived of their humanity. It would be easy to continue favoring the big camp in the distribution of food, as has been done in the past, and, more important for the wretches of the small camp, in the distribution of medicine." Anonymous, emaciated, naked or in rags, speaking strange languages, and often displaying craven behavior, Little Camp prisoners could easily be both pitied and avoided. These worst cases became symbols of horror, the stuff of nightmares, but otherwise remained in dangerous anonymity. . . .

One Polish Jew, Mordecai Stiegler, a writer, . . . was thirty, had lived in Warsaw, and indeed had manned the barricades with the Polish home guard when the Nazis entered the city in 1939. No sooner had the Germans taken over, however, than the Poles identified him as a Jew to the invaders. He was arrested, tortured, and one Nazi officer cut swastikas on his cheeks and forehead with a razor blade. Levin noted that the scars were still clearly visible on his thin face.

Stiegler was drafted into forced labor around the city and then shipped in a boxcar to a labor camp. It was the first of a series of such camps, and in each place many died and few survived. His luck held out, after a fashion. Sometimes he escaped, but always he was recaptured. This was the way Stiegler spent 1940. Oddly enough, so unorganized were Nazi plans for the Jews at this point that at times he was released, went home, and then was conscripted for a new slave labor assignment. By 1941 the decision to exterminate European Jewry had hardened; the massacres, once sporadic, became more and more predictable. At one point Stiegler was selected to be killed, but in the midst of the bedlam accompanying the machine-gun fire and the screams of the dying, he ran to a group selected for labor.

In 1942 he escaped a death march in the

Lublin area. He witnessed mass murders and incredible acts of sadism, but somehow survived. For sixteen months he worked in a munitions plant, but was evacuated at the approach of the Russians. He had managed to survive ten months at Buchenwald, even finding the energy to instruct in secret the children of the Little Camp in Yiddish and Hebrew. In addition, he held "literary evenings" for his fellow inmates, in which they shared poetry and history and literature.

Now Stiegler was free. To most who saw him he was just one of the animals, without history or future, part of the refuse of the Little Camp. For Meyer Levin, Mordecai Stiegler represented something else. "Slowly I was coming to understand," he commented with no little sense of awe, "what was indestructible in the human world."

Selection 3

The Liberation of Mauthausen

Albert J. Kosiek

Though the U.S. government knew quite a bit about the concentration camps by the end of the war, the soldiers fighting the Germans knew little or nothing about them. In most cases, the camps were liberated by a few soldiers or units that literally stumbled upon them. This was the case, for example, when Staff Sergeant Albert J. Kosiek ran into a group of Germans on a road in Austria and was told that a concentration camp was nearby. He then found the camp known as Mauthausen. Although Auschwitz is better known, Mauthausen may have been the worst concentration camp of them all, and that is where many prisoners of war were sent to be executed. The man mentioned in this article, Captain Jack Taylor, is referred to as an American naval officer. In fact, he was an agent for the Office of Strategic Services (OSS)—the forerunner of the CIA—and he had been captured and sent to the camp to be executed. During his time in Mauthausen, Taylor had a number of jobs, including building a crematorium. After the war he became a key witness at the war crimes trial that tried the Germans responsible for running Mauthausen. Kosiek served with the Eleventh Armored Division. After the war he became a barber.

Perhaps May 5th, 1945 was just another day to you. We thought it would be for us too but before the sun set that day we had participated in experiences that really taxed our imagination. We were awakened early that morning and the Commanding Officer (CO) gave all the platoon leaders their missions for the day and this is where my story begins.

I was platoon leader of the First Platoon of

Excerpted from Albert J. Kosiek, "Liberation of Mauthausen," an online article found at http://linz.orf.at/orf/gusen/kosiek1x.htm. Reprinted with permission from Gloria T. Kosiek.

Troop D, 41st Cavalry Reconnaissance Squadron, Mechanized [of 11th Ard Div, 3rd US Army]. . . . It was my platoon's mission to check the bridges at St. Georgen [the US Forces came in via the mountaineous Muehlviertel region to avoid heavy fighting with German troops at Linz and the major roads in the Danube valley] for intactness since they were on the route to be used by the combat command. Routes on maps were plotted, ammunition checked and everything else we could think of that goes along with being prepared. The sun was just becoming bright when we started out from the town of Katsdorf . . . in the foothills of the Austrian Alps . . . , the potential redoubt area of the diehard Nazis. We proceeded slowly and cautiously and everything seemed to be rather peaceful. We passed through the town of Lungitz but as we approached a bend in the road, Corporal Pickett, my acting scout section sergeant, spotted some Germans on the high ground above us. . . . I immediately gave orders to pull back to the town of Lungitz to spread out and set up a defense. We took cover and reported the situation to the CO, who suggested some persuasive artillery. Suddenly one of our men stumbled onto some people who seemed to be in some large cages [the KZ Gusen III camp with some 300 inmates]. He immediately informed me and while doing so a German soldier appeared and started coming toward me. That German soldier was in the sights of more assorted weapons than he had hairs on his head. In English he explained to us that up ahead was an annex of a concentration camp and that the refugee prisoners were Polish and Russian [also Italians]. We radioed the CO and told him that we would not need the artillery fire. . . .

Through our field glasses we were able to pick up a motorcycle and a white touring car with a red cross on the hood. As they approached we laid all our guns on them because no matter how innocent looking the Germans might appear you could not trust them. Out of the car stepped two SS captains, the driver and a man dressed in civilian clothes. The civilian was an International Red Cross affiliate, and the spokesman for this unholy mob. Fortunately one of my gunners, Rosenthal from Chicago, spoke and understood German. From what we could determine from these people there was a large concentration camp [KZ Gusen I, KZ Gusen II and KZ Mauthausen camps] beyond the bridge that we were supposed to check. The Red Cross man was trying to contact an American general to surrender this camp and 400 SS guards whom he pledged would give up. I made him believe that I was the direct representative of the commanding general of the 11th Armored Division. I then requested permission from my CO by radio to go to the camp and I stressed the fact that 1,600 prisoners were depending upon us for fast liberation [in fact he liberated some 25,000 prisoners at Gusen and some 12,000 prisoners at Mauthausen]. It was difficult for me to obtain his approval because this would bring us beyond our assigned mission, causing an unnecessary risk, as far as we were concerned. He finally consented but stressed that we remain in constant communication with him by radio.

Discovering Mauthausen

The situation was ticklish, for there was no guarantee that the roads to Mauthausen [via St. Georgen and Gusen] were undefended, in spite of the fact that we were assured we would not run into trouble at the camp. As a persuader we told the occupants of the white car heading the column that even so much as the breaking of a twig would spell their doom. With this understanding we finally reached the town of St. Georgen and continued to the outskirts finding the bridge [over Gusen River] intact. We also found, much to our surprise, German soldiers all over the place [maybe former guards of the Luftwaffe that were glad to become American Prisoners of War; the leading SS-men left Mauthausen and Gusen around April 28, 1945]. Fortunately they were the peace loving kind and didn't bother us too much. In the distance . . . we thought we saw our objective, namely Mauthausen [Gusen] Camp. Surprises seemed to be the order of the day, because we were in for another. This was a concentration camp alright, but not the one we were looking for. As we approached the camp an

SS captain came toward us and gave me an American salute, which I returned. After Rosenthal assured him I was an officer he explained to me that he was the commander of Gusen Camp. With the captain was an old buzzard in a Volkssturm uniform who spoke English perfectly [when the SS left at the end of April, Viennese Fire-Brigades and "the Volks-Sturm" (men of the area that were too old to serve in the German Army) were sent to Mauthausen-Gusen to guard the prisoners there; just some SS-key personnel and some low-ranking SS-guards were left at this time]. With the old man as my interpreter I explained to the SS captain that we were taking over his camp and expected him and all Germans to surrender. He evidently had the same idea in mind and he was very cooperative. He had quite a number of guards and I explained that I would have to pick them up on our way back from Mauthausen. He agreed to this but insisted that they would have to keep their weapons because he feared that they would not be able to keep order in the camp if they gave up their weapons. Frankly I had no choice but to agree but I warned him that not a shot was to be fired for if it was I would order the tank force forward which was not too far behind. . . .

As we continued we soon came upon Mauthausen. It was located on the highest ground in the area we were in and it was flanked on one side by the Danube. It looked like a series of factories from the distance [the barracks]. Tremendous cement walls surrounded it [granite walls] with large field cannons poking their ugly noses at us from everywhere [SS originally planned to defend the camps, but most of them left some days before]. On the other side of a patch of woods was the first entrance to the camp. The white car stopped and the occupants got out. At this section of the camp it was surrounded by a wire fence that was charged with 2,000 volts of electricity [the "Sanitaetslager" where thousands of exhausted KZ Gusen II inmates . . . were brought to die]. Behind that fence were hundreds of people who went wild with joy when they first sighted us. It's a sight I'll never forget. Some had just blankets covering them

and others were completely nude, men and women combined, making the most emaciated looking mob I have ever had the displeasure to look upon. I still shake my head in disbelief when that picture comes before me, for they hardly resembled human beings. Some couldn't have weighed over forty pounds. The place turned into an uproar and it was evident that if these people weren't stopped shortly bloodshed would be impossible to avoid. With the safety of my men in the back of my mind at all times I knew that the job of restoring order was mine. The platoon was tense, each man looking grimly down the sights of his gun ready for anything. It was too late in the game to be caught off guard, I heard the people yelling in Polish and I raised my hands for them to keep silent. I then told them in the tongue that they understood to go back to their quarters and to cooperate with me so that I could set them free as soon as possible by removing the German guards. They understood and thank God they did cooperate.

An American!

After quelling the fracas a young tall English speaking German came to me with the commander of the camp and through his interpreter the commander commended me on my quieting the mob. With the commander by my side we walked to the main part of the camp. . . . We came to a large gate in the cement wall [the Main Entrance to the *Schutzhaftlager*] and a German opened it. Walking in first I was greeted with the most spectacular ovation ever paid me. Behind that gate hundreds of prisoners were in formation and when I walked in they were so happy to see an American soldier that they all started yelling, screaming, and crying. To these people my appearance meant freedom from all torture and horror surrounding them. Never before have I felt such a sensation running through me as I did at that moment. I felt like some celebrity being cheered at Soldiers Field in Chicago. That was the first time I have had people so overjoyed at seeing me. As I stood there looking out at the mob I realized what this meant to them and I was glad we had made the effort to free the camp. We then walked on through the yard and through another gate and up a small stairway to where the inmates were quartered [the *Schutzhaftlager*]. By this time the prisoners were gathered all around me. At this point one of the prisoners stepped forward and introduced himself as Captain Jack Taylor of the United States Navy showing me his dog tags to prove it. Upon inquiring he told me that two other Americans were in the camp and one English flier in the hospital. . . .

We then looked for the English speaking German interpreter and upon reaching him he told me that the commander did not want to give up the camp until he was certain that we could keep the prisoners under control. . . . At the time a riot was going on in the kitchen and he wanted me to clear up the situation. When I got to the kitchen the door was blocked and I had to jump in through a window. The refugees were dipping soup out of large pots with their hands and drinking it. Others were stealing chickens and fighting over them among themselves. I yelled at them in Polish but it didn't do any good. Finally I fired a few rounds from my pistol into the ceiling and then they started to move out of the kitchen. Talking to them in Polish I told them that they were only making things more difficult for me and the German guards started pushing and hitting some of them. I felt like socking one of the guards but I couldn't do it at the time and end the riot. When I got outside again the refugees were all over the place and I started to plead with them to please get back to their quarters which was behind the gate.

Above the gate was a platform which overlooked a large courtyard [the Main Entrance to the *Schutzhaftlager* as it appears today]. On the side of the platform flags of the 31 nations represented in the camp were painted. We managed to get all the people in the courtyard and with an English speaking representative from each nation we got on the platform [there was established an International Prisoners Commitee at the Mauthausen camp a few days prior to the liberation]. I gathered the representatives together and asked them to explain to their people that they should stay in their quarters because by doing so it would facilitate my clearing the camp of the German guards and then the camp would be in command of the United States Army. While talking to the representatives some of the refugees were setting up a band down in the courtyard. The first representative to speak was Polish. When he finished he asked for three cheers for the Americans and the response was thunderous. Each representative went through this procedure and after 45 minutes all the speakers were finished. The band then played "The Star Spangled Banner" and my emotions were so great that the song suddenly meant more to me than it ever did before. Many of the refugees were crying as they watched our platoon standing at attention presenting arms. When we dropped our salute we found out that the Navy captain had taught the band our national anthem just the night before. The people cooperated and stayed in the courtyard or returned to their quarters.

In back of the courtyard were bodies piled up in one mass. . . . You wouldn't think they were human beings if you did not recognize certain features. They were being chewed up by rats and no one seemed to care. Then we were shown where they gassed the people, and then cremated them in big ovens. . . . We were told they shot Americans because they wanted them to be honored by shooting instead of gassing or other means of death. When they gassed women and children they made them believe they were going for a shower. The Germans would give them a bar of soap and a towel. Once in the shower room they would turn on the water for one minute and then let the gas in through the pipes that were near the base of the wall. I never saw so many dead people lying around in all my life. I saw things that I would never have believed if I hadn't seen them with my own eyes. I never thought that human beings could treat other human beings in this manner. The people that were alive made me wonder what kept them alive. They were only skin and bones.

The food rations for the prisoners was a loaf of bread a week for seven people. They slept on a cot the size of our Army cots. The difference was that we slept alone in one, and they had one for five people. I was talking to an eight year old Polish boy who told me that if he did not take his hat off and stand at attention when a guard passed by he would be shot. An older person verified the story and said there were many people shot because they refused to honor the Germans in this manner.

The English speaking German then asked me what I wanted the German guards to do. I told him to gather all the guards at the main gate and have them put their weapons in wagons that I would have there. Finding the Navy captain we went back to the main gate. We also had the other Americans with us, one a sergeant from the Air Corps, and the other a colored fellow. I told them to wait for me in a jeep until we had all the Germans rounded up. I hated to have them wait because it was raining and they were sickly. All of my platoon was busy keeping the Germans on the road and taking their weapons from them. . . .

I then went ahead with an armored car and a jeep and we proceeded to Gusen Camp where we went through similar experiences as we encountered at Mauthausen. We got the guards out of this camp and restored order among the prisoners. . . .

My platoon then went to the house I had selected and we brought the Navy captain with us. . . . The boys rustled up some food and the Captain enjoyed his meal. He told us he would never forget our platoon of 23 men as long as he lives. He told us he never expected to see Americans again. He was sentenced to death four times while at the camp but was spared by the refugees. He was to go to the gas chamber on May 6th which was the next day. He told us that 1,100 people a day were killed in Mauthausen. . . . We sat and talked with him until three o'clock in the morning. On May 5th we accomplished our mission and then some!

Selection 4

Bringing Nazis to Justice: The Nuremberg Trials

Robert E. Conot

Though the Allies could be criticized for not doing more to save the Jews, they did not ignore the Germans' actions. In fact, starting at the end of 1942, Roosevelt and Churchill expressed their horror at the behavior of the Nazis and vowed to bring the Nazi criminals to justice. The problem was that these statements seemed like little more than bluster and idle threats since no action was being taken. Slowly the idea evolved to gather evidence of the Nazis' crimes and bring them to justice. The United States led the effort to conduct a trial, in part to serve as a means of documenting everything for posterity. The British, at least initially, were more interested in summarily executing the men responsible for the war. This excerpt traces the development of the concept of holding a war crimes trial in Nuremberg and the process involved in choosing the defendants. The International Military Tribunal finished its work and handed down its verdicts on October 1, 1946. Of the twenty-two defendants, eleven were given the death penalty, three were acquitted, three were given life imprisonment and four were given imprisonment ranging from ten to twenty years.

*n*early two years had passed since President Roosevelt, on October 7, 1942, had first declared: "It is our intention that just and sure punishment shall be meted out to the ringleaders responsible for the organized murder of thousands of innocent persons in the commission of atrocities which have violated every tenet of the Christian faith." Two months later, on December 17, British Foreign Secretary Anthony Eden had told the House of Commons: "The German authorities are now carrying into effect Hitler's oft repeated intention to exterminate the Jewish people of Europe. From all the occupied centers of Europe Jews are being transported in conditions of appalling horror and brutality to eastern Europe. In Poland, which has been made the principal Nazi slaughterhouse, the ghettos established by the Nazi invaders are being systematically emptied of all Jews except a few highly skilled workers required for war industries. None of those taken away are ever heard of again. The able-bodied are slowly worked to death in labor camps. The infirm are left to die of exposure and starvation, or are deliberately massacred in mass executions."

The next year, Roosevelt, Churchill, and Stalin formally stated in the Moscow Declaration their determination to bring the guilty to justice. On October 26, 1943, the United Nations War Crimes Commission, composed of fifteen Allied nations (not including the Soviet Union) held its first meeting in London. Again, on March 24, 1944,

Roosevelt warned: "None who participate in these acts of savagery shall go unpunished. All who share in the guilt shall share the punishment."

Yet nothing had been done to implement the multitude of declarations. Morgenthau was bitter at the State Department for its bureaucratic bumbling and failure to facilitate the escape of Jews; and President Roosevelt was concerned about the possible loss of the Jewish vote in an election year. In the weeks following the Normandy landing on June 6, Eisenhower became more and more incensed as scores of British, Canadian, and American prisoners of war were shot by the Waffen SS in what seemed like calculated policy. In Washington, G-1, the Office of the Chief of Staff of the Personnel Division, was charged with collecting evidence on crimes committed against American servicemen. In July, the task was delegated to Lieutenant Colonel Murray C. Bernays; and Bernays was to prove the guiding spirit leading the way to the Nuremberg trial. . . .

On July 11, Churchill had written to Foreign Secretary Anthony Eden: "There is no doubt that this is probably the greatest and most horrible crime ever committed in the whole history of the world, and it has been done by scientific machinery by nominally civilized men in the name of a great State. . . . It is quite clear that all concerned who may fall into our hands, including the people who only obeyed orders by carrying out the butcheries, should be put to death after their association with the murders has been proved."

Morgenthau, who advocated the division and deindustrialization of Germany, concurred with Churchill and the British Lord Chancellor, John Simon, that the principal Nazi leaders should be charged with their crimes, then summarily shot. On the other hand, Colonel Mickey Marcus of the Army Civil Affairs Division, which was charged with formulating postwar policy for Germany, was disturbed by Morgenthau's emotional approach. At a meeting with Bernays, he agreed that retribution must not appear to be a Judaic act of revenge. Summary execution, no matter how justified, could never serve as a substitute for justice.

"Not to try these beasts would be to miss the educational and therapeutic opportunity of our generation," Bernays argued. "They must be tried not alone for their specific aims, but for the bestiality from which these crimes sprang.". . .

Bernays proposed that an international tribunal should be established to condemn violence, terror, racism, totalitarianism, and wanton destruction; the tribunal should arouse the German people to a sense of their guilt and a realization of their responsibility. Otherwise, Germany would simply have lost another war; the German people would not come to understand the barbarism they had supported, nor have any conception of the criminal character of the Nazi regime. The fascist potential would remain undiminished, and the menace remain. Only the

staging of a great trial—or, possibly, a number of trials—in which the conspiracy of the Nazi leadership would be proved and the utilization of the Nazi organizations in the furtherance of that conspiracy would be established, could all the objectives be attained, and all criminals, large and small, be caught in the same web. . . .

Churchill and Lord Simon stuck to the proposition that "it is beyond question that Hitler and a number of arch criminals associated with him [including Mussolini, Himmler, Goering, Ribbentrop, and Goebbels] must, so far as they fall into Allied hands, suffer the penalty of death for their conduct leading up to the war and for their wickedness in the conduct of the war. It being conceded that these leaders must suffer death, the question arises whether they should be tried by

Hans Frank, the governor of Nazi-occupied Poland, speaks at the Nuremberg Trials. The trials began on November 20, 1945 and judgment was handed down on October 1, 1946.

some form of tribunal claiming to exercise judicial functions, or whether the decision taken by the Allies should be reached and enforced without the machinery of a trial."

After weighing the pros and cons, the British concluded once more that the dangers of a trial outweighed the advantages and that "execution without trial is the preferable course.". . .

On April 30, however, Hitler had committed suicide and been followed by Goebbels. Mussolini was captured and executed by Italian partisans. Two weeks later Himmler bit into a capsule of cyanide. With these men dead, the British opposition to a trial softened. . . .

The British suggested that the trial might be held in Munich, the cradle of the Nazi movement; or, alternately, in Berlin or Leipzig. Jackson replied that he had no objection to Munich, which was in the American zone, but that the United States did not want the trial held in either of the other two cities, which were under Russian occupation. Fyfe proposed ten top Nazis as defendants: Hermann Goering, commander of the Luftwaffe, director of the Four Year Plan, founder of the Gestapo, and onetime heir apparent to Adolf Hitler; Rudolf Hess, party secretary and Hitler's right-hand man until 1941, when he had mysteriously parachuted from a Messerschmitt fighter over Scotland; Joachim von Ribbentrop, the foreign minister; Robert Ley, director of the German Labor Front; Alfred Rosenberg, party theoretician and minister for the Occupied Eastern Territories; Wilhelm Frick, interior minister; Field Marshal Wilhelm Keitel, chief of staff of the Wehrmacht; Julius Streicher, a gauleiter and notorious Jew baiter; Ernst Kaltenbrunner, head of the Reich Security Office, the second-ranking man in the SS after Himmler; and Hans Frank, governor of occupied Poland. . . .

The Anglo-American system of trial had little in common with the continental, followed by the French and Russians. Jackson was as ill-informed about continental practices as Major General I.T. Nikitchenko, the forty-five-year-old head of the Soviet delegation, was about American; and repeatedly one was unable to comprehend the other. Furthermore, it quickly became clear that the American and Soviet conceptions of the International Military Tribunal were startlingly at odds.

Nikitchenko maintained: "We are dealing here with the chief war criminals who have already been convicted by both the Moscow and Crimea [Yalta] declarations." The job of the court was merely to decide the degree of guilt of each individual, and to mete out punishment. The essence of the case would be determined before the start of the trial—in the continental system, the prosecutor assembled all evidence both against and in favor of the accused and presented it to an examining judge, who then decided whether the person should be brought to trial. If the judge ruled in the affirmative, he was, in effect, finding the person guilty, so that the burden of proof from then on rested on the defendant.

Unlike procedure in Anglo-American law, where the prosecutor and defense counsel are adversaries, with the judge acting as arbiter, in continental law prosecutor, defense counsel, and judge are all charged with the task of arriving at the truth. . . .

Nikitchenko's conception of the trial so shocked Jackson that he suggested, on June 29, that the best thing might be for each nation to go ahead and try the Nazis it held in custody according to its own customs.

The following day he recovered sufficiently to reiterate the American position that it was "necessary to authenticate by methods of the highest accuracy the whole history of the Nazi movement, its extermination of minorities, its aggression against neighbors, its treachery and its barbarism. . . . We envision it as a trial of the master planners.". . .

The next day produced new disagreement. SHAEF (Supreme Headquarters Allied Expeditionary Force) had conducted a survey of German cities as possible sites for the trial, Jackson revealed. The only undamaged facilities extensive enough to accommodate the trial were in Nuremberg, so Nuremberg should be selected as the location. . . .

The Nazi leadership was indicted for (1) Crimes Against Peace, including the launching of an aggressive war; (2) War Crimes, that is, acts contrary to acceptable usages and against the provisions of the Hague and Geneva conventions; and (3) Crimes Against Humanity, covering any and all atrocities committed by the regime during its reign. . . .

The most spectacular of the finds were the records of Alfred Rosenberg, providing a detailed description of German operations in the East and of the looting of the various occupied territories. Discovered hidden beneath wet straw behind a wall in a Bavarian barn by an OSS lieutenant seeking photographic material, the forty-seven crates were flown to Paris, where Jackson had set up his continental document-collecting center. Though, by the end of July, the contents of the crates had been only cursorily examined, one of Bernays's investigators wrote him: "This is an almost unbelievable admission of *systematic* killings, looting, etc.". . .

The Accused

During his stay in London, Bernays had compiled a master list of the major German war criminals; by the time he departed, the number stood at 122. On the first ten of these, Goering, Hess, Ribbentrop, Ley, Rosenberg, Frick, Keitel, Streicher, Kaltenbrunner, and Frank, suggested originally by the British, the Americans immediately agreed. Only Hess, because of his disoriented mental condition, posed a question mark. The Americans proposed five others: Admiral Karl Doenitz, head of the submarine service until his elevation to command of the entire Nazi navy in January 1943; Arthur Seyss-Inquart, an Austrian who had played a pivotal role in Hitler's Anschluss in 1938 and subsequently had been head of the German administration in the occupied Netherlands; Albert Speer, chief of Nazi war production during the last three and one-half years of the war; Hjalmar Schacht, economics minister and head of the Reichsbank during the first five years of the Hitler regime; and Walther Funk, who had replaced Schacht as minister of economics and president of the Reichsbank. The latter three primarily interested the Americans, with their emphasis on the economic aspects of the Nazi aggression; but the

British had no objection to them.

Almost everyone on the American and British delegations had his favorite candidate, and lists were compiled periodically. But by August 8, when the charter was signed, only Martin Bormann, who had succeeded Hess as party secretary, had been added. Since all the men were to be charged with a conspiracy, it was thought proper, and perhaps necessary, to list Hitler at the head of the group. The prosecutorial staff, nevertheless, hesitated to include him, for—although there was little doubt that he had killed himself—they feared that to do so might generate rumors of his survival.

No criteria had been established for inclusion in the list of defendants, and additions were arbitrary. The British suggested Baldur von Schirach, organizer and leader of the Hitler Youth, and subsequently gauleiter of Vienna. The Americans, adhering to the concept that each of the individual organizations should be represented by one or more of its leaders, had named Keitel for the armed forces, Doenitz the navy, and Goering the Luftwaffe, but were missing a man for the army. So General Alfred Jodl, the chief of the Wehrmacht operations staff, was included.

The OSS thought that to present a true panorama of Nazi crimes at least thirty defendants, including several industrialists, would have to be selected. The best known was Alfried Krupp, operating head of the world-famous armaments firm. His name was added, as was that of Fritz Sauckel, who had impressed workers from all over Europe into Hitler's labor program. By mid-August, however, no final determination had been made, and Jackson's list of potential defendants still contained seventy-three names.

After thinking the matter over, Jackson decided there was no point in trying a dead man, and dropped Hitler. However, Franz von Papen, who had preceded Hitler as chancellor and briefly been vice-chancellor in Hitler's cabinet, was tacked on.

When the tentative list was shown to the French and Russians in the third week of August, the French were chagrined that it contained no German held by them, and combed their roster for a candidate. They came up with Baron Constantin von Neurath, who had been living in retirement upon his estate in Württemberg, which was part of the French occupation zone. Neurath's tenure as Protector of Bohemia and Moravia and head of a "Secret Cabinet Council" placed him under suspicion. No one on the Allied staffs knew what this cabinet council had consisted of; but it sounded appropriately menacing.

On August 25, Jackson, Fyfe, Gros, and Nikitchenko agreed on a list of twenty-two defendants. Twenty-one were in custody. The twenty-second, Bormann, had, according to rumors, been captured by the Russians. Jackson repeatedly questioned Nikitchenko whether the Russians held Bormann; but Nikitchenko did not know, and apparently could not find out. A press release naming the accused was prepared, and about to be released on August 28, when Nikitchenko rushed in to announce that the Soviets did not hold Bormann, but that they had captured two Germans whom they wanted added to the list.

First was Admiral Erich Raeder, commander of the German navy until January 1943. Raeder had been a marginal candidate for the trial, so far as the British and Americans were concerned,

but had gained importance by the discovery of a document indicating he had been a prime instigator of the invasion of Norway.

The other was Hans Fritzsche, a popular newscaster and second-rank official in Goebbels' Propaganda Ministry, who had not been on any of the many lists of top war criminals. Had he been suggested by a member of the American or British prosecutorial staffs, he would have been summarily rejected. But since the Americans were contributing thirteen defendants, the British seven, and the French one, it was a matter of national pride to the Russians that they be permitted at least two.

In the interim, the Americans had second thoughts about naming thirty-eight-year-old Alfried Krupp, who had been active in the company's affairs only since the start of the war, rather than his seventy-five-year-old father, Baron Gustav Krupp von Bohlen und Halbach. At the last moment, Gustav's name was substituted for Alfried's. It turned out to be an incredible error, but one typical of a case in which the charges were prepared and the defendants chosen before the facts had been more than cursorily investigated.

On August 30, the list of Nazi leaders selected for the first trial was released to the press.

Selection 5

Odessa: Nazi Dreams of Future Power

Simon Wiesenthal

Hundreds of Nazis were tried after the war for their crimes, but thousands more escaped justice. Many of the higher-ranking officials had stolen millions of dollars in gold, art treasures, and other goods and hidden them in Swiss banks and other places. These funds helped them get away. Still, most needed help. By accident, during the Nuremberg trials Simon Wiesenthal learned about an organization called Odessa, composed of former members of the SS, which had been created to help their former comrades by providing money, jobs, documents, and assistance in establishing new identities in foreign countries, particularly Argentina. Frederick Forsyth's novel (which was later made into a movie) The Odessa File *dramatizes the events of this underground organization of Nazis who hoped the Reich would one day rise again. This excerpt discusses not only the operation of Odessa but also how the Nazis stole a fortune and hid it so well that much of the money has never been found. Simon Wiesenthal survived the concentration camps and dedicated his life to tracking down Nazi war criminals. Working mostly alone, Wiesenthal created a clearinghouse for information about Nazis and is responsible for bringing many war criminals to justice. This excerpt is from the Nazi-hunter's memoirs.*

*A*s early as 1947 I had begun to enter on maps the details of all escape routes known to me, and in so doing I found that a network of staging posts emerged similar to that in Austria and Germany. The escape routes invariably ran through particular German towns—Bremen, Frankfurt, Augsburg, Stuttgart and Munich—to converge in Memmingen, a small medieval town in the Bavarian Allgäu. There they divided again. One route continued to Lindau on Lake Constance, where it divided once more, to lead either to Bregenz in Austria or into Switzerland. The main route, however, lay from Memmingen to Innsbruck, and thence over the Brenner Pass into Italy. Later I discovered that the Nazis called this north-south route the 'B-B' axis, meaning the link from Bremen to

the Italian port of Bari. From there the escape routes continued to Spain, to various Arab countries, or, predominantly, to South America.

In all these countries the fugitives needed papers, and we knew from several cases that they evidently had no difficulty in obtaining forged documents. Nor did they seem to have any problems about establishing a new livelihood: the top-ranking ones, at least, immediately had substantial financial resources at their disposal wherever they arrived, sufficient to enable them to set up businesses, become partners in major enterprises, and, if necessary, bribe the authorities.

It was obvious that a secret organization of considerable magnitude, drive and exceptional wealth was at work here. At least certain preparations for such an organization must have been put in hand during the final years of the war: once the war was over the Nazis would have found it difficult to transfer such vast sums of money out of Germany. No doubt, as usually happens in history, the leaders responsible for the war were the first to transfer their loot abroad. . . .

The strangest document was the protocol of a secret conference of top German businessmen, held at the Maison Rouge hotel in Strasbourg in August 1944. Unbeknownst to [SS leader Heinrich] Himmler and Hitler, who still believed in final victory, a number of industrialists and financiers had met there, realizing that the war—which for so long had earned them great profits—was now lost: the coal baron Emil Kirdorf, the steel magnate Fritz Thyssen, Georg von Schnitzler of IG Farben, Gustav Krupp von Bohlen und Halbach, and the Cologne banker Kurt von Schroeder. All of them, having been among the first to turn to Hitler in 1933, were now also among the first to turn away from him. Even if Nazism were to survive—which all those at the conference hoped—it would be Nazism without Hitler. . . .

In actual fact, German industrialists had long begun to gradually transfer their money, giving preference to accounts in Switzerland and in Spain, from where, however, even then, large amounts were being transferred to Argentina. . . .

The protocol of the Strasbourg conference

contained this passage: "The party leadership is aware that, following the defeat of Germany, some of her best-known leaders may have to face trial as war criminals. Steps have therefore been taken to lodge the less prominent party leaders as 'technical experts' in various German enterprises. The party is prepared to lend large sums of money to industrialists to enable every one of them to set up a secret post-war organization abroad, but as collateral it demands that the industrialists make available to it existing resources abroad, so that a strong German Reich may re-emerge after the defeat." . . .

Uncommon Thieves

But where did the party get so much money? The answer is simple: the Nazis were not only murderers but robbers. This realization seems to me important, especially as in Germany and Austria there is a certain tendency to regard the mass murders as motivated by insanity. In reality it was never just a case of ensuring the hegemony of the Nordic race on the European continent; there was always the lure of the art treasures which might be stolen from Germany's neighbours. And it was never just a case of exterminating the Jewish race, but always also one of Aryanizing Jewish assets, plundering Jewish homes, and prising gold from the teeth of Jews after they had been gassed. . . .

The area around Aussee, in the northwestern corner of Syria, had been dubbed the "Alpine redoubt" by [propaganda minister Joseph] Goebbels, and many top Nazis did in fact seem to believe to the very end that it would be possible to "hibernate" there. About Christmas 1944 they began to set up their families there and send their looted possessions by the crateful. . . .

In its methodical way the SS, from March 1945, made records of the assets brought into the region. Only one of these records has fallen into American hands: it listed the assets of the Reich Security Directorate brought to Altaussee from Berlin . . . : 111 pounds of gold bars, fifty crates with gold coins and gold objects, each crate weighing 222 pounds, as well as two mil-

lion US dollars, two million Swiss francs, five crates of precious stones and jewelry, and a stamp collection valued at no less than five million Gold Marks.

In the early days of May 1945 a special department of the Reichsbank, which administered booty from concentration camps, sent several crates of "dental gold" to Aussee. And stored in the Altaussee salt mine were the art treasures pillaged from all over Europe. If discovery threatened, the Nazis intended to blow up these priceless cultural treasures—paintings by the greatest masters stolen from the major museums in France, Italy, Belgium and Holland—and blame the Allies for this act of barbarism. However, members of the Resistance got wind of the plan and succeeded in foiling it.

When the "Alpine redoubt" fell on 9 May 1945—Major Ralph Pierson took it with just five American soldiers in one tank and one jeep—the Nazi bigwigs were desperately retrieving the treasures which they had hidden. . . .

All in all, the fortune which the Nazis managed to hide and stow away is estimated at roughly four billion Gold Marks.

Who was able to dispose of these monies, whose signature authorized the withdrawal of funds from accounts in Switzerland, Spain or Argentina—these are some of the as yet unresolved secrets of the Third Reich. It is said that six lists exist, two of them in the keeping of well-known banking institutions. Two more may well have been held by the people who in 1947 set about creating the greatest escape organization in world history.

The Underground Nazi Railroad

By mere chance I learned of the existence of that organization at the very start. During the Nuremberg trials I made the acquaintance of a former member of German counter-espionage, who had been recommended to me by American friends and who evidently still had sufficient contact with his former comrades to be *au courant*.

"How did the big Nazis manage to disappear?" I asked him.

"Have you ever heard of Odessa?" he countered my question.

"A pretty town," I observed, a little nonplussed.

During the next four hours Hans (which is what I propose to call him) enlightened me about Odessa, the "Organization Der Ehemaligen SS-Angehörigen" (Organization of Ex-Members of the SS). It was only set up in 1946, when a number of top Nazis were already in prison camp or penitentiaries. Somehow they succeeded in making contact with old comrades who were still free, and "aid committees" were formed for prisoners' welfare. Under this humanitarian cover the committees conveyed letters, established contact with old comrades and, most important, raised money. Everything was done quite officially under the eyes of the unsuspecting Allies, who believed that even Nazis must be granted the benefits of a humanitarian society. The aid committees were promoted in particular by the Catholic Church, which suddenly remembered its humanitarian duties. Although during the Nazi period it had not done much for prisoners and virtually nothing for concentration-camp inmates, it was now evidently trying to make up for its omissions by looking after the inmates of POW camps.

In many instances, however, the assistance of the Church went far beyond the mere toleration of aid committees and actually amounted to abetting criminals: the most important escape route, the so-called "monastery route" between Austria and Italy, came into being. Roman Catholic priests, especially Franciscans, helped Odessa channel its fugitives from one monastery to the next, until they were received by the Caritas organization in Rome. Best known was a monastery on Via Sicilia in Rome, a monastery under the control of the Franciscans, which became a veritable transit camp for Nazi criminals. The man who organized this hideout was no less than a bishop and came from Graz: in his memoirs Alois Hudal subsequently boasted of the many top people from the Third Reich to whom he had been able to render "humanitarian aid."

It is difficult to guess the motives of these priests. Many no doubt acted from a misunderstood Christian love of one's neighbour—some of them, indeed, may have done the same for Jews under Nazi rule. The fact that of Rome's 8,000 Jews 4,000 survived the Third Reich is certainly due, above all, to the Church. Most of them had been living in monasteries, and a few dozen had actually been admitted into the Vatican. It seems to me probable that the Church was divided: into priests and members of the religious orders who had recognized Hitler as the Antichrist and therefore practised Christian charity, and those who viewed the Nazis as a power of order in the struggle against the decline of morality and Bolshevism. The former probably helped the Jews during the war, and the latter hid the Nazis when it was over.

While initially most fugitives used the Brenner-Bari route, the main link later ran between Bremen and Rome or Bremen and Genoa. At roughly every 25 miles staging posts were set up, organized as a rule by three people who, for their part, only knew the next two staging posts. The fugitives were passed on anonymously, as it were, and it was evidently easy to cross the various demarcation lines which at the time ran across Austria and Germany. The American forces newspaper *Stars and Stripes*, for instance, was transported by German civilian employees of the US army on trucks down the autobahn from Munich to Salzburg. As a rule these transports were simply waved through at the frontier because it was known what they were; very occasionally a military policeman would glance under the tarpaulin and would see there piles of batched newspapers. What he didn't see were the men crouching behind the papers, holding their breath to escape being heard; what he didn't know was that the truck driver belonged to Odessa. This particular escape route was subsequently cut because of a report I made . . . and the truck driver was arrested. But a dozen other routes remained open. . . .

Odessa . . . had at its disposal a second . . . escape route. This ran across Vorarlberg and profited from the casualness of the French occupation forces. As, in view of the beauty of their mother tongue, the French are in principle opposed to learning any other language, the French occupying officials had no clue what was happening around them. Thus Vorarlberg, in the triangle between Austria, Germany and Switzerland, became the Eldorado of fugitives from all parts of Germany. From Bregenz they effortlessly got across the Swiss frontier. Sometimes no doubt the Austrian and Swiss police turned a blind eye, and sometimes the fugitives had valid frontier passes: Odessa men were still, or again, working in all possible authorities and departments and evidently stole the required documents and rubber stamps.

Particularly astounding was the brazenness with which Nazis directly offered their services to the occupation armies. There seems to be a certain type of person who inspires confidence in officers: the haircut, the way of clicking one's heels, the readiness to lower one's head immediately in obedience—these presumably signal a certain kinship of souls. The Americans in particular had an incredible talent for being taken in by tall, blond, blue-eyed Germans, simply because they looked exactly like American officers in the cinema (whereas real American officers are, at least just as often, short, dark and of Italian descent). Quite recently the Office of Special Investigation revealed how many Nazis had found immediate reemployment as agents for the CIA after the war, merely because they were able to display the anti-Communism drilled into them under Hitler and to claim a detailed acquaintance with the east. In return for that, the Americans were willing to disregard the fact that these same people had previously served Adolf Hitler and that frequently their hands were still stained with fresh blood. It is just because I revere the Americans (and, God knows, have no sympathy for the Communists) that I

find this misjudgement incomprehensible: Communists are bad, but Nazis are worse. . . .

One of this type who immediately adjusted to the new age used the cover name of Haddad Said and was one of the most successful escape helpers. Later to become a respected Austrian businessman, he was then travelling on a Syrian passport, organizing transports from Munich or Lindau to Bregenz. All who travelled with him had valid frontier passes. From Bregenz they crossed the Swiss frontier, only a few miles away, and there they boarded the first train to Zürich or Geneva, to fly on to the Middle East or South America.

I discussed these matters at length with an Austrian police officer serving in Bregenz, but he thought not much could be done about it: "These people's papers are in order, for the most part they are in transit, and we're relieved when they're out of the country."

"And what are the French doing?" I enquired.

"Nothing," the officer said angrily.

I was subsequently able to discover who was hiding behind the pseudonym of Haddad Said: he was a former SS Hauptsturmführer and one of the leading lights in Odessa. He made his fortune by providing pretty holiday homes on Spain's Costa Brava for former SS leaders and party bigwigs. And for those who would find even Spain too hot to hold them, he obtained villas in Uruguay.

The more I discovered about the activities of Odessa the better I understood why it remained hidden from the Allies for so long. This was a Nazi enterprise run by professionals—former "illegals," members of the Security Service, former agents, men who had proved their worth and distinguished themselves in the administration of the Third Reich. Just as they had organized the mass murder to perfection, so did they perfectly organize the escape of the murderers.

The Trail and Trial of Adolf Eichmann

Alan Levy

Adolf Eichmann was an SS lieutenant-colonel and head of the "Jewish Section" of the Gestapo. Eichmann participated in the Wannsee Conference (January 20, 1942) and was instrumental in implementing the Final Solution by organizing the transportation of Jews to death camps from all over Europe. He was arrested at the end of World War II in the American zone but escaped, went underground, and disappeared. A concentration camp survivor named Simon Wiesenthal committed his postwar life to hunting down Nazi war criminals and was determined to find Eichmann. On May 11, 1960, members of the Israeli secret service uncovered his whereabouts. The Israeli agents smuggled him from Argentina to Israel. Eichmann was tried in Jerusalem (April–December 1961) in a trial considered crucial to the documentation of the truth of the Holocaust. Eichmann, who was put in a glass booth (hence the name of the film about the trial, The Man in the Glass Booth*), did not deny his role and was convicted of crimes against humanity. He was sentenced to death and was executed on May 31, 1962, the only person to ever receive the death penalty in Israel. This excerpt traces Eichmann's escape from Germany, Wiesenthal's efforts to find him, and the Nazi-hunter's view as to the appropriate punishment for one of the principal architects of the Final Solution. Alan Levy is an American-born journalist and freelance writer who moved to Prague and founded the English-language weekly newspaper, the* Prague Post.

*W*ith the extinction of the Warsaw Ghetto in 1943, the only large Jewish community left in the Third Reich was in Axis-allied Hungary, where territorial acquisition and an influx of refugees had doubled the Jewish population to more than three-quarters of a million. Half-heartedly but effectively, Admiral Miklos von Horthy, an ageing anti-Semitic, but not genocidal, regent had protected his Jews from deportation. On 19 March 1944, however, Hitler forced Horthy to appoint a more militantly anti-Semitic government which immediately stripped all Jews of their jobs, property, civil rights, and citizenship, ordered them to wear the Star of David, and herded them into ghettoes where they were systematically starved. German troops occupied friendly Hungary for the first time and Adolf Eichmann was dispatched to Budapest to expedite the Final Solution. As the

Axis war machine wore down, the German machinery of genocide sped up to fulfil at least one of Hitler's missions on earth. . . .

Whether Germany won or lost the war, Eichmann was convinced that if he could "succeed in destroying the biological basis of Jewry in the East by complete extermination, then Jewry as a whole would never recover from the blow. The assimilated Jews of the West, including America, would . . . be in no position (and would have no desire) to make up this enormous loss of blood and there would therefore be no future generation worth mentioning." So fanatical was Eichmann by the end of 1944, says Simon Wiesenthal, that "when even [SS leader Heinrich] Himmler ordered Eichmann to stop the killing in Hungary, he no longer understood the word 'Stop!' any more.". . .

"The worst story I can ever tell you about Adolf Eichmann," says Simon Wiesenthal, "took place during the time he was in Budapest. In the fall of 1944, a group of high-level SS officers were sitting in the SS casino there. And one of them asked Eichmann how many people had been exterminated already.

"Eichmann said: 'Over five million.'

"Well, because he was among comrades and they all knew it was only a matter of months before they would lose the war, one of them asked whether he was worried about what would happen to him.

"Eichmann gave a very astute answer that shows he knew how the world worked: 'A hundred dead people is a catastrophe,' he said. 'Six million dead is a statistic.'". . .

Adolf Hitler committed suicide in his Berlin bunker on 30 April 1945. . . .

Eichmann's Escape

Early that May, Eichmann . . . headed for Germany armed with . . . false papers. . . . These identified him as *Luftwaffe* (Air Force) Corporal Adolf Barth.

"Corporal Barth" was taken into custody in the Danube city of Ulm by the Americans, but escaped when Army Intelligence probed too deeply for his taste. He didn't go far, landing in another US prisoner-of-war camp in Weiden, where he managed to obtain a new identity for later use. Thrice transferred in the next month—to Camp Berndorf near Rosenheim in late May; to a special camp for SS men in Kemanten in early June; and to a work camp at Cham, a half-timbered medieval town in the Bavarian Forest near the Bohemian border, in mid-June—he recommissioned himself along the way as an officer: a "Lieutenant Eckmann," no less!

To Rudolf Scheide, the German civilian in charge of work details at Cham, "Lieutenant Eckmann" confessed that he really was a "Major Eichmann." The name meant nothing to Scheide. . . .

Eichmann worked on a thirty-man construction detail which was marched by a pair of American military policemen into the town to rebuild Cham. . . . On 30 June 1945, someone told Scheide who Eichmann was and a little of what he had accomplished in the war. This was too much for Scheide, who notified the camp's resident CIC (US counter-intelligence) man. He and Scheide were waiting for "Eckmann" when the work detail returned that night. Only twenty-nine men came back. Eichmann, alerted, had disappeared.

Under yet another alias, Otto Heninger, he found work with a farmer in Prien, on the Chiemsee, Bavaria's largest lake. Then he made his way north into the British Zone of Germany. In the spring of 1946, in the town of Eversen in Lower Saxony, "Heninger" registered with the police as a forestry worker and quickly found employment in that labour-starved timberland. A few months later, a currency reform bankrupted his employer, but "Heninger" headed north again—stopping just short of Hamburg at the Lüneburg Heath, where the brother of a friend found him work as a lumberjack. Later, "Heninger" leased a little land, on which he raised chickens, in Altensalzkoth, near the north German city of Celle.

The Hunters

Back in Eichmann's home town of Linz, Wiesenthal was keeping tabs on his quarry's relatives and had made his first contact with the future Israelis—then represented fairly furtively, but aggressively, in Austria by *Bricha* (which means *escape*), the Jewish organization that smuggled displaced persons into what was still Palestine, and *Haganah,* the secret Jewish defence army. Both were headed in Austria by a tall, slim, dapper man known only as "Arthur," . . . the former Arthur Pier, who, as a teenager early in Eichmann's 1938 tenure in Vienna, had applied by mail for his emigration papers rather than condescend to stand in line. In Palestine, he had joined *Haganah* while working as a journalist, changed his name to Asher Ben Nathan, and, in 1944, in a small office near the port in Haifa, started collecting the stories of arriving survivors and drawing up a list of Nazi criminals in order of importance. Returning to his native Vienna in November 1945, he'd reassumed his identity of Arthur Pier and arrived with a suitcase whose false bottom secreted not just gold to finance clandestine Jewish emigration to Palestine, but even more vital cargo: microfilmed dossiers on many of the major missing Nazi genocidists, with Adolf Eichmann at the top of the list. Under the auspices of the Association of Jewish Students, "Arthur" had set up the first Documentation Centre in Vienna. Most of his agents—including his eventual successor, Tuviah Friedman—were enrolled at the University of Vienna, which gave his operation a cloak of legitimacy.

"Arthur" preached to all his associates that they must never take the law into their own hands. "Only the legal authorities and properly appointed judges have the right to punish criminals," he told them. "Our job is to find wanted Nazis and have them arrested by the Allies. Acts of personal revenge can only harm our cause, which is not only justice, but sending as many Jews as possible to Palestine.". . .

Is Eichmann Dead?

Late in 1947, the CIC in Bad Ischl informed [Wiesenthal] that Veronika Liebl had applied to the district court for a death certificate for her "ex-husband" Adolf Eichmann "for the sake of the children." She had submitted an affidavit from one Karl Lukas of Prague, who swore that he had seen Eichmann shot to death during street fighting in the Czech capital on 30 April 1945. . . .

Wiesenthal sent a man to Prague, where he learned that the "eye-witness" to Eichmann's "death," Karl Lukas, an employee of the Czechoslovak Ministry of Agriculture, was married to Frau Eichmann's sister, Maria Liebl.

Upon examining Wiesenthal's evidence, the Austrian judge threw out Frau Eichmann's application. . . .

"I am convinced," says Wiesenthal, "that my most important contribution to the search for Eichmann was destroying the legend that he had died. If he had been legally declared dead, then his name would have disappeared from all the 'Wanted' lists and officially he would no longer exist. His case would be closed. Around the world the search for him would end. A man presumed dead is no longer hunted. Many SS criminals were never caught because they had themselves declared dead and then lived happily ever after under new names.". . .

Though he found himself bored to death in northern Germany, "Otto Heninger" stayed until he'd saved enough money to finance an ocean voyage. According to [Holocaust scholar] Hannah Arendt: "Early in 1950, he succeeded in establishing contact with ODESSA, a clandestine organization of SS veterans, and in May of that year, he was passed through Austria to Italy, where a Franciscan priest, fully informed of his identity, equipped him with a refugee passport in the name of Richard Klement and sent him on to Buenos Aires.". . .

With [the priest's] help, Eichmann arrived in Argentina in mid-July 1950 as "Ricardo Klement, thirty-seven, stateless, Catholic.". . .

Searching the Globe

"The 1950s were bad years for Eichmann-hunters," says Wiesenthal. "The Cold War had reached its climax and the former Allies were dug in on both sides of the Iron Curtain. The Americans had their hands full with the war in Korea. No one was interested in Eichmann or the Nazis.". . .

Simon never had nightmares, for his nights were waking hours spent with ghosts. A doctor he consulted told him he needed relaxation, diversion, a hobby.

"I have a hobby," Wiesenthal told him. "I collect witnesses."

"And from this hobby you are sick," the doctor said. "You are prolonging the concentration camp for yourself. When your witnesses cry, you cry, too. And when they suffer, you suffer. How many victims were there? Six million? Well, you will be number six million and one unless you get yourself a real hobby, like stamp-collecting.". . .

The matching up of Ricardo Klement with Adolf Eichmann was as painstaking a process as the mounting of a Penny Black or Twopenny Blue in a stamp album. And the breakthrough, though it wasn't recognized at the time, came from Wiesenthal's hobby. At a philately exhibition in Innsbruck in late 1953, he met an old baron who invited him home to his villa in the Tyrol to look at his collection. Over a bottle of wine, the baron—a lifelong Catholic and ardent monarchist who had suffered for his views under Hitler—told his Jewish guest how dismayed he was to see prominent Nazis regaining high positions in the Tyrol "as if nothing had changed. And it's not only here." Rummaging in a drawer for a recent letter from a friend in Argentina, he handed it, still in its envelope, to Wiesenthal. "Beautiful stamps, aren't they?" the baron remarked. "But read what's inside."

His friend, a former lieutenant-colonel in the German army who had never concealed his dislike for Hitler, had gone to Argentina as an instructor to Juan Perón's troops. He wrote to the baron:

> There are some people here we both used to know. . . . A few more are here whom you've never met. Imagine who else I saw—and even had to talk to twice: that awful swine Eichmann who commanded the Jews. He lives near Buenos Aires and works for a water company.

. . ."By late 1953," says Wiesenthal, "I had definite knowledge of where Eichmann was in Argentina and where he worked. I had everything but his name, which a trained, trustworthy Jewish investigator could have ferreted out easily from what else I had.". . .

The hunt for Eichmann would languish for at least five years. . . .

Was there no way to track down Eichmann when Wiesenthal came so close? "I was alone in Linz," he explained. "Suppose we did find Eichmann living near Buenos Aires and working for a water company, how could we get him? What would I, a private citizen half a world away, do? The Germans were a strong political force in Argentina. German soldiers were training Perón's army. German experts were running Argentine industries. Millions in German capital was invested in Argentine banks.". . .

Eichmann had hardly been in Buenos Aires during the first three years of his stay in Argentina. "Ricardo Klement" had arrived wearing dark glasses, a Hitler moustache, and a hat pulled low over his eyes, but had been met by SS friends who quickly put him in touch with the head of CAPRI, a firm founded by Germans to provide work for postwar refugees. . . .

CAPRI was a contractor to the Argentine government, prospecting for water power and planning hydroelectric plants and dams. "Klement" was put in charge of a crew of native workers and, determined organizer of labour that he was, soon excelled and was given promotions, responsibility, and raises that enabled him to send for his family within two years. Vera Liebl, the "ex-Frau Eichmann," had received a letter—from a "stranger" whose handwriting she recognized—saying that "your children's uncle, whom everybody believed to be dead, is alive and well." When she and her sons had joined "Uncle Ricardo" in Tucumán on 15 August 1952, the boys had been told that he was "your dead father's cousin," and they liked him so much that they rejoiced when their uncle married their mother and she had a fourth son: Ricardo Francisco, the middle name in honour of a Franciscan friar who had helped the proud father escape through Italy. . . .

In his first five years in Argentina, only a

handful of trusted SS friends knew that "Klement" was Eichmann. Anybody could guess that he was a Nazi fugitive, but there were thousands of those. . . . In financial distress, he turned to a couple of the Nazi help organizations in Argentina, even though they might be infiltrated by informers.

More of an "old boys' network," they quickly recognized Eichmann's growing notoriety and rewarded his past work with a job at the Mercedes Benz factory in Suarez, near Buenos Aires. Starting as a mechanic, he was quickly promoted to foreman and then department head.

Scarcely bothering to conceal his identity any more, Eichmann started cutting a celebrity's swath through Argentina's ample Nazi colony. . . .

On Wednesday morning, 22 April 1959, Simon Wiesenthal picked up the Linz newspaper *Oberösterreichische Nachrichten* (Upper Austrian News). On the back page was word that Frau Maria Eichmann, stepmother of his quarry, had died. . . . He cut out the article, put it atop his Eichmann file, and sent word to the Israeli consul in Vienna as well as to Tuviah Friedman, Asher Ben Nathan, Yad Vashem, and a few others in Israel who might care.

Ben-Gurion Gives the Order

Somebody high up in Israel *did* care. That summer, Wiesenthal's information went to Isser Harel, the head of Israel's secret services. Wiesenthal's information corroborated reports Harel was receiving from West Germany. He went to Prime Minister [David] Ben-Gurion and told him: "We have proof that Eichmann is in Argentina. Can I give orders for my men to get on his track?"

"Yes," said Ben-Gurion, "bring back Eichmann dead or alive. But I'd rather you brought him back alive. It would have great meaning for young people.". . .

Simon sent a man around to visit Maria Liebl in Germany in quest of the whereabouts of her daughter, Vera Eichmann. Frau Liebl shut the door in the man's face, but not before telling him Vera had married some man named "Klemt" or "Klems" in South America.

Wiesenthal reported this to Israel. Again, it corroborated a German source which said Vera Eichmann was living "in fictitious marriage" with a German named Ricardo Klement. . . .

"The Eichmann boys lived in Buenos Aires with their parents. It occurred to me that they would probably be registered there at the German embassy, since they would soon reach military age. I asked a friend to make a cautious inquiry. He notified me yes, the Eichmann boys were registered there, under their real name."

This was enough for the Israelis to move a team of three secret agents into a house on the Calle Chacabuco, opposite "Ricardo Klement's" residence. With telescopic lenses from their windows and attaché cases that were really hand cameras, they photographed "Klement" on the street, on buses to and from work, on his lunch hour, and every time he went into or out of his house or appeared at a window. In early 1960, when "Klement" and his family moved into a primitive brick house—with no electricity or running water—which he and his older sons had been building themselves, the Israelis moved with them and continued the surveillance. The house was on Garibaldi Street in San Fernando, one of the more run-down suburbs of Buenos Aires.

Because its agents were operating illegally on foreign soil, Israel needed to take every precaution before abducting Eichmann. They had to net the right man. A misfire or an embarrassing case of mistaken identity could rupture diplomatic relations with Argentina, an important trading partner and home of many thousands of Jewish refugees as well as Nazi fugitives. Despite the fact that they had photographed "Klement" up, down, and sideways, the Israelis were handicapped by the scarcity of early photos of Eichmann and by the fact that he had aged badly and lost weight. "Klement" had the same thin-lipped, cruel mouth, but none of the dapper arrogance of the high-living officer. . . . Even those who had known him personally in the past were reluctant to swear that this meek, shabby family man with the pallid, lined face was what had become of Adolf Eichmann. Until they were sure that Eichmann and "Klement" were one and the same, the Israelis would not move to seize him. . . .

On his way home from work on Monday, 21 March 1960, "Ricardo Klement" did something he had never done before in the months the Israelis had him under surveillance: he bought his wife a bouquet of flowers.

Checking his Eichmann file, the leader of the mission read that Adolf Eichmann had married Vera Liebl on 21 March 1935. This was their silver wedding anniversary—and his sentimental gesture did him in. That very night, a three-word cable reached Harel in Tel Aviv "HA'ISH HOU HA'ISH." ("The man is the man.")

In early April, while the surveillance team kept watch on Eichmann, a six-man "kidnap commando" was installed by Israel in Buenos Aires. Four were Israelis who had arrived via different routes and were equipped with false identification papers and cover stories that would hold water. Two were Argentinian Jews, recruited locally and warned they might have to leave Argentina for good—particularly if "Operation Eichmann" proved successful. . . .

On 11 May, the bus from the Mercedes Benz plant dropped Eichmann at his corner, as usual, at one minute before the half-hour. It was autumn in Argentina (in the southern hemisphere) and night was falling. A car was parked on Garibaldi Street with its hood raised and three men bent over the engine. A fourth man, apparently the owner, was pacing impatiently. Another car was parked nearby.

As Eichmann passed the "disabled" car, he reached into his pocket. The car's back door had just begun to open, but now—fearing he would produce a gun—the three "mechanics" who were supposed to abandon their engine to shove him inside couldn't risk waiting the extra fraction of a second. One of them made a flying tackle, diving to deflect Eichmann's hand, and knocked him to the ground. As they thrashed around, he and Eichmann rolled into a ditch, into which the other two "mechanics" jumped to subdue their quarry. The fourth man slammed the "disabled" car's hood shut and then stood lookout while the driver started the engine and the two men in the

back seat made room for a third.

Eichmann tried to shout for help, but his false teeth had been dislodged by the tackle and were rattling around his mouth, almost choking him. When his three assailants flung him on to the floor of the car, the two back-seat passengers pinned him down and searched him. The "weapon" he had been reaching for was a flashlight, which he would have used to find his way in the gathering dusk to his unlit door, which he never saw again. . . .

Only twenty-seven seconds had elapsed between the moment Eichmann had reached for his flashlight and the car's take-off with him being bound and gagged in the back. Opaque goggles served as a blindfold. Taking side streets rather than main arteries, [Zvi] Aharoni [chief interrogator for Israel's domestic equivalent of the Federal Bureau of Investigation and a key figure for the days of dialogue with Eichmann ahead] drove for an hour—with the second car checking that there were no pursuers—before arriving at a villa code-named "Tira" in the Florencio Varela district of Buenos Aires.

Inside the house, they searched their captive's mouth for a vial of poison and found none. Then they looked at his left armpit and found the telltale scars where his SS tattoo had been removed. Only then did Aharoni ask him in German: "Who are you?"

Eichmann didn't evade the question by pretending to be Ricardo Klement. "*Ich bin Adolf Eichmann*," he answered. After a pause, he added wearily but almost with relief: "I know I'm in the hands of Jews. I am resigned to my fate.". . .

The Trial

"I saw Adolf Eichmann for the first time on the opening day of his trial in the courtroom in Jerusalem," Simon Wiesenthal says in his 1967 memoir. *"For nearly sixteen years I had thought of him practically every day and every night. In my mind I had built up the image of a demonic superman. Instead I saw a frail, nondescript, shabby fellow in a glass cell between two Israeli policemen. . . . There was nothing demonic about him; he looked like a bookkeeper who is afraid to*

Adolf Eichmann stands in his glass booth as he receives the death sentence for crimes against humanity on December 16, 1961 in Jerusalem, Israel.

ask for a raise. Something seemed completely wrong, and I kept thinking about it while the incomprehensible bill of indictment ('the murder of six million men, women, and children') was being read. Suddenly I knew what it was. In my mind I'd always seen SS Obersturmbannführer [Major] Eichmann, supreme arbiter of life and death. But the Eichmann I now saw did not wear the SS uniform of terror and murder. Dressed in a cheap, dark suit, he seemed a cardboard figure, empty and two-dimensional.". . .

The trial would last eight months. . . . A dozen years after Adolf Eichmann was hanged in 1962, when Wiesenthal confessed to me that he wondered whether his quarry should have been exe-

cuted, it was on this same ground: "When you take the life of one man for the murder of six million, you cheapen the value of the dead. It means, if you look at it a certain way, that one German life is worth six million Jewish lives. In general, I am against the death sentence, though I can understand that Eichmann is a special case. But, in the moment they killed him, the case was closed. Yet, even today, there are people appearing with new testimony, new evidence against him. Maybe it would have been better to give him six or eleven million life sentences and kept him in prison as a warning to the murderers of tomorrow and, each time new charges surface, to bring him back into the glass booth and let him answer them and let a judge decide. The trial is a lesson. But I don't know."

What was the lesson of the Eichmann trial? At a time when the world was distancing itself from the Holocaust as a historical aberration and neo-Nazi revisionists were beginning to claim that Auschwitz and Anne Frank never really happened, Eichmann's testimony belied these lies. And, as Wiesenthal put it in the original German version of the 1988 memoir, *Justice, Not Vengeance*: "The Eichmann trial conveyed an essential deep understanding of the Nazi death machinery and its most important protagonists. Since that time, the world now under-stands the concept of 'desk murderer.' We know that one doesn't need to be fanatical, sadistic, or mentally ill to murder millions; that it is enough to be a loyal follower eager to do one's duty for a *Führer,* and that mass murderers absolutely need not be—indeed, cannot be!—asocial. On the contrary, mass murder on a large scale pre-supposes a social conformist for a murderer." To which he added in an interview: "These people were often good family men, good fathers. They gave to the poor. They loved flowers. But they killed people. Why? Because they had the idea that they did not need to think. Hitler would think for them. Not one was born a murderer."

Selection 7

Living with the Nightmares

William B. Helmreich

This encyclopedia is filled with horror sto-ries. They are difficult to read and it is im-possible to imagine what it must have been like to actually live through the war. How can anyone live with the memories of what hap-pened to them, what they saw in the camps, with the loss of loved ones? The resilience of humans is remarkable and is no more evident than in the lives of Holocaust survivors. Every one was deeply affected by his or her experience, but surprisingly few were inca-pacitated by it or driven to such despair that they would kill themselves. Most lived and are living what we would consider "normal" lives. Some were driven by their experiences to extraordinary success and wealth. Even these people, however, are different than their peers because of their past. This excerpt examines some of the ways that Holocaust survivors dealt with their experiences and how it affected their lives. William B. Helm-reich is a professor of sociology and Judaic studies at City University of New York Grad-uate Center and City College of New York and the author of several books.

Excerpted from William B. Helmreich, *Against All Odds: Holo-caust Survivors and the Successful Lives They Made in America.* Copyright © 1992 William B. Helmreich. Reprinted with permis-sion from the author.

"*I*f you've been through Auschwitz and you *don't* have nightmares, then you're not normal," a survivor once remarked to me. Her comment highlighted the importance of evaluating the survivors within the context of their own experience. If by normal we mean a happy, perfectly well-adjusted individual, then many survivors, as well as others who did not go through the Holocaust, could not be so described. But if we are referring to people who get up in the morning, go to work, raise a family, and enjoy a variety of leisure time pursuits, then an overwhelming majority of the survivors would qualify as normal.

Indeed, many survivors did quite well. They achieved financial security, raised families, and were active in community affairs. There is, however, another, more subtle yet crucial, measure of success that has not yet been looked at carefully—how the survivors live with their memories of what happened to them. What do years of incarceration in a world whose very raison d'être was inflicting pain and punishment do to the psyche? What are the long-range psychological effects and how do they influence the individual's outlook on life in general? In short, were the survivors able to resolve the turmoil and conflict that resulted from their ordeals? What insights into life did they gain because of what happened to them? . . .

A Viennese-born child survivor who is today a college professor [explains]:

> Many of us refuse to display symbols that identify us as Jews right off the bat; so that we will not wear a Star of David, for instance. . . . A few years ago my son, who had joined B'nai B'rith Youth Organization [BBYO], was going to have a simple march in support of the State of Israel . . . but that was the year of the massacres in Sabra and Shatila and I had received a nasty anonymous phone call, accusing me of being responsible for Sabra and Shatila. . . . So I called the regional leader for BBYO and asked him to cancel the march, because I was afraid. I told them I was a survivor . . . so yes, there is some fear. When I moved to this town and the Jewish stores were closed for the High Holidays, my thought was: "The next time they want to throw stones, they'll know exactly which ones are Jewish stores."

Nightmares are probably the most common symptom of disturbance among survivors. . . . Their frequency and intensity vary from one individual to the next but they are often accompanied by screaming and feelings of anxiety, as depicted in the well-known film *The Pawnbroker.* Most often the survivors dream about what happened to them during the war, but sometimes these memories intermingle with more current fears, such as running and hiding with their children, who were, in fact, born after their liberation. Some survivors awake, are comforted by their spouses, and go back to sleep; others find it necessary to read, walk around the house, or eat something. Most have learned to cope on their own, but a few require regular medication to help them. One man has been taking tranquilizers for almost forty years. Several survivors attributed an increase in nightmares to having read books and seen films on the Holocaust when the topic became very popular in recent years.

Living with Guilt

Of course, guilt is a normal emotion felt by most people, but, among survivors it takes on special meaning when related to the Holocaust. Most feel guilty about the death of loved ones whom they feel they could have, or should have, saved. Even if they could have done nothing to help their friends or relatives, they find themselves asking over and over: "Why did *I* live and not them?" Some feel guilty about situations in which they behaved selfishly even if there was no other way to survive.

Survivors, particularly males, also blame themselves for not having displayed bravery in the face of oppression. As David Jagoda, a survivor living in Minneapolis, put it:

> Sometimes I feel like I am really not a survivor. You know why? A lot of times, it came to my mind, like 100 Germans took 10,000 Jews. We could kill them in no time at all. If every one Jew would kill one German, they would be in trouble.

Jagoda makes no mention of the lack of arms, the physical condition of most Jews, or other factors, saying only, "I sometimes feel guilty because I survived; because I did not survive properly. I didn't do anything." In the following example, a survivor described how such guilt was engendered when individuals were forced to make impossible choices between those dear to them:

I remember a man whose wife and son were at the mercy of the Gestapo, and they told him that if he didn't tell them where his parents were in hiding, they would kill his young family. He went to his parents and asked them what he should do, and they said, "You must give us up"; so he did. And he survived the war, as did his wife and child. I have seen him a few times—he lives in New York now—but I can never meet him without thinking of the permanent agony those sadists condemned him to because of what they made him do.

Such agonizing dilemmas cannot ever be forgotten or ignored. In their happiest moments, the survivors remain aware of how human beings can be made to suffer. Moreover, it is an inner misery that remains with them no matter where they are. It affects their daily functioning and, most certainly, their judgments about people, not to mention their worldview. Even as they grapple with the implications of what they were compelled to do, they wonder whether others would have acted less nobly or more nobly were they in a similar situation. The words of a character in Sheila Levin's novel *Simple Truths* bring into sharp focus the horror of having to make such decisions. A father, he is responding to his daughter's question, "What is worse than death?":

Erosion. . . . To be nibbled away at, day after day. Not just from the beatings, the starvation, the fear of death. Worse than that is the mutilation of the spirit. The body can endure what the mind cannot. The brutality was unendurable because it was incomprehensible. . . .

The choices that that world allowed were a masterpiece of evil. Civilization was gone. Boundaries, parameters, limits, all canceled. "Shall we send these hundred-and-fifty boys to the ovens, or these? Tell me, sir, would you prefer us to rape your wife or your daughter? Which twin shall we castrate?" Those were the choices. Madness. Those were the choices.

Not once, but every day, every hour, day after day. Every day was the end of the world.

Guilt, depression, intense feelings of loneliness, withdrawal, anxiety, paranoia, all these formed part of the reaction known as Concentration Camp Survivors Syndrome. . . .

Nevertheless, only a minority of survivors found that these problems interfered with their ability to function on a daily basis and that in itself attests to their resiliency as a group. For those unable to cope, the support of friends and family greatly helped to cushion the impact of their suffering and many referred to it as a key factor in their ability to come to terms with what had happened. . . .

It is ultimately impossible to expect people to be like everyone else when the central event of their lives did not happen to anyone else and they know it. This perception of self is clearly and eloquently elucidated in a book by Cecilie Klein, a camp survivor currently living on Long Island.

A survivor will go to a party and feel alone.
A survivor appears quiet but is screaming within.
A survivor will make large weddings, with many guests,
but the ones she wants most will never arrive.
A survivor will go to a funeral and cry, not for the deceased but for the ones that were never buried.
A survivor will reach out to you but not let you get close, for you remind her of what she could have been,
but will never be.
A survivor is at ease only with other survivors.

When Memories Return

. . . In some instances, survivors are presented with an opportunity to respond openly and forcefully to those who participated in the war. Some are afraid to do so, others are not. The following story, told by a woman who survived Auschwitz, demonstrates how deep the scars can be:

I was shopping in Bloomingdale's and, as I held up a jacket, a man behind me commented that, in his country, the jacket was much more expensive. He kept saying that, so, out of courtesy, I asked: "Where is your country?" "Oh, Germany," he said. "Where are you from?" he asked. "You have an accent." "Hungary," I answered. "I was in Hungary, in 1944," the man said. Then the blood rushed to my head. "In what unit were you, in the Gestapo or the SS?" He said: "No, I wasn't in the Gestapo or the SS. I was in the Wehrmacht." Then I said: "In 1944, in Hungary, there were only SS or Gestapo." And he answered: "No, I wouldn't be ashamed to tell you if I was in the SS unit or the Wehrmacht. I am proud of my Führer. I always was proud. He was a very good man. I am very, very proud of him. He didn't do anything wrong." I started to shake. I started to scream: "You murderer!" And as I was screaming, two salesmen came over and in the meantime, he ran away down the escalator and disappeared. But in that moment I would have been able to kill him.

Of course, aggressive behavior need not be limited to the physical arena. Another form it took was that of the almost stereotypical, hard-driving survivor who worked long hours and fought tooth and nail to succeed in business. Indeed, many survivors did just that. . . . By succeeding, the survivor acquires the very power by which he feels threatened and gains control over his environment. To better understand the motivation involved, we need only consider the opposite of success. To require and receive assistance from others was often viewed by former camp inmates as a sign of weakness, something they could ill afford to have shown during that time. . . .

Not long after I began this project, I interviewed an elderly lady who had been in both ghettos and concentration camps. Her adaptation to life in America had been fairly smooth. She had raised two children and appeared to be happily married. Her demeanor was calm and she smiled often, especially when she spoke about her children and grandchildren. After I finished, her daughter happened to walk in. We spoke briefly about the study I was conducting. Then she called me aside and said, "I suppose you think my mother is well adjusted." "It would seem that way," I replied. "Well, she is, except for one thing. I live in Brooklyn and she lives in the Bronx. Every day she calls me at 3:30 sharp to ask if my kids came home, and if they haven't she goes crazy. One time, when the kids were twenty minutes late, she got into a cab and came over here, all the way from the Bronx, during the rush hour." "Why does she act this way?" I asked. "Because 3:30 is the exact time she was taken away from her parents in the ghetto in Poland and she never saw them again."

This woman's story made me realize early on that survivors can never really banish what happened to them from their minds. . . .

One general feature is that survivors' homes are very clean and neat. . . . Some researchers have noted that survivor women are compulsive house-cleaners. This seems to be related to life in the camps, where it was extremely difficult to stay clean, both personally and in general. "We had to live with dirt for so long, and every time I see a dirty place I remember those years," observed one former Dachau inmate. . . .

Since food was so basic to survival in the camps, survivors hate to see it wasted. Congressman Tom Lantos elaborated on this to me: "I cannot put food on my plate that I don't finish. In a restaurant I always have trouble ordering anything that is more than a reasonable portion because to send food back is a crime.". . .

Why Me?

The majority of believers did not become atheists, but there was a definite decrease in the number of believers. Moreover, for most the Holocaust created grave doubts about the nature of God and His relationship to human beings even as the survivors continued to believe in Him. . . .

For some survivors simply remaining alive during the Holocaust was enough of a miracle to justify continued faith in God. One man extended this view to the period after the war as well, saying: "I got through Auschwitz and nothing happened to me. I went through the Korean War and nothing happened to me, so somebody must be looking after me." Sam Halpern was more

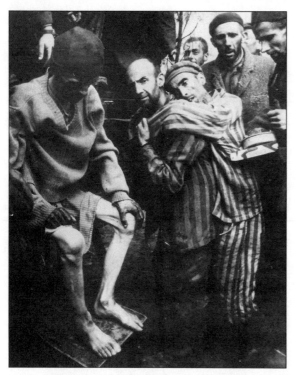

The horrors of the Holocaust caused some survivors to question their faith and others to abandon it completely.

specific: "I escaped from camp and didn't know whether to go right or left. Then I saw a pigeon flying and I said: 'I think I'll follow this pigeon.' Well, the pigeon was going to the front and that was the right direction." The proof is presented here in terms of personal survival. However, whenever I pressed respondents to explain why God had not chosen to save others in a similar manner, the response was invariably: "We can't understand God." No one claimed to have been saved because they were more worthy than someone else who died. Most simply asserted that they did not know why God had chosen to save them or why He had decided not to intervene on behalf of those who perished.

Some survivors justified their having been rescued from certain death conditionally, that is, God now expected certain things from them. One wealthy businessman, William Ungar, posed the dilemma in the following terms:

> Why did I survive and others didn't? Why was I only wounded and others were killed? I

survived to be a witness to what took place. And I also think God let me live to see what good I would do. This may be a very primitive way to answer the question but I feel that if I did survive, it was to do some good deeds in my lifetime. Of course, I wouldn't preach about it or advertise it. I'm not trying to elevate myself that I'm the only one who deserved to survive.

This individual clearly understood that he could not explain why he was, so to speak, "anointed" by God. He is active in the Jewish community and has given generously to charity. It is perhaps the best way for him to justify God's seeming faith in *him*. . . .

For most survivors, . . . the questions remain and are not so easily resolved. They believe in varying degrees, but they question, and often they are very angry. . . . And sometimes survivors act out their anger directly:

> A good friend of mine was in Bergen-Belsen and the first thing she did when she got out was she got a sandwich with some kind of meat and put cheese on it [a clear violation of the laws of kashruth]. Then she looked up at God and said, "See? Do me something!" Is that somebody who doesn't believe in God? No. She's *mad* at God.

Even those who remain steadfast in their religious observance can engage in behavior of this sort. One woman always places a drop of milk in her chicken soup and says, "This is to punish you, God, for what you have done."

Challenging and questioning God is not an act of heresy according to Jewish law. On the contrary, it is an ancient tradition, one first articulated in the Bible by Abraham when he wondered aloud whether God's desire to destroy Sodom and Gomorrah was just. Jonah defies God when told to go to Nineveh. . . .

For Jews who adhere to the teachings of the faith there is a causal connection between sin and punishment, even if its precise workings are not known. They read in the Bible of God's threats to the Jews of retribution if they forsake His commandments and they inevitably wonder what transgressions brought about the Holocaust. In [another] study 21 percent saw a direct relationship between the death of six million Jews and man's sinfulness. I asked one respondent who felt this way why so many of the Jews who were killed were observant. Her answer: "When it rains, everyone gets wet. On the other hand, the State of Israel was a reward to show the enemy that our Lord is alive.". . .

Some survivors find meaning in the tortures they endured by viewing them as a part of Jewish history, of which the Holocaust is simply the latest and most systematically brutal instance of cruelty to Jews. Hence they do not see it as a unique tragedy. . . .

For the survivors, ritual observance and cultural involvement became the vehicles for honoring and commemorating those no longer present. Miriam Brach summed it up best in the following words:

> I believe that it was my destiny to survive, to come back from the ashes and to be the link from the past that would begin life again and pass it on to future generations. My goal was to remain faithful to the religion into which I was born and to my upbringing. This upbringing gave me the strength to survive the war. When I live this way, I know I am living the kind of life my departed parents would have wanted me to live.

Nonbelievers

. . . When all is said and done, however, there is still a sizable segment of the survivor community whose members have either lost their faith and openly admit it, or who never believed to begin with. One unequivocally asserted: "I don't believe in anything and you wouldn't either if you went through what I went through.". . .

A number of nonbelieving survivors coupled their assertions with a wish that it could be otherwise. One such individual, who lived through Auschwitz, spoke of her doubts with sincere regret:

> It's easier to believe than not to, but I can't believe. I listened as my granddaughter read the story in synagogue of how the whale spit up Jonah after three days, and of course I couldn't say anything to the children about what a stupidity this is after we were in such a fire, in Auschwitz, where the sky was always black from the flesh of people they burned. There were a few Jews who tried to revolt; so they pushed them into the ovens alive. So I ask, couldn't there have been just one little miracle, something to show that there is justice in the world? I saw how the Nazis learned how to shoot by killing children. So that's why I never believed. There were no miracles. There were no miracles.

Selection 8

The Creation of a Jewish Homeland

Michael Berenbaum

The Jews who survived the Holocaust needed to first be rehabilitated from their weak and sickly condition and then required new homes. Some hoped to return to the homes they'd left behind, but, in most cases, those no longer existed or had been taken over by non-Jews after they left. No one was welcoming the Jews back to their old homes. On the contrary, the anti-Semitic attitudes that had allowed the Nazis to persecute the Jews remained strong. In Kielce, Poland, for example, returning Jews were massacred by the inhabitants. With no place to go, hundreds of thousands of Jews found themselves back in camps. The conditions were completely different and they were now supervised by Allied forces, but the survivors were still fenced in. Reluctantly, western nations, including the United States, began to allow some of them to immigrate, but the numbers were relatively small, and the quotas tended to still favor non-Jews. Many of the survivors hoped to go to Palestine where Jews were fighting to create a new independent Jewish state. The British controlled Palestine, however, and did not want thousands of Jews streaming into the country and

complicating their relations with the Arabs. Consequently, clandestine efforts were required to bring the Jews to Palestine. This article, by Michael Berenbaum, the former project director of the U.S. Holocaust Memorial Museum, describes what happened to many of the Jews who survived the Holocaust.

As the Allied armies swept through Europe in 1944 and 1945, they found seven to nine million displaced people living in countries not their own. More than six million returned to their native lands. But more than one million refused repatriation. Most of them were Poles, Estonians, Latvians, Lithuanians, Ukrainians, and Yugoslavs. Some had collaborated with the Nazis and were afraid of retaliation should they return home. Others feared persecution by the new Communist regimes in Eastern Europe.

Jewish survivors could not return home. Their communities were shattered, their homes destroyed or occupied by strangers. In the east, they were not welcome in the land of their birth. With nowhere to go, they were forced to live in camps set up on the sites where they had been imprisoned. For most of them, this meant a prolonged stay in Germany living in the midst of those who had sought to impose the Final Solution.

The beleaguered American army was hard pressed to juggle the multiple assignment of serving as both an occupation force and a counterforce in the new Cold War, and of dealing with the problems of the survivors. Short-term problems—housing, medical treatment, food, attempting to reunite families—were acute and demanding. The army had no long-range strategy for resettling those who could not or would not return home.

Most Jewish displaced persons wanted to begin a new life in Palestine. Although many would have preferred to emigrate to the United States, they were not willing to wait for years to qualify for admission. In 1945, most Jewish DPs were survivors of the concentration camps, partisans, or those who had spent the war in hiding. Life in the concentration camps had taken a hard toll. The survivors were destitute, and often sick. . . . They were haunted by nightmares and mistrusted authority—even the American authorities who were trying to help them.

Living conditions in the camps were unpleasant. Camps were overcrowded, and although the DPs were not starved, there was never enough food. Coping again with life, with the prospect of living after everything that had been endured, was the greatest difficulty. Major Irving Heymont who directed the Landsberg displaced persons camp wrote to his wife:

> The camp is filthy beyond description. Sanitation is virtually unknown. . . . The Army units we relieved obviously did nothing more than insure that rations were delivered to the camp. With few exceptions the people of the camp themselves appear demoralized beyond hope of rehabilitation. They appear to be beaten both spiritually and physically.

Britain was unwilling to permit Jewish emigration to Palestine. Trying to preserve the remnants of its empire, it was reticent to alienate the Arab world hostile to a potential Jewish state. The United States was not ready to receive an influx of refugees. Soldiers were coming home from the war. It was a time of transition from war production to a civilian economy, and there was a fear that refugees would consume scarce resources and take jobs away from Americans.

Nativistic thinking did not end with World War II, even if the isolationists were silenced. Within a few weeks of taking office as president, Harry Truman dispatched Earl Harrison, the dean of the University of Pennsylvania Law School, to report on the displaced-persons camps. The report was a bombshell. Harrison concluded that:

> We (the United States) appear to be treating the Jews as the Nazis treated them, except that we do not exterminate them. They are in concentration camps in large numbers under our military guard instead of SS troops. One is led to wonder whether the German people seeing this are not supposing that we are following or at least condoning Nazi policy.

His recommendations were sweeping: the special status of Jews must be recognized; they should be evacuated from Germany swiftly; and 100,000 Jews should be admitted to Palestine. Truman, who was later to become a hero to the Jews for recognizing Israel as a state, followed his humanitarian impulses. He endorsed the report, rebuked the army, and intensified the pressure on Britain to allow Jews to immigrate to Palestine. He also opened the United States to limited immigration. His personal sentiments were clear: "It is unthinkable that they should be left indefinitely in camps in Europe.". . .

On July 4, 1946, a mob of Poles attacked the one hundred and fifty Jews who had returned to the town of Kielce. Forty-two were killed and fifty wounded. Before the war, twenty-four thousand Jews had lived in Kielce; the one hundred and fifty who were targets of the pogrom were survivors who had come home looking for their families and their homes. The Kielce pogrom was inspired by the age-old blood libel that was part of the classic pattern of anti-Jewish violence: the mob believed hat Jews were killing Christian children and drinking their blood, or using the blood to bake Passover wafers. In Kielce, the Poles were also stirred up by fear that the Jews would reclaim their lost property. . . .

The news of the Kielce pogrom spread like wildfire throughout the remnant of the Jewish community in Eastern Europe. It was as though nothing had changed. Jews throughout Poland understood that it was not safe to return home; the future lay elsewhere.

On December 22, 1945, President Truman granted preferential treatment to displaced persons who wanted to immigrate to the United States. Within the next eighteen months, 22,950 DPs were admitted, 15,478 of them Jews. But the problem of what to do with the displaced persons could not be solved merely by a minor adjustment of the quotas. . . . In the summer of 1946, with the American zone of occupied Germany flooded by the 100,000 Polish Jews newly released by the Soviet Union and by Jews fleeing Eastern Europe after the Kielce pogrom, congressional action could no longer be avoided. . . .

In 1948, Congress passed a bill providing for the admission of 200,000 over four years. Truman called it "flagrantly discriminatory against Jews." In 1950, the act was amended to make it slightly less discriminatory. The change was too late: in 1949, most of the Jewish DPs had gone to the newly established state of Israel. . . .

During the three years after the war, only 41,000 DPs were admitted to the United States. Two-thirds of them were Jews. In the four years following the passage of the immigration law of 1948, 365,223 displaced persons were brought to American shores. Half the immigrants were Roman Catholic and only 16 percent Jews. Some of the DPs openly admitted to having collaborated with the Nazis. All in all, fewer than 100,000 Jews were able to reach the United States in the years between the end of the war and the closing of the last DP camp seven years later. . . .

Between 1944 and 1948, more than 200,000 Jews fled from Eastern and Central Europe to Palestine, crossing borders legally, semilegally, or illegally. The means did not seem to matter: the borders were crossed somehow.

The movement began spontaneously and in a small way. In the summer of 1944, three partisans, Abba Kovner of Vilna, Vitka Kempner, and Ruzhka Korczak, a former subordinate commander in Vilna, met in the Rudninkai Forest to discuss their future. They decided that every effort must be made to get to Palestine. At the same time, a survivor in Rovno, Eliezer Lidovsky, organized the first group to leave Poland, first to Romania and then to Palestine via the Black Sea. . . .

The pogrom in Kielce and other manifestations of continuing antisemitism, coming after the devastation of Jewish towns and villages in Eastern Europe, sent a clear message. Those who returned were convinced there was no future in what had been home. Poland was a vast Jewish graveyard, a place of bitter memories. Jewish life still seemed to hang by a thread.

Soon the inchoate movement was organized and given a name—Bricha, the Hebrew word for escape. Bricha facilitated the border crossings, but it did not initiate the migration. Operatives were brought in from the Jewish Brigade and the Hagana, the defense forces of Jews in Palestine. Two major routes were established. One went west from Lódź to Poznan and Szczecin, and then to the British or American zone in Germany. The other went south from Lódź to Katowice or Krakow, then through Czechoslovakia, Hungary, or Austria to Italy or Yugoslavia.

The borders were crossed by day and at night, on foot and by train. Some border guards had to be bribed. Others simply turned aside and pretended not to notice. Czechoslovakia cooperated with the refugees; at times Poland did as well. Most countries were quite pleased to be rid of the Jews and gladly helped them on their way. Much to the chagrin of the British, the Americans allowed Jews into their sector of Germany.

In the summer of 1945, when Earl Harrison wrote his report, there were about 50,000 Jews in Germany and Austria. At that moment, the Jewish DP problem could easily have been solved by the issuance of 100,000 entry permits to Palestine. In the next year and a half, the number of Jews in the American sector increased fourfold, creating political pressure on both the British and the Americans that led to the establishment of a Jewish state.

Meanwhile, Jews were not content to wait while the politicians decided their fate. They set out for Palestine on their own, assisted by a

Zionist underground network composed of Palestinian soldiers from the Jewish Brigade and Jews serving in Allied armies or working in Europe as civilians. Between 1945 and May 1948, 69,000 Jews made the journey by sea illegally on sixty-five boats. Only a few of the ships that ran the British blockade succeeded in reaching the coast of Palestine. Most were stopped by the British Royal Navy. The passengers were then sent to detention camps in Cyprus.

The movement of Jews to Palestine was known by several names. According to the British, it was illegal immigration. Palestinian Jews referred to it as Aliya Bet. (In Hebrew, *aliya* means a going up to the land, and *bet* is the second letter of the alphabet; hence, a second means of ascent to the land.)

Clandestine intelligence networks of Mossad (Mossad L'Aliya Bet, the agency for the Aliya Bet, which later evolved into the famed Israeli intelligence agency) operated most of the ships. The sailings, however, were anything but secret. Journalists were notified in advance. Pictures of the British forcibly removing Holocaust survivors from ships and imprisoning them yet again were sent to newspapers throughout the world as part of a campaign to discredit the British mandate over Palestine.

The most famous event in Aliya Bet was the journey of the *Exodus*, a ship that set sail from Marseilles in July 1947 carrying forty-five hundred passengers. After a brief fight, the ship was captured. Instead of sending the passengers to Cyprus, the British took a "get tough" policy and forced the ship back to Marseilles. The passengers refused to disembark in Europe. They went on a hunger strike, which captured international attention.

The British cabinet would not relent in a struggle they saw as a test of wills with the Jews. They feared losing control of the situation and did not understand the special sensitivity for Holocaust survivors that would galvanize world public opinion. The passengers would be taken to Germany and there returned to Bergen-Belsen against their will. It took tear gas to force the concentration camp survivors off the ship. For

two months the *Exodus* claimed the sympathy and attention of the world. The decision to send survivors back to a concentration camp caused international revulsion.

Aliya Bet dramatized the indomitable will of survivors to reach the land of Israel and broke the back of the British mandate over Palestine. Four months later, the United Nations voted for the establishment of an independent Jewish state in Palestine. Aliya Bet provided the means of migration to Palestine. The will to go to the Jewish homeland was pervasive among the survivors. I.F. Stone reported on the simple yearnings of the survivors: "I am a Jew," he was told. "That's enough. We have wandered enough. We have worked and struggled too long on the lands of other peoples. We must build a land of our own.". . .

On May 14, 1948, David Ben-Gurion proclaimed the state of Israel. That evening, the last British troops departed as the Union Jack was lowered. In its place rose the blue and white Star of David. That evening, Israel was also attacked by five Arab countries. A Jewish army was in place to defend its country.

In its Declaration of Independence, the provisional government of the new state ended all restriction on Jewish immigrants. In a few days, two ships, the *State of Israel* and *To Victory*, arrived with displaced persons now coming home. In the first days of independence, the Israeli government began the evacuation of the camps in Cyprus and the DP camps in Europe. It also began an intensive recruitment effort for the Israel Defense Forces among the young and able-bodied survivors, some of whom had fought in the Allied armies or as partisans. Resistance fighters from Warsaw and Vilna soon fought in Jerusalem and the Negev.

By the autumn of 1949, Jews were leaving the DP camps of Europe at a rate of ten thousand a month. On December 17, 1950, the Central Committee of Jewish Displaced Persons was disbanded. All those who wanted to settle in Israel had arrived. In 1950, Israel passed the Law of Return, granting Jews immediate citizenship upon their arrival. Once unwanted everywhere, Jews now had a country willing to open its borders to them. Israel offered itself as a haven to Jews fleeing persecution anywhere. Under the Law of Return, Jews fleeing Khomeini's Iran, segregated South Africa, starvation in Ethiopia, and persecution in the Soviet Union have found freedom in Israel.

Jewish survivors of the Holocaust finally found a place they could call home, a country that wanted them and that they wanted. The task of state-building was challenging and looked to the future. There were wars to be fought, cities and villages to be built, crops to be planted. These activities did not allow much time to dwell on the past. It would take a long time for the survivors to rebuild their lives from the ashes, and even more time to face the haunting memories of a painful past. . . .

The birth of the state of Israel was the most significant positive consequence of the Holocaust. The independent Jewish state might have come into being because of the impetus of Jewish nationalism and the Zionist movement of return to the land of Israel. But the presence of survivors in displaced-persons camps after the war increased worldwide support and sympathy for the Jewish state and hastened its formation. Yet Israel is not an answer to the Holocaust. Its formation could not undo the horror of the death camps. . . .

Could the Holocaust Have Been Prevented?

Chapter 8

*T*he persecution of the Jews by the Nazis beginning shortly after Hitler took power was no secret. Later, Hitler did not hide his desire to exterminate every Jewish man, woman, and child. Still, little was done to save the Jews. Before, during, and even after the war, severe restrictions were placed on the number of Jews who could immigrate to the United States and other countries. Even after it was clear the Jews were being liquidated, the Roosevelt administration (and its defenders today, represented here by Robert Herzstein's selection) took the position that the best thing it could do to help the Jews was to win the war.

Given the twenty-four-hour news coverage of today, and the doggedness with which journalists pursue stories about war and its human cost, it is difficult to imagine how the press could have failed to generate a public outcry over the mistreatment of the Jews. It is not true that the story was not covered; it is possible to find plenty of reports of tens of thousands of Jews being imprisoned or killed, but the stories were often buried in the newspapers or written in a way to discount their veracity.

One question that is always asked is, "What could have been done?" Some argue that nothing could have saved the Jews, but many ideas were raised at the time and some are described in this chapter. One of the most heated controversies is whether the Allies could have, and should have, bombed Auschwitz. Stuart Erdheim's article analyzes the questions.

Besides the question of what the United States and other governments could have done is the issue of Christian responses to the Holocaust, in particular the actions of Pope Pius XII. The title of David Cornwell's excerpt, "Saint or Sinner?" summarizes the arguments on each side.

Selection 1

Official Secrets

Richard Breitman

To answer the question of whether more could have been done to prevent the Holocaust, or to save more of the victims, it is essential to learn what *the Allied government knew and* when *they knew it. For many years, the claim was made that no one knew what the Nazis were doing until it was too late. Researchers have found that the U.S. government was aware of the large-scale murder of Jews by at least January 1942. In this article, Richard Breitman gives an overview of new evidence that has come to light from newly released classified British documents that proves the Allies did in fact have information very early in the war about Nazi atrocities and chose to keep it secret. Rather than make a concerted effort to save the Jews, the decision was made that they could best be helped by the more general war effort. Breitman is a professor of history at American University and editor of the journal* Holocaust and Genocide Studies.

*D*uring World War II, Hitler and his key subordinates were determined, one way or another, to destroy the Jewish "race." In chapter 1, I have traced some antecedents of this determination. I do not wish to suggest that, from the 1920s on, Hitler and Himmler were so rigid and fixated on Jews that the history of Nazi Germany and the history of the Holocaust were nothing more than an unfolding of pre-arranged ideas and ideology. Even if this were true, there would be no satisfactory way to demonstrate it empirically. But *Mein Kampf* was hardly empty rhetoric. Himmler certainly took it (and Nazi ideology generally) seriously enough before and after the Nazi takeover of power on January 30, 1933.

Hitler had broad political and foreign-policy goals that took priority during the 1930s and in peacetime circumstances would influence how far he would and could proceed against Jews. . . . Although, the idea of mass murder of Jews did not erupt suddenly in the middle of the war. It was very early regarded as conceivable—and not just by Hitler.

The radicalism of their hostility to Jews and the sweep of their racial vision set many Nazi leaders apart from the substantial anti-Semitic portion of the German public. That gap makes it important to investigate how large numbers of the Order Police came to participate in mass executions. Through a case study and suggestive

Excerpted from Richard Breitman, "Conclusion," from *Official Secrets: What the Nazis Planned, What the British and Americans Knew.* Copyright © 1998 Richard Breitman. Reprinted with permission from Hill and Wang, a division of Farrar, Straus and Giroux, LLC.

evidence, I have tried to show that popular anti-Semitism had some influence on police behavior, as it had some influence on German public reaction to the influx of information about genocide. But the authorities also heavily relied on orders, deception, and secrecy in handling both the police and the German public. If all German police had been "willing executioners," there would have been less official concern and far less urgency behind the push toward the use of gas chambers as a means of mass murder.

The first portion of this book contains a range of evidence, some of it available to Western scholars only in recent years, and certain British intelligence documents quite new, about the specific arrangements for the mass murder of Jews in Nazi Germany. This evidence modifies or complements our previous understanding of the Holocaust, most obviously by elevating the roles of several Nazi officials and the institutions they headed.

Nowhere else is Kurt Daluege considered a significant figure in the Final Solution, and other descriptions of the work of his Order Police have focused either on events and forces from 1942 on or on case studies of particular battalions. But it now appears that the Order Police was a major element even in the planning stage and that it clearly was a major element during the "first sweep" of Jews from the Soviet territories in 1941. This broad participation of non-elite units in the Germans' mass murders in the East raises some large political and philosophical questions.

The only substantial monograph on the Higher SS and Police Leaders concentrated on these officeholders within Germany. But Jeckeln, Bach-Zelewski, and, to a lesser extent, Prützmann and Korsemann—all of them in the Soviet territories—helped to direct the first phase of the Holocaust, and this work also clarifies their relationship with Daluege and his Order Police battalions, which has not generally been understood.

The Nazi regime planned, through the Higher SS and Police Leaders in the East, to construct stationary gas chambers using Zyklon B gas and crematoria to liquidate Soviet Jews, as well as

Jews deported from Germany and conceivably elsewhere. It is not certain that these plans went completely unrealized: the methods used to liquidate Jews at some sites remain obscure and in need of further research.

Some scholars have argued that the goal of Nazi Jewish policy was for a time uncertain, that deportations to the East simply meant removing the Jewish threat within Germany and getting Jews out of the way, that the deportations evolved into the Final Solution only under later wartime pressures. But Nazi officials envisioned deportations of European Jews to the East from at least early 1941, and Himmler worked on the arrangements for deporting German Jews to the East beginning in September of that year. The words and actions of Bach-Zelewski, Jeckeln, Prützmann, and others clarify what deportations of Jews meant—from the beginning.

This evidence tightens the intrinsic connection between the mass shootings of Jews in the Soviet territories and the assembly-line gassings of European Jews in the extermination camps, which only began at Chelmno at the end of 1941 and did not occur on a large scale elsewhere until mid-1942. In short, new evidence of Nazi plans for earlier extermination camps in the East fills a (partial) chronological gap in our reading of Nazi intentions and policies. This evidence suggests that the meaning of the term "Final Solution," used by Walter Schellenberg in May 1941 and again by Reinhard Heydrich on July 31, 1941, was exactly what it later became, even if all the locations and methods of mass murder were not determined in advance. This book is about the decodes in the strict sense of deciphering coded radio messages, but it is also about understanding evidence that is at times cryptic, partial, or even misleading on the surface.

Although I am no specialist in signals communication or cryptography, I have done my best to clarify how German forces in the Soviet territories communicated with high Nazi officials and vice versa. Much of this information is new, and this coverage had the side benefit of illustrating Nazi practices designed to maintain the secrecy of the Final Solution, as well as Britain's ability to penetrate Nazi cloaking devices.

Some decoding of the Allied response to the Holocaust is needed, too. The images of Winston Churchill and Franklin Delano Roosevelt remain so powerful and vivid that many people today tend to think of the history of British and American responses to the Holocaust primarily in terms of their individual reactions and policies. This tendency is not entirely sound: the history of any government policy in twentieth-century Western democracies must in good part be a study of bureaucracies. Still, we must look at the limited evidence about Churchill and Roosevelt themselves.

There are two explanations for the contrast between what Churchill said or wrote about Nazi killings of Jews and how British policy took shape: rhetoric is not always reality, and Churchill did not always (or even often) set British policy. Churchill's written comments are subject to more than one interpretation—something that becomes apparent if we think of them partly as the raw material for memoirs. High government officials not infrequently write their own memoirs or histories of events they were involved in (at times when others do not yet have access to the records they use), presenting themselves in the best possible light. Churchill once told his historical researcher Maurice Ashley: "Give me the facts, Ashley, and I will twist them the way I want to suit my argument." Although Ashley states that Churchill did not often follow through on this claim of twisting evidence, he admits that Churchill, in his writing, often presented his own case.

The eminent historian Gerhard Weinberg has noted that Churchill, while serving as Prime Minister, probably expected to write a history of the war (his history of World War I was already well known), and it is quite possible that he tailored some comments he made during his term as Prime Minister for the historical record. He was still an active politician when he wrote his history of World War II, and by the time the last volume appeared, he was again Prime Minister. One should not expect objectivity under such circumstances. Weinberg's general observa-

COULD THE HOLOCAUST HAVE BEEN PREVENTED? 399

tions—not specifically aimed at Churchill's reaction to the Holocaust—are, I believe, relevant
to this context.

Some of Churchill's statements suggest that
he recognized at the time the moral and historical significance of Nazi policy toward the Jews,
but he did not act as if he did, nor did Roosevelt.
Both Churchill and Roosevelt, but particularly
Churchill, deserve great credit for recognizing
the evils of Nazism at an early date; and both
men, especially Churchill, took tremendous risks
to oppose Nazi Germany, but during the war they
inevitably dealt far more with larger questions of
military and diplomatic strategy and of the Allied
partnership than with specific decisions about
rescue of Jews. There were some exceptions—
both men got involved with specific projects em-
anating from the Bermuda Conference—but the
general statement still holds.

It is, of course, asking a great deal of wartime
heads of government to recognize in the mael-
strom of events the significance of a moral crisis
and to initiate an appropriate response. Both
men directly involved themselves in managing
the military and diplomatic campaigns against
the Axis. For the most part, they depended on
subordinates and colleagues to handle Nazi
killings of Jews and other civilians, and occasionally they ratified—or disagreed with—the
recommendations that reached them from below.
In settling bureaucratic conflicts and dealing
with political issues, their behavior was more
similar than dissimilar. This makes it all the
more striking that Churchill enjoys a very positive reputation for his response to the Holocaust
and Roosevelt a very negative one. Apparently,
some believe that the buck and the pound stop at
different locations.

On both sides of the Atlantic, foreign-policy
officials failed badly. No Western action could
have come close to stopping the Holocaust, but
the Foreign Office and the State Department in
general decided to act as if the Allied Declaration of December 17, 1942, meant less than
nothing, that it was a move in the wrong direction which they had to correct. The Foreign Office's failure to use the information from the

German police decodes either during the war or
in postwar trial proceedings is consistent with
this broader assessment. While British officials
kept this irrefutable evidence secret, many State
Department officials chose not to believe or to
act on what evidence they had. With assistance
from Jan Karski, the Treasury Department
forced a major change of course in Washington
in 1943, and President Roosevelt, with some
limitations, accepted and followed it. But British
refugee policy did not significantly alter even
after decisive Allied military successes. If there
is a distinction between Churchill and Roosevelt
on rescue and relief issues, it is hard to see how
it is in Churchill's favor.

Given the basic similarities of British and
American foreign policy with regard to the
Holocaust until 1944, what were the significant
differences? There were some battles over Jewish issues within the State Department, particularly at the top, where Sumner Welles was more
liberal than Cordell Hull (or than most of the
specialists in the European Division and elsewhere). With Welles and Hull at odds and each
distracted (Welles by a looming scandal and
Hull by illness, as well as other issues of greater
concern to him), influence moved elsewhere.
Differences of opinion on Jewish issues within
the Foreign Office, on the other hand, were apparently few, and Anthony Eden was a powerful
foreign minister. Of all the officials mentioned
in this and other studies of Western wartime
policies, Eden had the most influence on his
government's policies.

David Dutton's recent political biography of
Eden, an excellent but selective account that unfortunately has little to say on Eden and Jewish
problems, presents him as a man hypersensitive
to his image and often eager to adjust it favorably throughout his political career and in retirement. He not only wrote three long volumes of
memoirs but tried to commission historians to
write appropriately about him. But there are significant discrepancies between Eden's image
and reality. The man who gained a reputation as
an opponent of appeasement—in part because
of his resignation from Neville Chamberlain's

government—had apparently quarreled with Chamberlain about other matters, and on a number of occasions Eden had expressed approval of the notion of coming to terms with Nazi Germany. In 1937, Eden had argued that Britain would join no anti-Communist bloc and no anti-Fascist block: "It is nations' foreign policies, not their internal policies, with which we are concerned." He also held a more favorable view of Hitler than of Mussolini. This orientation was quite different from Churchill's and helps to explain some of what happened after Churchill made Eden his foreign minister.

Whereas Churchill tried to make a close personal and political relationship with Roosevelt the center of his wartime strategy, Eden's anti-American streak made him far more independent. Churchill was impulsive; Eden was persistent and careful. According to Dutton, Eden often took Churchill on and got his way. Their political attitudes, their personalities, and the nature of their relationship partly explain why Churchill's occasional forays into rescue issues bore so little fruit. He used Eden and the Foreign Office to insulate him from political distractions, but a considerable price was paid for that strategy.

Victor Cavendish-Bentinck [British Foreign Office official who chaired the Joint Intelligence Committee] apparently represented Foreign Office views of Nazi killings better than he exploited the intelligence on the Holocaust that Bletchley Park made available. The police decodes, of course, did not provide continuous data about Nazi killings: one needed other sources to obtain an overall picture of the scale of Nazi policy. Yet during the war, Cavendish-Bentinck decided that Polish and particularly Jewish sources were unreliable because they had an interest in exaggerating the numbers of Nazi victims. Still, he wrote in 1943 that the Nazis had a policy of eliminating Jewish women, children, and the elderly, allegedly sparing only men capable of hard labor. This partial perception should have led him to conclude that the number of Jewish victims ran into the millions, an estimate for which Polish and Jewish reports gave added support. Yet Cavendish-Bentinck criticized the Political Warfare Executive for publicizing allegedly dubious information about Nazi atrocities. Later, he explained that his prewar experience of Germany had been limited, but it seems obvious that he found these conclusions politically inconvenient. Either he resisted the facts or he did nothing about them.

At the end of the war, Cavendish-Bentinck became British ambassador to Poland, and sometime thereafter he visited Auschwitz—a photo of him there appears in his biography, which is drawn largely from extensive interviews with him. He also related elsewhere that, after his visit to Auschwitz, when he told his Foreign Office colleagues that the Nazis had killed millions, they still did not believe him.

Overall, it remains difficult to assess in detail the response of American and British intelligence organizations to the Holocaust. Some intelligence records may have been destroyed, and many others remain unavailable to most scholars. There are, however, enough declassified Office of Strategic Services (OSS) records to allow historians to address the American side, and some scholars have already made important contributions there. The OSS, which had less information and less reliable information than London, was nonetheless able to get a reasonably accurate picture of the Final Solution, but probably not until late 1942. Even then, some knowledgeable people (such as the German émigré political scientist Franz Neumann) allowed ideological barriers to prevent them from understanding the obvious. The fact that two very committed American Jews (Charles Irving Dwork and Abraham Duker) worked in the Research and Analysis Branch of OSS helped to ensure attention there.

Which other agencies in Washington might have taken information about the Nazis' killings of Jews seriously enough to consider or take action? The Office of War Information (OWI) was for a long time opposed to publicizing Jewish issues, as we have seen, and the majority of State Department officials did not wish to get involved in rescue and relief. This situation changed fundamentally after the creation of the War Refugee Board, which cooperated well with the OSS, both in general and in at least one field office (Stockholm). Publicity was no longer taboo, and some rescue and relief measures received support.

To give an example of how government agencies might or might not react, the OSS representative in Switzerland, Allen Dulles, learned on May 18, 1944, that the Germans and Hungarians had just agreed on transportation arrangements for the deportation of about three hundred thousand Hungarian Jews to Poland "and to presumably their deaths." He immediately passed on the suggestion that Washington and London publicize this fact in radio broadcasts, warning that those who planned or carried out the deportations would be included among the war criminals. This information added to the pressure for continuing American broadcasts and threats against the Hungarian government, which apparently had some effect in Budapest.

It is still not possible to analyze the reactions of British intelligence in the way that others (and I) have done with the OSS, since many of the documents are not available. A study of British intelligence and the Holocaust should also cover intelligence specialists in MI 8 and MI 14, perhaps even the attitudes and reactions of Sir Stewart Menzies. One official who served in MI 14, Noel Annan, has written very interesting memoirs, but memoirs are not a substitute for original documents.

In a 1997 work based on little archival research, the historian William Rubinstein argued flatly that the Allies could not have saved any more Jews from the Holocaust. It was certainly possible to argue that some of the rescue schemes proposed at the time were unrealistic— particularly because they ignored the essential (but not absolute) rigidity of Nazi policy toward the Jews and also because they overlooked the difficulties and trade-offs involved in Allied military action for nonmilitary purposes when major battles were still raging.

In a larger sense, however, Rubinstein's argument is fundamentally misleading and methodologically flawed. The history of the American War Refugee Board, founded as late as January 1944, shows failures but also quite a few successes and partial successes. How much more difference would it have made if there had been a War Refugee Board and a comparable British one years earlier?

History is not a laboratory science, and we cannot give a precise answer to that question. But I have presented some of the nonmilitary ways in which Western governments could have made a considerable difference in saving Jewish lives earlier if there had been the will to do so. The mere distribution of information about Nazi killings itself had some positive effects.

Leon Kubowitzki, who worked in the Rescue Department of the World Jewish Congress, spoke in mid-1944 about a conspiracy of silence that had existed within OWI and that was reversed under pressure only after considerable time. New warnings broadcast to the satellite countries were, he said, very effective in Rumania in bringing about the cessation of killings there. But even after Kubowitzki's statement, OWI continued to be ambivalent about and somewhat resistant to the War Refugee Board in this regard. As late as December 1944, OWI told its London office: "Playing up atrocities that have been committed by the Germans may, on the part of the Germans, increase fear, feelings of guilt, and thus resistance . . . the advantage of our showing moral indignation does not outweigh this risk."

Before the founding of the War Refugee Board, there were a few positive Allied rescue efforts, such as an American and British effort to save five thousand Jewish children in France in late 1942. The British Political Warfare Executive and the BBC did for a time distribute essential information to Germany and Europe about the Final Solution and in general did a better job than their American counterparts. The high officials of the U.S. Treasury Department deserve special mention for their efforts in late 1943 and thereafter. But the record generally shows that in 1942 and 1943 the U.S. government and the British government did not try to do what might have worked. This makes it very difficult, long, long after the fact, to demonstrate that saving more Jews had been impossible.

Selection 2

The Gates Are Shut

Gary M. Grobman

It is easy to look back with hindsight and say, Why didn't the Jews leave Germany? Why didn't they flee Europe once the war started? Hundreds of thousands did flee, but even those who tried to escape discovered an often insurmountable hurdle: the unwillingness of any country to take them in. Even the land of immigrants, the great melting pot that is the United States, denied entry to thousands of Jews who sought refuge. In the case of imperial powers such as Britain, governments could block entrance to multiple countries; thus, for example, many Jews who desperately wished to escape to Palestine were prevented from doing so by the British. Why were governments so callous? A number of reasons exist. One is that most countries were just emerging from the Great Depression and did not want to admit mostly penniless refugees who would become welfare cases and compete for scarce jobs. Another reason was a dislike of foreigners in general and an anti-Semitic attitude toward Jews in particular. This article presents a summary of the immigration policies of the United States and several European nations. Gary Grobman is the author or coauthor of seven books. He served as executive director of the Pennsylvania Jewish Coalition and is cur-rently a Ph.D. candidate in Public Administration at Penn State.

Deteriorating economic conditions contributed to the political and social climate which both launched World War II and fueled the anti-Semitism which encouraged the destruction of the Jews of Europe. These same economic conditions world-wide resulted in barriers placed against those potential Jewish immigrants who sought refuge from the Nazi terror. Anti-Jewish sentiment in France, England, and even the United States resulted in hundreds of thousands of European Jews being denied a safe haven, which meant virtually certain death. Simple indifference to the plight of Jews, according to many historians, also played a role in the events which led to the Holocaust.

Thousands of Jews in Germany were successful in fleeing before the onset of hostilities in 1939, especially in the early years of the Nazi period. Many of these refugees were able to find their way aboard ships headed for American ports. There are, however, tragic stories of these ships being turned away by immigration officials, and their occupants returned to Europe to face the gas chambers. Each nation had its own story of how its government and citizens responded to the horrors of the Holocaust. The following are capsules of some of these stories.

United States. Despite the fact that the U.S. received early reports about the desperate plight of European Jewry, procrastination and inaction marked its policies toward rescue. Immigration quotas were never increased for the emergency; the existing quotas, in fact, were never filled.

Wagner-Rogers legislation. Legislation was introduced in the United States Congress in 1939 by Rep. Robert Wagner to admit a total of 20,000 Jewish children over a two-year period above the refugee quota applicable at the time. The legislation was inspired by similar efforts by the Dutch and British government to save Jewish children from Nazi terror. The legislation was amended in committee to admit the 20,000 children only if the number of Jewish refugees admitted under the regular quota was reduced by 20,000. The bill died in the House after the sponsor withdrew his support for the bill in frustration.

Bermuda Conference. As the Germans advanced through Europe, more Jews and others who were targets of Nazi racial policies came under Nazi control. By 1943, the war had created millions of refugees in Europe. The Bermuda Conference, jointly sponsored by the United States and Great Britain, was held in Bermuda in April 1943 to discuss solutions to the refugee problem. The conference failed. As Michael Marrus writes in *The Holocaust in History:*

> At the Bermuda Conference in April 1943 . . . the British and Americans proved most adept at postponing serious efforts to change matters. By this point, opinion was mobilized on behalf of several schemes for rescue and refuge. Such views were deflected, however; the press was kept at arm's length and little was achieved.

War Refugee Board. U.S. Secretary of the Treasury, Henry Morgenthau, presented a report to President Roosevelt in 1943 providing details about the Final Solution. It was not until January 1944, however, that the President responded by establishing the War Refugee Board as an independent agency to rescue the civilian victims of the Nazis. By then, most of these civilian victims had already been murdered. The Board joined a plea to the Hungarian Regent, Admiral Horthy, from Great Britain, Sweden, the Pope, and the International Red Cross to stop the deportations

of Hungarian Jews. While Admiral Miklós Horthy agreed on July 8, 1944, to discontinue the deportations, fewer than 200,000 Jews of the original number of more than 600,000 remained. Thousands of those permitted this reprieve from the death camps were eventually saved through the efforts of [Swedish diplomat] Raoul Wallenberg and other diplomats.

Spain and Portugal. As many as 40,000 Jews who were able to make their way to Spain and Portugal were saved from the Nazi death camps. More than 20,000 Jews made their way into Switzerland, but many thousands were turned back, according to Michael Marrus' *Holocaust in History.*

Denmark. The rescue of Denmark's 8,000 Jews serves as an example of an entire nation mobilized to rescue humanity from the abyss of German terror. While the story may be apocryphal that King Christian X threatened to abdicate and to wear the Nazi yellow Star of David as a badge of honor, it symbolizes his opposition to all anti-Semitic legislation. Almost all of the Jews of Denmark survived the war, while those in almost every other nation occupied by the Nazis had their ranks decimated.

A September 1943 decision by the Nazi occupiers of Denmark to round up all Danish Jews for shipment to the death camps was thwarted. Courageously acting on a tip from a German shipping official, Danes from all walks of life mobilized whatever would float and ferried 5,900 Jews, 1,300 part-Jews, and 700 Christians married to Jews to safety in Sweden. Of the 500 or so Jews left in Denmark on October 1, 1943, all were deported by the Germans to Theresienstadt. Eighty-five percent survived the war.

Historians have pondered why the citizens of Denmark resisted the war against the Jews, unlike most of their European neighbors. One reason is that Denmark did not have a history of anti-Semitism. Another was that nearby was neutral Sweden, willing to accept the Jews that could be saved.

Bulgaria. Forty-eight thousand Jews in Bulgaria were also spared the horror of the gas chambers as a result of the courage of the Bulgarian people. A public outcry by Bulgarian church officials and others against a deportation order directed at all Jews forced the Bulgarian government to rescind its order. Jews who had been rounded up in Bulgarian-occupied Thrace and Macedonia were not as lucky; virtually all perished in the Holocaust.

Several other governments resisted Nazi deportation orders, including Finland, Hungary, and Italy.

Several embassies in Hungary acted in concert to issue passports to Jews at risk. Yet many other European governments not only complied with the demand of the Germans to deport Jews to the death camps but facilitated the deportations.

France. Pre-war France had a Jewish population of over 300,000, out of a total population of 45 million. Many thousands of these were refugees, and only about 150,000 were native Frenchmen. In May 1940, the German army invaded France and occupied three-fifths of the country in accordance with an armistice signed on June 22nd.

A government was formed in unoccupied France at Vichy. The Vichy government was dominated by advocates for cooperation with the Germans. Many of the decrees of the Vichy government in 1940–41 paralleled the anti-Jewish edicts of Germany in the mid-1930s. Jewish property was expropriated, and Jews were stripped of their basic civil rights. Non-native French Jews were singled out in October 1940 for internment in labor camps, which resulted in a large number of deaths.

In March 1942, the Germans began deporting Jews from the occupied zones in France to the death camps. In July of that same year, they demanded that all Jews be rounded up in unoccupied France for deportation.

The Vichy government decided to protect French Jews, but handed over 15,000 foreign Jews from the internment camps for deportation to the death camps. Many hundreds of other Jews were executed, as described in Lucy Dawidowicz's *The War Against the Jews* in reprisal for partisan activities. By the time France was liberated, 90,000 of the pre-war Jewish population in France had been killed.

Selection 3

The Tragedy of the *St. Louis*

Jennifer Rosenberg

Why didn't Jews leave Germany when they had the chance? Didn't they foresee what was to come? Yes, many German Jews did realize that the future was grim, but it was not

so easy to leave. It cost money to move to another country. You needed documents. It was difficult to leave your home. And who would take you in? In 1939 a group of German Jews succeeded in getting tickets on a ship headed for Cuba where they hoped to either live or use the country as a transit point for the United States or some other country. This turned out to be one of the most tragic exam-

ples of the callousness of the Roosevelt administration, immortalized by the book and film, Voyage of the Damned. *The story is briefly retold here by Jennifer Rosenberg, the moderator of the Holocaust section of the About.com website.*

*a*fter Kristallnacht in November 1938, many Jews within Germany decided that it was time to leave. Though many German Jews had emigrated in the preceding years, the Jews who remained had a more difficult time because emigration policies had toughened. By 1939, not only were visas needed to be able to enter another country but money was also needed to leave Germany. Since many countries, especially the United States, had immigration quotas, visas were near impossible to acquire within the short time spans in which they were needed. For many, the visas were acquired after it was too late. The opportunity that the S.S. St. Louis presented seemed like a last hope to escape.

Boarding

The S.S. St. Louis, part of the Hamburg-America Line (Hapag), was tied up at Shed 76 awaiting its next voyage which was to take Jewish refugees from Germany to Cuba. Once the refugees arrived in Cuba they would await their quota number to be able to enter the United States. The black and white ship with eight decks held room for four hundred first-class passengers (800 Reichsmarks each) and five hundred tourist-class passengers (600 Reichsmarks each). The passengers were also required to pay an additional 230 Reichsmarks for the "customary contingency fee" which was supposed to cover the cost if there was an unplanned return voyage.[1] As most Jews had been forced out of their jobs and had been charged high rents under the Nazi regime, most Jews did not have this kind of money. Some of these passengers had money sent to them from relatives outside of Germany and Europe while other families had to pool resources to send even one member to freedom. On Saturday, May 13, 1939, the passengers boarded. Women and men. Young and old. Each person who boarded had

their own story of persecution.

One passenger, Aaron Pozner, had just been released from Dachau. On the night of Kristallnacht, Pozner along with 26,000 other Jews had been arrested and deported to concentration camps. While interned at Dachau, Pozner witnessed brutal murders by hanging, drowning, and crucifixion as well as torture by flogging and castrations by a bayonet.[2] Surprisingly, one day Pozner was released from Dachau on the condition that he leave Germany within fourteen days. Though his family had very little money, they were able to pool enough money to buy a ticket for him to board the S.S. St. Louis. Pozner said goodbye to his wife and two children, knowing that they would never be able to raise enough money to buy another ticket to freedom. Beaten and forced to sleep amongst bloody animal hides on his journey to reach the ship, Pozner boarded with the knowledge that it was up to him to earn the money to bring his family to freedom.

Many other passengers had either left family members behind while some were also going to be meeting relatives that had traveled earlier. As the passengers boarded they remembered the many years of persecution that they had been living under. Some had come out of hiding to board the ship and none were certain that they would not receive the same kind of treatment once aboard. The Nazi flag flying above the ship and the picture of Hitler hanging in the social hall did not allay their fears. Earlier, Captain Gustav Schroeder had given the 231 member crew stern warnings that these passengers were to be treated just like any others. Many were willing to do this, two stewards even carried Moritz and Recha Weiler's luggage for them since they were elderly. But there was one crew member who was disgusted by this policy and was ready to make trouble, Otto Schiendick the Ortsgruppenleiter. Not only was Schiendick ready to make trouble and was constantly trying, he was a courier for the Abwehr (German Secret Police). On this trip, Schiendick was to pick up secret documents about the U.S. military from Robert Hoffman in Cuba. This mission was code-named Operation Sunshine.

The captain, Gustav Schroeder, made a note in his diary:

> There is a somewhat nervous disposition among the passengers. Despite this, everyone seems convinced they will never see Germany again. Touching departure scenes have taken place. Many seem light of heart, having left their homes. Others take it heavily. But beautiful weather, pure sea air, good food, and attentive service will soon provide the usual worry-free atmosphere of long sea voyages. Painful impressions on land disappear quickly at sea and soon seem merely like dreams.[3]

At 8:00 p.m. on that Saturday (May 13) evening, the ship sailed. . . .

The Trip to Cuba

The passengers slowly started adjusting to life aboard a large ship. With lots of good food, movies, and swimming pools the mood began to relax a little. . . .

Several times Schiendick attempted to disturb this calm by posting copies of *Der Stürmer,* by substituting a newsreel with Nazi propaganda for the intended film, and by singing Nazi songs.

For Recha Weiler, who was helped by a steward with her luggage, her main concern was for her husband since his health continued to deteriorate. For over a week, the ship's doctor continued to prescribe medicine for Moritz Weiler but nothing helped. On Tuesday, May 23, Moritz passed away. . . . Recha agreed to a burial at sea for her husband. . . .

Once the Captain received a cable on May 23 which stated that the S.S. St. Louis passengers might not be able to land in Cuba because of Decree 937, he felt it wise to establish a small passenger committee. The committee was to explore possibilities if there were problems landing in Cuba.

Decree 937

In Cuba in early 1939, Decree 55 had passed which drew a distinction between refugees and tourists. The Decree stated that each refugee needed a visa and was required to pay a $500 bond to guarantee that they would not become wards of Cuba. But the Decree also said that tourists were still welcome and did not need visas. The director of immigration in Cuba, Manuel Benitez, realized that Decree 55 did not define a tourist nor a refugee. He decided that he would take advantage of this loophole and make money by selling landing permits which would allow refugees to land in Cuba by calling them tourists. He sold these permits to anyone who would pay $150. Though only allowing someone to land as a tourist, these permits looked authentic, even were individually signed by Benitez, and generally were made to look like visas. Some people bought a large group of these for $150 each and then resold them to desperate refugees for much more. Benitez himself had made a small fortune in selling these permits as well as receiving money from the cruise line. Hapag had realized the advantage of being able to offer a package deal to their passengers, a permit and passage on their ship.

The President of Cuba, Frederico Laredo Bru, and his cabinet did not like Benitez making a great deal of money—that he was unwilling to share—on the loophole in Decree 55. Also, Cuba's economy had begun to stagnate and many blamed the incoming refugees for taking jobs that otherwise would have been held by Cubans.

On May 5, Decree 937 was passed which closed the loophole. Without knowing it, almost every passenger on the S.S. St. Louis had purchased a landing permit for an inflated rate but by the time of sailing, had already been nullified by Decree 937.

Will They Be Turned Back?

After having crossed an entire ocean and fleeing a country where they suffered severe persecution, would the Cuban government disregard their Decree and let the passengers of the S.S. St. Louis land? . . .

Anticipation grew as the S.S. St. Louis neared the Havana harbor. . . . Passengers enjoyed their last remaining days on ship and wondered what their new lives would be like in Cuba.

Late Friday afternoon, the last full day before

the ship was to arrive, Captain Schroeder received a telegram from Luis Clasing (the local Hapag official in Havana) which stated that the St. Louis would have to anchor at the roadstead. Originally planning to dock at Hapag's pier, anchoring at the roadstead had been a concession by President Bru since he still disallowed the St. Louis passengers to land. Captain Schroeder went to sleep that night wondering about this change. . . .

Cuban police and immigration officials boarded the St. Louis Saturday morning. Then the immigration officials suddenly left with no explanation. The police stayed on board and guarded the accommodation ladder. Several officials boarded but then left without an explanation as to why they had to anchor in the harbor nor gave an assurance that the passengers would be allowed to disembark. As the morning elapsed, family and friends of the passengers who were in Cuba began renting boats and encircling the St. Louis. The passengers on board waved and shouted to those below, but the smaller ships weren't allowed to get too close.

The passengers remained anxious to disembark, not realizing the international and political negotiations which surrounded their fate.

Negotiations and Influences

Manuel Benitez. Though a major player in the fate of the refugees since it was he who had signed their landing permits, he continually underestimated President Bru's stance. Benitez constantly maintained that Bru would back down since the St. Louis was allowed in the harbor. He wanted $250,000 in bribes so that he could try to amend his relations with Bru and rescind Decree 937. President Bru refused to listen to Benitez' requests. Though he no longer had access to Bru, he continued to espouse his assurance that Bru would back down. His confident attitude and slick talk convinced a number of influential people that the circumstances were not as serious as they seemed, thus action was not taken.

Luis Clasing and Robert Hoffman (local Hapag officials in Havana). Clasing met several times with Benitez, hoping that Benitez could assure

that the passengers would be allowed to disembark. Benitez wanted $250,000—enough to pay President Bru what would seem a share in the landing permit profits. This was too much for Hapag to pay. Hapag had already given Benitez many "bonuses"; Benitez' request was in response to his lack of influence to change Bru's opinion.

Hoffman needed the ship to land so that he could meet with Schiendick and give him the secret documents. Captain Schroeder had refused to give shore leave to the crew so Hoffman needed to find a way on to the ship or a way to get Schiendick off.

Milton Goldsmith (director of the Relief Committee in Cuba which was financed by the American Jewish Joint Distribution Committee). Before the St. Louis arrived in Havana, Goldsmith had repeatedly asked the Joint for additional funds to help the refugees already in Cuba and those about to arrive. The Joint refused. The local Jewish community donated to the Relief Committee but felt that the world should be helping. After the St. Louis arrived, the Joint began to realize the seriousness of the predicament. They would send two professionals to negotiate—but they would not arrive until four days later.

Joseph Goebbels and Anti-Semitism. Goebbels had decided to use the S.S. St. Louis and her passengers in a master propaganda plan. Having sent agents to Havana to stir up anti-Semitism, Nazi propaganda fabricated and hyped the passengers' criminal nature—making them seem even more undesirable. The agents within Cuba stirred anti-Semitism and organized protests. Soon, an additional 1,000 Jewish refugees entering Cuba was seen as a threat. . . .

Stuck in Cuba

On Monday, two days after arriving in Cuba, Hoffman found a way to board the St. Louis. Clasing had allowed Hoffman to go aboard in his place since Clasing was currently occupied about what he was to do with the 250 passengers who were supposed to board the St. Louis on a return voyage to Germany. Would President Bru allow 250 refugees to land so that these passengers waiting in Havana could make their return journey?

Hoffman had already hidden the secret documents in the spine of magazines, inside pens, and inside a walking cane, so he brought these with him to the ship. At the accommodation ladder, Hoffman was told he was allowed onto the ship but that he couldn't bring anything on board. Leaving his magazines and cane behind, Hoffman boarded with the pens. Sent directly to Captain Schroeder, Hoffman used the influence of the Abwehr to force Schroeder into allowing the crew to go to shore. Schroeder, shocked that the Abwehr was connected to his ship, acquiesced. After a quick meeting with Schiendick, Hoffman left the ship. With the change in shore leave policy, Schiendick was able to pick up the magazines and cane and reboard the St. Louis. Now, Schiendick became a major push to head back to Germany with no stop in America for fear of being caught with the secret documents.

On Tuesday, Captain Schroeder called the passenger committee for a meeting for only the second time. The committee had become distrustful of the captain. The St. Louis had sat in the harbor for four days before they were called. No good news had come forward and the passenger committee was asked to send telegrams to influential people, family, and friends asking for help. . . .

The days continued to progress and the passengers all became increasingly suspicious and fearful. If they were forced back to Germany, they would surely be sent to concentration camps. The possible consequences of their return were loudly suggested in German newspapers and magazines.

For anyone thinking about jumping overboard, the chances were slim of their success with the increased number of police crafts, the searchlights that scanned the ship, and the dangling lights used to illuminate the water.

The world followed the fate of the passengers aboard the St. Louis. Their story was covered around the world. The U.S. Ambassador to Cuba met with an influential member of the Cuban government and spoke diplomatically about the precarious position the Cubans were now in.

The Ambassador had spoken without direct instructions from the President but he made the concerns of the U.S. known. The Cuban Secretary of State stated that the subject was to be determined by the cabinet.

On Wednesday, the cabinet met. The passengers aboard the St. Louis would not be allowed to land, not even 250 to allow room for return passengers.

Captain Schroeder began to fear mass suicides on board. Mutiny was also a possibility. With the help of the passenger committee, "suicide patrols" were created to patrol at night.

The two Americans from the Joint had arrived in Havana and by Thursday, June 1, had befriended a couple of influential people who convinced President Bru to reopen negotiations. To their shock though, Bru would not negotiate until the St. Louis was out of Cuban waters. The St. Louis was given notice to leave within three hours. Pleading by Schroeder that he needed more time to prepare for departure, the deadline was set back until Friday, June 2, at 10 a.m.

No options were left for the St. Louis, if they did not leave peacefully, they were to be forced out by the Cuban navy.

Leaving Cuba

On Friday morning, the S.S. St. Louis roared up its engines and began to take its leave. Farewells were shouted overboard to friends and family in rented boats below.

The St. Louis was going to encircle Cuba, waiting and hoping for the conclusion of negotiations between the Joint representative, Lawrence Berenson, and President Bru.

The Cuban government wanted $500 per refugee (approximately $500,000 in total). The same amount as required for any refugee to obtain a visa to Cuba. Berenson didn't believe he would have to pay that much, with negotiations, he believed, it would only cost the Joint $125,000.

During the following day, Berenson was approached by several men claiming affiliation with the Cuban government, one identified himself as having powers to negotiate bestowed by Bru. These men insisted that $400,000 to

Reporters converge on a ship carrying German Jewish refugees in 1939.
Most members of the press were skeptical of accounts of Nazi atrocities.

$500,000 were needed to ensure the St. Louis passengers' return. Berenson believed that these men just wanted a cut in the profit by negotiating a higher price. He was wrong.

While the negotiations continued, the St. Louis milled around Cuba and then headed north, following the Florida coastline in the hopes that perhaps the United States would accept the refugees. At this time, it was noticed that because of the lack of time to prepare for leaving port, the St. Louis would run into food and water shortages in less than two weeks. Telegrams continued to arrive insisting the possibility of landing in Cuba or even the Dominican Republic. Once a cable arrived stating the S.S. St. Louis passengers could land on the Isla de la Juventud (formerly Isle of Pines), off of Cuba, Schroeder turned the ship around and headed toward Cuba.

The good news was announced to those on board and everyone rejoiced. Ready and awaiting a new life, the passengers prepared themselves for their arrival the next morning.

The next morning, a telegram arrived stating that landing at the Isla de la Juventud was not confirmed. Shocked, the passenger committee tried to think of other alternatives.

Around noon on Tuesday, June 6, President Bru closed the negotiations. Through a misunderstanding, the money allotment had not been agreed upon and Berenson missed a 48 hour deadline that he didn't know existed. One day later, the Joint offered to pay Bru's every demand but Bru said it was too late. The option of landing in Cuba was officially closed.

With a diminishing supply of food and pressures from Hapag to return to Germany, Captain Schroeder ordered the ship to change heading to return to Europe.

The Return Voyage

The following day, Wednesday, June 7, Captain Schroeder informed the passenger committee that they were returning to Europe. Though the situation was desperate there was still hope that negotiations for their landing in Europe somewhere other than Germany could be possible.

While massive negotiations were beginning, Aaron Pozner rallied some youths aboard to participate in a mutiny. Though they succeeded in capturing the bridge, they did not capture the other strategic locations of the ship. The mutiny was overcome. . . .

Through miraculous negotiations, the Joint committee was able to find several countries that would take portions of the refugees. 181 could go to Holland, 224 to France, 228 to Great Britain, and 214 to Belgium.

The passengers disembarked from the S.S. St. Louis from June 16 to June 20. Other ships were transformed to carry the passengers to their locations.

Having crossed the Atlantic Ocean twice, the passengers' original hopes of freedom in Cuba and the U.S. turned into a forlorn effort to escape sure death upon their return to Germany. Feeling alone and rejected by the world, the passengers returned to Europe in June 1939. With World War II just months away, many of these passengers were sent East with the occupation of the countries to which they had been sent.

Notes

1. Gordon Thomas and Max Morgan Wittes, *Voyage of the Damned* (New York: Stein and Day, 1974) 37.

2. Thomas, *Voyage* 31.

3. Gustav Schroeder as quoted in Thomas, *Voyage* 64.

Selection 4

Bargaining for Jewish Lives

Yehuda Bauer

This encyclopedia contains several articles critical of the behavior of the Allies, American Jews, and others for their failure to do more to help the Jews of Europe. Some people have argued that Hitler was so intent on murdering every last Jew that nothing could have been done; however, it may have been possible to bargain for the lives of Jews. One question is how far the West should have gone in attempting to make a deal with the

enemy. We know, for example, that the Germans exchanged Americans held in concentration camps for German nationals held by the United States. Officials in the State Department were not happy with many of the proposals because they were afraid they involved recognition of Nazi conquests or might allow German spies to enter the United States. One of the most famous deals was Adolf Eichmann's proposal to exchange 1 million Jews for trucks the Nazis wanted to use in their war with the Soviets. This selection discusses the proposal and the reasons why it was not successful. Yehuda Bauer is one of the foremost authorities on the Holo-

Excerpted from Yehuda Bauer, *Jews for Sale?* Copyright © 1994 Yale University. Reprinted with permission from Yale University Press.

caust, the Jona M. Machover Professor of Holocaust Studies, and a permanent academic chair of the Institute of Contemporary Jewry at Hebrew University. He has also served as chair of the Vidal Sassoon International Center for the Study of Anti-Semitism.

7 n 1918–19 a short-lived communist government ruled Hungary, headed by Bela Kun, a Jew; a majority of the Ministers had Jewish parentage but totally repudiated their Judaism. The right-wing reaction to this regime brought to power the government of Adm. Miklos Horthy, who assumed the title of Regent. . . .

Between the world wars, antisemitism was part of the government creed, even though Horthy and his clique had Jewish connections, and the titled landowners and gentry had in no small part intermarried with Jews. Rich Jewish families and the upper level of the Jewish intelligentsia were accepted into Hungarian society, and a *numerus clausus* act of 1920 (limiting Jews in the professions to their percentage in the general population) was later disregarded. As Hungary began moving into the German orbit in the 1930s, antisemitic propaganda increased. To accommodate to German thinking and also to take the wind out of the sails of the rising fascist right wing, the government passed discriminatory legislation in 1938 and again in 1939, which reimposed the *numerus clausus*. Legislation was passed in 1940 to remove Jews from the officer corps of the Army, and a labor service under humiliating conditions was instituted for Jews instead of regular Army service. For the Hungarian Jews who had fought bravely for the Austro-Hungarian monarchy in World War I, this was a serious blow. . . .

The situation of the Jews went from bad to worse, but compared with the fate of Polish or German Jewry, they were incomparably better off. The Jewish labor battalions that the Army set up numbered 52,000 men in 1940. Hungary joined Nazi Germany on June 27, 1941, to attack the Soviet Union, partly, no doubt, because its neighbor, fascist-dominated Romania, had joined the Nazis, too, and Hungarian nonparticipation

would have endangered Hungary's hold over newly acquired northern Transylvania, which the Romanians wanted back. The Jewish labor battalions, mostly commanded by rabidly antisemitic officers, were sent into the Ukraine. Of the roughly 40,000 sent, some 5,000 returned in 1943, and a few thousand were taken prisoner or escaped to the Russians. The rest were killed, mostly by Hungarian and German troops, or starved and beaten to death. The result was that young Jewish men were simply not there when the German onslaught on Hungarian Jewry came in 1944.

After Hungary entered the war, the government of Laszlo Bardossy decided to deport those Jews who could not prove Hungarian citizenship, especially from the new areas in the north and east. A decree of July 12, 1941, provided legal cover, but many of the 18,000 Jews who were deported to German-occupied Ukraine did in fact have Hungarian citizenship. . . . On August 27–28, some 14,000–16,000 Hungarian Jews and several thousand local Jews were machine-gunned by the SS, Ukrainian collaborators, and Hungarian sappers. When Hungarian Interior Minister Ferenc Keresztes-Fischer, one of the few liberals still in power, learned of the massacre, he ordered a stop to the deportations. . . .

Hungary Falls

On March 19, a Sunday, relatively weak German forces occupied Hungary. There was no resistance. . . .

On March 17–18, Hitler had summoned Horthy to a series of discussions at Klessheim castle in Austria. . . . The Jewish question occupied an important part of Hitler's attention. It was clear to him that the influence of the Jews was anti-German and that it was growing. Hungary would have to deal radically with its Jews. The broad hint was made by Ribbentrop that in Poland the Jews were being killed. . . .

German industry was starved of workers. Germans were being recruited into the Army because of the very heavy losses on the Russian front. Labor tsar Fritz Sauckel was recruiting workers from all over Nazi Europe, by persuasion at first, but then mostly by force. Millions of workers were forced into Germany, and they were treated in accordance with their origins: the *Ostarbeiter* (Eastern workers) from the Soviet territories were treated worst, then came the Poles, then the others. But all this recruitment was insufficient. In the spring of 1944, Hitler himself was involved in consultations regarding a radical increase in aircraft production. Germany was developing jet fighters and missiles, as well as trying to replace the losses incurred in defending Germany from ever heavier attacks by Anglo-American bombers. The so-called *Jäger* plan for aircraft production and related war matériel was developed, which required more unskilled and semiskilled workers. The idea of demanding 50,000, then 100,000 Jewish workers from Hungary arose. The SS policy of murder and the demand for Jewish labor coalesced, but they appear to have been adopted separately as far as Hungary was concerned. The SS plan was the application of the "Final Solution" to Hungary, whereas the Jäger demand for workers was a temporary need. The two accidentally came together. From the Nazi point of view, the coalescence helped, because it made a good excuse to demand of the Hungarian government, especially Horthy, an agreement to the deportation of Jews: 100,000 Jews and their families, or, in other words, all of Hungarian Jewry, would be deported for labor in Germany. The physically fit would become slave labor; the rest would be murdered.

On April 28 the first train with Hungarian Jews left for Auschwitz; large-scale deportations started on May 14. . . .

Between May 14 and July 7, according to German figures, 437,000 Jews were deported to Auschwitz. What was left were the 250,000 Budapest Jews, the men in the labor battalions, and converts trying to escape deportation by hiding as Christians. Of those deported to Auschwitz, about a fourth were either introduced into the Auschwitz concentration camp or, more usually, sent to Germany to work there in armament factories. The exact number cannot be stated, but after the war a total of 72,000 Jews returned

A loaded deportation train in Koszeg, Hungary, prepares to depart for Auschwitz. It is estimated that over 300,000 Hungarian Jews died at Auschwitz.

from German camps, including those who had been in the labor battalions. If at least 50 percent had died in the camps and on the death marches at the end of the war, and if a proportion of these people had been in labor battalions, then the probable number of those selected for work was about 100,000–110,000, or 25 percent of those deported. This figure would also accord with the postwar testimonies of Rudolf Hoess, the commander of Auschwitz. The other three-fourths were murdered: children, older people, mothers with children, and many men were gassed and cremated, and their ashes were strewn over the grounds at Auschwitz. . . .

No Chance to Escape

The option of flight from Hungary seemingly existed. The youth movements, with the agreement of the Vaada [Hungarian Aid and Rescue Committee], tried the borders to Yugoslavia and Romania. . . . Yugoslavia was German occupied, but the Tito partisans were gaining ground, and attempts were made to find a way to reach them. Almost all these failed, and the people who tried were mostly caught or died in the attempt. No more than fifty to seventy youths made it through. The Germans were guarding the approaches to partisan territory very closely indeed. Hungarian Jews also faced language barriers and the understandable distrust that the partisans had of all Hungarians. . . .

If the Vaada wanted to save all or at least many of the Hungarian Jews, the alternatives of hiding, flight, and resistance had to be ruled out. . . .

These, then, were the options that had to be discounted. What remained? Two choices, basically: either despair and attempts to save individuals, as many of them as possible, or negotiations with the murderers. . . .

Trucks for Jews

On April 16 or 25, according to [Joel] Brand [the emissary for a Jewish rescue organization], Eichmann summoned him to his headquarters on the Schwabenberg in Budapest and there offered him the famous "trucks for blood" proposal. Or did he? What he apparently said was that he would be prepared to release one million Jews in return for an appropriate payment in kind or otherwise. The trucks, as well as other items, such as tea, coffee, and soap, came up only as examples of the kind of things the Nazis might request. Krumey, Eichmann's underling, spoke to Brand about machine tools, leather, and other commodities. But the demands soon solidified into 10,000 trucks and quantities of consumer staples. Brand was asked where he wanted to go to offer the proposal to the Jews and the Allies, and he chose Istanbul. . . .

Eichmann offered to blow up Auschwitz and free the first "ten, twenty, fifty thousand Jews" after receiving information from Istanbul that agreement had been reached in principle, or so Brand put it in his June 22 interview with the U.S. emissary Ira Hirschmann. In Brand's postwar book and in the [Rudolf] Kasztner trial in 1954, this offer became a promise to free 100,000 Jews. Eichmann also added that the trucks should be properly winterized and that they would not be used against the West. Eichmann himself—in the interview that he granted to the Dutch journalist Stassen prior to his capture by the Israelis—said that the "basic objective of Reichsführer [Heinrich] Himmler [was] to arrange if possible for a million Jews to go free in exchange for 10,000 winterized trucks,

with trailers, for use against the Russians on the Eastern Front. . . . I said at the time, '[W]hen the winterized trucks with trailers are here, the liquidation machine in Auschwitz will be stopped.'" It is dangerous to place any credence in Eichmann, but something of the sort must have been said. Whether that was Himmler's basic objective may be doubted. . . .

Some interpreters of the evidence have argued that the whole thing was a maneuver to outwit the Jews or a trick to sow discord between the West and the Soviets. The first argument is unacceptable because the SS did not need to outwit the powerless and helpless Jews, who in any case knew by that time precisely what was awaiting them—murder. The second point certainly is true, but it has to be seen in a much larger context, which we have already discussed. Another argument is that if the Allies had rejected the proposal, they would have been accused of not saving Jews when it was possible to do so.

The clumsiness of the approach has been a wonderment to all observers. An analysis of the available material leads us to a number of conclusions. For one thing, it seems very obvious that Eichmann was Himmler's reluctant messenger; his own inclination clearly was to carry on with the murders and not be diverted to negotiations with the Jews. On the very day that Brand left for Vienna and Istanbul, Eichmann traveled to Auschwitz to make sure that the Auschwitz commander, Rudolf Hoess, would be ready to receive the first transports, which began leaving Hungary on May 14. . . .

The Jews, in Himmler's ideology, were the real enemies of Nazism. They ruled the Western Allies and they controlled Bolshevik Russia. They had to be exterminated, but if Germany was in an unfavorable military situation, could this war of annihilation against them not be temporarily suspended in order to gain a breathing space? A basic desire to murder all the Jews does not contravene a readiness to use them, or some of them, as hostages to be exchanged for things that Germany needed in its crisis; the negotiations could be held with either the foreign Jews themselves or with their non-Jewish puppets. There would be plenty of time to return to the murder policy once Germany was on its feet again. . . .

From later developments it appears that Himmler really thought he might get trucks or goods of some kind or, as a last resort, money. During the negotiations with the Swiss in 1943 he and Eichmann had insisted on an exchange of four Germans for one Jew; that offer was meant seriously and was no less preposterous than the trucks idea a year later. Himmler's total misunderstanding of Western politics and of the psychological frame of mind of Western military and political leaders was evidenced by the proposal not to use the trucks against the West. . . .

Would he have let the million Jews go free? In the Cairo interrogations and in the discussions that took place later within the British government an issue came up that may have played a part in Himmler's calculations. If large numbers of Jews had been released—let us say only the first 10,000

or more promised by Eichmann in return for the agreement in principle by the Western Allies—the result would have been, in effect, the stopping of some, if not all, military activity, especially in the air, as these people were being gathered and then transported through Central Europe. . . .

Brand, as we have noted, did not believe that the Allies would give the Nazis trucks, but the very fact of negotiating might save many lives. . . .

The Western powers responded in the context of the Normandy invasion, which occurred in the middle of the events that we are dealing with, on June 6, 1944, and the end phase of the Soviet offensive, which brought the Soviet armies to the Vistula River in Poland and the Carpathian mountains in the south, on the edge of Hungary itself. At that crucial moment, to antagonize the Soviets because of some harebrained Gestapo plan to ransom Jews was totally out of the question.

Selection 5

Could Auschwitz Have Been Bombed?

Stuart Erdheim

Could the Holocaust have been prevented? Could more people have been saved? These are two of the big questions that will be debated forever. One of the enduring controver-

Excerpted from Stuart Erdheim, "Could the Allies Have Bombed Auschwitz-Birkenau?" *Holocaust and Genocide Studies*, Fall 1997. Reprinted with permission from the author.

sies has focused more specifically on the issue of whether the concentration camps could have been bombed to either stop or slow down the killing. As mentioned in this article, Buchenwald was bombed, though the damage to the camp was an inadvertent by-product of a raid on an adjacent factory. The Allies also bombed targets near Auschwitz, so the question arises: Why did they not bomb the death camp? This article offers a response to some of the arguments given for the failure to bomb Auschwitz and suggests that the answer to the question had little or nothing to do with military matters and everything to do with the mindset of the Allied leaders. Stuart Erdheim has both a master's degree in philosophy and a doctorate of divinity from Yeshiva University. He is an independent researcher.

Several works dating from the late 1970s onward have explored the question of whether the Allies had the knowledge and technical capability needed to bomb the killing facilities at Auschwitz-Birkenau. Beginning with a 1978 article in *Commentary* (later incorporated into a 1984 book, *The Abandonment of the Jews*), David Wyman argued that the failure to bomb the death camp did not result from any cogent assessment of military infeasibility, but rather was yet another example of Allied indifference to the ongoing destruction of European Jewry. More recently, two critics have sought to undermine Wyman's thesis by focusing on the operational obstacles that confronted a potential bombing mission over Auschwitz-Birkenau (hereinafter Birkenau). In separate articles, James H. Kitchens III and Richard H. Levy deflect criticism from the Allies by examining military complexities such as intelligence, target distance and placement, bomber availability and accuracy, and defenses. This article is a direct challenge to their assessment of the military practicality of bombing the death camp. Although the operational issue is clearly a complex one, the research presented below will show that, at least from a military standpoint, bombing Birkenau itself was no more complex than numerous other missions undertaken by the Allied powers during the Second World War. . . .

Photo Reconnaissance and Intelligence

If the Allies had considered Birkenau a potential target, they would have immediately ordered aerial reconnaissance in order to determine the capacity of the air forces to bomb the camp effectively. Photo intelligence was indispensable to the planning of bombing missions, and Birkenau would have been no exception. In order to make any operational assessment, then, we must first apply the same photo reconnaissance techniques to Birkenau that the Allies would have applied to any other target.

Any photo reconnaissance efforts might have been requested on the basis of earlier intelligence about the camp, but certainly by June 1944, when it became available to the Allies, the Vrba-Wetzler report established itself as the most crucial source. The testimony provided by Rudolf Vrba and Alfred Wetzler, who escaped from Auschwitz in April 1944, contained detailed information about the camp, including sketches of its layout. Yet Kitchens dismisses this evidence out of hand, arguing that it "had minimal utility for military intelligence purposes," did not "reliably locate" the gas chambers and crematoria, and that the "maps included with the report contained at least one error which could have puzzled those seeking to correlate the report with aerial photographs.". . .

While Kitchens openly criticizes the Vrba-Wetzler report for not providing detailed information on the size and design of the crematoria, he fails to discern valuable information that the report did provide. The escapees indicated, for example, that Birkenau prisoners worked outside the camp, thus lowering estimates of potential collateral deaths from a bombing raid. Their report also contained relevant corroborating material for several 1943 reports on gas chambers and crematoria. Finally . . . there was enough intelligence in the report that experts would have had little difficulty locating the extermination facilities, if only they had had aerial imagery with which to correlate it. . . .

"[Prior to 1944] there was enough generally accurate information [obtained through the Polish underground] about Auschwitz-Birkenau to preclude the argument that the Allies did not bomb the camp because they got the necessary information too late." If this information had evoked enough curiosity, if not horror, to have justified just one PR [photo reconnaissance] sortie, Birkenau could have been photographed much sooner. Indeed, as early as October 6, 1942, and August 20, 1943, photo reconnaissance Mosquitos obtained imagery of the oil refinery at Blechhammer, Germany, forty-seven miles from the death camp. When the Joint Chiefs of Staff received reports of crematoria at Oświecim in June 1943 from Polish Military Intelligence, for example, the area could have been included on the August 20 Blechhammer mission. . . .

Allied Intelligence on the Final Solution

Another important issue concerns the level of military intelligence on the Final Solution in general. On this point Kitchens argues that intelligence authorities were not alerted to look for gas chambers and crematoria since genocide was still unknown. Kitchens writes that "before the end of 1944, at least, the Allies lacked enough solid intelligence about the 'Final Solution' to adequately comprehend its hideous import." In support of this, he quotes an October 10, 1944, British War Office Report which, he informs readers, was an attempt to "summarize the concentration camp intelligence then in hand" and indicates that the Allies "had no exact knowledge of the number of camps the Germans were operating, where the camps were located, how many internees there were, or to what overall purpose the detainees were being held.". . .

In the case of the Oct. 10 report, Kitchens completely ignores what it had to say about Auschwitz, which is important not only in an informative sense, but as to the quality of this report itself. First, it provides a great deal of information on the concentration camp system (including identifying and locating all six death camps) and gassing facilities. It correctly locates the Auschwitz camp, states that it had been "mentioned frequently since 1939," and lists the estimated annual population since 1940. The report notes too that the "Birkenau camp is definitely connected, as Auschwitz makes use of

Birkenau's gas chambers, though it is said to have ten crematoria and four lethal gas chambers itself." Moreover, the report identifies the leading SS personnel by rank for December 1943 and March 1944 and classifies Birkenau as a "Special KL" (*Konzentrationslager*) and annihilation camp for women, where the inmates are said to be "mostly Hungarian Jews." Under the "remarks" section, it asserts bluntly: "Most likely controlled by AUSCHWITZ, where Jews are sent to keep the four crematoria busy." In short, though they did not get each and every fact exactly right, Allied Intelligence knew the location of an extermination camp that utilized gas chambers and crematoria to murder human beings and efficiently dispose of their remains. . . .

In August 1942, Churchill also learned from decrypts that 8,000 men and women had died in one month at Auschwitz. Although unable to reveal that they were all Jews (that would have exposed the intelligence coup of ULTRA), Churchill nonetheless announced in a radio broadcast to the British people (August 25, 1942) that "whole districts are being exterminated," and that the Germans were perpetrating "the most frightful cruelties." "We are in the presence of a crime without a name," the great wartime leader concluded, leaving no doubt that he understood all too well the "hideous import of the Final Solution."

This "crime without a name" was officially denounced by the Allied Declaration of December 17, 1942, signed by the United States, Britain, the Soviet Union, and the governments of eight occupied countries. It condemned the German government's "intention to exterminate the Jewish people in Europe," and denounced in the strongest possible terms this "bestial policy of cold-blooded extermination." Putting aside its prior hesitations to believe the reports on genocide the Allied governments now publicly confirmed what they had known for over a year.

Why did the Allies wait so long? According to William J. Casey, the former head of the CIA and an OSS agent during the war, the numerous reports on the Jewish genocide "were shunted aside because of the official policy in Washington and London to concentrate exclusively on the defeat of the enemy." Yet many of these reports contained reliable information on the gas chambers and crematoria at Birkenau. One of them, which came from Polish military intelligence in London, reached Washington by diplomatic pouch in May 1943 and the joint Chiefs of Staff by June. Updating information for Auschwitz-Birkenau, the report noted that: "A huge new camp crematorium consumes 3,000 persons daily." A summary of this and similar reports was made public on March 21, 1944, when the Associated Press in London released a report from the Polish Ministry of Information confirming that "more than 500,000 persons, mostly Jews, had been put to death at a concentration camp at Oświecim, southwest of Kracow." The report also stated that "three crematoria had been erected inside the camp to dispose of 10,000 bodies a day." The *Washington Post* published the AP release on the following day on page 2 under the banner, "Poles Report Nazis Slay 10,000 Daily." On March 24, 1944, five days after the Nazis installed a puppet government in Hungary and less than two months before the deportation of Hungarian Jews was to begin, Franklin Delano Roosevelt declared: "In one of the blackest crimes of all history . . . the wholesale systematic murder of the Jews of Europe goes on unabated every hour. . . . [The Jews of Hungary] are now threatened with annihilation. . . . All who knowingly take part in the deportation of Jews to their death in Poland . . . are equally guilty with the executioner.". . .

Based upon the evidence presented above, there no longer can be any question as to what the Allies knew and whether or not they had enough time to act upon it. We must now turn to the question of what they might have done. . . .

Risks to Prisoners

A common argument long marshaled by critics of the notion of bombing Auschwitz is that any concentrated high-altitude air attack on the death camp would have killed many prisoners in the process. We can never know for sure the extent of the prisoner casualties that would have

resulted. But by comparing such an attack to raids like that on Buchenwald, we can judge the degree to which this factor should have played a role in any potential bombing decision.

While Kitchens cites the August 24, 1944, raid on Buchenwald as proof that the inaccuracy of heavy bombers would have killed many Birkenau prisoners, the mission itself proves the exact opposite. The Buchenwald raid was, in fact, an extremely accurate one, successfully avoiding the concentration camp during a bombing of the Gustloff Works adjacent to it. According to the *Buchenwald Report*, the attack "completely destroyed the 'industrial development work' of the SS in Buchenwald in one single, well aimed blow." The *Report* further stated that "there were only two large fires caused by incendiary bombs," and an inmate wrote that "no [heavy] bombs struck the camp itself; only one bomb fell adjacent to the crematorium." The 384 prisoners killed were working in the factory areas at the time of the raid and were not allowed to retreat to the camp or to use bomb shelters during an air-raid alarm or attack, prompting another inmate to write: "The sole responsibility for the unfortunate deaths of several hundred prisoners in this attack falls on the SS, which at the time forbade prisoners to evacuate into the camp during an air raid alarm. . . ." The same prisoner also made it a point to note the effort of the Allied pilots to avoid collateral damage: "The Allied pilots in particular did all they could in order not to hit prisoners. The high number of prisoners killed is to be charged exclusively against the debit accounts of the Nazi murderers.". . .

A final aspect of this raid also is useful in conceptualizing what might have happened at Birkenau. The Buchenwald factories were believed by the Allies to be producing V-2 rocket parts and were thus attacked as part of the Crossbow offensive, despite the fact that the Allies knew well of the adjacent concentration camp. Whether they knew too that over 82,000 inmates were there is unclear, though even assuming a far lesser figure the decision to bomb was made with full knowledge that numerous prisoners could be killed if accuracy was below average (and this for a questionable strategic and tactical objective). Indeed, if the accuracy had not been up to standards, it is conceivable that more inmates would have been killed in this one raid than the total number of British civilians killed by all V-2 rocket attacks. To be consistent in their reasoning, then, those opposed to high-altitude bombing of Birkenau because of collateral deaths would have to consider this raid unconscionable. The British government, however, had its own priorities. . . .

Kitchens dismisses any attack by heavy bombers, arguing that their limited accuracy would have killed too many prisoners, thus resulting in unacceptable collateral damage. The problem, in this case, is not so much Kitchens' argument as his reasoning. He ignores, for example, the fact that most of these prisoners would be killed anyway, focusing only on how many Jews might have been killed by the bombing, rather than how many could have been saved. . . .

On July 7, 1944, British Foreign Secretary Anthony Eden wrote to the Secretary of State for Air, Sir Archibald Sinclair, inquiring "if anything could be done by bombing to stop the murder of Jews in Hungary." Sinclair and his staff replied on July 15 that due to various operational problems the RAF could do nothing. And though he did propose bringing the question up with the Americans, Sinclair added "I am not clear that it would really help the victims." Next to this remark, Eden scribbled: "He wasn't asked his opinion of this; he was asked to act," and then summed up the letter as "characteristically unhelpful.". . .

First, Sinclair argued that bombing the camp was "out of bounds of possibility for [RAF] Bomber Command, because the distance is too great for the attack to be carried out at night." Levy quotes Air Marshal Harris (a.k.a. "Bomber" Harris) for confirmation that "the extent of darkness" affects range. In other words, the major operational obstacle for the RAF in attacking Birkenau was the inability of British bombers to return to their bases in England under cover of darkness. Yet this same inability of airlift bombers to leave from and return to Italian bases at night did not prevent them from being sent in August and

September to Warsaw, 150 miles farther than Birkenau was from Allied bases in Italy. . . .

Conclusion

Both Sinclair and John J. McCloy, the U.S. Assistant Secretary of War, indicated that the target could not be bombed, thus putting an end to any further discussion on the matter. Yet their determination was not based upon standard operational procedure. As we have seen above, neither the British nor the Americans ever deliberately took a single photograph of Birkenau, though it would hardly have stretched their resources to do so. Further, no one ever bothered to make a simple request to the photo library for imagery of the Auschwitz area. The "could not" assessment, in short, appeared the most expedient way to implement the already established policy of not using the military to aid "refugees."

Even if the death camp could have been bombed, as this paper has sought to prove, the next line of argument against doing so was that it would have required, as McCloy indicated the "diversion of considerable air support essential to the success of our forces now engaged in decisive operations." This term "diversion can be applied to those actions which are (1) not directly related to military operations, or (2) not expressly ordered by the proper authority. Thus if Churchill (and the War Cabinet) or Roosevelt or any high-ranking commander had ordered an attack, then that mission would not be considered a diversion. . . .

From a simple comparison with other missions, there can be no question that the Birkenau extermination facilities could have been attacked by P-38 or Mosquito fighters using low-level precision bombing and causing minimal collateral damage. . . .

Also indisputable is the fact that both USAAF and RAF heavy and medium bombers had the range to attack the camp, though the inconsistent bombing accuracy of the heavies made it necessary to consider the cost/benefit ratio in human terms. In other words, how many would have to die to prevent the slaughter of how many others? Such a judgment, of course, was not unique to Birkenau, but constituted a decision taken even for strictly military operations. . . .

Such a cost/benefit analysis was simply never made in the case of Birkenau. The judgment that many inmates may have been killed was decided upon without any feasibility study and in complete ignorance of the location of the extermination facilities in relation to the camp. For all the Allies knew, the crematoria were situated in a field a mile from the camp and could have been destroyed with a few well placed bombs, as Cheshire suggests. In short, moral values and political considerations were tragically neglected in the case of the Holocaust. . . .

Richard Breitman argues that with intelligence reports received in 1943, enough could have been known about Birkenau to plan a raid in early 1944, had there been the will to act. If we consider a scenario in which Roosevelt ordered an attack at the time of his March 24, 1944, speech and it took place sometime in May (just as the Hungarian deportations were beginning), destroying at least Crematoria II and III (which constituted 75% of the capacity), would the killing process have been impeded? First, as Wyman points out, it took eight months to build these complex "industrial structures" at a time when Nazi Germany was at the height of its power. To organize the skilled labor and refashion highly specialized parts in the spring/summer of 1944 would have been difficult, if not impossible.

Kitchens' suggestion that the Jews could have been sent to Mauthausen, Belsen, or Buchenwald, none of which were extermination camps (or capable of accepting a few hundred thousand inmates on short notice), shows a lack of full knowledge of the camp system. Without the extermination facilities, the SS undoubtedly would have been forced to slow or altogether halt the deportations (which in the spring/summer of 1944 amounted to 70–80,000 Hungarian Jews a week) while they resorted to other, less efficient means of killing and body disposal. Cremation ditches, like those used for a short period in 1944 for the overflow of corpses, were hardly a practical alternative due to the problems posed by contamination as well as the threat of disease. It was for these very reasons, in fact, that Himmler had ordered the crematoria built in the first place. . . .

Doris Kearns Goodwin, a noted Roosevelt historian, once said that she thought bombing Auschwitz would have been worthwhile "if it had saved only one Jew. FDR somehow missed seeing how big an issue it was." With the kind of political will and moral courage the Allies exhibited in other missions throughout the war, it is plain that the failure to bomb Birkenau, the site of mankind's greatest abomination, was a missed opportunity of monumental proportions.

Selection 6

The Allies and the Holocaust

Gerhard L. Weinberg

Several articles in this volume are critical of the failure to help Europe's Jews, but Gerhard L. Weinberg, a history professor at the University of North Carolina, cautions that the situation was far more complex and that the opportunities for changing events were far more limited than other authors suggest.

*I*n the fall of 1941 German planning, which had originally anticipated a drive into the Middle East in the winter of 1941–1942 as a follow-up to the defeat of the Soviet Union, shifted the timetable to 1942. There was, however, one aspect of this project which, at least in Hitler's thinking, had not changed. In late July he had assured the Croatian minister of defense that all Jews would disappear from Europe; and he had predicted that Hungary would be the last country to give up its Jewish inhabitants. In November he made it clear that the project of killing Jews was by no means confined to Europe. As he explained to the Grand Mufti of Jerusalem, the Jews not only of Europe but everywhere else were to be killed. . . . Since the Mufti was presumably more interested in the Middle East than, say Australia or Latin America, Hitler spelled out for him that Germany intended the destruction, "Vernichtung" is the word recorded by the interpreter, of Jews living in the Arab world. What this latter term meant at the time was the Jewish community in Palestine and the then still substantial Jewish communities in Syria, Iraq, Iran, the Arabian peninsula, Egypt, and French Northwest Africa. And the Germans were indeed expecting to take over these areas so that, among other things, their Jewish inhabitants could be killed as was already being done in the newly occupied portions of the USSR. . . .

The way in which the Allied victory restricted Germany's program should be obvious but is rarely mentioned. The turning of the tide in the war, obvious in the Mediterranean theater in the winter of 1942–1943 meant that Nazi expectations of victory and the slaughter of all the world's Jews had been thwarted. In effect, the Allies had saved about two-thirds of the globe's Jews from the fate the Germans intended for them. On the other hand, the collapse of the Fascist regime in Italy, which was both an expected

and an obvious by-product of the Allied victory in North Africa, would open up to the Germans the opportunity to kill many Jews in Italy and in Italian-controlled portions of Europe—Jews who had hitherto been protected by the general unwillingness of the Italian diplomatic and military leadership to cooperate in the German murder program. As is well known, the Germans utilized what they saw as the opportunity opened up by the Italian surrender to try to include the Jews of Italy, the Italian islands in the Aegean, and the Italian occupation zones in France, Yugoslavia, and Greece in their killing program, and many thousands of Jews lost their lives as a result. Although this aspect of the Mediterranean campaign has received the attention it quite properly deserves, one ought not to overlook the fact that literally millions of Jews were saved by the same success of the Allies. . . .

German propaganda throughout the war years took the line that the Jews had caused the war and either controlled the countries aligned against Germany or influenced those who did exercise power. The expectation that in any new war the Jews would be killed had been part of the phrasing of Hitler's original public declaration on January 30, 1939. This propaganda line was a central one in subsequent years, and for a very good reason: it was correctly believed in Berlin that it was an effective one. Although the antisemitic sentiments of large portions of the British and American public certainly did not extend to any wish for the Jews to be killed, on the other hand any hint that their government was taking major steps to assist the Jews at their time of greatest danger was certain to evoke the strongest opposition.

The Western Powers were losing the war on land until the end of 1942, losing the war at sea until the fall of 1943, and were unable to assure victory in the war in the air until February–March 1944. So at a time when there was in practice very little that could be done to assist Germany's Jewish victims, the leadership in both London and Washington wanted nothing to happen on the home fronts that might discourage their peoples. Victory over the Axis was the

Excerpted from Gerhard L. Weinberg, "The Allies and the Holocaust," in *The Holocaust and History*, edited by Michael Berenbaum and Abraham J. Peck (Bloomington: Indiana University Press, 1989). Reprinted with permission from Indiana University Press.

first priority. . . . The Soviet Union, of course, had made it a matter of national policy to disregard the antisemitic policies and actions of the German government. Obsessed with the fatuous notion that fascism was the tool of monopoly capitalism, there was neither understanding of nor reaction to the persecution of Jews by the Nazis at the time—and, one might add, after the war until the collapse of the Soviet system. . . . It can, in fact, be argued that the official Communist Party line, sedulously spread throughout the Soviet Union, combined with the Nazi-Soviet Pact of 1939, contributed to the early successes of the German killing program during 1941 in that it led many citizens of the Soviet Union to expect that the Germans would behave in any occupied portions of the country rather the way they had in the preceding war when huge Russian territories had also been under temporary German occupation. By the time people discovered that this was a serious mistake, many Jews who might have made a greater effort to escape the Germans were already dead.

But just as the Soviet policy that had this effect as a terrible by-product was adopted for reasons having nothing to do with the Holocaust, so the major contribution that the Red Army made toward the containment of the German killing program was also unaffected by any consideration for the prospective Jewish victims. Keeping the German army away from a substantial proportion of the Jews living in the USSR as well as contributing to the defeat of Germany's attempt to control the globe obviously made for the saving of Jewish lives inside and outside the country. . . . The Soviets were mainly concerned about defending their country, and the Western Allies were terrified, to put it mildly, that the Axis might gain control of the oil resources of that region; the survival of the Jews of Palestine, Syria, Iran, and Iraq was, however, as surely due to the Soviets holding the Germans in the Caucasus as to the British holding in the Western Desert of Egypt.

Little Hope for Rescue

There were some minimal possibilities of rescuing Jews, but they were minimal indeed. . . .

Whatever the details of the various rescue schemes, there were very tight limits on what could be done. These limits were largely the result of German insistence on the sorts of trades and concessions that were impossible—and that they knew to be impossible—for the Allies to accept. A tiny number were saved in a variety of projects in which Jewish organizations, the War Refugee Board, and various neutral agencies and persons such as [Swedish diplomat] Raoul Wallenberg played significant roles; and it is entirely possible that more might have been done. The major obstacle, however, arose from the German side, a point that is too often overlooked.

The fixation on rescue attempts and their very limited success has tended to divert attention from the enormous efforts made by the Germans—including practically every agency of the German government—to maximize the killing and minimize any rescues. This is not to minimize the resistance of the British to most rescue attempts that involved getting the rescued into Palestine, and of the Americans to most rescue attempts that were likely to bring Jewish refugees to the United States. It is in this context that the title of Monty Penkower's book *The Jews Were Expendable* seems entirely appropriate. But such a title should not divert attention from those primarily responsible for the killing: the killers. This is a major aspect too often omitted from consideration of the other issue now frequently discussed, namely the possibilities of interfering with the killing process, primarily by bombing. This question is really appropriate only when considering the period beginning in the summer of 1944, when the Western Allies had finally defeated the German air force, had succeeded in establishing a firm bridgehead in Normandy, and had taken the airfields in central Italy from which airplanes could reach almost any portion of Europe still controlled by the Germans.

What could have been done and should have been done is essentially what the United States . . . did with the dropping of air supplies to some isolated portions of Bosnia: the clear and public indication of a policy preference opposed to the established policy of one side, even if there is little or no prospect of providing substantial practical assistance. An excellent example of this from World War II is the attempt by the Allies to drop supplies from the air to the Polish resistance forces that had risen against the Germans in Warsaw. These efforts no doubt showed where the British and Americans stood, and they also certainly helped the morale of those active in the uprising; but the practical effect was virtually nil. Perhaps the effort enabled the Poles to prolong their resistance a few days longer than otherwise would have been possible, but the outcome could not be in doubt.

One further point should be made in this connection. When the Western Allies sent planes to Warsaw, it was done over the strong objections of the commanders in the affected theaters of war. They always had other targets and priorities; this is particularly obvious from the records of the Allied command in Italy. In wartime there are invariably competing demands for all military resources, and the diversion of such resources in the fall of 1944 to the futile effort to assist the Polish uprising in Warsaw was ordered from the top.

German Commitment

One aspect of the debate over the possible bombing of Auschwitz or the railways leading to it has been too readily overlooked. That is the German side. By 1944 the murderers were both hardened and experienced. They were, it should be noted, proud of their activities and what they considered their great accomplishment. The notorious Stroop report on the destruction of the Warsaw Ghetto should be reread from this perspective: it shows men who boasted of what they were doing. They were completely committed to their careers as professional killers, and not only because of their ideological stance. By 1944 it was obvious to all of them that this was their road to advancement and to medals. It is not a coincidence that promotions and decorations invariably occupy such a central place in military and pseudomilitary hierarchies; these are the visible signs of success.

Furthermore, every individual involved in the program to kill all the Jews the Germans could reach knew very well, most especially by the summer of 1944, that this was not only the route to higher rank and higher decorations but the best chance of exemption from conscription if he was still in a civilian position and from far more dangerous duty at the front if he was in uniform. It may be a nasty picture, but these were nasty people. For them, killing Jews, most of whom had no weapons, was vastly preferable to serving at the front, where those with whom one had to deal had plenty of weapons, especially in this stage of the war.

Those active in the killing program had by this time an enormous vested interest in its continuation and in their own participation in it. There are signs that, even in the preceding year, 1943, the vast number of Jews killed in 1941 and 1942 had led those inside the apparatus of murder to search Europe for new categories of victims. Among them were Jews still protected in some way by Germany's satellites and allies; additional grist for the death mills was to be provided by the Sinti and Roma (Gypsies), persons of mixed ancestry (the so-called Mischlinge), and others.

The idea that men who were dedicated to the killing program, and who saw their own careers and even their own lives tied to its continuation, were likely to be halted by a few cuts of railway lines or the bombing of a gas chamber is preposterous. By the summer of 1944 these people had managed by one means or another the deaths of well over four million, and quite probably over five million, Jews; the notion that they lacked the persistence, ingenuity, and means to kill the majority of Hungary's 700,000 Jews defies all reason. It would have required greater exertions and more ingenuity on their part—and would perhaps have produced additional promotions and medals for those who in the face of great obstacles had carried out their Führer's design. On the other hand, interference by the Western Allies would have been an important assertion of policy, would have encouraged desperate victims in their last days and hours, might have inspired a few additional persons to provide aid and comfort to the persecuted, and might even have enabled a tiny number to escape the fate planned for them by the Germans. As it is, the absence of such essentially symbolic action leaves a blot on the record of the Allies and, possibly more effectively than any other development of those horrendous years, gives the lie to the endless stories about the alleged power of the Jews in the world: in the hour of supreme agony, all the Jewish organizations on earth could not get one country to send one plane to drop one bomb.

The Importance of Victory

In connection with the last stage of the war and of the Holocaust, one additional significant aspect of the policy of Britain and the United States needs review. To those who urged more drastic steps to assist the victims of the German killing program, time and again both governments responded that the most important thing was to win the war as quickly as possible. Victory would end the killing, and anything that might delay victory would only hurt, not help, those whom the Germans had marked out as victims. It is frequently claimed that this was not only a silly answer but that there was something mendacious about it because most of Europe's Jews were killed before victory was in fact attained. . . .

Given the determination of the Germans to fight on to the bitter end, and given their equally fierce determination to slaughter Jews to the last moments of the Third Reich, there were, as is well known, thousands of deaths every day into the final days of the war; and many of the surviving camp inmates had been so weakened by hunger and disease that thousands more died even after liberation. In this connection, it might be worthwhile to consider how many more Jews would have survived had the war ended even a week or ten days earlier—and conversely, how many more would have died had the war lasted an additional week or ten days. Whatever numbers one might put forward in such speculations, one thing is, or ought to be, reasonably clear: the number would be greater than the total number of Jews saved by the various rescue efforts of 1943–1945.

Every single life counts, and every individual saved counts. There cannot be the slightest doubt that more efforts could have been made by an earlier establishment of the War Refugee Board and by any number of other steps and actions. The general picture in terms of overall statistics would not have been very different; but the record of the Allies would have been brighter, and each person saved could have lived out a decent life. The exertions of the Allies in World War II saved not only themselves but also the majority of the world's Jews. But the shadow of doubt whether enough was done will always remain, even if there really were not many things that could have been done.

Any examination of the failure to do more must, however, carefully avoid a most dangerous shift in the apportioning of responsibility. It is the killers, whether in an office, a murder squad, or a killing center, who bear the central responsibility for their deeds. Any general distribution of blame, the "we are all guilty" syndrome, only serves to exculpate the truly guilty. And they were not to be found among the Allies.

Press Coverage of the Holocaust

Deborah E. Lipstadt

It is hard to imagine how the press could have failed to report the Nazi campaign to annihilate the Jews, yet the conventional wisdom is that little was known about Hitler's Final Solution until late in the war or after the concentration camps were liberated. In truth, a great deal was known, from at least 1942 on, and the major press did publish stories about the murder of thousands and sometimes millions of people. The problem was these stories were often buried in the paper, suggesting that they were not as important, or credible as those on the front page. Today when a madman goes on a shooting spree and kills nine people it merits banner headlines across the country; yet no such headlines were given to the stories of mass murder during World War II. Why? The answer is not as simple as the absence of a CNN. As Deborah E. Lipstadt found, the problem had a lot to do with the inability of editors to believe what their reporters were telling them. Many people had been conditioned to be skeptical of atrocity stories because World War I propaganda had contained many such stories, which were fabricated purely to provoke sym-

pathy for the war effort. Perhaps in the modern age when "ethnic cleansing" has become common enough that the Holocaust is viewed by many as just one of many examples of genocide, it is difficult to appreciate how shocking it was to discover what humans could do to other humans in World War II. In this excerpt, Lipstadt, the Dorot chair in modern Jewish and Holocaust studies at Emory University, offers an explanation for why the Holocaust was beyond belief.

Since the onset of Nazi rule Americans had greeted almost all the news of Nazi Germany's persecution of the Jews skeptically. Inevitably, their first reaction was to question whether it was true. Before, during, and even *after* the war many Americans, including those associated with the press, refused to believe the news they heard. . . .

In a January 1943 Gallup poll nearly 30 percent of those asked dismissed the news that 2 million Jews had been killed in Europe as just a rumor. Another 24 percent had no opinion on the question. Informal polls taken by the *Detroit Free Press* and the *New York Post* in 1943 found that a broad range of Americans did not believe the atrocity reports.

Journalists who had been stationed in Germany were among those most distressed by the

American refusal to believe that the Germans were engaging in physical persecution. In March 1943 William Shirer, writing in the *Washington Post*, castigated the public for thinking that the stories of the atrocities were untrue or had been magnified for "propaganda purposes." He attributed this attitude to a "silly sort of supercynicism and superskepticism" which persisted despite the fact that there was "no earthly reason" for people not to believe. . . .

In January 1944 Arthur Koestler also expressed his frustration that so many people refused to believe that the "grim stories of Nazi atrocities are true." Writing in the Sunday *New York Times Magazine*, Koestler cited public opinion polls in the United States in which nine

out of ten average Americans dismissed the accusations against the Nazis as propaganda lies and flatly stated that they did not believe a word of them. How, he wondered, could Americans be convinced that this "nightmare" was reality? The *Christian Century* responded to Koestler by arguing that there really was no point in "screaming" about the atrocities against the Jews because this would only "emotionally exhaust" those who wanted to devote their energies "*after*" the war to "building peace.". . .

In October 1944 Averell Harriman, American Ambassador to the Soviet Union, felt compelled to reassure the press that the reports of massacres and atrocities committed by the Germans and their supporters in Russian territory "have

Although journalists reported that Nazi genocide had taken thousands and even millions of lives, many Americans believed that the stories were either untrue or exaggerated.

not been and cannot be exaggerated." Though a December 1944 Gallup poll revealed that 76 percent of those queried now believed that many people had been "murdered" in concentration camps, the estimates they gave of the number who had died indicated that they had not really grasped the scope of the tragedy. Furthermore, while more Americans were now willing to believe that many people had been killed, they generally did not believe in the existence of gas chambers and death camps. . . .

The victims themselves recognized the difficulty they faced in piercing the barriers of incredulity. A Polish underground courier who, in August 1944, reached London with news of the stepped-up pace of the slaughter of Hungarian Jews was shocked to find that despite the fact that he brought news from within Auschwitz itself, "nobody will believe." As late as 1944 eyewitness accounts—particularly those of victims—were not considered irrefutable evidence even if they came from independent sources and corroborated one another. The press often categorized them as prejudiced or exaggerated. At the end of the war Kenneth McCaleb, war editor of the *New York Daily Mirror*, admitted that whenever he had read about German atrocities, he had not taken them seriously because they had always come from "'foreigners' who, many of us felt, had some ax to grind and must be exaggerat[ing].". . .

Associated Press staff member Daniel De Luce admitted that prior to the visit [to Maidanek] most of the other American and British correspondents in the group "could not even begin to imagine the proportions of its frightfulness." Now they had no doubts.

Edgar Snow of the *Saturday Evening Post*, Richard Lauterbach of *Time* and *Life*, and Maurice Hindus of the *St. Louis Post Dispatch* and the *New York Herald Tribune* all found the storehouse for the personal possessions of the victims more "terrifying" than even the gas chambers and the crematorium. In them they found rooms filled with shoes—one for men's shoes and one for women's—kitchenware, clothes, books, pocketknives, and other items that the unsuspecting victims had brought with them to facilitate their "relocation." Maidanek "suddenly became real" to Lauterbach when he stood on top of a "sea" of 820,000 pairs of shoes which had cascaded out of a warehouse. . . . In the introduction to his detailed description of this camp, Snow explained why he broke with his magazine's norm and wrote about a subject which was fully reported by the daily press. Maidanek was evidence of the way Nazi ideology enabled people to commit "crimes almost too monstrous for the human mind to accept.". . .

Even this news of Maidanek and the eyewitness accounts by reputable American correspondents did not significantly change the way the American press treated this story: momentarily attention was paid, but all too quickly the news was forgotten. . . . After a brief wave of interest, reports once again appeared in short articles on inner pages. But this pattern of deprecating the importance of the news regarding the Final Solution did not originate with the press. In fact the press was faithfully duplicating an Allied policy of obfuscation and camouflage.

Universalizing the Victims

Part of the responsibility for both American skepticism and the press's ambiguous treatment of this news can be traced directly to Allied opposition to publicizing reports of atrocities against Jewish victims. On many occasions when atrocities against Jews were discussed, the identity of the victims was universalized. In other words, Jews became Poles or Russians or innocent civilians. American and British leaders had been intent on avoiding mention of Jews as the specific victims of Nazi hostility as early as 1938 at Evian, and their policy had not substantially changed since. The Allies argued that if they treated Jews as a separate entity, it would validate Nazi ideology. A truer explanation for this behavior was American and British fear that singling out the unique fate of the Jews would strengthen the demands of those who wanted the Allies to undertake specific rescue action on their behalf. The Americans worried that they might be asked to admit more Jewish refugees, and the British were concerned that pressure would be put upon them to open Palestine to Jews.

It therefore became Allied policy to refer to "political refugees" and not Jews, even when these refugees were clearly Jews. Rarely did any reporters or editorial board take note of this policy. . . .

Probably the most outrageous example of this explicit policy of ignoring the Jewish aspect of the tragedy occurred in Moscow in the fall of 1943. There Churchill, Roosevelt, and Stalin met and affixed their signatures to what is known as the Moscow Declaration, which warned that

> Germans who take part in the wholesale shooting of *Italian* officers or in the execution of *French*, *Dutch*, *Belgian* or *Norwegian* hostages or of *Cretan* peasants, or who have shared in slaughters inflicted on the people of *Poland* or in the territories of the *Soviet Union* . . . will be brought back to the scene of their crimes and judged on the spot by the peoples whom they have outraged.

Nowhere in the declaration were Jews even obliquely mentioned, a phenomenon the press simply ignored. While there were some exceptions to this Allied policy, e.g., the December 1942 statement confirming the Nazi policy of exterminating the Jews, they were few. When declarations did contain references to Jews, as was the case in March 1944 when Roosevelt referred to the Hungarian situation, the President's advisers vigorously worked to ensure that they were not too prominently mentioned. . . .

Deputy Director of the Office of War Information Arthur Sweetser sent a memorandum to Leo Rosten, who was Deputy Director in charge of information on the enemy, on the "impending Nazi extermination of the Jews." In it he argued that the story of atrocities would be "confused and misleading if it appears to be simply affecting the Jewish people," and therefore news of the particular fate of the Jews should be contained and even suppressed. Consequently, when the news of German atrocities was publicized, the Jewish aspect was often eliminated. . . .

Even when war had virtually ended and the camps were being liberated, reporters continued to incorporate the fate of the Jews into that of all other national groups that had been incarcerated and murdered at the camps. For example, Edgar Snow wrote that at Maidanek "Jews, Germans and other Europeans were all robbed in common and were all fed to the same ovens." Other reports described the victims as "men, women and children of 22 nationalities"—some citing Jews as constituting "half" or "most" of the victims, others simply listing them along with Russians, Poles, Frenchmen, Italians, Czechs, Yugoslavs, Greeks, Belgians, Germans, and Dutchmen. *Time* correspondent Sidney Olsen, who accompanied the U.S. Seventh Army as it liberated Dachau, described its inmates as "Russians, French, Yugoslavs, Italians, and Poles." In this camp, Olsen observed, were "the men of all nations whom Hitler's agents had picked out as prime opponents of Nazism; here were the very earliest of Nazi-haters. Here were German social democrats, Spanish survivors of the Spanish Civil War." But nowhere in his article was there a Jew. . . .

The News About Auschwitz: An Eyewitness Account

The extent to which certain American officials were opposed to focusing on the murder of Jews was demonstrated in the fall of 1944 when John Pehle of the War Refugee Board received from American officials in Switzerland a full text of the eyewitness account of Auschwitz. The report contained precise details on the number and national origins of the victims, the process of moving newly arrived victims from the freight trains to the gas chambers, the kinds of work done by the inmates, the physical plant of the camp, the physical dimensions of the barracks, gas chambers, and crematorium, and the way in which the "selections" for the gas chambers were conducted. The escapees who were the eyewitnesses had also witnessed the preparation of the camp for the "handling" of Hungarian Jewry.

When Pehle received the report—he had previously only seen a summary—he did two things. First, he urged John McCloy, Assistant

Secretary of War, to "give serious consideration to the possibility of destroying the execution chambers and crematoria in Birkenau through direct bombing action." McCloy rejected Pehle's request with the incorrect but familiar explanation that it would pose too great a risk to American bombers and would divert critically needed air power. Pehle then decided to release the report to the press as a means of awakening public support for action.

Not since *Kristallnacht* had a story been so widely featured or prompted such extensive comment. Many papers carried it on the front page or in a prominent position elsewhere. The headlines alone encapsulated the press's horrified reaction.

New York Herald Tribune:
U.S. CHARGES NAZIS TORTURED MILLIONS TO DEATH IN EUROPE

War Refugee Board Says 1,765,000 Jews Were Killed by Gas in One Camp Alone; Witnesses' Testimony Gives Details of the Atrocities

Louisville Courier Journal:
THE INSIDE STORY OF MASS MURDERING BY NAZIS

Escapees Give Detailed Accounts of the Gassing and Cremating of 1,765,000 Jews at Birkenau
FROM AN OFFICIAL PUBLICATION OF THE WAR
REFUGEE BOARD

Philadelphia Inquirer:
1,765,000 JEWS KILLED WITH GAS AT GERMAN CAMP

New York Times:
U.S. BOARD BARES ATROCITY DETAILS TOLD BY WITNESSES AT POLISH CAMPS

Washington Post:
TWO MILLION EXECUTED IN NAZI CAMPS
Gassing, Cremation Assembly-Line Methods Told by War Refugee Boards

The Board appended a one-page preface attesting to its complete faith in the report's reliability. It stressed that all the information—both dates and death tolls—tallied with the "trustworthy yet fragmentary reports" previously received and therefore the eyewitness statements could be considered "entirely credible." The *New York Herald Tribune* described the report as the "most shocking document ever issued by a United States government agency." Virtually every news story on the report emphasized not only that this was an eyewitness report but that it had been released by the War Refugee Board, an official government body, composed of "the three highest ranking Cabinet officials." This was, according to Ted Lewis of the *Washington Times Herald*, "the first American official stamp of truth to the myriad of eyewitness stories of the mass massacres in Poland." The *Louisville Courier Journal*, which devoted an entire page to excerpts from the report, observed in its article that "there is no longer any need to speculate on the mass murdering of millions of civilians.". . .

One of the few papers to inject an explicit note of skepticism into its report was the *Chicago Tribune*, which prefaced its news story with the observation that there have been numerous reports on German atrocities, "some of which have been verified." While previous reports had been accompanied by photographs, "no pictures were released to corroborate the atrocity story released today." The extensive detail was still not enough for the *Tribune*, it wanted pictures. It never mentioned to readers that Auschwitz, the subject of the report, was still in German hands and consequently no pictures were available. . . .

On October 30 *Yank* magazine, published by the armed forces for their members, contacted the War Refugee Board and asked if it "dealt in German atrocity stories." A reporter for the magazine, Sgt. Richard Paul, had been assigned to prepare an article about German atrocities in order to "show our soldiers the nature of their enemy." Paul arranged to meet with Pehle to gather information for the story. At their meeting Pehle gave Paul a copy of the report for use by *Yank*.

A few days later Paul informed the War

Refugee Board that the report would appear in the next issue of the magazine. But Paul's superiors intervened, told him that the story was "too Semitic," and instructed him to get a "less Jewish story" from the Board. Pehle's assistant at the War Refugee Board refused to give him one, and in her explanation she explicitly stated something neither the Allied governments nor the Allied press ever really made clear: most of the victims in the German death camps were Jews. . . .

Americans prided themselves on their skepticism. The *Baltimore Sun* tried to explain how, despite so much evidence, Americans had been able to reject the reports as untrue. "Atrocities? Americans, a sophisticated people, smiled at this idea. . . . When it came to atrocities, seeing, and seeing alone, would be believing, with most Americans.". . .

But the press had been shown. It had been shown by reporters who had been stationed in Germany until 1942 and who had heard numerous reports including those of participants in the persecution of Jews. Sigrid Schultz, for example, sat in the train station listening to returning soldiers describe the massacres on the eastern front. In 1942 UP's Glen Stadler, who had just returned from Germany, described what was being done to the Jews as an "open hunt." By 1944 captured soldiers were confessing to atrocities that Harold Denny, the *New York Times* reporter assigned to the American First Army, called "so wantonly cruel that, without such confirmation, they might have been discounted as propagandist inventions." Reporters had seen places such as Babi Yar, where the soil contained human remains, and Maidanek, where mass graves were visible. The American government had released a documented report on Auschwitz. Yet these editors, publishers, and reporters claimed not to believe what they heard.

The truth is that much of the press had not rejected as propaganda all that it heard, but it had erected barriers which enabled it to dismiss parts of it. It accepted a portion, often quite grudgingly, and rejected the rest as exaggeration. It adhered to a pattern which I have chosen to call "Yes but." At first it argued, *Yes*, bad things may be happening *but* not as bad as reported. Subsequently it was willing to acknowledge that *Yes*, many Jews may be victims *but* not as many as claimed. *Yes* many may have died, *but* most probably died as a result of war-related privations and not as a result of having been murdered. *Yes*, many may have been killed *but* not in gas chambers. *Yes*, some Jews may have died in death camps, *but* so did many other people.

As this sequence of events progressed, the press seemed willing to believe a bit more, but rarely was it willing to accept the full magnitude of the atrocities. This was as characteristic of the press's behavior in 1945 as it was in 1933. In 1933 it could not believe that Jews were being indiscriminately beaten up in the streets, and in 1945 it could not believe that they had been singled out to be murdered. When it came to atrocity reports, particularly those concerning the annihilation of the Jewish people, skepticism always tempered belief. By responding in such a fashion, the press obscured the true picture for itself and its readers. . . .

We have seen how the reporters, editors, and publishers who visited the camps generally claimed that until that moment they had simply not believed that the stories were true. After their visits any vestiges of doubt had been eradicated. Now they knew such things could happen, but they could not fathom how. Their amazement had, in fact, only increased. In a front-page story in the *Baltimore Sun* Lee McCardell, the Sunpapers' war correspondent, voiced his confusion and disorientation after touring a camp.

> You had heard of such things in Nazi Germany. You had heard creditable witnesses describe just such scenes. But now that you were actually confronted with the horror of mass murder, you stared at the bodies and almost doubted your own eyes.
>
> "Good God!" you said aloud, "Good God!"
>
> Then you walked down around the corner of two barren, weatherbeaten, wooden barrack buildings. And there in a wooden shed, piled up like so much cordwood, were the naked bodies

430 THE COMPLETE HISTORY OF THE HOLOCAUST

of more dead men than you cared to count.

"Good God!" you repeated, "Good God!"

McCardell's reaction to what he found at this camp, Ohrdruf, which was far from the worst scene of German atrocities, was similar to that of the American major who first entered the camp:

"I couldn't believe it even when I saw it," Major Scotti said, "I couldn't believe that I was there looking at such things.". . .

The magnitude of the horror was unfathomable. The tales of horror beggared the imagination. They were just "too inconceivably terrible." This was certainly a critical factor in allowing the press to suspend belief. There were many failures in America's behavior during this period, and a failure of the imagination was one of them.

But there is a problem with explaining or excusing the press treatment of this news by relying on the fact that this was a story which was "beyond belief." While the unprecedented nature of this news made it easier, particularly at the outset, to discount the news, by the time of the Bermuda conference in 1943 and certainly by the time of the destruction of Hungarian Jewry in 1944 even the most dubious had good reason to know that terrible things were underway. Numerous eyewitness accounts which corroborated one another had been provided by independent sources. Towns, villages, and ghettos which had once housed millions now stood empty. The underground had transmitted documentation regarding the freight trains loaded with human cargo which rolled into the death camps on one day and rolled out shortly thereafter, only to be followed by other trains bearing a similar cargo. Where could these people be going? Where were the inhabitants of the towns and villages? Had they simply disappeared? There was only one possible answer to these questions. And most members of the press—when they stopped to consider the matter—knew it.

Given the amount of information which reached them, no responsible member of the press should have dismissed this news of the an-

nihilation of a people as propaganda, and the fact is that few did. In the preceding pages we have seen numerous examples of papers and journals acknowledging that millions were being killed. By the latter stages of the war virtually every major American daily had acknowledged that many people, Jews in particular, were being murdered. They lamented what was happening, condemned the perpetrators, and then returned to their practice of burying the information.

There was, therefore, something disingenuous about the claims of reporters and editors at the end of the war not to have known until the camps were open. They may not have known just *how* bad things were, but they knew they were quite bad. . . .

There is, of course, no way of knowing whether anything would have been different if the press had actively pursued this story. The press did not have the power to stop the carnage or to rescue the victims. The Allies might have remained just as committed to inaction, even if they had been pressured by the press. But in a certain respect that is not the question one must ask. The question to be asked is did the press behave in a responsible fashion? Did it fulfill its mandate to its readers? . . .

We still cannot answer the question that Malcolm Bingay's colleagues asked one another as they saw the remains of the Nazis' work—"how creatures, shaped like human beings, can do such things." Nor can we explain how the world of bystanders—particularly those with access to the news—were able to treat this information with such apathy. Both the Final Solution and the bystanders' equanimity are beyond belief.

Today we do not doubt that millions of people can be massacred, systematically and methodically, or that millions more can bear witness and do nothing. Over the past forty years we have lost our innocence and have become inured not only to the escalating cycle of human horror but also to the human indifference. Then the news shocked and confounded us. Today similar news, whether it come front Biafra, Cambodia, Uganda, or any one of a number of other places, does not shock us and sometimes it does not even interest us. It has become an "old," all too familiar, and therefore relatively unexciting story.

Our reaction is among the more tragic legacies of the Final Solution. The inability of re- ports of extreme persecution and even mass murder in foreign lands to prompt us to act almost guarantees that the cycle of horror which was initiated by the Holocaust will continue.

Selection 8

What American Jews Knew and Did About the Holocaust

Raul Hilberg

More than fifty years after World War II, the American Jewish community remains traumatized by its failure to prevent the Holocaust. It is often said the community was silent during the war and that was one reason nothing was done, but this was not really true. Efforts were made to publicize the plight of European Jewry, to protest Allied inaction, and to solicit help from the Roosevelt administration. Given Hitler's success in exterminating 6 million people, however, it is impossible to avoid the conclusion that more could have been done. Today, Jews are considered politically powerful and the pro-Israel lobby is, in fact, the most powerful foreign policy interest group in the country, so it is easy to assume this was always the case, but it was not. In the 1940s Jews were not powerful. This was a time when anti-Semitism was prevalent, quotas prevented Jews from attending many universities, and few Jews held positions of political influence. In this excerpt, Raul Hilberg discusses what the Jewish community knew about the Final Solution and how it responded to the news. Hilberg, a retired political science professor, is considered one of the leading authorities on the Holocaust.

Excerpted from Raul Hilberg, *Perpetrators, Victims, Bystanders: The Jewish Catastrophe*. Copyright © 1992 Raul Hilberg. Reprinted with permission from HarperCollins Publishers, Inc.

*a*merican Jewry was free and safe. It had grown from a small community of Portuguese Jews in the seventeenth century. In the middle of the nineteenth century, there was a noticeable immigration, mainly from Germany. Between 1881 and 1932, the Eastern European Jews arrived. The number of Jewish immigrants who settled in the United States during those five decades was over 2,300,000, and many of these Jews were still alive when the Second World War broke out. They had left parents, siblings, nephews, nieces, and cousins in Europe, although few had ever seen their relatives since youth. . . .

American Jewry was hemmed in geographically, economically, and psychologically. In the nineteen thirties, when the U.S. Jewish population was approximately 4,800,000, nearly 2,000,000 Jews lived in New York City. All over the United States, Jews were effectively barred from living in many neighborhoods. Quotas for Jews were established in colleges and medical schools. By and large, Jews were excluded from management and employment in heavy industry, the large banks, and the major insurance companies. Jewish business activity gravitated to the retail trade, the manufacture of clothing, and communications. The trade unions of the Jews were the International Ladies Garment Workers Union, the Amalgamated Clothing Workers, and the Fur Workers. The vast majority of the Jews did not own their own homes and struggled to pay rent. Even as their income rose to the levels of non-Jews in the cities, their capital and net worth were still relatively low. Moreover, American Jewry was uneasy about its status. The Jews read and listened nervously to open anti-Semitic statements that seemed to multiply in number and intensity of tone even as the situation of the European Jews was worsening. The American Jews were on the defensive and they proclaimed their undivided loyalty to America. There was to be no conflict between an American interest, such as the restrictive immigration laws adopted in the 1920s, and a Jewish need. America would always have priority.

As officeholders Jews were not numerous. The Secretary of the Treasury, Henry Morgenthau, Jr., was a Jew. The House of Representatives contained nine Jews, and after the election of 1940, just six. No Jew served in the Senate. As voters, American Jews overwhelmingly backed the Democratic party of Franklin Roosevelt in 1932, 1936, 1940, and 1944. Roosevelt—articulate reformer and trusted liberal—was Jewry's greatest hero. Like America, Roosevelt came first.

Two major political organizations had been formed by American Jews before Hitler came to power. The older of the two was the American Jewish Committee, which was established in 1906. . . . In the 1930s it was headed by one of its founders, the Arkansas-born Cyrus Adler, then in his seventies. . . . From 1941 to 1943, the committee was headed by Maurice Wertheim, an investment banker, and thereafter by the Alabama-born Judge Joseph Proskauer, who had immersed himself in New York Democratic party politics. The American Jewish Committee was anti-Zionist before and throughout the Second World War. In asserting Jewish rights or protesting against injustice, its style was always restrained. The committee did not organize public demonstrations.

The second political grouping was the American Jewish Congress and its outgrowth, the international World Jewish Congress. Originally an assembly of Jewish organizations, the American Jewish Congress became in the 1930s a society of individual members. The World Jewish Congress, founded in 1936, was formed of delegations from Jewish organizations and communities around the world, with sections in Great Britain, Latin America, and so forth. The principal figure in the American Jewish Congress and the World Jewish Congress was Stephen Wise, a Reform rabbi who was also a Zionist. Wise was born in 1874 in Budapest but was brought to the United States as a small child. His Zionist activity began early. As a young man he knew the founder of modern Zionism, Theodor Herzl, and helped organize the Zionist movement in the United States. Between 1936 and 1938 he also served as President of the Zionist Organization of America. Wise, perhaps more than any other Jewish public figure, identified himself with Roosevelt, whom he backed unreservedly and to whom he wrote letters addressing him as "Dear Chief.". . .

Both organizations had opposed a resolution introduced by Representative Samuel Dickstein in 1933 to liberalize the immigration law, preferring the less conspicuous approach of lobbying for more permissive applications of existing legal provisions. When the Jewish War Veterans of America and other small groups organized a boycott of German goods during the same year, the leadership of the American Jewish Committee and the American Jewish Congress again had similar reactions. Adler and Proskauer were dismayed, while Wise hesitated to support the movement in the absence of "the sanction of our government." Wise understood that the pressure was rising in the Jewish community and therefore he wrote to a colleague that he was trying to "resist the masses." In the end, his own administrative committee overruled him. By November 1938 the deterioration of Jewry's position in Germany prompted the representatives of the American Jewish Committee, the American Jewish Congress, the fraternal organization B'nai B'rith, and the Jewish Labor Committee to weigh the advisability of advocating a change in the immigration law and of organizing protest parades in the streets. Once again, the decision was in favor of restraint and inactivity. . . .

Several Jewish organizations established offices in Switzerland. When these outposts were created, before the German march across Europe, Switzerland was not considered an important location. The offices were to distribute some relief and gather some basic information. Their budgets were small and their personnel sparse.

The Jewish Agency in Palestine appointed as its representative in Switzerland the Berlin-born Richard Lichtheim. . . .

Warning Signs

Lichtheim's letters from Geneva are replete with warnings. Seeing darkness with every glance, he noted as early as October 1939 that in the newly occupied western portion of Poland, "we shall have to face the fact that under German rule 2,000,000 Jews will be annihilated in not less a cruel way, perhaps even more cruel, than 1,000,000 Armenians have been destroyed by the Turks during the last war." By November 1941, after the beginning of deportations of German Jews to Poland, he was full of forebodings. The fate of the Jews from Germany, he wrote, would be even more dreadful than that of the Polish Jews shut off in the ghettos, because the deportees did not have money, food reserves, or bedding. In the same letter he observed the "curious" fact that President Roosevelt never mentioned Jews in re-

marks about German oppression. The "studied silence" of the democracies was not making it easier for the victims. On February 11, 1942, he wrote: "The number of [Jewish] dead after this war will have to be counted not in the thousands or hundreds of thousands but in the several millions," and on May 13, 1942, he reiterated his demand that the persecutions be given publicity in the British and American press and over the radio. Two weeks later he predicted flatly that at the end of the war, two or three million Jews would be "physically destroyed."

The World Jewish Congress placed its office in Geneva under the direction of Gerhart M. Riegner. In 1939, Riegner was twenty-eight years old. . . .

The World Jewish Congress also operated a small rescue organization (Relico) in Geneva, which was headed by Adolf Silberschein, a former member of the Polish Parliament. . . .

The Truth Is Learned

At first, the information obtained by Riegner was the sort that could be culled from legal gazettes and newspapers. When the shootings in Eastern Europe and deportations from Germany began in 1941, the contents of his messages changed radically. The first deportations of the German Jews were mentioned in a telegram on October 16, 1941, and by March 23, 1942, Riegner sent a cable to Wise, Rabbi Maurice Perlzweig, and Rabbi Irving Miller in the World Jewish Congress headquarters in New York stating:

> GRAVEST POSSIBLE NEWS REACHING LONDON PAST WEEK, SHOWS MASSACRES NOW REACHING CATASTROPHIC CLIMAX PARTICULARLY POLAND ALSO DEPORTATIONS BULGARIAN ROMANIAN JEWS ALREADY BEGUN STOP EUROPEAN JEWS DISAPPEARING. . . .

Riegner had only pieces of information, some inaccurate, but he collected them. On June 17, 1942, he wrote to Goldmann that "some weeks ago" Silberschein had received a telephone call from a German Red Cross representative in Kolomea (eastern Galicia). The man, with whom no one in the Geneva office had ever been in contact, had even introduced himself by name. He informed Silberschein that the situation of the Jews in Kolomea had become catastrophic. A great many men had died a violent death, and women and children needed help. The caller said that his human feelings moved him to contact the Geneva office to alleviate his conscience. During the following month Riegner sent word that thirty thousand of forty thousand Jews in Vilnius were gone, that some of the Bialystok Jews had been deported, and that in eastern Galician villages serious "pogroms" had taken place in March and April. By June and July reports of this nature were increasing in frequency and volume, but they still did not trigger a suspicion that Nazi Germany had embarked on a final solution.

During July 1942, however, several Germans crossed into Switzerland with fundamental revelations. One of them was Ernst Lemmer, a founder of the German Democratic party in 1918 and Minister in West Germany during the 1950s and 1960s. Lemmer spent the wartime years as a newspaper correspondent in Budapest, Brussels, and Switzerland. According to Walter Laqueur, who made a search of these messengers, Lemmer met with several Swiss public figures in Zurich that July and told them about "gas chambers, stationary and mobile, in which Jews were killed." He wanted this news to be disseminated, but he was somewhat mistrusted and no one was inclined to do as he asked.

On or about July 27, 1942, a German lieutenant colonel, Artur Sommer, who was an economist and Deputy Director of the "Allied and Neutral States" Group in the Economy Office of the Armed Forces High Command, traveled to Switzerland on official business. Sommer had been in Switzerland before and had visited another economist, Professor Edgar Salin, at the University of Basel. On those occasions Sommer had freely talked about German behavior in the USSR, once leaving packets of photographs showing emaciated and dead Soviet prisoners of war. This time Salin found a note without an envelope in his box. It stated:

In the East camps are being prepared in which all the Jews of Europe and a large part of the Soviet prisoners of war are to be gassed. Please send messages immediately to Roosevelt and Churchill. If the BBC will warn daily against the gas ovens, their use may be prevented, since the criminals will do everything to make sure that the German people will not find out what they are planning and what they can surely carry out as well.

The information in Sommer's note was already old. Gas had been considered for the European Jews during the early fall of 1941. . . . Nevertheless, Sommer's message has considerable significance, first because it was sent by someone in Berlin who was likely to be close to the truth, and second because it was an unambiguous statement to the effect that European Jewry was to be gassed to death.

Salin was a convert to Christianity from Germany and he was sensitive to the unfolding events across the border. Nevertheless he did not know how to reach Roosevelt and Churchill. He contacted the American President of the Bank for International Settlements, Thomas H. McKittrick, in Basel, who subsequently assured Salin that he had gone to the American Minister in Bern immediately and that the Minister had cabled the news to "Roosevelt." No cable containing the contents of Sommer's communication from the American Minister to any Washington address has been found in any archives. . . .

A third informant was Eduard Schulte, who was an industrialist in Breslau, where he headed a large mining concern, Bergwerksgesellschaft Georg von Giesche's Erben. His connections in Germany included a German colonel and a Giesche manager who was close to Gauleiter Karl Hanke of Lower Silesia. Like Sommer, Schulte had previously been in Switzerland on business and had given information to various people about German policies and plans. This time, his visit was prompted by something he had heard about the Jews: they were going to be annihilated. On July 30, 1942, he talked to a business associate, Isidor Koppelmann, who contacted the press officer of the Swiss Jewish community, Benjamin Sagalowitz. Schulte wanted his message to be transmitted to America and Britain, and Sagalowitz turned to Riegner in Geneva. . . . On the morning of August 8, Riegner set out to meet with the British and American consuls in Geneva. Riegner, who had not met Schulte and had not been given his name, drafted a notice containing the substance of Schulte's statement. It was addressed to Sydney Silverman, a member of the World Jewish Congress in London and member of Parliament, and to Wise in New York. Its text is as follows:

> RECEIVED ALARMING REPORT STATING THAT IN FUEHRERS HEADQUARTERS A PLAN HAS BEEN DISCUSSED AND BEING UNDER CONSIDERATION ACCORDING TO WHICH TOTAL OF JEWS IN COUNTRIES OCCUPIED CONTROLLED BY GERMANY NUMBERING THREE-AND-HALF TO FOUR MILLIONS SHOULD AFTER DEPORTATION AND CONCENTRATION IN EAST BE AT ONE BLOW EXTERMINATED IN ORDER TO RESOLVE ONCE FOR ALL JEWISH QUESTION IN EUROPE STOP ACTION IS REPORTED TO BE PLANNED FOR AUTUMN WAYS OF EXECUTION STILL DISCUSSED STOP IT HAS BEEN SPOKEN OF PRUSSIC ACID STOP IN TRANSMITTING INFORMATION WITH ALL NECESSARY RESERVATION AS EXACTITUTE CANNOT BE CONTROLLED BY US BEG TO STATE THAT INFORMER IS REPORTED HAVE CLOSE CONNECTIONS WITH HIGHEST GERMAN AUTHORITIES AND HIS REPORTS TO BE GENERALLY RELIABLE
>
> WORLD JEWISH CONGRESS
> GERHARD RIEGNER

. . . When Vice Consul Howard Elting met with Riegner in the American consulate, he found the World Jewish Congress representative in great agitation. Riegner brought up the prussic acid and Elting interjected that the report seemed fantastic to him. Riegner replied that it had struck him the same way, but that he had to consider the recent mass deportations from Paris, Holland, Berlin, Vienna, and Prague. The report was so serious and alarming that he felt it his duty to request that the Allied governments and Rabbi Wise be informed and the governments "try by every means to obtain confirmation or denial."

Who Will Believe?

For Riegner the pieces were already falling into place. They were not so convincing to the Allied governments. The Department of State decided that, pending corroboration of the information, the message should not be delivered to Rabbi Wise. . . .

By October Riegner and Lichtheim had pooled their information. They met with the American Minister in Switzerland, Leland Harrison, and handed him an aide-mémoire, dated October 22, in which they pointed out that the "prominent German industrialist" (Schulte) who had originally conveyed the message of an intended annihilation was now in possession of a new report indicating that at the end of July Hitler had signed an order to destroy the Jews of Europe. The informant, according to the memoire, had stated that he had seen this order himself. He even had details, such as the attribution of the annihilation plan to State Secretary Herbert Backe of the Food Ministry and opposition to it from Generalgouverneur Hans Frank in Poland.

No order of this nature, signed by Hitler, has been found in archives, and no reference to such a document has been spotted in the wartime German correspondence, but Hitler's veiled oral utterances had been quoted by his underlings on more than one occasion. . . .

Riegner and Lichtheim had already come to the conclusion that European Jewry was in the grip of annihilation. The indefatigable Riegner, a bachelor, spent many hours with the reports, interpreting them and thinking about their implications. The profoundly pessimistic Lichtheim had sent his own stream of warnings to the Jewish Agency. Lichtheim was not immediately informed about Schulte's message, but as early as August 27 he had convinced himself that Hitler had killed or was killing 4 million Jews in continental Europe, that not more than 2 million had a chance of surviving, and that every month even this chance was becoming smaller. In their joint memorandum of October 22, Lichtheim and Riegner pointed out that 4 million Jews were on the verge of complete destruction. They went on to make a distinction between Jews under direct German control and those in satellite countries. They urged that measures be taken to save the Jews still living in the "semi-independent" states of Hungary, Italy, Romania, Bulgaria, and Vichy France. They indicated that the Jewish population in these countries was 1,300,000.

Outside continental Europe, the Jewish leadership was slow in assessing the import of the messages it received. . . .

In Jerusalem there was no room for doubt anymore. At a meeting of November 22, 1942, the Jewish Agency devoted its entire attention to European Jewry. No other item was on the agenda, and the conferees decided to make the news public. On the next day, banner headlines appeared

in the Hebrew press, and the Jewish population was stunned and paralyzed. "The entire reaction," wrote the American Consul in Jerusalem, "is pathetic in its helplessness.". . .

Publicizing what had been learned was another agonizing process. When Rabbi Wise of the World Jewish Congress had received the Riegner telegram through London at the end of August, he agreed with the State Department to withhold the information until it could be substantiated. Together with the heads of other Jewish organizations, he had "succeeded" in keeping his promise. At the end of November he finally approached the press with State Department concurrence, but the news was buried in the inside pages. Wise and four colleagues did

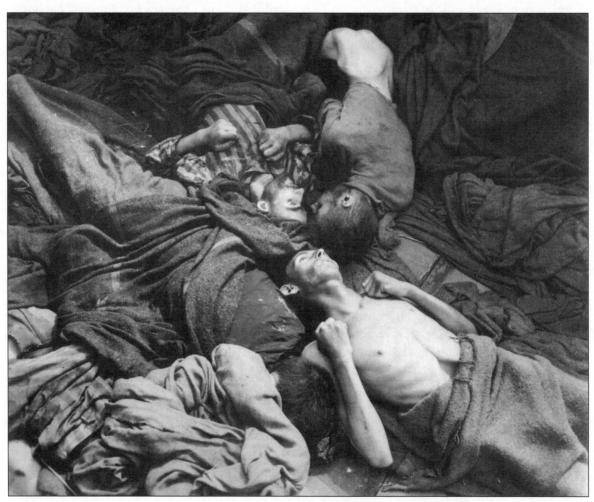

The shocking news of Hitler's campaign to annihilate Jews made headlines in Hebrew newspapers in 1942.

manage to see President Roosevelt. To this meeting, which took place on December 8, 1942, the Jewish delegation brought two memoranda, one with a summary of events, the other with recommendations. The compilers of the factual recapitulation. . . . said that almost 2 million Jews had died, an estimate that was half of the actual number at that time. They mentioned "mass murder, planned starvation, deportation, slave labor and epidemics in disease-ridden ghettos, penal colonies and slave reservations," but not gas. They named Mauthausen, Oswiecim (Auschwitz), and Chelmno (Kulmhof), but they did not identify Belzec, Sobibor, or Treblinka. They still referred to mass shootings in Kiev and other cities as "pogroms." In the recommendations there were only two requests: (1) warnings to be issued to Nazi Germany and its allies and (2) a commission to be created by the government to collect more information. There was no list of individuals to be warned, and there was no listing of questions about Jewry's fate to which answers might have been sought.

At the end of the half-hour meeting, the five Jewish leaders left without even a promise that the government would establish a fact-finding agency. Yet Wise was satisfied. . . . The five visitors "were all moved by the earnestness and vigor with which the President reacted to our pleas for his help." It was evident, Wise went on, that the President and the State Department "comprehend the magnitude of the crime against our brother Jews throughout the land occupied by Hitler, and that our Government is determined to avert by all possible means the continuance of the wrong which has been and is being done the Jewish people." Not all of the five delegates formed such an impression of the meeting. Adolph Held of the Jewish Labor Committee noted in a memorandum that the President had received them in a buoyant mood, listened to the recommendations, and told the delegation that he already had most of the facts, with confirmations from many sources. He assented to the warning proposal and asked whether the delegates had other recommendations. When the Jewish leaders could not think of anything, Roo-sevelt switched to other topics. In this way he used up 80 percent of the allotted half-hour. . . .

In January a description of the remnant ghetto of Warsaw was received: debilitated women in dilapidated houses. "One speaks with stubborn certainty about gassings." In Berlin, working parents returned home to discover that their children had been seized. Two thousand Berlin Jews were in hiding. Many committed suicide with veronal, but inasmuch as this product was expensive, some victims had used poisonous mushrooms. The Polish ambassador, Ciechanowski, wrote to [Arie] Tartakower [head of relief effort for World Jewish Congress] on March 24, 1943, enclosing a note from a "Jewish National Committee" in Poland addressed to Wise, Goldmann, and the American Jewish Joint Distribution Committee:

> The remnants of the Jewish communities in Poland exist in the conviction that during the most terrible days of our history you have not brought us help. Respond at least now in the last days of our life. This is our final appeal to you.

Shortly thereafter, when the Jews of Bulgaria were threatened with deportation, Wise and the American Jewish Committee's Proskauer, backed by the State Department, made an unsuccessful appeal to the British Foreign Secretary, Anthony Eden, in Washington to join with other Allied nations in a declaration calling upon Hitler to let the Jews leave occupied Europe. . . .

One more possibility arose in 1944. . . . Just when the deportations from Hungary began, the Germans themselves allowed an emissary of a Jewish rescue organization, Joel Brand, to carry a message to the Jewish Agency in Palestine for the ransoming of the remaining Jews. The price was ten thousand trucks. Brand met with Chaim Barlas, the Jewish Agency representative in Istanbul, before boarding a slow train across Turkey to British-occupied Syria, where he was held for many days. [Head of the political department of the Jewish Agency Moshe] Shertok saw him there. Hearing the figure "6 million" for the first time from Brand, he sat in disbelief.

Travel to London was not simple, even for Shertok. Eventually he arrived there and, accompanied by [Jewish Agency president Chaim] Weizmann, presented the proposal along with the bombing suggestion to the British Foreign Office. He had done his duty and the British refused the request. There was not to be even a simulated attempt to negotiate with the Nazis, and the Jews were not saved.

Selection 9

America and the Holocaust

David S. Wyman

The persecution of Jews began in the 1930s, and the killings began before the United States entered the war. It is possible the United States would never have gone to war if Japan had not attacked Pearl Harbor in 1941, and it is clear President Franklin D. Roosevelt was not prepared to go to war to save the Jews. Once in the war, victory became the paramount goal and the rescue of Jews was thought to be a by-product. During the years preceding that victory, however, millions were murdered. Could the United States have done anything to save them? If so, what measures could have been taken? David S. Wyman, a historian who taught at the University of Massachusetts from 1966 to 1991, wrote the seminal work documenting what the U.S. government did and did not do to rescue the Jews. This excerpt highlights some of the Roosevelt administration's failures and ways it could have saved more of Europe's Jews.

Excerpted from David S. Wyman, *The Abandonment of the Jews*. Copyright © 1994 David S. Wyman. Reprinted with permission from the author and The New Press.

*a*merica's response to the Holocaust was the result of action and inaction on the part of many people. In the forefront was Franklin D. Roosevelt, whose steps to aid Europe's Jews were very limited. If he had wanted to, he could have aroused substantial public backing for a vital rescue effort by speaking out on the issue. If nothing else, a few forceful statements by the President would have brought the extermination news out of obscurity and into the headlines. But he had little to say about the problem and gave no priority at all to rescue.

In December 1942, the President reluctantly agreed to talk with Jewish leaders about the recently confirmed news of extermination. Thereafter, he refused Jewish requests to discuss the problem. . . .

It appears that Roosevelt's overall response to the Holocaust was deeply affected by political expediency. Most Jews supported him unwaveringly, so an active rescue policy offered little political advantage. A pro-Jewish stance, however, could lose votes. American Jewry's great loyalty to the President thus weakened the leverage it might have exerted on him to save European Jews.

The main justification for Roosevelt's conduct in the face of the Holocaust is that he was absorbed in waging a global war. . . .

Years later, [Congressman] Emanuel Celler charged that Roosevelt, instead of providing even "some spark of courageous leadership," had been "silent, indifferent, and insensitive to the plight of the Jews." In the end, the era's most prominent symbol of humanitarianism turned away from one of history's most compelling moral challenges. . . .

Secretary [of State Cordell] Hull did issue public statements decrying Nazi persecution of Jews. Otherwise he showed minimal interest in the European Jewish tragedy and assigned no priority to it. Ignorant of his department's activities in that area, and even unacquainted with most of the policymakers, he abandoned refugee and rescue matters to his friend Breckinridge Long. Long and his co-workers specialized in obstruction. . . .

The State Department closed the United States as an asylum by tightening immigration procedures, and it influenced Latin American governments to do the same. When calls for a special rescue agency arose in Congress, Long countered them with deceptive secret testimony before a House committee. . . . It is clear that the State Department was not interested in rescuing Jews.

The War Department did next to nothing for rescue. Secretary [of War Henry] Stimson's personal opposition to immigration was no help. Far more important, however, was the War Department's secret decision that the military was to take no part in rescue—a policy that knowingly contradicted the executive order establishing the WRB [War Refugee Board]. . . .

The Office of War Information [OWI], for the most part, also turned away from the Holocaust. It evidently considered Jewish problems too controversial to include in its informational campaigns aimed at the American public. Its director, Elmer Davis, stopped at least two plans for the OWI to circulate the extermination news to the American people. . . .

Eleanor Roosevelt cared deeply about the tragedy of Europe's Jews and took some limited steps to help. But she never urged vigorous government action. She saw almost no prospects for

rescue and believed that winning the war as quickly as possible was the only answer.

Except for [Secretary of the Treasury Henry] Morgenthau, Jews who were close to the President did very little to encourage rescue action. David Niles, a presidential assistant, briefly intervened in support of free ports. The others attempted less. Bernard Baruch—influential with Roosevelt, Congress, the war time bureaucracy, and the public—stayed away from the rescue issue. So did Herbert Lehman, director of UNRRA [the United Nations Relief and Rehabilitation Administration]. Supreme Court Justice Felix Frankfurter had regular access to Roosevelt during the war, and he exercised a quiet but powerful influence in many sectors of the administration. Although he used his contacts to press numerous policies and plans, rescue was not among them.

As special counsel to the President, Samuel Rosenman had frequent contact with Roosevelt, who relied heavily on him for advice on Jewish matters. But Rosenman considered the rescue issue politically sensitive, so he consistently tried to insulate Roosevelt from it. For instance, when Morgenthau was getting ready to urge the President to form a rescue agency, Rosenman objected. He did not want FDR involved in refugee matters, although he admitted that no one else could deal effectively with the problem. Rosenman also argued that government aid to European Jews might increase anti-Semitism in the United States.

The President, his administration, and his advisers were not the only ones responsible for America's reaction to the Holocaust. Few in Congress, whether liberals or conservatives, showed much interest in saving European Jews. Beyond that, restrictionism, especially opposition to the entry of Jews, was strong on Capitol Hill.

Congressional attitudes influenced the administration's policies on rescue. One reason the State Department kept the quotas 90 percent unfilled was fear of antagonizing Congress. . . . The State Department was sufficiently worried about this that, when it agreed to the entry of 5,000 Jewish children from France, it forbade all publicity about the plan. . . .

Except for a weak and insignificant resolution condemning Nazi mass murder, Congress took no official action concerning the Holocaust. . . .

Of the seven Jews in Congress, only Emanuel Celler persistently urged government rescue action. Samuel Dickstein joined the struggle from time to time. Four others seldom raised the issue. Sol Bloom sided with the State Department throughout.

One reason for the government's limited action was the indifference of much of the non-Jewish public. It must be recognized, though, that many Christian Americans were deeply concerned about the murder of European Jewry and realized that it was a momentous tragedy for Christians as well as for Jews. In the words of an official of the Federal Council of Churches, "This is not a Jewish affair. It is a colossal, universal degradation in which all humanity shares." The message appeared in secular circles as well. [Newspaper publisher William Randolph] Hearst, for instance, stressed more than once in his newspapers, "This is not a Christian or a Jewish question. It is a human question and concerns men and women of all creeds."

Support for rescue arose in several non-Jewish quarters. And it came from leading public figures such as Wendell Willkie, Alfred E. Smith, Herbert Hoover, Fiorello La Guardia, Harold Ickes, Dean Alfange, and many more. But most non-Jewish Americans were either unaware of the European Jewish catastrophe or did not consider it important.

America's Christian churches were almost inert in the face of the Holocaust and nearly silent too. No major denomination spoke out on the issue. Few of the many Christian publications cried out for aid to the Jews. Few even reported the news of extermination, except infrequently and incidentally. . . .

The Press Buries Holocaust News

One reason ordinary Americans were not more responsive to the plight of the European Jews was that very many (probably a majority) were unaware of Hitler's extermination program until well into 1944 or later. The information was not readily available to the public, because the mass media treated the systematic murder of millions of Jews as though it were minor news.

Most newspapers printed very little about the Holocaust, even though extensive information on it reached their desks from the news services (AP [Associated Press], UP [United Press], and others) and from their own correspondents. In New York, the Jewish-owned *Post* reported extermination news and rescue matters fairly adequately. *PM*'s coverage was also more complete than that of most American papers. The *Times,* Jewish-owned but anxious not to be seen as Jewish-oriented, was the premier American newspaper of the era. It printed a substantial amount of information on Holocaust-related events but almost always buried it on inner pages. The *Herald Tribune* published a moderate amount of news concerning the Holocaust but seldom placed it where it would attract attention. Coverage in other New York City newspapers ranged from poor to almost nonexistent.

The Jewish-owned *Washington Post* printed a few editorials advocating rescue, but only infrequently carried news reports on the European Jewish situation. . . . The other Washington newspapers provided similarly limited information on the mass murder of European Jewry.

Outside New York and Washington, press coverage was even thinner. All major newspapers carried some Holocaust-related news, but it appeared infrequently and almost always in small items located on inside pages.

American mass-circulation magazines all but ignored the Holocaust. Aside from a few paragraphs touching on the subject, silence prevailed in the major news magazines, *Time, Newsweek,* and *Life.* The *Reader's Digest, American Mercury,* and *Collier's* released a small flurry of information in February 1943, not long after the extermination news was first revealed. From then until late in the war, little more appeared. . . .

American filmmakers avoided the subject of the Jewish catastrophe. During the war, Hollywood released numerous feature films on refugees and on Nazi atrocities. None dealt with the Holocaust. Despite extensive Jewish influence in the movie industry, the American Jewish Congress was unable to persuade anyone to produce even a short film on the mass killing of the Jews. . . .

In August 1944, a month after the Red Army captured the Majdanek killing center, near Lublin, Soviet authorities permitted American reporters to inspect the still-intact murder camp—gas chambers, crematoria, mounds of ashes, and the rest. One American voiced the reaction of all who viewed Majdanek: "I am now prepared to believe any story of German atrocities, no matter how savage, cruel and depraved."

The newsmen sent back detailed accounts, which were widely published in American newspapers and magazines, in many cases on the front pages. A few reports pointed out that Jews were the main victims, but most mentioned them only as part of a list of the different peoples murdered there. And none of the correspondents or their editors connected Majdanek with the extensive information available by then about the systematic extermination of European Jewry. . . .

In the last analysis, it is impossible to know how many Americans were aware of the Holocaust during the war years. Starting in late 1942, enough information appeared that careful followers of the daily news, as well as people especially alert to humanitarian issues or to Jewish problems, understood the situation. Probably millions more had at least a vague idea that terrible things were happening to the European Jews. Most likely, though, they were a minority of the American public. . . .

Throughout the war, most of the mass media, whether from disbelief or fear of accusations of sensationalism or for some other reason, played down the information about the Jewish tragedy. As a result, a large part of the American public remained unaware of the plight of European Jewry. Hesitation about giving full credence to reports of the systematic extermination of an entire people may be understandable. But those who edited the news surely realized, at the very least, that European Jews were being murdered in vast numbers. That was important news. But it was not brought clearly into public view.

Popular concern for Europe's Jews could not develop without widespread knowledge of what was happening to them. But the information gap, though extremely important, was not the only limiting factor. Strong currents of anti-Semitism and nativism in American society also diminished the possibilities for a sympathetic response. . . .

What Might Have Been Done

What could the American government have achieved if it had really committed itself to rescue? The possibilities were narrowed by the Nazis' determination to wipe out the Jews. War conditions themselves also made rescue difficult. And by mid-1942, when clear news of the systematic murder reached the West, two million Jews had already been massacred and the killing was going forward at a rapid rate. Most likely, it would not have been possible to rescue millions. But without impeding the war effort, additional tens of thousands—probably hundreds of thousands—could have been saved. What follows is a selection of twelve programs that could have been tried. All of them, and others, were proposed during the Holocaust.

(1) Most important, the War Refugee Board should have been established in 1942. And it should have received adequate government funding and much broader powers.

(2) The U.S. government, working through neutral governments or the Vatican, could have pressed Germany to release the Jews. If nothing else, this would have demonstrated to the Nazis—and to the world—that America was committed to saving the European Jews. It is worth recalling that until late summer 1944, when the Germans blocked the Horthy offer, it was far from clear to the Allies that Germany would not let the Jews out. On the contrary, until then the State Department and the British Foreign Office feared that Hitler might confront the Allies with an exodus of Jews, a possibility that they assiduously sought to avoid. . . .

(3) The United States could have applied constant pressure on Axis satellites to release their

Jews. By spring 1943, the State Department knew that some satellites, convinced that the war was lost, were seeking favorable peace terms. Stern threats of punishment for mistreating Jews or allowing their deportation, coupled with indications that permitting them to leave for safety would earn Allied goodwill, could have opened the way to the rescue of large numbers from Rumania, Bulgaria, Hungary, and perhaps Slovakia. Before the Germans took control of Italy, in September 1943, similar pressures might have persuaded the Italian government to allow its Jews to flee, as well as those in Italian-occupied areas of Greece, Yugoslavia, and France. . . .

(7) A campaign to stimulate and assist escapes would have led to a sizable outflow of Jews. Once the neutral nations had agreed to open their borders, that information could have been publicized throughout Europe by radio, airdropped leaflets, and underground communications channels. Local currencies could have been purchased in occupied countries, often with blocked foreign accounts. These funds could have financed escape systems, false documentation, and bribery of lower-level officials. Underground movements were willing to cooperate. . . . Even without help, and despite closed borders, tens of thousands of Jews attempted to escape to Switzerland, Spain, Palestine, and other places. Thousands succeeded. With assistance, and assurance of acceptance into neutral nations, those thousands could have been scores of thousands.

(8) Much larger sums of money should have been transferred to Europe. . . . Besides facilitating escapes, money would have helped in hiding Jews, supplying food and other essentials, strengthening Jewish undergrounds, and gaining the assistance of non-Jewish forces. . . .

The measures taken by Raoul Wallenberg in Budapest should have been implemented by all neutral diplomatic missions and repeated in city after city throughout Axis Europe. And they should have begun long before the summer of 1944.

The United States could also have pressed its two great allies to help. The Soviet Union turned away all requests for cooperation. . . . An American government that was serious about rescue might have extracted some assistance from the Russians. . . .

(11) Some military assistance was possible. The Air Force could have eliminated the Auschwitz killing installations. Some bombing of deportation railroads was feasible. The military could have aided in other ways without impeding the war effort. It was, in fact, legally required to do so by the executive order that established the WRB.

(12) Much more publicity about the extermination of the Jews should have been disseminated through Europe. . . . This might have influenced three groups: the Christian populations, the Nazis, and the Jews. Western leaders and, especially, the Pope [Pius XII] could have appealed to Christians not to cooperate in any way with the anti-Jewish programs, and to hide and to aid Jews whenever possible.

Roosevelt, [Prime Minister Winston] Churchill, and the Pope might have made clear to the Nazis their full awareness of the mass-murder program and their severe condemnation of it. If, in addition, Roosevelt and Churchill had threatened punishment for these crimes and offered asylum to the Jews, the Nazis at least would have ceased to believe that the West did not care what they were doing to the Jews. That might possibly have slowed the killing. And it might have hastened the decision of the SS, ultimately taken in late 1944, to end the extermination. . . .

The European Jews themselves should have been repeatedly warned of what was happening and told what the deportation trains really meant. (With good reason, the Nazis employed numerous precautions and ruses to keep this information from their victims.) Decades later, Rudolf Vrba, one of the escapees who exposed Auschwitz to the outside world, remained angry that the Jews had not been alerted. "Would anybody get me alive to Auschwitz if I had this information?" he demanded. "Would thousands and thousands of able-bodied Jewish men send their children, wives, mothers to Auschwitz from all over Europe, if they knew?" Roosevelt,

Churchill, other Western leaders, and major Jewish spokesmen should have warned Jews over and over against the steps that led to deportation and urged them to try to hide or flee or resist. To help implement these actions, the Allies could have smuggled in cadres of specially trained Jewish agents.

None of these proposals guaranteed results. But all deserved serious consideration, and those that offered any chance of success should have been tried. There was a moral imperative to attempt everything possible that would not hurt the war effort. If that had been done, even if few or no lives had been saved, the moral obligation would have been fulfilled. But the outcome would not have been anything like that barren. The War Refugee Board, a very tardy, inadequately supported, partial commitment, saved several tens of thousands. A timely American rescue effort that had the wholehearted support of the government would have achieved much more.

FDR's Excuses

A commitment of that caliber did not materialize. Instead, the Roosevelt administration turned aside most rescue proposals. In the process, government officials developed four main rationalizations for inaction. The most frequent excuse, the unavailability of shipping, was a fraud. When the Allies wanted to find ships for nonmilitary projects, they located them. In 1943, American naval vessels carried 1,400 non-Jewish Polish refugees from India to the American West Coast. The State and War departments arranged to move 2,000 Spanish Loyalist refugees to Mexico using military shipping. In March 1944, blaming the shipping shortage, the British backed out of an agreement to transport 630 Jewish refugees from Spain to the Fedala camp, near Casablanca. Yet at the same time, they were providing troopships to move non-Jewish refugees by the thousands from Yugoslavia to southern Italy and on to camps in Egypt.

When it was a matter of transporting Jews, ships could almost never be found. This was not because shipping was unavailable but because the Allies were unwilling to take the Jews in. . . .

Two refugees from Nazi Germany step ashore from the SS President Roosevelt in New York City on December 31, 1938.

Another stock excuse for inaction was the claim that Axis governments planted agents among the refugees. Although this possibility needed to be watched carefully, the problem was vastly overemphasized and could have been handled through reasonable security screening. It was significant that Army intelligence found not one suspicious person when it checked the 982 refugees who arrived at Fort Ontario. Nevertheless, potential subversion was continually used as a reason for keeping immigration to the United States very tightly restricted. Turkey, Latin American nations, Britain, and other countries used the same exaggerated argument. It played an important part in blocking the channels of rescue.

A third rationalization for failing to aid European Jews took the high ground of nondiscrimination. It asserted that helping Jews would improperly single out one group for assistance when many peoples were suffering under Nazi brutality. Equating the genocide of the Jews with the oppression imposed on other Europeans was, in the words of one of the world's foremost churchmen, Willem Visser 't Hooft, "a dangerous half-truth which could only serve to distract attention from the fact that no other race was faced with the situation of having every one of its members . . . threatened by death in the gas chambers."

The Roosevelt administration, the British government, and the Intergovernmental Committee on Refugees regularly refused to acknowledge that the Jews faced a special situation. One reason for this was to avoid responsibility for taking special steps to save them. Such steps, if successful, would have confronted the Allies with the difficult problem of finding places to put the rescued Jews.

Another reason was the fear that special action for the Jews would stir up anti-Semitism. Some asserted that such action would even invite charges that the war was being fought for the Jews. Congressman Emanuel Celler declared years later that Roosevelt did nearly nothing for rescue because he was afraid of the label "Jew Deal"; he feared the political effects of the accusation that he was pro-Jewish. . . .

The fourth well-worn excuse for rejecting rescue proposals was the claim that they would detract from the military effort and thus prolong the war. This argument, entirely valid with regard to projects that actually would have hurt the war effort, was used almost automatically to justify inaction. Virtually none of the rescue proposals involved enough infringement on the war effort to lengthen the conflict at all or to increase the number of casualties, military or civilian.

Actually, the war effort was bent from time to time to meet pressing humanitarian needs. In most of these instances, it was non-Jews who were helped. During 1942, 1943, and 1944, the Allies evacuated large numbers of non-Jewish Yugoslavs, Poles, and Greeks to safety in the Middle East, Africa, and elsewhere. Difficulties that con-

stantly ruled out the rescue of Jews dissolved. Transportation somehow materialized to move 100,000 people to dozens of refugee camps that sprang into existence. . . . Most of these refugees had been in desperate straits. None, though, were the objects of systematic annihilation. . . .

In all, Britain and the United States rescued 100,000 Yugoslav, Polish, and Greek refugees from disastrous conditions. Most of them traveled by military transport to camps where the Allies maintained them at considerable cost in funds, supplies, and even military staff. In contrast, the United States (with minimal cooperation from the British) evacuated fewer than 2,000 Jews to the three camps open to *them,* the ones at Fedala, Philippeville, and Oswego. . . .

It was not a lack of workable plans that stood in the way of saving many thousands more European Jews. Nor was it insufficient shipping, the threat of infiltration by subversive agents, or the possibility that rescue projects would hamper the war effort. The real obstacle was the absence of a strong desire to rescue Jews. A month before the Bermuda Conference, the Committee for a Jewish Army declared:

> We, on our part, refuse to resign ourselves to the idea that our brains are powerless to find any solution. . . . In order to visualize the possibility of such a solution, imagine that the British people and the American nation had millions of residents in Europe. . . . Let us imagine that Hitler would start a process of annihilation and would slaughter not two million Englishmen or Americans, not hundreds of thousands, but, let us say, only tens of thousands. . . . It is clear that the governments of Great Britain [and] the United States would certainly find ways and means to act instantly and to act effectively.

But the European Jews were not Americans and they were not English. It was their particular misfortune not only to be foreigners but also to be Jews.

Christian Responses to the Holocaust

Guenter Lewy and John M. Snoek

One of the enduring controversies associated with the Holocaust is the behavior of Pope Pius XII. What did he do to help the Jews and others? What could he have done? Jewish historians have judged the pope and many other Christian leaders harshly while Catholics, especially, have rushed to the pope's defense. As this article notes, the pope's silence may not have made things worse, but his failure to take a public stand against the Nazi atrocities meant that he did not do all that he could have to try to improve the situation for Jews and others persecuted by the Nazis. The article also shows that many clergymen did stand up to the Nazis. One of those, Martin Niemöller, left behind perhaps the most poignant statement ever written about the consequences of failing to help others:

> *In Germany they came first for the communists, and I didn't speak up because I wasn't a communist. Then they came for the Jews, and I didn't speak up because I wasn't a Jew. Then they came for the trade unionists, and I didn't speak up because I wasn't a trade unionist. Then they came for the Catholics,*

> *and I didn't speak up because I was a protestant. Then they came for me, and by that time no one was left to speak up.*

This article was written by Guenter Lewy, who was a professor of government at the University of Massachusetts, and Reverend John M. Snoek, secretary of the World Council of Churches' Committee on the Church and the Jewish People in Geneva.

The elevation of Cardinal [Eugenio] Pacelli to the papacy as Pius XII in the spring of 1939 brought to the throne of St. Peter a Germanophile who, in contrast to his predecessor, was unemotional, dispassionate, and a master of the language of diplomatic ambiguity. The Vatican received detailed information about the murder of Jews in the concentration camps from 1942 on, but Pius XII restricted all his public utterances to carefully phrased expressions of sympathy for the victims of injustice and to calls for a more humane conduct of hostilities. In his Christmas message of 1942, the pope spoke of his concern for the hundreds of thousands who, without personal guilt and merely on account of their nationality or descent, were doomed to death. Again, addressing the College of Cardinals in June 1943, the pontiff mentioned his twofold duty to be impartial and to point out moral errors. He had given special attention, he recalled, to the plight of those who were still being harassed because of their nationality or descent and who, without personal guilt, were subjected to measures that spelled destruction.

The pope's policy of neutrality encountered its crucial test when the Nazis began rounding up the 8,000 Jews of Rome in the autumn of 1943. Prior to the arrests, the Nazis told the Jewish community that unless it raised 50 kilograms of gold within 36 hours, 300 hostages would be taken. When it seemed that the Jews themselves could raise only part of this ransom, a representative of the community asked for and received an offer of a loan from the Vatican treasury. The pope approved of this offer of help, which, as it later transpired, did not have to be invoked.

During the German authorities' hunt for the Jews of Rome, Pius XII, contrary to German fears, remained silent. On Oct. 18, 1943, over 1,000 Roman Jews—more than two-thirds of them women and children—were transported to the death camp, Auschwitz. About 7,000 Roman Jews were able to elude their hunters by going into hiding. More than 4,000, with the knowledge and approval of the pope, found refuge in the numerous monasteries and houses of religious orders in Rome, and a few dozen were sheltered in the Vatican itself. The rest were hidden by their Italian neighbors, among whom the anti-Jewish policy of the Fascists had never been popular. Pius' failure to publicly protest against Nazi atrocities, especially against the murder of the Jews, drew criticism. In July 1942, Harold H. Tittmann, the assistant to [President Franklin D.] Roosevelt's personal representative at the Holy See, Myron C. Taylor, pointed out to the Vatican that its silence was endangering its moral prestige. In January 1943, Wladislaw Raczkiewicz, president of the Polish government-in-exile, appealed to the pope to issue an unequivocal denunciation of Nazi violence in order to strengthen the willingness of the Poles to resist the Germans and help the Jews. Bishop Preysing of Berlin, a man of courage and compassion urged the pope on at least two occasions to issue a public appeal on behalf of the Jews. A similar request with regard to the Hungarian Catholics was directed to Pope Pius in September 1944 by Isaac Herzog, the chief rabbi of Palestine.

Could the Pope Stop the Killing?

After the end of World War II, Pius XII was again criticized for his silence. It has been argued—among others, by the German playwright Rolf Hochhuth—that the pope could have saved numerous lives, if indeed he could not have halted the machinery of destruction altogether, had he chosen to take a public stand and confront the Germans with the threat of an interdict or with the excommunication of Hitler, Goebbels, and other leading Nazis belonging to the Catholic faith. As an example of the effectiveness of public protest, it is possible to cite the resolute reaction of the German episcopate to the euthanasia program. In Slovakia, Hungary, and Rumania, the forceful intervention of papal nuncios, who threatened the pro-Nazi governments with public condemnation by the pope, was also able, albeit temporarily, to halt the deportations. At the very least, it has been suggested, a public denunciation of the mass murders by Pius XII broadcast widely over the Vatican radio, would have revealed to Jews and Christians alike what deportation to the east actually meant. Many of the deportees might thus have been warned and given an impetus to escape, many more Christians might have helped and sheltered Jews, and many more lives might have been saved.

No way of proving or disproving these arguments exists, of course. Whether a papal decree of excommunication against Hitler would have dissuaded Hitler from carrying out his plan to destroy the Jews is doubtful, and revocation of the Concordat by the Holy See would have bothered Hitler still less. However, a flaming protest against the massacre of the Jews, coupled with an imposition of the interdict upon all of Germany, or the excommunication of all Catholics in any way involved with the apparatus of the "Final Solution" would have been a more formidable and effective weapon. This was precisely the kind of action that the pope would not take, however, without risking the allegiance of the German Catholics. Given the indifference of the German population to the fate of the Jews and the highly ambivalent attitude of the German Church toward Nazi anti-Semitism, a forceful stand by the pope on the Jewish question might well have led to a large-scale desertion from the Church. The pope had other, perhaps still stronger, reasons for remaining silent. In a world war that pitted Catholics against Catholics, the Holy See, as Mr. Tittmann was told by highly placed officials of the Curia, did not want to jeopardize its neutrality by condemning German atrocities, and the pope was unwilling to risk later charges of having been partial and contributing to a German defeat. Moreover, the Vatican did not wish to undermine Germany's struggle against Russia. Late in the summer of 1943, the papal secretary of state declared that the fate of Europe was dependent upon a German victory on the Eastern front. The Apostolic delegation in Washington warned the American Department of State in a note dated August 20, 1943, that Communism was making steady headway in Italy and Germany, and Europe was in grave peril of finding itself overrun by Communism immediately upon the cessation of hostilities. Father Robert Leiber, one of Pius XII's secretaries, later recalled (in *Stimmen der Zeit,* March 1961) that the pope had always looked upon Russian Bolshevism as more dangerous than German National Socialism. Hitler, therefore, had to be treated with some forbearance.

The reluctance of Pius XII to be drawn into a public protest against the "Final Solution" stands in contrast to the often energetic rescue activities of several of the papal nuncios in Slovakia, Hungary, Rumania, and Turkey. Monsignor Roncalli, the nuncio in Istanbul, who later became Pope John XXIII, in particular helped save many thousands of lives. The extent to which these men acted upon instructions from Rome is not clear, but the motives for the Vatican's solicitude seem to have been mixed. It appears that from late 1942 on, the Vatican was well aware that an ultimate Allied victory was inevitable. Considerations of expediency began

to reinforce whatever moral revulsion the pope may have felt at the massacre of the Jews, and Pius began to drop hints to the bishops of Germany and Hungary that it was in the interest of their people, as well as that of the Church, to go on record against the slaughter of the Jews. For example, he wrote an Austrian churchman on Oct. 15, 1942, that to intercede for those suffering in the conquered territories was not only a Christian duty but ultimately could only be of advantage to the cause of Germany.

A History of Hostility

The Nazis' assault on European Jewry occurred in a climate of opinion conditioned by centuries of Christian hostility to Jewish religion and people. At the same time, other factors, such as varying patterns of nationalism, had an important bearing on the attitude of the Catholic churches of different European countries toward the Jewish tragedy. Thus it is important to differentiate between the situation in Germany and in the various Nazi-occupied countries of Europe. During the 19th century some elements of German Catholicism contributed toward the emergence of modern anti-Semitism, and in the 1920s many Catholic publicists agreed with the Nazis on the importance of fighting Jewish liberalism and the Jews' alleged destructive influence in German public life. This trend received great impetus after Hitler's accession to power in 1933. Seeking to counter the Nazis' offensive against the Catholic Church, as a rival for the loyalty of the German people, churchmen attempted to gain favor with the Nazi regime and its followers by adopting certain aspects of Nazi ideology. They stressed the elemental values of race and racial purity, and limited their dissent to insisting that this National Socialist goal be achieved without resort to immoral means. The sacred books of the Old Testament, it was argued, were not only beyond the Jewish mentality but in direct conflict with it. Jesus, it was conceded, had been a non-Aryan, but the son of God was fundamentally different from the Jews of his time, who hated and eventually murdered him. They also said that the Jews had had a demoralizing effect on Germany's national character; the press, literature, science, and the arts had to be purged of the "Jewish mentality."

In the face of the Nazis' anti-Semitic legislation the Church retreated, even when the ordinances touched on vital domains of ecclesiastical jurisdiction, such as matrimony. The diocesan chancelleries helped the Nazi state to detect people of Jewish descent by supplying data from Church records on the religious background of their parishioners. The bishops facilitated the emigration of non-Aryan Catholics, but little, if any, solicitude was shown for non-Aryans who were not of the Catholic faith. Similarly, when mass deportations of German Jews began in October 1941, the episcopate limited its intervention with the government to pleading for Christian non-Aryans. When the bishops received reports about the mass murder of Jews in the death camps from Catholic officers and civil servants, their public reaction remained limited to vague pronouncements that did not mention the word Jews. An exception was the Berlin prelate Bernhard Lichtenberg, who prayed publicly for the Jews. The joint pastoral letter of the German episcopate of August 1943, for example, spoke of the right to life and liberty, which should not be denied even to "men of foreign races and descent" but such statements could be interpreted as referring to the Slavs. Almost half the population of the greater German Reich (43.1% in 1939) was Catholic and even among the S.S., despite Nazi pressure to leave the Church, almost a quarter belonged to the Catholic faith. While in the past the episcopate had issued orders to deny the sacraments to Catholics who engaged in dueling or agreed to have their bodies cremated, the word that would have forbidden the faithful, on pain of excommunication, to go on participating in the massacre of Jews was never spoken. The bishops had demonstrated their willingness to risk a serious clash with the Nazi regime by protesting the extermination of the insane and retarded in the "euthanasia" program. This intervention had been successful in large measure because it had had the backing of public opinion. In the case of the Jews, however, it was far from clear whether the episcopate could count on the support of the faithful, and this was probably one of the main reasons why a clear public protest against the "Final Solution" was never issued. Only a handful of Jews were hidden by the clergy or helped by individual Catholics in Germany. In Poland, where no official policy on the part of the Catholic Church has been discerned, it would seem that, as in Germany, the initiative to help Jews was taken only by individuals. This situation stands in marked contrast to that prevailing in Nazi-occupied Europe. In Western Europe declarations of solidarity and help for the Jews were almost universally regarded as signs of patriotism and resistance to the Germans. Here some of the highest Church dignitaries condemned the persecution of the Jews. In Holland, where the Church as early as 1934 had prohibited the participation of Catholics in the Dutch Nazi movement, the bishops in 1942 immediately and publicly protested the first deportations of Dutch Jews, and in May 1943, they forbade the collaboration of Catholic policemen in the hunting down of Jews, even at the cost of losing their jobs. In Belgium members of the episcopate actively supported the rescue efforts of their clergy, who hid many hundreds of Jewish children. Several French bishops used their pulpits to denounce the deportations and to condemn the barbarous treatment of the Jews. Throughout Western Europe numerous priests and members of the monastic clergy organized the rescue of Jews, and hid them in monasteries, parish houses, and private homes. French priests issued thousands of false certificates of baptism. Many lay Catholics in France, Holland, Belgium, and Italy acted similarly, thus saving thousands of Jewish lives. The concern of the population of these countries for Jewish fellow-countrymen was undoubtedly a key factor behind the bold protests of the French, Dutch, and Belgian bishops. . . .

Protestant and Greek Orthodox Churches

Protestant churches and their leaders in Britain, the United States, France, Switzerland, and Sweden protested against the first anti-Semitic measures in Germany, the promulgation of the Nuremberg Laws, and *Kristallnacht of* 1938. In Germany, Hitler's supporters within the Protestant Church complied with anti-Jewish legislation, applying it even within the Church by going so far as to exclude Christians of Jewish origin from membership. Although the "Confessing Church" (Niemoeller's dissident *Bekenntniskirche)* defended the rights of Christians of Jewish origin within the Church, it generally neither publicly opposed discrimination against them outside the Church, nor condemned the persecution of Jews. An exception to this rule was the memorandum sent by the "Confessing Church" to Hitler (May 1936), which stated that "when, in the framework of the National-Socialist ideology, anti-Semitism is forced on the Christian, obliging him to hate the Jews, he has nonetheless the divine commandment to love his neighbor." A number of ministers of the "Confessing Church" were sent to concentration camps because they did not cooperate with anti-Jewish directives. During the war, the Protestants in Germany maintained their silence, the notable exception being Bishop Wurm of Wuerttemberg, who intervened on behalf of the so-called "privileged non-Aryans," in 1943.

In the occupied countries, however, the situation was different. The Lutheran churches in Norway and Denmark issued a public protest when the deportations from their countries began. The Protestant churches in the Netherlands, together with the Roman Catholic Church, sent several protests, some of which were read from the pulpits. In France, the president of the Protestant Federation, the Rev. Marc Boegner, sent letters to the French chief rabbi, to [defense and foreign minister] Admiral [Jean] Darlan, Marshal [Philippe] Pétain, [head of the Vichy regime] Pierre Laval, and others. A message was read from the pulpits twice. . . .

Individual Christians rendered practical help, though the importance of this fact should not be overrated: only a small minority of the Protestant and Orthodox Christians in occupied Europe risked their lives on behalf of the persecuted Jews. It is difficult to assess the practical results of interventions and protests by churches and church leaders. In satellite countries, where they could turn to their own governments, the interventions of church leaders were of some avail. In the occupied countries, the protests hardly influenced the German authorities; but, in so far as they were read out from the pulpits, the protests contributed to breaking the silence and complacency that surrounded the extermination of the Jews and stirred the faithful to noncooperation with the Germans and to render individual aid to the Jews.

Selection 11

Pope Pius XII: Saint or Sinner?

John Cornwell

Eugenio Pacelli (1876–1958), better known as Pope Pius XII (elected 1939), is currently being considered for canonization, or sainthood, by the Catholic Church. One point being raised against the pope is his record during World War II. John Cornwell's book, provocatively titled Hitler's Pope, *accuses the pope of failing to speak out or take actions that might have ameliorated the plight of European Jewry. The Jewish community and the Catholic Church have a long-standing dispute over the pope's wartime record, which Jews hold was, at best, one of benign neglect, and Catholics maintain was morally exemplary. Now Cornwell has exacerbated tensions by supporting the Jewish view of the pope's failures and attributing them for the first time to anti-Semitism. Had this book been written by a Jewish scholar, it probably would have received only a fraction of the attention it has. Cornwell, however, is not Jewish. He is an award-winning journalist, author, and senior research fellow at Jesus College in Cambridge who set out to write a book sympathetic to the pope but was shocked by what he discovered in secret Vatican archives. This ex-*cerpt gives an overview of what has been written on the subject and Cornwell's conclusion.*

The earliest and most notorious attack on Pacelli's wartime conduct occurred in 1963 with the staging of Rolf Hochhuth's play *The Representative* in Berlin. It also appeared that year in London, and the following year in New York as *The Deputy,* and was subsequently translated into more than twenty languages. Written in blank verse, . . . it forms to this day the basis of a popular perception of Pacelli, even among people who have never seen or read the play.

The attitude of the Holy See is established in the first scene when a historical character, Kurt Gerstein, who has been an eyewitness to the gas chambers, reports what he has seen to the nuncio in Berlin, Archbishop Orsenigo. Orsenigo, however, declines to acknowledge anything he has heard, and refuses to pass on the information to the Pope. Eventually an emissary of Gerstein reaches the Vatican and is granted an audience. But Pacelli, who first appears in the fourth act, proves indifferent. Hochhuth's papal portrait is of a heartless, avaricious cynic, angry with the West and friendly toward Germany, preoccupied with his investments, which are suffering as a result of Allied bombing raids on Italian factories. Hochhuth's Pacelli speculates about the advantage of selling off some of his investments to influential Americans in the hope that this might deter further bombing of Rome. Informed about the death camps in Poland, he turns a deaf ear. The point is dramatically reinforced by the coincidence that the Jews of Rome are being rounded up even as Gerstein's messenger makes his plea for help.

The Deputy is historical fiction based on scant documentation. . . . . The characterization of Pacelli as a money-grubbing hypocrite is so wide of the mark as to be ludicrous. Importantly, however, Hochhuth's play offends the most basic criteria of documentary: that such stories and portrayals are valid only if they are demonstrably true. *The Deputy* was nevertheless given significant credence; and the eradication of such a powerful, simple view of the man was going to prove difficult if not impossible.

Hochhuth's play, however, had another far-reaching outcome for historians. The war of words, condemnations, and counter-condemnations that followed Hochhuth's production gave impetus to the pursuit of authentic documentation. . . . [Saul] Friedländer, born in 1932, was a historian of the Nazi period; his parents had died in Auschwitz, and he himself had survived the war hidden in a Catholic monastery in France. . . .

Friedländer's *Pius XII and the Third Reich* was published in Paris in 1964. . . . It is a rigorous attempt to let the available documents speak for themselves. Based mainly but not exclusively on reports passing through the German ambassadors at the Holy See during the war, it had a profound effect on the Vatican, for it revealed, as Friedländer cautiously states in the book's conclusion, that "the Sovereign Pontiff seems to have had a predilection for Germany which does not appear to have been diminished by the nature of the Nazi regime and which was disavowed up to 1944.". . .

Missing Secrets?

In 1964 Paul VI had directed a group of Jesuit scholars to edit the Vatican's wartime documents for speedy publication. The work appeared in eleven volumes published between 1965 and 1981. Collected under the overall title of *Actes et Documents du Saint Siège relatifs à la Seconde Guerre Mondiale,* the documents were published in their original languages with accompanying apparatus in French; only one volume, the first, appeared in English. The scope of evidence thus made available was impressive and scholarly— but was it complete? Amid the battle of words over what Pius XII knew and when, was it not possible that incriminating documents were withheld by the Vatican? . . .

Gerhard Riegner, . . . who coordinated information in Switzerland from all over Europe during the war, calls attention to the absence in the Holy See's documents of a crucial memorandum he had given to the papal nuncio in Berne, Monsignor Filippe Bernadini, for transmission to the Vatican on March 18, 1942. "Our memorandum," writes Riegner, "revealed the catastrophic situation of the Jews in a number of Catholic countries, or countries with large Catholic populations, such as France, Romania, Poland, Slovakia, Croatia. . . . The situations were exposed in detail country by country. We were able to show the measures taken by the Nazis to destroy the entire Jewish people."

The Vatican-published documents—*Actes et Documents*—show that the memorandum from Riegner and his colleague, Richard Lichtheim, had been received in the Secretariat of State, and that the document has survived and is in their keeping, for there is a bland description of its contents *"des mesures antisemites"* in a footnote in Volume 8. And yet the actual text of the document is omitted.

Riegner adds that the omission is all the more regrettable since he and his colleagues had stressed that "in some of these countries the political leaders were Catholics susceptible to a Vatican initiative." But he alleges that only in the case of Slovakia, where the Catholic priest Josef Tiso was president, did the Vatican intervene and bring about a "moderation of these anti-Semitic policies.". . .

The issue next received compelling treatment by journalist and former priest Carlo Falconi in *The Silence of Pius XII. . . .* Falconi's overall conclusions on Pacelli and the Final Solution, however, are cautious: he was not prepared to go beyond the story the documents told—"the Vatican was very well informed and . . . the Pope was continually being urged to speak out. . . . They certainly do not favor a justification of Pius XII's caution and silence.". . .

An Israeli Sees Pius as a Hero

Falconi's book was followed by an enthusiastic exoneration of Pacelli in Pinchas E. Lapide's *The Last Three Popes and the Jews* (London, 1967). Lapide . . . was Israeli consul in Milan in the early 1960s. Lapide had ransacked the Yad Vashem Archive, the Zionist Central Archives, and the Jewish Historical General Archives in Jerusalem for details of Vatican assistance to Jews during the war. Armed with tributes from many Jewish quarters, he claimed that the Holy See had done more to help the Jews than any other Western organization, including the Red Cross. He calculated that Pius XII, directly and indirectly, saved the lives of some 860,000 Jews. He was eager in particular to acknowledge Pope John XXIII's efforts to apologize for the long tradition of Catholic anti-Judaism, and gave prominence to John's prayer for forgiveness by printing it on the book's title page: "Forgive us for the curse we falsely attached to their name as Jews. Forgive us for crucifying Thee a second time in their flesh. For we knew not what we did.". . .

Lapide's book was a formidable and scholarly riposte to those who would paint Pius XII and the Holy See as villains, but it carried the taint of diplomatic self-interest. Yet, reading between the lines, Lapide does not seem entirely convinced of his own case. Perhaps its saddest reflection was the passing disclaimer that Pius XII was merely less lacking in courage than others, that he was merely less infected by the "sickness that lay in the soul of the free world."

Three years after Lapide's book, the writer Robert Katz undertook a reconstruction of [events] in his book *Black Sabbath.* (Earlier, Katz had published *Death in Rome,* about the murder of 335 Romans, including seventy Jews, in the Ardeatine Caves on March 24, 1944. Katz suggested Pacelli knew of the Nazi reprisal and failed to sympathize with its victims.) The more Katz studied Pacelli's reaction to Nazi atrocities in Rome during the German occupation, the more he was convinced that the papacy had a case to answer. . . . Katz's subtle exposition of Pacelli's reticence concludes that he had colluded with the Nazi system, which rewarded his silence with a semblance of honoring the extraterritorial status of the Vatican and key institutions around Rome. Katz argues that in order to protect the institutional Church, Pius was prepared to expend the lives of a handful of Jews. Katz was sued in Italy, where it is possible to bring libel actions on behalf of the dead, by Pacelli's sister and nephew after a film of his *Death in Rome* was made by Carlo Ponti. The Pacellis lost, but appealed, and the case was eventually judged inconclusive.

What Did Pacelli Know?

The next set of allegations against Pacelli's wartime conduct was published in 1980, in Walter Laqueur's *The Terrible Secret* (London, 1980), focusing on what was known about the Final Solution and when. . . . Laqueur was convinced that the Vatican "was better informed than anyone else in Europe" by reason of its "superior organization and more extensive international connections." Laqueur alleged that the Vatican systematically lied about its early ignorance of the Final Solution, a policy that is not far-sighted, he writes, "for sooner or later at least some of the facts will become known." A calculated guess, albeit from a distinguished scholar and historian, Laqueur was banking on the emergence of damning evidence from Italian and German espionage archives that had stored intercepted Vatican information, incoming and outgoing. Eighteen years on, no such evidence is forthcoming, although the Riegner memorandum is proof sufficient that the Vatican held back important documents. Laqueur's judgment on Pacelli was similarly guesswork. Why did Pacelli not speak out? "Probably," wrote Laqueur, "it was a case of pusillanimity rather than anti-Semitism. If the Vatican did not dare to

Pope Pius XII

come to the help of hundreds of Polish priests who also died in Auschwitz, it was unrealistic to expect that it would show more courage and initiative on behalf of the Jews.". . .

The first and, up to this time of writing, the only serious and extended portrait of the wartime Pacelli by a nonpartisan scholar is that attempted by the British Church historian Owen Chadwick in his book *Britain and the Vatican during the Second World War* (Cambridge, 1986). . . .

Pacelli, for Chadwick, was a timid, sensitive, holy man trapped in an imponderable dilemma. Should he speak out and make things worse for both Jews and Christians? Chadwick's verdict is underpinned by an unquestioning conviction that Pacelli was incapable of guile, narcissism, ambition, interest in power, or cowardice. If Pacelli erred, and Chadwick is not at all sure that he did, then it must have been with the best of intentions. . . .

Sainthood Considered

While these "secular" studies of Pacelli were appearing over a span of more than twenty years, an investigation of a rather different kind was in progress in Rome at the headquarters of the Jesuits in Borgo Santo Spirito, and continues at the time of this writing. This is the research and writing of a *positio,* a special "sacred" biography, in support of the beatification and, ultimately, the canonization of Pacelli. Beatification and canonization are infallible declarations by the Pope that a dead individual has led a life of heroic virtue and resides in Heaven. Beatification indicates that the Pope has sanctioned a local cult of the individual's "sainthood," and that this person may be prayed to; canonization indicates the celebration of a worldwide cult. The *positio,* which can run to many thousands of pages, is a story of an individual's holiness; it must be accurate and must reflect the views of many people who knew the "servant of God.". . .

Having come to the end of my own journey through the life and times of Pacelli, I am convinced that the cumulative verdict of history shows him to be not a saintly exemplar for future generations, but a deeply flawed human being from whom Catholics, and our relations with other religions, can best profit by expressing our sincere regret.

The Roosevelt Administration and the Politics of Rescue

Henry Feingold

Franklin Roosevelt is revered as one of America's greatest presidents. Jews are among his most vigorous fans, and yet it was during FDR's watch that the Holocaust occurred. What did he do? What could he have done to prevent the slaughter of millions? By leading the Allies to victory, Roosevelt may have saved the world and millions more, but the evidence that more could have been done to save European Jewry is overwhelming. This excerpt discusses some of the measures the Roosevelt administration took and offers explanations for why the president did not take others. Henry Feingold, at the time a historian at the City University of New York, was one of the first to write about FDR's role in the Holocaust.

*O*n those occasions during the Holocaust years when mass rescue appeared possible, it required of the nations a passionate commitment to save lives. Such a commit-

ment did not exist in the Roosevelt Administration, although there were many individuals who wanted to do more.

Between 1938 and 1941 refugee-rescue advocates, most of whom were supporters of the New Deal, undoubtedly believed that the humanitarian concern which characterized Roosevelt's handling of domestic problems could be projected to the refugee crisis. That assumption was buttressed by the statements of concern which accompanied each White House announcement that visa procedures had been liberalized. Those who might have questioned the authenticity of the Administration's concern would have been hard pressed to explain other steps taken by Roosevelt in this early period. The President had, after all, taken the initiative in calling an international refugee conference to meet at Evian. The establishment of the IGC which resulted from that conference was primarily an Administration-supported endeavor as were the Rublee-Schacht negotiations, which were designed to bring order into the refugee chaos. Moreover, a special procedure to rescue the cultural and scientific elite of Europe had been established and the Administration was busily occupied in searching for areas where the refugees might find new homes. What more could be asked?

Promise and Reality

What refugee-rescue advocates could foresee only with some difficulty at the time was that all these steps would remain largely gestures which the Roosevelt Administration would not and sometimes could not follow up. There developed a gulf between the professed good intentions of the Administration and the implementation of policy. The hope of bringing refugees to the United States was severely circumscribed by the seemingly immutable immigration law. The invitation to the nations to meet at Evian was so qualified that from the outset there seemed little hope of solving the problem of where to put the growing number of refugees. Once at the Conference the American delegation was in the embarrassing position of lacking the bargaining power to convince others to undertake a serious effort to provide for refugees or the will to do so itself. The Intergovernmental Committee for Political Refugees which grew out of the Conference became a monument to the Administration's impotence on the rescue front. The IGC remained throughout those years to clutter and confuse the effort. The attempt by Breckinridge Long to resurrect this ineffective agency after the Bermuda Conference was little more than an effort to thwart more energetic rescue activity. . . .

A proposal to make Alaska and the Virgin Islands available to a limited number of refugees was ultimately rejected. When the political risk of circumventing the immigration laws was finally taken in July 1944 by the establishment of a temporary haven in Oswego, New York, it was too late to make a difference.

The struggle over the administration of the visa procedure and the special visa lists throws some light on the conflicting tendencies within the Administration. The visa system became literally an adjunct to Berlin's murderous plan for the Jews. The quotas were underissued until 1939 and after June 1940 a skillful playing on the security fear resulted in ever more drastic reduction of refugee immigrants. In the critical year of 1941 only 47 percent of the German-Austrian quota was filled. A similar pattern is discernible in the procedure by which prominent refugees could receive special visitors' visas. Here again, the good intentions of the Administration were thwarted by the State Department and the consuls.

The calling of the Bermuda Conference in mid-1943 marks the fullest development of what might be called a politics of gestures. Held in inaccessible Bermuda, officials in London, where the initiative to hold such a conference developed, and Washington saw in the idea of holding another refugee conference the possibility of muting the growing agitation for a more active effort. The State Department confined the delegates to dealing with a group it called "political refugees," a euphemism for Jews, who bore the brunt of the Nazi liquidation program. The Conference was thereby confined to discussing ways and means of "rescuing" a handful of refugees who had found a precarious safety in Spain and other neutral havens and who were, in fact, already rescued, while those who faced death in the camps were ignored. . . .

The coterie of middle echelon career officers headed by Breckinridge Long and located primarily in the Special Problems Division of the State Department consistently opposed the professed humanitarian intentions of the Administration. The mobilization of a countervailing influence within the Administration which might have come from the Department of Interior, the Justice Department, and the Treasury Department, as well as numerous Jewish officials, did not materialize until the final months of 1943 when Henry Morgenthau, Jr., took up the cause. Before that time, Breckinridge Long, by his own account, usually had his way. He was able to capitalize on the weakness of White House leadership, so that the making and the administration of what amounted to the rescue program fell naturally in the purview of the State Department. An effective coalition of restrictionists and conservative legislators and Long's control of the flow of information to the White House abetted anti-rescue activities. After 1940, Breckinridge Long, by use of what I have called the security gambit, a playing on the fear that spies had infiltrated the refugee stream, was able to curtail the humanitarian activity of the Roosevelt Administration. . . .

Much of the inconsistency between the rhetoric of the Administration and the actual implementation of policy can be traced to the chief executive's uncertain mandate. Bound by a restrictive immigration law and perhaps an oversensitivity to the "Jew Deal" label which had been applied to his Administration on the one hand, and yet anxious to help the Nazi victims on the other, Roosevelt sought a balance between the opponents and advocates of a more active rescue policy. Such a middle road was never found, and to this day it is difficult for researchers to determine Roosevelt's personal role. . . .

The Role of American Jewry

On the surface, few groups appeared better equipped to exert pressure on the Roosevelt Administration than American Jewry. Yet between 1938 and 1943 Jews were not notably successful in influencing the establishment on rescue ground rules and that failure proved catastrophic. . . .

The role that fell to American Jewry was difficult, perhaps impossible, to fill. It was called upon not only to attempt to change restrictive immigration policies which a majority of American Jews had supported in 1938, but also to challenge the State Department's administrative fiat further limiting the number which might come to these shores. They had to counteract a hysterical fear of Nazi espionage which was abetted by Congress, the State Department, the White House, and the communications media. . . . The rescue case concerned the disposition and treatment of a foreign minority, took place largely during the war years and, most important, required Roosevelt to tangle with powerful restrictionists in Congress and his own Administration. The kind of influence required was not available to Jewish leaders. . . .

Much of their formidable organizational resources were dissipated in internal bickering until it seemed as if Jews were more anxious to tear each other apart than to rescue their coreli-gionists. One has only to read Long's description of the numerous Jewish delegations, each representing a different group, to realize how tragic the situation of American Jewry was. That a community which desperately needed to speak to Roosevelt with one voice remained in an organizational deadlock is no small tragedy, and when one realizes how appallingly irrelevant the issues and personalities dividing them were, one can only shake one's head in disbelief. The Jews had achieved higher positions in the New Deal than in any prior Administration, but even with such resources they could not fully mobilize. . . .

Perspective on the Roosevelt Administration

The rescue of European Jewry, especially after the failure to act during the refugee phase (1939 to October 1941), was so severely circumscribed by Nazi determination that it would have required an inordinate passion to save lives and a huge reservoir of good will toward Jews to achieve it. Such passion to save Jewish lives did not exist in the potential receiving nations. In the case of the United States, one can readily see today that a projection of human concern inwards to its own domestic problems such as alleviating the misery of its own Negro minority had barely been begun by the New Deal. What hope of better treatment could be held for a foreign minority? But this was not the only reason that the energy and organization of the Administration's rescue effort, even at its apogee in January 1944, never remotely approached the effort Berlin was willing to make to see the Final Solution through to its bitter end.

There were factors on the domestic political scene that further circumscribed action on the Administration's part. We have noted the continued strength of the restrictionists who remained alert during the refugee phase to the slightest infringement of the quota system. The anti-Jewish thrust of the anti-refugee sentiment did not escape the notice of Jewish leadership, who had become sensitized to the mood in the nation in the thirties. . . .

In October 1939 Roosevelt told Ickes about his hope to admit ten thousand refugees to Alaska on the same nationality ratio by which the quota system admitted immigrants to the mainland. That would limit entrance to one thousand Jews, a figure which Roosevelt hoped "would avoid the undoubted criticism" which would surely result "if there were an undue proportion of Jews.". . .

In those rare cases where governments are able to make human responses to catastrophes they do so at the behest of an aroused public opinion. . . . In the case of the Jews the Roosevelt Administration had no popular mandate for a more active rescue role. Public opinion was, in fact, opposed to the admission of refugees, because most Americans were not aware of what was happening. A Roper poll taken in December 1944 showed that the great majority of Americans, while willing to believe that Hitler had killed some Jews, could not believe that the Nazis, utilizing modern production techniques, had put millions to death. The very idea beggared the imagination. Perhaps there is such a thing as a saturation point as far as atrocity stories are concerned. In the American mind the Final Solution took its place beside the Bataan Death March and the Malmedy massacre as just another atrocity in a particularly cruel war. Not only were the victims unable to believe the unbelievable, but those who would save them found it extremely difficult to break through the "curtain of silence." The State Department's suppression of the details compounded the problem of credibility.

The Administration's reluctance to publicly acknowledge that a mass murder operation was taking place went far in keeping American public opinion ignorant and therefore unaroused while it helped convince men like Goebbels that the Allies approved or were at least indifferent to the fate of the Jews. Psychological warfare techniques such as threats of retribution and bombing did have some effect in Hungary. A statement by Washington that the massive raid on Hamburg in July 1943 was made in retribution for a Treblinka or better yet a bombing of the rail lines and crematoria would have gone far to pierce the "curtain of silence," not only in the United States but among the people of occupied Europe. Specific mention of the crime against Jews was omitted from war-crimes statements and not until March 1944 could Roosevelt be prevailed upon to make some correction in the Moscow War Crimes Declaration. That statement promised vengeance for crimes against Cretan peasants but neglected to mention the Final Solution. From that point of view the failure of John J. McCloy, then Assistant Secretary of War, to favorably consider a joint request by the World Jewish Congress and the WRB to bomb the crematoria because it would be of "doubtful efficacy" was especially tragic. It might have gone far to alert world opinion to the mass murder operation as well as disrupting the delicate strands which made it possible. Washington maintained its silence for fear, in McCloy's words, that it might "provoke even more vindictive action by the Germans." Berlin, it was felt, was fully capable of escalating the terror. But for European Jewry, at least, it is difficult to imagine a terror greater than that of Auschwitz. . . .

The Holocaust was part of the larger insanity of World War II. . . . There was a certain annoyance at the priority demanded by the Jews when the entire civilized world hovered on the brink of totalitarian domination. It was difficult for France to muster enthusiasm for a mass resettlement for refugees, which was suggested by Roosevelt at the meeting of the officers of the IGC in Washington in October 1939, when the existence of the French nation itself hung in the balance. Nor was Britain, while fighting for its life, anxious to accept more refugees. The priorities were for national survival and victory, and the rescue of Jews would be considered only if it could be accommodated to these priorities. . . .

By June 1941 a nonbelligerent United States had more rigid screening procedures for refugees than Britain, which had been at war for almost two years. The security psychosis which was generously abetted by the State Department was the Administration's version of the national survival argument and had much the same effect on rescue activity. Once the war began the mania about spies having been infiltrated among the largely Jewish refugees could be muted in favor of the argument that the fastest road to rescue was to defeat Hitler. Nothing must be done to divert energy and resources from that goal. As it turned out, almost anything that could be done for rescue would cause such a diversion. Ships to transport refugees, which came back empty, could not be diverted because they were in short supply. Relief supplies could not be sent to camps because, according to Breckinridge Long, it would relieve the Reich from responsibility of feeding people under its control. Camps could not be bombed because aircraft could not be diverted to tasks of "doubtful efficacy." If one argued, as many rescue advocates did, that by the time victory came all Jews in Europe would be dead, one revealed a greater concern for Jewish survival than for the survival of the United States. Breckinridge Long's diary is full of charges that the rescue advocates, in pressing for a more humanitarian visa procedure or relief shipments to the camps, were really acting as Berlin's agents and subverting the nation's war effort. Counteracting such arguments proved to be a nigh impossible task. . . .

Appalling as it may sound, the saving of lives was a far more formidable task than the practice of genocide. Even a passionate will to save lives could prove insufficient, given Nazi determination to liquidate the Jews of Europe. Something more was required, something to soften the hearts of those in Berlin who were in physical control of the slaughter. Such a miracle was never in the power of the Washington policy makers. It belongs to a higher kingdom whose strange indifference has become an overriding concern of the theologians.

Selection 13

Roosevelt Saved the World

Robert Edwin Herzstein

Roosevelt and Hitler, *excerpted here, is critical of President Roosevelt and his administration for failing to do enough to save the victims of the Holocaust. Still, even among Jews, Roosevelt is held in high esteem and is regarded as one of the greatest presidents in U.S. history. How can this be explained? In Roosevelt's case, he saved the world, but* could not save every life. This brief excerpt, written by Robert Edwin Herzstein, a professor of history at the University of South Carolina, explains how the pursuit of the larger goal of winning the war helped the Jews and insured Roosevelt's high standing in history.

Excerpted from Robert Edwin Herzstein, *Roosevelt and Hitler: Prelude to War.* Copyright © 1989 Robert Edwin Herzstein. Originally published by Paragon House, New York. Reprinted with permission from the author and his literary agent, Susan Ann Protter.

Thanks in large measure to Roosevelt's policies, the United States became involved in a faraway quarrel, among nations viewed with suspicion by a large majority of the citizenry. Roosevelt's mix of economic, ideological, ethical, and political motives led him to pursue a policy representing a violent break with recent American attitudes, including his own.

Roosevelt believed that active intervention by the White House on behalf of Jewish refugees and victims of Hitler would endanger his strategy. By isolating and politically castrating the Jew-haters, through means both fair and foul, Roosevelt helped to rake the United States in an anti-Nazi direction in foreign policy. . . .

The president refused to support changes in the immigrant quota system so as to provide sanctuary for Austrian and German Jewish refugees. He feared congressional reaction, as well as a domestic anti-Semitic backlash. Roosevelt viewed a battle with Congress over the refugee question as a diversion, one that would only give respectability to fringe groups and assorted anti-Semites. . . .

Roosevelt was thus too cautious when dealing with the refugee question, and at times betrayed a lack of humanitarian compassion. In making such assertions, his critics have been right. Nevertheless, the prime interest of the Jews, and of all humanity, was to rid the world of Hitlerism. Roosevelt's policy toward the immigration issue must be put in the broader context of his revolutionary foreign policy. This interventionist initiative, developed when the country was economically troubled, isolationist, and at peace, is our best guide to Roosevelt's intentions, and to his greatness or failure. Jewish refugees were tragic pawns, for FDR sacrificed them to a strategy calculated to ensure American global hegemony in a world free of the Nazis. . . .

Had Roosevelt not discredited the far-right and anti-Semitic movements between 1938 and 1941, would the United States have been willing to accept his forward policy in the North Atlantic after March, 1941? If Roosevelt had not helped to secure an anti-Nazi alliance and begun to prepare the United States for war in 1940 and 1941, would any Jews have been alive west of Moscow in 1945? If Roosevelt had taken the easy way out, there would have been no Grand Alliance, no extermination of Hitler. The most likely outcome would have been a German victory, or a strategic stalemate in Europe. . . .

Franklin Delano Roosevelt

In 1935, . . . the great German novelist Thomas Mann visited President Roosevelt. He recalled, "When I left the White House after my first visit [on 30 June 1935], I knew Hitler was lost." The imagination of the novelist saw more deeply than the observers who accused Roosevelt of timidity or lack of direction. Mann later avowed, "I passionately longed for war against Hitler and 'agitated' for it; and I shall be eternally grateful to Roosevelt, the born and conscious enemy of l'Infame [the infamous one, i.e., Hitler], for having manoevered his all-important country into it with consummate skill." A "born and conscious enemy"—this is what Hitler saw, and why he hated FDR so.

Another observer, who had reason to revile Roosevelt for his inaction during the Holocaust, says something of even greater significance. No one spent more time trying to tell the world about the Holocaust than the Polish resistance courier Jan Karski. He had been inside a Nazi camp and had seen the Warsaw Ghetto. Forty years later, he was still haunted by his inability to awaken the West to the full horror of his story. This Jan Karski visited Roosevelt on 28 July 1943, and spoke with him for eighty minutes. FDR asked a lot of questions about the Jews, "but he didn't tell me anything." Surely Karski would be bitter about this man, who viewed the military destruction of the Reich as the great aim of the Allied cause? No. Karski still views FDR as the embodiment of "[g]reatness. Power. I saw in him the height of humanity. Everyone did—

all the people of Europe. Roosevelt was a legend. So much so that when I left his office, I walked out backwards." Karski does not accept nor does he condemn the military explanation for Allied failure to save the Jews. He concludes in sorrow more than anger: Yes, "[s]ix million Jews perished. Six million totally helpless, abandoned by all." But Karski adds, "What do I know about strategy. They won the war, didn't they? They crushed Germany. If it were not for this victory, all of Europe would be enslaved today. That I know."

Selection 14

Was Enough Done?

Haskel Lookstein

American Jews, in particular, are haunted by feelings of guilt over their failure to do more to save European Jewry. More and more books are written every year about what was done, could have been done, or should have been done. If six hundred Jews had been murdered instead of 6 million, fewer books would be written, but people would still want to know why those Jews were not saved. In this excerpt, Haskel Lookstein focuses on the response of American Jews to several episodes during the Holocaust, including Kristallnacht *and the voyage of the* St. Louis. *He also offers some explanations for why American Jews did not do more to help their brothers*

and sisters in Europe. Lookstein is a rabbi and a principal of a Jewish school in New York. He has also taught at Yeshiva University. Lookstein has served as a leader of a number of Jewish communal and philanthropic organizations and was active in the effort to free Soviet Jews.

W e must stand as a generation, not only condemned to witness the destruction of a third of our number but guilty of having accepted it without any resistance worthy of the name.

Nahum Goldmann, *The Autobiography of Nahum Goldmann: Sixty Years of Jewish Life,* p. 148.

Looking back on the public Jewish response . . . , one reluctantly comes to the conclusion that Nahum Goldmann's assessment, twenty-five years after the events, was probably accurate. In these periods the Nazi effort appeared to be maximal and unrelenting, the Allies' response seemed minimal and ineffective, while the American Jews' public resistance was weak and sporadic. A retrospective view of this study may provide some insight into the reasons for the weak response.

In the two prewar periods, the critical issue facing the Jewish people was finding a refuge for Jews who wanted, and were able, to flee from the Nazis. The doors to the receiving nations were rapidly closing. Entry to America was governed by a quota system that was rigidly enforced. The American Jewish response to this pathetic situation was a muted one, as demonstrated in both the *Kristallnacht* and *St. Louis* episodes. In part this muted response resulted from the fact that American Jews did not fully appreciate the danger to which their German co-religionists were exposed. They certainly had no idea of the impending Final Solution, upon which even the Nazi regime did not decide until some time in 1941.

But the weakness of this early American Jewish response was more the result of fear than of incomplete knowledge. The American Jew of 1938–1939 was a cowed figure, who was destined to remain in that state for most of the war years. His timorousness, however, was at its height before America's entry into the war. The anti-Semites were at their most brazen. Jews were publicly vilified, accused of warmongering, and castigated as public menaces. Aside from the normal shivers that anti-Semites gave to Jews, American Jews were particularly sensitive in those days to the strident tones of hate because they could see what one unbalanced bigot had accomplished in Germany. . . .

The public consensus was so overwhelmingly anti-alien that Senator Lewis B. Schwellenbach, Democrat of Washington, confided in 1940 that condemnation of aliens "is perhaps the best vote-getting argument in present-day politics. The politician can beat his breast and proclaim his loyalty to America. He can tell the unemployed man that he is out of work because some

alien has a job." The real effort of Jewish groups in those days, therefore, had to be directed not at expanding the quotas but at opposing the restrictionist forces who wanted to stop immigration altogether. The strategy was to mute the refugee issue entirely. Magazines like the *National Jewish Monthly, Opinion,* and *Congress Bulletin,* which regularly denounced Britain for closing the doors of Palestine, were silent on urging America to open her own doors. . . .

They Knew, but Did Not Act

The situation had changed drastically for the worse by December 1942 when the issue was no longer one of providing havens for immigrants but rather finding ways to rescue the intended victims of the Nazis. By the end of December 1942, any American Jew who had read *The New York Times* or a Jewish newspaper or periodical knew that 2 million Jews had been murdered and about 4 million more were threatened with a similar fate. An immediate, strong public Jewish campaign for dissemination of the facts and a pressing for rescue effort might have been expected. Such a campaign did develop, but it was neither immediate nor strong. . . .

It is possible that the tentative nature of the response was the result of an inability on the part of many to comprehend the "facts" of the Final Solution, despite the numerous news reports. Why should American Jews have believed something that was inherently unbelievable— namely, that Jews were being killed by the millions for the crime of being Jewish? . . .

In January 1943, the month following the United Nations' announcement of the murder of 2 million, a public-opinion poll reported that less than half the American population believed the announcement. Most labeled it a rumor or expressed no opinion. Almost two years later, in December 1944, 75 percent believed that the Nazis had "murdered many people in concentration camps," but when asked to guess how many, most gave figures of under 100,000, perhaps the largest figure they could humanly conceive of. By May of 1945, when all of the camps had been liberated, the median figure was still only

1 million. Americans, it would appear, could not comprehend genocide on so immense a scale. Is it possible, then, that Jews were unable to believe it either? . . .

In addition to the problem of disbelief, a realistic distraction mitigated against an adequate Jewish involvement with the Jews of Europe. American Jews had their own personal concerns with regard to the war—husbands, fathers, brothers, and loved ones were in the armed forces, facing danger and possible death. By the end of World War II there were 16 million American men in the armed forces, among them 550,000 American Jews. They were the object of the most immediate concern and worry for their families in the United States, a personal concern and worry that transcended in importance the plight of European Jews.

Trust in FDR

Still another factor inhibited the Jewish response in this period and throughout the Holocaust: the implicit trust placed by American Jewry in Franklin D. Roosevelt. . . . The attitude toward Roosevelt, as revealed in the Jewish press, was reverential and subservient, obsequious in requests and fawning in gratitude for small favors. No matter how little the United States government did for Jews, . . . there was hardly a word of direct criticism of the President in all the Jewish press. . . .

One of the most bitter critics of American Jewish inaction during the Holocaust, Elie Wiesel, seems to have come sadly to the same conclusion that this press study suggests:

> What happened after Rabbi Wise was released from his pledge [to Welles about keeping the reports of the exterminations secret until they were confirmed]? Not much. Not much at all. Did he and the other Jewish leaders proclaim hunger strikes to the end? Did they organize daily, weekly marches to the White House? They should have shaken heaven and earth, echoing the agony of their doomed brethren. Taken in by Roosevelt's personality, they, in a way, became accomplices in his inaction. . . .

There are several responses that might be given to the agonizing questions posed by Wiesel. But the basic answer was supplied by the questioner himself. An act of civil disobedience would have been directed ultimately against the President. This was unthinkable to Jews at that time. Whatever the President's failings, Jews believed that in a world filled with enemies, Roosevelt represented the best that Jews could hope for. He was, after all, winning the war against the arch enemy. There was not even a possibility of exerting pressure on him in 1944, an election year, because, as Marie Syrkin, who lived through the Holocaust, writes:

> [There was] a genuine conviction held by most Jews at the time that in a world of enemies, Roosevelt represented the best Jews could hope for. He was the man who had recalled the American ambassador to Germany after *Kristallnacht* and had finally managed to get the United States to join the fight against Nazi Germany. The fact that an election was in the offing made American Jews all the more nervous. . . . I recall the near panic that would seize many of us for fear that Roosevelt might fail of election, because the forces against him were viewed as actively dangerous and inimical, whereas we believed that though Roosevelt could perhaps be more daring he was probably judging what the traffic would bear. The last thing the Jews wanted to do was to attack him in an election year and in any way jeopardize his victory.

Roosevelt, then, could not be challenged. He had to be supported. Thus did American Jews become "accomplices to his inaction.". . .

Was Enough Done?

To ask "was enough done" may be to engage in a futile rhetorical exercise. How can enough be done if 6 million were killed? And if 1 million had been saved, could one say enough was done? When a people is victimized by genocide, no help can be considered enough. America could have done much more. Roosevelt had many options he failed to use, from temporary havens to mortgaging immigration quotas for future years, from warning the murderers more often to bombing the camps and the rail lines leading to them. But Roosevelt was concerned about winning the war. He was not going to be distracted from the war effort without strong Jewish pressure. That pressure never came. Had it come, had Roosevelt acted accordingly, had America's power been exerted in behalf of rescue, there is still no guarantee that many lives would have been saved. Ultimately, the key to saving lives lay with the murderers rather than with even the best intentioned rescuers. . . .

Judah Piltch looked ahead to a time of spiritual accounting and asked a troubling question:

And what will happen when my son asks me tomorrow: "What did you do while your brothers were being exterminated and tortured by the Nazi murderers?" What will I say and what will I be able to tell him? Shall I tell him that I lived in a generation of weaklings and cowards who were neither moved nor shocked when they heard of hundreds of thousands of their brothers being led to the slaughter hour by hour, day by day, year by year? Shall I describe this chapter in the annals of American Jewry and admit that our people did not meet the test of history? Shall I tell him that the forces of destruction which enveloped their European brothers did not disturb the slumber of American Jews or arouse them from their inertia? Or shall I defend my generation, saying that we did not have the guts to launch a strong campaign because we knew well that our efforts would be unavailing and that we had no power to affect the situation. I shall, however, certainly not dare to tell my son about the "business as usual" conduct of our lives at a time when the press was informing us about the extermination of complete communities. I would be ashamed to face him with such a description.

And my heart pounds within me because I am sure that I shall have to give an accounting some day. Of course I will tell him of the public fast that the rabbis called for the people in order to mourn their dead. But then I shall have to admit the truth and add that from 5,000,000 Jews less than 30,000 came to the *shuls* and fewer than 50,000 came to the protest meetings called that day by the Jewish organizations.

Apparently our hearts are like stone. We do not tremble at the reports of the European Holocaust. We are still mired in the 49 levels of indifference and passivity, as if nothing has happened in our world.

One looks in vain . . . for a sign that American Jews altered some aspect of their lifestyle to indicate their awareness of the plight of their European brothers. There was no need for civil disobedience; some small gesture would have sufficed to keep the matter at the forefront of their consciousness and to generate feelings of sympathy and solidarity. Why, for example, was there not a regular fast day each month or a special prayer circulated by the Synagogue Council of America to be recited at sabbath services every week? Why could not the Holy Ark in each synagogue have been draped in black, so that an American Jew entering a house of worship would be reminded that European Jews were being slaughtered even as his prayers were being recited. There were other suggestions similar to these made by young rabbinical students at the Jewish Theological Seminary. But none of them was adopted. The result was a painful reenactment of a scene described by the poet Chaim Nachman Bialik in his "City of Slaughter":

The sun was shining
The trees were flowering
And the murderer kept on killing

Among the many tragic lessons of the Holocaust, this may be one of the most instructive. The Final Solution may have been *unstoppable* by American Jewry, but it should have been *unbearable* for them. And it wasn't. This is important, not alone for our understanding of the past, but for our sense of responsibility in the future.

What the Holocaust Means Today

Chapter 9

Introduction

The Holocaust is a historical event. Many history books relegate it to a paragraph or two, suggesting it is not that significant in the grand scheme of things. Studying the events that led up to the Holocaust, the Final Solution, and the reaction to Hitler's extermination campaign, however, provide important insights into human nature and can teach lessons for the future.

The belief that we can learn from the past to prevent mistakes in the future, and that we must honor the memory of the dead, is why the United States took the remarkable step of building a Holocaust Memorial Museum in Washington, D.C., in the shadow of the capital's greatest monuments and museums. The popularity of the museum, which is second only to the Smithsonian's Air & Space Museum, has defied all expectations and shown that people are very interested in learning about this dark period of human history.

Some people, such as Peter Novick in his book excerpted here, argue that studying and talking about the Holocaust has become an unhealthy obsession, particularly for American Jews. This is a minority view, but it is certainly the case that the Holocaust now attracts a tremendous amount of attention. Each year hundreds of new books are published, movies are released, and museums and memorials are constructed.

One reason this attention is important is that the Holocaust is becoming an increasingly distant memory. More than half a century has passed and soon there will be no one who lived through that period to provide eyewitness testimony. Who talks about World War I now, for example? How much longer will it be before World War II becomes a part of ancient history? The danger of forgetting is highlighted by the handful of neo-Nazis and fanatics who try to convince the naive and uninformed that the Holocaust never happened. These Holocaust deniers are active on college campuses and increasingly on the Internet. Deborah Lipstadt documented the activities and dangers of the deniers in the book excerpted here. If history is not to repeat itself, each person must remember the horrible events of the Holocaust and how they came to be.

The U.S. Holocaust Memorial Museum

Mitchell G. Bard

For most Americans, the Holocaust is little more than a fragment of history. Polls indicate many people know little or nothing about it, some doubt it even occurred. Relatively few Americans died in the Holocaust, so the event seems all the more "foreign." Nevertheless, President Jimmy Carter decided the Holocaust should be commemorated in some way in the United States. The commission he appointed recommended the construction of a museum in one of the most prime locations in Washington, D.C., near the memorials to Lincoln, Washington, and Jefferson; the White House; Congress; and the museums of the Smithsonian Institution. Many people questioned the appropriateness of spending any government funding on a memorial to victims of the Holocaust, and when the museum opened in 1993, no one knew how much interest it would generate. Sure, Jews could be expected to visit, but would non-Jews also come? In a city with so many places to visit, would tourists want to spend hours immersed in the history of one of the most terrible periods in human history? The answer is a resounding yes. The museum has exceeded all

expectations and become one of the most popular tourist attractions in Washington. This article describes what it is like to visit the museum and the care given to even the smallest architectural detail to convey a message about the Holocaust. In addition to editing this volume, Mitchell G. Bard is a foreign policy analyst in Washington, the executive director of the nonprofit American-Israeli Cooperative Enterprise (AICE), and the author of several books and hundreds of articles. He is also the webmaster for the Jewish Student Online Research Center (JSOURCE), which has an extensive collection of articles and documents pertaining to the Holocaust.

V isitors to Washington, D.C., are always emotionally touched by the symbols of democracy, the Capitol and the White House. Monuments to people who changed history for the better impress. One of the world's great museum systems, the Smithsonian, glorifies human triumphs. In April [1993], the counterpoint to these symbols opened in their shadow. The U.S. Holocaust Memorial Museum depicts the darker side of humanity, and the danger associated with the breakdown of democracy.

So why should anyone choose to visit a museum that is likely to depress them, with such uplifting shrines nearby?

Excerpted from Mitchell G. Bard, "Holocaust Museum Gives Portrait of World Gone Awry," *Woman's World*, Spring 1993. Reprinted with permission from the author.

Some people may indeed shy away, but as the Vietnam Memorial has proven, tourists are not hesitant to confront the uncomfortable past. . . .

The idea for the museum is said to have originated in the late 1970's after President Jimmy Carter saw the film, *Holocaust,* and decided something needed to be done to commemorate the event. With unanimous congressional approval, he appointed a 55-member U.S. Holocaust Memorial Council, originally headed by Elie Wiesel. Congress then gave the council a mandate to create a museum and donated nearly two acres for it. The catch was that the council had to privately raise $168 million for the building. . . . Private fundraising continued after the museum opened, but most operating funds will come from a congressional appropriation.

The decision to build a museum was one thing, but determining what it should contain was another. One of the first questions was whether it should be a "Jewish museum." Elie Wiesel's philosophy was that you could not tell the story of the disaster that befell the Jews without presenting the entire context. Thus, one of the first exhibits visitors see relates to the mentally and physically disabled who were the earliest groups murdered by the Nazis. The technology developed to kill them was later used in the Final Solution.

Still, most of the museum is devoted to what happened to the Jews. "There exists a moral imperative for special emphasis on the six million Jews," Wiesel wrote to President Carter in the cover letter of his report from the Commission on the Holocaust. "While not all victims were Jews, *all* Jews were victims, destined for annihilation solely because they were born Jewish . . . they were sentenced to death collectively and individually as part of an official and 'legal' plan unprecedented in the annals of history."

Why a National Museum?

People will undoubtedly ask why the government should spend money for what many will see as a museum for the Jews. Wiesel believed four reasons could be given. First, that the killers wanted to destroy the memory of the vic-

tims. Failing to remember the dead, he said, would grant the murderers a posthumous victory. Second, the last wish of the victims was to bear witness. Third, "indifference to the victims would result, inevitably, in indifference to ourselves." Finally, and most importantly, the lesson that must emerge from the Holocaust is that not enough people cared when the enemy of the Jewish people and mankind split human society. A quote inside the museum by George Washington sums up the U.S. interest in such a memorial: "The government of the United States . . . gives to bigotry no sanction, to persecution no assistance."

Even smaller issues are not without controversy. In planning a museum on such a sensitive subject, seemingly trivial details had to be considered, such as whether to have a cafeteria and what kind of food to serve (a vegetarian restaurant was built in the annex next to the museum) and whether the museum should stay open on Jewish holidays (as part of the Federal Museum system, it has the same hours as other museums: 10 A.M.–5:30 P.M., every day except Christmas).

The museum is designed to give visitors an emotional experience, but one that does not overwhelm them. Psychiatrists and psychologists were consulted to identify areas where feelings may get the best of people. Approximately 200 trained staff and volunteers are available to help people who have difficulty with any of the exhibits. Sensitivity has been incorporated throughout the museum, from "modesty" walls that conceal more graphic exhibits so that parents can decide whether their children should see them, to detours that allow survivors to avoid areas that may be too traumatic for them.

Education Through Architecture

Everything about the museum is meant to convey some sense of life under the Nazis. For example, visitors entering from 14th Street will see two doors. Groups go to the left, individuals to the right. It is a form of selection.

Traversing the Eisenhower Plaza (dedicated

to his years as Supreme Allied Commander) to the Raoul Wallenberg Place entrance, visitors immediately see the outside of the hexagonal Hall of Remembrance. What they might not notice is that the Hall's outer walls are freestanding and look like headstones. The stark brick and limestone exterior is supposed to remind people of a German factory.

Inside the museum, James Freed's architecture seems flawed: Rooms do not always have right angles; the windows above the atrium are different sizes and shapes; the floor is fractured; and the interior brick walls are uneven in shape and color as were the bricks used in the crematoria. Freed intentionally wanted to convey the sense of a world gone awry.

Nothing about the museum is comfortable. It is cramped in most places and dimly lit. Throughout, visitors must move through gates and cross bridges symbolizing those used in the ghettos to separate Jews. Passages often narrow as you move along. In the atrium, for example, the stairs to the third floor visibly narrow and lead to a gate resembling the entrance to Birkenau.

Though the Hall of Remembrance, a memorial to the victims, is the first glimpse many visitors get of the museum, it is the last thing they will visit. The philosophy is that unlike visitors to Yad Vashem in Jerusalem, who are generally knowledgeable about the subject, most people who come to Washington will have less familiarity with the Holocaust. Only after going through the exhibits will they feel a personal connection to the victims. . . .

During the ride up in a steel, factory-like elevator, a 30-second testimony of an American who liberated the camps is shown on a TV monitor. When the doors open, a photo of charred corpses found in Ohrdruf concentration camp immediately assaults you.

How could this happen?

The first clues are provided on this floor, covering the rise of Nazism in 1933–39 and the evolution of Hitler's racist doctrine. The boycott of Jewish businesses, the Nuremberg Laws and the burning of books are all illustrated. This trail of bigotry leads to a barrier at a border crossing.

Visitors must turn sharply and take a different route, a subtle reminder of the uncertainty of life for Jews in the '30s.

It is also on this floor that other victims are introduced: the mentally and physically handicapped who were murdered in euthanasia centers, gypsies, homosexuals, labor leaders and Jehovah's Witnesses. Another exhibit explains how Polish children were taken to Germany for "aryanization" after their country was overrun.

Walking through the exhibit, the silence was striking. Visitors behaved as though it was indeed a memorial. Perhaps this was partly because it was a weekday and no children were in the museum (it is *not* a place for young children). But, more likely, it was because the material is consuming, arranged in a way that is dense and intense, allowing no opportunity to catch your breath or engage in idle chatter. . . .

Descending to the third floor, which covers the 1940–44 period, a low bridge takes you over stones from the Warsaw ghetto to a cast of the ghetto walls (in the few instances where it was impossible to obtain artifacts, castings were made). Opposite them are large monitors showing films of life in the ghettos. Three images stand out. One shows a small girl huddling over a dead boy. A second is of Pawiak Prison in Warsaw where Americans were among the Jewish prisoners. And the last, and most haunting, the Hebrew words for "Jews-Revenge!" written in blood by a man murdered in the Kovno ghetto.

Walking past a Krakow synagogue window and exhibits on mobile killing squads, Babi Yar and the Wannsee Conference (where the details of the Final Solution were worked out), the bridge narrows from 16 to 5 feet, symbolizing how choices for ghetto residents dwindled.

Stepping into the Train

You identify with the victims as you walk past photographs of happy people carefully packing their belongings, believing that they are merely being resettled in another part of the country. But then you must pass through a boxcar, believed to have been one used to take people to Treblinka. Inside it is small and claustrophobic.

It is difficult to imagine how 40–60 people could fit into such a space. As you exit, you feel a burst of cool air, a sensation that the prisoners must have felt when the doors finally opened at their destination. This relief was fleeting, however, as they immediately came face to face with the infamous—and capricious—selections.

Like the prisoners, visitors have no choice about what direction they will go next. First, you see how those lovingly packed suitcases were taken away. Then, inexorably, you are led through the gates of Auschwitz under the ominous sign, *Arbeit Macht Frei.*

Inside, the exhibit is designed to give people a sense of what a day in the camp was like. Survivors provide graphic testimony in a video area where visitors must sit on blocks rather than the typical cushy seats, an inkling of the discomfort of the camp experience.

A mockup of a woman's barracks from Birkenau contains some of the artifacts from the camp, objects such as a bowl that one inmate kept tied to her body because it was her most valuable possession. A pile of 186 stones, one for every step inmates of Mauthausen had to take to and from the quarry, sit in a corner near a model of a crematorium. The most gruesome pictures in the museum, of medical experiments and suicides and executions, are shown on monitors behind a modesty wall.

The Tower of Faces

The more gruesome exhibits are not necessarily the most powerful. Like the simple black granite of the Vietnam Memorial, the Tower of Faces— a three-story room of photos of every man, woman and child from the town of Ejszyszki, Poland—is a reminder the victims were people, not just statistics. A woman standing beside me said: "I have photos just like these." Perhaps the most lasting message of a visit to the museum will be that the victims were people just like us.

The 3,000 Jews of Ejszyszki were killed in two days. Only 27 people survived. Yaffa Eliach, one who survived, went back and collected the photos. It is an amazing memorial to the townspeople; what is disturbing, however, is that this was just one of nearly 5,000 such towns that were made *judenrein* (free of Jews). . . .

The last floor of exhibits focuses on resistance and rescue from 1944 on. A Danish fishing boat used to take Jews to safety is on display. One can also read the story of Raoul Wallenberg who rescued thousands of Hungarian Jews and see names of 10,000 other people who were not perpetrators, collaborators or bystanders but saviors. Though the stories of resistance are reminders the Jews did not all go like sheep to slaughter, the events of those last months were rarely heroic. This was the time when thousands died on death marches as camps were evacuated. The horror did not end when the Allies overran the concentration camps. In Bergen-Belsen alone, 30,000 people died *after* liberation.

One of the most powerful exhibits is the hall where the perpetrators face their victims. On one side, the murderers are shown at the dock during the Nuremberg trials. Opposite them are drawings by children from Theresienstadt. Of the 10,000 children in that camp, fewer than 100 survived.

As I walked through the museum, questions haunted me: What would I have done if I had been a non-Jew in Germany? As a Jew, would I have fled, hid, resisted? The pictures by the children of Theresienstadt are a chilling reminder that Jewish children had no choices.

The main exhibits end with displays on the American response to the Nazis, how the Holocaust created impetus for the establishment of Israel, and a theater where survivors, liberators and resistors offer videotaped testimony. . . .

Remember

Now, after being immersed in the world of the European Jew, it is time to go to the Hall of Remembrance, a 60 foot-high empty chamber. As in other parts of the building, subtle architectural features, like triangular holes in the walls, reinforce the museum's message. A single quote from Deuteronomy is engraved on the wall above the flickering eternal flame: "Only guard yourself and guard your soul carefully, lest you forget the things your eyes saw, and lest these

The eternal flame in the Hall of Remembrance at the U.S. Holocaust Memorial Museum in Washington, D.C.

things depart your heart all the days of your life. And you shall make them known to your children, and to your children's children."

But the educational process does not end here. In the Wexner Learning Center visitors have the opportunity to learn much more through the use of state-of-the-art interactive computer systems. By touching the computer screen, it is possible to access information on almost every conceivable aspect of the Holocaust, to see photos and maps, hear survivor testimonies and watch documentary film footage.

The museum has more than 30,000 objects in its permanent collection. Some items were donated by survivors and individual donors, but a majority have been given on indefinite loan by the museums at Auschwitz and Majdanek. About 5,000 objects will be on display at any one time, the rest are kept in a warehouse whose location has been kept secret for security reasons.

While there is a massive amount of information in the museum, visitors should not expect to come away with answers to the most salient question: Why did it happen? You are left to ponder this after you leave.

It is fitting that Abraham Lincoln, who presided over America's bloodiest conflict, should look out and see out of the corner of his eye the monument to the world's greatest atrocity. Even now, one feels that he would get out of that great chair of marble in which he sits to protest what is memorialized within his sight. If he did, he might dedicate it with the same words he used 130 years ago at Gettysburg:

We cannot dedicate—we cannot consecrate—we cannot hallow—this ground. The brave men, women and children, survivors and victims, have consecrated it far above our poor power to add or detract. The world must note and long remember what we memorialize here, and never forget what was done to those who suffered. It is for us, the living, rather to be dedicated here to their memories and to insure that they are not forgotten and that the lessons of this terrible period in our history do not go unlearned.

Selection 2

The Holocaust in American Life

Peter Novick

Throughout this encyclopedia, authors have emphasized the importance of remembering and understanding what happened during the dark years of World War II. Several articles have also highlighted what the authors believe is the uniqueness of the Holocaust and why the mass murder of 6 million Jews should not be equated with other instances of genocide. In 1999 Peter Novick, a history professor at the University of Chicago, caused a stir with his book challenging some of these notions. As this excerpt illustrates, he asks why the Holocaust should receive as much attention as it does, why Americans in general, and American Jews in particular, should care so much about the subject and why the event needs to be regarded as unique.

*T*he Holocaust in American Life had its origin in curiosity and skepticism. The curiosity, which engaged me as an historian, had to do with why in 1990s America—fifty years after the fact and thousands of miles from its site—the Holocaust has come to loom so large in our culture. The skepticism, which en-

gaged me as a Jew and as an American, had to do with whether the prominent role the Holocaust has come to play in both American Jewish and general American discourse is as desirable a development as most people seem to think it is. . . .

Part of my puzzlement about how Americans became so "Holocaust conscious" had to do with timing: why now? Generally speaking, historical events are most talked about shortly after their occurrence, then they gradually move to the margin of consciousness. It was in the 1920s and 1930s, not the l950s and 1960s, that novels, films, and collective consciousness were obsessed with the carnage of Passchendaele and the Somme. By the fifties and sixties—forty years and more after events of the Great War— they had fallen down a memory hole where only historians scurry around in the dark. The most-viewed films and the best-selling books about the Vietnam War almost all appeared within five or ten years of the end of that conflict, as did the Vietnam Veterans Memorial in Washington. With the Holocaust the rhythm has been very different: hardly talked about for the first twenty years or so after World War II; then, from the 1970s on, becoming ever more central in American public discourse—particularly, of course, among Jews, but also in the culture at large. What accounts for this unusual chronology?

The other part of my puzzlement was: why

here? There is nothing surprising about the Holocaust's playing a central role in the consciousness of Germany, the country of the criminals and their descendants. The same might be said of Israel, a country whose population—or much of it—has a special relationship to the victims of the crime. To a somewhat lesser extent, this could be said of nations occupied by Germany during the war which were the scene of the deportation to death (or the actual murder) of their Jewish citizens. In all of these countries the parents or grandparents of the present generation directly confronted—resisted, assisted, in any case witnessed—the crime; in all cases, a fairly close connection. In the case of the United States none of these connections are present. The Holocaust took place thousands of miles from America's shores. Holocaust survivors or their descendants are a small fraction of 1 percent of the American population, and a small fraction of American Jewry as well. Only a handful of perpetrators managed to make it to the United States after the war. Americans, including many American Jews, were largely unaware of what we now call the Holocaust while it was going on; the nation was preoccupied with defeating the Axis. The United States was simply not connected to the Holocaust in the ways in which these other countries are. So, in addition to "why now?" we have to ask "why here?"...

What Is Different About American Jews?

What *does* differentiate American Jews from other Americans? On what grounds can a distinctive Jewish identity in the United States be based? These days American Jews can't define their Jewishness on the basis of distinctively Jewish religious beliefs, since most don't have much in the way of distinctively Jewish religious beliefs. They can't define it by distinctively Jewish cultural traits, since most don't have any of these either. American Jews are sometimes said to be united by their Zionism, but if so, it is of a thin and abstract variety: most have never visited Israel; most contribute little to, and know even less about, that country. In any case, in recent years Israeli policies have alternatively outraged the secular and the religious, hawks and doves—a less than satisfactory foundation for unity. What American Jews *do* have in common is the knowledge that but for their parents' or (more often) grandparents' or great-grandparents' immigration, they would have shared the fate of European Jewry. Within an increasingly diverse and divided American Jewry, this became the historical foundation of that endlessly repeated but empirically dubious slogan "We are one."...

The Holocaust, as virtually the only common denominator of American Jewish identity in the late twentieth century, has filled a need for a consensual symbol. And it was a symbol well designed to confront increasing communal anxiety about "Jewish continuity" in the face of declining religiosity, together with increasing assimilation and a sharp rise in intermarriage, all of which threatened demographic catastrophe. The Holocaust as central symbol of Jewishness has furthered in the late twentieth century what German Jews in the early nineteenth century had called *Trotzjudentum*. "Jewishness out of spite": a refusal to disappear, not for any positive reason, but, nowadays, so as not to grant Hitler a "posthumous victory."

Many Jewish commentators have warned that a Holocaust-centered Judaism would not work to ensure Jewish survival—that it would be a turnoff, alienating the young. Whether or not this proves to be true in the long run, so far this hasn't happened. At bar and bat mitzvahs, in a growing number of communities, the child is "twinned" with a young victim of the Holocaust who never lived to have the ceremony, and by all reports the kids like it a lot. Adolescent Jews who go on organized tours to Auschwitz and Treblinka have reported that they were "never so proud to be a Jew" as when, at these sites, they vicariously experienced the Holocaust. Jewish college students oversubscribe courses on the Holocaust, and rush to pin yellow stars to their lapels on Yom Hashoah (Holocaust Remembrance Day). And it's not just the young. Adult Jews flock to Holocaust events as to no others and give millions unstintingly to build yet another Holocaust memorial. . . .

Uniqueness

Every historical event, including the Holocaust, in some ways resembles events to which it might be compared and differs from them in some ways. These resemblances and differences are a perfectly proper subject for discussion. But to single out those aspects of the Holocaust that were distinctive (there certainly were such), and to ignore those aspects that it shares with other atrocities, and on the basis of this gerrymandering to declare the Holocaust unique, is intellectual sleight of hand. The assertion that the Holocaust is unique—like the claim that it is singularly incomprehensible or unrepresentable—is, in practice, deeply offensive. What else can all of this possibly mean except "your catastrophe, unlike ours, is ordinary; unlike ours is comprehensible; unlike ours is representable.". . .

Finally, there is the question of how we present ourselves to, how we wish to be thought of by, that vast majority of Americans who are not Jewish. The principal "address" of American Jewry—the representation of Jewishness and the Jewish experience visited by more Americans than any other, and for most the only one they'll ever visit—is the Holocaust museum on the Mall in Washington. There surely isn't going to be a *second* Jewish institution on the Mall, presenting an alternative image of the Jew. And there surely isn't going to be *another* set of legislatively mandated curricula about Jews in American public schools, besides the proliferating Holocaust curricula zealously promoted by Jewish organizations—something to balance the existing curricula, in which, for enormous numbers of gentile children (Jewish ones too, for that matter), the equation Jew-equals-victim is being inscribed.

So I wind up asking a traditional question—a question often mocked but sometimes appropriate. I ask about our centering of the Holocaust in how we understand ourselves and how we invite others to understand us: "Is it good for the Jews?". . .

Whatever its origin, the public rationale for Americans' "confronting" the Holocaust—and I don't doubt that it is sincerely argued and sincerely accepted—is that the Holocaust is the bearer of important lessons that we all ignore at our peril. Where once it was said that the life of Jews would be "a light unto the nations"—the bearer of universal lessons—now it is the "darkness unto the nations" of the death of Jews that is said to carry universal lessons. There is a good deal of confusion, and sometimes acrimonious dispute, over what these lessons are, but that has in no way diminished confidence that the lessons are urgent. Individuals from every point on the political compass can find the lessons they wish in the Holocaust; it has become a moral and ideological Rorschach test.

The right has invoked the Holocaust in support of anti-Communist interventions abroad: the agent of the Holocaust was not Nazi Germany but a generic totalitarianism, embodied after 1945 in the Soviet bloc, with which there could be no compromise. On a philosophical level, the Holocaust has been used by conservatives to demonstrate the sinfulness of man. It has provided confirmation of a tragic worldview, revealing the fatuousness of any transformative—or even seriously meliorative—politics. For other segments of the right, the Holocaust revealed the inevitable consequence of the breakdown of religion and family values in Germany. And, as is well known, the "abortion holocaust" figures prominently in American debate on that question.

For leftists, the claim that American elites abandoned European Jewry during the war has been used to demonstrate the moral bankruptcy of the establishment, including liberal icons like FDR [Franklin D. Roosevelt]. For liberals, the Holocaust became the locus of "lessons" that teach the evils of immigration restriction and homophobia, of nuclear weapons and the Vietnam War. Holocaust curricula, increasingly mandated in public schools, frequently link the Holocaust to much of the liberal agenda—a source of irritation to American right-wingers, including Jewish right-wingers like the late Lucy Dawidowicz.

For the political center—on some level for all Americans—the Holocaust has become a moral reference point. As, over the past generation, ethical and ideological divergence and disarray in the United States advanced to the point where Americans could agree on nothing else, all could join together in deploring the Holocaust— a low moral consensus, but perhaps better than none at all. . . .

Holocaust Lessons

The idea of "lessons of the Holocaust" seems to me dubious on several grounds, of which I'll here mention only two. One might be called, for lack of a better word, pedagogic. If there are, in fact, lessons to be drawn from history, the Holocaust would seem an unlikely source, not because of its alleged uniqueness, but because of its extremity. Lessons for dealing with the sorts of issues that confront us in ordinary life, public or private, are not likely to be found in this most extraordinary of events. There are, in my view, more important lessons about how easily we become victimizers to be drawn from the behavior of normal Americans in normal times than from the behavior of the SS in wartime. In any case, the typical "confrontation" with the Holocaust for visitors to American Holocaust museums, and in burgeoning curricula, does not incline us toward thinking of ourselves as potential victimizers—rather the opposite. It is an article of faith in these encounters that one should "identify with the victims," thus acquiring the warm glow of virtue that such a vicarious identification brings. (Handing out "victim identity cards" to museum visitors is the most dramatic example of this, but not the only one.) And it is accepted as a matter of faith, beyond discussion, that the mere act of walking through a Holocaust museum, or viewing a Holocaust movie, is going to be morally therapeutic, that multiplying such encounters will make one a better person. The notion that lessons derived from such encounters are likely to have any effect on everyday personal or political conduct seems to me extremely dubious on pedagogic grounds. . . .

Another ground on which I find the idea of lessons of the Holocaust questionable can be called pragmatic: what is the payoff? The principal lesson of the Holocaust, it is frequently said, is not that it provides a set of maxims, or a rule book for conduct, but rather that it sensitizes us to oppression and atrocity. In principle it might, and I don't doubt that sometimes it does. But making it the benchmark of oppression and atrocity works in precisely the opposite direction, trivializing crimes of lesser magnitude. It does this not just in principle, but in practice. American debate on the bloody Bosnian conflict of the 1990s focused on whether what was going on was "truly holocaustal or merely genocidal"; "truly genocidal or merely atrocious." A truly disgusting and not a merely distasteful mode of speaking and of decision-making, but one we are led to when the Holocaust becomes the touchstone of moral and political discourse.

Selection 3

The Holocaust Deniers

Deborah E. Lipstadt

As the years pass and World War II becomes a distant memory with few living witnesses to the terrible events of that time, it becomes easier for people to challenge the facts associated with the Holocaust. A number of people, some associated with neo-Nazi or other anti-Semitic and racist movements, claim the Holocaust never happened. They offer a variety of theories, some crackpot, others more plausible to the uninformed, to suggest that Jews either made up the whole thing or have greatly exaggerated what happened for their own political purposes. These "revisionists," as they are often called, have had great success in propagating their ideas over the Internet and on college campuses. This article discusses some of the arguments these Holocaust deniers use, the ways in which they try to spread their ideas, and the responses to what Deborah E. Lipstadt calls "the growing assault on truth and memory." Lipstadt holds the Dorot chair in modern Jewish and Holocaust studies at Emory University. Her first book, Beyond Belief, *examined the press coverage of the Holocaust and offered explanations for why it did not receive the publicity it deserved.*

Excerpted from Deborah E. Lipstadt, *Denying the Holocaust: the Growing Assault of Truth and Memory.* Copyright © 1993 The Vidal Sassoon International Center for the Study of Antisemitism, The Hebrew University of Jerusalem. Reprinted and abridged with permission from The Free Press, a division of Simon & Schuster.

*T*he producer was incredulous. She found it hard to believe that I was turning down an opportunity to appear on her nationally televised show: "But you are writing a book on this topic. It will be great publicity." I explained repeatedly that I would not participate in a debate with a Holocaust denier. The existence of the Holocaust was not a matter of debate. I would analyze and illustrate who they were and what they tried to do, but I would not appear with them. (To do so would give them a legitimacy and a stature they in no way deserve. It would elevate their antisemitic ideology—which is what Holocaust denial is—to the level of responsible historiography—which it is not.) Unwilling to accept my no as final, she vigorously condemned Holocaust denial and all it represented. Then, in one last attempt to get me to change my mind, she asked me a question: "I certainly don't agree with them, but don't you think our viewers should hear the *other side?*" . . .

The attempt to deny the Holocaust enlists a basic strategy of distortion. Truth is mixed with absolute lies, confusing readers who are unfamiliar with the tactics of the deniers. Half-truths and story segments, which conveniently avoid critical information, leave the listener with a distorted impression of what really happened. The abundance of documents and testimonies that confirm the Holocaust are dismissed as contrived, coerced, or forgeries and falsehoods. . . .

Deniers have found a ready acceptance among increasingly radical elements, including neo-

Nazis and skinheads, in both North America and Europe. Holocaust denial has become part of a mélange of extremist, racist, and nativist sentiments. Neo-Nazis who once argued that the Holocaust, however horrible, was justified now contend that it was a hoax. As long as extremists espouse Holocaust denial, the danger is a limited one. But that danger increases when the proponents of these views clean up their act and gain entry into legitimate circles. . . .

Denial and Free Speech

In response to student and faculty protests about the decision of the *Duke Chronicle* to run an ad denying the Holocaust, the president of Duke University, Keith Brodie, said that to have done otherwise would have "violated our commitment to free speech and contradicted Duke's long tradition of supporting First Amendment rights." Brodie failed to note that the paper had recently rejected an ad it deemed offensive to women. No one had complained about possible violations of the First Amendment.

Let this point not be misunderstood. The deniers have the absolute right to stand on any street corner and spread their calumnies. They have the right to publish their articles and books and hold their gatherings. But free speech does not guarantee them the right to be treated as the "other" side of a legitimate debate. Nor does it guarantee them space on op-ed pages or time on television and radio shows. . . .

Why Denial Has Grown

While Holocaust denial is not a new phenomenon, it has increased in scope and intensity since the mid-1970s. It is important to understand that the deniers do not work in a vacuum. Part of their success can be traced to an intellectual climate that has made its mark in the scholarly world during the past two decades. The deniers are plying their trade at a time when much of history seems to be up for grabs and attacks on the Western rationalist tradition have become commonplace.

This tendency can be traced, at least in part, to intellectual currents that began to emerge in the late 1960s. Various scholars began to argue that texts had no fixed meaning. The reader's interpretation, not the author's intention, determined meaning. . . . It became more difficult to talk about the objective truth of a text, legal concept, or even an event. In academic circles some scholars spoke of relative truths, rejecting the notion that there was one version of the world that was necessarily right while another was wrong. Proponents of this methodology, such as the prominent and widely read philosopher Richard Rorty, denied the allegation that they believed that two incompatible views on a significant issue were of equal worth. But others disagreed. Hilary Putnam, one of the most influential contemporary academic philosophers, thought it particularly dangerous because it seemed to suggest that every conceptual system was "just as good as the other." Still others rightfully worried that it opened the doors of the academy, and of society at large, to an array of farfetched notions that could no longer be dismissed out of hand simply because they were absurd. . . .

Holocaust denial is part of this phenomenon. It is not an assault on the history of one particular group. Though denial of the Holocaust may be an attack on the history of the annihilation of the Jews, at its core it poses a threat to all who believe that knowledge and memory are among the keystones of our civilization. Just as the Holocaust was not a tragedy of the Jews but a tragedy of civilization in which the victims were Jews, so too denial of the Holocaust is not a threat just to Jewish history but a threat to all who believe in the ultimate power of reason. It repudiates reasoned discussion the way the Holocaust repudiated civilized values. It is undeniably a form of antisemitism, and as such it constitutes an attack on the most basic values of a reasoned society. Like any form of prejudice, it is an irrational animus that cannot be countered with the normal forces of investigation, argument, and debate. The deniers' arguments are at their roots not only antisemitic and anti-intellectual but, in the words of historian Charles Maier, "blatantly racist anthropology." . . .

Casting Doubt on the Truth

What claims do the deniers make? The Holocaust—the attempt to annihilate the Jewish people—never happened. Typical of the deniers' attempt to obfuscate is their claim that they do not deny that there was a Holocaust, only that there was a plan or an attempt to annihilate the Jewish people. . . . They begin with a relatively innocuous supposition: War is evil. Assigning blame to one side is ultimately a meaningless enterprise. Since the central crime of which the Nazis are accused never happened, there really is no difference in this war, as in any other, between victor and vanquished. Still, they assert, if guilt is to be assigned, it is not the Germans who were guilty of aggression and atrocities during the war. The real crimes against civilization were committed by the Americans, Russians, Britons, and French against the Germans. The atrocities inflicted on the Germans by the Allies were—in the words of Harry Elmer Barnes, a once-prominent historian and one of the seminal figures in the history of North American Holocaust denial—"more brutal and painful than the alleged exterminations in the gas chambers." Once we recognize that the Allies were the aggressors, we must turn to the Germans and, in the words of Austin App, a professor of English literature who became one of the major "theoreticians" of Holocaust denial, implore them "to forgive us the awful atrocities our policy caused to be inflicted upon them."

For some deniers Hitler was a man of peace, pushed into war by the aggressive Allies. According to them, the Germans suffered the bombing of Dresden, wartime starvation, invasions, postwar population transfers from areas of Germany incorporated into post-war Poland, victors' vengeance at Nuremberg, and brutal mistreatment by Soviet and Allied occupiers. Portrayed as a criminal nation that had committed outrageous atrocities, Germany became and remains a victim of the world's emotional and scholarly aggression.

But it is showing the Holocaust to have been a myth that is the deniers' real agenda. They contend that the ultimate injustice is the false accusation that Germans committed the most heinous crime in human history. The postwar venom toward Germany has been so extreme that Germans have found it impossible to defend themselves. Consequently, rather than fight this ignominious accusation, they decided to acknowledge their complicity. This seeming contradiction—namely that the perpetrators admit they committed a crime while those who were not present exonerate them—presents a potential problem for the deniers. How can a group that did not witness what happened claim that the perpetrators are innocent while the perpetrators acknowledge their guilt? The deniers explain this problem away by arguing that in the aftermath of World War II the Germans faced a strategic conflict. In order to be readmitted to the "family of nations," they had to confess their wrongdoing, even though they knew that these charges were false. They were in the same situation as a defendant who has been falsely convicted of committing horrendous crimes. He knows he will be more likely to receive a lenient sentence if he admits his guilt, shows contrition, and makes amends. So too the innocent Germans admitted their guilt and made (and continue to make) financial amends.

The defendants at the war crimes trials adopted a similar strategy. They admitted that the Holocaust happened but tried to vindicate themselves by claiming they were not *personally* guilty. . . .

Deniers acknowledge that some Jews were incarcerated in places such as Auschwitz, but, they maintain, as they did at the trial of a Holocaust denier in Canada, it was equipped with "all the luxuries of a country club," including a swimming pool, dance hall, and recreational facilities. Some Jews may have died, they said, but this was the natural consequence of wartime deprivations.

The central assertion for the deniers is that Jews are not victims but victimizers. They "stole" billions in reparations, destroyed Germany's good name by spreading the "myth" of the Holocaust, and won international sympathy because of what they claimed had been done to them. In the paramount miscarriage of injustice, they used the world's sympathy to "displace" another people so that the state of Israel could be established. This contention relating to the establishment of Israel is a linchpin of their argument. It constitutes a motive for the creation of the Holocaust "legend" by the Jews. Once the deniers add this to the equation, the essential elements of their argument are in place.

Some have a distinct political objective: If there was no Holocaust, what is so wrong with national socialism? It is the Holocaust that gives fascism a bad name. Extremist groups know that every time they extol the virtues of national socialism they must contend with the question: If it was so benign, how was the Holocaust possible? Before fascism can be resurrected, this blot must be removed. At first they attempted to justify it; now they deny it. This is the means by which those who still advocate the principles of fascism attempt to reintroduce it as a viable political system. For many falsifiers this, not antisemitism, is their primary agenda. It is certainly a central theme for the European deniers on the emerging far right.

When one first encounters them it is easy to wonder who could or would take them seriously. Given the preponderance of evidence from victims, bystanders, and perpetrators, and given the fact that the deniers' arguments lie so far beyond the pale of scholarly argument, it appears to be ludicrous to devote much, if any, mental energy to them. They are a group motivated by a strange conglomeration of conspiracy theories, delusions, and neo-Nazi tendencies. The natural inclination of many rational people, including historians and social scientists, is to dismiss them as an irrelevant fringe group. Some have equated them with the flat-earth theorists, worthy at best of bemused attention but not of serious analysis or concern. They regard Holocaust denial as quirky and malicious but do not believe it poses a clear and present danger.

There are a number of compelling reasons not to dismiss the deniers and their beliefs so lightly. First, their methodology has changed in the past decade. Initially Holocaust denial was an enterprise engaged in by a small group of political extremists. Their arguments tended to appear in poorly printed pamphlets and in right-wing newspapers such as the *Spotlight, Thunderbolt,* or the Ku Klux Klan's *Crusader.* In recent years, however, their productivity has increased, their style has changed, and, consequently, their impact has been enhanced. They disguise their political and ideological agendas. Their subterfuge enhances the danger they pose. Their publications, including the *Journal of Historical Review*—the leading denial journal—mimic legitimate scholarly works, generating confusion among those who . . . do not immediately recognize the *Journal*'s intention. Their books and journals have been given an academic format, and they have worked hard to find ways to insinuate themselves into the arena of historical deliberation. One of the primary loci of their activities is the college campus, where they have tried to stimulate a debate on the existence of the Holocaust. It is here that they may find their most fertile field, as is evident from the success they have had in placing advertisements that deny the Holocaust in college newspapers. . . . They have also begun to make active use of computer bulletin boards, where they post their familiar arguments. Certain computer networks have been flooded with their materials. Their objective is to plant seeds of doubt that will bear fruit in coming years, when there are no more survivors or eyewitnesses alive to attest to the truth.

There is an obvious danger in assuming that because Holocaust denial is so outlandish it can be ignored. The deniers' worldview is no more bizarre than that enshrined in the *Protocols of the Elders of Zion,* a report purporting to be the text of a secret plan to establish Jewish world supremacy. The deniers draw inspiration from the *Protocols,* which has enjoyed a sustained and vibrant life despite the fact it has long been proved a forgery. . . .

Reason Versus Myth

The vast majority of intellectuals in the Western world have not fallen prey to these falsehoods. But some have succumbed in another fashion, supporting Holocaust denial in the name of free speech, free inquiry, or intellectual freedom. An absolutist commitment to the liberal idea of dialogue may cause its proponents to fail to recognize that there is a significant difference between reasoned dialogue and anti-intellectual pseudo-scientific arguments. They have failed to make the critical distinction between a conclusion, however outrageous it may be, that has been reached through reasonable inquiry and the use of standards of evidence, on the one hand, and ideological extremism that rejects anything that contradicts its preset conclusions, on the other. Thomas Jefferson long ago argued that in a setting committed to the pursuit of truth all ideas and opinions must be tolerated. But he added a caveat that is particularly applicable to this investigation. Reason must be left free to combat error. One of the ways of combating errors is by making the distinctions between scholarship and myth. In the case of Holocaust denial, we are dealing with people who consciously confuse these categories. As a result reason becomes hostage to a particularly odious ideology.

Reasoned dialogue, particularly as it applies to the understanding of history, is rooted in the notion that there exists a historical reality that—though it may be subjected by the historian to a multiplicity of interpretations—is ultimately found and not made. The historian does not create, the historian uncovers. The validity of a historical interpretation is determined by how well it accounts for the facts. Though the historian's role is to act as a neutral observer trying to follow the facts, there is increasing recognition that the historian brings to this enterprise his or her own values and biases. Consequently there is no such thing as value-free history. However, even the historian with a particular bias is dramatically different from the proponents of these pseudoreasoned ideologies. The latter freely shape or create information to buttress their convictions and reject as implausible any evidence that counters them. They use the language of scientific inquiry, but theirs is a purely ideological enterprise. . . .

History matters. Whether the focus be the Middle East, Vietnam, the Balkans, the Cold War, or slavery in this country, the public's perception of past events and their meaning has a tremendous influence on how it views and responds to the present. Adolf Hitler's rise to power was facilitated by the artful way in which he advanced views of recent German history that appealed to the masses. It did not matter if his was a distorted version—it appealed to the German people because it laid the blame for their current problems elsewhere. Although history will always be at a disadvantage when contending with the mythic power of irrational prejudices, it must contend nonetheless. . . .

And if history matters, its practitioners matter even more. The historian's role has been compared to that of the canary in the coal mine whose death warned the miners that dangerous fumes were in the air—"any poisonous nonsense and the canary expires." There is much poisonous nonsense in the atmosphere these days. The deniers hope to achieve their goals by winning recognition as a legitimate scholarly cadre and by planting seeds of doubt in the younger generation. Only by recognizing the threat denial poses to both the past and the future will we ultimately thwart their efforts.

Appendix A

World War II Casualties

Country	Military	Civilian	Total
Soviet Union	13,600,000	7,700,000	21,300,000
China	1,324,000	10,000,000	11,324,000
Germany	3,250,000	3,810,000	7,060,000
Poland	850,000	6,000,000	6,850,000
Japan	1,506,000	300,000	1,806,000
Yugoslavia	300,000	1,400,000	1,700,000
Rumania	520,000	465,000	985,000
France	340,000	470,000	810,000
Hungary			750,000
Austria	380,000	145,000	525,000
Greece			520,000
Italy	330,000	80,000	410,000
Czechoslovakia			400,000
Great Britain	326,000	62,000	388,000
United States	295,000		295,000
Holland	14,000	236,000	250,000
Belgium	10,000	75,000	85,000
Finland	79,000		79,000
Canada	39,000		39,000
India	36,000		36,000
Australia	29,000		29,000
Spain	12,000	10,000	22,000
Bulgaria	19,000	2,000	21,000
New Zealand	12,000		12,000
South Africa	9,000		9,000
Norway	5,000		5,000
Denmark	4,000		4,000

Appendix B

Estimated Number of Jews Killed in The Final Solution

Country	Estimated Pre-Final Solution Population	Estimated Jewish Population Annihilated	
		Number	Percent
Poland	3,300,000	3,000,000	90
Baltic Countries	253,000	228,000	90
Germany/Austria	240,000	210,000	90
Protectorate	90,000	80,000	89
Slovakia	90,000	75,000	83
Greece	70,000	54,000	77
The Netherlands	140,000	105,000	75
Hungary	650,000	450,000	70
SSR White Russia	375,000	245,000	65
SSR Ukraine*	1,500,000	900,000	60
Belgium	65,000	40,000	60
Yugoslavia	43,000	26,000	60
Romania	600,000	300,000	50
Norway	1,800	900	50
France	350,000	90,000	26
Bulgaria	64,000	14,000	22
Italy	40,000	8,000	20
Luxembourg	5,000	1,000	20
Russia (RSFSR)*	975,000	107,000	11
Denmark	8,000	—	—
Finland	2,000	—	—
Total	8,861,800	5,933,900	67

*The Germans did not occupy all the territory of this republic.
Source: *Holocaust Denial: A Pocket Guide.* Anti-Defamation League, 1997.

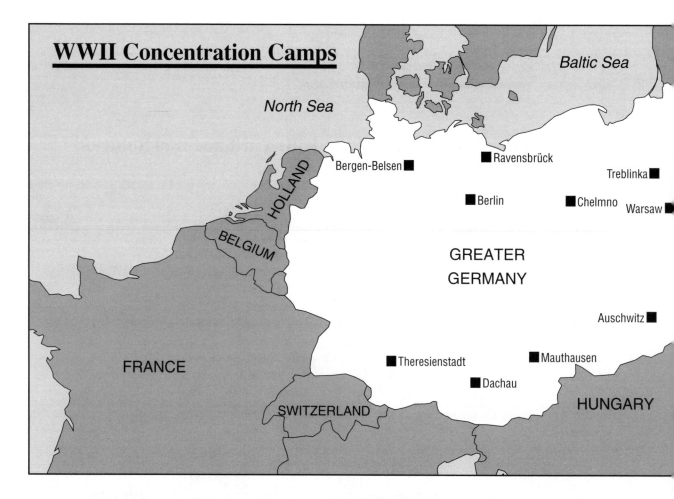

WWII Concentration Camps

North Sea

Baltic Sea

Bergen-Belsen ■

■ Ravensbrück

Treblinka ■

HOLLAND

■ Berlin

■ Chelmno   Warsaw ■

BELGIUM

GREATER
GERMANY

Auschwitz ■

FRANCE

■ Theresienstadt

■ Mauthausen

■ Dachau

SWITZERLAND

HUNGARY

---

1.   **Auschwitz**: Concentration and extermination camp established in 1940. Eventually, it consisted of three sections: Auschwitz I, the main camp; Auschwitz II (Birkenau), an extermination camp; Auschwitz III (Monowitz), the I.G. Farben labor camp, also known as Buna.

2.   **Babi Yar**: Kiev had a Jewish population of 175,000 on the eve of the Nazi invasion of the Soviet Union in 1941. On September 29 and 30, nearly 34,000 Jewish men, women, and children were brought to a ravine known as Babi Yar, where they were systematically machine-gunned.

3.   **Belzec**: One of the six extermination camps in Poland. Originally established in 1940 as a camp for Jewish forced labor, the Germans began construction of an extermination camp at Belzec on November 1, 1941, as part of Operation Reinhard. By the time the camp ceased operations in January 1943, more than 600,000 prisoners had been murdered there.

4.   **Bergen-Belsen**: Concentration camp erected in 1943. Thousands of Jews, political prisoners, and POWs were killed there. Liberated by British troops in April 1945.

5.   **Berlin**: The capital of the Third Reich.

6.   **Bialystok**: A ghetto in Lithuania. The final liquidation of the ghetto met with stiff resistance from the Jewish underground; nevertheless, more than 100,000 Jews were deported to Treblinka and other camps, where they were murdered.

7.   **Chelmno**: An extermination camp established in late 1941. It was the first camp where mass executions were carried out by means of gas. A total of 320,000 people were exterminated at Chelmno.

8.   **Dachau**: Erected in 1933, this was the first Nazi concentration camp. Used mainly to incarcerate German political prisoners until late 1938. Dachau was liberated by American troops in April 1945.

9.   **Kovno**: City in Lithuania whose population was 25 percent Jewish. When Germany invaded the Soviet Union, anti-Semitic Lithuanians attacked the Jews. As soon as the Germans occupied the

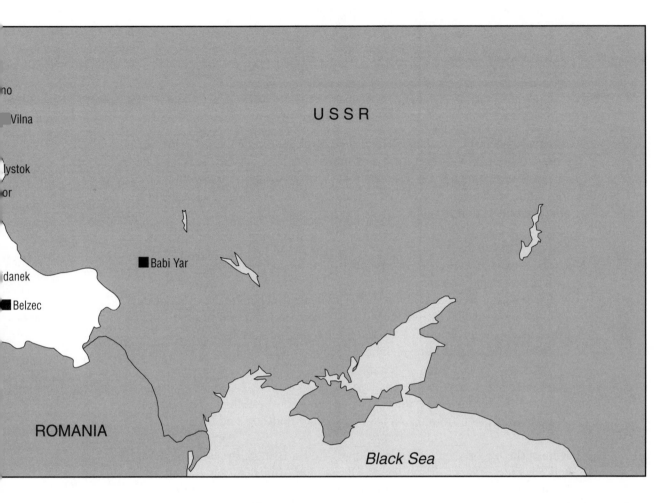

Map labels: no, Vilna, lystok, or, danek, Belzec, Babi Yar, USSR, ROMANIA, Black Sea

city, they established a ghetto for the Jews. Only 8 percent of the original population survived.

10. Majdanek: Originally a labor camp, Majdanek was transformed into a death camp. It is estimated that 1.5 million inmates were gassed at Majdanek. On July 23, 1944, Soviet troops liberated the camp; they found few survivors but a storeroom with 800,000 shoes.

11. Mauthausen: A camp for men, opened in August 1938. Conditions there were brutal, even by concentration camp standards. Nearly 125,000 prisoners were either worked or tortured to death at the camp before American troops liberated it in May 1945.

12. Ravensbrück: In 1939 the Nazis opened a special camp exclusively for female prisoners.The camp was liberated by the Soviets in May 1945.

13. Sobibor: Extermination camp built in May 1942 and closed one day after a rebellion of the Jewish prisoners on October 14, 1943. At least 250,000 Jews were killed there.

14. Theresienstadt: Established in early 1942 outside Prague as a "model" ghetto. The Nazis used the camp to deceive public opinion, but thousands of prisoners were deported to their deaths. On May 8, 1945, Theresienstadt was liberated by the Red Army.

15. Treblinka: An extermination camp established in May 1942 where 870,000 people were murdered. The camp operated until the fall of 1943, when the Nazis destroyed the entire camp in an attempt to conceal all traces of their crimes.

16. Vilna: A ghetto in Lithuania in which a revolt was staged. About 200 fighters escaped to the forests, where they became partisans. The remainder of the ghetto was liquidated.

17. Warsaw: Capital of Poland since 1596, with a Jewish population of 375,000 in 1939, representing 29 percent of the total city population. All Jewish institutions were destroyed by the Nazis and by Allied bombing. Site of the infamous Warsaw ghetto, which was established in November 1940 to confine nearly 500,000 Jews. From April 19 to May 16, 1943, a revolt took place in the ghetto before being suppressed by the Germans.

Glossary of Terms

Aktion Erntefest: "Operation Harvest Festival"; the code name for the liquidation and mass killings of the remaining Jews in the Lublin area that occurred on November 3, 1943. An estimated forty-two thousand people were shot while loud music was played to drown out the shootings. It was the last operation of Aktion Reinhard.

Aktion Reinhard: The code name of the operation that had as its goal the annihilation of the entire Jewish population of the General Government, the portion of Poland occupied by Germany. The operation was named by SS men in honor of Reinhard Heydrich, the main architect of the Final Solution, who was assassinated by members of the Czech underground in June 1942. Three death camps were built to accomplish the mass murder: Belzec, Sobibor, and Treblinka. Aktion Reinhard began in mid-March 1942 and ended in November 1943, during which more than 2 million Jews were killed.

Aktion T4 (Tiergarten Strasse 4): Code name for the euthanasia program. Its name was taken from the Reich chancellery building's address.

Allies: The nations, including the United States, Britain, the Soviet Union, and the Free French of Charles de Gaulle, that joined in the war against Germany and the other Axis nations. The Soviet Union was an ally of the Nazis between August 23, 1939, when the Molotov-Ribbentrop Pact was signed, and June 22, 1941, when Hitler attacked Russia. Britain became an ally of the Soviet Union only after Stalin and Hitler went to war. The United States became an ally of the Soviet Union only after Japan attacked Pearl Harbor. Hitler, allied to Japan, declared war on the United States.

Anschluss: "Annexation" of Austria to Germany on March 13, 1938.

anti-Semitism: Literally means "opposed to Semites" (which would include Arabic and other Semitic peoples as well), but usually applied specifically to opposition to Jews (anti-Judaism).

Appell: "Roll call"; within the camps, inmates were forced to stand at attention for hours at least twice a day while they were counted. This was always carried out no matter what the weather and often lasted for hours; often accompanied by beatings and punishments.

Appellplatz: "Place for roll call"; the location within the camps where the *Appell* was carried out.

"Arbeit Macht Frei": "Work Brings Freedom"; the sign over the gates of Auschwitz. It was placed there by Major Rudolf Höss, commandant of the camp.

Arbeitskommando: Forced labor detachment of prisoners of war.

Aryan: *Aryan* was a nineteenth-century linguistics term used to describe the Indo-European languages. The term was subsequently perverted to refer to the people who spoke those languages, which the Nazis deemed superior to those people who spoke Semitic languages. Thus, *Aryan* came to describe people of "proven" non-Jewish and purely Teutonic "racial" background.

Aryanization: The expropriation of Jewish businesses, enterprises, and property by German authorities and their transfer to Aryan ownership or control.

asocial: One of several categories of people targeted by the Nazi regime. People in this category included homosexuals, prostitutes, Gypsies (Roma), and thieves.

Auschwitz: A concentration and extermination camp in upper Silesia, Poland, thirty-seven miles west of Kraków. Established in 1940 as a concentration camp, it became an extermination camp in early 1942. Eventually it consisted of three sections: Auschwitz I, the main camp; Auschwitz II (Birkenau), an extermination camp; Auschwitz III (Monowitz), the I.G. Farben labor camp, also known as Buna. In addition, Auschwitz had numerous subcamps.

Axis: The Axis powers originally included Nazi Germany, Italy, and Japan, who signed a pact in Berlin on September 27, 1940. They were later joined by Bulgaria, Croatia, Hungary, and Slovakia.

Babi Yar: A ravine in Kiev where tens of thousands of Ukrainian Jews were systematically massacred.

badge: A symbol worn by Jews and others targeted by the Nazi regime for easy identification. Jews were ordered to wear a yellow Star of David; political prisoners, a red triangle; criminals, a green triangle; "asocials," a black triangle; Gypsies, a brown triangle; Jehovah's Witnesses, a purple triangle; and homosexuals, a pink triangle.

Baum Gruppe: "Herbert Baum Group"; a small, clandestine anti-Nazi organization founded in Berlin at the beginning of the Nazi regime by Herbert and Marianne Baum. It was composed of young people, primarily Jewish members of the Communist Party, as well as a number of Zionists. Its activities centered around increasing education, political, and cultural awareness, but it also engaged in one act of spectacular sabotage: the bombing of an anti-Soviet exhibit in Berlin. Most of the members were denounced, tried, and executed between July 1942 and June 1943.

Belzec: One of the six extermination camps in Poland. Originally established in 1940 as a camp for Jewish forced labor, the Germans began construction of an extermination camp at Belzec on November 1, 1941, as part of Aktion Reinhard. By the time the camp ceased operations in January 1943, more than six hundred thousand persons had been murdered there.

Bergen-Belsen: A Nazi concentration camp erected in northwestern Germany in 1943. Thousands of Jews, political prisoners, and POWs were killed there. It was liberated by British troops in April 1945, although many of the remaining prisoners died of typhus after liberation.

Bermuda Conference: An Anglo-American conference on refugees; it was held in Bermuda from April 19–30, 1943.

Birkenau: The death camp of Auschwitz II and III. Auschwitz II and Auschwitz III were mostly destroyed by the Nazis in 1945 before the Allied invasion.

"*Blut und Boden*": "Blood and Soil"; a phrase used by Hitler to mean that all people of German blood have the right and duty to live on German soil (i.e., in the German fatherland).

Boycott: An organized activity in Nazi Germany directed against the Jews to exclude them from social, economic, and political life.

Brunnlitz: The industrial town in German-occupied Czechoslovakia where Oskar Schindler relocated his Kraków factory in late 1944 as the Soviet Red Army advanced toward Kraków from the east. The weapons factory that Schindler established in Brunnlitz was a subcamp of the Gross-Rosen concentration camp. Labor camps exploiting Jewish and foreign labor like Brunnlitz were located throughout the Greater German Reich. Brunnlitz, under Schindler, was one of the few camps where Jews were not treated brutally.

Chelmno: An extermination camp established in late 1941 in the Warthegau region of western Poland, forty-seven miles west of Lodz. It was the first camp where mass executions were carried out by means of gas. A total of 320,000 people were exterminated at Chelmno.

concentration camps: Immediately upon their assumption of power on January 30, 1933, the Nazis established concentration camps for the imprisonment of all "enemies" of their regime: actual and potential political opponents (e.g., Communists, socialists, monarchists), Jehovah's Witnesses, Gypsies, homosexuals, and other "asocials." Beginning in 1938, Jews were targeted for internment solely because they were Jews. Before then, only Jews who fit one of the earlier categories were interned in camps. The first three concentration camps established were Dachau (near Munich), Buchenwald (near Weimar), and Sachsenhausen (near Berlin).

Cracow: See **Kraków.**

crematorium: A building that housed ovens used for the burning of bodies to be made into ashes, mostly found in the extermination camps.

Dachau: A Nazi concentration camp in southern Germany. Erected in 1933, this was the first Nazi concentration camp. It was used mainly to incarcerate German political prisoners until late 1938, when large numbers of Jews, Gypsies, Jehovah's Witnesses, homosexuals, and other supposed enemies of the state and antisocial elements were sent there as well. Nazi doctors and scientists used many prisoners at Dachau as guinea pigs for experiments. During the war, construction began on a gas chamber, but it never became operational. Dachau was liberated by American troops in April 1945.

death camp: Nazi extermination centers where Jews and others were brought to be put to death as part of Hitler's Final Solution.

death marches: Forced marches of prisoners over long distances and under intolerable conditions; they were another way that victims of the Third Reich were killed. The prisoners, guarded heavily, were treated brutally and many died from mistreatment or were shot. During the marches, prisoners were transferred to other ghettos or concentration camps or were sent to death camps.

deportation: The forced transport of people outside of the area where they live.

Der Stürmer: "The Assailant"; an anti-Semitic German weekly, founded and edited by Julius Streicher, which appeared in Nuremberg between 1923 and 1945.

Deutsche Email Fabrik (DEF): This is the factory that Oskar Schindler established in Kraków. The building still stands and houses yet another factory. When Schindler arrived in Kraków in September 1939, he purchased it at a very low price and by the process of "Aryanization." With the benefit of Jewish capital, Jewish labor, and Jewish expertise, he reorganized the factory and began producing enamel bowls and other kitchenware for the German army. Schindler named his new business Deutsche Email Fabrik, or German Enamel Factory. It became the haven for an estimated eleven hundred Kraków Jews. Schindler earned a fortune from his factory, but later spent much of it bribing Nazi officials on behalf of the Jews.

displaced persons (DPs): The term used to describe people who had been driven out of their homes as a result of Nazi decrees and World War II.

***Dolchstoss*:** "Stab in the back"; the myth that the German military had not been defeated in World War I, but rather had been "stabbed in the back" by Jews, socialists, and liberals who forced the Germans to surrender.

Dulag: The abbreviation for the German word *Durchgangslager*; a German transit camp for prisoners of war.

Dulagluft: The abbreviation for the German word *Durchgangsluftwaffelager*; a German transit camp for captured Allied airmen.

Einsatzgruppen: The four (A, B, C, D) mobile units of the security police and SS security service that followed the German armies into the Soviet Union in June 1941. Their charge was to kill all Jews as well as Soviet commissars and "mental defectives." They were supported by units of the uniformed German order police and used local Ukrainian, Latvian, Lithuanian, and Estonian volunteers for the killings. The victims were shot and buried in mass graves. At least 1.3 million Jews were killed in this manner.

Einsatzkommando: A company-sized component of the *Einsatzgruppen*.

***Endlösung*:** The "Final Solution" to the Jewish problem, the campaign of extermination against the Jews of Europe.

Erntefest: "Harvest Festival"; The Erntefest massacre was the single largest killing operation against the Jews in the entire war—forty-two thousand total, surpassing the thirty-three thousand who were killed in the Babi Yar massacre outside of Kiev.

Europa Plan: The scheme for the ransom of about 1 million Jews remaining in Europe to save them from extermination; initiated by the Working Group of Bratislava in the autumn of 1942.

euthanasia: The original meaning of this term was an easy and painless death for the terminally ill. However, the Nazi euthanasia program took on quite a different meaning: the taking of eugenic measures to improve the quality of the German "race." This program culminated in enforced "mercy" deaths for the incurably insane, permanently disabled, deformed, and "superfluous." Three major classifications were developed: 1) euthanasia for incurables; 2) direct extermination by "special treatment"; and 3) experiments in mass sterilization.

Évian Conference: A conference on refugee problems; it was attended by representatives of thirty-two countries and was held at Évian-les-Bains, France, in July 1938.

extermination camps: The six major extermination camps were established as part of the Final Solution in Poland. They were Chelmno, Belzec, Sobibor, Auschwitz-Birkenau, Treblinka, and Majdanek.

fascism: A social and political ideology with the primary guiding principle that the state or nation is the highest priority, not personal or individual freedoms.

Final Solution: "Endlösung"; in Nazi terminology, the planned mass murder and total annihilation of the Jews.

führer: "Leader"; Adolf Hitler's title in Nazi Germany.

Führerstaat: The "leader state," Germany after 1933.

gas chamber: The method used by the Nazis for "efficient" mass murder; originated in December 1939. The Nazis developed both mobile and stationary versions.

Gauleiter: The supreme territorial or regional party authority(-ies). The Nazi Party divided Germany and some annexed territories into geographical units called *Gaue*, headed by a *Gauleiter*.

General Government (*Generalgouvernement*): The territory in Poland administered by a German civilian governor-general with headquarters in Kraków after the German occupation in World War II.

genocide: The partial or entire destruction of religious, racial, or national groups.

Gestapo: "*Geheime Staatspolizei*"; the Nazi secret state police. The name was created from the first two letters of the German names *Geheime Staats Polizei*. Established in Prussia in 1933, its power spread throughout Germany after 1936. The Gestapo's chief purpose was the persecution of Jews and dissident political parties. Under Himmler's direction, the Gestapo was a prime force in the murder of the 6 million Jews.

ghetto: The Nazis revived the medieval ghetto in creating their compulsory "Jewish Quarter" "*Wohnbezirk*." The ghetto was a section of a city where all Jews from the surrounding areas were forced to reside. Surrounded by barbed wire or walls, the ghettos were often sealed so that people were prevented from leaving or entering. Established mostly in Eastern Europe (e.g., Lodz, Warsaw, Vilna, Riga, Minsk), the ghettos were characterized by overcrowding, starvation, and forced labor. All were eventually destroyed as the Jews were deported to death camps.

Gleichschaltung: "Coordination"; in Germany, everything was coordinated into the Nazi ideals.

Greater German Reich: The designation of an expanded Germany that was intended to include all German-speaking peoples. It was one of Hitler's most important aims. After the conquest of most of Western Europe during World War II, it became a reality for a short time.

Gypsies (Roma): A nomadic people, believed to have come originally from northwest India, from where they immigrated to Persia by the fourteenth century. Gypsies first appeared in Western Europe in the fifteenth century. By the sixteenth century, they had spread throughout Europe, where they were persecuted almost as relentlessly as the Jews. The Gypsies occupied a special place in Nazi racist theories. It is believed that approximately five hundred thousand perished during the Holocaust.

Haavara: A company for the transfer of Jewish property from Nazi Germany to Palestine, established in Tel Aviv in August 1933.

Häftlingspersonalbogen: Prisoner registration forms at the camps.

Heimwehr: German home defense force during World War II.

Herrenvolk: "Master Race"; Nazi term for the Aryan Germans who were destined to rule the world.

Holocaust: A Greek word meaning "entire burnt offering"; in recent times, the term *Holocaust* has come to refer to the Nazi policy to exterminate the Jewish people during World War II.

I.G. Farben: A German conglomerate of eight chemical companies, including BASF, Bayer, and Hoechst, that made extensive use of slave labor. In close partnership with Hitler, I.G. Farben established factories near concentration camps to take advantage of the large pools of forced laborers. Its Buna works near Auschwitz manufactured synthetic rubber from coal or gasoline. I.G. Farben was an important contributor to Hitler's rearming of Germany and the actual war effort.

IKL: *Inspektor der Konzentrationslager*; inspector of concentration camps.

Ilag: The abbreviation for the German word *Interniertenlager*; a civilian internment camp in World War II.

Jehovah's Witnesses: A religious sect, originating in the United States, organized by Charles Taze Russell. Jehovah's Witnesses base their beliefs on the Bible and have no official ministers. Recognizing only the kingdom of God, they refuse to salute the flag, bear arms in war, or participate in the affairs of government. This doctrine brought them into conflict with National Socialism. They were considered enemies of the state and were relentlessly persecuted.

Jewish ghetto police: In Poland, as in other occupied territories, the Nazis established Jewish police forces to control the Jewish population in the ghettos. In Kraków, the Jewish police, armed with truncheons, assisted the Nazis in the liquidation of the ghetto.

Jude: "Jew."

Judenfrei: "Jew-free"; one of Hitler's and the Nazis' war aims was a *"Judenfrei"* Europe.

Judengelb: "Jewish yellow"; the term for the yellow Star of David badge that Jews were ordered to wear.

Judenjagd: "Jew hunt"; the process of searching for any Jews who were in hiding after a massacre had occurred.

Judenrat: A council of Jewish representatives set up in communities and ghettos under the Nazis to execute their instructions.

Judenrein: A locality from which all Jews had been eliminated.

Kaddish: A classical Jewish prayer (mostly in Aramaic), with eschatological focus extolling God's majesty and kingdom, that is recited at the conclusion of each major section of each liturgical service; a long version (called rabbinic Kaddish) follows an act of study; also a prayer by mourners during the first year of bereavement and on the anniversary of the death of next of kin.

Kapo: A prisoner in charge of a group of inmates in Nazi concentration camps.

Kielce: A city in southeast Poland. Jews first settled there in 1868 and numbered twenty-four thousand by the year 1939. Most well known for its anti-Jewish pogrom on July 4, 1946, when an angry mob, incited by the rumor that Jews (recently returned to their hometown) had killed Polish children for their blood, killed forty-two Jews and wounded fifty others. The cemetery has a monument to the forty-two Jews, another one to forty-five very young children murdered in 1944, and a monument made of gravestones.

KL: An abbreviation for the German word *Konzentrationslager*, meaning "concentration camp."

Kommando: Labor squads made up of camp prisoners.

Konzentrations-Lager **(KZ-Lager):** Concentration camps, such as Dachau, used for political prisoners.

Kraków (or Cracow): This is the architectural gem of a city in southern Poland. The ancient seat of Polish kings, Kraków was designated the capital of Nazi-occupied Poland, the so-called General Government that was the administrative unit comprising those parts of Poland not incorporated into the German Reich. When German troops attacked Poland on September 1, 1939, fifty-six thousand Jews lived in Kraków, equivalent to the entire Jewish population of Italy. This number swelled as refugees from the countryside sought safety in Kraków. The Jews of Kraków were deported to the death camps in a series of brutal *Aktionen*. They had lived in Kraków for seven centuries, and many had become leaders in industry, the arts, and science.

Krieges: German for "soldiers" or "warriors"; also a reference to prisoners of war in World War II.

Kripo: "*Kriminalpolizei*"; the criminal police in Nazi Germany.

Kristallnacht: "Crystal Night," meaning "Night of Broken Glass"; the organized destruction of synagogues and Jewish houses and shops, accompanied by arrests of individual Jews, which took place in Germany and Austria under the Nazis on the night of November 9–10, 1938.

Lagersystem: The system of camps that supported the death camps.

lebensraum: "living space"; it was a basic principle of Nazi foreign policy. Hitler believed that Eastern Europe had to be conquered to create a vast German empire for more physical space, a greater population, and new territory to supply food and raw materials.

Lidice: A Czech mining village (population 700). In reprisal for the assassination of Reinhard Heydrich, the Nazis "liquidated" the village in 1942. They shot the men, deported the women and children to concentration camps, razed the village to the ground, and struck its name from the maps. After World War II, a new village was built near the site of the old Lidice, which is now a national park and memorial.

Lodz: A city in western Poland (renamed Litzmannstadt by the Nazis), where the first major ghetto was created in April 1940. By September 1941 the population of the ghetto was 144,000 in an area of 1.6 square miles (statistically, 5.8 people per room). In October 1941, 20,000 Jews from Germany, Austria, and the Protectorate of Bohemia and Moravia were sent to the Lodz ghetto. Those deported from Lodz during 1942 and June–July 1944 were sent to the Chelmno extermination camp. In August–September 1944, the ghetto was liquidated and the remaining 60,000 Jews were sent to Auschwitz.

Lublin: A city in eastern Poland that was the center of Jewish learning in Poland. In 1939 the Jewish population was forty thousand, 33 percent of the city total. In the spring of 1941 the ghetto was created. On March 17, 1942, deportations began to Belzec, and then to Majdanek, walking distance from the center of town. Only a few Jews live there today.

Luftlager: The abbreviation for the German word *Luftwaffelager*; a prisoner-of-war camp for Allied airmen.

Luftwaffe: The German air force.

Madagascar Plan: The Nazi plan to evacuate 4 million Jews to Madagascar over a period of four years. It was taken up in the summer of 1940 but was shelved February 10, 1942, after the Nazis decided to carry out the Final Solution.

Majdanek (also Maidanek): A mass murder camp in eastern Poland. At first a labor camp for Poles and a prisoner-of-war camp for Russians, it was turned into a gassing center for Jews. Majdanek was liberated by the Red Army in July 1944, but not before 250,000 men, women, and children had lost their lives there.

Marlag: A German prisoner-of-war camp for sailors.

Mauthausen: A camp for men, opened in August 1938, near Linz in northern Austria, Mauthausen was classified by the SS as a camp of utmost severity. Conditions there were brutal, even by concentration camp standards. Nearly 125,000 prisoners of various nationalities were either worked or tortured to death at the camp before American troops liberated it in May 1945.

Mein Kampf: This autobiographical book (*My Struggle*) by Hitler was written while he was imprisoned in the Landsberg fortress after the "Beer Hall Putsch" in 1923. In this book, Hitler propounds his ideas, beliefs, and plans for the future of Germany. Everything, including his foreign policy, is permeated by his racial ideology. The Germans, belonging to the "superior" Aryan race, have a right to living space (lebensraum) in the East, which is inhabited by the "inferior" Slavs. Throughout, he accuses Jews of being the source of all evil, equating them with Bolshevism and, at the same time, with international capitalism. Unfortunately, those people who read the book (except for his admirers) did not take it seriously, considering it the ravings of a maniac.

Mila 18: The underground bunker from which the battle of the Warsaw Ghetto Uprising was launched and in which Mordecai Anielewicz was killed. A monument stands today on top of a pile of rubble.

Munich Agreement: An agreement made at Munich between Hitler, Chamberlain, Mussolini, and Daladier on September 10, 1938, providing for the cession of the Sudetenland by Czechoslovakia to Germany.

Musselmann: Nazi camp slang word for a prisoner on the brink of death.

Mutterkreuz: "Mother's cross"; promoted Aryan mothers to produce more children. For every four kids, a mother received a bronze cross; for every six, she received a silver; and for eight kids, she got a gold cross.

"Nacht und Nebel": "Night and Fog"; the code name given to the decree of December 7, 1941, by the German high command of the armed forces, which directed that persons in occupied territories guilty of activities against Germany's armed forces were to be deported to Germany for trial by special courts and held in concentration camps.

Nazi Party (National Socialist German Workers' Party or NSDAP): Founded in Germany on January 5, 1919, it was characterized by a centralist and authoritarian structure. Its platform was based on militaristic, racial, anti-Semitic, and nationalistic policies. The Nazi Party membership and political power grew dramatically in the 1930s, partly based on political propaganda, mass rallies, and demonstrations.

Night and Fog Decree: A secret order issued by Hitler on December 7, 1941, to seize "persons endangering German security" who were to vanish without a trace into night and fog.

NSDAP: An abbreviation for the Nationalsozialistische Deutsche Arbeiterpartei, the National Socialist German Workers' Party, the party led by Adolf Hitler.

Nuremberg Laws: Two anti-Jewish statutes enacted in September 1935 during the Nazi Party's national convention in Nuremberg. The first, the Reich Citizenship Law, deprived German Jews of their citizenship and of all pertinent, related rights. The second, the Law for the Protection of German Blood and Honor, outlawed marriages of Jews and non-Jews, forbade Jews from employing German females of childbearing age, and prohibited Jews from displaying the German flag. Many additional regulations were attached to the two main statutes, which provided the basis for removing Jews from all spheres of German political, social, and economic life. The Nuremberg Laws carefully established definitions of Jewishness based on bloodlines. Thus, many Germans of mixed ancestry, called *Mischlinge*, faced anti-Semitic discrimination if they had a Jewish grandparent.

Nuremberg trials: The trials of twenty-two major Nazi figures in Nuremberg, Germany, in 1945 and 1946 before the International Military Tribunal.

Olag: A German prisoner-of-war camp for officers.

Operation Barbarossa: The code name for the German invasion of the Soviet Union, which began on June 22, 1941.

Operation Reinhard (Aktion Reinhard): The code name for the plan to destroy the millions of Jews in the General Government, within the framework of the Final Solution. It began in October 1941 with the deportation of Jews from ghettos to extermination camps. The three extermination camps established under Operation Reinhard were Belzec, Sobibor, and Treblinka.

Ordnungsdienst: "Order service"; the ghetto police who were made up of Jewish ghetto residents.

*Ostara***:** A series of anti-Semitic pamphlets published by Lanz von Liebenfels between 1907 and 1910. Hitler bought these regularly, and in 1909, Hitler sought out Liebenfels and asked for back copies.

Ostland: One of the two major administrative units of the German civil administration in the occupied territories of the Soviet Union, headed by Alfred Rosenberg, as Reich minister for the Occupied Eastern Territories; the other was Reichskommissariat Ukraine. Ostland included the three Baltic states—Lithuania, Latvia, and Estonia—as well as western Byelorussia and the western Minsk district in Soviet Byelorussia.

Oswiecim: A city in southern Poland that translates to "Auschwitz" in German. It was 80 percent Jewish in 1939, with eleven synagogues. The name also refers to the forced-labor camp that became a concentration camp in the suburbs of Kraków. Established in 1942, it was destroyed by departing Nazis on January 14, 1944, when the last of its prisoners went to Auschwitz.

Palestine: A Greek term meaning "Philistines," for the seacoast population encountered by early geographers; an ancient designation for the area between Syria (to the north) and Egypt (to the south), between the Mediterranean Sea and the River Jordan; roughly, modern Israel.

partisans: Irregular troops engaged in guerrilla warfare, often behind enemy lines. During World War II, this term was applied to resistance fighters in Nazi-occupied countries.

passive resistance: Opposition to oppression by means other than force, such as spiritual, religious, or cultural resistance.

perpetrators: Those who do something that is morally wrong or criminal.

pogrom: From the Russian word for "devastation"; an unprovoked attack or series of attacks on a Jewish community.

race violators: Anyone committing an act that is contrary to the anti-Semitic edicts of the Nuremberg Laws or of other anti-Semitic or racial orders by the German government.

Racien hygiene: "Racial hygiene"; this term relates to the eugenics aspect of the Holocaust, which the Nazis used to give a "scientific" backbone to their Final Solution.

Rassenschande: "Race treason"; a product of the Nuremberg Laws, it dealt with interracial marriages.

Reich: "Empire"; it also means "Federal" or "National."

Reichssicherheitshauptamt **(RSHA):** The National Central Security Department formed in 1939, combining the existing security police (Gestapo and *Kripo*) and the SD. It was the central office of the supreme command of the SS and the national Ministry of the Interior.

Reichstag: The German parliament. On February 27, 1933, a staged fire burned the Reichstag building. A month later, on March 23, 1933, the Reichstag approved the Enabling Act, which gave Hitler unlimited dictatorial power. After that the Reichstag became a rubber stamp for Hitler's policies.

***Reichszentrale für Jüdische Auswanderung*:** The Nazi central agency for Jewish emigration matters set up in the German Ministry of Interior on January 14, 1939.

rescuers: Those who helped rescue Jews without regard to the personal consequences.

resistance: The word commonly used to describe how Jews fought against the Nazis.

revisionists: Holocaust revisionists deny that the Holocaust ever happened.

Righteous of the Nations (Righteous Gentiles): The term applied to those non-Jews who saved Jews from their Nazi persecutors at the risk of their own lives.

SA: *Sturmabteilungen*; the storm troopers or Brownshirts of the early Nazi Party, organized in 1922.

SD: *Sicherheitsdienst;* the security service of the SS formed in 1932 as the sole intelligence organization of the Nazi Party.

selection (*Selektionen*): A euphemism for the process of choosing victims for the gas chambers in the Nazi camps by separating them from those considered fit to work.

Shoah: The Hebrew word for "catastrophe"; it denotes the catastrophic destruction of European Jewry during World War II. The term is used in Israel, and the Knesset (the Israeli parliament) has designated an official day, called Yom Ha-Shoah, as a day of commemorating the *Shoah* or Holocaust.

shtetl: A little Jewish village, especially of Ashkenazic Jews of Eastern Europe, prior to World War II.

***Sipo*:** An abbreviation for *Sicherheitspolizei*; the security police composed of the Gestapo and the *Kripo*.

Sobibor: An extermination camp in the Lublin district in eastern Poland. Sobibor opened in May 1942 and closed one day after a rebellion of the Jewish prisoners on October 14, 1943. At least 250,000 Jews were killed there.

Sonderbehandlung: "Special treatment"; a euphemism for rounding up Jews and deporting them to the extermination camps. In the exacting records kept at Auschwitz, the cause of death of Jews who had been gassed was indicated by *SB*, the first letters of the two words that form *Sonderbehandlung*.

***Sonderkommando* (special squad):** SS or *Einsatzgruppe* detachment; also refers to the Jewish slave labor units in extermination camps that removed the bodies of those gassed for cremation or burial.

SS: *Schutzstaffel*; the Nazi apparatus established in 1925, which later became the "elite" organization of the Nazi Party and carried out central tasks in the Final Solution. Headed by Heinrich Himmler, it became the most powerful organization of the Nazi Party, virtually a state within a state.

Stapo: The state police.

Star of David: The six-pointed star emblem commonly associated with Judaism. During the Holocaust, Jews throughout Europe were required to wear Stars of David on their sleeves or on the front or back of their shirts and jackets.

St. Louis: The steamship *St. Louis* was a refugee ship that left Hamburg in the spring of 1939, bound for Cuba. When the ship arrived, only 22 of the 1,128 refugees were allowed to disembark. Initially no country, including the United States, was willing to accept the others. The ship finally returned to Europe, where most of the refugees were finally granted entry into England, Holland, France, and Belgium.

swastika: A Sanskrit name for a hooked cross (*Hakenkreuz* in German) used by ancient civilizations as a symbol of fertility and good fortune. It has been found in the ruins of Troy, Egypt, China, and India. It was adopted by the Nazis and transformed into a symbol of Aryan supremacy.

Theresienstadt: Established in early 1942 outside of Prague as a "model" ghetto, Theresienstadt (or Terezin) was not a sealed section of town, but rather an eighteenth-century Austrian garrison. It became a Jewish town, governed and guarded by the SS. When the deportations from Central Europe to the extermination camps began in the spring of 1942, certain groups were initially excluded: invalids; partners in a mixed marriage and their children; and prominent Jews with special connections. These people were sent to the ghetto in Theresienstadt. They were joined by old and young Jews from the Protectorate and, later, by small numbers of prominent Jews from Denmark and Holland. Its large barracks served as dormitories for communal living; they also contained offices, workshops, infirmaries, and communal kitchens. The Nazis used Theresienstadt to deceive public opinion. They tolerated a lively cultural life of theater, music, lectures, and art. Thus, it could be shown to officials of the International Red Cross. Theresienstadt, however, was only a station on the road to the extermination camps; about eighty-eight thousand people were deported to their deaths in the East. In April 1945 only seventeen thousand Jews remained in Theresienstadt, where they were joined by fourteen thousand Jewish concentration camp prisoners who had been evacuated from camps threatened by the Allied armies. On May 8, 1945, Theresienstadt was liberated by the Red Army.

Third Reich: "Third regime or empire"; the Nazi designation of Germany and its regime from 1933–1945. Historically, the First Reich was the medieval Holy Roman Empire, which lasted until 1806. The Second Reich included the German Empire from 1871–1918.

Treblinka: An extermination camp in northeast Poland. Established in May 1942 along with the Warsaw-Bialystok railway line; 870,000 people were murdered there. The camp operated until the fall of 1943, when the Nazis destroyed the entire camp in an attempt to conceal all traces of their crimes.

Umschlagplatz: "Collection point"; it was a square in the Warsaw ghetto where Jews were rounded up for deportation to Treblinka.

underground: A secret network that is organized to resist authority.

Untermenschen: "Subhumans"; the Nazi categorization for the "lesser" races of Eastern Europe.

Va'ad Ha-Hazalah: Jewish rescue committees that functioned in different countries in Europe during the Holocaust.

Vernichtungslager: A death (or extermination) camp used for murdering Jews and other "racial undesirables."

Volk: "People"; in Nazi times, this term took on a more defined meaning: "People joined by blood."

Volksgemeinschaft: "People's community"; a community united by common German blood, i.e., no more social groups (Communists, Jews, political parties, Catholics, homosexuals, or Jehovah's Witnesses).

Volkswagen: "People's car"; Hitler wanted to make a cheap car for the lower-class Germans.

Waffen-**SS:** Militarized units of the SS.

Wagner-Rogers Legislation: Legislation introduced in the U.S. Congress in 1939 by Robert Wagner to admit a total of twenty thousand Jewish children over a two-year period above the refugee quota applicable at the time.

Wannsee Conference: A meeting held at a villa in Wannsee, Germany, on January 20, 1942, to coordinate the implementation of the Final Solution. Chaired by Reinhard Heydrich and attended by Adolf Eichmann and many other civilian and military leaders, the meeting established the administrative apparatus for accomplishing Hitler's dream of a Europe free of Jews.

War Refugee Board: A U.S. government agency for rescue of and aid to World War II victims. It was established on January 22, 1944, by President Franklin Roosevelt after receiving a report by Secretary of the Treasury Henry Morgenthau that provided details about the Final Solution. The board, which was headed by Morgenthau, was to take whatever steps were necessary to rescue the civilian victims of the Holocaust.

Warsaw: A city in central Poland that has served as the country's capital since 1596 and had a Jewish population of 375,000 in 1939, representing 29 percent of the total city population. All Jewish institutions were destroyed by the Nazis and Allied bombing; site of the infamous Warsaw ghetto.

Warsaw ghetto: Established in November 1940, the ghetto, surrounded by a wall, confined nearly five hundred thousand Jews. Almost forty-five thousand Jews died there in 1941 alone due to overcrowding, forced labor, lack of sanitation, starvation, and disease. From April 19 to May 16, 1943, a revolt took place in the ghetto when the Germans, commanded by General Jürgen Stroop, attempted to raze the ghetto and deport the remaining inhabitants to Treblinka. The uprising, led by Mordecai Anielewicz, was the first instance in occupied Europe of an uprising by an urban population.

Wehrmacht: The German armed forces.

Weimar Republic: Germany's political structure following World War I. The Constitution called for an elected president, a chancellor (prime minister) appointed by the president, a cabinet of ministers appointed by the chancellor, and an elected house of representatives, i.e. parliament, called the Reichstag. The governing powers rested with the chancellor through the ministry, with the president retaining veto powers and performing ceremonial duties. The Reichstag provided more of an advisory role than an actual legislative one.

Yad Vashem: The Israeli authority and museum for commemorating the Holocaust in the Nazi era and Jewish resistance and heroism at that time.

yellow badge: The distinctive sign that, by Nazi order, was compulsorily worn by Jews. See also **Star of David**.

Yom Ha-Shoah: Holocaust Remembrance Day.

Youth Aliyah: An organization founded in 1932 by Henrietta Szold to rescue Jewish children and young people and give them care and education in Israel.

Zegota: A small, unique organization clandestinely established in Nazi-occupied Poland for the purpose of rescuing Jews. The director of Zegota was Zofia Kossack, a devout Catholic and a prewar novelist whose writings were not without anti-Semitic overtones. Indeed, in a leaflet she published in September 1942 titled "Protest," Kossack wrote that the Jews were the enemies of the Polish people but that Poles could not stand by and watch the Jews be murdered by the Germans. It is estimated that twenty-five hundred Jewish children were saved as a result of Zegota's efforts. The children were smuggled out of the ghettos and transferred to Catholic orphanages and convents, where they pretended to be Christians. Zegota, which had a branch in Kraków (headed by Stanislaw Dobrowolski), also smuggled food into the Plaszow labor camp and, later, into Oskar Schindler's factory in Brunnlitz, Czechoslovakia.

Zentralstelle für Jüdische Auswanderung: "Central Office for Jewish Emigration"; set up in Vienna on August 26, 1938, under Adolf Eichmann.

Zyklon B: The commercial name for hydrogen cyanide, a poisonous gas used in the euthanasia program and at Auschwitz. The poison was produced by the firm DEGESCH, which was controlled by I.G. Farben. Zyklon B was delivered to the camps in the form of pellets in air-tight containers. When the pellets were exposed to the air, they turned into a deadly gas that would asphyxiate victims within minutes.

Chronology

1932

March 13
Presidential election under Weimar Republic in Germany gives 30.1 percent of the vote to Adolf Hitler, head of the NSDAP (National Socialist German Workers Party, i.e., Nazis). The incumbent president, Field Marshall Paul von Hindenburg, receives 49.6 percent.

April 10
Since a majority (more than 50 percent) was required by German law for the election of a president, another election is held in which incumbent president Hindenburg wins with 53 percent of the vote. Adolf Hitler increases his popular vote to 36.8 percent.

July 31
German national elections for delegates to the Reichstag (parliament) result in Nazis attaining 230 seats, or 38 percent. Social Democrats receive 21 percent; Communists, 15 percent; Catholic Center, 12 percent; numerous other parties combine to receive 14 percent.

1933

January 30
President Hindenburg appoints Adolf Hitler chancellor (prime minister).

February
The weekly publication *Der Stürmer*, devoted primarily to anti-Semitic propaganda and promoting hatred against the Jews, published since 1923 as the organ of the Nazi Party, becomes the official organ of the party in power. The motto of the paper is "The Jews are our misfortune."

February 27
The Reichstag building is burned.

March 5
During the last free election in Germany, ostensibly called to obtain a vote of confidence, the Nazi Party wins nearly 44 percent of the popular vote, more than twice as many votes as the next closest political party, the Social

Democrats, with 18 percent. In a coalition with another right-wing party, Hitler takes full control of Germany.

March 9
Rioting breaks out against German Jews by members of the SA storm troopers and Stahlhelm (an organization for former nationalist servicemen).

March 20
The first concentration camp, Dachau, is established.

March 23
The Law for Removing the Distress of People and Reich (commonly known as the Enabling Act) is passed, giving the chancellor (Hitler) legislative authority.

April 1
A boycott of all Jewish shops in Germany is instigated by the SA. This action was also directed against Jewish physicians and lawyers. Jewish students were forbidden to attend schools and universities.

April 7
Law "for the re-creation of civil service professionalism" removes many Jewish civil service employees. An exception is made for frontline veterans of World War I.

April 11
A decree is issued defining a non-Aryan as "anyone descended from non-Aryan, especially Jewish, parents or grandparents. One parent or grandparent classifies the descendant as non-Aryan . . . especially if one parent or grandparent was of the Jewish faith."

April 26
The Gestapo is formed.

May 10
Books written by Jews and opponents of Nazism are burned.

June
Dachau concentration camp opens.

July 14
A law pertaining to the revocation of naturalization and cancellation of German citizenship is passed; it is primarily aimed at Jews naturalized since 1918 from the formerly eastern German territories. The Nazi Party is declared the only party in Germany.

September 22
The Reich's Culture Ministry passes a law excluding Jewish writers and artists.

October 4
A law passes excluding Jewish editors.

October 14
Germany quits the League of Nations.

October 24
Nazis pass a law against "habitual and dangerous criminals" that justifies placing the homeless, beggars, unemployed, and alcoholics in concentration camps.

1934

January 24
Jews are banned from the German Labor Front.

May 17
Jews no longer are entitled to health insurance.

June 30
The "Night of the Long Knives" occurs when Hitler's rivals in the SA leadership are murdered.

August 2
President Hindenburg dies. Offices of president and chancellor are combined. Hitler becomes sole leader (führer) and commander in chief of the armed forces.

1935

May 21
The Defense Law passes, making "Aryan heritage" a prerequisite for military duty. During the summer "Jews Not Wanted" posters start to appear on restaurants, shops, and on village entrance signs.

September 15
National Day of the NSDAP. The Reichstag passes, during a special session, the anti-Semitic Nuremberg Laws, the Reich Citizenship Law, and the Law for the Protection of German Blood and Honor. These laws were the basis for the exclusion of Jews from all public business life and for the reclassification of the political rights of Jewish citizens.

November 14

First decree pertaining to the Reich Citizenship Law is issued, denying Jews voting rights and forbidding them from holding public office. All Jewish civil service employees are discharged, including World War I frontline veterans. Germans define what it means to be a "Jew." First decree pertaining to the Law for the Protection of German Blood and Honor prohibits the marriage of Jews to non-Jews. Work possibilities for Jews are narrowed to just a few professions. Jewish children were prohibited from using the same playgrounds as other children and from utilizing the same locker rooms.

1936

February 10

The German Gestapo is placed above the law.

March

The SS creates the Death's-head division to guard concentration camps.

March 7

German troops occupy the Rhineland.

June 17

Heinrich Himmler is appointed chief of the German police.

August 1

The opening of the Olympic Games in Berlin. Anti-Semitic posters are temporarily removed.

1937

The start of the Aryanization of the economy; Jewish owners are forced, without legal basis, to sell their businesses, in most cases considerably below the value of their goods.

June 12

A secret order by SS *Obergruppenführer* (lieutenant general) Reinhard Heydrich pertains to protective custody for race violators following the conclusion of the normal legal process.

July 16

Buchenwald concentration camp opens.

Autumn

Beginning of the systematic takeover of Jewish property.

November

Munich exhibition of "The Wandering Jew" depicts Jews as financial exploiters.

1938

March 13

"Annexation" (*Anschluss*) of Austria and start of persecution of Austrian Jews.

March 28

Law pertaining to the legal rights of Jewish cultural (ethnic) organizations is passed. Jewish communities are no longer legal entities enjoying civil rights; instead, they can only be legally created associations.

April 22

A decree is issued against the "camouflage of Jewish industrial enterprises." A decree is also passed requiring the declaration of all Jewish property greater than 5,000 Reichsmarks (approximately $1,190).

June 9

The Munich Synagogue is destroyed.

June 14

A decree requiring the registration and identification of Jewish industrial enterprises is issued. Lists are created identifying wealthy Jews at treasury offices and police districts.

June 15

All "previously convicted" Jews, including those prosecuted for traffic violations, are arrested and committed to concentration camps (approximately fifteen hundred persons).

July 15

An international conference is held in Évian-les-Bains, France, and is attended by delegates from thirty-two countries, including the United States, Great Britain, and France, to discuss the problem of Jewish refugees from Germany and results in no effective help for Jewish refugees.

July 21

Introduction of identity cards for Jews effective January 1, 1939.

July 28

A decree is issued for the cancellation of the medical certification of all Jewish physicians effective September 30. Thereafter, Jewish physicians are only allowed to function as nurses for Jewish patients.

August 10

The synagogue in Nuremberg is destroyed.

August 17

A decree is issued to carry out the law pertaining to the change of first and last names. Effective January 1, 1939, all Jews must add to their name either "Israel" or "Sara."

September 12

Jews are forbidden to attend public cultural events.

September 27

A decree is issued for the cancellation of the license to practice for all Jewish lawyers, effective November 30. Thereafter, Jewish lawyers can only practice in special instances as Jewish consultants for Jews.

September 29

The Munich Agreement: Britain and France accept German annexation of Sudetenland, part of Czechoslovakia.

October 5

A passport decree is issued, resulting in the confiscation of passports held by Jews. The procedure for the reissuance of passports is made more complicated. Newly issued passports are stamped *J*, designating Jewish ownership.

October 15

German troops occupy the Sudetenland.

October 28

Fifteen to seventeen thousand Jews of Polish origin are forced to relocate to Zbaszyn on the Polish border.

November 7

Herschel Grynszpan, whose parents were affected by the aforementioned expulsion, assassinates German consular aide Ernst vom Rath in Paris.

November 9–10

Kristallnacht: the Government-organized pogrom against Jews in Germany. It destroys synagogues, businesses, and homes. More than 26,000 Jewish men are arrested and committed to concentration camps—Dachau, Buchenwald, and Sachsenhausen. At least 91 Jews are killed, 191 synagogues are destroyed, and 7,500 shops are looted.

November 12

Decrees are issued for the "atonement payments" by German Jews in the amount of 1 billion marks, the elimination of German Jews from involvement in the economy, and the reconstruction of the facades of all Jewish shops. Jews have to pay for all damage caused during *Kristallnacht*. Jews are prohibited from attending movies, concerts, and other cultural performances.

November 15
Jewish children are expelled from German schools.

November 28
A police decree is issued pertaining to the appearance of Jews in public; it restricts the freedom of movement and travel, etc.

December 3
Jewish driver's licenses are confiscated. A ban against Jews is established in Berlin. A decree pertaining to the forced disposal (Aryanization) of Jewish industrial enterprises and businesses is issued.

December 14
Hermann Göring takes charge of resolving "the Jewish question."

1939

January 17
A decree is issued pertaining to the expiration of permits for Jewish dentists, veterinarians, and pharmacists.

January 24
A national central office for Jewish emigration is established with central offices in Vienna and Prague. SS leader Reinhard Heydrich is ordered by Göring to speed up emigration of Jews.

January 30
Hitler predicts in the Reichstag the "extermination of the Jewish race in Europe" in the event of war.

February 21
Nazis require Jews to relinquish all of their gold and silver.

March 15
Nazi occupy Czechoslovakia. The protectorate of Bohemia and Moravia is created. Anti-Semitic decrees, which are already in force in Germany, are introduced.

April 18
Anti-Jewish laws are passed in Slovakia. Cancellation of eviction protection.

April 30
A law pertaining to rent agreements with Jews is passed, calling for the combining of Jewish families into "Jewish houses." Cancellation of eviction protection.

May 13
Passengers board the SS *St. Louis* in Hamburg for trip to Cuba.

May 15
Ravensbrück concentration camp for women is established.

May 22
Nazis sign the Pact of Steel with Italy.

June 16–20
SS *St. Louis* returns to Europe and passengers disembark.

July 4
German Jews are denied the right to hold government jobs.

July 26
Adolf Eichmann (deputy to Heydrich) is placed in charge of the Prague branch of the emigration office.

September 1
Germany attacks Poland; World War II begins. Numerous pogroms in Poland. Curfews for Jews in Germany (9:00 P.M. in the summer, 8:00 P.M. in the winter).

September 3
Britain and France declare war on Germany.

September 21
Heydrich authorizes *Einsatzgruppen* in Poland. Ghettos are to be established in occupied Poland, each under a *Judenrat*, by order of Heydrich.

September 23
Radios are confiscated from Jews.

September 27
The *Reichssicherheitshauptamt* (National Central Security Department) is established. Warsaw surrenders.

September 29
Germans and Soviets divide Poland. More than 2 million Jews live in the German area and 1.3 million in the Soviet-controlled territory.

October
Nazis begin euthanasia on sick and disabled in Germany.

October 8
The first ghetto (unguarded and unfenced) is established in Piotrków, Poland.

October 12
The first deportations from Austria and the "protectorates" to Poland. The *Generalgouvernement* (General Government) is established in the German-occupied territories of Poland.

October 18
The wearing of the Star of David is first introduced in Wloclawek, Poland.

October 26
Forced labor for Jews in the General Government.

November 8
Hans Frank is appointed Governor of the General Government (headquartered in Kraków). An assassination attempt on Hitler fails.

November 23
The wearing of the Star of David is introduced in the entire General Government (occupied Poland).

November 28
A directive by Hans Frank establishes *Judenräte* in General Government.

1940

January 25
The Polish town of Oswiecim (Auschwitz) is chosen as the site of a new Nazi concentration camp.

February 10–13
The first deportations from Pomerania (Stettin, Stralsund, Schneidemuehl) to Lublin, Poland.

April 9
Germany invades Denmark and Norway.

April 20
A secret order by the high command of the armed forces discharges persons of mixed blood and husbands of Jewish women.

April 27
Himmler issues a directive to establish a concentration camp at Auschwitz.

April 30
The first guarded ghetto is established in Lodz, Poland.

May 1
Rudolf Höss is chosen to be commandant of Auschwitz.

May 10
Germany invades Holland, Belgium, and France.

June 14
The Nazis occupy Paris.

June 22
French army surrenders. Marshal Philippe Pétain signs an armistice with Germany.

August 8
Anti-Jewish laws are passed in Romania.

October 3
Anti-Jewish laws (*Statut des Juifs*) are passed by Vichy government in France.

October 7
German troops enter Romania.

October 16
The establishment of the Warsaw ghetto is ordered.

October 22
Aktion Burckel: Jews are deported from Alsace-Lorraine, Saarland, and Baden to southern France, then in 1942, to Auschwitz.

November 15
Hermetic sealing of the Warsaw ghetto occurs.

November 20–24
Hungary, Romania, and Slovakia join the Axis powers.

1941

January 22–23
The first massacre of Jews occurs in Romania.

February 22–23
Deportation of four hundred Jewish hostages from Amsterdam to Mauthausen.

February–April
Deportation of seventy-two thousand Jews into the Warsaw ghetto.

March 2
German troops occupy Bulgaria.

March 7
German Jews are inducted into forced labor.

April 6
Germany invades Yugoslavia and Greece.

May 14
Arrest of thirty-six hundred Parisian Jews. Romania passes law condemning adult Jews to forced labor.

May 16
French Marshal Pétain approves collaboration with Hitler in radio broadcast.

June
Vichy government revokes civil rights of French Jews in North Africa and decrees many restrictions against them. Nazi SS *Einsatzgruppen* begin mass murders.

June 22
Germany attacks the Soviet Union.

June–July
Mass shootings of Jews begin in Ponary Forest, the killing grounds near Vilna. By 1944 seventy to one hundred thousand Jews perish there.

June–August
Numerous pogroms occur in occupied Russian territories.

July 2
Anti-racist riots occur in Lvov; Ukrainian nationalists take part in riots.

July 8
The wearing of the Star of David is introduced into the Baltic countries.

July 17
Alfred Rosenberg is appointed Reich minister for the Eastern Occupied Territories to administer territories seized from the Soviet Union.

July 31
Göring assigns to Heydrich the task for "a complete solution of the Jewish question in the German sphere of influence in Europe," beginning the Final Solution.

August
Ghettos are established in Bialystok and Lvov.

September
Janówska, a labor and extermination camp near Lvov in Ukraine, opens.

September 1
A police order decrees that, effective September 19, all Jews age six and older in Germany must wear the Star of David.

September 3
The first gassing tests take place in Auschwitz using Zyklon B.

September 6
The Vilna ghetto is created with a population of forty thousand Jews.

September 19
German troops capture Kiev.

September 27
Heydrich is made protector of Bohemia and Moravia.

September 28–29
The mass murder of Jews occurs at Babi Yar near Kiev (thirty-four thousand victims).

October 3
Forced labor becomes mandatory for the Jews in the Reich.

October 10
The ghetto in Theresienstadt, Czechoslovakia, is established.

October 12–13
Jews are massacred at Dnepropetrovsk, Ukraine (eleven thousand victims).

October 14
German Jews are ordered to be deported from Germany, as defined by its 1933 borders.

October 16
Start of deportation of the Jews from the Reich.

October 23
Emigration of Jews is prohibited. Jews are massacred in Odessa (thirty-four thousand victims).

October 28
Jews are massacred in Kiev, Ukraine (thirty-four thousand victims).

October–November
Einsatzgruppen mass killings of Jews occur all over southern Russia.

November 6
Jews are massacred in Kovno (Kaunas), Lithuania (fifteen thousand victims).

November 25
A declaration is issued pertaining to the collection of Jewish assets through deportations.

December 7
The Japanese attack Pearl Harbor. Hitler issues Night and Fog Decree.

December 8
The United States and Britain declare war on Japan. Chelmno extermination camp is opened near Lodz, Poland; by April 1943, 360,000 Jews had been murdered there.

December 8–9
Jews are massacred in Riga, Latvia; victims include the first transport of Jews from Germany (twenty-seven thousand victims).

December 11
Germany declares war on the United States; America declares war on Germany.

December 30
Massacre of Jews in Simferopol in the Crimea (ten thousand victims).

1942

January 1
A declaration by the United Nations is signed by Allied nations.

January 15
Start of the "resettlements" from Lodz to the extermination camp Chelmno.

January 20
Wannsee Conference is held to solidify plans for deportation and extermination of European Jewry (Final Solution).

January 31
A report is issued from *Einsatzgruppen* A pertaining to the liquidation of 229,052 Jews in the Baltic states.

Late January
Start of deportations to Theresienstadt.

February–March
Jews are mass murdered in Charkow (Kharkov), Ukraine (fourteen thousand victims).

March 1
Extermination of Jews begins at Sobibor; by October 1943, 250,000 Jews had been murdered there.

March 6
First conference on sterilization: Definitions issued pertaining to sterilization of persons of mixed blood.

March 16–17
Extermination camp Belzec is established in Poland to murder Jews from Lublin, the Lublin district, and Galicia. Six hundred thousand Jews were murdered there.

Mid-March
Start of Operation (Aktion) Reinhard, the code name for the operation that had as its objective the physical destruction of the Jews in the interior of occupied Poland within the framework of the Final Solution.

March 21
Resettlement of the ghetto in Lublin, Poland: twenty-six thousand persons are sent to the extermination camps at Belzec, Majdanek, and other locations.

March 26
Public notices are posted pertaining to the identification of Jewish homes in Germany. Deportation begins of sixty thousand Slovakian Jews, some to Auschwitz, others to the extermination camp Majdanek.

Late March
Initial transports of Jews arrive at the concentration and extermination camps at Auschwitz (Auschwitz I and Auschwitz II).

April 24
Jews are prohibited from using public transportation. Exceptions are only made for forced laborers if their workplace is farther than seven kilometers from their place of residence. Taking a seat in the conveyance is not allowed. During the war, Jews were also forbidden to use public telephones and automatic ticket dispensing machines; to congregate in railroad stations or visit restaurants; to enter forests (parks) or step on lawns; to keep dogs, cats, birds, or other pets; to place orders with organized skilled trades; or to obtain newspapers or periodicals. All electrical or optical equipment had to

be turned in without compensation, as well as bicycles, typewriters, fur coats, and wool items. Jews could not obtain any seafood items or ration cards for meat, clothing, milk, or tobacco. They were not allowed any white bread, fruit, canned fruit, candy or sweets, or shaving soap.

May 27
SS leader Heydrich is mortally wounded by Czech underground agents.

June 1
Jews are ordered to wear the Star of David in France and Holland. Treblinka extermination camp is opened; mass exterminations by gassing start on July 23, 1942 (seven hundred thousand Jews murdered there by August 1943).

June 2
Start of deportation of German Jews to Theresienstadt.

June 4
Heydrich dies of his wounds.

June 10
Germans liquidate Lidice in retaliation for Heydrich's death.

June 30
Jewish schools are closed in Germany.

July 1
Jews are massacred in Minsk, Lida, and Slonim, all in Byelorussia.

July 2
Berlin Jews are sent to Theresienstadt.

July 4
Mass gassings start at Auschwitz.

July 7
Himmler grants permission for sterilization experiments at Auschwitz.

July 15
The first deportation train leaves Holland bound for Auschwitz. Major police raids occur in Paris.

July 19
Himmler orders Operation Reinhard, the mass deportation of Jews in Poland to extermination camps.

July 22
Start of the "resettlement" of the inhabitants of the Warsaw ghetto to the extermination camps at Belzec and Treblinka; by September 13, three hundred thousand Jews had been deported to Treblinka. Armed resistance takes place during liquidation of Nieswiez ghetto in western Byelorussia.

August 4
First deportations from Belgium to Auschwitz occur.

August 9
Armed resistance breaks out during the liquidation of the Mir ghetto in western Byelorussia.

August 10–22
"Resettlement" of the Lvov ghetto in Ukraine; forty thousand Jews are deported to extermination camps.

August 14
Arrest of seven thousand "stateless" Jews in unoccupied France.

August–September
Deportations occur from Zagreb, Croatia, to Auschwitz. Gassings take place near Minsk of Jews deported from Theresienstadt.

September 3
Armed resistance occurs during liquidation of Lahava ghetto in western Byelorussia.

September 9
Jews are massacred near Kislovodsk, Caucasus.

September 16
"Resettlement" of the Lodz ghetto concludes (fifty-five thousand victims).

September 23
Armed resistance occurs during the liquidation of the Tutzin ghetto in western Ukraine.

September 30
Hitler publicly repeats his forecast of the destruction of Jewry.

October 4
German concentration camps are ordered to be "free of Jews": All Jewish inmates are deported to Auschwitz.

October 18

The Ministry of Justice transfers responsibility for Jews and citizens of the eastern countries within Germany to the Gestapo.

October 22

Nazis suppress revolt at Sachsenhausen by Jews assigned for deportation to Auschwitz.

October 27

A second conference is held pertaining to sterilization.

October 29

Jews are massacred in Pinsk, Byelorussia (sixteen thousand victims).

November 25

The first deportation of Jews from Norway to Auschwitz occurs.

December 10

The first transport of Jews from Germany arrives at Auschwitz.

December 17

The Allies solemnly condemn the extermination of the Jews and promise to punish the perpetrators.

1943

January 18

The first armed resistance against deportation takes place in the Warsaw ghetto.

January 20–26

Jews from the Theresienstadt ghetto are transported to Auschwitz.

January 29

Germans order all Gypsies arrested and sent to concentration camps.

January 30

Ernst Kaltenbrunner succeeds Heydrich as head of the National Central Security Department.

February 2

German Sixth Army surrenders at Stalingrad. (This marks the turning point in the war.)

February 15

First "resettlements" occur in Bialystok ghetto in Poland; one thousand Jews are killed on the spot, ten thousand are deported to Treblinka.

February 18

Nazis arrest White Rose leaders in Munich.

February 27

Jewish armament workers are deported from Berlin to Auschwitz.

March

Jews are transported from Holland to Sobibor; from Prague, Vienna, Luxembourg, and Macedonia to Treblinka.

March 1

American Jews hold a mass rally at Madison Square Garden in New York to pressure the United States to aid European Jewry.

March 13

The ghetto in Kraków is disbanded.

March 15

Deportations occur in Salonika and Thrace.

March 22

The first new crematorium in Auschwitz-Birkenau is placed into operation.

March–May

Second "resettlement" occurs in Croatia.

April 19

The Bermuda Conference: fruitless discussions by U.S. and British delegates on deliverance of Nazi victims.

April 19–May 16

Revolt in and destruction of the Warsaw ghetto.

June 11

Himmler orders the liquidation of all Polish ghettos. By the edict of June 21, the order is expanded to the Soviet Union.

June 21–27

Liquidation of the ghetto in Lvov (twenty thousand victims).

June 25

Revolt in and destruction of the ghetto in Czestochowa, Poland.

July 1

The thirteenth order of the Reich's civil laws places Jews within Germany under police justice.

July 25–26
Benito Mussolini is arrested and the fascist government in Italy falls; Marshal Pietro Badoglio takes over and negotiates with Allies.

August 2
Revolts occur in Treblinka death camp and the Krikov labor camp in the Lublin district.

August 16–23
Revolt in and destruction of the ghetto in Bialystok.

September 11
German raids start against Jews in Nice, France.

September 11–14
Ghettos in Minsk and Lida are liquidated.

September 11–18
Families are transported from Theresienstadt to Auschwitz.

September 23
The Vilna ghetto is liquidated.

September 25
Smolensk is recaptured by Soviet troops. All ghettos in Byelorussia are liquidated.

October 2
An order calls for the expulsion of Danish Jews; due to the rescue operations by the Danish underground, some 7,000 Jews were evacuated to Sweden. Only 475 were captured by the Germans.

October 13
Italy declares war on Germany.

October 14
A revolt occurs in Sobibor.

October 18
The first transport of Jews from Rome to Auschwitz occurs.

October 20
UN War Crimes Commission is established.

November 3
The Riga Ghetto is liquidated. The remaining Jews in Majdanek are murdered (seventeen thousand victims).

November 6
Kiev is recaptured by Soviet troops.

November 28
Roosevelt, Churchill, and Stalin meet for a conference in Tehran.

December 15–19
The first trial of German war criminals takes place in Charkow (Kharkov), Ukraine.

1944

January 24
Roosevelt creates the War Refugee Board.

March 19
Germany invades Hungary.

April 10
Rudolf Vrba and Alfred Wetzler escape from Auschwitz and carry detailed information about the death camp to the outside world.

April 14
The first transport of Jews from Athens to Auschwitz occurs.

May 15–July 8
The deportation of 438,000 Jews from Hungary to Auschwitz occurs.

June
A Red Cross delegation visits Theresienstadt.

June 4
The Allies enter Rome.

June 6
D-Day, the Allied invasion in Normandy, begins.

June 14
Rosenberg orders forty thousand Polish children ages ten through fourteen kidnapped for slave labor in the Reich.

June 23
Start of the Soviet offensive.

July
Swedish diplomat Raoul Wallenberg arrives in Budapest, Hungary, and begins to issue diplomatic papers to save Hungarian Jews.

July 20
Soviet troops liberate the concentration camp at Majdanek. A German assassination attempt on Hitler fails.

July 25
The ghetto in Kovno, Lithuania, is evacuated.

August 4
Anne Frank's family is arrested by the Gestapo in Amsterdam.

August 6
Twenty-seven thousand Jews from camps east of the Vistula River are deported to Germany.

August 23
Drancy holding camp (Paris) is liberated. Romania capitulates.

September 5
The Lodz ghetto is evacuated.

September 11
British troops arrive in Holland.

September 13
Soviet troops are on the Slovakian border.

September
All Jews in Dutch camps are transported into Germany. New deportations send Jews from Theresienstadt to Auschwitz. The last transport from France to Auschwitz occurs.

September 14
American troops are on the German border.

September 23
Jews in the concentration camp in Kluga, Estonia, are massacred. Deportations from Slovakia resume.

October 7
Escape attempts occur in Auschwitz-Birkenau.

October 15
Germany installs new puppet Hungarian government, which resumes deporting Jews.

October 18
Hitler orders the establishment of the *Volksturms* (mobilization of all men between ages sixteen and sixty).

October 23
Paris is liberated by Allied armies.

Late October
The survivors of the Plaszow (Kraków) concentration camp are transported to Auschwitz.

October 31
Approximately fourteen thousand Jews are transported from Slovakia to Auschwitz.

November
Trial of the leaders of the Majdanek extermination camp are held in Lublin.

November 2
Gassings in Auschwitz are terminated.

November 3–8
Soviet troops are near Budapest.

November 18
Eichmann deports thirty-eight thousand Jews from Budapest to Buchenwald, Ravensbrück, and other concentration camps.

November 26
Himmler orders the destruction of the crematorium at Auschwitz-Birkenau, as Nazis try to hide evidence of the death camps.

December 17
The SS murders eighty-one U.S. prisoners of war at Malmédy.

1945

January 16
Soviet troops liberate 800 Jews at Czestochowa and 870 in Lodz.

January 17
Soviet troops liberate Warsaw. Eighty thousand Jews are liberated in Budapest. Auschwitz is evacuated; the death march of prisoners begins.

January 27
Soviet troops liberate Auschwitz.

February 4
A conference takes place in Yalta, Crimea, in which the three chief Allied leaders—Franklin D. Roosevelt, Winston Churchill, and Joseph Stalin—plan the final defeat and occupation of Nazi Germany.

March 3
American troops are on the Rhine River.

March 19
Hitler orders the destruction of all German military, industrial, transportation, and communications facilities to prevent them from falling into enemy control.

April
The Allies discover stolen Nazi art and wealth hidden in salt mines.

April 6–10
Fifteen thousand Jews are evacuated from Buchenwald.

April 12
Buchenwald is liberated by American troops. President Roosevelt dies; Truman becomes president.

April 15
The Bergen-Belsen concentration camp is liberated by British troops.

April 20
American troops occupy Nuremberg.

April 23
Soviet troops are in front of Berlin.

April 23–May 4
Inmates from the Sachsenhausen (Berlin) and Ravensbrück concentration camps are evacuated. The last massacre of Jews occurs by SS guards.

April 25
American and Soviet troops meet on the Elbe River.

April 28
Mussolini is captured and hanged by Italian partisans.

April 29
American troops liberate Dachau.

April 30
Hitler commits suicide.

May 2

Berlin capitulates. Representatives of the International Red Cross take over at Theresienstadt.

May 5

Mauthausen is liberated.

May 7–9

Germany concedes to unconditional surrender, ending the war in Europe.

May 8

V-E (Victory in Europe) Day.

May 9

Hermann Göring is captured by U.S. troops.

May 23

Himmler is captured and commits suicide.

June 5

The Allies divide up Germany and Berlin and take over the government.

June 26

The UN Charter is signed in San Francisco.

August 6

The first atomic bomb is dropped on Hiroshima.

August 15

Japan surrenders, ending World War II.

October 24

The United Nations is officially born.

November 22

Nuremberg trials start. They end January 10, 1946, with twelve defendants sentenced to death, three to life imprisonment, four to various prison terms, and three acquitted.

Prominent People

Anielewicz, Mordecai (1919–1943) Major leader of the Jewish resistance in the Warsaw Ghetto; killed May 8, 1943.

Baeck, Leo (1873–1956) Rabbi, philosopher, and community leader in Berlin. In 1933, he became president of the Reich Representation of German Jews, an organization responsible to the Nazi regime concerning Jewish matters. Despite opportunities to emigrate, Baeck refused to leave Germany. In 1943, he was deported to the ghetto of Terezin (Theresienstadt), where he became a member of the Council of Elders and spiritual leader of the Jews imprisoned there. After the liberation of the ghetto he emigrated to England.

Bormann, Martin (June 17, 1900–1945?) Adolf Hitler's personal secretary. One of the most powerful men in the Third Reich because he controlled access to Hitler; known as "the Brown Eminence" and "the man in the shadows." Helped the Führer with his personal finances. Hitler viewed him as an absolute devotee, but Bormann had high ambitions and kept his rivals from having access to Hitler. He was in the bunker during Hitler's last days; he left the bunker on May 1, 1945, and is believed to have died shortly thereafter either by a Soviet shell or by suicide. He was sentenced to death in absentia by the Nuremberg tribunal. The West German government officially declared him dead in 1973.

Chamberlain, Neville (1869–1940) British prime minister, 1937–1940. He concluded the Munich Agreement in 1938 with Adolf Hitler, which he mistakenly believed would bring "peace in our time."

Churchill, Winston (1875–1965) British prime minister, 1940–1945. He succeeded Chamberlain on May 10, 1940, at the height of Hitler's conquest of Western Europe. Churchill was one of the very few Western politicians who recognized the threat that Hitler posed to Europe. He strongly opposed Chamberlain's appeasement policies.

Czerniakow, Adam (1880–1942) The head of the Warsaw Judenrat. He committed suicide on July 23, 1942, to protest the killing of Jewish children. His diary consisted of 1,009 pages in eight notebooks, from September 6, 1939, until the day of his death.

Eichmann, Adolf   (1906–1962) An SS lieutenant colonel and the head of the Jewish Section of the Gestapo. Eichmann participated in the Wannsee Conference (January 20, 1942). He was instrumental in implementing the Final Solution by organizing the transportation of Jews to death camps from all over Europe. He was arrested at the end of World War II in the American zone, but escaped, went underground, and disappeared. On May 11, 1960, members of the Israeli Secret Service uncovered his whereabouts and smuggled him from Argentina to Israel. Eichmann was tried in Jerusalem (April–December 1961), convicted, and sentenced to death. He was executed on May 31, 1962.

Eicke, Theodor   (1928–1943) Eicke joined the Nazi Party and the SA in 1928. He transferred to the SS in 1930. Appointed commandant of Dachau in 1933, Eicke later became the inspector of concentration camps. He was known for his cruel treatment of prisoners, which became the norm in concentration camps. In 1939 Eicke was given command of the Death's Head division of the Waffen-SS. He was killed on the eastern front on February 16, 1943.

Eisenhower, Dwight D.   (1890–1969) An American general and thirty-fourth president of the United States (1953–1961). In 1942 he was named U.S. commander of the European theater of operations. He commanded the American landings in North Africa, and in February 1943, he became chief of all the Allied forces in North Africa. After successfully directing the invasions of Sicily and Italy, he was called to England to become chief commander of the Allied Expeditionary Forces. He was largely responsible for the cooperation of the Allied armies in the battle for the liberation of the European continent.

Frank, Hans   (1900–1946) The governor-general of occupied Poland from 1939–1945. A member of the Nazi Party from its earliest days and Hitler's personal lawyer, he announced, "Poland will be treated like a colony; the Poles will become slaves of the Greater German Reich." By 1942 more than 85 percent of the Jews in Poland had been transported to extermination camps. Frank was tried at Nuremberg, convicted, and executed in 1946.

Frick, Wilhelm   (1877–1946) A dedicated Nazi bureaucrat who was appointed minister of the interior in 1933, a position in which he was responsible for enacting Nazi racial laws. In 1946 he was tried at Nuremberg, convicted, and executed.

Ganzenmüller, Albert   (1905–1973) The state secretary of the Reich Transportation Ministry from 1942–1945, Ganzenmüller was responsible for overseeing the German railway system during the period in which approximately 3 million Jews were transported to the death camps by rail. After the war he escaped to Argentina but returned to Germany in 1955. In

1973 Ganzenmüller was brought to trial, but he died of a heart attack during the proceedings.

Gerstein, Kurt   (1905–1945) The head of the *Waffen* SS Institute of Hygiene in Berlin. While maintaining ties with the resistance, Gerstein purchased the gas needed in Auschwitz, officially for fumigation purposes, but actually used for the killing of Jews. He passed on information about the killings to Swedish representatives and Vatican papal nuncios. Overwhelmed with remorse he hanged himself in a French jail after the war.

Glücks, Richard   (1889–1945) In 1936 Glücks became chief aide to Theodor Eicke and eventually succeeded Eicke as the inspector of concentration camps. Glücks was responsible for the construction of Auschwitz and the creation of the gas chambers. In 1942 he was made head of an SS *Wirtschafts-Verwaltunghauptamt* unit. He died in May 1945, presumably a suicide.

Goebbels, Joseph   (1897–1945) Goebbels joined the Nazi Party in 1924 and became the party's chief of propaganda in 1930. He was responsible for garnering support for the Nazis among the general population. After Hitler's rise to power in 1933, Goebbels became the minister of propaganda and public information. He controlled the media and oversaw the "Nazification" of public discourse and written materials. He supervised the publication of *Der Stürmer* and conducted the propaganda campaign against the Jews. He was responsible for the book burning of May 10, 1933. On the day following Hitler's death, Goebbels and his wife committed suicide in Hitler's bunker, after first ordering the murder of their six children, all under the age of thirteen.

Göring, Hermann   (1893–1946) An early member of the Nazi Party, Göring participated in Hitler's Beer Hall Putsch in Munich in 1923. After its failure, he went to Sweden, where he lived (for a time in a mental institution) until 1927. In 1928 he was elected to the Reichstag and became its president in 1932. When Hitler came into power in 1933, he made Göring air minister of Germany and prime minister of Prussia. He was responsible for the rearmament program and especially for the creation of the German air force. In 1939, Hitler designated him his successor. During World War II he was virtual dictator of the German economy and was responsible for the total air war waged by Germany. Convicted at Nuremberg in 1946, Göring committed suicide by taking poison just two hours before his scheduled execution.

Grynszpan, Herschel   (1921–1943) A Polish Jewish youth who immigrated to Paris. He agonized over the fate of his parents, who, in the course of a prewar roundup of Polish Jews living in Germany, were deported to the Polish frontier. On November 7, 1938, he went to the German embassy, where he shot and mortally wounded Third Secretary Ernst vom Rath. The Nazis used this incident as an excuse for the *Kristallnacht* pogrom.

Hess, Rudolf (1894–1987) The deputy and close associate of Hitler from the earliest days of the Nazi movement. On May 10, 1941, he flew alone from Augsburg and parachuted, landing in Scotland, where he was promptly arrested. The purpose of his flight has never become clear. He probably wanted to persuade the British to make peace with Hitler as soon as he attacked the Soviet Union. Hitler promptly declared him insane. Hess was tried at Nuremberg, found guilty, and sentenced to life imprisonment. He was the only prisoner in Spandau Prison until he apparently committed suicide in 1987.

Heydrich, Reinhard (1904–1942) The head of the SS Security Service (SD), a Nazi Party intelligence agency. In 1933–1934 he became head of the political police (Gestapo) and later of the criminal police (Kripo). He combined Gestapo and Kripo into the Security Police (SIPO). In 1939, Heydrich combined the SD and SIPO into the Reich Security Main Office. He organized the *Einsatzgruppen,* which systematically murdered Jews in occupied Russia during 1941–1942. In 1941 he was asked by Göring to implement a "Final Solution to the Jewish Question." During the same year he was appointed protector of Bohemia and Moravia. In January 1942 he presided over the Wannsee Conference, a meeting to coordinate the Final Solution. On May 29, 1942, he was assassinated by Czech partisans who parachuted in from England.

Himmler, Heinrich (1900–1945) As head of the SS and the secret police, Himmler had control over the vast network of Nazi concentration and extermination camps, the *Einsatzgruppen,* and the Gestapo. Himmler committed suicide in 1945, after his arrest.

Hitler, Adolf (1889–1945) The *Führer und Reichskanzler* ("Leader and Reich Chancellor"). Although born in Austria, he settled in Germany in 1913. At the outbreak of World War I, Hitler enlisted in the Bavarian army, became a corporal, and received the Iron Cross First Class for bravery. Returning to Munich after the war, he joined the newly formed German Workers' Party which was soon reorganized, under his leadership, as the National Socialist German Workers' Party (NSDAP). In November 1923, he unsuccessfully attempted to forcibly bring Germany under nationalist control. When his coup, known as the Beer Hall Putsch, failed, Hitler was arrested and sentenced to five years in prison. It was during this time that he wrote *Mein Kampf.* Serving only nine months of his sentence, Hitler quickly reentered German politics and soon outpolled his political rivals in national elections. In January 1933 President Hindenburg appointed Hitler chancellor of a coalition cabinet. Hitler, who took office on January 30, 1933, immediately set up a dictatorship. In 1934 the chancellorship and presidency were united in the person of the *Führer.* Soon all other parties were outlawed, and opposition was brutally suppressed. By 1938 Hitler implemented his dream of a Greater Germany, first annexing Austria; then (with the acquiescence of the Western democracies), the Sudetenland (Czech province with ethnic German concentration); and, finally, Czechoslovakia itself. On September 1, 1939, Hitler's armies invaded Poland. By this time the Western democracies realized that no agreement with Hitler could be honored, and World War II had begun. Although initially victorious on all fronts, Hitler's armies began suffering setbacks shortly after the United States joined the war in December 1941. Although the war was obviously lost by early 1945, Hitler insisted that Germany fight to the death. On April 30, 1945, Hitler committed suicide rather than be captured alive.

Höss, Rudolf (1900–1947) A member of the SS, Höss held various positions in Dachau under Theodor Eicke before he was assigned to Auschwitz in May 1940. He became the camp's first commandant. At Auschwitz Höss oversaw the operation that murdered more than 1 million people. At the end of the war, he adopted the name Franz Lang and escaped detection by the Allies. In March 1946, however, he was recognized and arrested. He was tried in Poland and sentenced to death. Höss was hanged in Auschwitz on April 16, 1947.

Kaltenbrunner, Ernst (1899–1946) An Austrian, Kaltenbrunner was the head of the SS in Austria from 1935–1938, when Germany formally annexed the country. After the takeover he became undersecretary of state for public security. After Reinhard Heydrich's death, Kaltenbrunner became chief of the *Sicherheitspolizei* (Security Police, Sipo) and the SD (*Sicherheitsdienst*, Security Service). He, along with Heinrich Himmler, was responsible for Aktion Reinhard. After the war, Kaltenbrunner was tried at Nuremberg and sentenced to death. He was hanged on October 16, 1946.

Korczak, Dr. Janusz (1878–1942) An educator, author, physician, and the director of a Jewish orphanage in Warsaw. Despite the possibility of personal freedom, he refused to abandon his orphans and went with them to the gas chamber in Treblinka.

Krupp A German family firm that manufactured armaments for the Nazis. Krupp extensively used slave labor in its factories and operated a facility at Auschwitz.

Mengele, Josef (1911–1978?) An SS physician at Auschwitz, notorious for pseudomedical experiments, especially on twins and Gypsies. He selected new arrivals by simply pointing to the right or to the left, thus separating those considered able to work from those who were not. Those too weak or too old to work were sent straight to the gas chambers, after all of their possessions, including their clothes, were taken for resale in Germany. After the war he spent some time in a British internment hospital but disappeared, went underground, escaped to Argentina, and later to Paraguay, where he be-

530 THE COMPLETE HISTORY OF THE HOLOCAUST

came a citizen in 1959. He was hunted by Interpol, Israeli agents, and Simon Wiesenthal. In 1986 his body was found in Embu, Brazil.

Rath, Ernst vom (1909–1938) The third secretary at the German embassy in Paris who was assassinated on November 7, 1938, by Herschel Grynszpan.

Ringelblum, Emanuel (1900–1944) A famed historian and public leader, best known for his clandestine archive called the Oneg Shabbat, hidden in milk cans in the Warsaw ghetto.

Sauckel, Fritz (1894–1946) Sauckel joined the Nazi Party in 1921 and held senior honorary ranking in both the SA and the SS before World War II. In 1942 he was appointed plenipotentiary-general for labor mobilization and oversaw the seizure of millions of workers for the armaments and munitions production program. His harsh treatment of slave laborers caused the deaths of thousands of Jews in Poland. Sauckel was tried and convicted of his crimes at Nuremberg and was hanged on October 16, 1946.

Sennesh, Hannah (1921–1944) A Palestinian Jew of Hungarian descent who fought as a partisan against the Nazis. She was captured at the close of the war and was assassinated in Budapest by the Nazis.

Speer, Albert (1905–1981) Hitler's architect and the German minister of armaments from 1942–1945. Speer was appointed minister of armaments after Fritz Todt was killed in 1942. In this position, Speer dramatically increased armaments production through the use of millions of slave laborers. After the war Speer was tried at Nuremberg, found guilty of war crimes and crimes against humanity, and sentenced to twenty years in prison. At his trial Speer admitted his guilt and took responsibility for the actions of the Nazi regime.

Wallenberg, Raoul (1912–19??) A Swedish diplomat who, in 1944, went to Hungary on a mission to save as many Jews as possible by handing out Swedish papers, passports, and visas. He is credited with saving the lives of at least thirty thousand people. After the liberation of Budapest, he was mysteriously taken into custody by the Russians and his fate remains unknown.

Wiesel, Elie (1928–) A survivor of Auschwitz and Buchenwald, Wiesel won the Nobel Peace Prize in 1986. Starting with his first novel *Night,* his writings have inspired the world to understand the plight of the victims of the Holocaust.

Wiesenthal, Simon (1908–) A famed Holocaust survivor who has dedicated his life since the war to gathering evidence for the prosecution of Nazi war criminals.

Bibliography

Books and Articles

Robert H. Abzug, *Inside the Vicious Heart: Americans and the Liberation of the Nazi Concentration Camps*. New York: Oxford University Press, 1987.

American Jewish Historical Society, *When the Rabbis Marched on Washington*. Waltham, MA: American Jewish Historical Society, 1999.

Yitzhak Arad, "Operation Reinhard," *Yad Vashem Studies,* vol. 16, 1984.

Mitchell G. Bard, "Holocaust Museum Gives Portrait of World Gone Awry," *Women's World*, Spring 1993.

Mary Berg, *Warsaw Ghetto*. New York: L.B. Fischer, 1945.

Harry James Cargas, *When God and Man Failed*. New York: Macmillan, 1981.

Richard Chesnoff, *Pack of Thieves: How Hitler and Europe Plundered the Jews and Committed the Greatest Theft in History*. New York: Doubleday, 1999.

Maria Júlia Cirurgião and Michael D. Hull, "Aristides de Sousa Mendes: Angel Against the Blitzkrieg," *Lay Witness*, October 1998.

David Cornwell, *Hitler's Pope: The Secret History of Pope Pius XII*. New York: Viking, 1999.

Ruth Elias, *Triumph of Hope*. New York: John Wiley & Sons, 1998.

Stuart Erdheim, "Could the Allies Have Bombed Auschwitz-Birkenau?" *Holocaust and Genocide Studies*, vol. 11, no. 2, Fall 1997.

Benjamin Ferencz, *Less than Slaves*. Cambridge, MA: Harvard University Press, 1979.

Jack Fishman, *Long Knives and Short Memories*. New York: Richardson & Steirman, 1987.

Varian Fry, *Surrender on Demand*. Boulder, CO: Johnson Books, 1997.

Kitty Hart, *Return to Auschwitz*. New York: Atheneum Books, 1982.

William Helmreich, *Against All Odds: Holocaust Survivors and the Successful Lives They Made in America*. New York: Simon & Schuster, 1992.

Robert Edwin Herzstein, *Roosevelt and Hitler*. New York: Paragon House, 1989.

Eva Hoffman, *Shtetl*. Boston: Houghton Mifflin, 1997.

Marion Kaplan, *Between Dignity and Despair: Jewish Life in Germany*. New York: Oxford University Press, 1998.

Gerd Korman, ed., *Hunter and Hunted: Human History of the Holocaust*. New York: Viking, 1973.

Ota Kraus and Erich Kulka, *The Death Factory*. London: Pergamon, 1966.

Lawrence Langer, ed., *Art from the Ashes*. New York: Oxford University Press, 1995.

Primo Levi, *Survival in Auschwitz and the Reawakening*. New York: Summit Books, 1965.

Alan Levy, *The Wiesenthal File*. Grand Rapids, MI: William B. Eerdmans, 1993.

Guenter Lewy and John Snoek, "The Christian Churches," in *Holocaust*. Jerusalem: Keter, 1974.

Jane Marks, *The Hidden Children*. New York: Fawcett Books, 1995.

Arno Mayer, *Why Did the Heavens Darken?* Buffalo, NY: Pantheon Books, 1988.

Ernest Michel, *Promises to Keep*. New York: Barricade Books, 1993.

Peter Novick, *The Holocaust in American Life*. New York: Houghton Mifflin, 1999.

Carol Rittner and John Roth, eds., *Different Voices—Women and the Holocaust*. New York: Paragon House, 1993.

Richard Rubenstein and John Roth, *Approaches to Auschwitz: The Holocaust and Its Legacy*. Atlanta: John Knox, 1987.

Tom Segev, *Soldiers of Evil*. New York: McGraw-Hill, 1987.

Eric Silver, *The Book of the Just*. New York: Grove, 1992.

Jean-Francois Steiner, *Treblinka*. New York: Simon & Schuster, 1967.

John Toland, *Adolf Hitler*. New York: Anchor Books, 1976.

Isaiah Trunk, *Jewish Responses to Nazi Persecution*. New York: Stein and Day, 1979.

Elie Wiesel, *Night*. New York: Bantam Books, 1960.

Simon Wiesenthal, *The Sunflower*. New York: Schocken Books, 1998.

Mark Wyman, *DP—Europe's Displaced Persons, 1945–1951*. London: Associated University Presses, 1989.

Shalom Yoran, *The Defiant*. New York: St. Martin's, 1996.

Susan Zuccotti, *The Holocaust, the French, and the Jews*. New York: BasicBooks, 1993.

Internet Sources

Per Anger website, "The History of a Swedish Hero." www.raoul-wallenberg.com/per-anger/history.html.

Ben S. Austin, "An Introduction to the Holocaust," Holocaust/Shoah Page. www.mtsu.edu/~baustin/holo.html.

Yale Edeiken, "An Introduction to the Einsatzgruppen." www.pgonline.com/electriczen/index.html.

Ron Greene, "Visas for Life: The Remarkable Story of Chiune and Yukiko Sugihara." www.hooked.net/users/rgreene/Sug.html.

Gary M. Grobman, "Resisters, Rescuers, and Bystanders," *The Holocaust—A Guide for Teachers,* 1990. www.remember.org/guide/wit.root.wit.res.html.

Harry Herder Jr., "The Liberation of Buchenwald: The Forgotten Camps." http://www2.3dresearch.com/~June/Vincent/Camps/CampsEngl.html.

Jacob G. Hornberger, "The White Rose," Future of Freedom Foundation. www.execpc.com/~jfish/fff/.

Albert J. Kosiek, "Liberation of Mauthausen," KZ Mauthausen-Gusen Info-Page. http://linz.orf.at/orf/gusen/kosiek1x.htm.

Ruediger Lautmann, "Gay Prisoners in Concentration Camps as Compared with Jehovah's Witnesses and Political Prisoners," Nizkor Project. www.nizkor.org/ftp-cgi/micellany/homosexuals/homosexual.002.

Jennifer Rosenberg, "The Tragedy of the S.S. *St. Louis,*" About.com. http://history1900s.about.com-education/history1900s/library/holocaust/aa103197.htm.

William Shapiro, "A Medic Recalls the Horrors of Berga," Jewish Student Online Research Center. www.us-israel.org/jsource/Holocaust/Shapiro.html.

Southern Institute for Education and Research at Tulane University, "Schindler's List Teaching Guide." www.tulane.edu/~so-inst/slindex.html.

James Steakley, "Homosexuals and the Third Reich," *Body Politic*, January/February 1974. www.fordham.edu/halsall/pwh/.

U.S. Holocaust Memorial Museum, "Children and the Holocaust." www.ushmm.org/education/children.html.

———, "The Nazi Olympics." www.ushmm.org/olympics.zch002.htm.

Robert S. Wistrich, *Who's Who in Nazi Germany*. www.routledge.com/routledge/who/germany/hitler.html.

Yad Vashem, "The 'Righteous Among the Nations' Program." www.yad-vashem.org.il/righteous/index.html.

Holocaust-Related Websites

About.com Guide to the Holocaust (http://holocaust.about.com/). Contains many original articles related to the Holocaust, news about current events, and links to other sites.

American-Israeli Cooperative Enterprise (www.us-israel.org/). One of the most extensive collections of documents, articles, and photographs on the Holocaust.

The Anne Frank House (www.annefrank.nl/). This is the official website for the museum in the house where Anne Frank was hidden.

Auschwitz—Gate to Hell (http://home8.inet.tele.dk/aaaa/Auschwitz.htm). Offers a good collection of photos and brief descriptions of events during the Holocaust.

The Avalon Project (www.yale.edu/lawweb/avalon/avalon.htm). This Yale University project has a collection of World War II and Holocaust-related documents, including transcripts from the war crimes trials.

C.A.N.D.L.E.S. Holocaust Museum (www.candles-museum.com/frmain01.htm). Provides information about survivors—especially twins—lesson plans, and general information on the Holocaust.

Cybrary of the Holocaust (http://remember.org/). One of the best collections of materials and links on all aspects of the Holocaust.

The Einsatzgruppen (www.pgonline.com/electriczen/einsatz.html). A site devoted to material related to the Nazi mobile killing squads.

The Forgotten Camps (http://www2.3dresearch.com/~June/Vincent/Camps/CampsEngl.html). Contains detailed information on some of the lesser-known concentration camps.

Forgotten Victims: The Abandonment of Americans in Hitler's Camps (http://members.aol.com/bardbooks/ index.htm). A site with a syn-

534

opsis of study on what happened to American civilians and prisoners of war captured during World War II.

Hell of Sobibor (http://home.wirehub.nl/~mkersten/shoa/sobibor.html). A site devoted to telling the story of one of the Nazi death camps, which also was the scene of the most dramatic escape.

The History Place (www.historyplace.com/index.html). An excellent collection of materials on all aspects of the Holocaust.

Holocaust Educational Digest (http://idt.net/~kimel19/digest.html). Offers an excellent series of articles prepared by a survivor on all aspects of the Holocaust.

The Holocaust History Project (www.holocaust-history.org/). An archive of documents, photographs, recordings, and essays regarding the Holocaust, including direct refutation of Holocaust-denial.

Holocaust Memorial Center (www.holocaustcenter.com). A museum in Michigan that maintains a website with a good overview of the Holocaust and a chronology of events.

Holocaust Pictures Exhibition (www.fmv.ulg.ac.be/schmitz/holocaust. html). A collection of digitized Holocaust photographs.

The Holocaust\Shoah Page (www.mtsu.edu/~baustin/holo.html). An excellent collection of essays and documents on virtually every aspect of the Holocaust.

Internet Modern History Sourcebook (www.fordham.edu/halsall/mod/ modsbook.html). A good collection of links to documents and articles on the Holocaust.

Jewish Student Online Research Center (www.us-israel.org/jsource/). A comprehensive encyclopedia of Jewish history and culture that includes an extensive collection of Holocaust material.

KZ Mauthausen-GUSEN Info-Pages (http://linz.orf.at/orf/gusen/ index.htm). A collection of material related to the Mauthausen death camp and its subcamps.

March of the Living (www.bonder.com/march.html). A site that organizes an annual student trip to Israel and Eastern Europe.

Moreshet Mordechai Anielevich Memorial (www.inter.net.il/~givat_h/ givat/moreshet/moreshet.htm). A museum website devoted to the leader of the Warsaw Ghetto Uprising.

The Nizkor Project (www.nizkor.org). One of the largest collections of Holocaust documents, specializing in material aimed at debunking Holocaust deniers.

Raoul Wallenberg Website (www.raoul-wallenberg.com/). A site dedicated to telling the story of the Swedish diplomat who rescued thousands of Jews in Hungary before being arrested by the Soviets.

Schindler's List Teaching Guide (www.tulane.edu/~so-inst/slguide. html). An excellent website covering the story of Oskar Schindler, the rescuer featured in the movie *Schindler's List*.

Shamash (http://shamash.org/trb/judaism.html). An excellent collection of materials on a broad variety of topics related to Jewish history, Judaism, and the Holocaust.

The Simon Wiesenthal Center (www.wiesenthal.com). This site, named after the famed Nazi hunter, has an extensive collection of Holocaust material and entries from the *Encyclopedia of the Holocaust*. One of the best sources of information on all aspects of the Holocaust.

A Teacher's Guide to the Holocaust (http://fcit.coedu.usf.edu/holocaust/ default.htm). A comprehensive overview of the Holocaust with photos, maps, and links to other related sites.

United States Holocaust Memorial Museum (www.ushmm.org/). One of the best sources of Holocaust information. The site has a growing number of on-line exhibits and provides access to many of the museum's photographs.

Women and the Holocaust (www.interlog.com/~mighty/). A collection of articles related to women in the Holocaust.

Yad Vashem (www.yad-vashem.org.il/). Israel's Holocaust museum has a number of on-line exhibitions and document collections. One of the best sources of information on the Holocaust.

For Further Reading

Lucie Adelsberger, *Auschwitz: A Doctor's Story.* Boston: Northeastern University Press, 1995.

Alan Adelson and Robert Lapides, eds., *Lodz Ghetto: Inside a Community Under Siege.* New York: Penguin, 1991.

David A. Adler, *The Number on My Grandfather's Arm.* New York: Union of American Hebrew Congregations, 1987.

———, *We Remember the Holocaust.* New York: H. Holt, 1995.

Stanislav Adler, *In the Warsaw Ghetto.* Jerusalem: Yad Vashem, 1982.

H. Agar, *The Saving Remnant: An Account of Jewish Survival.* New York: Viking, 1960.

Zvi Aharoni et al., *Operation Eichmann: The Truth About the Pursuit, Capture, and Trial.* New York: John Wiley & Sons, 1997.

William Sheridan Allen, *The Nazi Seizure of Power: The Experience of a Single German Town, 1922–1945.* New York: Franklin Watts, 1984.

Stephen Ambrose, *Band of Brothers: E Company, 506th Regiment, 101st Airborne from Normandy to Hitler's Eagle's Nest.* New York: Touchstone Books, 1993.

———, *Citizen Soldiers: The U.S. Army from the Normandy Beaches to the Bulge to the Surrender of Germany, June 7, 1944, to May 7, 1945.* New York: Touchstone Books, 1998.

———, *D-Day June 6, 1944: The Climactic Battle of World War II.* New York: Simon & Schuster, 1995.

Per Anger, *With Raoul Wallenberg in Budapest: Memories of the War Years in Hungary.* New York: Holocaust Library, 1996.

Yitzhak Arad, *Belzec, Sobibor, Treblinka: The Operation Reinhard Death Camps.* Bloomington: Indiana University Press, 1987.

———, ed., *The Pictoral History of the Holocaust.* New York: Macmillan, 1991.

Yitzhak Arad, Shmuel Krakowski, and Shmuel Spector, eds., *The Einsatzgruppen Reports.* Washington, DC: U.S. Holocaust Memorial Museum Shop Memorial Council, 1990.

Hannah Arendt, *Eichmann in Jerusalem: A Report on the Banality of Evil.* 1965. Reprint, New York: Penguin, 1994.

Elliot Arnold, *A Night of Watching.* New York: Scribner, 1967.

Eugene Aroneanu, *Inside the Concentration Camps: Eyewitness Accounts of Life in Hitler's Death Camps.* Westport, CT: Praeger, 1996.

Linda Atkinson, *In Kindling Flame: The Story of Hannah Senesh, 1921–1944.* New York: Beech Tree Books, 1992.

Mitchell G. Bard, *The Complete Idiot's Guide to World War II.* New York: Macmillan, 1998.

———, *Forgotten Victims: The Abandonment of Americans in Hitler's Camps.* Boulder, CO: Westview, 1994.

Jorgen H. Barfod, *The Holocaust Failed in Denmark.* Copenhagen: Frihedsmuseets Venners, 1985.

A.J. Barker, *Behind Barbed Wire.* London: B.T. Batsford, 1974.

J.H. Barrington, *The Zyklon B Trial: Trial of Bruno Tesch and Two Others.* London: n.p., 1948.

Omer Bartov, *Murder in Our Midst: The Holocaust, Industrial Killing, and Representa-*

tion. New York: Oxford University Press, 1996.

Yehuda Bauer, *American Jewry and the Holocaust: The American Jewish Joint Distribution Committee, 1939–1945*. Detroit: Wayne State University Press, 1981.

———, *A History of the Holocaust*. New York: Franklin Watts, 1982.

———, *Jewish Reactions to the Holocaust*. Woodstock, NY: Jewish Lights, 1997.

———, *Jews for Sale? Nazi-Jewish Negotiations, 1933–1945*. New Haven, CT: Yale University Press, 1994.

———, *My Brother's Keeper: A History of the American Jewish Joint Distribution Committee, 1929–1939*. Philadelphia: Jewish Publication Society of America, 1974.

———, *They Chose Life: Jewish Resistance in the Holocaust*. New York: American Jewish Committee, Institute of Human Relations, 1973.

Judith Taylor Baumel, *Unfulfilled Promise: Rescue and Resettlement of Jewish Refugee Children in the United States, 1934–1945*. Juneau, AK: Denali, 1990.

Arieh L. Bauminger, *The Righteous Among the Nations*. New York: Gefen Books, 1996.

Michael Berenbaum, *The World Must Know: The History of the Holocaust as Told in the United States Holocaust Memorial Museum*. Boston: Little, Brown, 1993.

———, ed., *A Mosaic of Victims: Non-Jews Persecuted and Murdered by the Nazis*. New York: New York University Press, 1992.

———, ed., *Witness to the Holocaust*. New York: HarperCollins, 1997.

Michael Berenbaum and Abraham J. Peck, eds., *The Holocaust and History: The Known, the Unknown, the Disputed, and the Reexamined*. Bloomington: Indiana University Press, 1998.

Doris L. Bergen, *Twisted Cross: The German Christian Movement in the Third Reich*. Chapel Hill: University of North Carolina Press, 1996.

Israel Bernbaum, *My Brother's Keeper: The Holocaust Through the Eyes of an Artist*. New York: G.P. Putnam's Sons, 1985.

John Bierman, *Righteous Gentile: The Story of Raoul Wallenberg, Missing Hero of the Holocaust*. New York: Penguin, 1996.

Edwin Black, *The Transfer Agreement: The Dramatic Story of the Pact Between the Third Reich and Jewish Palestine*. New York: Dialog, 1999.

Joseph Borkin, *The Crime and Punishment of I.G. Farben*. New York: Free, 1979.

Elinor J. Brecher, *Schindler's Legacy: True Stories of the List Survivors*. New York: Plume/Penguin, 1994.

Richard Breitman, *The Architect of Genocide: Himmler and the Final Solution*. Hanover, NH: University Press of New England, 1992.

———, *Official Secrets: What the Nazis Planned, What the British and Americans Knew*. New York: Hill & Wang, 1998.

Richard Breitman and Allen Kraut, *American Refugee Policy and European Jewry, 1933–1945*. Bloomington: Indiana University Press, 1987.

Christopher Browning, *Ordinary Men: Reserve Police Battalion 101 and the Final Solution in Poland*. New York: HarperCollins, 1992.

———, *The Path to Genocide: Essays on Launching the Final Solution*. Cambridge: Cambridge University Press, 1995.

Alan Bullock, *Hitler, a Study in Tyranny*. New York: HarperCollins, 1994.

Central Commission for Investigation of German Crimes in Poland. New York: Howard Fertig, 1982.

Miriam Chaikin, *A Nightmare in History: The Holocaust, 1933–1945*. New York: Clarion Books, 1992.

Brewster Chamberlin and Marsha Feldman, eds., *The Liberation of the Nazi Concentra-*

tion Camps, 1945: Eyewitness Accounts of the Liberators. Washington, DC: U.S. Holocaust Memorial Council, 1987.

Richard Chesnoff, *Pack of Thieves: How Hitler and Europe Plundered the Jews and Committed the Greatest Theft in History*. New York: Doubleday, 1999.

Robert E. Conot, *Justice at Nuremberg*. New York: Harper & Row, 1983.

John Cornwell, *Hitler's Pope: The Secret History of Pius XII*. New York: Viking, 1999.

Lucy S. Dawidowicz, *A Holocaust Reader*. New York: Behrman, 1976.

———, *The War Against the Jews, 1933–1945*. New York: Bantam Doubleday Dell, 1991.

Leonard Dinnerstein, *America and the Survivors of the Holocaust*. New York: Columbia University Press, 1982.

Michael N. Dobkowski, ed., *The Politics of Indifference: A Documentary History of Holocaust Victims in America*. Washington, DC: University Press of America, 1982.

Deborah Dwork and Robert Jan Van Pelt, *Auschwitz: 1270 to the Present*. New York: W.W. Norton, 1996.

Abraham Edelheit and Hershel Edelheit, *History of the Holocaust: A Handbook and Dictionary*. Boulder, CO: Westview, 1995.

Dwight D. Eisenhower, *Crusade in Europe*. Baltimore: Johns Hopkins University Press, 1997.

Jack Eisner, *The Survivor*. New York: William Morrow, 1980.

Yaffa Eliach and Brana Gurewitsch, eds., *The Liberators: Eyewitness Accounts of the Liberation of Concentration Camps*. Vol. 1. *Liberation Day: Oral History Testimonies of American Liberators from the Archives of the Center for Holocaust Studies*. Brooklyn, NY: Center for Holocaust Studies Documentation and Research, 1981.

Konnilyn Feig, *Hitler's Death Camps: The Sanity of Madness*. New York: Holmes & Meier, 1981.

Helen Fein, *Accounting for Genocide: National Responses and Jewish Victimization During the Holocaust*. New York: Free, 1979.

Henry Feingold, *Bearing Witness: How America and Its Jews Responded to the Holocaust*. Syracuse, NY: Syracuse University Press, 1995.

———, *The Politics of Rescue: The Roosevelt Administration and the Holocaust, 1938–1945*. New Brunswick, NJ: Rutgers University Press, 1970.

Fania Fenelon, *Playing for Time*. Syracuse, NY: Syracuse University Press, 1997.

David Foy, *For You the War Is Over*. New York: Stein and Day, 1984.

Anne Frank, *Anne Frank: Diary of a Young Girl*. New York: Bantam Books, 1993.

Henry Friedlander, *The Origins of Nazi Genocide: From Euthanasia to the Final Solution*. Chapel Hill: University of North Carolina Press, 1995.

Saul Friedlander, *Nazi Germany and the Jews*. Vol. 1. *The Years of Persecution, 1933–1939*. New York: HarperCollins, 1997.

Philip Friedman, ed., *Martyrs and Fighters*. New York: Praeger, 1954.

———, *Roads to Extinction: Essays on the Holocaust*. Philadelphia: Jewish Publication Society, 1980.

Saul S. Friedman, *No Haven for the Oppressed: United States Policy Toward Jewish Refugees, 1938–1945*. Detroit: Wayne State University Press, 1973.

Arnold Geier and T.G. Friedman, *Heroes of the Holocaust*. New York: Berkley Books, 1998.

Haim Genizi, *American Apathy: The Plight of Christian Refugees from Nazism*. Ramat-Gan, Israel: Bar-Ilan University Press, 1983.

Miep Gies with Alison Gold, *Anne Frank Remembered: The Story of the Woman Who Helped to Hide the Frank Family*. New York: Simon & Schuster, 1988.

Martin Gilbert, *Atlas of the Holocaust*. New

York: William Morrow, 1993.

———, *Auschwitz and the Allies*. New York: Holt, Rinehart & Winston, 1981.

———, *The Boys: The Untold Story of 732 Young Concentration Camp Survivors*. New York: Henry Holt, 1997.

———, *The Day the War Ended: May 8, 1945: Victory in Europe*. New York: Holt, 1996.

———, *The Holocaust: A History of the Jews of Europe During the Second World War*. New York: Henry Holt, 1987.

———, *Holocaust Journey: Travelling in Search of the Past*. New York: Columbia University Press, 1997.

———, *Holocaust Maps and Photographs*. New York: Anti-Defamation League, 1992.

———, *The Second World War: A Complete History*. New York: Henry Holt, 1992.

Leo Goldberger, ed., *The Rescue of the Danish Jews: Moral Courage Under Stress*. New York: New York University Press, 1987.

Daniel Jonah Goldhagen, *Hitler's Willing Executioners: Ordinary Germans and the Holocaust*. New York: Alfred A. Knopf, 1996.

Howard Greenfeld, *The Hidden Children*. New York: Houghton Mifflin, 1997.

Alex Grobman and Daniel Landes, eds., *Genocide, Critical Issues of the Holocaust: A Companion to the Film, "Genocide."* New York: Rossel Books, 1982.

Leonard Gross, *The Last Jews of Berlin*. New York: Simon & Schuster, 1988.

Nerin E. Gun, *The Day of the Americans*. New York: Fleet, 1966.

Israel Gutman, *Resistance: The Warsaw Ghetto Uprising*. Boston: Houghton Mifflin, 1994.

———, ed., *Encyclopedia of the Holocaust*. 4 vols. New York: Macmillan, 1995.

David Hackett, trans., *The Buchenwald Report*. Boulder, CO: Westview, 1997.

Jorgen Haestrup, *Passage to Palestine: Young Jews in Denmark, 1932–1945*. Odense, Denmark: Odense University Press, 1984.

———, *The Secret Alliance: A Study of the Danish Resistance Movement, 1940–1945*. 3 vols. New York: New York University Press, 1985.

Philip Hallie, *Lest Innocent Blood Be Shed: The Story of the Village of Le Chambon and How Goodness Happened There*. New York: HarperPerennial Library, 1994.

Richard Hamilton, *Who Voted for Hitler?* Princeton, NJ: Princeton University Press, 1982.

Leslie H. Hardman, *The Survivors: The Story of the Belsen Remnant*. London: Valentine, Mitchell, 1958.

Isser Harel, *The House on Garibaldi Street*. New York: Frank Cass, 1997.

Max Hastings, *Victory in Europe: D-Day to V-E Day*. Boston: Little, Brown, 1992.

Gideon Hausner, *Justice in Jerusalem*. New York: Schocken, 1978.

Robert Headland, *Messages of Murder: A Study of the Reports of the Einsatzgruppen of the Security Police and the Security Service, 1941–1943*. Rutherford, NJ: Fairleigh Dickinson University Press. 1992.

Eugene Heimler, *Night of the Mist*. New York: Gefen Books, 1997.

Ernst C. Helmreich, *The German Churches Under Hitler: Background, Struggle, and Epilogue*. Detroit: Wayne State University Press, 1979.

Ivo Herzer, *The Italian Refuge: Rescue of Jews During the Holocaust*. Washington, DC: Catholic University Press, 1989.

Raul Hilberg, *Commandant of Auschwitz*. London: Weidenfeld and Nicholson, 1959.

———, *The Destruction of the European Jews*. New York: Holmes & Meier, 1985.

———, *Perpetrators, Victims, Bystanders: The Jewish Catastrophe, 1933–1945*. New York: HarperPerennial Library, 1993.

———, *The Politics of Memory: The Journey of a Holocaust Historian*. Chicago: Ivan R. Dee, 1996.

Peter Hoffman, *The History of the German Resistance: 1933–1945*. Montreal: McGill Queens University Press, 1996.

Rudolf Höss, *Death Dealer: The Memoirs of the SS Kommandant at Auschwitz*. Buffalo, NY: Prometheus Books, 1992.

Douglas D. Huneke, *The Moses of Rovno: The Stirring Story of Fritz Graeve*. New York: Dodd Mead, 1985.

International Military Tribunal, *Trial of the Major War Criminals*. Nuremberg: William S. Heine, 1947.

Kazimierz Iranek-Osmecki, *He Who Saves One Life*. New York: Crown, 1971.

Clara Isaacman, *Clara's Story*. Philadelphia: Jewish Publication Society, 1984.

Benjamin Jacobs, *The Dentist of Auschwitz: A Memoir*. Lexington: University Press of Kentucky, 1994.

Inge Jens, ed., *At the Heart of the White Rose: Letters and Diaries of Hans and Sophie Scholl*. New York: Harper & Row, 1987.

Michael Kater, *The Nazi Party: A Social Profile of Members and Leaders, 1919–1945*. Cambridge, MA: Harvard University Press, 1983.

Jacob Katz, *Out of the Ghetto: The Social Background of Jewish Emancipation*. New York: Schocken Books, 1978.

I. Kaufman, *American Jews in World War II*. New York: Dial, 1947.

Thomas Keneally, *Schindler's List*. New York: Simon & Schuster, 1994.

Ian Kershaw, *The Nazi Dictatorship: Problems and Perspectives of Interpretation*. 2nd ed. London and New York: E. Arnold, 1993.

Robert Kirschner, *Rabbinic Responsa of the Holocaust Era*. New York: Schocken Books, 1985.

Ernst Klee, Willi Dressen, and Volker Riess, *The Good Old Days: The Holocaust as Seen by Its Perpetrators and Bystanders*. New York: Free, 1992.

Eugen Kogon, *The Theory and Practice of Hell: The German Concentration Camps and the System Behimd Them*. Trans. Heinz Norden. 1950, Reprint, New York: Berkley, 1980.

Eugen Kogon, Hermann Langbein, and Adalbert Ruckerl, eds., *Nazi Mass Murder: A Documentary History of the Use of Poison Gas*. New Haven, CT: Yale University Press, 1994.

Claudia Koonz, *Mothers in the Fatherland: Women, the Family, and Nazi Politics*. New York: St. Martin's, 1988.

Isaac Kowalski, ed., *Anthology on Armed Jewish Resistance, 1939–1945*. Vol. 1. New York: Jewish Combatants, 1984.

George M. Kren and Leon H. Rappoport, *The Holocaust and the Crisis of Human Behavior*. New York: Holmes & Meier, 1994.

Julian E. Kulski, *Dying We Live: The Personal Chronicle of a Young Freedom Fighter, Warsaw, 1939–1945*. New York: Holt, Rinehart & Winston, 1979.

Lucette Matalon Lagnado and Sheila Cohn Dekel, *Children of the Flames: Dr. Josef Mengele and the Untold Story of the Twins of Auschwitz*. New York: Penguin, 1992.

David Lampe, *The Danish Resistance*. New York: Ballantine, 1960.

Jochen von Lang, ed., *Eichmann Interrogated: Transcripts from the Archives of the Israeli Police*. New York: Farrar, Straus, & Giroux, 1983.

Claude Lanzmann, *Shoah: The Complete Text of the Acclaimed Holocaust Film*. New York: Pantheon Books, 1985.

Walter Laquer, *The Terrible Secret: Suppression of the Truth About Hitler's Final Solution*. New York: Viking, 1982.

Vera Laska, ed., *Women in the Resistance and in the Holocaust: The Voices of Eyewitnesses*. Westport, CT: Greenwood, 1983.

Lucien Lazare, *Rescue as Resistance: How Jewish Organizations Fought the Holocaust in France*. New York: Columbia University Press, 1996.

F. Le Boucher, *The Incredible Mission of Father Benoit*. New York: Doubleday, 1969.

Evelyn Le Chene, *Mauthausen*. London: Methuen, 1971.

Olga Lengyel, *Five Chimneys: A Woman's True Story of Auschwitz*. Chicago: Academy Chicago, 1995.

Elenore Lester, *Wallenberg:The Man in the Iron Web*. Englewood Cliffs, NJ: Prentice-Hall, 1984.

Primo Levi, *The Drowned and the Saved*. New York: Vintage Books, 1989.

———, *Survival in Auschwitz: The Nazi Assault on Humanity*. New York: Collier Books, 1995.

Nora Levin, *The Holocaust: The Destruction of European Jewry, 1933–1945*. New York: Schocken Books, 1973.

Hillel Levine, *In Search of Sugihara: The Elusive Japanese Diplomat Who Risked His Life to Rescue 10,000 Jews from the Holocaust*. New York: Free, 1996.

Guenter Lewy, *The Catholic Church and Nazi Germany*. New York: McGraw-Hill, 1964.

Betty Jean Lifton, *The King of the Children: A Biography of Janusz Korczak*. New York: St. Martin's, 1997.

Robert J. Lifton, *The Nazi Doctors: Medical Killings and the Psychology of Genocide*. New York: Basic Books, 1986.

Deborah E. Lipstadt, *Beyond Belief: The American Press and the Coming of the Holocaust, 1933–1945*. New York: Free, 1986.

———, *Denying the Holocaust: The Growing Assault on Truth and Memory*. New York: Free, 1993.

John Loftus and Mark Aarons, *The Secret War Against the Jews: How Western Espionage Betrayed the Jewish People*. New York: St. Martin's, 1997.

Haskel Lookstein, *Were We Our Brothers' Keepers? The Public Response of American Jews to the Holocaust, 1938–1944*. New York: Hartmore House, 1985.

Charles S. Maier, *The Unmasterable Past: History, Holocaust, and German National Identity*. Cambridge, MA: Harvard University Press, 1997.

Ber Mark, *Uprising in the Warsaw Ghetto*. New York: Schocken Books, 1975.

Michael R. Marrus, *The Holocaust in History*. Hanover, NH: University Press of New England, 1987.

———, *Vichy France and the Jews*. Palo Alto, CA: Stanford University Press, 1995.

Robert Marshall, *In the Sewers of Lvov*. New York: Charles Scribner's Sons, 1990.

Rafael Medoff, *The Deafening Silence: American Jewish Leaders and the Holocaust*. New York: Caroll, 1986.

Vladka Meed, *On Both Sides of the Wall*. New York: Holocaust Library, 1979.

Lili Meier, ed., *Auschwitz Album: A Book Based upon an Album Discovered by a Concentration Camp Survivor*. New York: Random House, 1981.

Milton Meltzer, *Never to Forget: The Jews of the Holocaust*. New York: HarperCollins, 1991.

———, *Rescue: The Story of How Gentiles Saved Jews in the Holocaust*. New York: HarperCollins, 1991.

John Mendelsohn, *Relief and Rescue of Jews from Nazi Oppression, 1943–1945*. New York: Garland, 1982.

———, *Rescue to Switzerland: The Musy and Saly Mayer Affairs*. New York: Garland, 1982.

Judith Miller, *One by One by One: Facing the Holocaust*. New York: Simon & Schuster, 1990.

Alan S. Milward, *The German Economy at War*. London: Athlone, 1965.

Arthur D. Morse, *While Six Million Died: A Chronicle of American Apathy*. New York: Random House, 1968.

George Mosse, *Toward the Final Solution: A*

History of European Racism. New York: Howard Fertig, 1997.

Filip Müller et al., *Eyewitness Auschwitz: Three Years in the Gas Chambers*. New York: Stein & Day, 1979.

Nazi Conspiracy and Aggression. Vol. 4. Washington, DC: Government Printing Office, 1946.

Verne E. Newton, ed., *FDR and the Holocaust*. New York: St. Martin's, 1996.

Yehuda Nir, *The Lost Childhood*. New York: Berkley, 1996.

Jeremy Noakes and Geoffrey Pridham, *Documents on Nazism, 1919–1945*. New York: Viking, 1974.

———, *Nazism, 1919–1945, a Documentary Reader: The Rise to Power, 1919–1934*. Vol. 1. London: University of Exeter Press, 1998.

Zdenka Novak, *When Heaven's Vault Cracked*. London: Merlin Books, 1996.

Miklos Nyiszli, *Auschwitz: A Doctor's Eyewitness Account*. New York: Arcade, 1993.

Richard J. Overy, *The Origins of the Second World War*. London: Longman, 1998.

———, *War and Economy in the Third Reich*. New York: Oxford University Press, 1995.

———, *Why the Allies Won*. New York: W.W. Norton, 1997.

Mordecai Paldiel, *The Path of the Righteous: Gentile Rescuers of Jews During the Holocaust*. New York: Ktav, 1993.

———, *Sheltering the Jews: Stories of Holocaust Rescuers*. Minneapolis: Fortress, 1997.

Moshe Pearlman, *The Capture and Trial of Adolf Eichmann*. New York: Simon & Schuster, 1963.

Monty Noam Penkower, *The Holocaust and Israel Reborn: From Catastrophe to Sovereignty*. Urbana: University of Illinois Press, 1994.

———, *The Jews Were Expendable: Free World Diplomacy and the Holocaust*. Detroit: Wayne State University Press, 1988.

William R. Perl, *The Holocaust Conspiracy: An International Policy of Genocide*. New York: Shapolsky, 1989.

———, *Operation Action: Rescue from the Holocaust*. New York: F. Ungar, 1983.

Jonathan Petropoulos, *Art as Politics in the Third Reich*. Chapel Hill: University of North Carolina Press, 1996.

Michael Phayer, *Protestant and Catholic Women in Nazi Germany*. Detroit: Wayne State University Press, 1990.

Judah Pilch, ed., *The Jewish Catastrophe in Europe*. New York: American Association for Jewish Education, 1968.

Leon Poliakov, *Harvest of Hate*. New York: Schocken Books, 1979.

Gerald Posner, *Mengele: The Complete Story*. New York: Dell, 1987.

Lou Potter et al., *Liberators: Fighting on Two Fronts in World War II*. New York: Harcourt Brace Jovanovich, 1992.

Jean-Claude Pressac, *Auschwitz: Technique and Operation of the Gas Chambers*. New York: Beate Klarsfeld Foundation, 1989.

Robert Proctor, *Racial Hygiene: Medicine Under the Nazis*. Cambridge, MA: Harvard University Press, 1989.

Alexander Ramati, *The Assisi Underground: The Priests Who Rescued Jews*. New York: Stein & Day, 1978.

Hannau Rautkallio, *Finland and the Holocaust: the Rescue of Finland's Jews*. Washington, DC: U.S. Holocaust Memorial Museum Shop Memorial Council, 1988.

Gerald Reitlinger, *The Final Solution: The Attempt to Exterminate the Jews of Europe, 1939–1945*. New York: Jason Aronson, 1987.

Abraham Resnick, *The Holocaust*. San Diego: Lucent Books, 1991.

Carol Rittner and Sondra Myers, eds., *The Courage to Care: Rescuers of Jews During the Holocaust*. New York: New York University Press, 1989.

Jacob Robinson, *And the Crooked Shall Be Made Straight: The Eichmann Trial, the Jewish Catastrophe, and Hannah Arendt's Narrative*. New York: Macmillan, 1965.

———, *The Holocaust and After: Sources and Literature in English*. New Brunswick, NJ: Transaction, 1973.

Barbara Rogasky, *Smoke and Ashes: The Story of the Holocaust*. New York: Holiday House, 1991.

H. Rosenfeld, *The Swedish Angel of Rescue: The Heroism and Torment of Raoul Wallenberg*. Buffalo: Prometheus Books, 1982.

Robert Ross, *So It Was True: The American Protestant Press and the Nazi Persecution of the Jews*. Minneapolis: University of Minnesota Press, 1980.

Seymour Rossel, *The Holocaust: The World and the Jews, 1933–1945*. New York: Behrman House, 1992.

Morris Roy, *Behind Barbed Wire*. New York: Richard R. Smith, 1946.

Arnold P. Rubin, *The Evil That Men Do: The Story of the Nazis*. New York: J. Messner, 1981.

William D. Rubinstein, *The Myth of Rescue: Why the Democracies Could Not Have Saved More Jews from the Nazis*. London: Routledge, 1997.

Ward Rutherford, *Genocide*. New York: Ballantine Books, 1973.

Abram L. Sachar, *The Redemption of the Unwanted*. New York: St. Martin's, 1983.

David Schoenbaum, *Hitler's Social Revolution: Class and Status in Nazi Germany, 1933–1939*. New York: W.W. Norton, 1997.

Inge Scholl, *The White Rose: Munich, 1942–1943*. Middletown, CT: Wesleyan University Press, 1983.

Arnold Schwartzman, *Code Name: The Long Sobbing: The Allies, the Axis, and the Victims: An Anthology from D-Day to V-E Day: The Companion to the film "Liberation."* Los Angeles: Simon Wiesenthal Center, 1994.

Tom Segev, *The Seventh Million: The Israelis and the Holocaust*. New York: Hill & Wang, 1994.

Michael Selzer, *Deliverance Day: The Last Hours at Dachau*. Philadelphia: Lippincott, 1978.

William Shirer, *Rise and Fall of the Third Reich: A History of Nazi Germany*. New York: Fawcett Books, 1991.

Dawid Sierakowiak, *The Diary of Dawid Sierakowiak: Five Notebooks from the Lodz Ghetto*. Ed. Alan Adelson. New York: Oxford University Press, 1998.

Eric Silver, *The Book of the Just: The Unsung Heroes Who Saved Jews from Hitler*. London: Weidenfeld & Nicolson, 1992.

Dorrith Sim, *In My Pocket*. New York: Harcourt Brace, 1997.

Elizabeth R. Skoglund, *A Quiet Courage—Per Anger, Wallenberg's Co-Liberator of Hungarian Jews*. Grand Rapids, MI: Baker Book House, 1997.

Marcus Smith, *The Harrowing of Hell: Dachau*. New York: State University of New York Press, 1995.

Louis Snyder, *Encyclopedia of the Third Reich*. New York: McGraw-Hill, 1976.

Albert Speer, *Inside the Third Reich*. New York: Touchstone Books, 1997.

Art Spiegelman, *Maus: A Survivor's Tale*. 2 vols. New York: Pantheon Books, 1986, 1992.

R. Conrad Stein, *The Holocaust*. Chicago: Children's Press, 1986.

Alan Steinweis, *Art, Ideology, and Economics in Nazi Germany: The Reich Chambers of Music, Theater, and the Visual Arts*. Chapel Hill: University of North Carolina Press, 1996.

Jill Stephenson, *Nazi Organisation of Women*.

London: Barnes & Noble Books, 1980.

———, *Women in Nazi Society*. London: Barnes & Noble Books, 1975.

Barbara McDonald Stewart, *United States Government Policy on Refugees from Nazism, 1933–1940*. New York: Garland, 1982.

Adina Blady Szwajger, *I Remember Nothing More: The Warsaw Children's Hospital and the Jewish Resistance*. New York: Pantheon Books, 1992.

Telford Taylor, *The Anatomy of the Nuremberg Trials*. New York: Knopf, 1992.

Nechama Tec, *Dry Tears: The Story of a Lost Childhood*. New York: Oxford University Press, 1984.

———, *When Light Pierced the Darkness: Christian Rescue of Jews in Nazi-Occupied Poland*. New York: Oxford University Press, 1987.

Shabtai Teveth, *Ben-Gurion and the Holocaust*. New York: Harcourt Brace, 1996.

Irene Tomaszewski and Tecia Werbowski, *Zegota: The Rescue of Jews in Wartime Poland*. Montreal: Price-Patterson, 1994.

Trials of War Criminals. Washington, DC: Government Printing Office, 1950.

Henry A. Turner, *German Big Business and the Rise of Hitler*. New York: Oxford University Press, 1985.

Ann and John Tusa, *The Nuremberg Trial*. New York: McGraw-Hill, 1985.

U.S. Senate, *Report of the Committee Requested by Gen. Dwight D. Eisenhower Through the Chief of Staff. Gen. George C. Marshall to the Congress of the United States Relative to Atrocities and Other Conditions in Concentration Camps in Germany*. 79th Cong., 1st sess., May 15, 1945. S. Doc. 47.

John Vietor, *Time Out: American Airmen at Stalag Luft I*. New York: R.R. Smith, 1951.

Hermann Vinke, *The Short Life of Sophie Scholl*. Cambridge: Harper & Row, 1984.

Sam Waagenar, *The Pope's Jews*. LaSalle, IL: Alcove, 1974.

Raoul Wallenberg, *Letters and Dispatches, 1924–1945*. New York: Arcade, 1996.

Marek Web, ed., *The Documents of the Lodz Ghetto: An Inventory of the Nachman Zonabend Collection*. New York: Workman's Circle, 1988.

Gerhard L. Weinberg, *The Foreign Policy of Hitler's Germany: Diplomatic Revolution in Europe, 1933–36*. Chicago: University of Chicago Press, 1970.

———, *The Foreign Policy of Hitler's Germany: Starting World War II, 1937–1939*. Chicago: University of Chicago Press, 1980.

Frida Scheps Weinstein, *A Hidden Childhood: A Jewish Girl's Sanctuary in a French Convent, 1942–1945*. New York: Farrar, Straus, & Giroux, 1986.

Eugene Weinstock, *Beyond the Last Path*. New York: Boni and Gaer, 1947.

Leon Weliczker Wells, *Shattered Faith: A Holocaust Legacy*. Lexington: University Press of Kentucky, 1995.

———, *Who Speaks for the Vanquished? American Jewish Leaders and the Holocaust*. New York: Peter Lang, 1988.

Frederick E. Werbell and Thurston Clarke, *Lost Hero: The Mystery of Raoul Wallenberg*. New York: McGraw-Hill, 1985.

Charles Whiting, *The Hunt for Martin Bormann: The Truth*. New York: Combined Books, 1996.

———, *Massacre at Malmédy*. New York: Combined Books, 1996.

———, *Werewolf: The Story of the Nazi Resistance Movement, 1944–1945*. New York: Combined Books, 1996.

Elie Wiesel, *Dimensions of the Holocaust*. Evanston, IL: Northwestern University Press, 1990.

———, *Selected and Annotated Resource List of Materials on the Holocaust*. New York: Anti-Defamation League, 1991.

Simon Wiesenthal, *Justice Not Vengeance*. Trans. Ewald Osers. New York: Grove Wiedenfeld, 1989.

———, *The Murderers Among Us: The Simon Wiesenthal Memoirs*. New York: McGraw-Hill, 1967.

Robert S. Wistrich, *Antisemitism: The Longest Hatred*. New York: New York University Press, 1990.

———, *Who's Who in Nazi Germany*. New York: Routledge, 1995.

Jacqueline Wolfe, *Take Care of Josette: A Memoir in Defense of Occupied France*. New York: Franklin Watts, 1981.

E. Thomas Wood and Stanislaw M. Jankowski, *Karski: How One Man Tried to Stop the Holocaust*. New York: John Wiley & Sons, 1994.

David S. Wyman, *The Abandonment of the Jews*. New York: Pantheon Books, 1984.

———, *Paper Walls: America and the Refugee Crisis, 1938–1941*. New York: Pantheon Books, 1985.

———, *The World Reacts to the Holocaust*. Baltimore: Johns Hopkins University Press, 1996.

———, ed., *America and the Holocaust: A Thirteen-Volume Set Documenting the Acclaimed Book "The Abandonment of the Jews."* New York: Garland, 1989–1990.

Leni Yahil, *The Holocaust: The Fate of European Jewry, 1932–1945*. New York: Oxford University Press, 1991.

———, *The Rescue of Danish Jewry: Test of a Democracy*. Philadelphia: Jewish Publication Society, 1984.

Hiltgunt Zassenhaus, *Walls: Resisting the Third Reich—One Woman's Story*. Boston: Beacon, 1993.

Major Subject List

Index

and conformity, 110
planning for, 397–98, 420
Pope Pius XII's knowledge of, 452
shootings, 35, 86–90, 171
U.S. inaction on, 437, 438–39
see also gas chambers; Jews, rescue efforts
Masson, Andre, 320
Matisse, Henri, 319
Mauthausen camp, 132
liberation of, 363–67
Mayer, Arno J., 78
McCaleb, Kenneth, 426
McCardell, Lee, 429–30
McCloy, John J., 418, 427–28
McKittrick, Thomas H., 434
media, 22
on American disbelief, 424–25
burying information, 440–41
on eyewitness account of Auschwitz, 427–28
German, 135
ignoring reference to Jews, 426–27
killings proven to, 426, 429–30
on Nazi violence, 50
skepticism in, 426, 428–29
medical experiments, 18, 72–73, 356
dissection of corpses, 94–96
on Gypsies, 207
Jews as guinea pigs for, 96
location, 91
selecting twins for, 98–99
sterilization, 91–92
on twins, 100–102
selection of, 98–99
treatment of, 99–100
types of, 90–91
x-ray and surgical castration, 93–94
Mehring, Walter, 320
Mendes, Cesar, Jr., 324
Mengele, Josef
aim of experiments by, 99
charming side of, 102
experiments by, 100–102
selections by, 98–99, 150–51, 179
treatment of patients under, 99–100
mentally ill, 72, 73
mentally retarded, 72, 73, 184
Merin, Moses, 77
Messerschmidt, 163
Messersmith, George, 219
Metz, Erwin, 227–30
Metzler, David, 307
Meyer, Alfred, 79, 82
Meyerhof, Otto, 320

Michel, Ernest W., 164
Middle East, 420
Milejkowski, Israel, 117
military, U.S.
Buchenwald liberated by, 360–61
encountering concentration camps, 351–57
Mauthausen liberated by, 363–67
Milton, Sybil, 214–15
Minsk ghetto, 272
Mischlinge (German/Jewish offspring), 46, 59, 109
Morell, Theodor, 42
Morgenthau, Henry, 368, 403, 439
Morse, Arthur D., 345
Moscow War Crimes Declaration, 427, 457
Mozes, Eva, 99, 100
Muller, Heinrich, 80
Muller, Josef, 173
Munich Pact, 292
Muselmanner, 257
music, 122
Musmanno, Michael, 85, 87, 88, 90

names, Jewish, 55
National Central Office for Jewish Emigration, 19
National Citizens Law, 18
National Press Law, 44
National Socialist German Workers. *See* Nazis
National Socialist German Workers' Party (NSDAP), 39
Native Americans, 31
Natonek, Hans, 320
Nazis, 26
after the war
escape routes for, 373
organization for, 374–76
transferring money out of Germany, 373–74
brainwashing of, 109–10
Churchill on, 398–99
confession by, 248–52
conformity by, 110
dedicated to killing program, 422
disobeying orders, 108–109, 111
dissent against, 260–62
forgiving, 252–53
on homosexuality, 209–10
and Jehovah's Witnesses, 203–205
Jew defined by, 46–47
Jewish lack of action against, 48–49, 253–54

and *Judenrat*, 256
language of, 68–69
as "ordinary men," 21
Oscar Schindler belonging to, 292
punishment for, 382–84
racial policy, 52–53
resistance against
blowing up German trains, 277–80
in France, 273
in Hungary, 273–75
in Poland, 269–73
rise to power, 39–40, 49–50
Roosevelt on, 399
on social deviations, 200–201
song of, 27
stealing from Jews, 63–64, 87–88, 374
strategies of, 29–30
winning elections, 33
on women, 212
see also Einsatzgruppen (SS); legislation, anti-Jewish; mass killings; medical experiments; Nuremberg trials; propaganda, anti-Semetic; SS guards
neo-Nazis, 475–76
Netherlands, 37
Neudegg, L.D. Classen von, 209
Neumann, Erich, 80, 82
Neumann, Margita, 92
Newsweek (magazine), 440
New York Herald Tribune (newspaper), 224, 428
New York Times (newspaper), 428, 440
New York Times Magazine, 425
Niebuhr, Reinhold, 318
Night of Broken Glass. *See* Kristallnacht
Nikitchenko, I.T., 370, 372
Nilsson, Asta, 315
Nishri, Yehoshua, 333
Normandy, 42
North Africa, 42
Norway
German invasion of, 41, 313–14
Jewish deaths in, 37
Novick, Peter, 465, 471
Nuno, Pedro, 324
Nuremberg Laws, 34, 45, 65
discussed at Wannsee Conference, 82
including Gypsies, 206
see also legislation, anti-Jewish
Nuremberg trials, 24

Picture Credits

Archive Photos, 453

Central State Archive of Film, Photo, and Phonographic Documents, 185

Dover, 115

Estate of E. Harry James Cargas, 239, 241

FPG International, 219, 347

Government Press Office, Jerusalem, 383

Herbert Steinhouse, United States Holocaust Memorial Museum, 296

KZ Gedenkstatte Dachau, 79, 166

Library of Congress, 102, 146, 459

Main Commission for the Investigation of Nazi War Crimes, 93, 101

National Archives, 42, 51, 66, 86, 112, 207, 243, 267, 353, 369, 425, 436

PhotoDisc, 470

Simon Wiesenthal Center Library and Archives, 196, 207, 224, 239, 240, 252, 304, 322

UPI/Corbis-Bettmann, 310, 409

USHMM Photo Archives, 260

Yad Vashem Photo Archives, 412

YIVO Institute for Jewish Research, 45